Salomon Smith Barney Guide to Mortgage-Backed and Asset-Backed Securities

Founded in 1807, John Wiley & Sons is the oldest independent publishing company in the United States. With offices in North America, Europe, Australia and Asia, Wiley is globally committed to developing and marketing print and electronic products and services for our customers' professional and personal knowledge and understanding.

The Wiley Finance series contains books written specifically for finance and investment professionals, as well as sophisticated individual investors and their financial advisors. Book topics range from portfolio management to e-commerce, risk management, financial engineering, valuation, and financial instrument analysis, as well as much more.

For a list of available titles, please visit our Web site at www.WileyFinance.com.

Salomon Smith Barney Guide to Mortgage-Backed and Asset-Backed Securities

LAKHBIR HAYRE, Editor

John Wiley & Sons, Inc.

New York • Chichester • Weinheim • Brisbane • Singapore • Toronto

This publication is designed to provide accurate and authoritative information in regard to the subject matter covered. It is sold with the understanding that the publisher is not engaged in rendering professional services. If professional advice or other expert assistance is required, the services of a competent professional person should be sought.

ISBN 0-471-38587-5

Printed in the United States of America.

10 9 8 7 6 5

acknowledgments

Many people contributed to the successful completion of this book. Key among these are the contributing authors, without whose excellence and hard work this book would not have been possible.

A major vote of thanks is owed to the management of the fixed-income division of Salomon Smith Barney, particularly the heads of the mortgage department, currently Jeffrey Perlowitz and Mark Tsesarsky and previously Tom Maheras, for their encouragement and support of the research presented in this book. Many thanks also to the mortgage traders and salespeople, as well as our colleagues in Fixed-Income Research at Salomon whose comments and feedback invariably improve the quality and relevance of the research.

I would especially like to thank Ana Edwards, Vered Vaknin, and Eileen Contrucci for their immense hard work in preparing the chapters and their grace under pressure. Thanks also go to the fixed-income editorial group at Salomon for their help in retrieving old graphs and text. Finally, I want to thank the editorial and production staff at John Wiley & Sons, particularly Bill Falloon, for their many helpful comments and gentle cajoling in nudging this book along.

LAKHBIR HAYRE

contents

Introduction

Lakhbir Hayre

Mortgage-backed securities (MBSs) and asset-backed securities (ABSs)[1] constitute the largest sector of the bond market. They form a core holding of almost all U.S. institutional fixed-income investors, and Wall Street dealers trade billions of dollars of these securities every day. However, the complexity and variety of these securities, along with the dearth of easily available information, means that very few people in the financial industry or in academia have a detailed understanding of their characteristics.

The purpose of this book is to provide a comprehensive, sophisticated, and clear treatment of the MBS and ABS markets. The book brings together recent research conducted by analysts at Salomon Smith Barney (SSB), which (as Salomon Brothers) played a pioneering role in creating the secondary mortgage market in the late 1970s and early 1980s, and which remains the largest trader in the market.

WHAT ARE MORTGAGE- AND ASSET-BACKED SECURITIES?

In essence, MBSs and ABSs are securities entitled to the cash flows from a specified pool of assets. A majority of the market (close to $3 trillion) consists of securities backed by residential mortgage loans; however, a large variety of other types of assets have been securitized, including commercial

---

[1] In the United States, the term MBS is used to refer to securities backed by residential mortgage loans, while ABS denotes securities collateralized by other types of consumer loans, such as car loans. However, securities backed by home equity loans (HELs) or by manufactured housing loans (MHs) are usually labeled ABSs by convention. Outside the United States, the term ABS is used in a more general sense, with MBSs a subset of ABSs.

mortgage loans, car loans, credit card receivables, and so on. The cash flows from the assets can be channeled to investors in two ways: (1) they can simply be passed through to investors, after administrative or **servicing** fees are subtracted. This method produces a **pass-through security**, which comprises the bulk of MBSs; or (2) the cash flows can be allocated to investors according to specified rules, creating **structured securities**, such as **collateralized mortgage obligations** (CMOs).

Despite the variety of collateral types and cash flow allocation structures, most MBSs and ABSs share certain characteristics:

- In almost all cases, payments, both those received from the pool of assets and those paid to security holders, are monthly.
- The monthly payments from the assets typically consist of principal and interest. The principal can be *scheduled* and *unscheduled*.
- The scheduled principal reflects the **amortizing** nature of most consumer loans; in other words, the principal borrowed is paid back gradually over the term of the loan, rather than in one lump sum at the maturity of the loan.
- Unscheduled payments of principal, or **prepayments**, reflect the fact that most consumer loans can be paid off early, either in whole or in part. For example, most mortgage loans are paid off early because the borrower sells the house or refinances into a new, lower-rate mortgage.

Because we cannot predict with certainty when and how borrowers will make prepayments, there is cash flow uncertainty for MBSs and ABSs. In fact, prepayment uncertainty is key to the investment characteristics of most MBSs. As we discuss next, there is minimal credit risk for most MBSs and ABSs, whereas for traditional bonds, cash flow uncertainty arises from credit risk.[2]

DEVELOPMENT OF THE MARKET

The U.S. government has played a key role in the development of the secondary mortgage market in the United States, through the creation of three housing finance agencies—Ginnie Mae, Fannie Mae, and Freddie Mac—to

---

[2] It has been said that the difference between mortgage securities and corporate bonds is that in the case of corporate bonds investors know when they are supposed to get the principal back, but are not sure if they will, while in the case of MBSs, investors know that they will get the principal back, but are not sure when.

facilitate the flow of mortgage capital and make it easier for potential home buyers to obtain mortgages.[3] The agencies support the secondary mortgage market by buying mortgage loans from lenders, ensuring that lenders have funds to make additional loans. The agencies can pay cash for the mortgages and hold them in portfolio (only Fannie Mae and Freddie Mac) or issue an MBS in exchange for pools of mortgages from lenders. MBSs provide lenders with a liquid asset that they can hold or sell to Wall Street dealers who will then trade these MBSs:

- **Ginnie Mae** (formerly known as the **Government National Mortgage Association,** or GNMA) is still a part of the U.S. government, and MBSs guaranteed by Ginnie Mae carry the full faith and credit of the U.S. government. Hence, like U.S. Treasuries, Ginnie Mae MBSs are generally considered to have no credit risk.
- The other two agencies, **Fannie Mae** (formerly the **Federal National Mortgage Association,** or FNMA), and **Freddie Mac** (formerly the **Federal Home Loan Mortgage Corporation,** or FHLMC), are now private entities but maintain close ties to the U.S. government.[4] Although Fannie Mae and Freddie Mac MBSs do not have explicit U.S. government guarantees, they are not rated by any of the rating agencies, the implicit assumption being that they have negligible credit risk.

The *agency MBS market* refers to mortgage securities guaranteed by Ginnie Mae, Fannie Mae, or Freddie Mac, and at over $2.5trillion (as of late 2000), it constitutes the majority of the MBS/ABS market. *Private-label MBSs* refer to mortgage-backed securities not guaranteed by Ginnie Mae, Fannie Mae, or Freddie Mac, generally because the underlying mortgage loans do not meet certain necessary criteria for inclusion in agency MBSs (see Chapter 1). Since the mid-1980s, many nonmortgage asset types have been securitized—these securities are collectively referred to as asset-backed securities (ABSs)—as many institutions realized that securitization provided a means for both controlling risk and for efficient balance sheet management (see Chapter 2).

---

[3] To be precise, the agencies guarantee the timely payment of interest and principal to investors.

[4] These ties include a line of credit to the U.S. Treasury, a number of board members being appointed by the U.S. president, exemption from having to register publicly issued securities with the U.S. Securities and Exchange Commission (which other private institutions have to do), and an exemption from all state and local taxes (except real property taxes). Fannie Mae, Freddie Mac, and a few other similar entities are now commonly called government-sponsored enterprises, or GSEs.

The rapid growth in the MBS/ABS has been possible because of widespread investor sponsorship of these securities. Several factors are responsible for the rapid acceptance of MBSs and ABSs by institutional investors, with the main ones being their high credit quality and returns that have historically been superior to alternative high quality securities; these factors are discussed in more detail in Chapter 1.

ORGANIZATION OF THIS BOOK

The book is organized into parts, each covering a specific topic or sector of the market.

Part One: *An Overview of the Market* provides an introduction to the market. The three chapters in this section give a concise treatment of topics covered in more detail in the rest of the book. It is intended to provide a self-contained introduction to the market for readers who are not specialists in mortgage- and asset-backed securities, or for use in a brief course on the market in academia.

Part Two: *Prepayment Analysis and Modeling* discusses the modeling of prepayment rates on residential mortgage loans. Prepayment forecasts are critical in estimating security cash flows and investment characteristics. However, since prepayment behavior is influenced by a host of economic and demographic factors, modeling prepayments is as much art as science. Chapter 4 describes a general framework for modeling prepayments that has been applied at Salomon for developing models for many different types of mortgages; these models are used by traders at the firm and by several hundred institutional investors to manage portfolios of mortgage- and asset-backed securities. Chapter 5 discusses the effect of prepayment modeling errors on investment value. Chapter 6 gives a detailed description of the mortgage origination process, a knowledge of which is crucial for the understanding of prepayments, while Chapter 7 discusses how the Internet is changing the process, and the resulting implications for prepayment patterns.

Part Three: *Collateral Sectors* provides a description of several subsectors of the agency and non-agency MBS markets. Even within the agency MBS market, there are diverse types of loans, each characterized by specific prepayment and hence investment characteristics. The section describes these prepayment characteristics, and how they can be modeled.

Part Four: *Option-Adjusted Spreads and Durations* discusses the concept of *option-adjusted spreads* (OASs), a valuation methodology pioneered by Salomon Brothers in the mid-1980s, which combines prepayment and term structure models and which is now the standard method for analyzing

MBSs and ABSs. The section also discusses some issues that arise when estimating durations for MBSs.

Part Five: *Agency CMOs and Stripped MBSs* describes the many ways that mortgage cash flows have been structured to create bonds with specific maturity and prepayment profiles. The resulting bonds, generally termed *Collateralized Mortgage Obligations* (CMOs), form a large sector of the market, but it is important for investors to understand how the prepayment risk of the underlying pass-through securities is allocated among different types of CMO bonds, as these allocations are not generally equal.

Part Six: *Commercial Mortgage-Backed Securities* provides an introduction to commercial MBSs, or CMBSs, which, as the name implies, are securities backed by commercial mortgage loans. The section provides an introduction to the broad category of loans in CMBSs—on residential apartment buildings, retail stores, nursing homes, hotels, and so on—and describes basic methods of analyzing CMBSs. The section also gives a detailed description of two specific types of CMBSs: *interest-only* (IO) securities, which receive just a strip of the coupon interest payments from the collateral, and agency CMBSs backed by loans on multifamily housing.

Part Seven: *Mortgage-Related Asset-Backed Securities* is the first of two sections on asset-backed securities. By convention, securities backed by two types of mortgage loans—home equity loans and loans on manufactured housing—are classified as ABSs. This section gives a detailed description of these two types of ABSs, focusing on their prepayment characteristics and on the extensive modeling, based on loan level data, that Salomon Smith Barney has conducted in recent years.

Part Eight: *Nonmortgage-Related Asset-Backed Securities* discusses in detail several types of nonmortgage-related ABSs, including some recent innovations in credit card ABSs. There is a large variety of asset types that have been securitized, and it is difficult to provided descriptions of every type without making the book overly long. However, this section, along with the general overview of ABSs in Chapter 2, should provide the reader with an understanding of key asset types and of important structural developments in the market.

Part Nine: *Non-U.S. Markets* discusses important sectors of the MBS and ABS markets outside the United States. Perhaps the most important development in the market in recent years has been the surge of securitization outside the United States, and key growth areas have been Europe (especially the United Kingdom) and Australia. In this section, we describe the MBS and CMBS markets in the United Kingdom, and the rapidly growing MBS market in Australia.

The last part of the book includes a glossary of common terms (the MBS and ABS markets, like every specialized field, has its share of jargon), and a series of Appendixes, including basic mortgage mathematics; a guide to resources for investors, including useful Web sites; and some information on risk-based capital standards as they apply to MBSs and ABSs.

USING THIS BOOK

The book is designed to both provide a comprehensive and authoritative description of the MBS and ABS markets, and to serve as a reference source for specialists. A major strength of the book is that it is written by specialists with many years of experience in the field, working at a firm that was a pioneer in the market and that still trades the largest volume of MBSs and ABSs. Given the specialized nature of the market, the vast variety of collateral types and cash flow structures, the fact that trading is over-the-counter rather than on public exchanges, and the dearth of generally available information about the securities, this type of "hands-on" experience is critical for a realistic understanding of these complex instruments.

There are no prerequisites for this book, other than a basic knowledge of fixed-income concepts, such as coupon and principal payments, maturity, yield, and duration. We recommend that readers who are not already MBS and ABS specialists start with Part One, which provides an overview of the market. The rest of the book is self-contained and individual chapters can be read as desired. One exception is Part Three, which discusses the prepayment characteristics of various sectors of the market; a prior reading of Chapter 4, on prepayment modeling, will help make Part Three more rewarding.

An encouraging trend in recent years has been the increased attention paid in academia to MBSs and ABSs, as part of real estate finance courses or as courses offered in financial engineering programs. Part One, along with the Appendixes can be used for a brief course on the topic; parts of Chapters 4, 13, and 14 can be added if there is time. The whole book may be suitable for a two-semester course on the market.

An Overview of the Market

A Concise Guide to Mortgage-Backed Securities (MBSs)

Lakhbir Hayre

This chapter provides an introduction to mortgage securities and methods of analyzing them. While it lays the groundwork for the more detailed treatment of various topics in the rest of this book, it can also be used as a concise but comprehensive overview of the market for nonspecialists. The chapter is organized as follows:

- Section 1.1 describes the growth of the market.
- Section 1.2 reviews key features of agency mortgage pass-through securities, the most basic and most prevalent type of MBS.
- Section 1.3 discusses the basics of MBS analysis, such as prepayment estimation and modeling, and spreads over Treasuries.
- Section 1.4 describes option-adjusted spread methodology, which has become the standard way of evaluating MBSs.
- Section 1.5 gives an overview of structured MBSs, such as collateralized mortgage obligations and interest-only MBSs.
- Section 1.6 provides an introduction to the various types of non-agency MBSs.
- Section 1.7 gives a brief review of mortgage securitization outside the United States.

1.1 GROWTH OF THE SECONDARY MORTGAGE MARKET

The mortgage-backed securities (MBSs) market has experienced phenomenal growth over the past 20 years. The total outstanding volume of MBSs

EXHIBIT 1.1 Relative Size of U.S. Debt Sectors (Dollars in Trillions)

All Mortgage Debt	$6.32
Single-Family Mortgage Debt	4.76
Mortgage-Backed Securities	2.95
Treasury Securities	3.65
Corporate Bonds	2.06
Agency Debt	1.95

Note: Total for Treasuries includes Bills, while the total for Mortgage-Backed Securities includes those backed by nonresidential loans and home equity loans.
Source: Federal Reserve Bulletin, pp. A35 and A40, May 2000.

has increased from about $100 billion in 1980 to about $3 trillion, and as Exhibit 1.1 shows, mortgage-backed securities form a major component of the U.S. bond market.

Exhibit 1.2 shows a breakdown of Salomon Smith Barney's U.S. Broad Investment Grade (BIG) Index. Note that MBSs are a bigger proportion of the index than suggested by Exhibit 1.1, as almost half of all Treasury securities are Bills with maturities less than one year, and are hence excluded from the index.[1]

What accounts for the rapid growth of the MBS market? Increased securitization of mortgages and ready acceptance of MBSs by fixed-income investors are both key reasons. Mortgage originators became much more disposed to sell loans into the secondary market after the high-interest-rate environment of the late 1970s and early 1980s, when the disadvantages of holding fixed-rate long-term loans in their portfolios became apparent. The growing market share of mortgage bankers, who have little interest in holding onto mortgage loans, also has contributed to the increasing securitization of mortgages. In addition, many institutions have increasingly come to view securitization as a means of turning illiquid assets into liquid securities, and hence a tool for efficient balance sheet management.

The federal government has played an equally important role. Three agencies, the Government National Mortgage Association (Ginnie Mae), the Federal National Mortgage Associations (Fannie Mae), and the Federal Home Loan Mortgage Corporation (Freddie Mac) are major players in the

---

[1] Also excluded are various mortgage sectors, such as non-agency MBSs, and various corporate bond issues. See *Salomon Smith Barney Global Index Catalog—1999* edition, February 1999.

EXHIBIT 1.2 Breakdown of Salomon Smith Barney's U.S. Broad Investment Grade (BIG) Index (Dollars in Trillions)

Sector	Par Amount	% of Index
Treasuries	$1.634	29.1 %
MBSs	1.895	33.8
Coroporates	1.408	25.1
Agency Debt	0.627	11.2
BIG Index	$5.607	100.0 %

Source: Salomon Smith Barney, May 2000.

secondary mortgage market in issuing and guaranteeing MBSs.[2] These federal housing finance agencies were created to facilitate the flow of mortgage capital and, hence, to ensure that lenders have adequate funds to make new mortgage loans. The three agencies are generally credited with significantly reducing the cost of mortgage borrowing for American home buyers, as well as making mortgages more widely available. On the demand side, MBSs have come to represent a significant portion of fixed-income holdings for many types of investors over the past decade. In Exhibit 1.3 we show a breakdown of holdings of MBSs by investor type.

Why Institutional Investors Buy Mortgage Securities

MBSs have quickly become popular fixed-income investments for many reasons, including:

■ *Higher returns.* MBSs typically yield 100bp (basis points) or more over Treasuries and offer higher yields than comparable-quality corporate bonds. Although some of this higher yield compensates for their complexity and embedded prepayment options, MBSs still have outperformed comparable Treasuries and other corporate bonds in most years since the early 1980s, as shown in Exhibit 1.4.

---

[2] As discussed in the Introduction, although all three entities are commonly referred to as agencies, only Ginnie Mae is now a true agency. Fannie Mae, which the government established in 1938, and Freddie Mac, which Congress created in 1970, are now private entities, although both have strong ties to the government. The market convention is to refer to all three as agencies (although *Government Sponsored Enterprises* [GSEs] is becoming a more common term for Fannie Mae, Freddie Mac, and other such entities), and we will follow this convention.

EXHIBIT 1.3   Mortgage-Backed Securities—Holdings by Investor Type

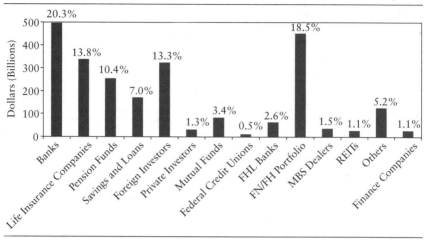

Note: Numbers shown at the top of the bars are holdings as a percentage of total outstanding MBSs, as of midyear 1998. Note that the total may not add up to the same as in Exhibit 1 because certain types of MBSs, such as those backed by nonresidential loans, are not included here. *Source: Inside MBS and ABS,* Salomon Smith Barney.

EXHIBIT 1.4   Mortgage, Corporate, and Treasury Securities—Historical Performance, 1982–1999

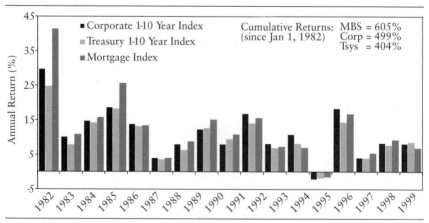

Source: Salomon Smith Barney Fixed-Income Index Group.

Exhibit 1.4 also shows cumulative returns on various Salomon Smith Barney fixed-income indices; MBSs have outperformed Treasuries and corporate bonds by substantial margins. Even during the 1990s, when conditions were ideal for Treasuries and corporate bonds—falling interest rates and a sustained recovery from the early 1990s recession—and the environment tough for MBSs, with several major refinancing waves, MBSs still did relatively well versus comparable fixed-income instruments.

■ *Credit quality.* Ginnie Mae MBSs are backed by the full faith and credit of the U.S. government and, hence, like Treasuries, are considered to carry no credit risk. Fannie Mae and Freddie Mac MBSs do not have U.S. government guarantees, but because of Fannie Mae's and Freddie Mac's close ties to the government, their MBSs are perceived to have minimal credit risk and do not seem to trade at a noticeable credit premium to Ginnie Maes. MBSs from other (private) issuers typically carry AAA or AA ratings from one or more of the credit rating agencies.

■ *Choice of investment profiles.* Given the variety of MBSs created, this sector provides a wider range of investment characteristics than most other parts of the fixed-income market. For example, MBSs are available with negative, short, or very long duration. Prepayment sensitivities can range from low to very high. Coupons can be fixed (from 0% to more than 1,000%) or floating (directly or inversely with a range of indices).

■ *Liquidity.* The amount of outstanding MBSs, trading volume (second only to U.S. Treasuries), and the involvement of major dealers provide an active, liquid market for most MBSs.

■ *Development of analytic tools.* Since the mid-1980s, many major dealers (and some buy-side firms) have devoted considerable resources to developing analytic models for evaluating MBSs. These efforts have led to a better understanding of mortgage cash flows and a higher level of comfort with the characteristics of mortgage securities.

1.2 AGENCY PASS-THROUGH SECURITIES

The basic mortgage-backed security structure is the pass-through. As the name implies, a pass-through passes through the monthly principal and interest payments (less a servicing fee) from a pool of mortgage loans to holders of the security. Thus, investors in the pass-through are, in effect, buying shares of the cash flows from the underlying loans. Structured MBSs, such as collateralized mortgage obligations (CMOs) and interest-only (IO) and principal-only (PO) stripped MBSs (or STRIPs), carve up mortgage cash flows in a variety of ways to create securities with given prepayment and maturity profiles. In this section we discuss pass-throughs; we describe structured mortgage securities (agency and non-agency) later in this chapter.

Development of the Pass-Through Market

The pass-through is the most common structure for mortgage-backed securities. A pass-through issuer acquires mortgages either by originating them or by purchasing them in the whole-loan market. Many mortgages with similar characteristics are collected into a pool, and undivided ownership interests in the pool are sold as pass-through certificates. The undivided interest entitles the owner of the security to a pro rata share of all interest payments and all scheduled or prepaid principal payments.

The growth of the pass-through market stems in large part from the active role of the U.S. housing finance agencies in the primary and secondary mortgage markets. Ginnie Mae, Freddie Mac, and Fannie Mae account for nearly all of the issuance and outstanding principal amount of mortgage pass-throughs.

The programs of the three major federal housing agencies reflect the historical development of U.S. housing policy. Fannie Mae was created in 1938 as a wholly owned government corporation. Its charter mandated that it purchase Federal Housing Administration (FHA)-insured and, (since 1948), Veterans Administration (VA)-guaranteed mortgages for its portfolio.[3] Congress intended to ensure that mortgage lenders would continue to be able to make residential mortgage loans, even in periods of disintermediation (when withdrawals by depositors are high) or when delinquencies and defaults are high. Fannie Mae's purchase activities encouraged the standardization of repayment contracts and credit underwriting procedures for mortgages.

In 1968, the government restructured its role in the housing finance market. Fannie Mae was privatized, although it retained its mandate to buy FHA/VA loans for its own portfolio. **Ginnie Mae** was spun off as a separate agency that would undertake some of Fannie Mae's previous activities; in particular, Ginnie Mae assumed the financing of home loans not ordinarily underwritten in the established mortgage market, such as loans to low-income families. Ginnie Mae's most important activity has been its mortgage pass-through program, which was instituted in 1970. Under this program, Ginnie Mae guarantees the payments of principal and interest on pools of FHA-insured or VA-guaranteed mortgage loans.

---

[3] The FHA and the VA are U.S. government entities that provide mortgage insurance intended to serve low and moderate-income home buyers.

The enhanced availability of credit to home owners who qualify for FHA and VA loans led to calls for similar treatment for nongovernment-insured (or *conventional*) mortgages. In 1970, Congress established Freddie Mac to develop an active secondary market for conventional loans, and in 1972, Fannie Mae began to purchase conventional mortgages. Thus, by 1972, lenders could sell their newly originated conventional mortgages to either Fannie Mae or Freddie Mac.

Freddie Mac issued a small volume of pass-throughs in the 1970s, while Fannie Mae began its MBS program in late 1981. As Exhibit 1.5 indicates, issuance volume from all three agencies increased tremendously in the 1980s, hit a peak in the refinancing waves of 1993, and recently hit record levels with the heavy volume of refinancing in 1998.

TERMINOLOGY

Exhibit 1.6. provides a description of a fairly typical mortgage pass-through, or pool, including key current pool characteristics which are updated each month by the agencies (through electronic tapes called *pool factor tapes)* for their pools (for non-agency MBSs, issuers provide updated tapes for their deals each month).

Ginnie Mae guarantees timely principal and interest payments on all of their pools. On Fannie Mae and Freddie Mac pools, the respective agencies guarantee principal and interest payments to investors. Private-label MBSs,

EXHIBIT 1.5   Agency Pass-Through Securities—Issuance, 1970–1999

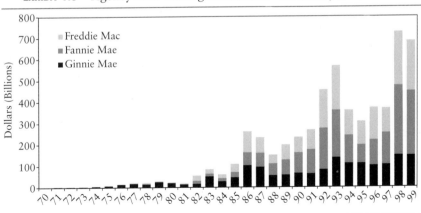

Source: Inside MBS and ABS.

EXHIBIT 1.6   Ginnie Mae Pool 301100

Issue Date:	03/01/1991	**Delay:**	45 Days
Collateral:	30-Year Fixed-Rate Loans	**Original Balance:**	$3,258,373
Net Coupon:	9.00%	**WAC:**	9.50%
Current Balance:	$341,431		
Factor:	0.10478598		
WAM:	20-05 Yrs.		
WALA:	9-04 Yrs.		

WAC: Weighted-average coupon, WALA: Weighted-average loan age, WAM: Weighted-average maturity.
Note: Current balances, Factor, WAM, and WALA as of June 8, 2000.
Sources: Ginnie Mae and Salomon Smith Barney.

which the rating agencies typically rate triple-A, are issued with various forms of credit enhancement, based on rating agency requirements.

Exhibit 1.6 also shows some of the terminology and information used to analyze MBSs:

- **Net coupon and WAC.** The net coupon of 9% is the rate at which interest is paid to investors,[4] while the weighted-average coupon (WAC) of 9.5% is the weighted-average coupon on the pool of mortgages backing the pass-through. The difference between the WAC and the net coupon is called the **servicing spread.** The majority of Ginnie Mae pools are issued under the so-called **Ginnie Mae I** program, and for such pools, the underlying mortgage loans all have the same note rate (9.50% for the pool in Exhibit 1.6) with a servicing spread of 50bp. Pass-throughs issued under an alternative program called **Ginnie Mae II**[5] and those issued by Fannie Mae and Freddie Mac allow for variations in the note rates on the underlying loans. In the latter case, the WAC could change

---

[4] This is the annualized rate. Mortgage cash flows are monthly, so each month investors receive interest at a rate of $\frac{9}{12}$%; in other words, 0.0075 times the balance outstanding at the beginning of the month.

[5] The Ginnie Mae II program allows for multiple-issuer pools (i.e., loans from a number of different issuers are pooled—in contrast, Ginnie Mae I pools contain loans from a single issuer), as well as for different note rates on the underlying pools. The Ginnie Mae II program has become well established in recent years, with issuance running at about 30% of that of Ginnie Mae I. For a recent update on the Ginnie Mae II program, see *Bond Market Roundup: Strategy,* Salomon Smith Barney, December 12, 1998.

over time (as loans are prepaid), and hence, the latest updated WAC would be shown.

■ **WAM and WALA.** The weighted-average maturity (WAM) is the average (weighted by loan balance) of the remaining terms on the underlying loans, while the WALA is the weighted-average loan age. Note that the sum of the WAM and WALA in Exhibit 1.6 is (20-05 + 9-04), or 29-09. If the underlying loans had original terms of 30 years, why is this figure not 30 years exactly? There are two reasons: (1) some of the loans may have had original terms of less than 30 years (e.g., 25 years) because pass-throughs backed by 30-year loans in fact may have mortgages with any original term of greater than 15 years (although the majority of loans will typically have 30-year original terms); and (2) some mortgagors are in the habit of sending in extra monthly payments, above and beyond the scheduled monthly payment, to build up equity in their properties at a faster rate. These extra payments, often referred to as *curtailments* or as *partial prepayments* (as opposed to a full prepayment of the whole mortgage) shorten the remaining term until the mortgage is paid off because the monthly payment remains unchanged (for fixed-rate loans) while the balance to be amortized decreases. The WAM will reflect the extent of this shortening.

■ **Delays.** Cash flows are passed through to investors with a delay to allow servicers time to process mortgage payments. For the Ginnie Mae pool shown in Exhibit 1.6, the stated delay is 45 days, which means that the principal and interest for September, say, is paid on October 15, rather than on October 1. Thus, the actual delay is 14 days. Fannie Maes have a stated delay of 55 days, while FHLMC Golds have a stated delay of 45 days.[6] Of course, these delays are factored into calculations of returns to investors.

■ **Pool factor.** The Ginnie Mae pool in Exhibit 1.6 had a factor of 0.10478598 as of June 8, 2000. The factor is the proportion of the original principal balance outstanding as of the stated factor date. The factor declines over time because of scheduled principal payments (amortization) and prepayments. In this case, amortization alone would have reduced the factor by less than 10% since the pool was issued in 1991; thus, this pool clearly has experienced heavy prepayments. As we discuss in the next section, a comparison of the actual

---

[6] Almost all Freddie Mac pass-throughs are issued now under its Gold program, which was started in 1990. Freddie Mac pass-throughs issued prior to the introduction of the Gold program have a delay of 75 days and, hence, are often labeled 75-day *Participation Certificates* (PCs).

factor with the factor under amortization alone is used to estimate pre-payment rates on mortgage pools.

TYPE OF AGENCY PASS-THROUGH COLLATERAL

In general, the agencies segregate loans into pools by the following categories:

- Type of property (single-family or multifamily);
- Payment schedule (*level, adjustable,* other);
- Original maturity; and
- Loan coupon rate.

Single-family loans, defined as loans on one- to four-family homes, provide the collateral for the great majority of agency pass-throughs. A brief description of agency multifamily programs is given later in this section. Here we review single-family collateral types.

Government and Conventional Loans

Loans insured by two U.S. government entities, the FHA and the VA, collateralize Ginnie Mae pools. Other loans are referred to as *conventional* loans. Conventional loans back almost all Fannie Mae and Freddie Mac pools, although both agencies have issued pools backed by FHA/VA loans.

Because of restrictions on loan size and lower downpayment requirements, FHA and VA borrowers tend to be less affluent than conventional borrowers, characteristics likely to lead to slower Ginnie Mae prepayment rates. However, because income levels and housing costs vary from region to region, certain regions have greater concentrations of FHA/VA loans. Hence, prepayment differentials between Ginnie Mae and Fannie Mae/Freddie Mac speeds can partly reflect regional housing market differences.

Conforming and Nonconforming Loans

Conventional loans may be segregated further into conforming and non-conforming loans. Conforming loans are those that are eligible for securitization by Fannie Mae and Freddie Mac, which means that the original loan balance must be less than the specified Fannie Mae/Freddie Mac limit (currently $240,000 and changed each year based on housing inflation) and that the loans must meet Fannie Mae/Freddie Mac underwriting guidelines (in terms of required documentation, borrower debt-to-income ratios, loan-to-value (LTV) ratios, etc.).

Nonconforming loans form the collateral for private-label MBSs. In most cases, these loans are nonconforming because they exceed the Fannie Mae/Freddie Mac loan size limit (jumbo loans). However, the sizes of a significant number of loans in private-label deals are below this limit, but are nonconforming because they do not meet Fannie Mae and Freddie Mac underwriting standards. An overview of non-agency MBSs is given in Part Six.

Payment Schedules and Loan Terms

Within each of these administrative categories, loans are further classified by payment type and term.

Fixed-Rate or Level-Pay Loans   These loans remain the basic collateral for pass-throughs. As the name implies, they are fully amortizing loans with fixed coupons and, hence, fixed monthly payments. The most popular loan term is 30 years, although 15-year loans appeal to those who want to build up equity faster in their homes and who can afford higher monthly payments. Smaller amounts of pass-throughs are backed by 20-year and 10-year loans, which were mainly issued as refinancing vehicles during the various refinancing waves of the past several years.

Adjustable-Rate Mortgages (ARMs)   ARMs became popular during the high-interest-rate period of the early 1980s. Since then, they have continued to account for a significant fraction of total mortgage originations. During periods of high fixed mortgage rates, as much as 60% of originations have been ARMs, but even when fixed rates are low, ARMs typically constitute at least 15% of originations. An explanation for their popularity is the low initial coupon (or teaser rate), that attracts borrowers (such as first-time home buyers) who want to minimize their starting monthly payments. After the teaser rate period is over, the coupon resets off a specified index, such as the one-year Treasury rate, subject to periodic caps (the maximum amount that the coupon can change at each reset date) and life caps (the upper limit on the ARM coupon). Securitization rates for ARMs are typically less than for fixed-rate loans, because some originators hold them in their portfolios.

A recent development is the **hybrid ARM.** As the name implies, a hybrid has features of both fixed-rate loans and ARMs: It has a fixed coupon for a specified number of years (typically three, five, seven, or ten), after which the coupon, as with a standard ARM, resets periodically off a specified index.[7]

---

[7] See Chapters 9 and 10 for a more detailed discussion of ARMs and hybrid ARMs.

Balloon Loans Fannie Mae and Freddie Mac securitize these loans. The loans amortize according to a 30-year schedule, with a balloon payment due at the end of five or seven years. Balloon MBSs were first issued in late 1990 and were quite popular in the refinancing waves of 1992 and 1993, but have declined in popularity since then, partly because of the growing popularity of hybrid ARMs.

There are various other payment types, such as *graduated payment mortgages* (GPMs), which typically have lower initial monthly payments and higher subsequent ones relative to a standard fixed-rate loan. The idea behind these mortgages is to make it easier to purchase a home for first-time buyers. Such types are a fairly minor segment of the market nowadays.

In Exhibit 1.7, we summarize some of the key features of the main agency pass-through programs.

TYPES OF PASS-THROUGH TRADING

Most agency pass-through trading is on a **to-be-announced** (**TBA**) basis. In a TBA trade, the buyer and seller decide on general trade parameters, such as agency, coupon, settlement date, par amount, and price, but the buyer typically does not know which pools actually will be delivered until two days before settlement. The seller is obligated to provide pool information

EXHIBIT 1.7 Through Programs—Characteristics

	Ginnie Mae	Fannie Mae	Freddie Mac
Types of Mortgage	FHA/VA	Conventional (Some FHA/VA)	Conventional (Some FHA/VA)
Guarantee	Timely payment of interest and principal	Timely payment of interest and principal	Timely payment of interest and principal
Guarantor	US Government	Fannie Mae	Freddie Mac
Amount (in Billions)			
• Issued to Date	$1,282	$1,674	$1,642
• Currently Outstanding	537	785	633
Main Collateral Types and Amounts Outstanding (in Billions)	30 Yr. F-R Ginnie I: $356 Ginnie II: $69 15 Yr. F-R Ginnie I: $23 Ginnie II: $1 ARMs: $79 Projects: $9	30 Yr. F-R: $533 15 Yr. F-R: $164 Balloons: $22 ARMs: $35 Multifamily: $31	30 Yr. F-R: $444 15 Yr. F-R: $146 Balloons: $18 ARMs: $24 Multifamily: $1
Servicing Spread	Ginnie Mae I: 50bp Ginnie Mae II: 50bp-150 bp	Up to 250bp, but typically 40bp-80bp	Up to 250bp, but typically 40bp-80bp
Delays (Days)			
• Stated	45 (Ginnie II: 50)	55	45
• Actual	14 (Ginnie II: 19)	24	14

ARMs: Adjustable-rate mortgages, bp: Basis points, BLNs: Balloons, FHA: Federal Housing Authority, F-R: Fixed-Rate, VA: Veterans Administration.
Notes: For Freddie Mac, delay shown is for Gold PCs; older PCs issued before the Gold program have a 75-day delay. Data as of February 1999.
Sources: Ginnie Mae, Freddie Mac, Fannie Mae, and Salomon Smith Barney.

by 3 P.M. two days prior to settlement (the 48 Hours Rule). The pools delivered are at the discretion of the seller, but must satisfy *Good Delivery* guidelines established by the Bond Market Association, a trade group representing bond dealers (formerly known as the Public Securities Association, or PSA). Good Delivery guidelines specify the allowable variance in the current face amount of the pools from the nominal agreed upon amount,[8] the maximum number of pools per $1 million of face value, and so on.

The TBA market facilitates liquidity in pass-through trading because most individual pass-through pools are small. Almost all newly issued pools trade as TBAs. Most price quotes shown for pass-throughs, and valuation analyses such as those in the next section, are for TBA coupons. Such pricing and analysis assume WACs and WAMs based on an estimate of what is most likely to be delivered at the time.

Pass-Through Vintages

Investors also can specify a particular loan origination year (or vintage, sometimes also referred to as a specific WAM) when buying a block of pass-throughs. For example, whereas a TBA trade might be for $100 million of 30-year Ginnie Mae 7s, a vintage trade might specify $100 million of 1993 30-year Ginnie Mae 7s. The investor would then receive Ginnie 7% pools collateralized by loans originated in 1993. Because the 1993 Ginnie 7s may have favorable prepayment characteristics relative to new production (e.g., more burnout or more seasoning), they would typically sell at a premium to TBAs. This blended market has become much more active in the past few years.[9]

Specified Pools

A large and active market also exists in specified pools, in which buyers know exactly which pools they are buying, and, hence, relevant characteristics such as WAC, WAM, age, prepayment history, and so on. With this

---

[8] Because the face amount of the pools could be any arbitrary amount (e.g., $341,431 in the example in Exhibit 1.6), it will generally be difficult to obtain pools whose outstanding amounts sum *exactly* to the agreed upon trade amount. Hence, some variance is allowed in the amount delivered. This variance was as one time 2% from the agreed upon amount, then 1%, and currently the BMA is in the process of implementing even tighter variances.

[9] For readers with access to Salomon Smith Barney's Yield Book® system or to SSB Direct, report MB712 gives market and theoretical prices for TBAs and specified origination year pass-throughs.

extra degree of certainty, specified pools typically trade at a premium to comparable TBA coupons.

Story Bonds While most trading in specified pools involves fairly seasoned bonds, a recent development is the trading of new pools with specific prepayment characteristics. Some examples include:

- *Prepay penalty pools,* which are backed by loans that carry a penalty (typically about six months of interest) if the loan is refinanced within the first three or five years.
- *Low WAC pools,* which are pools with WACs lower than the typical TBA average. For example, conventional TBA 7s currently are assumed to have a WAC of 7.60%, so 7% pools with a WAC of, say, 7.40% will trade at a premium to TBA 7s.
- *Low loan balance pools,* which are backed by "smaller than average" loans. Because refinancing costs are more of a hurdle for such loans and because smaller loan balances can imply less affluent borrowers, then other things being equal, such loans may prepay more slowly than average.

Combined Pools

Freddie Mac Giant PCs and Fannie Mae MegaPools, introduced in mid-1988, and Ginnie Mae Platinum pools, introduced in late 1994, are mortgage pass-throughs that the agencies create by combining already outstanding pass-throughs. Such pools benefit investors who own small pass-through pools or seasoned pools that have paid down. These investors can swap their holdings for a pro rata share of a new Giant PC, MegaPool, or Platinum pool. Similarly, these programs help lenders design more marketable securities. Lenders can take recently securitized smaller pools that are still held in portfolio and aggregate them into a bigger pool.

From the investor's perspective, large pools provide the following advantages in addition to greater liquidity:

- *Greater diversification.* When the combined pool is backed by pass-throughs from many investors, the geographic distribution of the underlying mortgages is typically greater. This diversification reduces the risk of random prepayment and default variations. Thus, the prepayment rates of combined pools would follow average mortgage sector prepayment rates more closely than would most standard pools.
- *Lower administration costs.* Investors can track the monthly payments and balances for a few large pools more efficiently than they can for a greater number of small pools.

■ *Lower reverse repurchase rates.* Investors can achieve lower financing rates when entering into reverse repurchase agreements by pledging bigger pools. Securities dealers and banks often pass on the administrative cost savings of larger pools to the customer.

MULTIFAMILY PASS-THROUGH PROGRAMS

Although small in comparison to the single-family MBS sector, passthroughs backed by multifamily mortgages comprise a sizable market as shown in Exhibit 1.7. Fannie Mae and Freddie Mac have securitized multifamily loans (defined as mortgages on five or more family homes) for many years, and their programs have gone through various revisions over the years. Investors should note some common features of multifamily MBSs:

■ Many multifamily loans have **prepayment penalties,** giving the investor a degree of call protection. The penalty is often in the form of *yield maintenance*; thus, the amount of the penalty depends on the decline in interest rates since issuance. The objective is to fully compensate the investor for the prepayment.
■ Many multifamily loans have balloon payments due, with the balloon date typically occurring between 5 and 15 years.

Project loans is a term that refers to FHA-insured mortgage loans made on a variety of property types such as multifamily housing, nursing homes, and hospitals. The loans are either securitized as Ginnie Mae passthroughs or sold as FHA PCs. Project loans typically have prepayment penalties. In addition, some project loans are putable; in other words, the investor has the option of selling the bond to the issuer for a specified price at specified times.

Multifamily pass-throughs and project loans are special cases of MBSs backed by **commercial real estate** loans. Commercial mortgage-backed securities (CMBSs) combine the features of standard MBSs with those of callable corporate bonds and are further discussed in Part Six.

1.3 BASICS OF MORTGAGE SECURITY ANALYSIS

In this section, we discuss the basics of MBS analysis, starting with prepayments. Standard bond valuation measures, such as yield spread, are also described. Although the dependence of mortgage cash flows on interest rates (through prepayments) makes traditional bond analysis of limited use for MBSs, such analysis is still a useful starting point.

Measuring Prepayments

Prepayments are calculated by comparing actual principal received with scheduled principal; the difference is the prepaid principal. The convention is to state prepayment rates in terms of the outstanding principal balance (as opposed to, for example, the initial balance). Observed prepayment rates can be stated in one of several different units.

Single Monthly Mortality (SMM)   This refers to the prepayment rate for a month and forms the basis for all prepayment calculations. The SMM is the fraction of the beginning-month balance that prepays during the month; by convention, the scheduled principal is subtracted from the balance before calculating the prepayment rate. (The SMM is defined mathematically in Equation D1 in Appendix D). For example, if the principal balance at the beginning of a month is $100, scheduled principal is $0.5, and total principal received is $1, then prepaid principal equals $0.5, and the SMM is $0.5 divided by ($100 − $0.5), or 0.5/99.5, which is 0.5025%.

Constant Prepayment Rate (CPR)   The CPR is the annualized version of the SMM; that is, it is the cumulative prepayment rate over 12 months given the same SMM each month. It is given by Equation D2 in Appendix D for small SMM (less than a few percent), the CPR is approximately 12 times the SMM.

Public Securities Association (PSA) Convention   The PSA benchmark curve was introduced in the mid-1980s to account for the seasoning (or aging) pattern typically observed with MBSs; new loans tend to have low prepayment rates, which gradually increase until the loans are seasoned. The PSA measurement convention adjusts the CPR for age, as shown in Exhibit 1.8. The base PSA curve, or 100% PSA, assumes the prepayment rate starts at 0% CPR at age 0 and increases by 0.2% CPR per month until month 30, after which the speed is a constant 6% CPR. A rate of 50% PSA means that the CPR in any month is half that implied by 100% PSA. A rate of 200% PSA means that the CPR in any month is twice that implied by 100% PSA, and so on. Formulae for converting from CPR to PSA, and vice versa, are given by Equations D3 and D4 in Appendix D. Prepayment speeds are rarely stated in SMMs. Instead, the speed is stated either in its annualized form (CPR), or in PSAs (which can be thought of as an age-adjusted CPR).

Which Is Preferable, CPRs or PSAs?   Investors should note that CPRs and PSAs are just different units for expressing a prepayment rate. Hence, provided we understand what the units are, it does not matter whether a given

EXHIBIT 1.8 The PSA Prepayment Convention

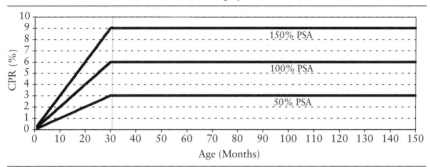

CPR: Constant prepayment rate.
Source: Salomon Smith Barney.

month's speed is stated as a CPR or as a PSA; both will translate into the same MBS cash flow.

The question becomes meaningful, however, if the loans are relatively new, and we are using actual speeds to assess likely future speeds. In this case, each method makes assumptions about the effect of age on speeds. The CPR in effect assumes no seasoning ramp: A CPR of 3% remains the same whether the loans are 10 months old or 100 months old. The PSA curve makes an explicit seasoning assumption: The speed is adjusted as if seasoning occurs at a linear rate over 30 months. Hence, a CPR of 3% at loan age 10 months is assumed to be equivalent to 9% CPR for loans more than 30 months old.

The PSA convention would be preferable if loan seasoning did take place as specified by the PSA ramp. However, while the PSA curve is based on historical data—average prepayment speeds on seasoned discount FHA loans have been around 6%, and mortgages in the past have seasoned over about 30 months—the data (the so-called FHA experience) is old, and seasoning patterns are now often quite different from the PSA assumption. For example, new premiums can prepay at rates of 30% CPR or more, which can translate into PSAs in the thousands. A PSA of 4,000% is clearly useless for assessing likely future speeds. However, a CPR of 1% on a new discount is equally lacking in predictive value.

To summarize, it does not matter whether CPRs or PSAs (or SMMs, for that matter) are used as prepayment measurement units. However, for new securities, we should be careful about extrapolating forward from actual CPRs or PSAs. For such securities, projected cash flows should be obtained

EXHIBIT 1.9 Ginnie Mae 6.5% Cash Flows with No Prepayments

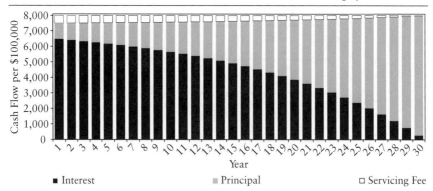

Source: Salomon Smith Barney.

using a vector of projected monthly speeds, with the projections incorporating the expected seasoning pattern of the MBS.[10]

The Effect of Prepayments on MBS Cash Flows

Exhibit 1.9 shows the cash flows from a new Ginnie Mae 6.5% in the (unlikely) case of zero prepayments; that is, all the underlying loans survive the full 30-year original term. Although the total monthly payment from the underlying loans is constant, the payment to the Ginnie Mae 6.5% holders is the total payment *minus* a servicing spread of 50bp; that is, the mortgagors pay a 7% coupon, while the Ginnie Mae investors receive a 6.5% coupon. Hence, the servicing amount is proportional to the remaining principal balance and declines as the remaining balance declines.

In practice, all MBSs will experience some prepayments. Exhibit 1.10 shows the Ginnie Mae 6.5% cash flows if prepayments occur at a constant rate of 100% PSA.

While actual speeds will vary from month to month, Exhibit 1.10 does give a good representation of the likely cash flow pattern from an MBS, with principal payments and total cash flows peaking and then declining over time, as the principal balance declines.

---

[10] Note that if a vector of monthly projections, such as the one generated by Salomon Smith Barney's prepayment model, is used to obtain projected MBS cash flows, the results will be the same whether the vector is stated in CPRs or PSAs.

EXHIBIT 1.10 Ginnie Mae 6.5% Cash Flows at a Constant Prepayment Rate of 100% PSA

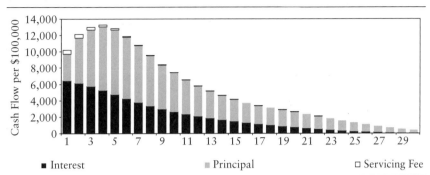

Source: Salomon Smith Barney.

A Brief Primer on Prepayment Analysis and Modeling

Prepayment projections are fundamental in valuing MBSs. We have published a comprehensive discussion of prepayment behavior in Chapter 4.[11] Here we briefly describe the main factors that influence prepayment rates.

Prepayments occur for several reasons, the most important of which are **home sales** and **refinancings.** Minor causes include **defaults,** which typically average less than 0.5% CPR, and **curtailments** or **partial prepayments,** referring to mortgagors' paying more than the scheduled payment each month to obtain a faster equity buildup. Like defaults, curtailments are typically low (less than 0.5% CPR), although some evidence exists that they are higher for very seasoned loans. When the loans are very seasoned and the remaining balance is small, some mortgagors may pay off their mortgage in full. (Full payoffs can also occur because of the destruction of the home from natural disasters such as hurricanes and earthquakes.)

Home Turnover The sale of a home in the United States typically leads to an attached mortgage being paid off.[12] Hence, prepayment rates on discount mortgages will depend on the turnover rate of existing homes. This rate has recently been running at around 7% per year, although the historical average

---

[11] See Chapter 4 for a detailed discussion of prepayments.

[12] The main exceptions are FHA and VA loans (the collateral for Ginnie Maes), which are assumable by the buyer of the house. However, except for new deep discount loans, few such mortgages are assumed, due to the expense of obtaining a second mortgage on top of the existing one.

is closer to 6%. Thus, 6% to 7% CPR can be considered an average overall baseline prepayment rate for discount mortgages. However, the prepayment rate for discounts will depend on several factors:

- Housing turnover rates will depend on mortgage rates and the general state of the economy. In addition, U.S. home sales have a pronounced seasonal pattern, with summer sales almost double those in the winter.
- Newer discount MBSs tend to have lower speeds than seasoned ones, because people typically do not change homes again soon after moving. The length of this **seasoning period** will depend on various factors, such as the difference between the current loan rate and prevailing rates, housing inflation and resulting equity buildup in the house, and loan type. FHA/VA loans are assumable, a characteristic that reduces the speeds on newer deep-discount Ginnie Maes and, in effect, lengthens the seasoning period.
- Because speeds on newer discounts will be much lower than on seasoned ones, speeds on seasoned discounts will be higher than the 6% to 7% average.
- Conventional (Freddie Mac/Fannie Mae) loans historically have somewhat higher turnover rates than FHA/VA (Ginnie Mae) loans, although the difference partly depends on the relative strengths of regional housing markets.[13]
- If a particular MBS has a concentration of loans in a particular geographic area (e.g., predominantly in California), speeds can vary from the average.
- As indicated earlier, defaults and curtailments can add 1% CPR or so to the prepayment rate.

Refinancings   Prepayments on premium coupons will consist of refinancings as well as housing turnover. Typically, refinancing rates tend to accelerate when mortgage rates drop about 100bp below the WAC on the loans, and to level out when the loans are several hundred basis points in the money, as further increases in refinancing incentive lead to little marginal increase in refinancing activity. Investors should note some other points regarding refinancing:

- Speeds on premium coupons exposed to refinancing opportunities for the first time can exceed 60% CPR. However, pools typically do not experience such high speeds for a sustained period of time. As the

---

[13] See Chapter 8.

mortgagors who are the most capable or anxious to refinance exit the pool, speeds typically slow down, a process known as **burnout**.

■ However, further drops in mortgage rates may temporarily cancel the effects of burnout, as we saw in 1992, 1993, and 1998. In fact, low levels of mortgage rates seem to cause a *media effect*, with publicity about low rates and proactive mortgage lenders spurring an extra degree of refinancing activity, even in burnt-out MBSs.

■ The seasoning period for premium coupons with ample refinancing incentive is very short. In 1993, for example, MBSs less than a year seasoned prepaid at more than 50% CPR.

■ In particular, loans originated with **no points** (so that the borrowers had little up-front expense when taking out the loan) tend to have almost no seasoning period. Such loans may be refinanced even when the incentive is minimal, as the borrower just goes from one no-point loan to another, incurring little expense in the process.

How Do We Project Speeds?   As this brief discussion indicates, projecting speeds is not a trivial task. Prepayment rates depend on a host of variables, such as interest rates and other economic factors; on borrower characteristics such as credit and demographics; and on mortgage characteristics such as coupon, loan age, type, previous exposure to refinancing opportunities, and so on. Recent actual speeds on a pool or a deal give some guidance, but may be misleading if interest rates have recently changed significantly.

Econometric prepayment models are the usual means now to estimate likely speeds in a given interest rate environment. The Salomon Smith Barney prepayment model[14] is one such model. It uses a number of variables, such as past and current interest rates, housing inflation, mortgage characteristics, and so on, to obtain prepayment projections. Exhibit 1.11 shows projections from Salomon Smith Barney's model for new **current coupon**[15] conventional pass-throughs for several projected interest rate levels.

■ At current rates, projected speeds will be due mostly to housing turnover, and increase for several years as the loans season.

---

[14] See Chapter 4. The model is available to investors through SSB's analytic system, Yield Book®.

[15] The current coupon refers to a pass-through priced at or close to par. For example, if 30-year mortgage rates are around 7%, then the typical WAC for newly issued pass-throughs will be around 7%. Assuming a servicing spread of about 50bp, this implies that 6.5% pass-throughs will be the current coupon.

EXHIBIT 1.11 Projected Monthly Prepayment Rates for a Conventional Current Coupon Pass-Through

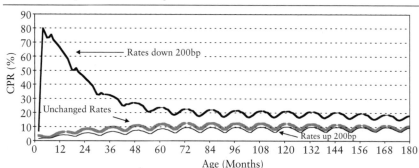

Source: Salomon Smith Barney.

- If rates drop by 200bp, speeds rise very sharply, peaking at close to 80% CPR, and then gradually decline over time because of burnout, as the most capable or able refinancers exit the pool.
- If rates rise by 200bp, speeds drop, as refinancings vanish and housing markets slow because of lower levels of affordability. The seasoning period of the pass-through lengthens, because the mortgagors, now holding a discount loan, have a disincentive to move. However, over time, speeds are projected to increase gradually, as housing markets adjust to higher rate levels and the pass-through becomes fully seasoned.

For practical purposes, the vector of monthly projections from the model is converted into a summary number, which is a weighted average of the monthly numbers, with more weight given to earlier speeds to reflect the higher, earlier balances.[16] Exhibit 1.12 shows one-year and long-term (life of security) projected CPRs for the current coupon pass-through for the three interest scenarios in Exhibit 1.12 and some additional scenarios.

The average speeds in Exhibit 1.12 reflect the same seasoning patterns that were shown in Exhibit 1.11. In the base case and in higher interest rate scenarios, projected speeds are lower in the short term (the next year) than in

---

[16] The convention used by Salomon Smith Barney is to calculate the single speed (either CPR or PSA) that gives the same *weighted average life* for the pass-through as the vector of monthly projections; this is termed the *WAL-equivalent* speed.

EXHIBIT 1.12 Projected One-Year and Long-Term CPRs for a Current-Coupon Pass-Through

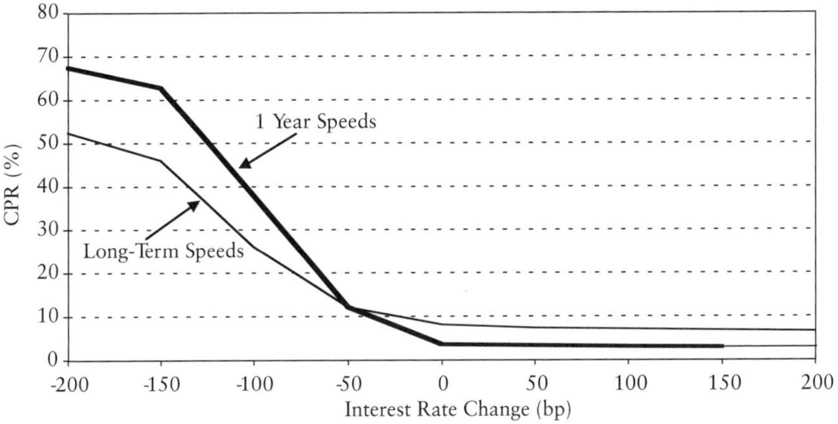

CPR: Constant prepayment rate.
Source: Salomon Smith Barney.

the long term. This reflects the increase in speeds over time due to turnover seasoning illustrated in the base and +200bp scenarios in Exhibit 1.11

If interest rates decline by 100bp or more, the loans become highly refinanceable, and this leads speeds to spike sharply. However, because rates are assumed to stabilize after the initial drop, *burnout* causes refinancing activity to decline over time, and thus, short-term speeds are faster than long-term ones.

Exhibit 1.11 also illustrates the distinctive S-curve that characterizes prepayment rates as a function of the economic incentive to refinance (i.e., the amount the coupon is *in the money*). Note that the S-curve is reversed in Exhibit 1.12 because the refinancing incentive increases as rates decline. For discounts (corresponding to unchanged or higher rates in Exhibit 1.11), speeds depend mostly on housing turnover, which (over longer periods of time) is relatively insensitive to interest rates; hence the S-curve is relatively flat for unchanged and higher rates. If interest rates decline, however, and the coupon becomes a premium, speeds accelerate sharply. As rates keep falling, the S-curve starts to flatten again, as the coupon is now well in the money and further increases in the refinancing incentive lead only to marginal increases in refinancing activity.

Yield, Average Life, and Spread over Treasuries

Given a prepayment projection, we can calculate an MBS's cash flows using standard formulae (see Appendix B). From the cash flows and a price, standard bond mathematics gives us the yield.

For U.S. fixed-income securities, the Treasury market is often used as a benchmark, and bond yields are typically quoted as a spread to a comparable Treasury. For MBSs, which return principal not in one lump sum (or *bullet payment*) but in uncertain monthly increments, the definition of a "comparable" Treasury is not transparent. The convention in the market is to compare MBSs to Treasuries with a maturity close to the Weighted Average Life (**WAL**) of the MBS. The WAL is defined as the average time that a dollar of principal is outstanding; it is calculated by multiplying the proportion of principal received at time t by t, and then summing over t (see Equation A6 in Appendix A). Exhibit 1.13 shows traditional bond analysis applied to TBA Ginnie Mae 6.5% pass-throughs.

It can be seen that both the yield and the WAL (and hence, the comparable Treasury) depend on the projected prepayment rate, which in turn depend on interest rate levels. Therefore, it is advisable to examine such measures over a range of interest rate scenarios. Exhibit 1.14 shows projected speeds, yields, and WALs for the Ginnie Mae 6.5% for parallel yield curve shifts of 100bp up and down, as well as the base case.

The results in Exhibit 1.14 illustrate both the usefulness and the shortcomings of static analysis when applied to MBSs. The analysis is useful for getting a sense of the shortening and extension of the MBS as rates change. For example, if rates drop 100bp, the Ginnie Mae 6.5% becomes a premium, prepayments surge, and the WAL shortens from 9.4 years to 3.2 years. Conversely, if rates increase 100bp, speeds slow slightly, and the WAL extends to 10.4 years. Note the asymmetry of the response, with a much

EXHIBIT 1.13   Traditional Analysis of TBA Ginnie Mae 6.5s

Price: 100-24, Assumed WAM: 29-08 Yrs., WALA: 2 months	
Projected Long-Term Speed	7.6% CPR
Yield @ Projected Speed	6.42%
WAL @ Projected Speed	9.4 Yrs.
Yield of WAL (9.4 yr) Treasury	4.90%
Spread over WAL Treasury	152bp

WAL: Weighted-average life, WALA: Weighted average loan age, WAM: Weighted-average maturity.
Source: Salomon Smith Barney.

EXHIBIT 1.14   Scenario Analysis for a Ginnie Mae 6.5% Pass-Through (WAC: 7.00%, WAM: 29-08 Years, Price: 100–75)

	Interest Rate Moves (bp)		
	-100 bp	**0 bp**	**100 bp**
Proj. LT CPR	25.7%	7.6%	6.7%
WAL	3.2 Yrs.	9.4 Yrs.	10.4 Yrs.
Yield	6.19%	6.42%	6.44%
WAL Treasury Yield	3.78%	4.90%	5.91%
Spread/WAL Treasury	241 bp	142 bp	53 bp

Initial Yield Curve	**1 Yr.**	**2 Yr.**	**3 Yr.**	**5 Yr.**	**10 Yr.**	**30 Yr.**
	4.63 %	4.77 %	4.78 %	4.79 %	4.91 %	5.35 %

bp: Basis points, CPR: Constant prepayment rate, LT: Long term, WAC: Weighted-average coupon, WAM: Weighted-average maturity, WAL: Weighted-average life.
Note: Interest rates are assumed to change instantaneously in parallel by the stated amount and then remain stable.
Source: Salomon Smith Barney.

bigger change in WAL if rates drop than if rates increase. This illustrates the fact that the Ginnie Mae 6.5%, because it is close to par and not subject to any significant refinancings at current rate levels, is at the lower end of the prepayment S-curve shown in Exhibit 1.12. Thus, if rates drop 100bp, the projected speed quickly climbs up the cusp of the S-curve; however, in the other direction, there is only a mild decline in speeds along the flat part of the S-curve. This indication of the WAL sensitivity with respect to prepayments can be especially useful for structured mortgage securities such as CMOs (described in Part Five), because it may not be obvious otherwise for complex structures.

However, scenario analysis has serious shortcomings for valuation analysis. In Exhibit 1.14, the yield of the MBS declines slightly as rates drop 100bp, because the security is priced slightly above par. However, because its WAL has shortened and the WAL Treasury has also dropped 100bp, the spread over the WAL Treasury has increased, to 241bp. This apparently strong performance versus Treasuries is misleading, of course; the high prepayments on the MBS have to be reinvested at lower prevailing rates. In addition, receiving principal back at par is a negative for the investor, because the MBS was priced above par. This problem would be more serious for a higher coupon priced well above par.

We describe a sounder methodology to estimate the impact of interest rate and prepayment variations in the next section.

1.4 OPTION-ADJUSTED ANALYSIS OF MORTGAGE SECURITIES

...The race is not to the swift, nor the battle to the strong, neither yet bread to the wise, nor yet riches to men of understanding, nor yet favor to men of skill; but time and chance happeneth to them all.

Ecclesiastes 9:11

Traditional bond analysis has serious limitations when applied to MBSs (or indeed any other type of callable bond). Among these limitations are:

- The **yield spread,** the standard measure of incremental return over a benchmark Treasury, compares an MBS to a single, somewhat arbitrarily chosen point on the yield curve. Because an MBS returns principal over a period of time, rather than in one lump sum, it would be preferable to compare it to an appropriate portfolio of Treasuries.
- MBS cash flows vary with interest rates, typically in a manner adverse to the MBS holder. The cost of such prepayment variation needs to be incorporated in any measure of the MBS's return relative to Treasuries.

In the mid-1980s, Salomon Brothers pioneered the development of option-adjusted analysis for MBSs.[17] This approach has since become widely used to analyze MBSs and other callable bonds. Here we give a brief description of the methodology and its application to MBSs.

Yield Curve Spread

Developing a more accurate static measure of incremental return over Treasuries—improving on the yield spread—is straightforward. Let us go back to the Ginnie Mae 6.5% example illustrated in Exhibits 1.13 and 1.14. In the base case, given the projected speed, the yield of the Ginnie Mae 6.5% was 6.43%, its WAL was 9.4 years, the interpolated 9.4-year Treasury yield was 4.90%, and hence, the Ginnie Mae 6.5's spread to its WAL Treasury was 142bp.

This analysis can be interpreted as assuming that the Ginnie Mae 6.5% returns all its principal after 9.4 years (i.e., it is a 9.4-year bullet security), and thus, the appropriate discount rate is the 9.4-year Treasury plus a spread (in this case, 142bp). Rather than making this assumption, we can

---

[17] See *Evaluating the Option Features of Mortgage Securities: The Salomon Brothers Mortgage Pricing Model,* Salomon Brothers Inc., 1986.

discount each cash flow from the Ginnie Mae 6.5% by an appropriate Treasury rate plus a spread. For example, the cash flow in month 64 can be discounted by the 64-month Treasury zero rate plus a spread. Instead of zero rates, we could use forward rates. If $f_1, f_2, \ldots$ are the one-month forward rates (based on the current yield curve) for months 1, 2, . . ., then for a given spread s the discount rate for month n is

$$\mathrm{DIS}(n, s) = \frac{1}{\left[(1+f_1+s)(1+f_2+s)\ldots(1+f_n+s)\right]} \qquad (1.1)$$

Hence, if CF(1), CF(2), . . . are the projected cash flows from the Ginnie Mae 6.5%, then their present value is

$$\mathrm{PV}(s) = C(1) \times \mathrm{DIS}(1,\ s) + \mathrm{CF}(2) \times \mathrm{DIS}(2, s) + \ldots \qquad (1.2)$$

The value of s that makes the present value PV(s) equal to the market price is the solution of

$$\mathrm{Price} = \mathrm{PV}(s) \qquad (1.3)$$

and is defined as the **yield curve spread (YCS)**.[18] In concept, it is similar to the standard spread over Treasuries, but it is clearly a more accurate measure of incremental return over Treasuries for securities that return principal not in one lump sum but over many periods. Rather than calculating the incremental return over a single Treasury, the YCS gives it relative to a portfolio of Treasuries chosen according to the timing of the MBS's cash flows.

For a flattish yield curve, the YCS and the spread/WAL will tend to be very close to each other. In general, the relationship between the YCS and the spread/WAL will depend on the shape of the yield curve and the dispersion of the MBS's cash flows. For the current mildly upward sloping yield curve, intermediate and longer forward rates are much higher than spot rates; hence, the YCS is lower than the spread/WAL for longer MBSs, such as discount pass-throughs, while it is about the same or slightly higher than the spread/WAL for shorter-average-life securities.

---

[18] Other names for the yield curve spread include yield curve margin and zero-volatility OAS.

Option-Adjusted Spread

The yield curve spread, while an improvement over the standard yield spread, is still a static measure; that is, it assumes that interest rates and cash flows remain unchanged. Of course, such an assumption is at variance with reality. Interest rates and prepayment speeds will vary over time in an uncertain manner.

In general, the MBS investor suffers a cost as a result of this variation. We can think of this cost as the value of the embedded option in the MBS resulting from the mortgagors' ability to prepay their loans at any time. However, it is a complicated effect, with several factors at work, and standard option pricing theory can be of limited use:

- The strongest factor is typically **reinvestment risk.** Prepayment speeds tend to increase when interest rates decline, so that the investor has to reinvest an increased amount of prepaid principal at lower prevailing rates. Conversely, if interest rates increase, prepayments will decline, reducing the cash flow that the investor can reinvest at prevailing higher rates.

- Changes in prepayments change the time until each dollar of principal is returned. Thus, for example, for MBSs priced at a deep discount, if there is a decline in interest rates and a corresponding pickup in speeds, the benefit of earlier return of principal at par may mitigate or even outweigh reinvestment risk. An example is provided by POs, which typically benefit from interest rate and prepayment volatility.

- The impact of typical prepayment patterns is often quite different from that implied by option valuation theory. For example, if speeds on a high premium security have reached an upper plateau, volatility can be a benefit, because speeds cannot increase much but can decline significantly; very high coupon IOs can provide an example. In addition, note that no matter how out of the money mortgage loans are, there will always be some prepayments, because of home sales.

How do we incorporate interest rate (and hence, prepayment) volatility in the valuation of MBSs? For a *given* path of interest rates and a *given* spread *s*, the projected value of the MBS is given by Equation 1.2. Financial theory tells us that the value of a stream of contingent cash flows is (under certain conditions) the expected present value of the cash flow stream. Hence, with PV(*s*) defined as in Equation 1.2,

$$\text{Value of MBS} = \frac{\text{Average value of PV}(s) \text{ over}}{\text{all possible interest rate paths}} \quad (1.4)$$

$$= \text{AVGPV}(s)$$

The option-adjusted spread (OAS) is defined as the value of s in Equation 2.4 that makes the value of the MBS equal to its market price; that is, it is the solution of

$$\text{Price} = \text{AVGPV}(s) \qquad (1.5)$$

Thus, conceptually, the OAS is a straightforward extension of the traditional yield spread over Treasuries. We start by replacing a single Treasury discount rate by a series of forward rates to determine the YCS and then factor in the effect of volatility by calculating this spread over the spectrum of possible future interest rates. However, the actual calculation of the OAS involves some complicated steps, as we discuss next.

Interest Rate Volatility and Calculation of OAS

To calculate the expected value over future interest rate paths, a **term structure model** is needed to describe the evolution of interest rates over time.[19] Such a model must be consistent with today's yield curve (this typically means that the set of benchmark Treasuries must be fairly priced under the model—they must have zero OASs), and it should generate interest rate paths that are internally consistent (that do not lead to arbitrage opportunities) as well as consistent with historical interest rate behavior.

A **one-factor** model has just one random factor that shocks the yield curve each period; hence, such a model assumes that different interest rates are perfectly correlated. A **two-factor** term structure model, such as the Salomon Smith Barney model, avoids this unrealistic assumption and is preferable, leading to more realistic simulated interest rate paths. In addition, Salomon Smith Barney's model includes another desirable characteristic of term structure models, namely **mean reversion**. This property prevents simulated rate paths from going to levels, such as more than 100%, that seem unlikely for a stable country such as the United States.[20]

Volatility   An important element in the term structure model is the specification of volatilities. A good model should give different volatilities for different maturity rates. For example, three-month Treasury yields tend to be more volatile than 10-year Treasury yields, and the interest rate paths generated by the term structure model should reflect this. A term structure

---

[19] More precisely, the model describes the evolution of the term structure of interest rates, hence, the name given to such models.

[20] For a more detailed description of Salomon Smith Barney's two-factor term structure model, see Chapter 13.

model that has different volatilities for different maturity interest rates is said to incorporate a **term structure of volatility.**

Two different sources of volatility inputs are, (1) empirical volatilities calculated from historical interest rates, and (2) the options markets. In the first case, the parameters within the term structure model are adjusted so that simulated interest rate paths display specified volatilities. The second method uses implied volatilities from the options markets. In this case, the model parameters are chosen so that the model reprices a chosen set of option instruments. Both methods provide useful insight into MBS value.

Calculation of OAS   Simulation is used to evaluate the expected value in Equation 1.5. The steps are as follows:

1. Using computer generated pseudorandom numbers and the term structure model, hundreds of hypothetical interest rate paths are simulated, including short-term rates for discounting and longer term rates that are important for prepayment analysis.
2. On each interest rate path the prepayment model is used to project prepayment rates and, hence, the MBS's cash flows.
3. For each path, the present value of the cash flows is calculated using Equation 1.2, with the discount rates being the short-term forward rates along that path plus a specified spread s. The average of these present values gives us an estimate for the AVGPV(s) term in Equation 1.4.

To find the OAS corresponding to a given market price, we start with an initial estimate for the OAS and use iteration to solve Equation 1.5. That is, we start with an initial spread s, calculate AVGPV(s), and keep adjusting s until AVGPV(s) equals the market price (within a given tolerance). Conversely, we can use Equation 1.5 to find the theoretical price corresponding to a given OAS.

Option Costs and Interpretation of OAS

Exhibit 1.15 shows a portion of a daily Salomon Smith Barney report,[21] illustrating a typical example of OAS analysis.

---

[21] For readers who have access to the Yield Book® and SSB Direct, the report is on the manifold system as MB713.

EXHIBIT 1.15   OASs for Ginnie Mae Pass-Throughs

Coupon	WAM	Price	Proj. LT CPR	Yield	WAL	Spread/ WAL	YCS	OAS	Option Cost
6.0%	29-10	98-17	5.3%	6.24%	11.4 Yrs	130 bp	110 bp	70 bp	40 bp
6.5	29-08	100-23	7.5	6.42	9.5	153	134	75	59
7.0	28-04	102-10	12.6	6.51	6.5	166	153	78	75
7.5	28-02	103-10	20.3	6.42	4.2	160	161	85	76
8.0	28-01	104-10	23.4	6.41	3.6	160	167	105	62
8.5	28-00	106-02	23.3	6.33	3.7	152	158	108	50

bp: Basis points, CPR: Constant prepayment rate, LT: Long term, OAS: Option-adjusted spread, WAL: Weighted-average life, YCS: Yield curve spread.
Note: Prices and Treasury rates as of the close of February 11, 1999, using market volatilities.
Source: Salomon Smith Barney.

The option cost is the difference between the zero volatility OAS (the YCS) and the OAS. It is a measure of the cost to the investor of volatility in interest rates and, hence, in prepayments. Thus, for the Ginnie Mae 6%, the YCS is 110bp, the OAS is 70bp, and, hence, the option cost is 40bp. The Ginnie Mae 6% is a discount. Thus, it has some degree of call protection (the option is out of the money), and the option cost is lower than for higher coupons. For the Ginnie Mae 7.5%, in comparison, the option cost is much higher, at 76bp; the Ginnie Mae 7.5% is a premium and on the "cuspy" part of the prepayment curve. Therefore, small interest rate changes can lead to sharp prepayment speed changes.

As shown in Exhibit 1.1, as the coupon increases, the option cost eventually starts to decline, even though, theoretically, the coupons are becoming deeper and deeper in the money. This illustrates the complex and multidimensional nature of prepayment behavior. The critical element is not the amount that the coupon is in the money, but the sensitivity of speeds to interest rate changes (or the slope of the prepayment curve). Recall that prepayment speeds, as a function of the coupon, resemble an "S" curve—they tend to be flat for discount coupons, increase sharply as the coupon becomes a premium, and then level out at very high premiums. Therefore, speeds on high premiums, like those on discounts, tend to be less affected by small interest rate changes than speeds on cuspy coupons.

What Does the OAS Represent and How Should It Be Used?   In the relatively short time since its development, OAS analysis has become an essential tool for MBS investors. Its widespread acceptance indicates that most investors are well aware of the optionality inherent in MBSs. However, while OASs are a critical component in analyzing MBSs, investors should be aware of their limitations and of the many assumptions that go into an OAS calculation.

The OAS has been derived here as an extension of the standard spread over Treasuries, to account for the dispersion and uncertainty associated with the return of principal from MBSs. Can it be realized as a return over Treasuries? Theoretically, with dynamic hedging, the answer is yes, *provided all the assumptions in the model (for term structure movements, prepayments, volatility, etc.) hold true.*[22]

From a practical point of view, it is perhaps best to think of the OAS playing the same role for MBSs (and other callable bonds) as the standard spread does for noncallable bullet bonds; that is, it acts as a useful measure of relative value, allowing an assessment of an MBS's value relative both to other MBSs and to its own past levels. In fact, various studies have shown that, applied consistently over time, OASs can be good indicators of cheap or rich MBSs.[23] However, while the OAS can act as an initial filter in identifying seemingly rich or cheap securities, it is a single, summary number and investors should supplement it with other analyses such as holding-period returns to obtain a more complete risk/reward profile of the security.

Assumptions in OAS Models   Although widely used, market participants maintain some skepticism about OASs. Much of this skepticism derives from the often wide differences in OASs produced for the same securities by different firms' models. However, given the steps involved in the OAS calculation, it would be surprising if such disparities did *not* occur. Recall that the two main steps are:

1. Generating a set of interest rate paths.
2. Projecting prepayment rates along each such path.

The first step involves using a term structure model and making a set of volatility assumptions. No consensus exists as to the correct term structure or volatility model, and thus, it is natural that models differ. Similarly, it goes without saying that prepayment projections, which involve assumptions about future demographic trends, housing markets, and economic conditions, will differ from model to model.

Given that it is inevitable that different models will produce different numbers, investors should become comfortable with one or two well-formulated and consistent models—in particular, understanding key assumptions—and use these models.

---

[22] This is discussed in more detail in Chapter 13.

[23] For example, see *Using OAS to Enhance Mortgage Portfolio Returns,* Salomon Brothers Inc., April 1989.

Effective Duration

Standard duration measures, such as Macaulay or modified, can be misleading for MBSs, because of the dependence of MBS cash flows on interest rates. OAS methods provide a more useful measure, generally known as *effective duration*.

The standard formula to calculate effective duration is given by Equation A9 in Appendix A. Effective duration is defined as the percentage price change for a 100-basis point parallel change in yields, assuming the OAS remains unchanged. The calculation is illustrated in Exhibit 1.16 for a Ginnie Mae 7.5%.

As interest rates change, the usual impact of changing discount rates on fixed-income securities tends to be reduced in the case of mortgage securities by changes in prepayments. This effect is most pronounced for cuspy premiums. As interest rates decline, the positive effect of lower discount rates is partly balanced by the negative effect of higher prepayment speeds, resulting in a smaller price increase. Conversely, if rates rise, declines in speeds can mitigate the discount-rate-related price decline. The net effect is that the effective duration is lower than the modified duration for prepayment-sensitive securities. In the case of the Ginnie Mae 7.5% shown in Exhibit 1.16, the modified duration is about 3 years, compared with the effective duration of 1.8 years. IOs represent an extreme case for which the effect of prepayment changes overwhelm the discount rate effect, leading to negative durations. However, deep discounts and seasoned high premiums may have similar effective and modified durations, because speeds on these coupons change little for a small change in interest rates.

EXHIBIT 1.16   Calculation of Effective Duration for a Ginnie Mae 7.5% Pass-Through

1) Current price = 103-10	⟶ OAS = 85bp
2) Interest rates move down 50bp in parallel: OAS = 85bp	⟶ Price = 103.93
3) Interest rates move up 50bp in parallel: OAS = 85bp	⟶ Price = 102.08
4) Effective Duration = pct. price change per 100bp change in yields	

$$= 100 \times (103.93 - 102.08) / 103.31$$

$$\cong 1.8$$

bp: Basis points, OAS: Option-adjusted spread.
Note: Based on closing prices and market volumes as of February 11, 1999.
Source: Salomon Smith Barney Inc.

Effective Durations and Market Price Moves Market price moves for MBSs often differ from those predicted by effective durations, even for good OAS models. This should not be surprising, given the assumptions used in calculating effective durations. Major assumptions include:

- Constant OAS
- Parallel yield curve shifts
- No change in other relevant factors, such as mortgage rate to Treasury spreads and volatilities
- Symmetric price changes

These assumptions rarely hold in practice, leading to deviations between effective and empirical durations.[24] Furthermore, interest rate changes can lead to substantial shifts in a particular MBS's effective duration. For example, the effective duration of a conventional 6.5%, the current coupon at the time of writing, is projected to drop from about four to about one if interest rates decline by 100bp (other things being equal). However, over a longer period of time, as deviations from assumptions average out, effective durations from a good OAS model should track empirical durations.[25]

Convexity

As with duration, OAS methodology leads to more meaningful convexity estimates for MBSs than traditional measures. The formula used to calculate convexity for MBSs is given by Equation A10 in Appendix A. As with the effective duration calculation, price changes are calculated assuming parallel yield curve shifts and a constant OAS, with the convexity calculated by comparing the relative price change in up-rate moves with that in down-rate moves.

Noncallable bonds have positive convexity; that is, the percentage price increase if interest rates decline is greater than the percentage price decline if rates increase by the same (small) amount. In other words, if the price is plotted against various interest rates, the curve will be convex. For MBSs, convexity is often negative, because rising prepayment rates dampen the price increase in declining rate scenarios. Exhibit 1.17 plots projected prices, effective durations and convexities for a conventional 6.5% for various interest rate levels.

---

[24] Empirical durations refer to those calculated from market price changes.
[25] A detailed discussion of this topic is given in Chapter 14.

EXHIBIT 1.17 Conventional 6.5s—Projected Speeds, Prices, Durations, and Convexities for Various Interest Rate Changes

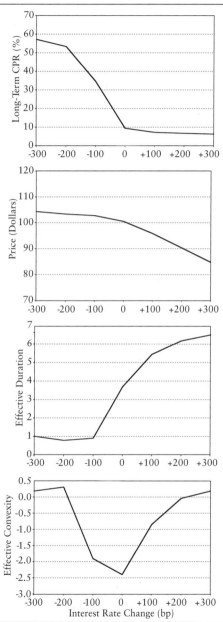

Source: Salomon Smith Barney.

As interest rates drop, prepayments on the conventional 6.5s accelerate, leading to a slowdown in price appreciation, which is reflected as a decline in duration. This decline in turn is reflected in the negative convexity of the bond. As rates keep dropping and projected speeds on the 6.5s level off, the duration and the convexity start to increase. In fact, for a 200bp drop, the convexity becomes positive; the 6.5% is a high premium, speeds have leveled off, and it assumes some of the characteristics of a short fixed-cash-flow bond.

If interest rates increase, prepayments on the 6.5% slow down and become less sensitive to rate change. As a result, the duration and convexity both increase, with the convexity again eventually becoming positive.

What Does Negative Convexity Mean for Investors?   Convexity is a method to estimate the impact of prepayment variation on the likely price appreciation of an MBS. For an MBS, negative convexity dampens the price appreciation if interest rates fall. Thus, even though the MBS may have significantly higher returns than a comparable Treasury under unchanged rates, it may underperform the Treasury if rates drop.

However, subject to the assumptions in the model, the OAS incorporates the impact of prepayment volatility and, hence, of negative convexity. Does this mean that two bonds with the same OAS should be treated the same, even if one has much more negative convexity than the other? To some extent, yes, because presumably the MBS with the greater negative convexity had a higher nominal yield, in order to arrive at the same OAS. However, to the extent that reality deviates from the assumptions in the OAS model and given that it is difficult to dynamically hedge the MBS so as to fully realize the OAS, higher negative convexity does imply a greater degree of uncertainty about the OAS. This observation reinforces the point made earlier, that investors should supplement OAS with scenario and holding period analysis to obtain a more complete risk/reward profile for the MBS, as well as stress-testing the results by changing some of the assumptions (e.g., refinancing sensitivity) in the model.

1.5 STRUCTURED MORTGAGE-BACKED SECURITIES

Despite the dramatic growth of the mortgage pass-through market, the cash-flow characteristics of pass-throughs did not meet the needs of some institutional investors. To broaden the range of potential investors, structured mortgage-backed instruments with a variety of maturity and prepayment profiles have been created out of basic mortgage cash flows.

EXHIBIT 1.18 CMO Issuance, 1983–1999

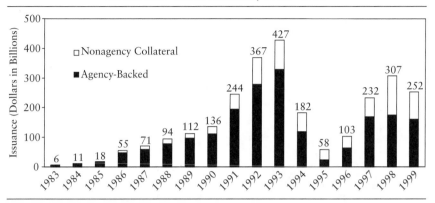

Source: Inside Mortgage Finance Publications, Salomon Smith Barney.

A landmark in the development of the MBS market occurred in June 1983, when Freddie Mac issued the first CMO. Since then, the CMO market has grown rapidly, and as of year-end 1998, more than $2.3 trillion of CMOs have been brought to market by Freddie Mac and Fannie Mae, investment banks, mortgage bankers, thrifts, home builders, insurance companies, and commercial banks (see Exhibit 1.18). In recent years, the majority of CMOs have been issued under the Fannie Mae and Freddie Mac name.[26]

Development of the CMO Market

CMOs comprise a number of classes of bonds issued against specified mortgage collateral. The collateral can be agency pass-through pools, whole loans (typically, nonconforming loans), or classes from other CMO deals (termed Re-REMICs). Early CMO structures, which typically had three or four classes, illustrate well the basic CMO principle. Exhibit 1.19 shows a hypothetical CMO with four classes labeled A, B, C, and D. These classes, or *tranches*, are retired sequentially. All principal payments are directed first to the bonds with the shortest maturity, the class A bonds. When the A bonds are retired, the principal payments are directed to the bonds with the next shortest maturity, the class B bonds. The process

---

[26] The term real estate mortgage investment conduit (REMIC) is often used synonymously with CMOs. The Tax Reform Act of 1986 allowed CMOs to be issued in the form of REMICs, which have certain tax and accounting advantages for the issuer. Most CMOs are issued now as REMICs.

EXHIBIT 1.19 Principal Payments to CMO Bonds with a Four-Class
Sequential Structure

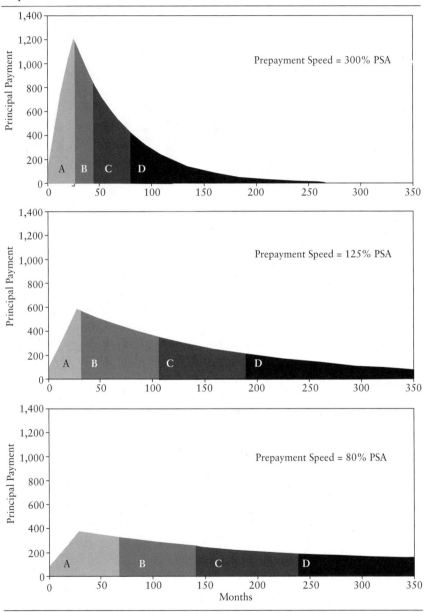

Source: Salomon Smith Barney.

continues until all of the bond classes have been paid off. The allocation of cash flows from a pool of mortgages among the classes of this type of CMO is illustrated in Exhibit 1.19 at several different prepayment rates.

The CMO structure shown in Exhibit 1.19 creates short-, intermediate-, and long-term MBSs from the underlying collateral, giving investors a choice of maturities. Class A remains a relatively short-term security even if prepayment speeds slow down, while the later classes obtain a degree of call protection because the earlier classes act as a buffer against prepayments.

In addition to more choice in maturity characteristics, several other factors played a role in the expansion of the CMO market:

- The size of typical CMO deals means that monthly speeds are less erratic than for a typical pass-through pool. CMO deals are typically collateralized by several hundred pools, which leads to geographical diversification in the underlying loans as well as a reduction in the degree of "noise" in monthly prepayments.
- Agency CMOs offer the same high credit quality as corresponding agency pass-throughs.
- CMO classes often offer attractive yields relative to other comparable credit quality fixed-income instruments.

Another major factor in the expansion of the CMO market is the development of numerous CMO bond types, catering to different investor needs—in essence, customizing mortgage cash flows.

CMO Bond Types

The classes in the hypothetical CMO deal shown in Exhibit 1.19 is usually labeled **sequential** bonds, for the obvious reason that principal is allocated sequentially to the classes. A detailed description of the structure of MBS is given in Chapter 15, and a glossary of standard agency definitions of the many different bond types developed over the years is given in Appendix B. Here, we provide a brief description of the main types.

Accrual or Z-Bonds The Z-bond was the first departure from standard sequential bonds. As the name implies, Z-bonds receive no interest until their principal payment window starts. Instead, the interest due is accrued and added to the Z-bond's principal balance, which, as a result, increases until earlier classes are retired, and collateral cash flows are directed toward making interest and principal payments to the Z-bond. The Z-bond was typically the last bond in a CMO deal, although in recent years many deals placed Z-bonds earlier in the structure.

A Z-bond has a beneficial effect on the cash flow stability of earlier bonds, because the interest that should have been paid to the Z-bond is used to pay down the other bonds. Hence, if prepayment speeds slow, the growing balance on the Z-bond and the increasing amount of Z-bond interest available for paying down the other bonds can partially balance the effect of slower collateral principal payments.

PACs, TACs, and Companions Planned amortization class (PAC) bonds are perhaps the most important innovation in the CMO market to date. First issued in 1986, PAC bonds and their various offshoots have dominated CMO issuance since early 1989. Because of their central role in the CMO market, PACs will be discussed in somewhat more detail here than other CMO bond types.

PACs expand on the basic rationale behind CMO bonds. Whereas the early CMO bonds used sequential segmentation of principal to offer investors a better defined maturity profile than pass-throughs, PAC bonds go further and essentially remove maturity uncertainty *provided prepayments stay within a given range.* A PAC bond is characterized by a specified principal payment schedule (much like a sinking fund on a corporate bond). In allocating principal paydowns from the collateral to the CMO bonds, priority is given to meeting the PAC principal schedule; thus, other bonds in the deal, termed **support** or **companion** bonds, for obvious reasons, absorb prepayment variations as much as possible. As might be expected, companion bonds typically have a high degree of WAL sensitivity to prepayment changes and tend to be priced at higher yields as compensation.

A PAC bond's degree of prepayment protection is typically characterized by a **PAC band,** such as 100% to 300% PSA. The PAC's principal payment schedule is derived by taking the minimum of the collateral principal payments at two constant speeds (in this example 100% PSA and 300% PSA), as shown Exhibit 1.20; these two speeds will constitute the PAC band. The shaded area in Exhibit 1.20 represents the maximum available principal paydown schedule for the specified PAC band. The PAC's payment schedule will be met as long as the collateral prepays at a *constant* prepayment rate that is within the stated PAC band. The schedule may not be met if speeds vary over time, even if they stay within the PAC band.

Offshoots of PAC bonds include **Targeted Amortization Class (TAC)** bonds, **reverse TACs, PAC Is, PAC IIs,** and so on. TAC bonds are in essence one-sided PACs; they provide a degree of call protection if prepayment speeds increase from pricing assumptions. Reverse TACs, as the name implies, provide protection against a slowdown in speeds. PAC Is, PAC IIs, and so on are PAC bonds with progressively narrower PAC bands than standard PAC bonds.

EXHIBIT 1.20 Creating a PAC Principal Payment Schedule with a PAC Band of 100%–300% PSA

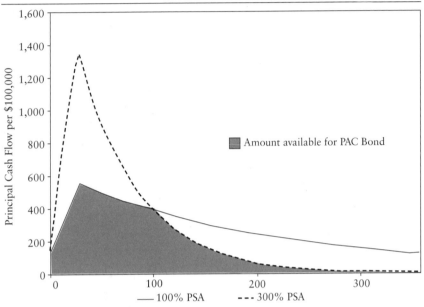

PAC: Planned amortization class.
Source: Salomon Smith Barney.

A more detailed analysis of PAC structures is given elsewhere.[27] Some general rules should be kept in mind:

■ PAC bonds typically have more call risk than extension risk. The lower PAC band—typically 80% to 100% PSA for conventional collateral and lower for Ginnie Maes—is unlikely to be broken to any appreciable degree, because normal housing turnover implies that average speeds are unlikely to fall below the lower PAC band for any length of time. However, if interest rates drop, speeds may well exceed the upper band (typically in the 250%–400% PSA), especially for coupons exposed to refinancing opportunities for the first time.

---

[27] For example, see "Anatomy of PAC Bonds," Michael Bykhovsky and Lakhbir Hayre, *Journal of Fixed Income*, June 1992, and Chapter 15.

■ As prepayments vary from the pricing speed and support bonds are paid down at rates different from initial pricing assumptions, the effective PAC bands will change, a phenomenon known as *PAC band drift.* This drift is typically small and gradual, with the lower and the upper bands rising. However, the effect does emphasize that it is essential to evaluate PAC (and other CMO) bonds using a vector of monthly projections rather than a single (or scalar) projected CPR or PSA.

■ In most cases, short-term PACs (WALs less than two to three years) have low prepayment uncertainty. Even if prepayment speeds pick up significantly, the companion classes will still be there to absorb the extra principal payments.

It is difficult to make general statements about PACs (or other CMO bonds). Much depends on the collateral and its prepayment profile as interest rates change. Also important is the structure of the CMO—-for example, the amount of support classes remaining in the deal. Although CMO bonds are typically priced at a spread over a benchmark Treasury, OAS analysis is critical in evaluating the effect of changing interest rates and prepayments on a particular CMO structure.[28]

Floating-Rate Bonds   Floating CMO bonds were first issued in September 1986. The coupons typically reset monthly at a stated spread over an index (LIBOR being the most common) subject to a cap on the coupon. Floating-rate CMOs appeal to many European and Japanese investors, as well as U.S. commercial banks and thrifts.

The cap on floating CMO bonds is typically higher than the coupon on the fixed-rate collateral, because a low cap would diminish the floater's appeal to investors. In structuring such bonds, it is necessary to ensure that the coupon income from the collateral is sufficient to make the coupon payments on the floaters for any combination of the index and prepayment rates.

The usual solution is to pair the floater with an **inverse floater,** which pays down simultaneously with the floater. As suggested by the name, the coupon on the inverse floater moves inversely with the index, such that the combination of the floater and the inverse floater is a fixed-rate bond with a coupon equal to or less than the collateral coupon. This constraint still

---

[28] Also useful is a technique called **distribution analysis,** which involves examining WALs and other bond characteristics over the hundreds of paths used to calculate OASs, for example, examining the WAL stability of a PAC bond over varied and realistic interest rate paths. A description of distributional analysis is given in "Anatomy of PAC Bonds." SSB's Yield Book®, allows distributional analysis for CMOs.

allows a fair degree of flexibility in the structuring of the bonds. For example, if we issue $80 million of the floater and $20 million of the inverse, it is not difficult to see that for every basis point increase in the index (and, hence, in the floater coupon), the coupon on the inverse has to decline by a factor of 80/20, or four. This number is termed the **multiplier** or **leverage** of the inverse floater coupon. Alternatively, we could issue $66.67 million of the floater and $33.33 million of the inverse floaters, in which case the inverse floater would have a multiplier of two.[29] Floaters can be structured, in terms of principal paydown types, as sequential-pay bonds, PACs, TACs, companions, and so on.

Conceptually, CMO floaters are straightforward extensions of standard floating-rate bonds, with prepayment variability adding a new dimension. OAS methodology provides a means of estimating the net combined effect of the cap and of prepayment variations. Typically, CMO floaters offer cap- and prepayment-adjusted returns superior to those of similar credit quality standard floaters.

Inverse floaters are an unusual type of instrument. Properly used, they provide a unique means of reducing the interest rate exposure of a fixed-income portfolio, and they have the potential to provide very high returns. However, inverse floaters are exposed to a variety of interest-rate and prepayment risks and are recommended only for investors possessing the background and analytic tools to understand these risks.

Stripped Mortgage-Backed Securities

First issued in 1986, mortgage STRIPs are created by dividing the cash flows from a pool of mortgages or mortgage securities and allocating specified percentages of interest and principal to each new STRIP. For example, a Fannie Mae 9% pass-through can be stripped to produce two securities, one with a 6% coupon and the other with a 12% coupon, simply by directing more of the interest from the underlying collateral to the higher coupon and less of the interest to the lower coupon.[30] If the ratio of interest to principal is varied, STRIPs with a wide range of coupons and performance characteristics can be created.

The predominant types of mortgage STRIPs (constituting almost all the issuance in recent years), and the most elementary, are IO and PO STRIPs.

---

[29] The coupons have to be modified for caps and the inverse floater coupon has a floor.

[30] For example, if each security receives 50% of the principal, then by directing one-third of the interest to the first security and the remaining two-thirds to the second security, we create 6% and 12% coupons.

IO STRIPs receive all of the interest payments from the underlying collateral and none of the principal. PO STRIPs receive all of the principal and none of the interest.

IOs and POs are much more sensitive to prepayment rate changes than the underlying collateral. Faster prepayments reduce the principal balance of the underlying collateral more rapidly, leading to smaller interest payments in future periods and hurting the IO, but returning principal at par at a faster rate, helping the PO. Conversely, slower prepayments help IOs but hurt POs.

Exhibit 1.21 shows projected speeds, prices, and effective durations under changing interest rates for hypothetical IOs and POs and for the underlying current coupon pass-through collateral. The graph illustrates the complex combined effects of changing discount and prepayment rates on IOs and POs.

- As interest rates decline, speeds on the collateral begin to accelerate. For the PO, higher speeds combined with lower discount rates boost the price, leading to a high positive duration and also giving the PO positive convexity. For the IO, the price actually falls as interest rates decline, as higher speeds overwhelm the effect of lower discount rates; hence, the IO displays negative duration.
- As interest rates continue to drop and prepayments begin to level off, the rate of price appreciation for the PO begins to slow, while for the IO the price begins to level off. Fairly stable speeds means that the discount rate effect becomes relatively more important. Thus, the duration of the PO starts to decline, while that of the IO begins to increase.
- Increasing interest rates lead to slower prepayments, which hurt the PO and help the IO. The IO price increases as slower prepayments outweigh higher discount rates. Again, however, as interest rates keep increasing and speeds level off at the lower end of the prepayment S-curve, the effect of lower discount rates begins to dominate, and the IO price levels off and eventually declines as rates continue to increase, thus displaying positive duration.[31]

---

[31] The analysis in Exhibit 1.21 was done at a time when interest rates were at historically low levels, with the 10-year Treasury yield at 5%. Hence, the declining rate scenarios in Exhibit 1.21(with a drop of 200bp corresponding to a 10-year rate of 3%) take interest rates to levels not seen in recent decades and may correspond to a severe recession. In this case, the projected prepayment speeds for these scenarios may be too fast.

EXHIBIT 1.21 Projected Speeds, Prices, and Durations for Hypothetical Current-Coupon IOs and POs

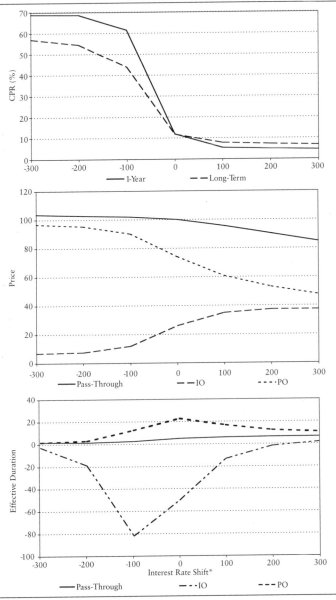

*Parallel shift in basis points.
CPR:Constant prepayment rate, IO: Interest only, PO: Principal only.
Source: Salomon Smith Barney.

The IO and PO market acts as a barometer of market perceptions and expectations of prepayment speeds, and the unusual duration characteristics of these instruments make them among the most versatile and useful vehicles in the fixed-income markets. Investors can use IOs and POs to hedge prepayment or interest rate risk or combine them with other securities to create synthetic instruments or portfolios with desired investment or duration profiles. They also can be used simply to take a position on prepayments. However, their extreme sensitivity to prepayments implies a high degree of risk, and investors in these instruments should have a correspondingly high degree of understanding of prepayment and OAS analysis.

1.6 THE NON-AGENCY MARKET

In this section we give an overview of non-agency (or nonconforming) mortgage securities, including commercial MBSs (CMBSs). This is a large and diverse sector, covering the complete spectrum of borrower demographics and credit characteristics, as well as loan sizes and types.

Cash Flow Structure of Non-Agency Mortgage Securities

Despite the many different types of collateral backing non-agency deals, the cash flow structures of these deals tend to be fairly similar. With agency MBSs, agency guarantees assure investors that they will receive timely payment of interest and principal, regardless of the delinquency or default rates on the underlying loans. Because non-agency MBSs have no such guarantees, some other form of protection (or credit enhancement) is needed to protect investors from borrower delinquencies. Most deals now have *internal credit enhancement* through a senior/subordinated structure.[32] In its most basic form, there is a *senior* class and a *subordinated* (or *junior*) class; the latter absorbs principal shortfalls from liquidation (hence, it is sometimes called a first-loss piece). Rating agency requirements determine the amount of the subordinated class, but typically, for the senior class to be rated AAA, 4% to 20% of the deal, depending on the collateral, tends to be in the junior classes. The AAA class is then typically structured as a CMO,

---

[32] *External Credit Enhancement,* infrequently used in recent years, means obtaining insurance of some sort from an external source to cover shortfalls and losses resulting from delinquencies and defaults.

EXHIBIT 1.22   Typical Structure for a Non-Agency Deal

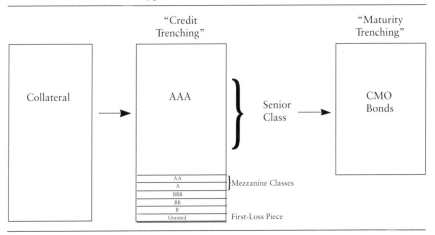

Source: Salomon Smith Barney.

with PACs, sequential bonds, and so on. The junior class itself is often tranched, but along credit lines, from AA or A (sometimes called *mezzanine* classes) down to an unrated piece. As the ratings imply, any principal losses are absorbed in reverse order (i.e., the unrated class is the first-loss piece). Exhibit 1.22 shows a typical structure for a non-agency MBS deal.

Non-agency MBSs, particularly those with lower ratings, tend to trade at much wider spreads than comparable corporate bonds. For example, recent spreads on BBB-rated non-agency MBSs have been close to 300bp, or more than 150bp higher than BBB-rated corporates.[33] We could, in fact, argue that the law of large numbers implies less uncertainty about credit losses for a large geographically diversified group of mortgage loans than for a single corporation, in which the investor has greater exposure to event risk. This implies that, for example, a BBB-rated bond from a deal backed by such a group of loans should trade *tighter*, not wider than a BBB-rated corporate bond.

---

[33] Although the subordinated MBS classes have some prepayment risk, it tends to be relatively minor, because prepayments are directed to the senior classes, and in fact, the junior classes typically have prepayment lock-outs for a number of years.

Types of Nonconforming Residential Mortgages

Exhibit 1.23 gives a rough schematic representation of some of the main sectors of the nonconforming market.[34] Also shown are some major issuers in the various sectors.

Traditional Jumbo Loans   Deals backed by such loans (generally termed whole loan [WL] deals) constitute the largest sector of the non-agency market, with issuance in 1998 of about $105 billion, and a total outstanding market size of $265 billion. As might be expected, such loans are characterized by the following:

- Affluent, financially sophisticated borrowers.
- Large loan sizes, with a current average of around $325,000, compared to an average of about $120,000 for agency loans.
- A heavy California (and to a lesser extent, Northeast) concentration, with most deals having 30% to 50% of the loans from California.
- Generally high credits, and LTV ratios below 80%.

These factors imply:

- Very efficient refinancers and, hence, fast speeds in an interest rate rally;
- Strong geographical effects—for example, speeds on WL deals were generally slower than on comparable agency pools from 1994 to 1997 because of the California housing recession of the time;
- Generally low default rates, although, again, geographical effects could outweigh demographic factors for a period.

The prepayment characteristics of jumbo loans means a greater degree of negative convexity for WL MBSs relative to comparable agency MBSs. However, many firms (such as Salomon Smith Barney) have developed prepayment models for jumbos that take into account these characteristics,[35] so that valuation measures such as OAS reflect these specific prepayment

---

[34] We say *rough* because the nuances of the distribution of borrower credits is difficult to represent in a simple table. For example, many loans in Ginnie Mae pools could be considered to be below A credit, based on LTVs, debt-to-income ratios, and so on; however, a U.S. government guarantee makes this a nonissue for investors. Also note that some Manufactured Housing borrowers may be rated A, based on criteria such as credit history and debt ratios.

[35] For a description of Salomon's WL prepayment model, see Chapter 11.

Exhibit 1.23   The Spectrum of Residential Mortgage Loans

	Credit	
A	**Nontraditional A**	**Subprime**
Traditional Jumbos Average balance ≅ $325,000 Higher CA % Affluent borrowers **Major Issuers** *Countrywide, Norwest, RFC, GE Capital, Chase, Citicorp Mfg.* Conforming Limit Agency MBS		Poor credit history High debt ratios **Larger Loans (B & C)** Average balance > $80,000 Higher CA % More A−, B Credits **Major Issuers** *RASC, Option One, Long Beach, New Century* **Home-Equity Loans (HEL)** Average balance ≅ $40,000–$60,000 More B, C and D credits Shorter terms Some second liens **Major Issuers** *EquiCredit, Advanta UCFC, IMC, Money Store, ContiMortgage, Gree Tree*
	Alt-As Average balance ≅ $130,000, but large dispersion Investor loans Limited documentation Good credit, higher debt **Major Issuers** *Indy Mac, Norwest RALI*	
	Manufactured Housing (MH) Average balance. ≅ $30,000–$40,000 Lower-income borrowers *Major Issuers* *Gree Tree, GreenPoint, Associates First, Vanderbilt, Oakwood*	

Higher Loan Balances ↑

RFC: Residential Funding Corporation, RALI: Residential Accredit Loans, Inc., RASC: Residential Assets Securities Corp., UCFC: United Companies Financial Corporation.
Source: Salomon Smith Barney.

characteristics. OASs on WL CMO bonds have recently been 10bp to 20bp wider than those on comparable agency CMOs.

Alternative-A Loans   The alternative-A (alt-A) sector has grown in recent years. Total issuance was about $20 billion in 1998, more than double 1997 volume, and the total outstanding volume of alt-A MBSs is about $30 billion. Salomon Smith Barney recently published a comprehensive discussion of the alt-A market,[36] so we will keep the discussion here brief.

Alt-A loans tend to be of moderately high credit quality. Although the average loan balance is not much higher than for agency loans, loan sizes vary widely with significant percentages—typically 30% to 40%—above the agency conforming limit. The loans that are below agency loan size limits may be *nonconforming* —that is, not eligible for agency pools—for a variety of reasons, the main ones being that the loans are on investor properties, are underwritten using limited or alternative documentation (for example, the borrower may be self-employed and not have a history of regular income), or are cash-out (or equity take-out) loans with a new LTV that exceeds agency guidelines for such loans. In some cases, the loans may qualify for agency pools, but the borrower may obtain a better rate through a non-agency program. On average, recent alt-A loans have been originated at about 70bp to 80bp above standard conforming loans.

The nature of alt-A loans leads to distinctive prepayment patterns:

- Baseline speeds tend to be high, because of ongoing "curing"; that is, borrowers' situations improve so that they are able to refinance at a lower rate. This implies an ongoing stream of refinancings even if mortgage rates do not change. Dispersion in WACs tends to accentuate this phenomenon.
- The high proportion of refinancings in total alt-A speeds leads to a short seasoning period relative to agency collateral.
- However, sensitivity to interest rate moves tends to be lower for alt-As, because most alt-A borrowers face extra hurdles in refinancing their loans relative to standard conforming or jumbo borrowers.

These patterns imply a flatter prepayment curve for alt-As relative to conforming or jumbo loans, giving them attractive convexity characteristics.

A recent development has been increasing agency purchases of alt-A loans, as both Fannie Mae and Freddie Mac have relaxed certain underwriting guidelines in an effort to increase market share. There has been

---

[36] See Chapter 12 for a more detailed discussion of the alternative A sector.

some concern that this could lead to lower alt-A rates and, hence, higher refinancings for alt-A securities. However, early indications do not seem to warrant such concerns.[37] In fact, agency involvement could actually improve the favorable convexity characteristics of new alt-A deals, as the agencies skim off the cream of the alt-A borrower pool leaving in the alt-A pools those borrowers who face the greatest hurdles in obtaining a loan.

The Subprime Sector: B and C and Home Equity Loans   The term B and C is used as a synonym for subprime loans. These are loans made to borrowers with imperfect credit histories and higher debt-to-income ratios than those allowed by the agencies. Based on the degree of these deficiencies, the loans are classified as being of A (or A−), B, C, or D credit quality, although an A rating does not by any means imply that the loan is of the same quality as agency loans. Subprime loans tend to be originated at several hundred basis points above conforming agency (i.e., prime quality) loans. However, there is no industry standard for classifying loans by credit quality, and hence, the loan rate on, for example, C loans may vary from issuer to issuer.[38] Our studies indicate that, typically, subprime lenders originate A− loans at 100bp to 200bp above agency conforming rates, while note rates on B loans tend to be about 100bp higher, and those on C and D loans are each about 150bp higher than the preceding category.

Home Equity Loan (HEL) nominally refers to a second mortgage (or lien) on a property. Indeed, at one time HEL MBSs were collateralized mostly by second liens. However, the collateral for HEL deals issued in the past several years typically has had a majority of first liens; these have constituted 75% or more of the collateral in most cases. These first liens are typically subprime loans, ranging from A− to D.

Since both B and C and HEL securities are backed by subprime loans, what is the main difference between B and C and HEL securities?[39] The main difference is in the distribution of credits. Despite the terminology, B and C deals tend to have mostly A− and B quality loans, while HEL deals tend to contain the full spectrum of credits from A− to D. This difference is reflected in typical loan sizes: The loan balance in HEL deals tends to average between

---

[37] See Chapter 12.

[38] For a description of typical criteria used by a few major B and C lenders to categorize borrowers, see *"B" and "C" Borrowers: A New Frontier in the Nonagency Market,* Salomon Brothers Inc., May 1994.

[39] Apart from the fact that B and C loans tend to be labeled MBSs while HELs are called asset-backed securities (ABSs).

$40,000 to $60,000, while for B and C deals it is typically $80,000 or higher.[40] In addition, more B and C loans have prepayment penalties.

Salomon Smith Barney has developed issuer-specific HEL prepayment models based on extensive data analysis.[41] The main characteristics of HEL speeds, relative to agency collateral, are:

- **High base case speeds,** typically averaging 25% to 35% CPR. This is mainly due to credit-curing; that is, borrowers improving their rating, and, hence, being reclassified from, say, a C to a B loan. As indicated above, such a reclassification can lower the coupon rate by up to 200bp, providing ample refinancing incentive even if interest rates do not decline.
- **A short seasoning ramp,** because of the high proportion of refinancings in total speeds.
- **Lower sensitivity to interest rates,** which is a result of the small loan balances and the extra refinancing hurdles faced by subprime borrowers.
- **Higher levels of defaults,** as might be expected given the nature of the loans. Our studies indicate that annual default rates peak at about 3% on average, or more than six times typical rates on conventional agency loans.

B and C loan speeds follow a similar pattern, with minor variations resulting from the differences in loan characteristics just described:

- Baseline speeds are a little lower (by 5% to 10% CPR). B and C borrowers have higher credit quality on average, and hence, credit-improvement related speeds play a smaller role. Prepayment penalties also help to slow speeds.
- Sensitivity to interest rates is about the same, maybe a tad higher. The higher average loan quality and larger loan balances may be balanced by the effect of prepayment penalties.

These attributes lead to attractive convexity characteristics for MBSs backed by subprime loans. In addition, subordinate pieces of subprime collateral provide a challenging but potentially rewarding opportunity for investors.

---

[40] The difference in loan balances, however, could partly be due to geographical reasons. The lenders typically termed B and C have a California concentration, while traditional HEL lenders do not.

[41] See Chapters 19 and 20 for a discussion of HELs.

Manufactured Housing Loans   Manufactured housing (MH) refers to homes constructed in a factory and transported to a land site. Although the size and quality of MH has increased in recent years, the homes still tend to be much less expensive than site-built homes. Hence MH loans tend to be much smaller than most other types of mortgage loans, with average balances of $30,000 to $40,000 in recent deals, and $20,000 or so for older deals. In addition, borrowers tend to have lower than average incomes.

These factors imply among the most favorable prepayment characteristics of all mortgage product. Indeed, prepayments on seasoned MH loans tend to be relatively stable, averaging about 12% CPR in the base case (i.e., when there is little or no refinancing incentive) and rarely rising much above 20% to 25% CPR.[42] Salomon Smith Barney recently released an MH prepayment model based on a detailed analysis of almost one million loans originated by Green Tree Financial Corporation, the largest lender in this sector. The model shows that the option costs for bonds backed by MH loans tend to be a fraction of those for comparable CMO bonds backed by agency or jumbo loans.[43]

Summary of Prepayment Characteristics   Exhibit 1.24 is a simplified guide to the effect of various loan characteristics on prepayments defaults, based on these discussions.

Commercial Mortgage-Backed Securities

The term *commercial mortgages* is used to denote loans on multifamily housing,[44] as well as loans on a variety of nonresidential property types, such as *office, retail, hotel/motel,* and various others (such as *industrial* and *nursing home*). The total outstanding amount of such loans at the end the third quarter of 1998 was about $1.25 trillion, compared with $4.3 trillion of one- to four-family mortgage debt.[45] Issuance of securities backed by commercial mortgages has grown tremendously in recent years, with about $78 billion in public issuance in 1998, compared with roughly $45 billion in 1997, and only $17 billion in 1993. The size of CMBS deals has increased,

---

[42] As with subprime loans, defaults are a more significant part of the total speed for MH loans than is the case for agency loans, peaking at about 3% CPR after several years.

[43] See Chapter 21 for a more detailed description of the MH sector.

[44] Loans on one- to four-family properties are included in the agency definition of single-family mortgages.

[45] *Federal Reserve Bulletin,* February 1999, page A35.

EXHIBIT 1.24 Major Factors Influencing Prepayments and Defaults

	Refinancings			
Factor	Turnover	Rate-Driven	Other*	Defaults
Collateral and Borrower Related				
Larger Loan sizes	—	↑	↑	—
Higher Credit Score, Lower Debt	↑	—	↓	↓
More Second Liens	—	↓	↑	—
Higher LTV	↓	↓	↓	↑
Macro Economics				
Lower Rates	↑	↑	—	↓
Healthier Economy	↑	↑	↑	↓
Higher Home Prices	↑	↑	↑	↓

*Refinancings on lower credits that are insensitive to rate moves, driven by debt consolidation and credit improvement.
Source: Salomon Smith Barney.

from an average of just over $400 million in 1997, to almost $900 million in 1998, reflecting a trend toward deals backed by many loans from several issuers and investor interest in secondary market liquidity.[46]

Most commercial loans have payments based on an amortization schedule of 25 to 30 years, but have a balloon payment due, usually after 10 or 15 years. Prepayment risk is low compared to that for other mortgage sectors. Commercial mortgage loans typically have severe restrictions on prepayments, such as a complete prohibition (or *lock-out*), a *yield maintenance* provision (which means that if the loan is prepaid, the borrower has

---

[46] The term *fusion deal* is used to refer to transactions containing some large loans; the industry convention currently is to define a fusion deal as one where an individual loan is more than 10% of the collateral, or loans of greater than $50 million constitute more than 15% of the deal.

to compensate the lender for the loss of an above-market coupon), *defeasance,*[47] or a gradually declining penalty proportional to the loan balance (e.g., a "5-4-3-2-1" schedule, which means 5% for a year, then 4% for a year, and so on). These penalties are often combined; for example, a loan may have a lock-out period of five years, followed by a declining penalty proportional to the loan balance for the next five years. Such penalties, combined with the considerable expense and time involved in refinancing a commercial loan, means that CMBSs are unlikely to be exposed to a sudden spike in refinancings, at least during the prepayment penalty period.[48]

CMBSs constitute an unusual sector in the mortgage market, combining features of both MBSs and corporate bonds. A key difference between residential and commercial mortgage loans is that the latter are non-recourse; that is, if the borrower defaults, the lender cannot seize any other assets of the borrower. In other words, the income-producing capabilities and value of the underlying asset is key to CMBS analysis. Hence, evaluation of the credit risk in CMBSs depends on specific property characteristics, such as the ability to make mortgage payments (a commonly used measure is the *debt service coverage ratio* (DSCR), which is the net operating income divided by debt payments), and the ability to refinance the loan at the balloon date (hence rating agencies attach importance to initial LTV). In addition, general relevant business trends, such as apartment or office vacancy rates, have to be analyzed.

For senior CMBS classes, the likelihood of losses from defaults is negligible, even under extreme scenarios, because of the stringent subordination amounts required by the rating agencies; typically, there is 28% to 30% of credit support for triple-A CMBS classes, compared to 10% or less for triple-A bonds from non-agency deals backed by prime quality, single-family loans. In fact, spreads on senior CMBS classes currently seem to be driven primarily by capital market developments. An example is provided by the events in the fall of 1998, when CMBSs spreads widened with other spread product despite good commercial real estate fundamentals. Since then, CMBSs spreads have tightened sharply as the fixed-income markets have stabilized. However, as has been the case historically, they still offer substantially higher spreads relative to comparable quality corporate bonds, even though one could argue that CMBSs backed by a diversified pool of

---

[47] A defeasance provision allows the borrower to obtain a release of the mortgaged property by pledging U.S. Treasury securities whose cash flows equal or exceed that of the mortgage loan.

[48] In fact, for CMBSs the term *refinancing risk* typically refers to the possibility that the borrower will not be able to refinance the loan at the balloon date.

loans have less credit uncertainty and event risk than a similarly rated corporate bond.[49]

1.7 MBS MARKETS OUTSIDE THE UNITED STATES

An important trend over the past ten years has been the development of
secondary mortgage markets outside the United States. The factors behind
this trend are similar to the ones that drove the development of the market
in the United States. At a governmental and social policy level, there is a
desire to replicate the perceived success of the United States in making
housing finance cheaper and more easily available to home buyers. For
lending institutions, competitive and regulatory pressures have grown for
efficient balance sheet management, and securitization of assets facilitates
this process.

The largest MBS market outside the United States, and the one with the
most potential, is Europe, and we discuss the European market in more detail later. Other countries with developing secondary markets include
Canada, where the market has grown steadily since its inception in 1987,
helped by the establishment of a Ginnie Mae-type entity, the Canadian
Mortgage and Housing Corporation; **Australia** and **New Zealand,** where a
total of about $18 billion in loans were securitized in 1997 and 1998; **Hong
Kong,** where an agency-type entity, the Hong Kong Mortgage Corporation,
has been established; and **Argentina,** where several MBS deals have been issued. While these markets are small compared to that in the United States,
a potentially large market exists in **Japan,** which has about $1.5 trillion in
mortgage loans outstanding and where an MBS deal was recently priced.
There is pressure on Japanese banks to remove loans from their balance
sheets, to meet capital adequacy requirements, and hence, a continuing
stream of securitizations is expected.

The Danish MBS Market

Before discussing the development of the European MBS market, we note that
a well-established secondary mortgage market already exists, in Denmark. In
fact, the Danish market is older than the U.S. MBS market: A mortgage credit
system has been in existence in Denmark for 200 years. Although there are

---

[49] This is illustrated by the fact that investors prefer CMBS deals backed by a large
number of small loans to those backed by a few large loans. Part Six of this book provides a comprehensive description of CMBSs.

other established types of mortgage bonds in Europe, notably the *Pfandbrief* sector in Germany,[50] Danish MBSs are the closest to U.S. pass-through securities in cash-flow characteristics.[51] They are mostly fixed-rate, level-pay loans (called annuity loans in Denmark), with original maturities of 10, 15, 20, or 30 years, and can be prepaid without penalty at any time. However, mortgage payments are quarterly rather than monthly. In addition, residential and commercial mortgage loans are mixed in the same pools.

The amount of outstanding Danish fixed-rate MBSs was DKr 970 billion at the end of the second quarter 1998, or about $150 billion, a remarkable amount for a nation of only five million people. Danish mortgage pools (or series) tend to be large in size, typically $1 billion or more initially (some issues are more than $10 billion). This size is achieved by keeping a series open for up to three years; that is, new loans can be put into the pool anytime during a period of three years.

Prepayments in Denmark show extreme efficiency, because of very low refinancing costs, a national awareness of refinancing opportunities (a strong media effect), and the ability to prepay discount loans at market value (rather than at par). However, as in the United States, considerable resources have been devoted to developing prepayment and OAS models to capture prepayment risk.[52]

Securitization in Europe

The first MBS deals in Europe (not counting the Danish MBS market) were done in the mid-1980s, with United Kingdom mortgages as collateral. There

---

[50] *Pfandbriefs* are collateralized bonds, with a total market size of close to $1 trillion, of which a quarter are backed by residential mortgages (although because the LTV cannot exceed 60%, only a fraction of German mortgages are eligible for *Pfandbriefs*). However, prepayments are not allowed, and even if a loan is prepaid, the issuer typically does not pass on the prepayment to investors. For a description of the sector, see *The Jumbo-Pfandbrief and its Future*, Udo Herges, Salomon Smith Barney, July 1998.

[51] For an introduction to Danish MBSs, see *Mortgage Bonds*, by Den Danske Bank, September 1998. The figures on the Danish market are taken from this publication.

[52] There is one difference in the way prepayments are passed through to investors: Instead of the pro rata system used in the United States, prepayments in Denmark are distributed by a lottery system, each bond (nominal value Dkr 1,000) being one lot. Investors with large holdings would expect to see prepayments on their bonds close to the rate for the pool (or series), given the law of averages, but smaller investors may see deviations.

EXHIBIT 1.25   European MBS/ABS Issuance by Asset Type, 1997 and 1998
(Dollars in Billions)

Asset Type	1997	% of Total	1998	% of Total
MBS	$11.0	24	$22.7	49 %
CMBS	2.6	6	2.6	6
CBO/CLO	14.6	32	8.5	18
Other ABS	17.3	41	12.9	27

Source: Moody's Investors Services.

have also been securitizations of other asset-classes, such as credit cards and
auto loans. According to estimates by Moody's Investors Services, annual issuance of European MBS/ABS was less than $10 billion until 1996, when it
jumped to $30 billion, then further increased to $45.4 billion in 1997. Volume for 1998, however, was about the same as 1997, at $46.6 billion, as the
flight to quality last fall led to a dramatic widening in ABS spreads and reduced issuance to a trickle. Despite the increase in issuance in 1996 and
1997, volume is still low relative to the United States and relative to the
amount of mortgage loans outstanding in Europe. However, as the jump in
volume in the past few years implies, many of the impediments to securitization have been diminishing, and volume is expected to surge in coming years.

Mortgages continue to form the bulk of collateral for European deals.
Exhibit 1.25 shows a breakdown of European issuance by collateral type
for 1997 and 1998. The total outstanding volume of European MBS/ABS
has been estimated to be about $130 billion,[53] of which perhaps half are
MBSs.

For MBSs, the United Kingdom has been the major source of collateral;
in fact, until the past year or two, three countries (the United Kingdom,
France, and Spain) provided the collateral for almost all MBS issues. However, in a sign of the gradual progress of securitization, in 1998 seven other
countries were also represented in MBS deals (although the United Kingdom, France, and Spain still accounted for two-thirds of the collateral). A
notable entry into the MBS market was Germany, the largest mortgage market on the continent in terms of amount of loans outstanding, where three
large deals were issued in 1998.

Raw Material: Amount of Loans Outstanding   What is the volume of European
mortgage loans outstanding? A study by a consulting firm estimated that
"retail" mortgage loans outstanding in 1996 totaled about $2.6 trillion in

---

[53] These estimates exclude Danish MBSs and mortgage bonds, such as *Pfandbriefs.*

16 western European countries.[54] This compares with $3.8 trillion in one-to four-family mortgages outstanding in the United States at the end of 1996. However, the term retails, according to the study, "does not include loans to self-employed businessmen," an exclusion that would knock out a significant fraction of the loans in the United States. We can probably conclude that the size of the primary mortgage market in western Europe is comparable to, or a tad smaller than, the U.S. mortgage market.

Why Has the European MBS Market Not Developed Faster? Despite steady issuance since the mid-1980s, securitization volume in Europe has lagged U.S. rates, for a variety of reasons:

- Many institutions have not faced strong incentives to remove assets from balance sheets, due to favorable funding rates and excess capital.
- The severe recession in Europe in the early 1990s led to a sharp drop in loan originations, further diminishing pressure on balance sheets.
- A lack of legal and regulatory frameworks hinder securitization.
- Few analytic tools and an infrastructure exist for timely reporting of deal information to investors.
- A diversity of mortgage terms and conditions, such as prepayment penalties, from country to country diminish the appeal of MBSs backed by loans from one country to investors in other countries.
- Currency differences hindered cross-border transactions in the past.
- Many European investors have tended to focus on sovereign debt, rather than spread products.

Faster Growth Expected Many of these impediments to growth have been diminishing, as indicated by the substantial jump in issuance starting in 1996 mentioned earlier. The general expectation is for more rapid development of the European MBS and ABS markets over the next several years. Several factors are expected to contribute to this trend:

- The introduction of the Euro is expected to have a major impact, as it will gradually eliminate much of the existing sovereign bond markets, shift investor attention to spread products, especially MBSs and ABSs because of their high credit quality, and eliminate currency concerns.
- In the past few years, various countries have made legal and regulatory changes that facilitate securitization, and this trend is expected to continue.

---

[54] *European Mortgages Report*, Datamonitor, 1997.

- Competitive and regulatory pressures on institutions are mounting, leading to more focus on measures such as return-on-equity and on efficient balance sheet management.
- Gradual improvements in MBS deal information reporting systems, and more familiarity with cash-flow characteristics, both contributing to increasing investor comfort levels with MBS and ABS products.[55]
- A continuing broadening of the types of assets being securitized—for example, subprime mortgages, student loans, soccer receivables, pub leases, and so on.

However, before the European MBS and ABS markets approach United States levels (more than $3 trillion in MBSs and ABSs outstanding), some impediments have to be removed. One is the variety of rules and regulations (or lack of them in some cases) governing securitization from country to country. Some securitization professionals expect that with a common currency and a single central bank, standardization will occur, although it may take a while. Second, and perhaps most important, there is no equivalent of Ginnie Mae, Fannie Mae, or Freddie Mac in Europe. These entities have not only played a critical role in the growth of the secondary mortgage market in the United States; the establishment of Fannie Mae in 1938 by the federal government also led to standardization of mortgage terms and underwriting practices in the United States. The establishment of a pan-European housing finance agency would likely have a similar effect in Europe.

---

[55] As an indication of this trend, we note the Bond Market Association (formerly the PSA), a trade group in New York representing fixed-income dealers, has recently set up a European Securitization Forum to "promote the continued growth and development of securitization throughout Europe."

CHAPTER 2

An Introduction to the Asset-Backed Securities Market

Mary E. Kane

"**D**iscovery consists of seeing what everybody has seen and thinking what nobody else has thought."[1] It is hard to imagine why the ABS market did not begin until 1985, when the corporate bond market is so well developed and relatively speaking, ancient. Despite its more recent nascence, the ABS market is now an important sector in its own right. In this chapter, we provide an introduction to the asset-backed securities market, its origins, product types, investor base, market size and composition. We describe the motivation for corporations to issue ABSs and the benefits for ABS investors. We also describe the structural and legal framework for securitization. We then focus on two major sectors of the ABS market: autos and credit cards. Together, these two sectors comprise 40% of outstanding issuance in the ABS market and 52% of new issue volume.

2.1 BACKGROUND

Asset-backed securities (ABS) are securities collateralized by the cash flows of a variety of receivables or loans. ABSs are mostly shorter-term assets, and in many respects, less complex than mortgage securities.[2] ABSs have an element

---

[1] Albert von Szent-Gyorgyi, *The Scientist Speculates*. In Elizabeth Knowles. Ed. *The Oxford Dictionary of Phrases, Sayings, and Quotations*, Oxford, United Kingdom: Oxford University Press.

[2] As mentioned in the Introduction, in the United States, the term ABS refers to securities backed by assets other than mortgage loans, although Home Equity Loans (HELs) and Manufactured Housing (MH) Loans are exceptions. Outside the United States, the term logically includes all securities products, including MBS.

of credit risk, unlike U.S. government agency-backed MBS, but less prepayment and cash flow volatility. In the dawn of the new millenium year 2000, triple-A ABSs are taking on increasing importance as a high quality alternative to U.S. Treasury securities, and to highly rated corporate securities.

The origins of the ABS market are actually derived from nonmortgage ABSs. In 1985, Chrysler Financial issued the first public ABS deal, in a securitization of its auto loan portfolio. In the early years, auto loans, particularly the big 3 auto manufacturers, dominated ABS issuance. Publicly issued credit cards securitizations were introduced in 1987, as the market expanded and diversified. By 1988, the ABS markets had many securitized asset classes, including home equity loans, manufactured housing and even boat loans. Maturation of the market has led to:

- Standardization
- Innovative structures
- Changes in accounting, regulatory and tax matters
- Development of a deep investor base
- Wide maturity spectrum
- Ratings changes, both upgrades and downgrades due to collateral performance (but less volatility than the unsecured corporate market)

The size of the ABS market in relation to other fixed income markets can be seen in Exhibit 2.1. The much smaller outstanding size of the ABS market is a clear function of the shorter history than that of the other markets.

WHY DO CORPORATIONS ISSUE ABSS?

Issuers with a below-investment-grade unsecured debt rating are able to sell investment-grade, even triple-A-rated debt. The debt costs far less than a non-investment-grade firm would be able to access in the capital markets on

EXHIBIT 2.1   Relative Size of U.S. Debt Markets

All Mortgage Debt	$6.50 trillion
Single Family Mortgage Debt	$4.86 trillion
Mortgage-Backed Securities	$3.00 trillion
Asset-Backed Securities	$ 813 billion
U.S. Treasuries	$3.63 trillion
Agency Debentures	$1.62 trillion
Corporate Bonds	$2.00 trillion

Source: Federal Reserve Bulletin, Bloomberg, August 2000.

an unsecured basis. Securitization diversifies sources of capital, reduces the size of the balance sheet and frees up capital associated with the securitized assets.

The released capital can be put back to work and the issuer may replace the securitized assets with new receivables. A higher volume of originations would, therefore, provide the issuer with the potential to generate higher revenues and earnings. In effect, this allows the issuing corporation to leverage off its capital base. It should be noted, however, that many issuers retain a portion of risk from securitization, generally the most subordinated risk. Therefore, a securitization strategy does not generally release 100% capital.

Issuers need to weigh the cost of issuance versus the benefits of securitization. There are up-front legal and professional fees, and on-going administrative costs. Therefore, the issuer will need to weigh these and other expenses versus the cost savings of triple-A issuance. Capital cost savings as well as tax implications are carefully analyzed. A critical mass of securitized receivables are beneficial and economies of scale are relevant. Larger size is more cost-effective for the issuer to amortize fixed up-front costs.

For investment-grade companies, the benefits are similar. As there are very few triple-A unsecured issuers, the cost of issuance is attractive for most investment-grade firms, even after issuance costs. The nonrecourse sale of assets enables issuers to reduce exposure to higher risk-weighted assets, and to fund portfolio growth through off-balance sheet treatment.

How Do Investors Benefit from Securitization?

- *High Quality Ratings Universe.* Investors enjoy a wide universe of triple-A and other investment-grade assets. Many investors find that liquidity in the ABS market, especially in the more generic asset classes, is superior to the corporate bond market.
- *Lower Ratings Volatility.* Investors benefit from consistently lower ratings volatility than the unsecured corporate debt market. In the 15-year history of the ABS market, until 1998, the only downgrades to occur were caused by third party credit enhancement deterioration. To date, the CBOs/CLOs sectors experienced the majority of the ratings downgrades for collateral performance. Those sectors contained most of the negative ratings volatility. Certain third-party risks, however, have caused prior ABS downgrades.
- *De-Linkage from Servicer Bankruptcy Risk.* ABSs are bankruptcy-remote. Investors are insulated from a bankruptcy of the underlying seller of the receivables. Shelter is given to ABS investors from the event risks routinely faced by corporate bond investors.

WHAT IS THE MARKET SIZE AND COMPOSITION?

The ABS market has grown impressively since its inception in the mid-1980s. Issuance grew exponentially in the early years of the market as investors familiarized themselves with structured product and its applications. The market developed new asset classes. Legal and accounting developments facilitated new and more efficient structures. The market evolved in response to issuer and investor needs. Exhibit 2.2 illustrates the growth of the market since its inception, along with the breakdown of asset classes.

We show a breakdown by asset type of public ABS issuance from 1995 to present in Exhibit 2.3. Growth has leveled off, and it appears the market may be in a more mature phase. The chart illustrates the contribution of the different sectors of ABSs in each year. For comparative evaluation, we include the home equity and manufactured housing sectors' contributions to issuance. The largest segments of the ABS market are typically autos, credit cards, and home equities." Other" asset classes such as recreational vehicles, collateralized bond and loan obligations, and stranded assets are growing in significance. There are also many off-the-run or one-off transactions that fall in the "other" category. These include such diverse transactions as the securitization of sports arenas, entertainment royalties, film profits, franchise loans and mutual fund fees.

The ABS market has also evolved from being exclusively a U.S. domestic market, to being a global, multi-currency market. Foreign corporations have issued in U.S. dollars in the United States, and U.S. corporations have

EXHIBIT 2.2   ABS Issuance Statistics 1985 through August 2000

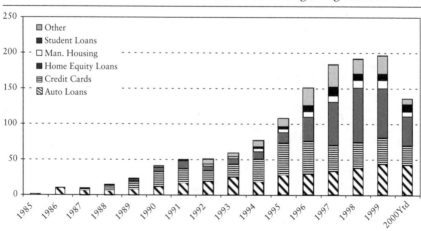

Source: McCarthy, Crisanti, and Maffei, Inc.

EXHIBIT 2.3   ABS Issuance 1995 through August 2000 (Dollars in Billion)

	1995	1996	1997	1998	1999	2000Ytd
Auto Loans	28.2	29.2	33.1	37.6	43.3	42.0
Credit Cards	45.3	47.2	37.5	37.1	38.0	28.2
Home Equity Loans	14.4	33.2	60.3	76.5	68.9	40.6
Man. Housing	5.4	7.9	8.9	10.7	12.0	6.9
Student Loans	3.3	8.9	12.8	9.2	8.8	10.6
Other	11.8	24.9	30.8	20.3	25.2	7.3
Total	108.4	151.3	183.4	191.4	196.2	135.6

Source: McCarthy, Crisanti, and Maffei, Inc.

issued global notes distributed on other continents, and in alternate currencies. Examples of this are U.K. and Australian mortgages issued in the United States, and U.S. credit cards issued in the United Kingdom. Asia is also a developing market for securitized products.

Exhibit 2.4 shows the volume outstanding in the ABS market by asset type. The three largest sectors are credit cards, HELs and car loans. The "other" category includes recreational vehicles, collaterized bond and loan obligations, stranded costs and many diverse off-the-run products, such as franchise loans and mutual fund fees, for example.

WHO INVESTS IN ABSs?

ABS investors are far more diverse than the investor base for conventional corporate bonds. This is because of the nature of structured product. ABS structures allow rating and maturity profiles to be more closely matched to

EXHIBIT 2.4   ABSs Outstanding as of September 2000—$881 Billion

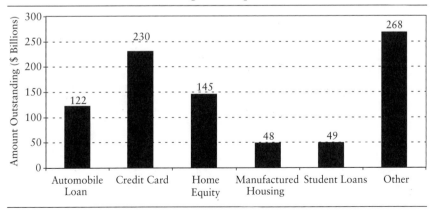

Source: Salomon Smith Barney.

investors needs than the conventional corporate bond market. This enables an issuer to simultaneously access short-term money market investors and term investors. The same issue may contain both fixed and floating-rate interest rates. In this case, the issue is structured for different investor bases.

As a result, in the corporate bond market, the issuer would have to bifurcate such issuance and separately tap the commercial paper, medium term note, and corporate underwritten market to achieve the same flexibility and to access as diverse an investor base. The increased globalization of the ABS market adds further diversity to the range of potential investors in a typical ABS transaction. We see the diversity of the investor base in Exhibit 2.5, showing Salomon Smith Barney's placement of fixed and floating rate credit card securitizations in 1999.

THE LEGAL STRUCTURE

The main objective of a securitization is to isolate the pool of assets from the seller in a true sale (see Conditions for Sale Treatment next) and to allow accounting off-balance sheet treatment of assets for the seller. Assets are sold into a bankruptcy-remote structure on a nonrecourse basis to the issuer and the cash flows are pledged to the investors. In addition, investors receive a perfected security interest in the receivables and proceeds. This means that a lien is filed in the appropriate jurisdictions to legally recognize the trust collateral interest. A true sale and nonconsolidation opinion and

EXHIBIT 2.5 Salomon Smith Barney 1999 Credit Card Investors Fixed and Floating Rate

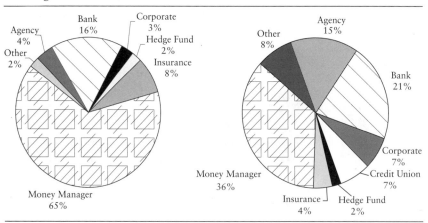

Source: Bloomberg, LP.

security interest perfection are key legal opinions issued for the benefit of investors. With this transfer of risk, the seller-servicer is able to account for the assets off-balance sheet and the investor is isolated from a bankruptcy of the underlying seller-servicer.

Conditions for Sale Treatment

The following conditions must be met to achieve the off-balance sheet treatment of financial assets and to have what is legally considered to be a "true sale" (has the seller *truly* sold the assets?):

- Legal isolation from the seller (transferred assets put "presumptively beyond the reach of the transferor and its creditors");
- The new owner of the assets has the right to pledge or to exchange the assets (or the beneficial interests in the assets if the new owner is a *qualifying* Special Purpose Vehicle (SPV); and
- The seller doesn't have the right to buy the assets back.

Legal and Cash Flow Mechanics

We show the legal and cash flow dynamics of a typical securitization in Exhibit 2.6. The seller originates a pool of assets and sells them into a

EXHIBIT 2.6 How a Typical Transaction Works

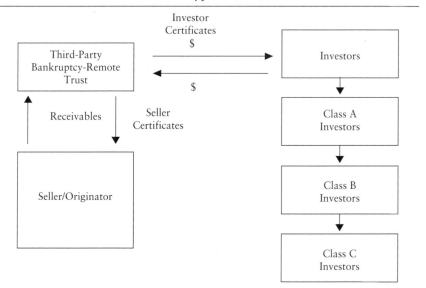

Source: Salomon Smith Barney.

bankruptcy-remote trust or SPV. The trust or SPV issues notes or certificates to investors and pledges the cash flows from the receivables to the trust. A security interest is perfected by the trust in the receivables and proceeds. Other collateral may also be pledged—auto loans, for example, have a lien on the financed vehicles.

The two-way arrows at the top of the figure show that investors pay cash up-front to purchase the securities and the right to receive the cash flow of the assets to the trust. The security is structured into three classes, Classes A, B and C in order of seniority. Cash flows will be paid in order of priority, first to Class A, then to Class B and finally to Class C. Generally, interest is paid first, then principal. Class B could not receive any interest payments unless Class A is current. The same would apply to principal payments.

With this general framework in place for ABSs, the rest of this chapter provides a more detailed description of the two largest sectors of the non-mortgage related ABS market—autos and credit cards.

2.2 A PRIMER ON THE AUTO LOAN MARKET

Vehicles are the most widely held nonfinancial assets in America—86% of families either own or lease a vehicle.[3] Commensurate with their importance in the economic and social fabric of America, auto loan ABSs are a major and very liquid sector of the ABS market. The importance of auto loans to the new issue market is indicated in Exhibit 2.7. We see that in the year 2000 (through August 31, 2000), auto loans are 31% of new issue volume. Outstanding securities are actually smaller as a percent of the market, because auto loans are constantly amortizing assets. The term *auto* loans includes light trucks and SUVs, that are very popular among U.S. vehicle sales.

Benefits of Auto Loans

Auto loans were one of the earliest products in the securitization market. Investors favored auto loans as a result of their many benefits:

- Large and diversified pools of consumer obligations
- Security interest in underlying vehicles and receivables
- Bankruptcy-remote from underlying seller-servicer
- Short-term exposure—average life generally less than two years

---

[3] See "1998 Survey of Consumer Finances," A.B. Kennickell, M. Starr-McCluer, and B.J. Suretts, published in the January 2000 *Federal Reserve Bulletin*.

EXHIBIT 2.7 ABS New Issue Volume from January 1, 2000 through August 31, 2000—$135.6 Billion

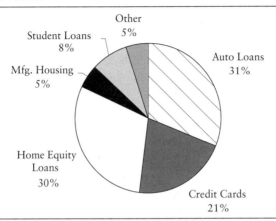

Source: Salomon Smith Barney.

■ Losses in the prime sector have a very stable track record with low losses

■ Stable and consistent prepayment speeds with little volatility

Market Segmentation

Many investors originally supported auto loans as a result of the security interest in hard collateral, and this remains a positive aspect of this class. This is in contrast to unsecured obligations such as credit cards. The nature of the obligation is also a positive attribute. A vehicle ranks highly in the consumer "hierarchy of needs." Many people will make paying their monthly vehicle loan payment a priority, even in hard times, as consumers need vehicles to get to work and for basic transportation. It was not until several years after the ABS market began that investors developed a more sophisticated understanding of structured product. It was then that the market evolved with successful offerings of unsecured credits, such as credit card receivables.

The auto loan market is segmented according to different types of lenders, so named because of the asset underwriting risk characteristics:

■ *Prime*—Top quality obligors, least likely to default
■ *Nonprime*—Higher risk than prime obligors, may have some slow-paying credit history

■ *Subprime*—Highest default probabilities—obligors may have low income, a prior bankruptcy, or poor credit history

It is best to compare and contrast the sectors of the auto loan market by examining differences in pool underwriting characteristics shown in Exhibit 2.8. We list a range of average pool yields, FICO scores and expected cumulative losses for prime, nonprime and subprime auto issuers.

FICO scores are a risk ranking system developed by Fair Issacs, a consumer credit modeling firm. FICO scores are reported by many credit bureaus in compiling consumer credit reports. (Auto lenders will typically pull the credit bureau report for a loan applicant.) A FICO score measures the probability of an individual to default given his or her credit file. The lower the probability that an individual is likely to default, the higher the FICO score. Weighted average FICO scores of auto loan pools are a strong indication of the credit quality of the underlying loan contracts. Issuers do not generally report average FICO scores in ABS prospectuses. However, issuers sometimes reference FICO scores in discussions of underwriting credit quality. Many issuers rely on proprietary internal risk models to underwrite loans. However, FICO scores are a convenient way to compare underwriting risks among issuers.

Many auto lenders rely on risk-based pricing models that adjust yield for credit risk. Contract yield, therefore, is an additional strong indicator of the probability of default. Yield ranges delineate differences among high and lower quality obligations. Interest rates change over time and with market conditions. However, in general, lower yields are indicative of higher credit quality and lower default probabilities. Lastly, cumulative losses measure total net losses for a given static pool. Higher risk paper will incur greater cumulative losses. Therefore, cumulative loss experience helps to identify which sector a particular issuer belongs in.

Loss Curves

Prime, nonprime and subprime paper will incur losses at different points in their life cycle, and their respective loss curves will look quite different. We

EXHIBIT 2.8 Underwriting Characteristics of Auto Issuers

Underwriting Criteria	Prime	Nonprime	Subprime
Average pool yield	8%–10%	12%–18%	19%–21%
Avg. FICO range	680-800	600-680	500-600
Expected cumulative losses	Less than 2%	6%-9%	8% - 15%

Source: Salomon Smith Barney.

EXHIBIT 2.9 Typical Prime and Subprime/Nonprime Automobile Loss Curves

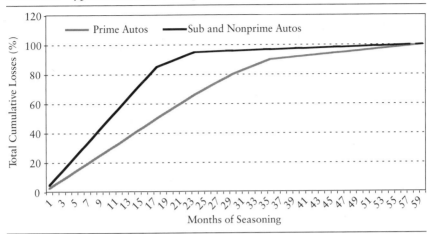

Source: Moody's.

show prime versus subprime/nonprime loss curves in Exhibit 2.9.[4] Moody's plots loss curves over 60 months, which correspond to the terms of a typical vehicle installment loan sales contract. The curves depict differences in the timing of loss recognition. Therefore, even though we show prime and subprime/nonprime loss curves on the same chart, total cumulative losses are not equal to each other. The chart shows losses equal to 100%. Therefore, if total cumulative losses will equal 1% for a prime loan, the chart plots the timing of loss recognition during the life of the pool. The same applies for subprime/nonprime vehicles. Total cumulative losses may total 10%, and the curve shows the difference in timing of loss recognition from a prime issuer. Losses are recognized earlier for subprime/nonprime lenders and are more evenly distributed for prime auto lenders.

Prime

Losses are distributed fairly symmetrically along the curve for prime auto loans. As the underwriting risks are fairly low, losses are initially low, and are gradual over the life of the pool. Peak losses occur about mid-cycle and level off later in the life of the pool.

---

[4] *Moody's Approach to Rating Automobile-Backed Securitizations: The Driving Force,* August 11, 1995.

Subprime/Nonprime

We also show a typical subprime/nonprime loss curve in Exhibit 2.9. Non-prime/subprime loss curves look quite different, exhibiting a phenomenon many people in the industry call "spike and burn." Losses tend to occur early in the life of the pool, then level off. This is because of the lower credit quality of the individuals in these pools—credit problems surface early, but then the defaults abate. Subprime/nonprime obligors tend to have lower incomes, little credit history or poor prior credit records, maybe a bankruptcy.

The loss curve rises early in the life of the transaction—typically, approximately 75% to 85% of the losses occur by month 18 and 95% by month 24, with the remaining fairly evenly distributed over the remaining life of the transaction. We note, however, that Moody's[5] and other industry experts affirm, that loss curves are becoming more back-ended than typical subprime/nonprime benchmark curves.

Why Look at Loss Curves?

Auto loan loss curves are worth a look in order to measure pool performance during the life of the deal versus expected losses. If the issuer is expected to incur 1.00% cumulative losses over the transaction life, and has a pattern of repetitive loss curves, it is possible to forecast early on how the pool will perform. Let's look at a specific example for a subprime issuer. We assume a cumulative loss forecast of 10%, and the loss curve typically is 75% complete by month 18. At month 18, the pool ought to have no more than 7.50% cumulative losses. If cumulative losses exceed 7.50% at that point, total cumulative losses will likely exceed 10%. Let's assume that losses are actually 8.50% at month 18. The adjusted total cumulative loss forecast is approximately 11.33% instead of 10%.

An accurate forecast hinges on loss curves with repetitive patterns. Loss curves are generally consistent among prime issuers. However, if Moody's statement—that loss curves are becoming more back-ended—is correct, an adjustment to the forecast is required. The adjustment must coincide with the new shape of the loss curve. Using the same example, if the loss curve is more back-ended, and we now assume that by month 18 only 50% of losses have occurred, with a 10% cumulative loss forecast, cumulative losses should not exceed 5%. If actual cumulative losses are 7.50%, the forecast must be adjusted to 15% total cumulative losses. With the trend among

---

[5] Moody's Subprime Auto Loan Credit Indexes: 1st Quarter 2000—Static Indexes Continue To Rise: More Back-Ended Loss Curve May Be The Cause, July 14, 2000.

some finance companies in the subprime arena to make longer-term loans up to 72 months, it is certainly possible to see more back-ended losses.

Loss curve forecasting is useful for investors to monitor pool performance during the life of the transaction, and particularly important for those investors that buy subordinated classes of auto deals, which have less credit enhancement against losses than senior classes.

Structures

Two structures are commonly used—grantor trusts and owner trusts. The primary difference between grantor and owner trusts is the allocation of cash flow among the different classes of securities:

- *Grantor trusts* accommodate a pass-through structure and were the original structures in the market. The cash flow is paid simultaneously to all classes. The grantor trust structure mirrors the actual cash flows of the majority of auto loan contracts. Auto loans typically pay monthly over a period of 36 to 60 months. (As previously stated, some lenders have been lending up to 72 months in recent years but the significance is generally small).
- *Owner trusts* provide the ability to time tranche and to re-allocate cash flow among senior and subordinate investors. This structure has a series of classes in staggered maturity. There is typically a short-term money-market class, a one-year, a two-year, and a three-year class. The owner trust allows sequential (instead of pro-rata) payment of cash flows, and repays investors in order of maturity and seniority.

First, the trust pays interest, typically to all classes. Next, the trust directs principal payments to each class in order of maturity instead of pro rata. Therefore, the trust allocates all principal payments (typically monthly) to the money market class until it is repaid, then directs all principal payments to the one-year class until it is retired, and so on. Although referred to as money market, one-year, two-year and three-year classes, there is generally monthly amortization within a narrow window in each of the classes, corresponding to the cash flow of the collateral. In the event of default, cash flows would revert to a pro-rata allocation of cash flows.

Typical Auto Loan Structures

We show a typical auto loan structure in Exhibit 2.10. The seller/servicer originates a pool of auto loans and sells the receivables, the rights to receive proceeds, and the lien on the vehicles into a bankruptcy-remote grantor or

EXHIBIT 2.10 Typical Auto Loan ABS Structure

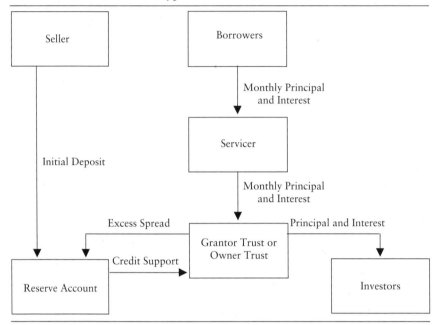

Source: Salomon Smith Barney.

owner trust. The sale is a true sale of assets, meaning that the conditions for sale treatment have been met.

The principal and interest is passed along to investors. Most auto deals have a *cash reserve account,* with the initial deposit provided by the seller. The cash reserve account provides additional credit enhancement, and the seller pledges the account to the trust. The structure generates *excess spread* and pays it into the cash reserve account, if required. Excess spread is cash flow that remains after the payment of all deal expenses. Deal expenses include the coupon, servicing and trustee fees and the absorption of losses.

Excess spread may be required to fully fund the required reserve account amount, provide additional credit enhancement if the pool performance deterioration trips any triggers, or else it may be paid out to the seller.

Alternative Structures

Prefunding   Some issuers choose to prefund vehicle loan origination (borrow in advance of contract origination). Market conditions may be especially attractive, or the issuer needs a critical mass of loans to securitize. In an ABS, prefunding may cover up to six months of future originations, but generally terminates within two to three months. In the event that the originator fails to originate sufficient receivables, the funds in the escrow fund are returned to the investors as a prepayment. The undercollateralized prefunded portion is deposited into a prefunding escrow account. The trustee may release the escrow account upon substitution of qualified receivables. The new receivables must be consistent with the underwriting standards in the rest of the pool, and may have other restrictions, such as maximum maturity and minimum coupon, so that the integrity of the receivables pool is maintained.

Soft Bullet Structures Two of the top three auto companies began to issue a new structure in late 1999 and early 2000. In lieu of a conventional amortizing deal, the new structure provides for a soft bullet repayment of the term notes. The trust simultaneously issues a series of term notes and asset-backed commercial paper notes. The same receivables pool collateralizes both series. The trust cash flow is first directed to the commercial paper notes, and all principal collections are applied against reduction of the commercial paper notes. The targeted maturity of the first series of term notes coincides with the expected reduction of the first series of commercial paper notes to zero (based on historical prepayment speeds). To repay the first series of term notes when due, the trust issues a new series of ABS commercial paper, and with the proceeds repays the terms notes in a bullet. The sequence begins again until the deal is fully repaid (see Exhibit 2.11).

The collateral may pay *faster than expected* and the trust may reduce the commercial paper notes to zero before the bullet term note is scheduled to mature. A designated account will accumulate collections from the receivables pool until the term note matures. The accumulated funds in the account and proceeds from new commercial paper issuance will repay the term note.

If the collateral pays *more slowly than expected,* and the commercial paper is still outstanding upon maturity of the soft bullet, the trust may still issue a new series of commercial paper notes to retire the term notes. The two series of commercial paper notes are then simultaneously outstanding, and principal collections repay the two series of commercial paper on a sequential basis.

The bullet classes maturity dates are "targeted" dates. The notes will extend if the trust is unable to sell commercial paper to retire that class on its targeted distribution date. A disruption in the commercial paper market, for example, might cause such an event. While this is extremely unlikely, the trust would then apply principal collections pro-rata to the commercial paper notes outstanding and to the class next targeted for maturity. The trust would

EXHIBIT 2.11 ABS Commercial Paper Notes Absorb Principal Amortization and Allow Soft Bullet Term Notes Structure

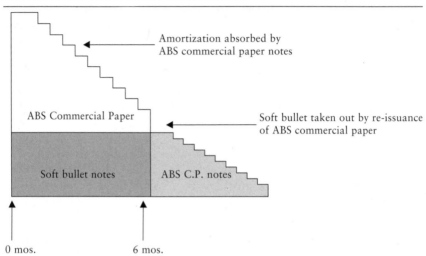

Source: Salomon Smith Barney.

attempt to get back on track with the bullet structure for the next class. However, if two consecutive bullet maturities are not paid in full, the structure begins sequential amortization, with pro-rata application of principal against the bullet notes and any outstanding commercial paper.

The commercial paper notes are floating rate, yet the collateral is fixed rate. The trust enters into an interest rate swap with a swap counterparty to remove the interest rate risk of the trust floating liability. If the swap were to terminate, the commercial paper interest rate will automatically become a fixed rate payable by the trust, and the trust will not be permitted to issue future commercial paper notes.

Credit Enhancement

Auto loan securities typically have combinations of several of the following types of credit enhancement:

- *Cash reserve account*—The seller generally makes an up-front cash deposit into a cash reserve fund. This cash reserve may be fully or partially funded up-front. Excess spread retention over time would complete full cash reserve funding requirement. Cash reserve funds are usually allowed to invest in permissible investments until the cash is required. Some structures allow the use of cash investments in additional receivables. (That generates a higher yield than money market investments). This, however, creates additional risk that some of those receivables will incur losses.

■ *Excess spread*—Excess spread is additional credit enhancement that is available to the trust to absorb losses, if needed. Excess spread is cash flow remaining in any given month after payment of all the deal expenses, including losses. The seller may receive payment of the excess spread in any month it is not needed in the deal. The formula for excess spread is

$$\text{Pool yield} - \left(\frac{\text{Servicing fee} + \text{Coupon interest}}{\text{expense} + \text{Losses}} \right) = \text{Excess spread}$$

Excess spread on prime auto loans is generally between 1.50% to 3.00% after losses. Excess spread on subprime auto loans is generally higher, between 4% to 7% p.a. after losses. Higher excess spread from a subprime pool provides a larger cushion to absorb greater variability of expected losses than that of a prime pool. On a risk-adjusted return basis, cash from the excess spread varies over the life of a transaction, depending on the timing of losses (loss curve), and prepayments, especially of higher coupon loans.

■ *Subordination*—Investors and the seller/servicer generally share ownership of the trust. Each owns a proportional undivided interest in the auto loans, and the seller's interest is subordinate to the senior interest in its right to receive payments. The trust may sell subordinate classes in the public market to third party investors and reduce its "subordinate interest."

■ *Turbo payments*—The trust may accelerate repayment of the senior classes by the application of excess spread to the senior tranches. The effect of this is that the remaining subordinated class as a proportion of the outstanding deal is greater than the original structure.

■ *Overcollateralization*—If the receivable pool balance exceeds the notes issued under the security structure, this is overcollateralization. This is another form of subordination—cash flows generated by the larger pool balance are available to absorb losses.

■ *Triggers*—Triggers are provisions in place to capture more credit enhancement in the event of pool deterioration. Triggers are usually tied to levels of pool delinquency and losses. They are generally based on a variance to historical pool performance, and generally require the spread account to build to a certain level by trapping excess spread. The worse the pool performance, the higher the required cash reserve account level.

Alternatively, excess spread could also be applied to "turbo" the senior classes in lieu of building the cash reserve account. That would increase the subordination as a percent of the transaction by reducing the senior classes disproportionately as previously discussed.

■ *Monoline insurance*—Third party insurance may be used to guarantee repayment of auto loan (and other) ABS, and monoline insurance is frequently utilized by subprime auto issuers. Monolines are mostly triple-A rated insurance companies whose sole purpose is to guaranty payment of principal and interest to investors. In addition to a repayment guaranty, many monolines indemnify investors against the bankruptcy risk, in the event that the court did not uphold the structure's bankruptcy-remoteness. Investors ought to have a clear understanding of precisely what the monoline guaranties, and the timing of claims payments. Some monolines guaranty for full principal and interest when due, while others guaranty timely interest and ultimate principal.

Other Risk Factors

Servicing risk addresses the concern that the servicer will survive the full life of the securitization in order to service the collateral. Several points ought to be considered in relation to servicing risk:

■ *Financial stability of seller-servicer and access to liquidity.* Seller-servicers are not always investment-grade companies, and the investor should spend some time to understand the servicer. It is especially important that the seller should have access to a continuing source of liquidity and capital. Finance companies need liquidity in order to continue to originate new business. This is most critical in a high portfolio growth environment where the servicer has negative cash flow (originates more contracts than mature in any period). Funding requirements may exceed the cash flow produced by the servicer's managed portfolio. Therefore, investors should spend some of their due diligence to gain an understanding of the seller's access to capital and liquidity.

■ *Servicing intensity of collateral.* How much servicing intensity needs to be applied to the collateral? Subprime accounts, or the "underserved" market requires frequent and intensive servicing. Investors need to factor in the competence and experience of the servicer, and the adequacy of the resources devoted to servicing. Higher losses and a delay in servicing transfer should be factored into stress tests run by investors.

■ *Ability of a third-party servicer to assume collateral servicing, if neces-sary.* In the event of a servicer failure, how generic is the collateral and how many other servicers would be able to assume servicing the port-folio? If the servicer is non-investment grade, investors may consider having a "hot" back-up servicer that runs a parallel set of books and is able to assume servicing on little notice. "Hot" back-up servicers are generally found mostly in the private markets.

Underwriting and Collections Risks

A servicer's underwriting policies determine the credit profile of the collat-eral pool. Collections policies outline how the servicer manages the pool collateral. Greater underwriting risks require more collections and servicing intensity.

In reviewing the collateral pool in a securitization, the following infor-mation is generally provided in a prospectus:

■ *Delinquency and net loss history.* This information is generally avail-able for the managed pool, not for static pools. Check to see if the is-suer reports static pool information on a Web site or on Bloomberg. Delinquencies and losses affect the cash flow of the pool. Delinquencies arise from obligors that fail to make a payment by the due date. Delin-quencies provide an early warning signal for upcoming losses. A per-centage of delinquencies will most likely become uncollectable. It is important to examine the stability and level of delinquencies and net losses and their trends in order to evaluate the sufficiency of credit en-hancement versus expectations. The servicer's *collections policy* for payments that are behind is generally outlined in the prospectus. Gen-erally, the collections policy outlines when and how often the servicer contacts the borrower and when they will charge-off an account. The servicer may also describe some of the systems used to originate and to collect auto loans.

Collections need to be much more intensive for a subprime obligor base than for a prime obligor base. The servicer is likely to describe the timing and frequency of contact for slow accounts and repossession policies. They may provide general details about their origination and collections systems. Subprime collateral is more servicing intensive than prime collateral and warrants closer inspection of the servicing and col-lections issues.

■ *New versus used mix.* Most auto lenders grant credit for the purchase of used as well as new vehicles. New vehicles depreciate more quickly than used vehicles, but generally hold up their collateral value better over the life of a transaction. In addition, a higher quality obligor generally purchases a new vehicle over a used vehicle. Therefore, prime lenders tend to finance a greater mix of new versus used vehicles. Subprime lenders tend to finance mostly used vehicles.

- *Minimum, maximum, average loan balance.* It is useful to examine the distribution of loan balances. Concentrations in large loan balances may result in higher severity of losses for those loans. Changes in any of the averages from prior deals may signal a change in underwriting policies.
- *Weighted average original maturity, weighted average remaining maturity and mix of contracts.* This measures the seasoning of the pool (how long ago the servicer made the loans) and the remaining term to maturity. The contract maturities are usually well-distributed to provide a pool with short average life characteristics.
- *Geographic diversity.* A geographically well-balanced pool is desirable. Large regional or state concentrations might invite further inquiry into the laws or loss patterns peculiar to that region. The rating agencies will generally require extra credit enhancement to compensate for any unusual geographic concentrations.

Other Information   The following information is generally *not* provided in prospectuses, but investors may have opportunities to ask for this information in issuer meetings or in site visits:

- *Average FICO score, range and mix of scores.* This provides a general idea of the obligor quality of the pool and is comparable across issuers. The minimum FICO score acceptable to the servicer provides insight into the range of obligor quality.
- *Average advance on vehicle value.* This is more important for subprime lenders. Higher losses are generally experienced on high advance rates. Most lenders will generally advance no more than 105% to 110% of NADA wholesale value, plus tax, tags and insurance.
- *Number of first payment defaults (for subprime issuers).* This should be a low number, even for subprime lenders. First payment defaults should be in a range of 1% or less.
- *Contract extensions policies.* The servicer ought to have a policy concerning extensions on contracts. The investor wishes to ensure that extensions will not unduly lengthen the average life of the pool. Another concern is that extensions may disguise credit problems. Monoline insurers of subprime vehicle pools generally limit the amount of extensions that may be granted by the servicer, and the proportion of extended contracts in the pool.

■ *Number of accounts serviced per collector.* Subprime collateral is more servicing-intensive than prime collateral. The servicer needs to call higher risk delinquent accounts more frequently than a prime account. The nature of the obligor is such that they are often more leveraged, and the lender often needs to call the obligor to remind them to make a payment. Sixty-day delinquent accounts are more serious than 30-day delinquent accounts. Some servicers specially handle the more serious delinquency buckets. It is useful to compare and contrast among similar issuers the resources they devote to covering delinquent accounts and their process to manage collections.

■ *Underwriting decision model—automated or subjective.* Many lenders have risk-based proprietary decision-making systems. It is interesting to find out the lenders strategy, how long it has been in place, and what their success is. It is also useful to ask how often policy exceptions are made and whether exceptions are tracked for performance.

■ *Average discount (applicable for subprime paper).* Many subprime lenders do not purchase the vehicle contract at face value, but at a discount to face value. The average discount provides an idea how "deep" the servicer lends. The more deeply discounted contracts are riskier credits.

Credit Enhancement Analysis

We discussed the various types of credit enhancement commonly used for auto securitizations earlier. For most transactions, the credit enhancement is typically a cash reserve account, subordination and excess spread. The credit enhancement is sized appropriately for the rating level to cover the expected pool losses during the securitization life. The amount of credit enhancement will vary according to the expected pool losses and the historical volatility of the issuer's losses. Therefore, prime issuers will have the lowest credit enhancement, followed by nonprime issuers, and finally subprime issuers will have the most credit enhancement (and additionally, often a monoline wrap).

Cash reserve accounts are not always fully funded up-front. The rating agencies will take into consideration the timing of losses—it generally takes time for a pool to season—there are typically no delinquent accounts in the pool in excess of 30 days at the time of new issue. Therefore, excess spread has a chance to build in the structure to augment the credit enhancement when losses begin to occur.

Triggers are built into many transactions to increase credit enhancement in the event of performance deterioration. Performance is usually tied to delinquencies and losses. If performance falls below defined levels, the servicer may not receive excess spread unless they fortify the cash reserve account.

Payment Speeds

Payment speeds of auto loan ABS are extremely stable due to the short final maturity (generally within five years), and disincentive to refinance. There is generally no benefit for borrowers to refinance in order to obtain a lower rate for auto loans, consequently, there is little prepayment volatility. This is because the interest rate is generally much higher for used vehicles than for new autos. Payment speeds are generally expressed as an asset-backed speed. Transactions generally pay between a 1.5 to 1.7 asset-backed speed.

Other Auto Products

Dealer Floor Plan Loans   The practice of lenders that provide loans to auto dealers for the purpose of financing vehicle inventory is called dealer floor planning. This provides working capital for dealers financing inventory in the showroom and on the dealer lot before selling it to retail customers. Floor plan lenders may be the vehicle manufacturer, a bank or finance company, and the loans are generally made to franchised new vehicle dealers.

Vehicles and proceeds secure these loans, and they generally require interest only until the vehicle is sold. The advance rate on the loans may include the wholesale vehicle price plus destination charges. The dealer repays the loan on the sale of the vehicle.

These structures look very much like credit card ABS. A bankruptcy-remote vehicle purchases the floor plan loans, and is secured by the vehicles and proceeds. Transactions mirror the dynamics of the underlying receivables with a bullet or soft bullet maturity. As vehicle inventory turns over fairly quickly, the receivables pool revolves and new advances replace runoff until the security maturity. Losses are low on dealer floor plan transactions, and diversification generally good, but investors should be aware of the consolidating trend in the auto dealer business that may affect the diversification of these pools. Investors are typically well protected, however, by concentration triggers in the structure.

Fleet Financing

Daily rental car companies found a cost-effective solution in the ABS market to finance their vehicle inventory. Daily rental car companies purchase vast amounts of vehicles from the big three auto manufacturers and foreign manufacturers. It is their largest corporate investment, requiring a significant amount of capital. In fact, the daily rental companies are some of the largest global customers of the vehicle manufacturers. Actually, several of the vehicle manufacturers used to own rental car companies. Most of them were spun-off in the mid-1990s, however, in the belief that the rental companies may operate more effectively independently.

Program Vehicles The rental companies generally keep vehicle inventory for about 10 to 15 months, and then replace the vehicle with a new one. This exposes the rental companies, potentially, to a lot of residual value risk. Since the rental car companies are such major customers of the vehicle manufacturers, many of them have a contractual buyback arrangement with vehicle manufacturers. The manufacturer will repurchase the vehicle at a predetermined price. This eliminates the residual value exposure for the rental company.

The contracts are usually renewable annually, and it is a symbiotic relationship that encourages contract renewals. For the manufacturer, the rental firms are their largest customers. The rental companies will absorb some vehicle models that may be difficult for the manufacturers to sell elsewhere. The rental company is able to achieve cost savings by bulk purchases and immunity from residual value risk.

The rental company will depreciate the vehicle during the expected holding period, amortizing it to the manufacturer's buyback price. (The depreciation expense is typically 1.50% to 2.00% monthly.) The vehicle manufacturer (many of them investment-grade) has the unconditional obligation to repurchase the "program vehicle" at a stated price. There is a minimum holding period and penalties apply for early returns. This arrangement is called a *program* vehicle and eliminates residual value losses for the rental company.

Nonprogram Vehicles Inventory that rental companies purchase *without* a buyback guaranty is called *at risk* or *nonprogram* vehicles. Some vehicle rental companies prefer to take the residual value risk on a portion of their vehicle fleet, while utilizing the manufacturers' buyback guaranty on other portions of their inventory. The goal of firms that manage nonprogram vehicles is to dispose of the vehicles at a profit. The rental companies will depreciate nonprogram vehicles at a rate that is expected to yield a profit or to at least break even on the sale of the vehicles. This exposes the company to residual value fluctuations, however.

Transactions Structures The credit enhancement is a dynamic borrowing base, greater for nonprogram than for program vehicles. Program vehicles rely on the manufacturer repurchase agreement that creates a receivable from an investment-grade auto manufacturer. Nonprogram vehicles rely on the cash flow from selling the nonprogram vehicles in the used car market. Credit enhancement is typically subordination, overcollateralization and a letter of credit, and takes into account the length of time that would be required to liquidate the inventory.

Transactions are structured as a revolving asset pool with a bullet or soft bullet. A special-purpose bankruptcy remote vehicle (SPV) will purchase the vehicles from the manufacturer and lease them back to the daily rental company. The transaction is secured by a lien on program and nonprogram vehicles, and proceeds due under the lease agreement between the SPV and the rental company.

Cash flows come from two sources:

1. Lease payments due from the rental company;
2. Sale of vehicles from the buyback programs or sale of the vehicles in the used car market.

The lease payments are equal to all the expenses incurred by the SPV. The SPV expenses include interest expense, vehicle depreciation, and any incidental charges such as early return fees on program vehicles, salvage and the like. Depreciation and interest expense are the largest monthly expenses.

Similar to a credit card revolving pool, the trust may replace repayments under the lease with purchases of additional vehicles during the revolving period. Prior to maturity, the pool will cease to revolve, and the transaction will pay down in a bullet or soft bullet.

The vehicle lease and vehicles secure the SPV. It is not intended that investors absorb the residual value risk of the borrowing base. The depreciation expense is supposed to adequately cover fluctuations in vehicle values at any point in time. This is accomplished in several ways. Some structures provide that the vehicles are marked-to-market each month based on national auction market (NADA) results. If the depreciation charge for the pool is insufficient for the nonprogram vehicles, the rental company must pay a higher adjusted lease payment. Another protection sometimes used is a *Residual Value Realization Test*. If the rental car company experiences an aggregate loss upon the disposition of nonprogram vehicles, the required credit enhancement levels will increase for those vehicles.

Credit Enhancement   The rating agencies establish separate credit enhancement requirements for program and nonprogram (risk) vehicles. The total credit enhancement of the pool is dynamic, calculated as a weighted average of the credit enhancement for the program and nonprogram vehicles. The mix of program and nonprogram vehicles may change over the life of the transaction as the trust disposes of and purchases new vehicles. The rating agencies generally cap the amount of nonprogram vehicles allowed in the pool.

A point to note is that the rating agencies do not give any credit to vehicles with a contractual manufacturer buyback agreement if the manufacturer's rating is below a certain level, generally single-A. The credit enhancement for those vehicles is treated as nonprogram vehicles. This provides a certain amount of over-enhancement.

Some market transactions have utilized monoline insurance guarantees.

Credit Risk   The credit risk of the transaction weighs on the ability of the rental company to make payments under the lease and the manufacturer's ability to honor its obligations. In the event of an early amortizing event, the trustee would take action against its security interest in the collateral and the vehicle inventory would be sold in the auction market. The credit enhancement is sized for the amount of time it would be necessary for the trustee to take the necessary action against the collateral and to sell it in the auction market without incurring any losses, including all carrying charges.

The credit enhancement is sized to cover very adverse circumstances. The rating agencies took into account a liquidation bankruptcy for the rental company, as well as a stay period greater than the 60 days required by bankruptcy codes. The credit enhancement assumes that the rental company suspends lease payments to the trust during the stay period. The bondholder's risk is greater the longer it takes to liquidate the vehicles, as the vehicles in the pool continue to depreciate and to accrue financing charges.

The credit risk is very dependent on the ability of the auto rental company to make uninterrupted lease payments to the trust. The rental company is the sole obligor in the transaction. Therefore, a careful analysis of the auto rental company as an unsecured stand-alone entity is warranted.

Auto Leases

Some captive finance companies and banks have used the securitization market to finance their vehicle lease portfolios. Leasing now accounts for a substantial proportion of all U.S. vehicle sales—between 35% to 45%. Closed-end leases are the most common consumer vehicle leases. In a closed-end lease, the lessor retains ownership of the vehicle. The consumer pays some up-front costs—a capitalized cost reduction (small down payment equivalent), taxes, registration and other fees and charges.

The monthly lease payment is lower than it would be on a comparable loan for same purchased vehicle. This is because the lease payment depreciates the vehicle only to the lease termination date, and assumes a "residual" value at the lease maturity. For example, a 36-month lease payment may cover about 40% of the vehicle cost. The lessor forecasts that the value of that vehicle will be worth 60% of the original cost at the lease maturity in 36 months. That forecast is called *residual valuation*. The lease payment also includes charges for interest, taxes and other fees. On the other hand, a vehicle loan payment covers the entire vehicle cost in the loan period. Even with a longer repayment period, loan payments are generally higher than lease payments.

Credit Losses   Credit losses are very low on vehicle leases because the criteria are very stringent to obtain a lease. Credit losses on leased vehicles are much lower than even prime auto loans, and is not a great risk in leased transactions.

Residual Value   The greatest risk in a lease-backed transaction is the residual value risk. At the lease maturity, the lessor has the option, but not the obligation, to purchase the vehicle at the preestablished residual value price. If the vehicle residual value at lease maturity is *less* than the market value of the vehicle (i.e., lessee can sell the car for more than residual value), many lessees will exercise their option to purchase the vehicle at the residual option price. However, some lessees prefer to always drive a new vehicle, and will return the car even if there is a profit on the residual. On the other hand, if the residual value price *exceeds* the market price (i.e., market price is less than the residual), lessees will usually return the vehicle to the lessor. If the lessee terminates the lease prior to maturity, the lessee is responsible for the residual value. Therefore, the leasing company will only be at risk for residual value exposure for leases that go to full term.

Turn-Ins   Leased vehicles that are returned to the manufacturer are called *turn-ins*. Turn-ins create the possibility for the manufacturer to incur a loss on the residual value. In the early 1990s, turn-in rates as a proportion of managed lease pools were in the low 30% range among major vehicle manufacturers. In recent times, turn-in percentages have increased, and are in the 60% to 70% range.[6] This is partially because in the strong economy, many people are turning back leased vehicles for another new one.

Turn-ins are not a bad thing. The manufacturer has another opportunity to lease a new vehicle to the customer and to sell the used vehicle to a new customer. Turn-ins increase the chances that there will be a loss on the vehicle, but proper initial residual value setting and effective vehicle disposal management mitigate the risks of greater turn-ins.

---

[6] Lease-backed ABS prospectuses.

Losses Frequency and Severity   Moody's looks at the frequency and severity of losses to size credit enhancement in their approach to rating lease-backed transactions. Turn-ins addresses the *frequency* component of the risk, where the manufacturer may incur a loss on the residual in reselling the vehicles. *Severity* of loss is addressed by whether or not the vehicle manufacturer incurs a loss on the returned vehicle in resale. Losses on residual valuations have been mixed in recent years. Many banks and manufacturers have experienced higher turn-ins and higher losses on the re-sale of vehicles. However, healthy credit enhancement protects the higher turn-ins and expected losses in ABS lease securitizations (see next section).

Structure

A special purpose, bankruptcy remote vehicle called a "titling trust" purchases and owns the vehicles. The trust has a beneficial interest in a designated portfolio of leases and vehicles in the titling trust, also known as a *special unit of beneficial interest* (SUBI). It is the SUBI and the rights associated with it that are securitized. Neither ownership of the leased vehicles nor lease receivables are part of the securitized trust estate but remain in the titling trust. The SUBI is a claim on the designated portfolio of contracts and leased vehicles and gives the securitization trustee a right to cash payments received from these assets.

Deals may be structured as pass-throughs or sequential cash flows. Credit enhancement looks very similar to auto loan transactions, although credit enhancement is greater to cover potential residual value losses. There is generally a cash reserve account, subordination or overcollateralization and excess spread. Several deals have incorporated dynamic credit enhancement where the cash reserve account is nondeclining. This builds credit enhancement over the life of the transaction, as the cash reserve account is a greater proportion in relation to the declining balance of the security.

Some issuers have chosen to cover the residual value risk with residual value risk insurance from a highly rated insurer, and to assign it for the benefit of the SUBI interests.

2.3 A PRIMER ON CREDIT CARD ASSET-BACKED SECURITIES

The securitization market recognized the potential of credit cards receivables early on. They were one of the first sectors to develop in the ABS market, and are among the most liquid products. In terms of outstanding issuance, credit cards represent the largest single sector of the ABS market, with $228 billion outstanding as of August 31, 2000, about 26% of the market (see Exhibit 2.12).

EXHIBIT 2.12 ABS Outstanding Volume by Sector as of August 31, 2000

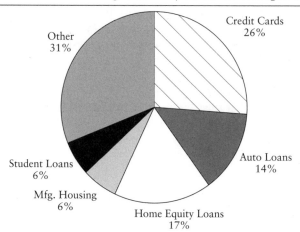

Source: Bloomberg.

Credit cards receivables are pools of largely unsecured obligations[7] owed by individuals to the issuer of the card, generally a bank or finance company under the auspices of the Master Card or Visa Associations. These are known as *bank* credit cards. Obligors may repay credit cards on extended terms. Some retail organizations also issue their own proprietary credit cards for the purchase of merchandise or services (*private label* credit cards). Credit cards are sometimes a misnomer for Charge cards. Firms that allow charges for goods and services, but require payment of the full balance each month issue charge cards. They do not allow repayment on extended terms like a credit card. American Express and Diners Club issue well-known charge cards. The ABS market has a few charge card issuers, and hereinafter the term *credit card* is used generically and may also refer to a *charge card*.

Credit Cards Charge Mechanics

Credit card receivables arise through purchases of services or merchandise, or cash advances via credit placed on the card. Some firms also issue checks that may utilize the available credit limits. Card companies generally bill clients monthly and the customer is not charged an interest rate if they

---

[7] Some issuers have secured or partially secured accounts.

repay the balance in full within a defined grace period following billing. An interest rate applies on the outstanding balance should the client choose to revolve the account, with a small monthly principal and interest payment typically required. There are no penalties to pay more than the minimum amount due.

The monthly principal as a percentage of the outstanding pool repaid by the credit card issuer's account base is referred to as the *principal payment rate*. The payment rate is generally calculated monthly to correspond with the billing cycle for credit card usage. This indicates how quickly the receivable base can liquidate the pool assuming a constant pool balance. It would take approximately two to three years to liquidate a constant pool with receivables paying only the minimum payment each month. Payment rates vary among issuers depending on their customer strategy, but usually range from 8% to 20% monthly. Some encourage *revolving* customers (card users that pay less than the total monthly balance), while others encourage *convenience* usage (balances paid in full each month).

Competition has intensified among credit card issuers, and most offer a range of interest rate plans based on some sort of risk-based pricing model. Interest rates typically range from high single digits to the maximum allowed under the bank's home state usury ceilings. Additionally some issuers offer very low "teaser" rates to attract new accounts. Some banks charge an annual fee for card usage, although in today's competitive environment, this is becoming less commonplace. Other fees may apply, for late payments, insufficient funds checks, and so on. Card issuers also charge merchants a fee for processing an account. So, if an individual charges a $100 item, the merchant will typically only receive $96 to $98 and the fee is split between the card association and the issuing card bank. This fee income is called *interchange* and is typically an additional 1% to 2% in revenue. Therefore, credit card issuers derive additional sources of revenues besides interest income in the form of credit card fees and interchange.

In a credit card securitization, the combination of these items: card fees, interest and interchange income, finance charges income, and equal *pool yield*. Many issuers also add recoveries on charged-off loans back into pool yield, and monthly pool performance reports often include this number.

Losses and *delinquencies* also affect the performance of a securitization. Delinquencies and losses have a direct impact on the cash flow of the pool. *Delinquencies* refer to accounts with receivables balances that have failed to make a payment when due. Losses arise from receivables the servicer considers uncollectable. Losses are typically net of recoveries. Charge-offs are before recoveries. The seller-servicer will establish a policy for the period of time by which the receivable must make a payment. This is typically within 90 to 120 days past the due date. Accounts that fail to make any payments within this period will be charged-off by the master trust, or sooner in the event an obligor files for bankruptcy.

Many credit card issuers are experiencing a significant amount of losses from bankruptcies that often occur without any prior warning signals. Therefore, unlike in a static pool such as auto loans, where higher delinquencies are an early radar sign for impending losses, credit card pool delinquencies do not always signal upcoming charge-offs. Bankruptcies account for a large proportion of major credit card issuers losses.[8]

Industry Consolidation

There is increasing consolidation among issuers in the market. As of August 2000, about 50% of the entire credit card market is concentrated among the top 4 or 5 issuers, and about 75% of the market is among the top 10 issuers.[9] Some credit card banks find it increasingly difficult to compete for market share, and others lack the necessary infrastructure to efficiently process applications and to service the account once it is in place. The consolidation in the banking sector is another factor responsible for this trend.

Attracting New Card Holders

Credit card issuers have traditionally sought new accounts by direct mail solicitation, and many have competed for the business by offering subsidized balance transfers, also known as "teaser rates." For example, the issuer may invite a customer to apply for a new account and offer them the first three months of a balance transfer, at 5.6% pa, where the standard market rate would be 18% for that customer. The subsidized program would allow the customer to transfer the balance and to borrow at 5.6% pa for the first three months, and then the rate would revert to the market rate. This is becoming an increasingly expensive method to attract new customers unless losses on the portfolio are commensurate with the income generated by the lower rate.

The Internet is a natural new account application source. However, many credit card issuers are approaching the Internet cautiously until they are able to analyze a greater sample of results over a meaningful time period. The potential for fraud is one concern, and credit quality is another.

Additionally, credit card issuers source new accounts from other avenues, such as university students and affinity groups. They may offer additional incentives for merchandise or the like in exchange for opening the account and

---

[8] Salomon Smith Barney.
[9] Ibid.

utilizing the card. Well-known programs along these lines are airlines mileage programs and automobile purchase programs.

How Do Credit Card Securitizations Work?

Like any securitization, the basics start with a sale of receivables into a special purpose entity to achieve off-balance sheet accounting treatment for the "real" issuer and to de-link the receivables from the underlying seller-servicer. In today's environment, the important factor for off-balance sheet treatment is (1) legal isolation of the receivables and (2) proof that the seller-servicer no longer "controls" the receivables. The seller sells the receivables and proceeds to the trust, and the trustee takes a perfected security interest in the collateral.

A credit card pool, unlike an amortizing asset pool (i.e., auto loans and home equity loans), is a *revolving pool* of assets. Repayments may be replaced by new charges and the credit limit may continually be utilized to the maximum limit. The credit card securitization mirrors the revolving nature of the underlying asset pool. Each month, receivables are repaid and new charges replace repayments, enabling the issuer to maintain a level pool balance, (assuming active utilization of the accounts in the receivables pool). Prior to the securitization maturity, the structure ceases to revolve and begins to accumulate monthly repayments in a designated account to repay investors in a single payment called a *soft bullet* payment.

Master Trusts

Most credit card securitizations are issued today out of a *master trust,* meaning that multiple issuances can be supported by one "master" receivables pool. The seller-servicer will designate a group of accounts, and pledge the receivables thereof to the trust. Because accounts tend to change over time, the trust may need to replace accounts that provide the receivables to the trust, and there is generally a provision to enable the seller to add accounts. Master trusts may have *static* or *dynamic* account additions. Static account additions provide for a limited number of times when accounts can be added to a pool. Dynamic account additions may be added continuously to a master trust pool.

The rating agencies generally limit the amount of additional accounts that can be added to a master trust in order to preserve the consistency of the underwriting standards applied to the receivables in the trust. Static and dynamic account additions will each have a different effect on the pool. Static one-time new account additions tend to initially understate delinquencies and losses, as it takes a while for a new account to season. Dynamic account additions tend to dilute the ability to analyze the underwriting characteristics of the pool because of the delayed seasoning effect.

The structural mechanics of a Master Trust with a revolving/bullet structure are illustrated in Exhibit 2.13. The different ownership interests are shown by the *transferor's interest* and *investors interest*. The transferor's interest (also known as *sellers interest*) is the least amount required by the rating agencies to absorb dilution (referred to as the *required sellers interest*) but is typically a much larger amount. Dilution is amounts related to disputes or returns. For example, someone may not recall charging an item and will ask the credit card issuer to investigate the item. If the item is a bona fide charge incurred by the cardholder, the cardholder will be required to pay for the disputed charge. If the item is a mistake, the card issuer will not charge the cardholder and will settle up with the merchant. Most card issuers typically have a small amount of the pool always in dispute. Thus, the rating agencies require the issuer to allocate an proportion of the trust to absorb dilution, that is typically 5% to 10% of the pool balance, depending on the historical rates.

The wave-like lines across the top of the chart demonstrate the month-to-month fluctuations in the trust pool. The step-like lines illustrate the cessation of the revolving period and the accumulation of the repayments in an account (controlled amortization can also be used, but is less common in today's market) to retire the securitization.

EXHIBIT 2.13 Credit Card Securitization Structure—Master Trust

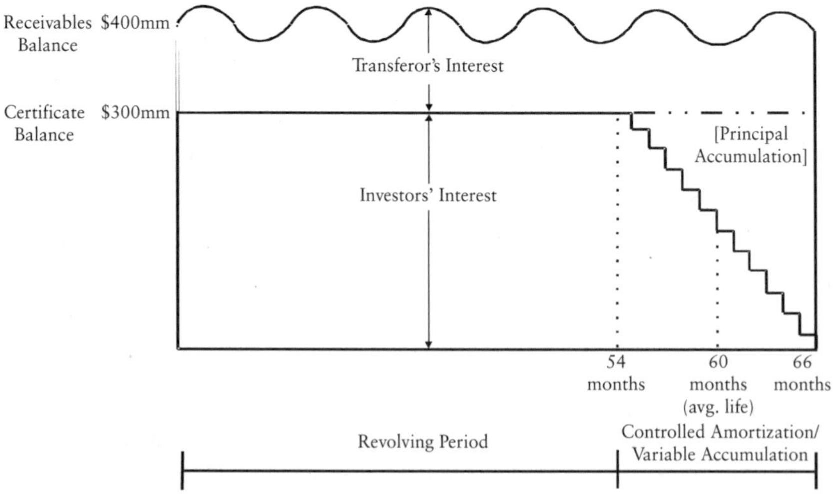

Important Factors for Investors to Analyze in a Master Trust   Investors ought to regularly analyze the characteristics of the receivables in the master trust. Pool yield, payment rate, delinquencies, losses and excess spread are the most important numbers to evaluate. These are monthly numbers that are released by the issuers to the investors via the trustee of the master trust. Additionally, many major issuers report these statistics on Web sites or on Bloomberg. To access this information on Bloomberg, type CCR <GO>.

Average account balance, line utilization, seasoning, account additions and new accounts yields are also useful to evaluate. Investors may sometimes find such information in the firm's 8K reports or in prospectuses.

Cash Flow Allocation and Impact on Master Trusts

In a master trust, most of the cash flow-impacting factors will be identical— pool yield, losses, delinquencies, payment rate. That is, the pool yield will be the same for all issues in the same master trust, losses the same, and so on. However, a master trust will most likely have differences among coupon interest expenses, which will cause excess spreads (net interest margin minus servicing expense) to be different across individual issues in the same master trust. This is because the master trust may issue various series of securities from the same master trust structure.

The timing of issuance and coupons are likely to be different for each issue. Some issues may be fixed, some floating. Coupons will be issued in different interest rate environments, high and low. A typical master trust structure with various issuance, called series, is illustrated in Exhibit 2.14. The illustrated master trust has four issues outstanding, two fixed and two

EXHIBIT 2.14 Master Trust Cash Flow Allocation

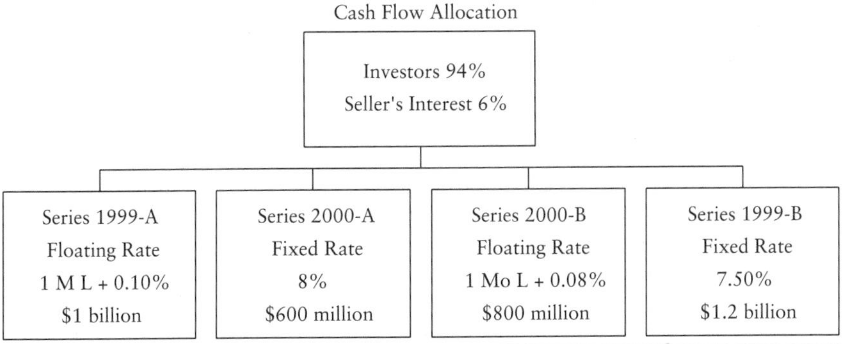

Cash Flow Allocation

Investors 94%	
Seller's Interest 6%	

Series 1999-A	Series 2000-A	Series 2000-B	Series 1999-B
Floating Rate	Fixed Rate	Floating Rate	Fixed Rate
1 M L + 0.10%	8%	1 Mo L + 0.08%	7.50%
$1 billion	$600 million	$800 million	$1.2 billion

Source: Salomon Smith Barney.

floating. The coupons are different for each issue. The 8% coupon issue will have a lower excess spread than the 7.50% coupon issue. *These differences in coupons impact cash flow and potentially the timing of triggers and early amortization* (see the glossary at the end of this book).

Recognizing that cash flow allocation may have a substantial impact on ABS investors, we describe two types of common structures that allocate finance charges according to different methods: (1) *Socialized finance charges* and (2) *Excess sharing.* The socialized finance charges method is not commonly used and most trusts allocate by subordinated excess sharing. We explain these methods in detail later.

There are several steps to calculate cash flow allocations:

1. Allocate finance charges between the investor interest and the seller interest. This is a proportionate split, in relation to the amount of receivables each is assigned in the trust.

2. The second step is to allocate and to re-allocate the investor interest portion of the finance charges across the various outstanding series. *It is this component that lacks uniformity, due to differences in the way different master trusts allocate finance charges.* Coupon differences among the various issues in the master trust may produce a different excess spread for any individual issue in the master trust. This would produce greater excess spread for the lower coupon issues than for the higher coupon issues in the master trust.

   As described in more detail next, finance charges can be allocated pro-rata (socialized) or may be allocated in accordance with the respective coupon for that individual issue (excess sharing).

3. Allocate principal collections. The master trust may share principal collections as described next.

Finance Charges Allocation Methods

1. *Excess sharing.* Cash flows are first allocated to each series based on the series proportion to the total investor's interest. As each series has a different coupon, there may be finance charges collected in excess of that required to service a low interest rate coupon, and these cash flows are available to service other higher coupon series. These "excess" collections from low coupon issues are generally available on a pro-rata basis to share among all series with a shortfall.

   In a high interest rate environment where the trust structure cannot support the weighted average pool coupon, there is a way to enhance the yield on the portfolio to preserve the mechanics of the structure. The seller may sell receivables into the trust at a discount. As we have been in a relatively stable interest rate environment for some time, the sale of discounted loans is more commonly used to improve the yield on a low-yielding portfolio. Alternatively, the seller may designate a portion of the finance charges collections as principal collections, reducing the outstanding principal balance.

2. *Socialized finance charges.* The servicer allocates the interest expense for all series as if one pool. The calculation is made on a weighted average cost basis and "excess" collections are allocated pro-rata among all series.

As there are differences between fixed and floating-rate coupons, the trust is generally credit enhanced and managed to a prespecified average coupon rate (the *managed rate*) and as long as the outstanding series rate is below the managed rate, the outstanding series will have some excess credit enhancement. In either situation, if excess cash flow exists after servicing all the required payments, the seller may receive excess spread payments. We summarize highlights of each structure and the pros and cons of each in Exhibit 2.15.

Principal Allocations

In most cases, principal is allocated in proportion to the outstanding amount of indebtedness. To the extent that any series is in a revolving period and does not require the full amount of its principal collections, excess principal collections can be used to offset pro rata deficiencies in other series that are in an amortizing or controlled amortization period.

As master trusts are dynamic entities in that the seller constantly issues or retires new series, investors ought to monitor the amounts outstanding, that is, monthly cash flows and debt service requirements. The sharing of principal collections is very beneficial to investors and allows

EXHIBIT 2.15 Master Trust Cash Flow Allocation Comparisons

		Socialization Structure	Excess Sharing Structure
Pros		Accommodates the issuance of series in high Interest rate environments.	Efficient utilization of credit enhancement
		Will delay the occurrence of early amortization in the trust.	
Cons		May result in over enhancement.	May require costly modifications to issue series in high interest rate environment (i.e., discount option)
		Will result in all series early amortizing simultaneously.	May result in the occurrence of an early amortization of individual series when the trust could otherwise support the series.
		Difficult to issue uncapped floating rate certificates.	

Source: Salomon Smith Barney.

trusts to pay back outstanding series more quickly than its monthly payment rate would imply.

APPENDIX
COMMON CREDIT CARD TERMS, TRIGGERS, AND TERMINOLOGY

Credit Card Securities	*Typical Terms*
Coupon	Fixed- or floating-rate
Floating Rate Index	1-month LIBOR or 3-month LIBOR
Average Life	3-years to 15-years
Payment Structure	Bullet or controlled amortization
Payment Frequency	Monthly, quarterly, or semi-annually
Credit Enhancement	Senior/subordination, cash collateral account or loan (CCA), class C notes, reserve account
Rating	Senior: triple-A
	Subordinate: single-A, triple-B and double-B
Trust Structure	Master trust
Receivables	Affinity/co-brand
	Bank card (Visa and MasterCard)
	Discover Card
	Retail (e.g., Target, JCPenney, Sears)
	Private label
	Charge card (American Express)

Typical Early Amortization Triggers:

- Failure to pay interest or principal;
- Failure to perform any covenant in any of the relevant agreements having a material adverse effect on the investors;
- Insolvency or bankruptcy events;
- Failure to make an addition of credit card receivables to the master trust when required;
- Master trust becomes an "investment company" under the Investment Company Act of 1940;
- Servicer default;
- False representations or warranties that remain unremedied;
- 3 months average excess spread declines below 0%; and
- Seller participation falls below required level.

CHAPTER 3

The Mechanics of Investing in Mortgage- and Asset-Backed Securities

Robert Young and Lakhbir Hayre

The same factors that make the investment characteristics of mortgage-backed securities challenging also lead to certain complications in their cash flow and settlement mechanics. In this chapter, we address these "back-office" issues, using examples to illustrate the mechanics involved. The chapter is organized as follows:

- Section 3.1 describes settlement procedures and how subsequent cash flows are calculated and paid to investors.
- Section 3.2 discusses the structure and conventions of mortgage securities lending.
- Section 3.3 describes clearance and settlement in the back-office.

3.1 SETTLEMENT PROCEDURES

In this section, we give several examples of MBS and ABS trades. In each example, the trade is followed from initiation to when investors start to receive cash flows to illustrate the steps involved in the process.

An Agency Pass-Through Trade

Most agency pass-through trading occurs on a **to-be-announced (TBA)** basis. In a TBA trade, the buyer and seller agree on general trade parameters, such as agency, type, coupon, par amount, and price (e.g., $100 million of Ginnie

EXHIBIT 3.1 A TBA Freddie Mac Gold 30-Year 7% Trade

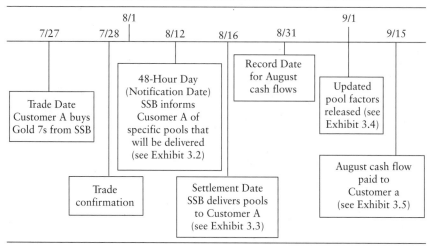

Source: Salomon Smith Barney.

Mae 30-year 7% pass-throughs at a price of 98-14[1]), but the buyer does not know the specific pools that will be delivered until two business days before the settlement date, when the seller is obligated to provide the information. However, the pools have to satisfy **good delivery** requirements (see following heading: 48-Hour Day and Good Delivery Requirements).

TBA trading is the norm in the agency pass-through market for several reasons. It greatly improves market liquidity, allowing trades of large size to take place (most MBS pools are relatively small, typically less than $10 million). It also helps mortgage lenders to hedge interest rate exposure after a borrower locks in a rate.[2] Between the lock-in date and the loan closing date, the lender has interest rate exposure on a future loan that the lender is committed to making, but that has not yet been finalized.[3] As an example, we follow a TBA trade for $2 million face value of Freddie Mac Gold 30-year 7% pass-throughs. Exhibit 3.1 shows a time line of the steps in the process.

---

[1] 98 and ¹⁴/₃₂nds, or, in decimal terms, $98.4375 per $100 of face or par value.

[2] When a bank decides to loan money to a home owner, the borrower does not have to commit immediately to take out a loan at that day's mortgage rate. Instead, the borrower typically has a period of time (for example, 60 days) during which he has a one-time option to "lock in" the current mortgage rate.

[3] For example, if interest rates fall, the borrower may not want to close at the locked-in rate. This risk of a loan not closing is called **fallout risk.**

Trade and Confirmation Dates   On Tuesday, July 27, 1999, a portfolio manager at Customer A tells his salesperson at SSB that he wishes to purchase $2 million face value of 30-year Gold 7s.[4] The salesperson checks with the desk and quotes a price of 98-03 for standard August settlement. The customer accepts, and a **trade confirmation** is sent out within one day of the trade date (in fact, the trade confirmation is normally sent out immediately).

48-Hour Day and Good Delivery Requirements   TBA trades normally settle according to a monthly schedule set by the Bond Market Association, a trade group of fixed-income dealers (formerly called the Public Securities Association, or PSA). For Gold 7s, the August 1999 settlement date is Monday, August 16, 1999 (see Appendix E). The buyer has to be notified as to which pools will be delivered before 3 P.M., two business days prior to the settlement date, or Thursday, August 12, in this case. This is the **48-hour rule;** hence, the **notification date** is often called the **48-hour day.**

The pools have to satisfy requirements for **good delivery** established by the Bond Market Association. These requirements have changed over time, but at present, for each $1 million **lot** (trades are usually transacted in terms of $1 million units, called lots), the following constraints apply:

■ A maximum of three pools per lot;[5] and
■ **Variance** refers to the difference between the face amount of the pools delivered and the agreed-upon face amount. Some variance is allowed in recognition of the fact that the face amount of a pool, which is the sum of the current balances of the underlying mortgage loans, is unlikely to be a nice round number, such as $1 million. The allowable variance is 0.01% per lot (i.e., for a $1 million lot, the sum of the par amounts of the pools in each lot should be within 0.01% of $1 million, or between $999,900 and $1,000,100).

On Thursday August 12, Salomon Smith Barney notifies Customer A of the pools that will be delivered, sending the information shown in Exhibit 3.2.

Settlement Calculations   Exhibit 3.3 shows financial details of the settlement, which takes place on Monday, August 16, 1999. Account A pays Salomon

---

[4] Although TBA trades are typically larger than $2 million, we have used a small amount for simplicity's sake.
[5] Slightly more liberal good delivery requirements are allowed for very old pools. See the Bond Market Association's *Uniform Practices* manual for complete details, or contact your SSB salesperson.

EXHIBIT 3.2 48-Hour Day—Notification of Pools to Be Delivered for $2 Million Freddie Mac Gold 7% TBA Trade

Lot 1. Freddie Mac Gold Pool #111

Issue Date	June 1, 1999
Original Face	$1,020,000
Current Factor	0.98044118
Current Face	= Original Face * Current Pool Factor
	= $1,020,000 * 0.98044118 = $1,000,050

Lot 2. Freddie Mac Gold Pools #222 and #333

	Pool #222	Pool #333
Issue Date	August 1, 1999	August 1, 1999
Original Face	$499,910	$500,000
Current Factor	1.0000000	1.0000000
Current Face	$499,010	$500,000

Note: Current factors and face amounts as of August 1, 1999.
Source: Salomon Smith Barney.

Smith Barney an amount equal to the current face amount times the agreed-upon price of 98-03, plus accrued interest from the beginning of the month. Accrued interest is computed on a 30/360 basis.

Clearing Trades The clearing process refers to the mechanism by which trades are settled (i.e., how money is exchanged and changes in ownership of the securities are recorded). Almost all trades are now settled electronically, or **book-entry; physical delivery,** in which certificates of ownership are delivered, is now rarely used. In Section 3.3 we provide a detailed description of the clearing and settlement process from more of a back-office perspective.

Record Date The owner of an agency pool on the last day of a month (the record date) is entitled to the cash flows for that month. For August, the record date is August 31, 1999. Account A is recorded as the owner of the three pools shown in Exhibit 3.2 and, hence, will receive the August cash flow, consisting of interest and principal for the month. As Exhibit 3.1

EXHIBIT 3.3 $2 Million Gold 30-Year Trade: Settlement

Current Face Amount	= $1,000,050 + $499,910 + $500,000 = $1,999,960
Accrued Interest	= Current Face Amount * Coupon Rate * (Settlement Day of Month − 1)/360
	= $1,999,960 * 7% * (16 − 1)/360 = $5,833.22
Total Amount Due	= Current Face Amount * (Price / 100) + Accrued Interest
	= $1,999,960 * (98.09375 / 100) + $5,833.22 = $1,967,668.98

Source: Salomon Smith Barney.

EXHIBIT 3.4 Agency Pool Factor Monthly Release Schedule

	Factors Released on	Factors Incorporate Prepays
Freddie Mac	Evening of Last Business Day of Month	Up to 15th of Month
Fannie Mae	Evening of 4th Business Day of Month	Up to End of Previous Month
Ginnie Mae	Morning of 5th Business Day of Month	Up to End of Previous Month

Source: Salomon Smith Barney.

indicated, the August payment is actually made in September. Payments for most Ginnie Mae and Freddie Mac MBSs are made on the 15th of each month, and for Fannie Mae MBSs, on the 25th of each month (see the definition of **delay** in the Glossary).

Pool Factor Updates and Principal and Interest Calculations   Interest due to investors for the month of August is based on the principal balance at the beginning of August and is determined on a 30/360 basis. The principal payment is calculated by comparing the pool factors on August 1 and September 1. All three agencies release updated factors for their pools near the beginning of each month according to a set schedule, shown in Exhibit 3.4.

In our example, Freddie Mac releases an updated pool factor at the end of the last business day of August. This is termed the **September 1 factor,** even though it reflects prepayments received between July 16 and August 15. This factor is used to calculate payments due to the investor for the month of August and to be paid on September 15. Exhibit 3.5 shows details of the calculations. For Fannie Mae, which releases pool factors on the evening of

EXHIBIT 3.5 $20 Million Gold 30-Year Trade: Interest and Principal Payments for August (Paid on September 15)

Principal Paydown	= Original Face Amount * (Previous Pool Factor – New Pool Factor)
Interest Payment	= Face Amount as of Aug 1 * Coupon Rate / 12
Pool A	Sep 1 Factor = 0.97941177, Aug 1 Factor = 0.98044118
Principal Paydown	= $1,020,000 * (0.98044118 – 0.97941177) = $1,050.00
Interest Payment	= $1,000,050 * 7% / 12 = $5,833.63
Pool B	Sep 1 factor = 0.99500000, Aug 1 factor = 1.0000000
Principal Paydown	= $499,910 * (1.00000000 – 0.99500000) = $2,499.55
Interest Payment	= $499,910 * 7% / 12 = $2,916.14
Pool C	Sep 1 factor = 0.99500000, Aug 1 factor = 1.0000000
Principal Paydown	= $500,000 * (1.00000000 – 0.99500000) = $2,500.00
Interest Payment	= $500,000 * 7% / 12 = $2,916.67
Total Payment Received by Investor on 15 Sep 99	= $1,050.00 + $2,499.55 + $2,500.00 + $5,833.63 + $2,916.14 + $2,916.67 = $17,715.99

Source: Salomon Smith Barney.

the fourth business day of each month, and Ginnie Mae, which releases pool factors on the morning of the fifth business day of each month, the September 1 factors incorporate prepayments received during the calendar month of August. Updated pool factors are posted on MBS analytic systems such as Salomon Smith Barney's Yield Book.

TBA Trade "Fail"   In a TBA transaction, the seller does have the costly option to be late (or fail) in delivering securities to the buyer. For example, if collateral is needed for new CMO deals, this additional demand could cause a temporary shortage of the coupon being used to back the new deals. However, in the case of a "fail," the buyer benefits by not having to pay the seller until the securities are delivered. The price of the securities, including accrued interest that is to be paid, does not change. Therefore, the buyer receives both of the following:

■ Interest on the money that was to be paid for the security; and
■ Interest (as well as principal if a record date is passed) on the security that will eventually be delivered.

To summarize, although the security has not been delivered, the buyer does "own" the security in the sense that cash flows that would have gone to the buyer (if a "fail" had not occurred) still must be passed to the buyer by the seller. And the buyer receives the "extra" of interest earned on the funds that were to be paid to the seller (compensation for the inconvenience of the fail).

Other Types of Pass-Through Trading

Although the bulk of trading in agency pass-throughs is done on a TBA basis, there are other types of trades. An investor can request specific characteristics that are deemed desirable, such as a loan origination year—for example, 1993 Ginnie Mae 30-year 7s (this is the so-called **TBA vintage market**). An investor may do this if he feels that seasoned 1993 Ginnie Mae 7s have more desirable prepayment characteristics than the new Ginnie Mae 7s that are likely to be delivered in a standard TBA trade. In addition, of course, there is an active market in **specified** (usually seasoned) pools, where the investor knows at the time of the trade the exact pools that will be purchased.

A New-Issue CMO Trade

On June 10, 1999, Salomon Smith Barney priced Ginnie Mae REMIC 1999-25, a $1.3 billion collateralized mortgage obligation (CMO) deal

EXHIBIT 3.6 New-Issue CMO Bond—Ginnie Mae REMIC 1999-25, Class PC: Purchase and Settlement

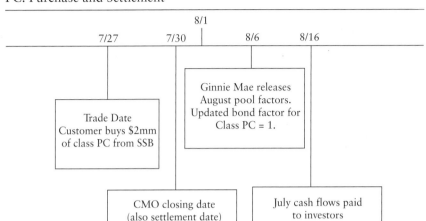

Source: Salomon Smith Barney.

backed by Ginnie Mae 7% and 7.5% pass-throughs. The CMO closing date (i.e., the day on which the CMO settles) is July 30, 1999. Among the bonds in this deal is Class PC, a four-year planned amortization class (PAC) bond with a coupon of 7%.[6] On July 27, 1999, a customer agrees to buy $2 million face value of Class PC at a price of 101-00. Exhibit 3.6 shows a timeline of the trade.

Settlement Date   Newly issued CMOs normally settle when the deal settles (issue date). (In secondary trading of CMO classes, the settlement is $T + 3$, or three business days after the trade date.) The **accrual date** for agency CMOs—the date from which interest starts to accrue on the bonds—is, as with agency pass-throughs, the first of each month, or July 1, 1999, in this case.

Settlement Calculations   Because this is a new issue, the current **bond factor** is 1.0, so the current face is equal to the original face of $2 million. Since the accrual date is July 1, 1999, the accrued interest is:

---

[6] See Chapter 1, Section 1.4 or Chapter 15 for a description of PAC bonds.

$$\text{Accrued interest} = \text{Current face} \times \text{Coupon rate} \times \frac{(\text{Day of month} - 1)}{360}$$

$$= \$2,000,000 \times 7\% \times \frac{(30 - 1)}{360}$$

$$= \$11,277.78$$

Hence, the total amount due from the investor is:

$$\text{Total amount due} = \text{Current face} \times \left(\frac{\text{Price}}{100}\right) + \text{Accrued interest}$$

$$= \$2,000,000 \times \left(\frac{101}{100}\right) + \$11,277.78$$

$$= \$2,031,277.78$$

Record Date   The record date is the last business day of the month, or July 30, 1999, in this case (July 31 is a Saturday). The customer is noted as the owner of $2 million of Class PC and, hence, entitled to July interest and principal payments, which are paid with a delay in August.

Updated Pool and Bond Factors and Investor Cash Flow Calculations   As shown in Exhibit 3.4, Ginnie Mae releases updated pool factors—which are as of August 1, 1999, in this case—on the morning of the fifth business day of the month, or August 6, 1999, in this case. The CMO deal trustee uses these pool factors, which reflect principal payments on the underlying loans in July, to calculate principal payments due to the various classes in the CMO, according to the principal allocation rules specified in the deal prospectus and, hence, to calculate updated (or current) bond factors for each class. In this case, all of the July principal payments were allocated to other classes in the deal, so the updated bond factor for Class PC remains at 1.00 (signifying that none of the principal backing this class has yet paid down). In other words, Class PC is not yet in its principal payment window.

Calculation of July Cash Flow for Class PC   Payment dates for agency CMOs usually correspond to the payment dates for the underlying pass-throughs. For Ginnie Maes, the payment date is the 15th of the month. However, because August 15, 1999, is a Sunday, the investor receives the July principal and interest on Monday, August 16, 1999. The interest paid is:

$$\text{Interest payment} = \text{Face amount (as of July 1, 1999)} \times \frac{\text{Coupon rate}}{12}$$

$$= \$2,000,000 \times \frac{7\%}{12}$$

$$= \$11,666.67$$

Because the updated bond factor for Class PC is one, it receives no principal (principal payments on the collateral are directed to other bonds in the deal, as specified in the prospectus).

A Secondary Market ABS Trade

On February 22, 1999, Salomon Smith Barney priced Citibank Credit Card 1999-2, a $798 million ABS deal backed by Citibank credit card receivables. Senior Class A is a triple A rated bond with a fixed coupon of 5.875% (Exhibit 3.7 provides some details about this bond). Even though the cash flows from the assets (credit card payments) are monthly, this bond is structured as a traditional semiannual pay bullet security.

Trade Date On Tuesday, July 27, 1999, a customer buys $2 million face of Class A at a price of 102-00. Trade confirmation is normally sent out immediately.

Settlement Date As with CMOs, secondary trades of ABS classes settle $T + 3$, that is, three business days after the trade date. Hence, the trade settles on Friday, July 30, 1999.

Settlement Amounts Accrued interest is calculated from the issue date of February 25, 1999. After the first coupon period, the accrued interest would be calculated from the previous payment date (September 10 or March 10). A

EXHIBIT 3.7 Citibank Credit Card 1999–2, Senior Class A

Issue Date	February 25, 1999
Rating	AAA (S&P), AAA (Fitch), Aaa (Moody's)
Coupon	5.875% (30/360 basis)
Frequency of Payments	Semiannual, on September 10 and March 10
Initial Accrual Date	February 25, 1999
Principal Payments	Soft Bullet Payment on March 10, 2009[*]

[*]Under certain circumstances, it is possible for principal to be paid earlier or later.
Source: Salomon Smith Barney.

30/360 basis gives 155 days from February 25, 1999, to the settlement date of July 30, 1999, so the calculation is as follows:

$$\text{Accrued interest} = \text{Current face} \times \text{Coupon rate} \times \frac{155}{360}$$

$$= \$2,000,000 \times 5.875\% \times \frac{155}{360}$$

$$= \$50,590.28$$

$$\text{Total amount due} = \text{Current face} \times \left(\frac{\text{Price}}{100}\right) + \text{Accrued interest}$$

$$= \$2,000,000 \times \left(\frac{102}{100}\right) + \$50,590.28$$

$$= \$2,090,590.28$$

Record Date (as Specified in the Prospectus)   The record date is one day before a payment date, or September 9, 1999, in our example. The owner of the security on this date receives semiannual interest.

Payment to Investor   The investor receives interest on September 10, 1999 (payment dates depend on the issuer and deal, and are specified in the prospectus). The semiannual interest payment usually would be:

$$\text{Normal interest payment} = \text{Current face} \times \frac{\text{Coupon rate}}{2}$$

$$= \$2,000,000 \times \frac{5.875\%}{2}$$

$$= \$58,750.00$$

However, for the first interest payment, the accrual period begins on the issue date, February 25, 1999, so the first interest payment on September 10, 1999, is:

$$\text{First interest payment} = \$2,000,000 \times 5.875\% \times \frac{195}{360}$$

$$= \$63,645.83$$

3.2 MORTGAGE SECURITIES LENDING

Securities lending markets, which in essence involve the temporary exchange of cash for securities, are huge and extremely active. For example, the Federal Reserve Bank of New York estimates the average **daily** amount of outstanding reverse repurchase and repurchase transactions in U.S. government securities was about $2.5 *trillion* as of June 30, 1999. The mortgage securities lending market, in particular, is very active because of the high credit quality and liquidity of most MBSs. In this section, we explain the mechanics of the transactions that take place in this important market.

Although there is a fair amount of variation in the transactions that are characterized as securities lending activity, mortgage securities lending essentially occurs through two channels: **repurchase transactions** and **dollar rolls.** We provide more precise definitions of these activities later, but in the broadest terms, repurchase transactions are securities transactions in which one party agrees to sell securities to another in return for cash, with a simultaneous agreement to repurchase the same securities at a specific price at a later date. At the termination of the transaction, the securities are resold at the predetermined price plus a previously determined interest rate. A dollar roll is analogous to a repurchase transaction except that the party borrowing the securities does not have to return the same securities, but can instead return "substantially similar" ones.

Why would two parties participate in such transactions? There is no single answer to this question because there are a number of participants in securities lending markets and their motivations may vary. The key point is this: Because the lending activity is secured by collateral, the borrowing rate is typically lower than the interbank short-term uncollateralized lending rate. So, for example, a hedge fund that wishes to increase its leverage may loan its securities for cash to finance its positions cheaply. An institutional investor, such as a pension fund, may lend out securities from its portfolio to boost income or to defray custodial fees. A broker-dealer may borrow and lend securities as part of its market-making activities. Such activities might include borrowing securities to cover a short position or simultaneously borrowing and lending securities to earn a higher rate on the securities loaned versus the securities borrowed.

Securities lending activities are a vital part of today's capital markets and provide an important source of liquidity and flexibility to all market participants. The factors that fueled the growth of these activities in the past—an increase in the amount of outstanding securities, the development of custodial and securities lending departments, and the active short-term cash management strategies employed by investors—should continue to provide a strong impetus into the future.

Repurchase Transactions

A **repurchase agreement** (**repo**) is an agreement between a **seller** and a **buyer,** in which the seller sells securities to the buyer with a simultaneous agreement to repurchase the securities at an agreed-upon price (**repurchase price**) at a future point in time (**repurchase date**).[7] The seller is charged interest (at the **repo rate**) for the use of funds and, typically, pays these interest costs at the maturity of the repo. The buyer of the securities is said to have entered into a **reverse repurchase** (**reverse repo**) agreement.

We previously discussed the economic rationale for a repo. To reiterate, because the repo is a form of secured lending it may provide a relatively inexpensive source of funding compared with other short-term money-market instruments of similar duration. In general, the following factors primarily determine the repo rate: (1) the credit quality of the underlying collateral; (2) the maturity of the repo; and (3) the liquidity of the collateral. In addition, to provide a buffer against a loss in the market value of the security, the lender of funds usually requires a **margin** amount. In practice, the margin amount is established by lending out a sum of money less than the market value of the underlying collateral. The difference between the market value of the collateral and the dollar proceeds lent out is called a *haircut.*

Mechanics

Collateral   A variety of collateral types are allowed in a repo, including agency pass-throughs (Ginnie Mae, Fannie Mae, and Freddie Mac), agency REMICs, double A and triple A non-agency CMOs, double A pass-throughs, and whole loans. The seller receives the *identical* collateral back at the maturity of the repo.

Haircut   The haircut deducted in a repo is used to set up a margin account that the buyer (i.e., the lender of funds) will use as a hedge against a decline in the market value of the securities. Haircuts range from 1% to 10%, but can be as high as 25% to 50% if the securities are perceived to have high price volatility or low liquidity. The haircut can also depend on the fiscal strength of the borrower (i.e., the seller of securities). The securities are

---

[7] The **seller** is also referred to as the **borrower** (of funds), and the **buyer** is also referred to as the **lender** (of funds).

typically **marked-to-market** on a daily basis. A decline in the market value of the securities can result in a **margin call**, whereas an increase will result in a payment to the borrower of funds. Margin calls must be settled promptly; $T + 0$ is typical.

Term   The length of a repo can extend from one day (**overnight repo**) to more than one day (**term repo**), or be **open**. An **open repo** is equivalent to a series of overnight repos on the same security, with the repo agreement effectively being renewed each day at a new rate. Term repos cover specified periods rarely extending beyond three months, with 30 days the most common term.

Title   The party entering into the repo (i.e., the borrower of funds) loses title to the security over the repo period. However, all payments of principal (scheduled or unscheduled) and interest are forwarded to the original owner. The transfer of title allows the buyer (i.e., the lender of funds) to now "repo out" the securities (i.e., sell the securities and, thus, borrow money) if it so desires. This activity of combining repos and reverse repos is commonly known as a "repo book."

Repo Calculations   Repo calculations are straightforward. The **repo principal** (the funds provided to the borrower) is simply the market value of the collateral obtained by the lender, reduced by the haircut. The interest cost of the loan (**repo interest**) is obtained by applying the repo rate to the repo principal. Exhibit 3.8 provides a sample calculation.

We note two points about the calculation in Exhibit 3.8. First, the bid price of the security is for cash settle ($T + 0$). Second, the cash flow characteristics of the repoed bond are *not* relevant to the transaction because the buyer (the lender of funds) does not retain any coupon or principal payments, but passes them on to the seller (the borrower of funds). The second

EXHIBIT 3.8 Sample Repo Calculation

Repo $52.6 Million Freddie Mac CMO 2180 Class G for 30 Days at 5.34% With a 5% Haircut on 11 Nov	
Repo Principal	= Par Amount * Factor * ((Bid Price + Accrued) / 100) * (1 – Haircut)
	= $52,555,848 * 1.000 * ((97-22 + 0-06) / 100) * (1 – 0.05)
	= $48,867,084.42
Repo Interest	= Repo Principal * Repo Rate * Repo Term in Days/360
	= $48,867,084.42 * 5.34 / 100 * 30/360
	= $217,458.53

Source: Salomon Smith Barney.

observation is not strictly true in the sense that the repo rate and the haircut charged are influenced, to some extent, by how volatile the cash flows of the MBS are, because this volatility, in turn, will affect how the market value of the security fluctuates. Exhibit 3.9 illustrates the flows of cash and securities in a representative repurchase transaction.

Cost of Carry   As discussed, repos constitute a form of secured lending, and as a result, repo rates are typically lower than other short-term (unsecured) borrowing rates. For example, Exhibit 3.10 shows that the one-month mortgage repo rate has on average been about 10bp (basis points) lower than one-month LIBOR over the past year. In other words, a mortgage investor could have earned an incremental return of approximately 10bp per year by funding his mortgage securities through repos versus simply holding them (assuming interim cash flows are invested in one-month LIBOR). This measure of determining the advantage of the funding position is often called the **cost of carry.**

Risks

Credit Risk   Credit risk refers to the possibility that one of the parties to a repo transaction may default, which in turn may result in the loss of the full value of the securities borrowed or funds loaned. For example, if the borrower of funds defaults, the lender can liquidate the collateral but may still not be able to recoup the full amount of the repo principal. To hedge against this particular risk, the lender charges the haircut. In addition, both parties usually evaluate the credit quality of their counterparties before entering into a repo transaction. Whatever the hedge employed, it should be kept in mind that hedge ratios often break down in extreme market conditions.

EXHIBIT 3.9 The Repo Transaction

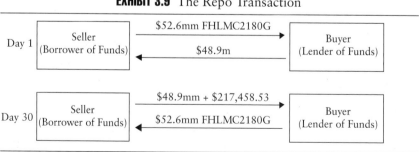

Source: Salomon Smith Barney.

EXHIBIT 3.10 The Repo Funding Advantage: One-Month LIBOR—One-Month Mortgage Repo

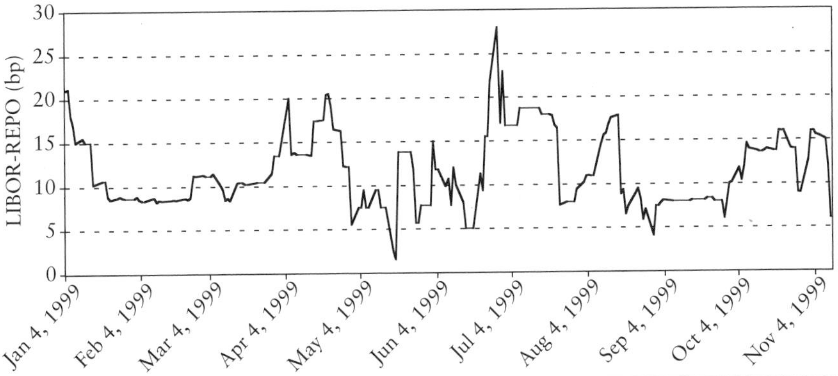

Source: Salomon Smith Barney.

Liquidity Risk A market disruption, such as a squeeze, may result in the lender's being unable to deliver the securities back to the borrower at settlement. This qualifies as a failed transaction, rather than a default, because the lender will typically be able to settle the transaction at a later date.

Market Risk The repo position may suffer because of an adverse move in the market prices of assets or interest rates. For example, a borrower locked into a fixed-term repo financing arrangement is subject to interest-rate risk, which is the risk that an initially attractive borrowing rate may become very costly if short-term interest rates fall substantially over the course of the repo.

Settlement Risk Both parties to a repo may risk the loss of the full value of the securities or funds if the exchange of securities for funds is not completed in both legs of a repo transaction. For example, such a situation may occur if it is possible to complete delivery of funds without simultaneously receiving delivery of collateral. To avoid these situations, settlement of a repo transaction usually takes place on a DVP delivery-versus-payment (DVP) basis, where delivery of securities takes place if and only if payment of cash occurs at the same time.

Dollar Rolls

Dollar rolls are another way to obtain financing via the mortgage market. Repurchase agreements do not involve the transfer of a security's cash flows;

principal and interest continue to be sent to the original owner. In contrast, in a dollar roll transaction, the original owner gives up principal and interest to the temporary holder of the securities (assuming record dates are passed during the period of the roll). In addition, the returned security does not have to be exactly the same as the original security, but instead should be "substantially similar" to qualify as a financing transaction (rather than a sale and purchase). "Substantially similar" has been defined in the American Institute of Certified Public Accountants *Statement of Position 90-3* as meaning that the original and returned security should be of the same agency/program, original maturity, and coupon (for example, 30-year Freddie Mac Gold 7.5s) and both should satisfy good delivery requirements. The dollar roll can be thought of as two simultaneous transactions, one buy and one sell order, for the same TBA security for different settlements.

For an investor with a long position in pass-throughs for forward settlement who wants to avoid actually taking delivery of bonds (and subsequently receiving principal and interest payments), rolling the position forward each month can be attractive from a financing as well as operations perspective. By continually rolling the position forward, he stays invested in mortgages, but never reaches settlement for receiving bonds and often obtains an attractive financing rate on the funds obtained during each roll period. Exhibit 3.11 compares the main features of repos and dollar rolls.

A Sample Dollar Roll Computation   Suppose an SSB pass-through trader "buys $2 million of the November/December roll" for Freddie Mac Gold 7s down ^{5}/32nds ("the drop") from an investor. If the price for Bond Market Association November settlement is 98-20, then the trader is simultaneously buying $2 million Gold 7s for November settlement (November 15, 1999) at a price of 98-20 and selling $2 million for December settlement (December 13, 1999) at a price of 98-15 (= 98-20 − 0-05). This transaction gives the trader a long position from November 15 to December 13, which could be used to collateralize a CMO deal settling at the end of November, for example. (The

EXHIBIT 3.11   Repo (Repurchase Agreement) versus Dollar Roll

	Repo	Dollar Roll
Security Type	Any	Pass-through
Financing Rate	Usually related to general collateral	Often lower than repo rate (at times, substantially lower)
Principal and Interest	Goes to original owner	Goes to holder on each record date
Used for Short Covering	No	Yes
Haircut	Yes	No
Identical Securities Returned	Yes	No
Prepayment Risk	No	Yes

Source: Salomon Smith Barney.

EXHIBIT 3.12 Dollar Roll Example per $100 Face (Period for Dollar Roll is 28 Days: November 15–December 13)

Date	Transaction	Trader	Investor
Nov 15	Trader buys from investor	Pays 98-20 + accrued interest = $98.897 for bonds.	Receives 98-20 + accrued interest = $98.897 for bonds and invests $98.897 in money market near Fed funds rate at 5.20%.
	Investment	$98.897 (in securities).	$98.897 (in cash).
Dec 13	Investor buys back from trader	Receives 98-15 + accrued interest = $98.702 for bonds. Also pays for 0.5% of 100 for Dec to make up for expected paydown (price is 98-15 + accrued interest = $98.702, transaction done simultaneous to dollar roll).[*]	Pays 98-15 + accrued interest = $98.702 for bonds (reestablishing original long position). Receives proceeds of 98.897 * (1 + 0.052 * 28/360) = $99.297 on money market investment.
Dec 15		Receives payment corresponding to November payment period, principal paydown 0.5% and one month of interest. (These cash flows are present valued back to December 13 to obtain net proceeds in Exhibit 3.13.)	

[*]Because of principal paydowns, the trader will not have the same amount of bonds to give back to the investor and so must purchase additional bonds to make up for these paydowns. In practice, this is not a concern.
Source: Salomon Smith Barney.

trader would subsequently need to go long to cover his short position for December settlement.) Exhibit 3.12 shows the mechanics of the roll for the trader and investor. Exhibit 3.13 shows the net proceeds for the trader and investor (for the cases of rolling and not rolling).

The investor can roll his position (as shown on the right side of Exhibit 3.12), or the investor can choose not to roll his bonds. In this latter case, the investor receives the principal paydown and coupon interest and pays for 0.5% of bonds to make up for the principal paydown (this 0.5% purchase just serves to make it easier to compare the two cases of rolling and not rolling bonds). As shown in Exhibit 3.13, the proceeds from not rolling ($0.590) are almost the same as those in the case of choosing to roll the bonds ($0.595). Put another way, the implied financing rate of 5.13% (calculated in Exhibit 3.13 under the Trader column) is very close to the 5.20% investment rate available. There is no significant advantage to rolling the Gold 7s in this example (the roll for these bonds is said to be

EXHIBIT 3.13 Dollar Roll Example: Net Proceeds per $100 Face

Date	Scenario	Trader	Investor
Dec 13	If investor does roll	(1 − 0.005) * 98.702 + (0.5 + 7.0 / 12) / (1 + 0.052 * 2 / 360) = $99.292, which implies (99.292 / 98.897 − 1) * 360 / 28 = 5.13% financing rate (annualized)	99.297 − 98.702 = $0.595
	If investor does not roll		−0.005 * 98.702 + (0.5 + 7.0 / 12) / (1 + 0.052 * 2 / 360) = $0.590

Source: Salomon Smith Barney.

trading at or near carry). Note that prepayment risk, which enters through the principal paydown, was not considered.[8]

3.3 CLEARANCE AND SETTLEMENT IN THE BACK OFFICE

The MBS and ABS market participants that typically receive the most attention are primary market originators, institutional investors, and broker-dealers such as Salomon Smith Barney that facilitate the flow of capital between originators and investors by establishing secondary markets. Missing in this picture are the roles played by other securities market service providers such as primary brokers, custodians, and clearing and settlement organizations. The back-office services provided by these entities—portfolio administration, risk management, "netting" trades, among others—considerably ease the administrative and operational complexities involved in securities lending and trading.

Clearance and settlement refer to the mechanics of the exchange of funds and securities resulting from trading activities. Completing a securities transaction involves the interaction of back-office departments, banks, clearing corporations, other depositories, and funds transfer systems. This section provides more of a back-office perspective on how money and securities are transferred between these organizations in consummating a trade. It also provides brief descriptions of some of the major organizations involved in clearing and settling MBS and ABS trades.

Our discussion is by no means definitive—the continued growth and globalization of securities markets, technological advances, and an increasing focus by investors on "putting their money to work" continue to alter the landscape of back-office services. In particular, modern financial institutions such as Salomon Smith Barney can assume multiple back-office roles, and offer their institutional clients a number of portfolio administration (clearing, custody, financing, and lending) and portfolio allocation services.

Clearing and Settling a Specified Pool Pass-Through Trade

To directly use a clearing organization such as Fedwire[9] which is operated by the U.S. Federal Reserve (or Fed), membership in that clearing organization is

---

[8] It was assumed that the principal paydown could be forecast perfectly accurately in the example. In practice, there is always some uncertainty about what the paydown will turn out to be. For a more comprehensive look at dollar rolls, see *A Review of Mortgage Dollar Rolls*, Salomon Smith Barney, September 1988.

[9] For further details about Fedwire, see the heading: Clearance and Settlement Providers.

normally required. In the case of Fedwire, banks and other depository institutions that are members of the Federal Reserve System have direct access, but other financial institutions such as broker-dealers do not. So, to trade securities that only clear through certain organizations like Fedwire, a non-member, such as a broker-dealer, must use an intermediary **clearing agent** (normally a bank).

Suppose Customer U, which uses bank V as its clearing agent, buys a specified Freddie Mac pool from broker-dealer SSB, which uses Bank T as its clearing agent. (Freddie Mac and Fannie Mae pools clear through Fedwire.) Exhibit 3.14 shows how the funds/securities are transferred.

On the settlement date:

1. Customer U instructs bank V to (a) receive the pool from Broker-Dealer SSB via SSB's clearing agent Bank T (the pool is taken from Bank T's Fedwire account), and (b) make the appropriate payment to Bank T.
2. Bank T, acting on instructions from Broker-dealer SSB, transmits a message to Fedwire authorizing delivery of the Freddie Mac pool to Bank V's Fedwire account versus payment of the agreed-upon price.

EXHIBIT 3.14 Payment for a Security

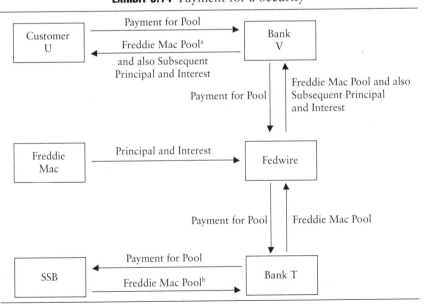

[a] Bank V holds the Freddie Mac pool on behalf of Customer U, the beneficial owner.
[b] SSB's clearing agent, Bank T, holds the Freddie Mac pool (prior to the trade) on behalf of SSB, the original beneficial owner.
Source: Salomon Smith Barney.

3. The Federal Reserve executes these instructions by making the appropriate security and cash entries to the Fed accounts of Banks V and T. More specifically, Bank V's account is debited with cash, and credited with securities, while the opposite flows are recorded for Bank T.
4. Bank V in turn makes the appropriate entries to Customer U's account, and Bank T does the same for SSB.

As far as Freddie Mac and the Federal Reserve are concerned, Bank V is the holder of the security and should receive payments of principal and interest on it. Customer U is the beneficial owner (i.e., the true owner) of the pool through its Clearing Bank V. Therefore, principal and interest from the pool is received first by Bank V and is subsequently credited to Customer U's account.

If Bank T and Bank V happen to be the same clearing bank (denoted as Bank TV for clarity), then Fedwire is not directly involved in the trade. Instead, Bank TV clears the trade internally by crediting to Customer U's account securities obtained by debiting Broker-Dealer SSB's account. In addition, cash is debited from Customer U's account and credited to Broker-Dealer SSB's account. There is no need to change anything in Bank TV's Fed accounts because Bank TV's security/cash position at the Fed is unchanged.

Special Considerations for TBA Pass-Through Trades

The previous section describes the settlement process for specified pool pass-through trades. The description also applies to TBA pass-through trades. However, particularly in the case of TBA trades, several additional activities often take place between the trade date and the settlement date. Because trades often settle forward (on one of the Bond Market Association settlement dates), there is a relatively long time between the trade date and settlement date. This means that there is a relatively longer period of time during which a trade should be monitored to guard against one party's not fulfilling its trade obligations.

Assuming both parties in a trade are participants of the Mortgage-Backed Securities Clearing Corporation (MBSCC)[10] and the trade is executed through MBSCC, the trade is marked to market on a daily basis because both parties must meet daily margin requirements, which help to ensure that the trade is completed. MBSCC, to some extent, acts as a huge back office for its participants. It nets the trade activity for each participant involved in a TBA trade category (such as 30-year Freddie Mac Gold 7s for

---

[10] See the heading: Clearance and Settlement Providers later in this section.

October settlement, for example) and provides a summary net position to each of its member participants. For example, a firm with offsetting long and short positions (possibly with different counterparties) has no net security position and can settle its position by paying or receiving cash depending on the prices at which the offsetting trades were executed.

For participants with net securities positions, MBSCC matches net sellers with net buyers and provides a service, called Electronic Pool Notification, that helps the matched parties exchange pool information in preparation for delivery of securities. When settlement is reached, net positions are paid off and pools must be delivered. This happens as discussed in the previous subsection.

When outstanding trades are marked to market or must satisfy margin requirements, as in cases in which MBSCC is involved, for example, the basic cash flow mechanics presented in Section 3.2 become more complicated. For a trade that is marked to market, cash will be paid or received in all likelihood prior to the settlement date. On the settlement date, payment is made **net** of all the prior cash paid or received due to margin requirements. When MBSCC is involved, the final price paid at settlement is further complicated by the netting process (which averages out prices across different trades in determining the price to be paid on the settlement date).

Clearance and Settlement Providers

Here we provide brief descriptions of the various organizations that clear MBS and ABS trades:

- The **Mortgage-Backed Securities Clearing Corporation (MBSCC)** deals primarily with TBA transactions. Although the MBSCC does not act as the counterparty guaranteeing a trade, it does provide TBA trade position reports, netting services, margin protection, and Electronic Pool Notification.
- **Fedwire,** operated by the Federal Reserve Banks, settles Freddie Mac and Fannie Mae pools and CMOs. Fedwire collects and distributes interest and principal on these securities. Note that in addition to clearing securities, it serves as a funds transfer system, acting as an intermediary for large-dollar wire transfers.
- **Depository Trust Company (DTC)** settles asset-backed securities and non-agency CMOs. DTC collects and distributes interest and principal on these securities. DTC is a private sector service company owned by members of the financial industry.
- **Participants Trust Company (PTC)** settles Ginnie Mae securities (pools and CMOs backed by Ginnie Mae collateral). PTC collects and distributes

interest and principal on these securities. PTC has become the Mortgage-Backed Securities Division of DTC.

■ **Euroclear** and **Cedel** settle internationally traded securities. For example, Citibank Credit Card 1999-2 can be held with Euroclear and Cedel, as well as DTC.[11] Note that settlement practices may differ for these international depositories. For example, according to the Citibank Credit Card 1999-2 prospectus, secondary trading between investors holding securities through Euroclear and Cedel should be conducted in accordance with conventional Eurobond practices.

These institutions interact with one another. For example, DTC maintains securities accounts at the Federal Reserve Bank of New York, holding Fedwire-eligible securities for transfers against payment on DTC's system.

Custodial and Prime Broker Services

Custodial banks and Prime brokers are among the chief intermediaries involved in the securities trading and lending markets. Brief descriptions of the various services provided by these entities follow:

■ **Custodial banks** have historically been the chief intermediary service provider for institutional investors. The administrative, accounting, and operational complexities of the mortgage securities market require a significant amount of costly infrastructure. Many firms do not have the resources to invest in this infrastructure and, therefore, prefer to outsource these services to a custodial service. Although custodians are essentially portfolio administrators, they will also arrange trades, provide collateral management services, and basically manage all operational and administrative aspects associated with mortgage securities trading and lending.

■ **Prime brokers** provide a range of clearance, custodial, financing, and reporting services for large retail and institutional accounts. The idea behind prime brokerage is that the customer can centralize at one broker (namely, the *prime* broker) the administrative tasks associated with maintaining his trading account, while executing trades through several brokers. This strategy leads to competitive execution and helps disguise trading strategies.

---

[11] Euroclear and Cedel do not actually hold Citibank Credit Card 1999-2 securities, but indirectly through the accounts of banks that are DTC participants.

Accounts at Salomon Smith Barney

A new customer must go through a credit check to start trading. Customers who have a bank clearing agent to handle transfers of funds and securities processing should provide SSB (the broker-dealer) with a tax identification number, various account numbers including that of their bank clearing agent, an address to which confirmations and statements are to be sent, and clearing instructions. Clearing instructions specify the entities (DTC, PTC, Fedwire, see previous heading: Clearance and Settlement Providers) through which trades are to be cleared.

Investors concerned about the back-office issues associated with investing in MBS and ABS can open a custodial account with a prime broker such as SSB. The prime broker will manage all administrative aspects of maintaining the investor's trading account. In particular, SSB's Fixed Income Prime Broker leverages the firm's proprietary fixed-income technology infrastructure to provide clients with flexible clearance, custody, financing, and reporting for all trading activity. Moreover, SSB's Prime Broker has developed a niche for servicing funds that employ strategies that invest in mortgage pass-through securities. For these clients, Prime Broker can arrange for accounts at the Mortgage Backed Securities Clearing Corporation (MBSCC) to take advantage of netting and electronic pool notification services. In addition, the prime broker works with clients to optimize allocation strategies. Contact information for SSB Prime Broker is provided in Appendix E.

Prepayment Analysis and Modeling

Anatomy of Prepayments

The Salomon Smith Barney Prepayment Model

Lakhbir Hayre and Robert Young

Prepayment projections are at the center of all mortgage security valuation and analysis. Since Salomon Brothers pioneered the development of the Street's first prepayment model in the mid-1980s,[1] such models have come to be widely used in the mortgage market and are critical for valuation techniques such as option-adjusted spread (OAS) analysis.

However, projecting prepayments is not an exact science. A large body of data now exists on prepayments, but it still only partially covers the range of interest-rate and macroeconomic environments that is possible over the term of a mortgage-backed security (MBS). In addition, there are other difficulties in developing prepayment models, including the following:

- As with any econometric model, a basic premise is that the conditions and relationships observed in the past will hold going forward. In fact, the factors that determine prepayments—borrower demographics, loan origination and servicing practices in the mortgage lending industry, the costs and ease of refinancing, borrower responsiveness, and so on— change over time, often in unpredictable ways.
- There is substantial diversity in the types of collateral backing MBSs, both in mortgage contractual terms and in borrower demographics. To compound the problem, critical information, such as the loan-to-value

---

[1] See *The Salomon Brothers Prepayment Model: Impact of the Market Rally on Mortgage Prepayments and Yields*, Salomon Brothers Inc., September 4, 1985.

ratio (LTV) and the mortgagor's credit status and other demographic characteristics, is often not available.

These observations suggest that a prepayment model should possess two critical characteristics. First, the model should be dynamic and flexible, with time-varying values of key inputs, such as the costs of refinancing, in order to capture "environmental" changes over time. Second, the model should be based on fundamental relationships that are likely to persist over time, and that apply whatever the borrower demographics or mortgage type; relationships derived solely from a statistical fit to the data are unlikely to have these attributes. Such an approach allows for a plausible model to be developed, even when there is missing formation. With these considerations in mind, let us start by examining the basic reasons for prepayments.

Why Do Prepayments Occur?

Most readers are familiar with mortgages and home ownership in general and with the various causes of prepayments. We use four categories to classify prepayments:

1. *Home sales.* The sale of a home generally will lead to the prepayment of a mortgage. Exceptions will arise if the home has a Federal Housing Administration or Veterans Administration (FHA/VA) loan and the new buyer decides to "assume" the obligations of the existing loan, or if the home does not carry a mortgage.[2]
2. *Refinancings.* The second major cause of prepayments refers to mortgagors refinancing out of an existing loan into a new one. This is generally undertaken to take advantage of lower rates, but can also occur because the mortgagor wants to access increased equity in the house, or, in the case of borrowers with initially poor credit, wants to take advantage of an improvement in credit. As we will discuss shortly, refinancings tend to be the most volatile component of speeds, and constitute the bulk of prepayments when speeds are very high.
3. *Defaults.* These are prepayments caused by the foreclosure and subsequent liquidation of a mortgage. Defaults are a relatively minor component of aggregate prepayments in most cases, but can be significant for certain types of loans.

---

[2] According to the U.S. Census Bureau, 61% of all owner-occupied housing units were mortgaged as of 1997.

EXHIBIT 4.1 Turnover Rate on Existing Homes and Speeds on 1977 Ginnie Mae 7.5s, 1977–2000

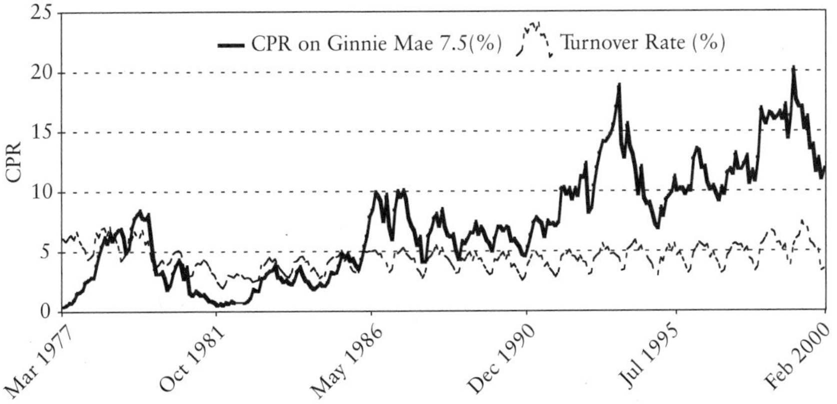

Sources: Salomon Smith Barney, National Association of Realtors, and U.S. Census Bureau.

4. *Curtailments and full payoffs.* Some mortgagors are in the habit of sending in more than the scheduled payment each month, as a form of forced savings and to build up equity in their homes faster. The extra payments are referred to as curtailments, and show up as partial prepayments of principal. Full payoffs refer to mortgagors paying off their mortgage completely, usually when it is very seasoned and the remaining loan balance is small. Full payoffs can also occur because of the destruction of the home from natural disasters such as hurricanes and earthquakes.

A Case Study: Speeds on 1977 Ginnie Mae 7.5% MBSs

An example helps in understanding the various components of prepayment speeds, and their relative importance and evolution over time. Exhibit 4.1 shows prepayment speeds on 1977 origination Ginnie Mae 7.5s, along with the turnover rate on existing homes. The turnover rate is obtained by dividing the number of existing homes sold in a given month[3] by the estimated number of single-family homes in the United States at that time.[4]

---

[3] This data is provided by the National Association of Realtors. Note that we are using the actual, rather than the seasonally adjusted number of homes sold.
[4] This is based on U.S. Census Bureau data.

In the late 1970s, the housing market was very strong, and speeds increased rapidly, reflecting fast *seasoning*.[5] In the early 1980s, mortgage rates rose sharply into the teens, leading to a substantial proportion of *assumptions*[6] on the Ginnie Mae 7.5s. This resulted in the prepayment rate on Ginnie Mae 7.5s declining more than the turnover rate for existing homes. In 1986 and early 1987, a period of heavy refinancing activity, speeds on the Ginnie Mae 7.5s jumped to well above the turnover rate. However, the weighted-average coupon (WAC) on the Ginnie Mae 7.5s is 8%, while mortgage rates in 1986 and 1987 were generally 9% or higher. This discrepancy suggests that the 1977 Ginnie Mae 7.5s experienced *cash-out refinancings*[7] in 1986 and 1987, as some homeowners refinanced into larger loans to make use of the equity in their homes, even if it meant a small increase in the loan rate.

From 1988 through early 1991, speeds on the Ginnie Mae 7.5s tracked the turnover rate quite closely, on average being about 1% to 2% Constant Prepayment Rate (CPR) higher. This trend indicates that over this period speeds were driven mostly by home sales, few assumptions occurred (because the balances on the underlying loans, originated in 1977, were by then small compared with the cost of a new home), and some curtailments occurred. Defaults were quite low (about 0.25% CPR, according to FHA data), reflecting the fact that few loans default once they are seasoned more than ten years.

Starting in late 1991, the 1977 Ginnie Mae 7.5s began to experience refinancings, reflecting declining mortgage rates. Note however, that the 1977 Ginnie Mae 7.5s did not experience the sky-high prepayment rate of newer coupons, probably because the small remaining balances on 1977 loans reduced the incentive to refinance the loans. The same phenomenon occurred in the refinancing waves of 1998, with peak speeds on these pools very briefly reaching 20% CPR. With mortgage rates climbing upward through most of 1999, speeds on the 7.5s have declined from their late-1998 highs, but remain about 5% to 10% CPR above the turnover rate. At this point, these coupons are out of the money, but the balances on these loans are low

---

[5] See the heading: The Seasoning Process in Section 4.1 for a discussion of seasoning.
[6] A mortgage is said to be assumable if, when the house is sold, the new buyer can take over the payments on the old mortgage. In this case, the home sale does not result in a prepayment of the existing mortgage. See the heading: The Lock-in Effect in Section 4.1 for details.
[7] A refinancing in which a borrower increases the existing loan amount to borrow more money is known as a cash-out refinancing. See the heading: Cash-Out and Credit-Driven Refinancings in Section 4.2 for details.

enough that an increasing number of households are resorting to curtailments or full payoffs to reduce the level of their mortgage indebtedness.

A Framework for Modeling Performance

As the previous case study suggests, a successful prepayment model needs to take into account the fact that the different sources of prepayments can vary significantly in their contribution to aggregate prepayment speeds at any given point in time. The magnitude of these contributions will depend upon borrower incentive, credit, equity, and loan age, among other factors. These considerations naturally lead to a modeling framework in which a separate submodel is estimated for each of the four sources of prepayments. Projections from the four submodels are then summed to obtain the total projected prepayment rate. This modular approach has, we feel, a number of benefits, including the following:

- The same model applies to all mortgage types. Whereas different mortgage types may vary in the relative importance of the sources of prepayments, the fundamental causes of prepayments apply to all types.
- Similarly, the same model can be applied to different regions or countries, though the relative importance of the different components will vary depending on local cultural and market conditions.
- The time-dependent nature of key parameters, such as refinancing costs and intrinsic borrower propensities to refinance, means that the same model applies across time, despite significant changes in the mortgage industry and in borrower behavior.
- Each submodel depends in an economically sound manner on the variables likely to influence mortgagor behavior or response. This allows plausible models to be developed even when there is missing information (such as LTVs) or a lack of historical prepayment data.
- Within each component, relationships can be easily modified to explore the effects of unanticipated demographic or mortgage market changes on prepayments, and hence on MBS value.[8]

Organization of Chapter

The rest of this chapter expands on this capsule description of our modeling approach, and, in particular, describes in detail each of the four causes of

---

[8] Readers who have access to the Salomon Smith Barney analytic system, the Yield Book™, can use the "Dials" facility to do this.

prepayments. The chapter is organized as follows: The next four sections detail the four components of our modeling framework; namely the turnover, refinancing, default, and curtailment submodels. We then describe how this framework has been applied in several cases, covering a diverse range of loan and borrower types. A final section provides a "User's Guide" to prepayment models, in particular discussing the limitations of such models. The chapter concludes with two appendixes that provide some additional technical detail on modeling turnover and refinancings.

4.1 HOUSING TURNOVER

In the absence of refinancings, prepayments will be caused mostly by home sales, as Exhibit 4.1 illustrates. Hence, the critical component of discount speeds is housing turnover. For a specific pool, the contribution of housing turnover to aggregate prepayment speeds will depend on a number of factors:

- *The overall turnover rate,* which is the percentage of all existing homes likely to be sold in a given period;
- *Relative mobility,* which for an overall turnover rate refers to differences in the likelihood of moving between different types of borrowers because of demographic factors;
- *Seasoning,* which refers to how the likelihood of moving varies with the time since the loan was taken; and
- *The lock-in effect,* which refers to the dampening effect on the likelihood of moving due to having a loan rate that is below current mortgage rates.

In the rest of this section, we discuss these factors in detail, and describe how they are captured in the Salomon Smith Barney Prepayment Model.

The Overall Turnover Rate

A number of housing industry statistics are published each month, but the one that is most relevant for prepayment analysis is *sales of existing homes.* While other statistics, such as housing starts or new home sales, often receive more publicity, they do not have the direct relationship with prepayments that existing home sales do. Unless the mortgage is assumed or the home has no mortgage, the sale of an existing home leads to a prepayment. Given data on the number of existing homes sold nationally, we can compute the overall turnover rate—it is the number of existing homes sold as a percentage of the stock. This statistic can be thought of as the overall prepayment rate resulting from home sales. Exhibit 4.2 summarizes mortgage rates and annual values of some of the data series we have just discussed, from 1978 to 2000. The exhibit shows that annual turnover rates on existing homes have generally hovered between 4% and 6%, with somewhat lower rates in the early 1980s, when high mortgage rates and a severe recession severely depressed the housing markets.

While mortgage rates do affect housing activity through affordability levels, other factors can also play an important role. For example, the turnover rate in 1986 was about the same as that in 1993, despite mortgage rates being several hundred basis points higher in 1986. Economic growth and the business cycle, the federal taxation of home sales, and changes in household situations (the arrival of children, divorce, retirement) can all affect a household's decision to move. Levels of turnover

EXHIBIT 4.2 Housing Turnover Rates, 1978–2000

Year	Average Mortgage Rate	Sales of Existing Homes	Single-Family Housing Stock	Turnover Rate
1978	9.64 %	3.99	55.98	7.12 %
1979	11.19	3.83	57.37	6.67
1980	13.77	2.97	58.80	5.05
1981	16.64	2.42	60.03	4.03
1982	16.09	1.99	61.15	3.25
1983	13.23	2.70	62.27	4.31
1984	13.87	2.83	63.39	4.44
1985	12.42	3.31	64.52	4.84
1986	10.18	3.47	65.64	5.30
1987	10.20	3.44	66.76	5.14
1988	10.33	3.51	67.48	5.16
1989	10.32	3.35	67.86	4.99
1990	10.13	3.21	68.24	4.70
1991	9.25	3.22	68.63	4.69
1992	8.40	3.52	69.22	5.09
1993	7.33	3.80	70.04	5.43
1994	8.36	3.95	70.91	5.57
1995	7.93	3.81	71.92	5.29
1996	7.81	4.09	73.06	5.74
1997	7.60	4.21	74.31	5.90
1998	6.94	4.99	75.47	6.58
1999	7.44	5.20	76.58	6.78
2000 YTD	8.25	4.60	77.24	5.96

Note: Total housing stock is estimated by using U.S. Census Bureau data on single-family residences. Units for home sales and housing stocks are in millions. YTD: Year-to-date.
Source: Freddie Mac, National Association of Realtors, U.S. Census Bureau, and Salomon Smith Barney.

activity in 1998 to 1999 were close to all-time highs, with a booming housing market fueled by low mortgage rates, a strong economy, and high levels of consumer confidence.

Projecting Housing Turnover   If housing turnover largely drives speeds on discount MBSs, then we need to understand how turnover rates vary over different interest-rate cycles. Mortgage rates clearly affect the overall level of home turnover and hence speeds, and our turnover model computes an affordability measure to capture the variation in discount speeds as interest rates change. We defer a detailed discussion of the explanatory variables included in the model and our modeling assumptions to Appendix 4A, and focus on the projections produced by the model here. The model is fitted to historical data over the past 20 years. Its projections include the influence of current interest rates as well as the lingering influence of recent interest-rate history on the present level of home sales.

Exhibit 4.3 depicts the turnover model's predictions for various interest-rate changes. The model realistically captures mortgagors' real-life response to interest-rate changes. For example, if rates rise by 2.0% and hold steady, it projects that turnover rates will fall initially but subsequently revert toward historical means as consumers adjust to the new economic situation. Conversely, a drop in rates leads to an initial surge in turnover, followed by a gradual drop, as satiation of demand causes a reversion toward historical

EXHIBIT 4.3   Projected Housing Turnover Rates

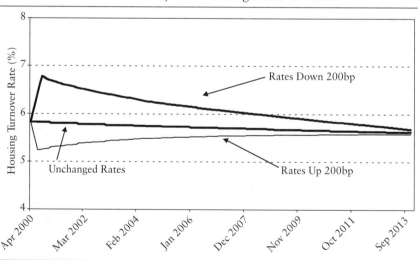

Sources: National Association of Realtors, U.S. Census Bureau, and Salomon Smith Barney.

EXHIBIT 4.4 Existing Home Sales, 1995–2000

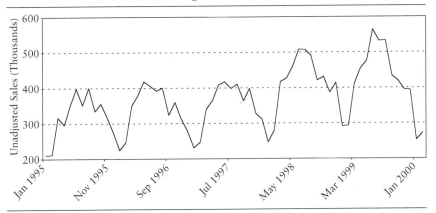

Source: National Association of Realtors.

means. However, as discussed earlier, factors other than mortgage rates do affect turnover rates. For example, turnover rates dipped significantly in 1990/1991 (see Exhibit 4.2), as a result of the recession that occurred at that time.

Seasonal Variation in Turnover Rates   Home sales volume exhibits a pronounced but consistent seasonal pattern, which obviously passes through to turnover speeds. The extent and consistency of the seasonal cycle is indicated in Exhibit 4.1 and it is also shown in Exhibit 4.4, which plots the (unadjusted) existing home sales data released by the National Association of Realtors (NAR) over the period 1995 to 2000.[9]

As one might expect, the seasonal highs occur in the summer and the lows in the winter, with the school year calendar and the weather the driving forces behind the seasonal cycle. MBS investors need to be aware of the magnitude of the seasonal variation. There is almost a two-to-one ratio between summer highs and winter lows and some significant month-to-month changes. Exhibit 4.5 shows an average seasonal factor for each month, along with the change from the previous month.

The largest one-month change is from February to March, when home sales typically increase by about 42%. In the fall and winter months, a series of double-digit percentage declines occurs until the seasonal cycle reaches its

---

[9] The NAR also releases seasonally adjusted existing home sales volume. The seasonal adjustments are estimated using the U.S. Census Bureau's X-11 statistical program.

EXHIBIT 4.5 Estimated Seasonal Adjustments for Sales of Existing Homes

Month	Seasonal Adjustment	Pct. Change from Previous Month
Jan	0.66	−21 %
Feb	0.72	+10
Mar	1.01	+42
Apr	1.07	+5
May	1.18	+11
Jun	1.22	+2
Jul	1.14	−7
Aug	1.19	+3
Sep	0.99	−16
Oct	1.07	+8
Nov	0.92	−13
Dec	0.83	−9

Sources: National Association of Realtors and Salomon Smith Barney.

low in January. These adjustments can form the basis for incorporating seasonal factors in prepayment projections; however, readers should be aware of one or two complications. First, in reporting sales volume to the NAR, local realtors do not consistently define a sale. The majority defines a sale as a closing, which implies an immediate mortgage prepayment, but a small fraction[10] defines it as a sales contract, which implies a mortgage prepayment a couple of months later. Second, depending on the servicer and servicing agreement, for some closings that take place near the end of the month, the prepayment may not actually show up in pool factors until the following month. The Salomon Smith Barney Prepayment Model starts with the NAR adjustments and uses historical correlations between home sales changes and discount speed changes to derive monthly seasonal factors for each agency.

Relative Mobility

The overall turnover rate on discounts tends to vary by loan type. Relative mobility describes the extent to which these differences are determined by the self-selection of borrowers who opt for certain types of loans. For example, balloon discounts typically prepay faster than conventional discounts, which in turn usually prepay faster than Ginnie Mae discounts.

---

[10] As of 1999, the NAR received the bulk of the data on its sales transactions from Multiple Listing Services, which are almost all computerized, and report only closed transactions. Thus, the NAR estimates that currently about 99% of its sales transactions represent closings. The figure is likely less for previous years.

EXHIBIT 4.6 The Effect of Loan Type: Speeds on 1996 Freddie Mac 30-Year 6.5s and 7-Year Balloon 6s

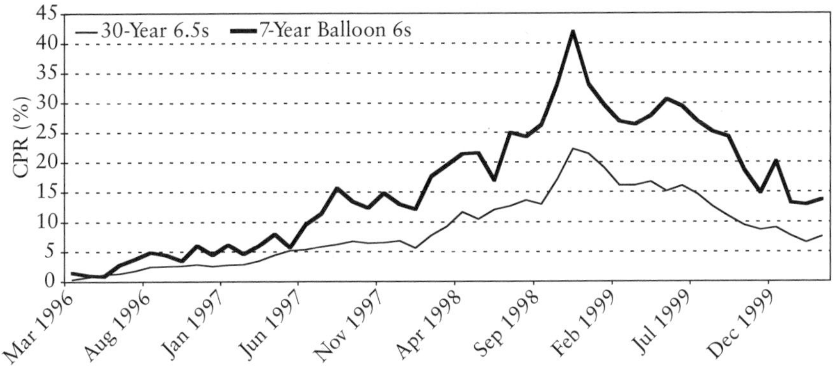

Sources: Freddie Mac and Salomon Smith Barney.

Anecdotal evidence from originators indicate that borrowers who select balloon loans—or adjustable-rate mortgages (ARMs)—often expect to move again soon, leading to a higher base-line mobility rate (as well as faster seasoning) than the average.

An example of such loan-specific differences may be found by comparing Freddie Mac 30-year 6.5% mortgages from 1996 with 7-year 6% balloons from the same origination year, as shown in Exhibit 4.6.[11] While the overall pattern of prepayments is the same for the two classes, the higher level of speeds on the balloon MBS is an indication of differences in relative mobility.

The Seasoning Price

Seasoning refers to the gradual increase in prepayment speeds on a pool of new mortgages over time until a reasonably steady-state speed is reached. A pool of mortgages that has reached this steady-state level is said to be *fully seasoned*. In addition to loan age, seasoning also depends on several other variables, most notably the strength of the housing market and amount of equity that has been accumulated in the home. Since a majority of currently

---

[11] We have chosen to compare a 6% balloon pool with 6.5% 30-year pool because balloon mortgage rates have recently been 25bp to 40bp lower than 30-year mortgage rates.

EXHIBIT 4.7 Seasoning Patterns for Conventional 30-Year Discounts

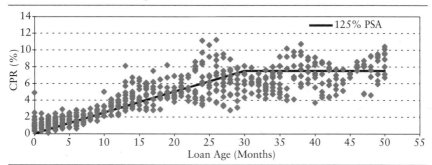

Source: Salomon Smith Barney.

outstanding MBSs are new discounts, many of which were originated in the refinancing waves of 1998 and early 1999, a critical question for MBS investors concerns the rate at which the underlying loans will season.

The Base, or Age-Dependent, Seasoning Ramp   The traditional approach to modeling the seasoning process was to assume that the seasoning curve depended only on loan age. The industry standard, the PSA aging ramp, assumes that loans season linearly over the first 30 months. The PSA ramp is based on historical data that show that discount speeds tend to increase for the first few years, before leveling off.[12] This is what one would expect—the transaction costs incurred in a home purchase are substantial, amounting to several percentage points of the purchase price. Most home purchases are therefore followed by a quiescent settling-in period, when the family avoids relocation unless compelled by circumstances. Hence, prepayments associated with newly originated purchase loans are initially quite small, and increase to the "natural" level implied by the housing turnover rate gradually over the seasoning period.

As an illustration, Exhibit 4.7 graphs speeds on discount conventional 30-year MBSs as a function of age. Also shown is an appropriate multiple (125% PSA) of the industry-standard PSA curve. Note that speeds do not quite follow the PSA ramp. Speeds are above the PSA curve in the initial months of the mortgage, but then drop below it, leading to the so-called PSA *elbow,* which is most pronounced around the age of 30 months. This

---

[12] The old *FHA Experience* survivorship table showed this pattern as well, and was in fact the predecessor of the PSA ramp.

EXHIBIT 4.8 The Effect of Housing Inflation: Speeds on Colorado and California 1993 Conventional 30-Year 6.5s

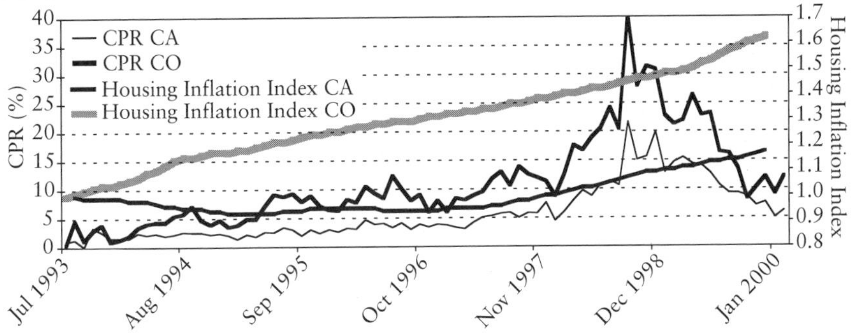

CA: California, CO: Colorado
Source: Salomon Smith Barney.

type of seasoning ramp leads to high initial PSAs, which then decrease, but eventually start increasing again until the collateral is fully seasoned.

Housing Inflation   While discount speeds *on average* will tend to follow the seasoning pattern shown in Exhibit 4.7 local economic conditions will tend to affect the *rate of seasoning*. For example, strong home price increases and the resulting build-up in equity can affect the ability of a homeowner to move. Rapid price appreciation leads to a quick increase in the amount of equity in the home, which can spur "trade-up" moves, as well as reflect a generally vigorous housing market. In contrast, price depreciation will dampen the ability to move and overall housing activity. These points are illustrated in Exhibit 4.8, which shows speeds on 1993 conventional 6.5s from Colorado and from California. Colorado experienced a much stronger housing market until recently, as illustrated by the housing inflation indices for the two states (normalized to 100 in 1993) that are also shown in Exhibit 4.8. The faster seasoning (as well as higher overall turnover rates) of the Colorado 6.5s is clearly evident in Exhibit 4.8.[13]

To capture the effect of regional housing markets on prepayments, we compute **Housing Inflation Indices** for each group of loans or "cohort." To calculate the Housing Inflation Index for any cohort at any point in time, we need two items of information:

---

[13] Note that refinancing rates in 1998 were also higher for the Colorado 6.5s. As we discuss in Section 4.2, home equity growth also plays a key role in refinancings.

1. The percentage of the surviving loans that were originated in each state; and
2. The average home price appreciation experienced in each state since the loans were originated.

The data for item 1 are released at the pool level by the agencies (they are usually available in even greater detail for non-agency MBS). For item 2, we utilize the Conventional State-Level Home Price Indices that are released by Freddie Mac and Fannie Mae on a quarterly basis. Items 1 and 2 are then combined to create a weighted-average housing inflation index for each cohort over its entire life span.

The Combined Seasoning Curve   The seasoning curve for a cohort is thus a function of two variables: (1) the average loan age, and (2) the cohort's Housing Inflation Index. The inclusion of the Housing Inflation Index allows the model to capture the differences in seasoning between, for example, 1993 California and Colorado discount pools or between conventional discounts originated in 1987 (which experienced a strong housing market and seasoned quickly) and those originated in 1993 (which because of the weak California and Northeast housing markets seasoned slowly).

Other Factors Affecting the Seasoning Ramp   A number of other factors can affect the rate of seasoning. The most important of these variables are as follows:

The percentage of refinanced loans in the pool. The presence of a substantial number of refinanced loans in a mortgage pool can indicate higher prepayments during the seasoning period. It could be argued that refinanced loans should season faster than purchase loans, because many of the elements that determine seasoning (a growing family, expanding income, etc.) are already developed to some extent in a refinanced loan. In addition, the very act of purchase sends a much stronger message than a refinancing that the mortgage holder plans to put down some roots. Moreover, the circumstances that tend to make the purchasers of a home unwilling/unable to move immediately, such as a high LTV ratio, the fresh memory of the joys of moving, and the typically higher transaction costs of relocation continue to distinguish purchase loans from refinanced loans.

However, the view that refinanced loans season faster is not universally held. Homeowners who plan to move in the near future may decide not to refinance, or if they do, they can now refinance into a balloon or ARM. Therefore, it is possible that mortgage holders refinancing into 30-year loans nowadays might actually be sending the opposite message, namely that they plan to stay in their current home for a while.

On balance, we believe that a high percentage of refinanced loans in a pool is still likely to lead to a somewhat faster seasoning process. Our loan-level studies indicate that when other factors are controlled for, refinanced loans appear to season about 10% faster than purchase loans. Our model conservatively projects a slightly higher trajectory of prepayments during the seasoning period based on the percentage of refinanced loans at origination.

The number of points paid at origination. Another distinguishing feature useful in predicting seasoning characteristics is the estimated points paid at origination. It has become common for lenders to offer loans with differing amounts of points. At one extreme are low-point or no-point loans, with which the borrower accepts a higher coupon rate in exchange for lower up-front costs. As discussed later in the section on refinancings, such borrowers tend to be "fast" refinancers. At the other extreme, borrowers can pay extra points to obtain a lower coupon rate. Both theory and empirical evidence indicate that borrowers who choose to put down points to lower their rates are signaling an intent to stay for some period of time. Although the number of points paid are not part of the available data for agency mortgage pools, we can estimate it from the difference between the prevailing mortgage rate at the time of origination and the WAC of the pool. As with the percentage of refinanced loans in a pool, the points paid statistic is used by our prepayment model to modify the baseline seasoning ramp: The more points a borrower pays, the more slowly they are expected to season.

The Lock-In Effect: Modeling the Disincentive to Move

The lock-in effect refers to the borrower's disincentive to move because of the existing loan rate being below prevailing market rates. In this situation, moving to a new home would increase the borrower's mortgage coupon rate, in addition to the other expenses incurred. Thus, the more a borrower is locked-in (the greater the difference between the borrower's below-market rate and prevailing mortgage rates) the lower the turnover rate of the borrower.

How do we model the lock-in effect? An economic argument suggests that the disincentive to move (and as the section **Refinancing Behavior** will show, the incentive to refinance) is a function of two quantities:

1. The present value cost per dollar of changing from the existing loan rate to a new loan rate (reflecting prevailing market rates)—the greater the cost, the more the borrower is locked in.
2. The current loan balance as a proportion of the likely amount of a new loan—as this proportion declines over time due to amortization and home price increases the lock-in effect will diminish.

Exhibit 4.9 shows the balance of an existing loan as a fraction of the *likely* value of a new loan, and thus illustrates how the lock-in effect will weaken over time due to the combined effects of amortization and housing inflation, which we assume to be a constant 3% per year.

To summarize, we model the lock-in effect as a function of the relative coupon differential between the loan rate and current rates, housing inflation, and to a lesser extent, amortization.

Using the Lock-In Effect to Model Assumable Mortgages   If a home seller is currently financing a house with an *assumable* mortgage, the new buyer can "assume" the obligations of the existing mortgage, thereby not triggering a prepayment. In general, whenever the current market rate exceeds the contract rate on the assumable mortgage, the home seller can pass on the below-market rate loan to the buyer, and capture the value of the assumability option through a higher selling price. The seller and the buyer thus both benefit at the expense of the lender, who continues to carry a low-rate loan in a period of high market rates.

EXHIBIT 4.9 Existing Loan Balance as a Proportion of the Likely Balance of a New Loan

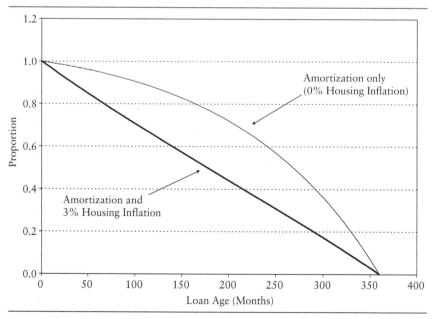

Source: Salomon Smith Barney.

FHA and VA loans have always been assumable, although the FHA has periodically tightened the requirements for making an assumption. Until the 1970s, most conventional loans were assumable but this began to change in the 1980s. In the high-rate environment of the early 1980s, lenders became increasingly aware of the value of the assumability option and began to remove it for conventional mortgages through a due-on-sale clause. Essentially, a due-on-sale clause stipulates that the entire amount of the remaining loan balance is due to the lender in the event of a sale of the property. By the 1990s, virtually all conventional mortgages had this clause. In practice, the assumability of FHA and VA loans can be modeled by assuming these loans experience an enhanced lock-in effect. Technically, having an assumable mortgage has little additional bearing on a borrower's economic disincentive to move. However, the value of the assumability option is directly proportional to the lock-in effect, and depends on the same two factors:

1. The greater the relative rate differential between the existing below-market loan rate and the market rate, the more attractive the existing loan is as a candidate for assumption.
2. The smaller the current loan balance as a proportion of the likely amount of a new loan the less attractive the existing loan is as a candidate for assumption.

Thus, the more locked-in a borrower is, the more likely it is that their mortgage is an attractive candidate for assumption, and vice-versa. This explains why prepayment rates on FHA/VA discount loans initially appear as if the borrower were experiencing a strong lock-in effect.

4.2 REFINANCING BEHAVIOR

Very high prepayment speeds are primarily a result of refinancings. Housing turnover by itself will rarely lead to prepayment rates above 10% to 12% CPR. Hence, an accurate modeling of prepayments during market rallies such as those from 1991 to 1993, and in 1998, when speeds sometimes exceeded 50% CPR, requires a sound understanding of refinancing behavior.

A refinancing is an economic prepayment and can be thought of as an exercise of a call option on the existing loan by the mortgagor. However, traditional option theory is of limited use in analyzing refinancings, because mortgagor behavior represents an inefficient exercise of the option. This observation is illustrated in Exhibit 4.10, which shows prepayment rates versus

EXHIBIT 4.10 Conventional Prepayment Speeds versus Refinancing Incentive, December 1998 and December 1999

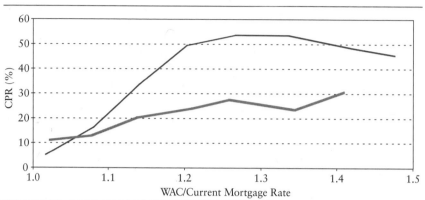

Source: Fannie Mae and Salomon Smith Barney.

a simple measure of refinancing incentive (the ratio of WAC to the current mortgage rate) at two different points in time.[14]

Both sets of speeds follow the familiar S-curve typically displayed by prepayment rates. This curve bears some resemblance to the "0-1" step-function that represents an efficient option exercise by the mortgagor; that is, do not refinance if the savings from a refinancing is less than some hypothetical transaction cost and refinance otherwise. A striking feature of Exhibit 4.10 from an option-theoretic point of view, albeit one very familiar to anyone who has looked at prepayment speeds, is the difference between the speeds in December 1998 and December 1999. For the same refinancing incentive, speeds in December 1999 were about half of what they were 12 months earlier.

This phenomenon, whereby refinancing rates decline over time even if no change occurs in the refinancing incentive, is known as *burnout*. This term is used to describe the empirically observed phenomenon that a pool of mortgages that has experienced previous exposure to refinancing opportunities will, other things being equal, have lower refinancing rates than a pool with no such prior exposure. Burnout can be explained (as discussed in detail later) as the effect of changes in the composition of the pool caused by refinancings, which remove the most capable or eager refinancers from

---

[14] The calculation of refinancing incentive is discussed in further detail later in this chapter under the heading: Refinancing Incentive in Section 4.2.

the pool, so that the remaining borrowers have lower tendencies to refinance. Burnout also explains why the speeds in Exhibit 4.10 can actually begin to decline for higher refinancing incentives; these coupons have had greater past exposure to refinancing opportunities.

The burnout process is evident in Exhibit 4.11, which shows speeds of Freddie Mac Gold 1991 8.5s and 9.0s. In 1992, the greater refinancing incentive of the 9.0s resulted in speeds that were much higher than the 8.5s. But, as rates continued to rally into 1993, speeds on the 8.5s overtook the 9.0s by the fall of 1993. Speeds on both issues were high (60% CPR or more), but the earlier higher speeds of the 9.0s had depleted more of the most capable and eager refinancers from the 9.0 borrower population compared to the 8.5s. In other words, the 9.0s were more burnt-out than the 8.5s by September 1993. Furthermore, speeds in 1998 for both issues were substantially lower than in 1993 even though mortgage rates reached new historical lows in 1998. Both issues had already been exposed to many refinancing opportunities over the years, resulting in substantial burnout and the slower speeds in 1998 compared to 1993.

However, refinancing patterns are more complex and dynamic than the relatively simple population decay model of burnout described so far. In between the massive refinancing waves of 1993 and 1998, a mini-refinancing wave occurred in 1996, when mortgage rates rallied to levels not far from the lows previously reached in 1993. However, prepayment speeds were surprisingly subdued, as shown in Exhibit 4.11, and were not even half of the fast

EXHIBIT 4.11 Prepayment Speeds of 1991 Freddie Mac 8.5s and 9.0s, 1991–2000

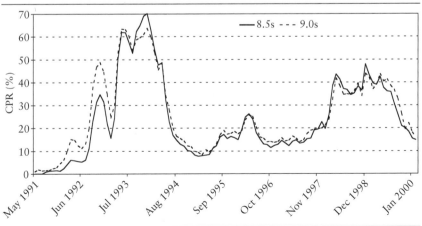

Source: Salomon Smith Barney.

speeds recorded in most of 1993. Burnout accounts for some of the slowness in 1996 (indicated by peak speeds of the 8.5s and 9.0s being about the same despite the roughly 45bp [basis points] of additional rate incentive of the 9.0s), but it is difficult to believe that the subsequently lower rates of 1998 could then boost speeds of these even more burnt-out issues so much higher. More likely, gains in the equity in their homes from strong home price appreciation put more borrowers in a position to be able to refinance in 1998, and the borrower psychology of reacting to historical lows in rates kept borrowers on the sidelines in 1996, when no such historical low was reached.[15]

As we discuss later, we feel that burnout, and refinancing patterns in general, are best modeled within a behavioral or statistical framework.

Some Basic Issues for a Refinancing Model

The previous discussion highlights just some of the complexities in trying to model refinancing behavior. A refinancing model has to address a number of issues, including:

- *Refinancing incentive.* What are borrower decisions to refinance based on? A simple answer might be that the decision simply involves comparing the rate on the existing loan with that available on a new loan. However, there are several complications. First, there is not a single "mortgage rate," but many, varying by lender, by region, by mortgage term, by the credit of the borrower, and so on. Second, different borrowers will use different means to reach a decision on whether to refinance— remember that we are not dealing with an efficient corporation. And, third, there are substantial costs involved in taking out a mortgage, and these costs can vary from lender to lender and may also depend on borrower or loan characteristics (such as LTV and credit).
- *Burnout.* As discussed above, burnout is not a simple, monotonic process. Rather, it is dynamic, subject to external influences such as multi-year lows in mortgage rates (the **media effect,** discussed later under the heading: Media Effect and Borrower Migrations in Section 4.2) and changes in borrower circumstances.
- *Diversity in borrower types.* Assumptions about refinancing behavior that hold for one type of MBS may not hold for another, even within the same sector. However, for consistency and relative value analysis, it is desirable to apply the same model to all types of MBSs.
- *Changes in the refinancing environment.* Refinancing behavior and patterns have changed over the years, and will no doubt continue to do so

---

[15] In addition, rates did not stay low for very long in 1996.

going forward, because of **regulatory, technological, market,** or **borrower** changes—a prime example being increases in refinancing efficiency over the years due to reductions in the cost of taking out a mortgage. This means that care has to be taken in using historical prepayment data to project prepayments. In the rest of this section, we discuss these issues in more detail, and explain how they are handled in the Salomon Smith Barney Prepayment Model.

The Refinancing Incentive

What Is the "Mortgage Rate"?   Anyone who has taken out a mortgage, or even simply looked at the real estate section of the Sunday paper, will be aware of the differences in mortgage rates and terms offered by lenders in the same area. In addition, there are regional variations in rates, and, perhaps most important, differences in rates based on borrower credit, LTVs, and the size of the loan.[16] Finally, there are a variety of mortgage loan types available to a prospective refinancer: ARMs, hybrid ARMs, balloons, and fixed-rate mortgages ranging in term from 10 to 30 years. Since the decision to refinance depends critically on some perceived mortgage rate, how do we calculate such a rate?[17]

The weekly Freddie Mac Survey rate (the average from a large group of lenders) is a widely used reference for the industry. However, this rate applies only to *conforming conventional* loans with LTVs of 80% or less. Rates for FHA/VA loans, which collateralize Ginnie Mae MBSs, tend to be slightly higher, while rates for "jumbo" loans (i.e., loans larger than the agency limits) are typically 25bp or more than on conforming loans. Mortgage rates for borrowers with poor credit histories, who form the collateral for *Home Equity Loan (HEL)* and *Subprime* (or *B&C*) MBSs, tend to be several hundred basis points higher than the Freddie Mac Survey rate.

The point is that it is important to estimate mortgage rate series for each loan type, and use the appropriate rate in obtaining projections. In addition, especially in the case of agency MBSs, we need to factor in the availability of loans of different terms. For example, many 30-year mortgagors refinance into 15-year loans, which typically have rates that are between 30bp and 50bp below 30-year loans.

---

[16] Mortgage rates will also depend on the points paid by the borrower, but points represent a borrower choice on how much to pay up-front versus over the term of the loan, rather than true differences in mortgage costs.

[17] Another complication is that mortgage rates change continuously within a month, and resulting prepayments will reflect all the rates in a particular month. For practical purposes, we have to assume some average rate for a month to feed into the prepayment model.

How Do We Calculate the Refinancing Incentive? Traditionally, the refinancing incentive for a pool of mortgages was measured as the difference, or spread, between the WAC and prevailing mortgage rates. A related measure is the ratio of these two rates. These measures are simple and easily understood, but have the following drawback. Loans with different ages or balances—a new loan, a seasoned one close to maturity, a small loan, and a large one—but with the same loan rate, would all have the same incentive. The number of payments remaining and the loan balance do not enter into the calculation.

A preferable approach is to compare the monthly payments under the existing and new mortgages, or, alternatively, the present values of the payments, factoring in costs of refinancing in both cases. While the present value comparison might seem theoretically preferable,[18] a comparison of monthly payments seems to be how most borrowers actually reach a decision.[19] However, as we now show, under reasonable assumptions the two approaches give the same incentive.

Let B = Current loan balance
W = Remaining term of loan (in months)
C = Rate on existing loan
M = Prevailing mortgage rate (on new loans)

$$x = \frac{1}{(1+C)}$$

$$y = \frac{1}{(1+M)}$$

where C and M are expressed as monthly decimals. Then

$$\text{Monthly payment on existing loan} = \frac{BC}{1-x^W} \qquad (4.1)$$

There are W equal remaining payments, given by Equation 4.1. The present value of these payments, at a discount rate M, is:

---

[18] An even more theoretical approach would be to calculate the value of the existing mortgage using a stochastic (OAS) approach, which would incorporate the effects of volatility and the embedded prepayment option. Apart from being computationally cumbersome, this approach may also not really mimic how ordinary people make a prepayment decision.
[19] A calculation of the number of months until costs are recouped seems to be the way many decisions are evaluated.

$$\text{Present value of payments at discount rate } M = \frac{BC}{M} \times \frac{1 - y^W}{1 - x^W} \qquad (4.2)$$

Assume the borrower takes out a new loan, with a coupon M, with the same balance B as the existing loan; then by definition, the *present value of the new payments at a discount rate M will be just B*.

Refinancing Costs While the mortgage lending process has been getting more efficient over the years, there are still significant costs associated with refinancing a loan. Costs include origination fees, and fees for a credit report, appraisal, and title search and insurance.[20] It is convenient to divide refinancing costs into two types: (1) *fixed costs* and (2) *variable costs*, which vary with the loan size. For example, the attorney's fee would typically be considered a fixed cost while the origination fee normally is a percentage of the loan size. Let v be the variable cost (expressed as a decimal), and let F be the fixed cost (expressed in dollars). Then the savings (in present value terms) from a refinancing equal

$$\begin{aligned} \text{SAV} &= \frac{BC}{M} \times \frac{1 - y^W}{1 - x^W} - B - Bv - F \\ &= \frac{BC}{M} \times \frac{1 - y^W}{1 - x^W} - B\left(1 + v + \frac{F}{B}\right) \end{aligned} \qquad (4.3)$$

As our refinancing incentive, we use the percentage savings,[21] or Equation 4.3 divided by Equation 4.2, which equals

$$\%\text{SAV} = 1 - \frac{M}{C} \times \frac{1 - x^W}{1 - y^W}\left(1 + v + \frac{F}{B}\right) \qquad (4.4)$$

Equivalence to Savings in Monthly Payments If the new loan is assumed to have a term equal to the remaining term of the old loan (W in the above formulation), and costs are rolled into the new loan (so that the new loan

---

[20] See Chapter 6 for a detailed discussion of refinancing costs.
[21] An argument can be made that the absolute dollar savings, given by Equation 4.3, is also relevant. The use of the percentage savings reflects the belief that a larger loan size is indicative of a greater level of borrower affluence and that an absolute dollar of savings is worth less to a wealthier borrower. Dividing by B normalizes the savings to account for differences in the affluence of borrowers.

balance is $B(1 + v + F/B))$ then it is straightforward to show that the percentage savings in monthly payments is equal to Equation 4.4, the percentage savings in present values. Hence, our refinancing incentive measure has the advantage of also being meaningful for borrowers who base decisions in terms of changes in monthly payments.

The refinancing incentive defined in Equation 4.4 is dependent on loan size and on the remaining term (i.e., number of remaining payments). This is consistent with observed prepayment behavior. As loan size increases, the fixed costs F divided by the loan balance B decreases so that the percentage savings increases. In other words, fixed costs represent a lower hurdle for larger loans. Conversely, fixed costs are a greater hurdle to refinancing for borrowers with smaller loans.[22] The dependence on remaining term is consistent with the empirical observation that seasoned loans tend to have dampened refinancing rates, even after controlling for burnout. Exhibit 4.12 shows how the refinancing incentive changes with loan age for a 30-year and a 15-year mortgage. Fifteen-year loans tend to have lower balances than 30-year loans; our assumptions are based on recent average loan balances in conventional pools.

In Exhibit 4.12, we assume that, due to inflation, fixed costs increase 3% per year. Hence, the term F/B will increase over time due both to inflation driving the fixed costs F higher, and amortization driving the loan balance, B, lower. The effect of amortization becomes pronounced for the 15-year loan after just a few years. The incentives shown in Exhibit 4.12 explain the slower refinancing rates of both seasoned loans and of 15-year MBSs.

Transient Costs, or the Refinancing Seasoning Ramp The time and inconvenience involved in refinancing a mortgage (even nowadays) implies that a borrower who has just completed a refinancing may be reluctant to immediately enter the process again. In addition, since a refinancing normally involves upfront costs, there may be reluctance to write off those costs right away by taking out a new mortgage. A high initial LTV may also represent a hurdle for some loans. At the same time, it is clear that if rates fall far enough, borrowers would most likely refinance even a very recent mortgage.

---

[22] While the incentive of the borrower is the most important driver of refinancings, the incentive of the mortgage originator can also have an effect. Mortgage brokers are usually paid a fixed percentage of the size of the loan (e.g., one *point*, which is one percent of the loan size). So, for example, when refinancing activity is extremely high and mortgage brokers are inundated with customers, they have more incentive to serve their larger loan size customers (all the customers may eventually refinance, but the larger loan size customers may prepay earlier).

EXHIBIT 4.12 Refinancing Incentive for 30-Year and 15-Year Mortgages

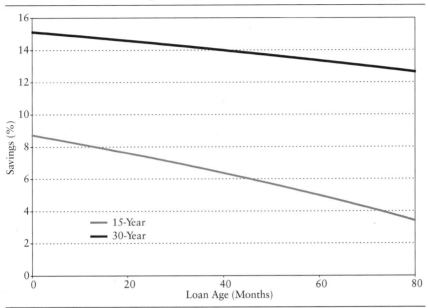

Assumptions: Coupons on both mortgages = 9%; Prevailing mortgage rate = 7%; Balance of 30-year loan = $130,000; Balance of 15-year loan = $100,000; Fixed costs = $1,500; Variable costs = 1.5%. Fixed costs are assumed to increase by 3% per year.
Source: Salomon Smith Barney.

Prepayment models have typically handled refinancing seasoning by applying a ramp that is a function of not just loan age but also of how much the loan was in the money. The ramp would thus shorten as rates fell and the refinancing incentive increased. We take a different approach, by introducing two transient costs. The first cost, which we label the *Fatigue Factor,* declines with loan age. As the name implies, this cost captures the reluctance to re-enter the mortgage process soon after taking out a loan. The second cost, which we call the *LTV Effect,* declines with the *Housing Inflation Indices* defined in the previous section; it captures the effect of low equity in the home. Note that if the mortgage is well in the money, and near the higher end of the prepayment S-curve, these costs will have little impact. Improvements in the mortgage process have reduced the costs and inconveniences over the years, and a high LTV is not the handicap that it used to be. Hence, *we assume that the initial magnitudes of these transient costs have declined over time.*

Lags Obtaining a mortgage takes a reasonable amount of time in most cases, even nowadays. After an application is filed, it will typically take several weeks to complete the steps involved (credit checks, income verification, title search, etc.) and close on the mortgage. The traditional assumption has been a two-month lag between an application and the resulting closing and prepayment. However, it is clear that several factors determine lags. First, a refinancing takes less time than a home purchase. Second, the lag will depend on the age of the loan; refinancing a newer loan, where the paperwork is fresher, will usually involve less time. Third, borrowers with good credit characteristics will generally be able to refinance in a shorter period of time than those with poorer credit. Finally, lags have shortened over time, due to better technology such as automated underwriting systems, and due to streamlined refinancing programs.

The Basic Dynamics of the Refinancing Model

In previous publications, one of the authors outlined a statistical approach to describing burnout patterns.[23] Appendix 4B gives a mathematical description of this approach. Its basic elements are as follows:

- *A diverse pool of mortgagors.* The mortgagors in a given pool are assumed to differ in their intrinsic propensity to refinance. The simplest case is to assume that each person is either a "slow" or a "fast" refinancer. At the other extreme, we could assume that there is a continuous spectrum of borrower types. Different borrower types have different response rates (likelihoods of refinancing) for a given level of refinancing incentive, as illustrated in Exhibit 4.13, in which we assume that borrowers fall into one of four refinancing types.

   All of the refinancing curves in Exhibit 4.13 have the familiar empirically observed S-shaped curve that speeds tend to follow, and that is also displayed in Exhibit 4.10. The refinancing rate is low for a low incentive, accelerates as the incentive increases (the *cuspy* part of the refinancing curve) and levels off, as further incentive increases seem to have little incremental impact. However, the rate at which the refinancing response rate rises with incentive, and the cuspiness, or steepness, of the curve, varies according to borrower type.

   The observed refinancing rate for the pool will be the average of the refinancing rates for the different categories of borrowers, weighted by

---

[23] See, for example, "A Simple Statistical Framework for Modeling Burnout and Refinancing Behavior," Lakhbir Hayre, *Journal of Fixed Income*, December 1994.

EXHIBIT 4.13 Refinancing Curves for Different Borrower Types

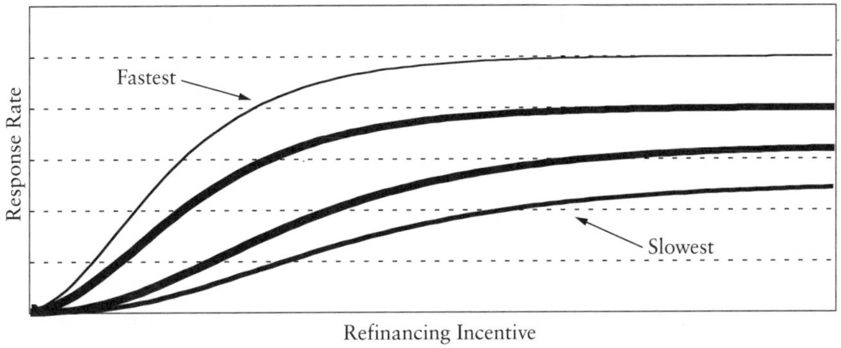

Source: Salomon Smith Barney.

the proportion of the pool in that category in that particular month. For example, if in month one, half the mortgagors are "slow" refinancers with a refinancing rate (for a given level of refinancing incentive) of 2% per month, and the other half are "fast" refinancers with a rate of 18% per month, then the expected refinancing rate for the pool in month one will be 10%.[24]

■ *Evolution of the pool composition over time.* As the pool undergoes refinancings, faster refinancers will leave the pool at a faster rate. For example, in the simple "slow/fast" case discussed previously, 18% of the fast refinancers, but only 2% of the slow refinancers, will leave the pool each month. Hence, the slow refinancers will form an increasingly larger proportion of the remaining population, and other things being equal, the refinancing rate of the pool will gradually slow down toward the 2% rate of the slow group.[25] Exhibit 4.14 illustrates this for a hypothetical case where there are four types of borrowers. The gradual slowdown in the pool refinancing rate, caused solely by the change in the pool's composition as faster refinancers leave at a faster rate, is what we term burnout.

---

[24] In general, the pool refinancing rate is the expected value across the probability distribution of borrower types and is given by Equation (4.5) in Appendix 4B.

[25] Equation (4.6) in Appendix 4B gives a mathematical model of the evolution of the population mix.

EXHIBIT 4.14 Evolution of Pool Population Mix

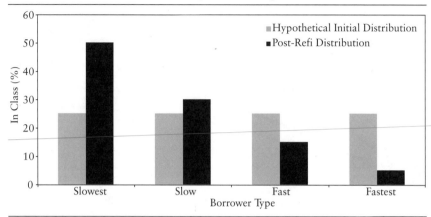

Source: Salomon Smith Barney.

The Media Effect and Borrower Migrations

From April 1997 to the end of that year, mortgage rates fell by over 100bp, but refinancing activity stayed muted. Then, at the beginning of 1998, mortgage rates fell below the 7% level for the first time since 1993, and refinancing activity surged. This is illustrated in Exhibit 4.15, which shows 30-year mortgage rates and the Mortgage Bankers Association (MBA) Refinancing Index (a widely followed measure of overall refinancing volume) from early 1997 to the end of 1998.

What happened during the rest of 1998 is even more instructive. Rates rose a little, and then fell below 7% again in June of 1998. However, this time nothing happened. Then, in October 1998, when rates fell *well* below 7%, to the 6.5% range—the lowest mortgage rates in a generation—there was another explosion in refinancing activity.

These refinancing patterns, also illustrated by the pick-up in 1998 of speeds on Freddie Mac 8.5s and 9.0s shown in Exhibit 4.11, cannot be explained by consideration of refinancing incentives alone. Instead, they reflect a turbo-charging of speeds, and rejuvenation of burntout pools, caused by mortgage rates hitting certain new lows. In our statistical framework, this can be interpreted as a temporary increase in intrinsic borrower refinancing propensities, caused by several factors, including the following:

■ A blitz of media publicity about refinancing opportunities after a big market rally (especially pronounced when rates hit generational lows in 1992, 1993, and in 1998), which creates a refinancing "buzz";

EXHIBIT 4.15 Mortgage Rates and the MBA Refinance Index, April 1997–December 1998

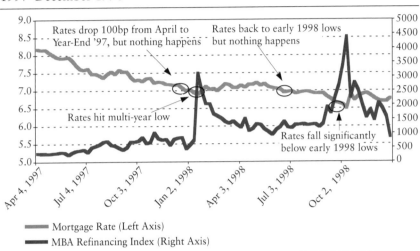

Mortgage Rate (Left Axis)

MBA Refinancing Index (Right Axis)

Sources: Mortgage Bankers Association, Freddie Mac, and Salomon Smith Barney.

- More proactive mortgage lenders when refinancing rates are at attractive levels; and
- Dormant accumulated changes in the personal circumstances of borrowers (improved credit, more equity in the home, etc.), which are brought to the surface by the first two factors.

The first two factors will lead to a higher overall level of refinancing activity, while the combination of all three will lead to a pickup in the speeds of even very seasoned, burnt-out coupons. This phenomenon has been labeled the *media effect.*

How Do We Actually Capture the Media Effect? Clearly, the media effect will be high when a widespread impression prevails that mortgage rates are low relative to "historical levels." Thus, 7% mortgage rates created a buzz in early 1998, since borrowers had not seen rates below 7% for five years, but these levels were no big deal in June 1998 (people had seen 7% rates just six months earlier). In addition, we clearly need a large pool of refinancible loans; in other words, a significant proportion of outstanding loans need to be in the money. Hence, the media effect in the Salomon Smith Barney model is based on two factors:

1. The time since mortgage rates were this low; and
2. A term that approximates the ratio of the average coupon in the mortgage universe to current mortgage rates.

The first variable is an attempt to capture the psychological or "buzz" effect of new rate lows, while the second measures the "overhang" of refinancible coupons.

Migrations of Borrowers   In addition to the temporary change in refinancing tendencies caused by the media effect, there will also be ongoing changes in borrowers' personal circumstances or characteristics, which may change the likelihood that they will refinance. Examples include changes in credit or in the amount of equity in the home. The term *curing* is often used to denote this process, reflecting the fact that in most cases, the process leads to an improvement in the borrower's ability to refinance. However, the reverse can also happen; for example, steep declines in home prices, such as those that occurred in California in the first half of the 1990s, may impair the ability to refinance. To capture such ongoing changes, the Salomon Smith Barney Prepayment Model allows borrowers to shift between the refinancing groups described earlier. There are two types of such migrations:

1. A constant trickle to faster classes, resulting from improvements in borrower credit or financial circumstances; and
2. Movements to other classes based on changes in LTV, which are calculated using the housing inflation indices described earlier.[26]

For example, some California borrowers who saw sharp declines in their home prices in the early 1990s, and hence an increase in LTVs, would have shifted down to slower classes. However, over the last few years, as California home prices recovered, there would have been migrations back to faster classes.

Choosing the Initial Population Mix

The initial distribution of borrowers reflects the characteristics and demographics of the population *that are not explicitly included as inputs to the model*. For example, in the case of agency MBSs, for which little loan-level information is available, this would include LTVs, credit, and so on. For

---

[26] For agency MBSs, we do not have initial LTV information, and hence the migrations are based on *changes* in LTVs.

standard agency MBSs, choosing the initial proportion of borrowers in the various refinancing classes is mostly an empirical exercise, with iteration being used to find a mix that works well.[27] For other types of MBSs, a reasonable population mix can be estimated by adjusting the agency mix based on loan-level and demographic differences relative to agency collateral (a couple of examples are given next). For non-agencies, in fact, more extensive loan-level information is often available, which can be used to decide on the initial population mix.[28]

Our approach allows the model to capture both changes in borrower behavior over time, and diversity in borrower types. Changes over time can simply be modeled by making the initial population mix time-dependent; for example, if we feel that agency borrowers who took out a loan in 1998 are likely to be more savvy about refinancing opportunities than those who took out an agency loan in, say, 1986.

Handling Collateral Diversity   We give two examples of how the agency, or "standard" population mix, can be modified to handle diverse types of collateral.

Above-Market Premiums   This term refers to agency pools of mortgages that have WACs significantly above (often 100bp or more) prevailing mortgage rates. Why do borrowers take out such loans? One reason could be that they want to pay little or no upfront costs—that is, take out a no point/no cost loan (the zero points/costs are exchanged for a higher loan rate). Such borrowers could be opportunistic fast refinancers, who would react quickly to even a small drop in rates. At the other extreme in terms of refinancing propensities, they could be people who cannot afford to pay up-front costs, or the high rate could indicate borrowers who contributed a very small downpayment (i.e., have high LTVs), or have questionable credit, and so on—such borrowers will tend to face extra hurdles in refinancing, and hence will tend to be slow refinancers. Thus, as illustrated in Exhibit 4.16, relative to standard agency pools, above-market premiums will have more very fast refinancers and more slow refinancers, and less in the middle—hence, they are sometimes referred to as *schizophrenic premiums*.

The population mix in Exhibit 4.16 implies an initial burst of fast speeds, and then a dampened responsiveness after the very fast refinancers have left

---

[27] Note that we have to choose only the initial mix; the subsequent evolution of the mix is completely determined by refinancing rates and migrations.

[28] An example is our model for Manufactured Housing loans, based on extensive loan level data supplied by Green Tree (see Chapter 21).

EXHIBIT 4.16 Initial Population Mix for Above-Market Premiums

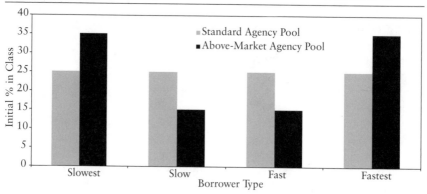

Source: Salomon Smith Barney.

the pool. This indeed has been the pattern observed on such pools. However, in the absence of loan-level information such as LTVs or credit scores, it is difficult to estimate the precise fractions of very slow and very fast borrowers, and continuing changes in agency underwriting policies (such as their entry into the alt-A market) in fact make these fractions moving targets.

Subprime Collateral   This term refers to loans given to borrowers with poor credit histories. The loans tend to have note rates well above (often several hundred basis points higher) those offered to "prime" borrowers, and are also characterized by lower loan balances. Such borrowers face many extra hurdles in refinancing, and often lack financial sophistication. As might be expected, there is a much higher concentration of slow refinancers in the initial population mix. A typical initial mix is shown in Exhibit 4.17.

Despite the high proportion of "slow" refinancers in subprime pools, speeds still tend to be high. This is because of continuing improvements in borrower credit, which allows a refinancing into a more advantageous rate. Such *credit-driven* refinancings are discussed in more detail later.

Changes in the Refinancing Environment

The factors that drive prepayment patterns change over time. New and better technology (most recently, the Internet) can lower the costs and inconvenience in taking out a loan. New products (such as no-point loans, high LTV loans, hybrid ARMs, etc.) can influence peoples' decisions to refinance.

EXHIBIT 4.17 Initial Population Mix for Subprime Loans

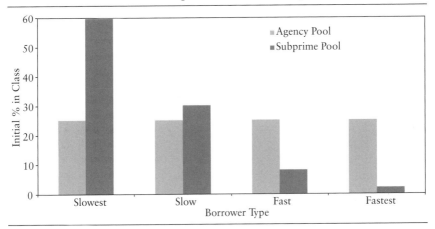

Source: Salomon Smith Barney.

Changes in underwriting policies (for example, to meet affordable housing targets) can change borrower demographics, and hence prepayment patterns. Regulatory changes (such as new mortgage fees on FHA loans) will affect the decision to refinance. Finally, borrower behavior may change; for example, the pervasiveness of "consumer finance" columns in newspapers and programs on television, implies that borrowers are more likely to become aware of refinancing opportunities when mortgage rates fall. Exhibit 4.18 illustrates changes in prepayment patterns over the years. The graph shows the prepayment S-curve during the peak of four prepayment waves: April 1987, November 1993, March 1998, and November 1998. The coupons had comparable seasoning and burnout in all four cases.

The changes in the curves reflect various changes in the infrastructure of the "refinancing process":

■ The most dramatic change has been the upward shift in the lower end of the S-curve between 1987 and 1993. We believe this is largely due to the advent of **no-point** and **no-cost loans** during the refinancing waves of the early 1990s. Such loans dramatically reduce the up-front costs that need to be paid by the borrower, making a refinancing much more appealing for loans with marginal incentive. The effect of the introduction of these new products was to shift the S-curve leftward, effectively throwing out the old rule about refinancing a loan only if it is at least 200bp in the money;

EXHIBIT 4.18 The Evolution of the Prepayment S-Curve

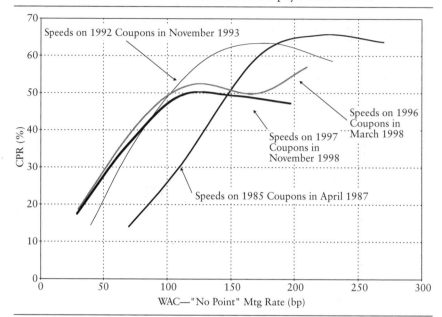

Source: Salomon Smith Barney.

■ Between 1993 and 1998, there was a slight shift upward at the low end of the S-curve. We believe that this shift reflects declines in refinancing costs, due to better technology and less "friction" in the system, and agency initiatives such as *automated underwriting* systems and *streamlined refinancing programs;*[29]

■ Perhaps surprisingly, peak speeds (for large cohorts) did *not* increase from the 1980s to the 1990s, remaining at between 60% and 70% CPR, even though presumably lenders had better processing capabilities in the 1990s. In fact, speeds for higher premiums actually *declined* from 1993 to 1998. This decline reflects, we think, the increasing *diversity* in agency pools discussed earlier, as a result of *affordable housing initiatives* and other *changes in underwriting policies.*

The model handles these changes over time by making key inputs time-dependent. For example, costs of refinancing are assumed to have declined

---

[29] See Chapter 6.

over the years, and the initial borrower mix has shifted toward faster borrowers.[30] Going forward, refinancing costs and friction will likely decline further, as the Internet aids borrowers in finding the best terms, and Internet originations grow. The model assumes that refinancing costs will continue declining.[31]

Cash-Out and Credit Driven Refinancings

Most refinancings result from borrowers taking advantage of declines in interest rates to lower their mortgage coupon. However, refinancings can also occur for other reasons.

Cash-out refinancings have been popular in the last couple of years. As the name implies, a cash-out refinancing is used to access equity in the home; mortgage debt represents an attractive tax-deductible form of borrowing. While the majority of cash-out refinancings occur for in-the-money loans, and hence are usually accompanied by a lowering of the coupon rate, this is not always the case. Loan-level data from a major lender indicate that some borrowers are willing to accept a higher rate in order to access the equity in their homes. In fact, these data indicate that the high speeds seen on 6s and 6.5s in late 1998 and early 1999 were explained by cash-out refinancings.

For a specific MBS, the model assumes that cash-out refinancings depend on three variables:

1. The *Housing Inflation Index* for the collateral,[32] which gives an indication of the amount of equity in the home;
2. The refinancing incentive for the MBS; and
3. The *media effect,* the assumption being that when people are more prone to refinance, they might well decide to obtain a larger loan, to access the equity in their house.

Credit-driven refinancings are an important component of prepayments for subprime loans. Borrowers who have less than pristine credit histories are generally given a letter grade, typically A–, B, C, or D, with lower letters denoting poorer credits; for example, D credits are considered the highest risks, and loan rates for such borrowers tend to be as much as 600bp above

---

[30] As mentioned earlier, we also assume that transient costs, which lead to a refinancing "seasoning ramp," have also declined over time, and that lags have shortened.

[31] An important caveat: We cannot anticipate all the changes that may affect prepayment behavior in the future. Users should keep this uncertainty, and resulting model risk, in mind.

[32] See Section 4.1 for a description of how Housing Inflation Indices are calculated.

standard "prime" mortgage rates (for example, as measured by the weekly Freddie Mac Survey rate). Many lenders will move borrowers to a higher letter grade if they make timely mortgage payments for a specified number of months (typically 12). This makes the borrower eligible for a lower mortgage rate, often 200bp or so lower. Thus, even if there has been no change in interest rates, there will typically be an ongoing stream of refinancings as borrowers improve their credit.

The credit-driven refinancing model is based on loan-level data from a number of originators. There is a seasoning ramp, as clearly there will be very few such refinancings in the first few months. The ramp begins to decline after about five years; if a borrower has not improved in credit by this time, then the chances they will still do so begin to diminish. There is also some dependence on interest rates. Increases in interest rates will obviously dampen credit-driven refinancings, and in a major sell-off, if the increase in rates is comparable to the difference in coupons between different letter credits, it will almost eliminate them. In a rally, the model assumes some increase in credit-driven refinancings, but attributes most of the increase in a major rally to interest-rate-driven refinancings.[33]

4.3 DEFAULTS

A borrower **defaults** on their mortgage obligation when they stop making the monthly payments due on the mortgage. For agency MBSs, the investor realizes the default as a full prepayment of the outstanding balance of the loan because of the agency guarantee. This prepayment typically occurs a few months after the borrower is officially in default status. For non-agency MBSs, **credit enhancement** is typically used to protect investors from borrower defaults, so that investors will again generally realize a default as a prepayment.[34]

Determinants of Mortgage Credit   In order to control and assess the risk of default, borrowers usually undergo a process of qualification by which a lender gauges their ability and willingness to repay the mortgage debt. Not surprisingly, the factors that they hold to be the most important in making the decision whether to underwrite the loan or not, also turn out to be good

---

[33] For more details, see Chapter 19.

[34] A discussion of the mechanisms used to provide credit enhancement in non-agency MBSs can be found in Chapter 1.

predictors of default rates. The factors considered most important in the decision to extend mortgage credit are:

- *Original loan-to-value ratio (OLTV)*. This is probably the most important variable influencing defaults. Theoretically, no borrower with positive equity would default, since even if they were unable to make their monthly payments, they could sell the property and capture the positive equity accumulated in it. Negative equity is therefore a necessary though not sufficient condition for default. A borrower might continue making payments even with negative equity if they did not want to lose their homes, or held the view that in the long term home prices would begin increasing again, or out of fear of a bad credit rating, among other reasons.
- *Credit history*. Lenders will look at a borrower's prior mortgage delinquencies and a credit score in order to assess a borrower's credit status. There are several different types of credit scores as many of the major mortgage lenders have developed their own proprietary scoring methods. The most commonly used credit score in the industry is the FICO credit score developed by Fair, Isaac & Co. While the FICO score is based solely on information from consumer credit reports, it has been found to be heavily correlated with the likelihood of mortgage default. The use of FICO scores in mortgage underwriting has become commonplace after Fannie Mae and Freddie Mac endorsed the use of credit scores in underwriting decisions in 1995.
- *Debt-to-income ratios*. Two ratios are commonly calculated—the borrower's monthly mortgage payments divided by gross monthly income, and the total monthly debt payments divided by gross monthly income.
- *Liquid reserves*. This is computed by taking the amount of liquid assets (such as cash in a checking account) remaining after a loan closing and dividing by the monthly mortgage payment.

Other factors considered in the mortgage credit analysis include the borrower's work status (self-employed borrowers are judged to be more risky than salaried borrowers), the loan term (longer loan terms are considered more risky), the property type (co-op or condos are more risky than single-family detached residences), and so on. All these factors may be utilized as inputs to a default model, with the four factors highlighted previously being given the most weight.[35] Unfortunately, no information is released on these variables at either the loan- or pool-level by the agencies.

---

[35] A detailed description of one such model can be found in Chapter 21.

EXHIBIT 4.19 The 100% Standard Default Assumption (SDA) Curve

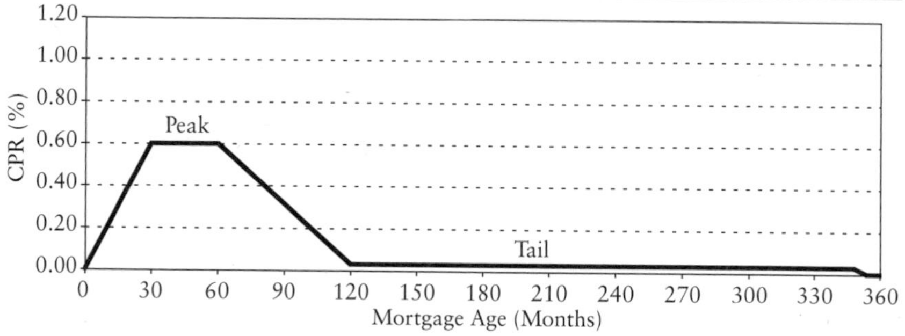

Source: Salomon Smith Barney.

The modeling of defaults on agency pools thus usually proceeds by assuming the existence of a typical "default curve" for all agency pools.

The Standard Default Assumption (SDA) Curve   Is there a typical pattern to default-related prepayments? The answer turns out to be yes—default rates on mortgages show a distinctive dependence on the age of the mortgage. Default rates tend to be low early on in the life of a pool of mortgages, and then gradually ramp up before peaking at two to five years after origination. Default rates then taper off over the next two to three years, and typically remain very low for the rest of the life of the pool. The intuitive economic rationale for this pattern of default behavior is easy to understand. First, default rates start out low since lenders will not underwrite borrowers whom they suspect will default immediately. Next, default rates ramp up gradually the first two or three years after origination because it is over this period that borrowers are most vulnerable to losing all their equity if home values decline. Finally, default rates start tapering off five years or so after origination since increases in home prices[36] and an increasing loan amortization effect decrease the likelihood of negative equity.

The SDA curve was developed by the Bond Market Association (formerly, the PSA) to capture this default experience and provide a standard for the market in the same way that the PSA prepayment curve helped standardize the agency market in 1985. Exhibit 4.19 graphs a 100% SDA curve,

---

[36] Over an extended period of time, most single-family homes will appreciate in value.

which may be interpreted as a simple but realistic model for default-related prepayments for typical agency pools.[37] Beginning with a CPR of 0.02%, default rates increase by 0.02% CPR per month until month 30, when the peak value of 0.60% is reached. Defaults remain at this value for the next 30 months. Starting in month 61, defaults decrease by 0.0095% per month until month 120, where the tail value of 0.03% is reached. The defaults remain constant at that level for the remaining life of the security. By convention, the last 12 default rates are set to zero, assuming it takes 12 months to liquidate a property.[38]

The 100% SDA curve is a reasonable model for the typical default rates experienced on 30-year conventional pools under "normal" circumstances. However, as one might expect, it is not an appropriate benchmark for default rates experienced on conventional mortgages in regions undergoing prolonged recessions, or for the default rates seen on 30-year FHA loans or subprime mortgages in "normal" circumstances. Stated differently, the appropriate SDA curve for a pool of mortgage loans depends strongly on the *loan type*. For example, default rates on 15-year conventional loans will typically be much lower than 100% SDA, while the default rates on 30-year FHA loans will be much higher than 100% SDA.

4.4 CURTAILMENTS AND PAYOFFS

When a borrower sends in a monthly payment that is larger than the one due on their level payment mortgage, they are said to *curtail* or *partially prepay* their mortgage. A borrower may also opt to reduce their mortgage indebtedness completely through a *full payoff*.[39]

By making a partial prepayment, the borrower is effectively shortening the term of the mortgage,[40] thus leading to the weighted average maturity (WAM) shortening that is commonly observed on agency pools. Pool WAMs are calculated using the current pool balance and the scheduled monthly payments. Thus, a balance that has been reduced by partial prepayments will,

---

[37] Strictly speaking, the SDA curve applies to fully amortizing with original terms greater than or equal to 15 years.

[38] If one month to liquidation were assumed, then only the last rate would be set to zero.

[39] Full payoffs can also occur because of the destruction of the home from natural disasters such as hurricanes and earthquakes.

[40] The monthly payment due on a level payment mortgage is fixed, regardless of the amount of the outstanding balance that has been prepaid.

EXHIBIT 4.20 Speeds on Conventional Discounts by Age

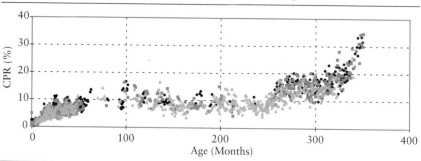

Source: Salomon Smith Barney.

for a fixed monthly payment, be amortized in less time than the nominal remaining term implies.[41]

Curtailment and Payoff Rates

For the sake of clarity, in what follows we will phrase our discussion mostly in terms of curtailment rates, although it should be kept in mind that full payoffs may contribute significantly to prepayments when the loan is very seasoned and the remaining balance is small.

Based on information from mortgage servicers, we estimate that the prepayment rates resulting from curtailments are typically very small. They average about 0.5% CPR early on in the life of an agency pool, consistent with the prepayment rates implied by WAM shortenings, but can ramp up sharply to as much as 15% to 20% CPR in the tail end of the mortgage term. Exhibit 4.20 illustrates this trend by graphing *aggregate* prepayment speeds on conventional discount pools by age and relative coupon. As discussed in previous sections, the total contribution of housing turnover and defaults to aggregate speeds on seasoned conventional discount loans probably averages

---

[41] A detailed analysis of the impact of partial prepayments on mortgage age calculations, cash flows, and investment characteristics can be found in "Partial and Full Prepayments and the Modeling of Mortgage Cash Flows," Lakhbir S. Hayre and Kenneth Lauterbach, *The Journal of Fixed Income*, Vol. 1 No. 2, September 1991.

between 6% to 8% CPR. We may therefore assume that after subtracting this contribution from the aggregate speeds in Exhibit 4.20, what remains are the prepayments due to curtailments and payoffs.[42] Prepayment rates resulting from curtailments and payoffs thus appear to range from 0.5% CPR to 2% CPR during the first two-thirds of the life of a 30-year conventional mortgage pool, and then ramp up rapidly to average as much as 15% to 20% CPR during the last third of the pool term. In other words, there is a pronounced dependence on age. According to Exhibit 4.20, there is also a somewhat less-pronounced relative coupon effect—more in-the-money mortgage holders appear to curtail at a greater rate.

Why Borrowers Curtail

At first glance, curtailing a mortgage does not appear to be an optimal strategy for a borrower. If a borrower's mortgage rate is above prevailing mortgage rates, they derive maximum benefit from a full refinancing, and if their mortgage rate is below the market rate, it is not economic for them to send in an additional amount over their monthly payment. This analysis ignores two important factors though. First, the transaction and hassle costs incurred in the refinancing process can be significant. If a borrower cannot refinance because of the costs involved, curtailment represents the optimal strategy.[43] Second, the "optimal" strategy assumes that the typical borrower will always act to minimize the present value of the monthly mortgage payments. However, a greater imperative for some households may simply be to reduce the amount of their indebtedness by paying off as much of their mortgage debt as they can. This would explain why even the discount mortgages depicted in Exhibit 4.20 experience significant curtailments.

The patterns to curtailment behavior seen in Exhibit 4.20 can now be interpreted in the light of these considerations. If a borrower cannot refinance, the more in the money the mortgage is, the more likely the borrower is going to curtail. This explains the dependence of curtailments on relative coupon. The dependence of curtailments on age may be explained by the

---

[42] The implicit assumption that these mortgages are not refinancible is reasonable, given how out of the money most of them are. However, a small number of borrowers will raise their mortgage rates by doing cash-out refinancings in order to take equity out of their homes. Empirical data suggest that such refinancings may contribute as much as 1% to 2% CPR to the speeds on discount pools.

[43] This observation is likely to be particularly true for mortgages in which a significant penalty is incurred for refinancing.

increasing risk-aversion of aging householders to holding debt, and their increasing financial ability[44] to make extra payments.

4.5 APPLYING THE MODELING FRAMEWORK

The prepayment modeling framework we have described has been applied to a wide variety of mortgage types—Salomon Smith Barney has developed over 40 different prepayment models using the framework, which are extensively used both internally and by clients (through Salomon Smith Barney's analytic system, the Yield Book). We describe five applications, covering a range of mortgage terms and borrower demographics, to illustrate the issues discussed in earlier sections and how they are handled by the model.

Tracking Speeds over the Years: 1980 Origination 11.5s

Exhibit 4.21 shows actual and projected speeds on conventional 1980 11.5s, a cohort that has been through several economic cycles, multiple refinancing waves, and profound changes in the refinancing process. Through all of this, the model tracks actual speeds reasonably well. As discussed earlier, changes in the mortgage industry have lowered costs and increased the efficiency of the mortgage refinancing process over the years. The Salomon Smith Barney Prepayment Model reflects the changes that have occurred through the use of *time-dependent parameters* such as costs, chosen to decline over time, and the strength of the media effect, chosen to increase over time.[45]

The 11.5s experienced a heavy round of refinancings in 1986 and 1987, when mortgage rates reached lows of around 9%. Burnout and, to a lesser extent, smaller loan sizes resulted in lower speeds on these pools during the 1992 to 1993 refinancing wave. However, speeds would have been even lower if not for declining costs, a stronger media effect, and the curing of

---

[44] For example, even if the borrower's monthly income were to remain the same, they would be more able to make the $50 payment since the inflation-adjusted value of $50 decreases with time.

[45] These choices reflect the belief that declining costs and an increasingly powerful media effect are primarily responsible for the generally higher speeds that have been observed over the years, especially for "cuspy" coupons (as noted earlier, peak refinancing wave speeds have not changed much). Exhibit 4.18, for example, provides evidence for costs having declined over time. The increasing use of mortgage brokers by borrowers and the increased initiative taken by lenders to solicit refinances (aided by advances in technology) points to a stronger media effect, and consequently to higher refinancing rates in a refinancing wave.

EXHIBIT 4.21 Actual and Projected Speeds on 1980 Conventional 11.5s

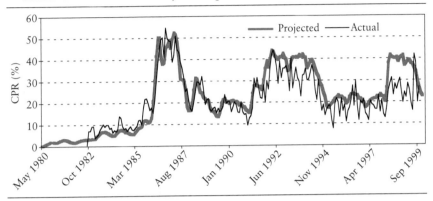

Source: Salomon Smith Barney.

borrowers previously unable to refinance (recall that the model mimics curing by assuming migrations between borrower populations based on changes in LTV). Similar remarks apply to the 1998 refinancing waves, but note that this class had dwindled to a very small size by then, resulting in very noisy month-to-month speeds.

Capturing Term and Balance Difference: 15-Year versus 30-Year Loans

A 15-year mortgage requires substantially larger monthly payments than a 30-year with the same balance, but offers a lower rate (usually 30bp to 50bp lower) and faster amortization (and hence faster equity build-up). Hence, 15-year borrowers tend to be older and more affluent and put down larger down payments. In addition, 15-year loans are a popular choice for borrowers refinancing out of 30-year loans. As a result, 15-year loans tend to be smaller than 30-year loans. In our modeling framework, these differences have several implications:

- In the *turnover component,* the greater affluence of the 15-year borrower implies *higher relative mobility;* however, the higher average age of the 15-year borrower, and the higher chance that this is the "final" home before retirement, partially offsets this. In fact, in recent years, the difference in turnover rates between 15-year and 30-year loans has been shrinking.

- In the *refinancing component,* the lower loan balances and shorter terms for 15-year collateral imply lower refinancing incentives, with the difference increasing over time (see Exhibit 4.12); however, this effect is partially balanced by the greater affluence of the 15-year borrower, which implies an initial population mix with a higher concentration of faster refinancers.
- As indicated earlier, 15-year rates tend to be lower than 30-year rates, and in addition 15-year borrowers are more likely to refinance into a 15-year loan than 30-year borrowers. The greater importance of shorter maturity mortgage rates is modeled by placing greater weight on shorter rates when calculating the refinancing incentive for 15-year loans.
- *Defaults* are lower for 15-year loans, as a result of greater borrower affluence and lower LTVs.

These differences are illustrated in the top panel of Exhibit 4.22, which shows actual prepayment speeds of 1992 conventional 15-year 7.5s and

EXHIBIT 4.22 Actual and Projected Speeds on 1992 15-Year 7.5s and 30-Year 8s, 1992–2000

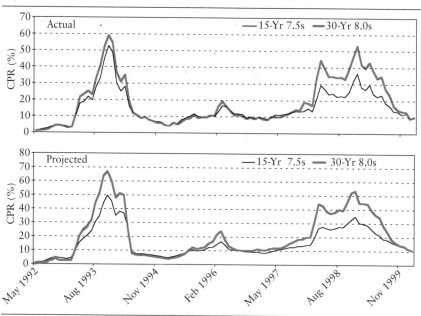

Sources: Fannie Mae and Salomon Smith Barney.

30-year 8s.[46] In 1993, the 15-year 7.5% speeds reached levels that were about 5% CPR lower than the corresponding 30-year 8% speeds, consistent with the relatively lower refinancing incentive of 15-year loans owing to their smaller loan size and shorter term. Over time, the faster amortization of 15-year loans accentuated these differences, and the differences in the 1998 refinancing waves were well over 10% CPR. The model prepayment projections for these two classes, shown in the lower panel in Exhibit 4.22, exhibit the same pattern as the actual speeds, with the differential increasing over time.

Home Equity Loans (HELs)

At one time, the term *HEL* denoted an asset-backed security collateralized by second mortgages. In recent years, however, the term HEL typically denotes a security backed by *subprime* loans. As discussed under the heading Choosing the Initial Population Mix in Section 4.2, such loans are made to borrowers with poor credit, often from lower socio-economic strata, that cannot qualify for standard conforming loans.[47]

Apart from impaired credit and lower socio-economic demographics, two other important factors are *low loan balances*, which are typically about half those for agency loans, averaging between $40,000 and $70,000, implying that fixed costs of refinancing will be a significant hurdle; and second, *high loan rates*, which tend to average between 250bp to 300bp higher than those on standard conforming loans. Exhibit 4.23 shows a HEL current coupon series that Salomon Smith Barney has constructed using the WACs on new-issue HEL deals. Also shown is the 30-year conforming mortgage rate from Freddie Mac's weekly survey, and the spread between the two rates. The spread between HEL and conforming rates changes over time, emphasizing that it is important to use the appropriate mortgage rates available to HEL borrowers, rather than a simple spread to conforming rates, to correctly measure the refinancing incentive.

---

[46] It is standard practice, when comparing 15-year and 30-year MBSs, to use a 30-year coupon that is 50bp higher, reflecting the higher 30-year mortgage rates mentioned previously. The aim is to compare coupons that are roughly equivalent in how much they are in-the-money.

[47] See Chapter 19 and 20, for a detailed description of HELs and their prepayment characteristics.

EXHIBIT 4.23 HEL and 30-Year Conforming Mortgage Rates

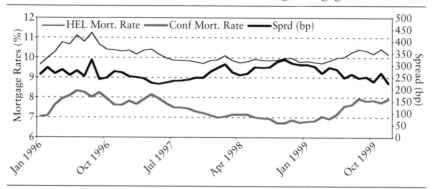

Sources: Freddie Mac and Salomon Smith Barney.

We have used loan-level data from several issuers and our general pre-payment modeling framework to develop issuer-specific HEL prepayment models. Key features of the HEL model include the following:

- In the **turnover component, the relative mobility is low** and there is a **long seasoning ramp,** reflecting HEL borrower demographics.
- In the **refinancing component,** the *initial borrower mix* resembles that shown in Exhibit 4.17, with a heavy concentration of slow refinancers, but the exact mix varies from deal to deal.
- The combination of low loan balances and the impaired credit characteristics of the borrowers means that **rate-driven refinancings** are relatively muted.
- **Credit-driven refinancings** typically constitute the largest component of HEL speeds, and depend on borrower credit—the poorer the credit, the higher the level.
- **Default rates** are significant, averaging 2% to 5% per year, but again vary from deal to deal based on borrower credit.

Exhibit 4.24 shows actual and projected speeds for Advanta 1997-1, a HEL deal priced in 1997. The model tracks the actual speeds quite well. Noticeable is the fast seasoning of speeds, which level out after 12 to 18 months. This reflects both the dominant role of credit-driven refinancings, and the industry practice of typically requiring 12 timely mortgage payments for an upgrade in borrower credit.

EXHIBIT 4.24 Actual and Projected Speeds for Advanta 1997-1

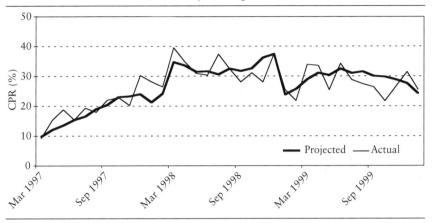

Source: Salomon Smith Barney.

Hybrid ARMs

As the name implies, hybrids combine elements of fixed-rate loans and adjustable-rate mortgages (ARMs). The coupon is fixed for a specified period of time—typically three, five, seven, or ten years—after which it resets annually at a specified spread over a specified index (the one-year Treasury in almost all cases). Hybrids are a relatively new product,[48] being relatively rare before the 1990s, and the paucity of historical prepayment data and uncertainty about borrower behavior at the first coupon reset adds an extra challenge in prepayment modeling. However, our prepayment modeling framework is well suited to handling such challenges.

For traditional (one-year) ARMs, we assume there are two types of borrowers: *ARM-to-Fixed Refinancers,* and *ARM-to-ARM Refinancers.*[49] The former type comprises the traditional ARM borrowers, who choose an ARM to obtain the lowest monthly payments, but who plan to either sell the house before too long (i.e., have a short tenure horizon) or eventually refinance and lock in the security of a long-term fixed-rate loan; refinancing

---

[48] In many countries outside the United States, hybrid mortgages are either the norm (e.g., in the Netherlands), or in countries where variable rate loans are the norm (e.g., in England), a "fixed-rate" loan usually means a hybrid (e.g., the coupon is "fixed" for a specified period).

[49] Within each type, there is the usual mix of slow and fast refinancers.

decisions are hence driven by the level of long-term fixed mortgage rates. The second type is a more recent development, representing aggressive refinancers who take out a *teasered* ARM (i.e., one with an initial low below-market coupon) and then refinance into another teasered ARM as soon as the coupon starts resetting upward; refinancing decisions are driven by the level of short-term rates. The refinancing incentive is hence based on different mortgage rates for the two types of borrowers.[50] Hybrid ARMs will also have both types of borrowers, but the longer the first reset, the lower the fraction of ARM-to-ARM refinancers. The main components of the model are summarized next.

Housing Turnover   A *high relative mobility* and *fast seasoning* is assumed, based on the shorter tenure horizons of many ARM borrowers.[51] However, the longer the time until the first reset, the lower the relative mobility factor.

Refinancings   There are several distinctive features of this component:

- Since the loan coupon is not fixed for the term of the security, but will eventually reset until it is fully indexed, a weighted average of the coupon path going forward (the *Effective WAC*) is used in calculating the refinancing incentive, both for ARM-to-Fixed and ARM-to-ARM refinancings.
- Sensitivity to refinancing opportunities into a fixed-rate loan is high during the period until the first reset, as many borrowers will be anxious to lock in a fixed rate.
- At and around the first coupon reset, which may mean a sharp increase in the coupon due to the teasered nature of the initial coupon, there tends to be an extra spurt in refinancing activity.

Exhibit 4.25 shows actual and projected speeds for 1992 6.5% 5 × 1 hybrids (the 6.5% is the initial net or MBS coupon, while the 5 × 1 means that the time until initial reset is five years, with annual resets after that), which had their first coupon reset in 1997.

The model tracks speeds quite well both during the "fixed coupon" period (before the first reset in 1997), and after the first reset, when the loans became one-year ARMs, over several interest-rate cycles. There was an initial burst of refinancing activity in late 1993 and early 1994, when mortgage

---

[50] See Chapters 9 and 10 for a more detailed discussion of ARMs.

[51] In fact, many borrowers choose a hybrid as an alternative to a balloon mortgage, and the growth of the hybrid market has come at the expense of balloons.

EXHIBIT 4.25 Actual and Projected Speeds for 1992 6.5% 5 × 1 Hybrids, 1992–2000

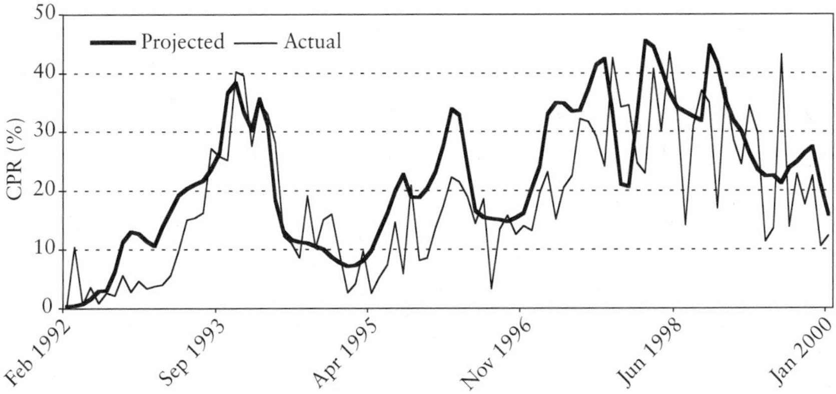

Source: Salomon Smith Barney.

rates fell to multiyear lows. There was another burst in refinancings in the middle of 1997, but this spike illustrates the impact of first coupon reset: Even though mortgage rates were relatively high around this time, many borrowers still chose to refinance. Finally, the spikes in 1998 reflect the interest-rate rallies that year, with borrowers taking advantage of low rates to refinance their now one-year ARMs.

Prepayment-Penalty Mortgages

A prepayment-penalty mortgage imposes a penalty on the borrower for early prepayment of the mortgage (not including the sale of the house). The most common penalty is a 5-year penalty with the following features:

- The penalty period is 60 months from the origination of the loan. The penalty is 6 months of interest on the amount by which the prepayment exceeds 20% of the original loan balance.
- There is no penalty if the house is sold.
- During the penalty period, the borrower can prepay up to a maximum of 20% of the original loan amount each 12-month period without penalty.
- The servicer retains the prepayment penalty.

In return for agreeing to pay the penalty, the borrower typically receives a rate concession (about 15bp–25bp) or cash up front (typically three-fourths of a point).

The penalty materially affects the economics of refinancing a mortgage. For example, a borrower with an original loan balance of $150,000 and a mortgage rate of 8% would typically pay a penalty of $4,800 for refinancing at any time in the first 60 months from loan origination. The efficacy of the penalty in curbing refinancing can be seen in Exhibit 4.26, which compares speeds on pools of agency prepay-penalty mortgages versus speeds on ordinary pools with the same WAC seasoning. Exhibit 4.26 shows that, at the peak of the refinancing wave in late 1998, 1997 vintage 7% prepay-penalty pools prepaid at less than 50% of the equivalent no-penalty pools. As we would expect, in recent months speeds have begun to converge as refinancings have started to ebb, thus increasing the importance of housing turnover-related prepayments. To model agency prepayment-penalty pools, we begin with our agency model and then make the following modifications:

- Since the prepayment penalty increases the transaction costs associated with refinancing, prepay-penalty borrowers have less incentive to refinance than ordinary borrowers. Our prepayment-model assumes that these borrowers effectively face a higher mortgage rate for refinancing their mortgages during the penalty period. The magnitude of this effective refinancing rate varies as a function of the **remaining penalty period** (borrowers become increasingly reluctant to refinance as penalty expiration approaches) and of the **media effect** (borrowers are willing to pay the penalty to lock in a historically attractive mortgage rate).
- The model assumes that **pent-up demand** for refinancing opportunities exists when the penalty expires, leading to a significant spike

EXHIBIT 4.26 Actual Prepayment Speeds on 1997—7% Agency Penalty and No-Penalty Pools

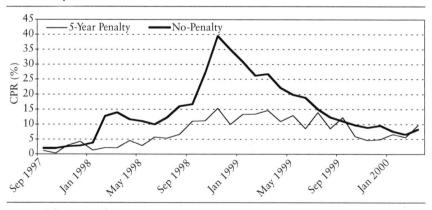

Source: Salomon Smith Barney.

in prepayment speeds at the end of the penalty period if the loans are in the money. We also assume that six months to one year after the expiration of the penalty, speeds on the penalty and no-penalty transactions converge.

■ The model assumes that turnover rates are the same for penalty and no-penalty borrowers because there is no penalty for selling the house.

Exhibit 4.27 shows projected speeds for the 7% penalty and no-penalty pools in 1997. The effect of the penalty is accurately captured by the model, which tracks actual speeds quite well.

4.6 PREPAYMENT MODELS: A USER'S GUIDE

Despite the many assumptions and uncertainties embedded in prepayment models, MBS investors have little choice but to use them—to calculate mortgage cash flows, and hence even basic valuation measures such as yields, one needs a prepayment projection. Given this imperative, what do users need to be aware of concerning the limitations of prepayment models?

Some Basic Properties of Model Projections

Exhibit 4.28 shows projections for a Ginnie Mae 8% pass-through under three assumed interest-rate scenarios: rates unchanged, rates up by 200bp,

EXHIBIT 4.27 Projected Prepayment Speeds on 1997—7% Agency Penalty and No-Penalty Pools

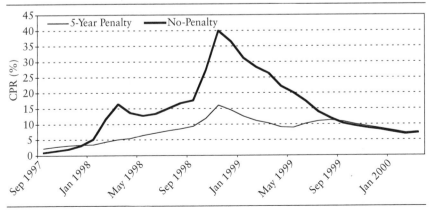

Source: Salomon Smith Barney.

EXHIBIT 4.28 Prepayment Projections for 1992 Ginnie Mae 8.0s

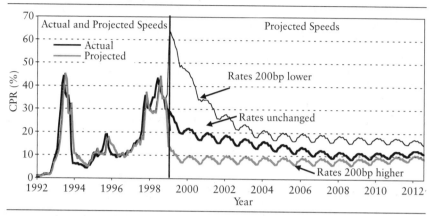

Source: Salomon Smith Barney.

and rates down by 200bp.[52] The numbers shown are the vectors of monthly projections from the model.

There are several points to note from Exhibit 4.28, including:

- *The conditional nature of projections.* Projections from a prepayment model are for a *specified path of interest rates.* In other words, projections are conditional upon the realization of the prescribed path of interest rates—a path that in reality is never going to be *exactly* realized. Although this observation will not be news to most investors, two implications are worth noting. First, prepayment projections should always be obtained for a variety of bullish and bearish interest-rate scenarios. Second, in evaluating the accuracy of a model, it is necessary to determine what its projections were for interest-rate scenarios approximating those that actually occurred. For example, while many models did fail to accurately predict the high speeds that occurred in 1991 to 1994, investors should remember that mortgage rates fell by approximately 300bp between 1990 and 1993; hence, the relevant predictions from 1990 would be those for a 300bp drop in rates.

- *Use long-term projections with care.* Even if interest rates were to stay unchanged forever, prepayments (actual and projected) would still vary over time, for a variety of reasons. Premium speeds tend to decline over time because of burnout; newer discount speeds tend to increase as a

---

[52] We are assuming parallel shifts in interest rates.

EXHIBIT 4.29 Monthly Projections and the Long-Term Average Projection for 1992 Ginnie Mae 8s if Rates Drop 200bp

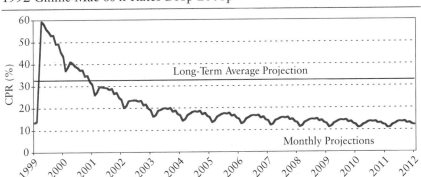

Source: Salomon Smith Barney.

result of seasoning. On a month-to-month basis, seasonal factors can lead to double-digit percentage changes. Changes in speeds over time will be even greater in changing interest-rate scenarios. For convenience and practicality, a long-term average of the projected speeds is typically reported as the model's projection.[53] The somewhat obvious point here is that a single long-term projected speed is inadequate in most cases. Exhibit 4.29 shows the vector and the long-term average speed for the Ginnie Mae 8s in the "down-200" rally scenario.

The long-term average projection is below model projections for the first few years and above in later years. For an investor analyzing, for example, a short-term Collateralized Mortgage Obligation (CMO) bond, the long-term projection can be quite misleading. Yet a surprising proportion of investors still seem to evaluate MBSs using a single speed.[54]

■ *Prepayment model error.* Model projections represent a statistical estimate of the *expected* prepayment rates along a specified path of interest rates. Hence, random variation (noise) means that actual month-to-month speeds will differ from projections even if the model is perfectly

---

[53] The long-term projection is a weighted average of the vector of month-by-month projections. The method used by Salomon Smith Barney is to find the single speed that gives the same average life as the vector; another common method is to find the single speed that gives the same yield as the vector.
[54] Bloomberg® and the Bond Market Association both publish dealer estimated long-term speeds.

accurate (in this context, *perfectly accurate* just means that the average deviation will be zero; in other words, the model is *unbiased*). This is a particularly important point for CMO or Interest Only/Principal Only (IO/PO) deals; even for relatively large deals, the random errors can be significant.[55]

However, our research[56] shows that the effect of purely random variation in speeds has almost no impact on OASs of pass-throughs and a minimal impact for OASs of IOs and POs. In other words, if the model is accurate on average, then the averaging over many interest-rate paths involved in OAS calculations minimizes the effect of noise.[57] No model is ever likely to be perfectly accurate for any length of time; projections incorporate a number of assumptions (explicitly or implicitly) about various factors (such as housing sales rates and housing inflation) that are unlikely to hold forever. In practice, even for an unbiased model, errors can persist for a while before actual and projected speeds converge again. For example, for a particular group of loans, housing activity may be stronger or weaker than the average used in the model, leading to speeds that are either too fast or too slow for a period of time. Such *runs* of errors have been analyzed in a separate paper;[58] as with purely random noise, the effect on OASs is minimal as long as actual and projected speeds eventually converge.

Finally, a model can be misspecified, either because it was wrong to start with or because conditions have changed, resulting in systematic errors that do not go away. However, distinguishing between errors that will persist only for a while and more systematic errors is difficult, since, for example, it will not generally be known in advance whether the conditions leading to the errors are temporary or permanent. We next discuss ways of quantifying the impact of such systematic and persistent errors.

Prepayment Model Risk: Partial Prepayment Durations

We use the term *prepayment model risk* to signify the risk that the market price will reflect prepayment assumptions that differ from model projections. This risk measure is distinct from the risk associated with interest-rate

---

[55] For a discussion of random variation in speeds, see "Fact and Fantasy About Collateral Speeds," Michael Bykhovsky and Lakhbir Hayre, *Journal of Portfolio Management,* summer 1992.

[56] See Chapter 5.

[57] Random variations can have an impact on a CMO that is asymmetric with respect to prepayments (e.g., if speeds are centered at the end of a PAC band range).

[58] See Chapter 5.

movements causing changes in prepayments. We note that prepayment model risk may arise either because actual prepayments are substantially different from projected levels (for example, because of structural changes in the mortgage finance industry and housing market) or because market expectations about prepayment prospects differ from model projections.

A useful measure of prepayment model risk is the concept of *prepayment duration*. This is defined as the percentage change in price, holding OAS constant, for a given percentage deviation in speeds from some defined base level projection.[59] The base level could be the straight model projections, or some market-implied multiple of the projections—for example, the multiple of the projections that would equalize OASs on the IO and PO of a chosen benchmark strip issue.

An extension of this concept is to calculate partial prepayment durations; that is, price sensitivity with respect to deviations from the projections for a specific component of speeds. One can define partial prepayment durations for any of the important variables discussed in the previous few sections. The most important ones are:

- *Housing turnover rate.* The impact of higher- or lower-than-projected home sales.
- *Refinancing rate.* The impact of refinancing rates being higher- or lower-than-projected refinancing rates.

We have computed overall prepayment durations as well as partial durations associated with these two components using the Salomon Smith Barney prepayment model projections as the base. Exhibit 4.30 shows prepayment durations and partial prepayment component durations for these two components for a range of representative conventional 30-year pass-throughs. The durations are calculated using the following formula:

$$D_c = \frac{P_{-10} - P_{+10}}{20P_0} \times 100$$

where D_c = Prepayment partial duration w.r.t. component C
P_d = Price when projections for component C are changed by $d\%$ in the Salomon Smith Barney prepayment model, holding OAS constant.

---

[59] See Chapter 14.

EXHIBIT 4.30 Prepayment Component Partial Durations, March 27, 2000

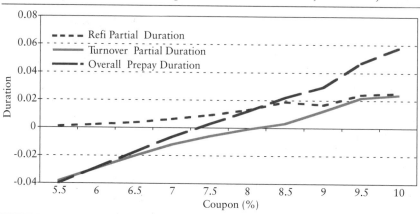

Note: Current coupon is about 7.5%.
Source: Salomon Smith Barney.

The durations represent the estimated change in price for a 1% change in prepayments associated with the total prepayment or prepayment component. From the formula on the previous page, if slower-than-expected speeds lead to an increase in price, the prepayment duration will be positive. Note that the current coupon for the calculations in Exhibit 4.30 is approximately 7.5%. We may draw a number of interesting observations from these durations.

The overall prepayment durations and partial durations for the turnover component are negative for discounts and current coupons, while they are positive for the premiums. This is because slower-than-projected speeds hurt mortgage pass-throughs in discount scenarios but help them when they are premiums. However, the partial durations for the refinancing component are always positive, because the refinancing component is zero except in premium scenarios, in which lower prepayments lead to higher prices. Newer premiums that have had less exposure to refinancing opportunity have the highest durations, because refinancing represents the largest component of prepayments for such coupons. Note that the overall prepayment duration is approximately, although not exactly, the sum of the partial durations for the turnover and refinancing components.

The durations are most significant for deep discounts (about −0.03 for the turnover component) and substantial premiums (about +0.02 each for the turnover and the refinancing components). These levels imply a price change of roughly one tick and two-thirds of a tick, respectively, per 1%

change in prepay component projections. For seasoned premiums, the partial durations for the turnover and refinancing components are more or less of equal importance. Although this pattern is reasonable, given that long-term projections for each of those components is roughly the same (around 6%–10% CPR), it may come as a surprise to those accustomed to thinking of refinancing rates as posing the major prepayment risk for premiums. At the same time, the partial durations associated with deep discounts for the turnover component are quite high, suggesting that there is substantial prepayment risk associated with that sector. The risk is accentuated by the common divergence in predictions about the strength of the housing market and the seasoning rates of discounts among Wall Street firms.[60]

If desired, these prepay components may be dissected further, and partial durations computed for other more specific factors:[61]

- *Turnover seasoning length.* The length of time after origination required for seasoning of the turnover component.
- *The refinancing elbow.* The degree of refinancing incentive at which refinancing rates begin to accelerate.
- *Steepness (or "cuspiness") of the refinancing curve.* The slope of the refinancing response curve.
- *Refinancing amplitude.* Peak speeds when premium coupons are first exposed to significant refinancing opportunities.
- *Degree of burnout.* The rate at which speeds slow after a refinancing peak.

These more elaborate measures can be very useful in certain contexts, such as risk management or in evaluating complex mortgage derivatives.

APPENDIX 4A
THE SALOMON SMITH BARNEY HOUSING TURNOVER MODEL

As discussed in Section 4.1, housing turnover may be defined as the ratio of existing (single-family) home sales to single-family housing stock. This

---

[60] The actual price risk could be thought of as the **product** of the partial duration with some measure of dispersion or volatility for the projected prepayment component. Disagreement and uncertainty among market players would tend to increase the volatility of the component's projected levels.

[61] Readers who have access to Salomon Smith Barney's Yield Book will recognize these as some of the "Dials" available for customizing the prepayment model.

definition makes the relationship of housing turnover rates to prepayment speeds very clear. Salomon Smith Barney has performed an analysis of housing turnover rates over the past 20 years, leading to a model that may be used to project turnover rates into the future under different interest-rate scenarios. This Appendix outlines this model.

We believe that explicitly modeling home turnover rates offers a number of advantages. It leads to a more dynamic and realistic depiction of the evolution of turnover and hence prepayment rates over time, capturing in particular the path dependence of such rates. For example, if a sudden and sustained rise in mortgage rates occurs, an initial drop in home sales (and hence in speeds) will take place, but eventually pent-up demand and a gradual adjustment to the higher mortgage rates will lead to a pickup in sales and in speeds (as happened, for example, in the first half of the 1980s). The model also allows easier sensitivity testing; for example, it allows us to project what happens if for a given level of interest rates, home inflation is significantly different from historical norms. Finally, an explicit projection for the housing turnover rate furthers our goal of increasing the transparency of the prepayment model; users can determine for themselves if they agree with the model's projections for home turnover rates along given interest-rate paths.

Factors Affecting Housing Turnover

Demographics and population mobility, as well as macroeconomic and social factors all combine to influence home sales:

- *Affordability.* This refers to the home buyer's ability to make a monthly mortgage payment. Affordability can be approximated by the ratio of median income to the monthly mortgage payment on a median home. Affordability is often cited as an important predictor of home sales, and correctly so. However, the effect of affordability is subtler than it first appears, in that home sales depend not only on the current affordability of housing, but also on the recent history of affordability. For example, when mortgage rates rallied after hitting all-time highs above 16% in 1981 to 1982, the pickup in home sales was immediate. Turnover averaged 4.31% and 4.44% in 1983 and 1984, respectively, although affordability was still quite low by historical standards, with rates still several hundred basis points above mean 1970s levels. It is likely that pent-up demand for housing from prospective buyers who could not afford a house in 1981 to 1982 was a factor.
- *Desirability.* Another socioeconomic factor that helps explain historical variations in turnover is the desirability of homeownership. We use this

term in a general sense, to include a perception of the likely economic return from buying a home and a perception as to whether it is currently prudent to do so. In our model the variable influencing this desirability is the prospective inflation in home prices, for which a good proxy might be a weighted average of nominal home price changes in recent years. High levels of price inflation, which tend to lower the **real** (inflation-adjusted) mortgage interest-rate are acknowledged in the literature as a key factor behind the sharp rise in turnover rates from 1973 to 1978, which bucked the sustained drop in affordability during the same period.[62]

Another important influence on housing activity is the level of *consumer confidence*. However, although using this variable would improve the historical fit of our model, we have chosen not to use it, as we do not want to attempt to predict its levels going forward.

The Estimation of Turnover

Our analysis has thus shown that there are two intersecting populations of prospective buyers or movers: those who desire to buy or trade up and those who can afford to do so. The basic behavioral assumption behind the model is that the turnover rate is determined by the size of the intersection of these two groups. The size of the groups depends upon the levels of desirability and affordability, respectively. We capture these levels with two factors: (1) an **affordability factor** that depends upon the median income, median home price and mortgage rates, as described previously, and (2) a **desirability factor** that incorporates the effects of home price inflation. The model also accounts for pent-up demand, or the lack of demand due to past interest rates, by carrying forward an affordability "deficit" or "surplus" from previous periods.

For our projections, we make the assumption that income and home prices change at the same rate over time; hence, changes in affordability are just a function of changes in mortgage rates.

A discussion of the model's predictions for various interest-rate scenarios is included in the section on home sales (see Exhibit 4.3 and accompanying commentary). As shown there, the model provides realistic projections of the impact of interest-rate changes on future housing turnover levels.

---

[62] See, for example, *Urban Economics,* E.S. Mills and B.W. Hamilton, Chicago: Scott Foresman, Chapter 10.

APPENDIX 4B
A GENERAL STATISTICAL FRAMEWORK FOR MODELING
REFINANCING BEHAVIOR

Let x be a measure of refinancing incentive. Assume that, for a given x, the likelihood of a refinancing varies from person to person. Let Θ be a parameter that characterizes a mortgagor's propensity to refinance, and let

$$p(x;\theta) = \text{Probability of a refinancing, given } x \text{ and } \theta$$

Let $f_o(\theta) = $ Initial probability distribution of θ across the population of borrowers.

If $x_1 = $ Refinancing incentive in month one, then the refinancing rate in month one will be

$$\bar{p}_1 = \text{Average of } p(x_1;\theta) \text{ across the distribution of } \theta$$

$$= E[p(x_1;\theta)] = \int_{-\infty}^{\infty} p(x_1;\theta)f_o(\theta)d\theta$$

Evolution of the Population Mix and Refinancing Rate

Mortgagors with a higher propensity to refinance will leave the population at a faster rate. The *survival rate* in month one of a "type θ" mortgagor is the probability that the borrower does not refinance, which is $[1 - p(x_1;\theta)]$, and it follows that the new distribution of θ at the end of month one is

$$f_1(\theta) = A_1(x_1)(1 - p(x_1;\theta))f_o(\theta)$$

where $A_1(x_1)$ is a normalizing constant given by

$$A_1(x_1) = \left[\int_{-\infty}^{\infty} (1 - p(x_1;\theta))f_o(\theta)d\theta \right]^{-1}$$

Repeating the arguments above, if x_n is the refinancing incentive in month n, then the refinancing rate in month n will be

$$\overline{p}_n = \int_{-\infty}^{\infty} p(x_n;\theta) f_{n-1}(\theta) d\theta \tag{4.5}$$

where $f_{n-1}(\theta)$ is the distribution of θ at the beginning of the month. The distribution of θ at the end of the month is given by

$$\begin{aligned} f_n(\theta) &= A_n(1 - p(x_n;\theta))f_{n-1}(\theta) \\ &= A_n(1 - p(x_n;\theta))(1 - p(x_{n-1};\theta))...(1 - p(x_1;\theta))f_o(\theta) \\ &= A_n Q_n f_o(\theta), \text{ say} \end{aligned} \tag{4.6}$$

where $Q_n = (1 - p(x_n;\theta))(1 - p(x_{n-1};\theta))...(1 - p(x_1;\theta))$

and A_n is a normalizing constant given by

$$A_n = \left[\int_{-\infty}^{\infty} Q_n f_o(\theta) d\theta \right]^{-1}$$

Burnout

Note that, from Equation 4.6, as the population undergoes refinancings, the population distribution will shift toward those with the lowest propensities to refinance (or highest survival likelihoods). Hence, even for a constant refinancing incentive, the refinancing rate will decline, at a rate proportional to the average across θ of the cumulative survival factor Q_n (note the similarity to the traditional Wall Street practice of modeling burnout using some sort of pool factor).

The Media Effect and Borrower Migrations

Refinancings lead to faster borrowers exiting the pool at faster rates, causing a change in the population composition toward a slower average mix. In addition, the population mix (i.e., the distribution of θ) can change due to two other phenomena:

1. The **media effect** (see the heading: The Media Effect and Borrower Migrations in Section 4.2) can cause a *temporary* change in intrinsic borrower propensities to refinance;

2. **Borrower migrations,** resulting for example from changes in LTVs or in borrower credit.

Note: A simple version of this framework, in which θ can take only two values (so that mortgagors are either *slow* or *fast*), has been discussed in more detail in a previous publication.[63]

---

[63] See "A Simple Statistical Framework for Modeling Burnout and Refinancing Behavior," Lakhbir Hayre, *Journal of Fixed Income,* December 1994.

CHAPTER 5

Random Error in Prepayment Projections

Lakhbir Hayre

Prepayment models are used to obtain cash flows in the analysis of mortgage-backed securities (MBSs). Such models project expected prepayment rates on a given MBS for specified path of interest rates.[1]

Actual speeds will differ from projection almost every month. These differences can be categorized into two types:

1. **Random errors,** due to month-to-month erraticness (noise), or to temporary differences between model assumptions and reality.
2. **Permanent and fundamental errors,** due either to an initial misspecification of the model or to structural or demographic changes since the model was fitted. For example, future changes in the refinancing process (such as automation) may lead to a more efficient prepayment option than is assumed by the model.

In case (1), the basic assumption is that the model is right on average, and hence, deviations between actual and projected speeds will even out over time. The modeling of such deviations, and quantifying their effect on MBS valuation, is the subject of this chapter.

5.1 REASONS FOR RANDOM ERRORS

Random errors can be classified into two types: (1) errors that are uncorrelated from month to month and represent *noise;* and (2) errors that are

---

[1] See Chapter 4 for a discussion of prepayment modeling.

correlated from month-to-month, leading to model speeds that are either too high or too low for a period of time.

Noise

What causes noise in month-to-month prepayment speeds? For **pools** or **collateralized mortgage obligation** (CMO) deals, one cause of noise is *sampling error*. The loans in the collateral represent a sample from the generic class (or universe) of loans for which projections are made. For example, if a CMO deal is collateralized by 1993 origination GNMA 7s, then even if the collateral is identical to the universe of 1993 GNMA 7s with respect to Weighted Average Coupon (WAC), age, and so on, speeds on the deal are unlikely to equal those on the generic each month; instead they will fluctuate randomly around the generic speeds.[2]

For large generic classes (e.g., 1993 GNMA 7s), noise can arise for various reasons. Among those are the following:

■ The prepayment model assumes a specified value for mortgage rates in any given month. In reality, mortgage rates tend to vary by lender, by region and within a month. The prepayments resulting from mortgagors' experiencing these diverse rates likely will differ from those obtained if all borrowers experienced the same rate for the whole month, as assumed by the model.

■ The model assumes that given current and past rates, and other relevant factors, a certain fraction of the remaining borrowers in a given class will refinance in a given month. In fact, this fraction is a statistical estimate of the *expected* refinancing rate; even if the estimate is unbiased (i.e., right on average), we will still see noisy variation around the expected value each month.

■ Either explicitly or implicitly, the model assumes a given level of housing turnover for the specified level of interest rates. As with refinancing rates, this is an expected value; even if it is correct on average, deviations will occur between the expected and the actual turnover each month.

■ Projections are based on assumed lags between interest rate changes and resulting speed changes. Again, even if the assumptions are correct on average, actual lags will tend to fluctuate randomly around the assumed ones from month to month.

---

[2] For a discussion on how to estimate the degree of dispersion for a given deal, see "Fact and Fantasy about Collateral Speeds," Michael Bykohvsky and Lakhbir Hayre, *Journal of Fixed Income*, summer 1992.

The common theme in these examples is that of random month to month variation around expected values of key factors that influence speeds. Such variations are uncorrelated from month to month; that is, one month's error does not provide information on the direction of next month's error.

Correlated but Transient Errors

In practice, differences between model projections and actual speeds are often due to more than just random noise. If noise were the only source of differences, we would be unlikely to see an extended sequence of model speeds faster (or slower) than actual speeds. Such sequences are in fact often seen with most prepayment models.[3]

Such transient deviations are to be expected, even if the model is fundamentally sound in the long run. Prepayment rates on a group of mortgages will be determined by a myriad of factors, only a few of which are captured in any prepayment model. A prepayment model (like any statistically fitted model) effectively assumes "average" levels for factors not explicitly in the model (the average being defined as over the data used to fit the model). To the extent that actual levels of these factors differ from the data set averages, actual speeds will differ from projected ones. Two examples will help make these points more concrete:

1. The geographical mix of borrowers influences speeds, both through the level of home turnover and through home price appreciation (and hence ability to relocate and refinance). A particular region may be under- or overrepresented in a particular generic MBS, leading to speeds different from those of the model. However, given the cyclical nature of housing markets, such differences generally would be expected to average out over time.

2. Housing turnover depends on factors other than mortgage rates—for example, consumer confidence. To the extent that these factors will tend to differ from what is implicitly assumed in the model, projected speeds resulting from housing turnover will differ from actuals. Such deviations might persist for a while, but would average out over time, as periods with below average turnover (for a given level of rates) balance periods of above average turnover. The key assumption made in this paper is that over time, these deviations will average out; hence, while

---

[3] Graphs of historical actual versus projected speeds, over the period for which data is used to fit the model (i.e., within sample fits) often show deviations between actual and projected lasting for a year or longer.

actual and projected speeds may diverge for a while, they are expected to come back into line eventually.

5.2 A SIMPLE MODEL FOR RANDOM ERRORS

Let ERROR(t) denote the deviation between model and actual speeds in month t as a percentage of the model projection. In other words, if ACTUAL_SMM(t) and PROJ_SMM(t) denote the actual and projected speeds in month t (as SMMs), then

$$ACTUAL\_SMM(t) = PROJ\_SMM(t) \times [1 + ERROR(t)] \qquad (5.1)$$

It will be assumed that the error term changes randomly each month, with the error in one month related to the error in the previous month according to the equation

$$ERROR(t) = b \times ERROR(t-1) + NOISE(t) \qquad (5.2)$$

where b is a specified constant between 0 and 1 and NOISE(t) is a normal random variable with a zero mean, a fixed standard deviation and which is uncorrelated from month to month (that is, it is a noise term).[4]

Discussion of Model

Equation 5.2 states that the error in a given month is partly determined by the previous month's error and partly by a new random shock. The parameter b

---

[4] Statistically oriented readers will recognize ERROR(t) as a first-order autoregressive model. (We truncate ACTUAL_SMM(t) to keep it within reasonable bounds.) A more general model would be to have separate processes for correlated and uncorrelated errors, that is,

$$ACTUAL\_SMM(t) = PROJ\_SMM(t) \times [1 + ERROR(t) + NOISE2(t)]$$

where ERROR(t), given by Equation 5.2, represents correlated errors while NOISE2(t) represents uncorrelated errors. However, we have chosen to combine correlated and uncorrelated errors into Equation 5.2 both for simplicity and because in practice observed errors are an unknown mix of the two.

is for all practical purposes the correlation between monthly errors,[5] and, hence, represents how much one month's error depends on that of the previous month. If b is zero, the errors are uncorrelated and represent pure noise; for b close to one, the errors are highly correlated and hence can persist for a while. At the extreme, if b is one, ERROR(t) is a random walk and the model projections could drift further and further away from actual speeds.

Another interpretation is to think of the error as mean reverting toward zero. This point becomes clearer if we rewrite Equation 5.2 as

$$\text{ERROR}(t) - \text{ERROR}(t-1) = -(1-b) \times \text{ERROR}(t-1) + \text{NOISE}(t)$$

Hence, if ERROR($t - 1$) is negative, there is an upward trend in ERROR(t), while the trend is downward if ERROR($t - 1$) is positive. The mean reversion strength is equal to $(1 - b)$. A more comprehensive model could have separate error sequences for the turnover and refinancing components of prepayments. However, we feel that the present formulation is sufficient for illustrating the effects of random error on MBS valuation.

5.3 CHOOSING MODEL PARAMETERS

The sequence of errors given by Equation 5.2 depends on the correlation term b and on the standard deviation of the NOISE(t) term, which we will label σ. Exhibit 5.1 shows a graph of simulated sequence of errors for b set equal to 0.70 and σ equal to 10%, with the initial error ERROR(0) set equal to 0.

From Exhibit 5.1, it can be seen that two key characteristics of the errors are:

1. The duration of a sequence (or "run") of errors all of the same sign (i.e., the length of time the model can be off before it comes back into line)

---

[5] Assuming that ERROR(0) = 0 and that b is less than one, then the correlation between ERROR($t - 1$) and ERROR(t) is given by

$$\text{CORR}[\text{ERROR}(t), \text{ERROR}(t-1)] = b \left[\frac{\left(1 - b^{2t-2}\right)}{\left(1 - b^{2t}\right)} \right]^{1/2}$$

which converges rapidly to b as t increases.

EXHIBIT 5.1 A Simulated Error Sequence for b = 0.70 and σ = 10%

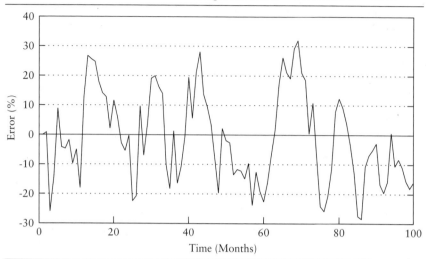

Source: Salomon Smith Barney.

(in Exhibit 5.1, such runs are the periods between crossings of the horizontal axis); and
2. The amplitude (or magnitude) of errors, which we measure by their
   standard deviations.

The likely duration of runs or errors has to be computed numerically,
and estimates obtained by simulation for various combinations of b and σ
are shown in Exhibit 5.2. We can, however, derive an analytic formula for

EXHIBIT 5.2 Average Length of Error Sequences and Standard
Deviations of Errors

| Noise Vitality | Correlation Between Month-to-Month Errors (b) | | | | | |
| | 0.50 | | 0.70 | | 0.90 | |
	Avg. Run Length	Std. Dev. Of Errors	Avg. Run Length	Std. Dev. of Errors	Avg. Run Length	Std. Dev. of Errors
0.05	6.7 Mths	5.8%	11.8 Mths	7.0%	28.6 Mths	11.5%
0.10	5.9	11.6	10.2	14.0	25.2	22.9
0.20	5.2	23.1	8.0	28.0	21.1	45.9

Note: The "Avg. Run Length" is the average number of months that a run of errors of the same
sign will persist, while the "Std. Dev." of Errors is the equilibrium standard deviation of the
error term given by Equation (5.4)
Source: Salomon Smith Barney.

the standard deviations of the errors. Working backward from Equation 5.2, we obtain

$$\text{ERROR}(t) = b^t\,\text{ERROR}(0) + b^{t-1}\,\text{NOISE}(1)$$
$$+ b^{t-2}\,\text{NOISE}(2) + \ldots + b\,\text{NOISE}(t-1) + \text{NOISE}(t)$$

Assuming that $\text{ERROR}(0) = 0$ and $0 < b < 1$, then since the NOISE terms are uncorrelated with zero means, we obtain that

$$\text{Expected Value of ERROR}(t) = 0$$
$$\text{Variance of ERROR}(t) = \sigma^2\left(1 + b^2 + b^4 + \ldots + b^{2(t-1)}\right)$$
$$= \sigma^2\,\frac{\left(1 - b^{2t}\right)}{\left(1 - b^2\right)} \tag{5.3}$$

Because b^{2t} approaches zero as t increases, the amplitude (or range) or error is given approximately by

$$\text{Standard Deviation of ERROR}(t) \cong \frac{\sigma}{\left(1 - b^2\right)^{1/2}} \tag{5.4}$$

Exhibit 5.2 shows some values for the standard deviation of the error term from Equation 5.4, along with simulated estimates for average error runs.

As might be expected, the average run length increases as b goes up, reflecting increasing correlations between month-to-month errors. Note also that the average run length declines as the noise volatility goes up, as greater erraticness lessens the chances of an extended run of positive or of negative errors. The standard deviation of the errors not surprisingly increases with s, and also increases with b; higher correlations between month-to-month errors increases the chances of a run of errors leading to a wider divergence between actual and projected speeds.

What are appropriate choices for b and σ? An examination of historical prepayment model errors can be somewhat misleading, because the errors may just reflect *within sample* accuracy. In other words, because the model was fitted using historical data from a given period, model errors within that period may understate likely errors in the future. The current Salomon Smith Barney prepayment model was completed in the spring of 1995, and has remained essentially unchanged since then. Hence a comparison of actual speeds versus projections from the model since then provide an (admittedly limited) indication of *out-of-sample* errors. Based on this data, values of around $b = 0.7$ and $\sigma = 0.1$ seem to be conservatively appropriate. This combination implies that the correlation between monthly errors is about 70%, that runs of positive or negative errors will last on average about 10 months, and that the standard deviation of monthly errors will be around 14% (giving a two standard deviation range of, approximately, the projected speed ±30%). However, investors may still want to use higher values of b and σ. First, the performance of the model could be worse in the future, and second, certain coupons have had more substantial errors than the average. As we discuss later, values for b of about 0.9 and 0.95 do lead to fairly wide dispersions between actual and projected speeds.

5.4 DISPERSION OF REALIZED PREPAYMENT RATES

In Exhibit 5.3, we show projected speeds for a new current coupon Ginnie Mae MBS from the Salomon Smith Barney prepayment model, for three interest rate scenarios: unchanged; down by 2000 basis points; and up by 200 basis points. Projections are given for the near term (one-year), medium term (three-years) and the long term (term of the security).

Suppose that actual speeds deviate from projections, as described by Equation 5.2. What is the range of speeds actually likely to be experienced? In Exhibit 5.4, we show a frequency curve of the realized one-year speeds, assuming unchanged rates, obtained from 500 simulated paths of error sequences with the error correlation b set equal to 0.70 and the noise volatility σ equal to 10%. Each of the 500 sequences of simulated error paths is applied to the vector of speeds, and 500 resulting one-year speeds.

From Exhibit 5.3, the projected one-year speed was 2.7% constant prepayment rate (CPR). Exhibit 5.4 indicates that the presence of random errors (as per our assumptions) means that the actual one-year speed can be up to about 0.5% CPR higher or lower, or a range of roughly 20% around the projected value. The standard deviation of the distribution of one-year

EXHIBIT 5.3 Projected Speeds for a New Current-Coupon GNMA

	Interest Rate Charge		
	Down 200bps	No change	Up 200bps
1 Year CPR	46.9%	2.7%	1.9%
3-Year CPR	39.9	4.9	3.1
Long –Term CPR	33.5	8.2	5.8

BPS: Basis points, CPR: Constant prepayment rate.
Source: Salomon Smith Barney.

EXHIBIT 5.4 Frequency Distribution of Realized One-Year Speeds

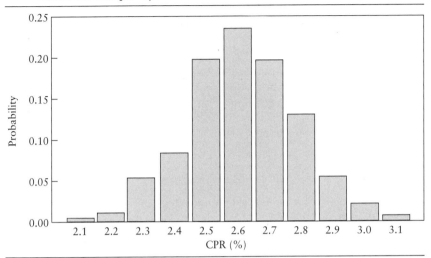

Source: Salomon Smith Barney.

CPRs (calculated from the 500 simulation runs) is 0.2% CPR. As a percentage of the projected CPR, the standard deviation is about 6.4%—note that this is less than 14%, the equilibrium error standard deviation derived from Equation 5.4 (see Exhibit 5.2). This is because Equation 5.4 gives that standard deviation of the error in a given month, where as the one-year CPR (or any other average speed) represents the cumulative effect of the month-to-month errors. This averaging process over time reduces the standard deviation of the cumulative error, because periods of underprediction balance periods of over prediction.

In Exhibit 5.5, we show the average CPR and the standard deviation of the CPR for the various scenarios and horizon periods given in Exhibit 5.3, using 500 simulated error paths.

Thus, for example, while the projected one-year speed if rates decline 200bp (basis points) is 46.9% CPR, the actual one-year speed, if $b = 0.7$ and $\sigma = 0.10$, is distributed around the projected value with a standard deviation of 3.3% CPR.[6] As a percentage of the projected CPR, the standard deviation of the realized CPR is 6.6%.

---

[6] The distribution is asymmetric, and the actual range of CPRs obtained from the 500 simulations was roughly 35% CPR to 55% CPR.

EXHIBIT 5.5 Realized Speeds for a New Current-Coupon GNMA

	Down 200bps			No Change			Up 200bps		
	CPR		%Std	CPR		%Std.	CPR		%Std.
	Avg.	Std Dev	Dev	Avg.	Std. Dev.	Dev.	Avg.	Std. Dev.	Dev.
Horizon									
1 Year	46.5%	3.1%	6.6%	2.7%	0.2%	6.7%	1.9%	0.1%	5.7%
3 Years	39.8	2.0	5.0	4.9	0.3	5.4	3.1	0.2	5.3
Long Term	33.5	1.8	5.3	8.2	0.2	2.2	5.8	6.1	2.1

BP: Basis points, CPR: Constant prepayment rate.
Note: Results are obtained by simulating 500 error sequences, with the initial error = 0, $b = 0.7$ and $\sigma = 0.10$. The "% Std. Dev." is the standard deviation of the CPRs divided by the projected model CPRs shown in Exhibit 5.3.
Source: Salomon Smith Barney.

The percentage standard deviation of the realized CPRs declines as the horizon lengthens, due to the averaging effect over time discussed previously. While this may strike some readers as odd, it follows from our basic assumption that prepay model errors are mean reverting. However, within our framework, choosing a value for b that is close to one will lead to more severe and sustained errors, essentially implying that the model is, or becomes, seriously flawed. Exhibit 5.6 shows percentage standard deviations of actual (realized) CPRs, in the base case, for various values of b.

For b close to 1, the percentage standard deviation initially increases with the horizon, but even for $b = 0.95$, mean reversion in the errors implies that eventually the standard deviation will begin to decline. In contrast, for the extreme case $b = 1$, the error is random walk, and does not mean revert to zero; in other words, actual and projected speeds can diverge for an indefinitely long period of time. As a result, as Exhibit 5.6 shows, the standard deviation of the cumulative errors tends to increase over time.

Investors who want to obtain very conservative estimates of the effect of model error on near-term performance probably should use a value of b of 0.9 or 0.95. From Exhibit 5.2, for example, $b = 0.9$ and $\sigma = 0.1$ implies error runs lasting an average of more than two years, with monthly errors

EXHIBIT 5.6 Percentage Standard Deviations of Realized CPR Distribution

	Error Correlation			
	0.70	0.90	0.95	1.0
Horizon				
1 Year	6.7	11.6	14.7	16.2
3-Years	5.4	14.5	19.9	38.5
Maturity	2.2	6.6	12.3	49.8

Source: Salomon Smith Barney.

having a standard deviation of around 23%. Cumulative errors are lower, but still substantial; for $b = 0.95$ and $\sigma = 0.1$, the three-year average CPR has a standard deviation of about 20% around the projected speed.

5.5 EFFECT ON OPTION-ADJUSTED SPREAD

The calculation of OASs involves generating a large number of interest rate paths, and then using a prepayment model to project speeds (and hence cash flows) along each path. However, what if the actual speeds come in different from projections? Exhibit 5.7 shows the effect on the OAS of various MBSs, assuming that prepayment errors occur according to the error model in Equation 5.2, for several values of b and with s set equal to 0.10.

The results in Exhibit 5.7 likely will surprise most people. First, little change occurs in the OAS for the pass-throughs, even for values of b close to 1; even for the IOs and POs, the OAS changes are relatively minor. However, this can be explained by the fact that OASs calculations involve averaging over time and across interest rate paths, and thus even wide divergences in speeds can cancel out. This result perhaps indicates a weakness of the OAS measure; it is an average, and often is not significantly affected by the variability of returns. For example, suppose we measure variability by the standard deviation of the present values of the cash flows along the different interest rate paths. Then for the Trust 240 IO, the standard deviation was about 4.4 without random errors, and was close to double this if we have random errors with b close to one (and $\sigma = 0.10$). However, the average present value (which is used in OAS calculations) remained about the same.

EXHIBIT 5.7 Effect of Prepayment Errors on OASs for Pass-Throughs and IOs/POs

		Price	Base OAS	Change in OAS for b Equal to		
				0.7	0.9	0.95
Pass-Throughs						
7%		95-10	61	1	1	1
8		100-03	61	0	1	1
9		103-31	59	-1	0	2
IOs and POs						
FN Trust 240	IO	34-30	42	0	4	13
	PO	61-68	76	1	-2	-6
FN Trust 237	IO	34-10	172	-1	5	18
	PO	66-03	21	1	-2	-8

IO: Interest only, OAS: Option-adjusted spread, PO: Principal only.
Note: OASs calculated using market volatilities and prices at close of June 26, 1996.
Source: Salomon Smith Barney.

EXHIBIT 5.8 Prices for FNMA Trust 237 IO at Various Prepayment Model Multiples

	Prepayment Model Multiple				
	0.80	**0.90**	**1.00**	**1.10**	**1.20**
Price	38.20	36.16	34.31	32.64	31.11
Price Change	3.89	1.85	0	-1.67	-3.20

IO: Interest only.
Source: Salmon Smith Barney.

Second, IOs seem to benefit (if only marginally) from prepayment errors. This seems to be counter-intuitive, given that IOs are generally perceived to have high prepayment risk. However, note that in our formulation, errors have equal chances of being positive or negative. Thus, because of the averaging involved in OAS calculations, the net effect of random errors will typically depend less on prepayment duration (how much the price is affected by changes in prepayments) than on prepayment convexity (the asymmetry of the impact).

To clarify this point, Exhibit 5.8 shows price changes for the FNMA Trust 237 IO as various multiples are applied to the prepayment model, holding OAS constant. The IO has positive prepayment convexity—it benefits more from a given percentage slowdown in speeds than it loses from the same percentage increase in speeds. Hence, on average it gains from random prepayment errors.

These same observations apply to structured products. The magnitude and direction of the impact of random prepayment errors depends to a large extent on the prepayment convexity of the security. Exhibit 5.9 shows two structured IOs, one which is hardly affected by random errors, and the other being a bond substantially impacted by them.

The price of the FNMA 94.50 PL IO changes little if multiples are applied to the prepayment model, explaining why the OAS is almost unaffected by random prepayment errors. On the other hand, the FNMA 93.5 MA IO has high prepayment duration and, more important, significantly

EXHIBIT 5.9 Effect of Random Prepayment Errors on OASs for Structured IOs

Bond	Price	OAS	Change in OAS for b Equal to		
			0.70	**0.90**	**0.95**
Fn 94.50 PL	59-30	138	0	-3	-2
FN 93.5 MA	34-21	460	-18	-63	-91

OAS: Option-adjusted spread.
Source: Salomon Smith Barney.

negative prepayment convexity: Its price drops by about 9.4 points if a multiple of 1.2 is applied to the prepayment model, but increases by only 5.5 points if a multiple of 0.8 is applied. Thus random errors have a noticeable negative impact on the OAS.[7]

Generally speaking, the impact of random prepayment errors is fairly minor even for structured MBSs. We ran a large number of structured bonds, and even for b close to one, the change in OAS typically less than 10% of the base OAS in almost all cases. However, as noted earlier, the *variability* of returns (as measured by the standard deviation of the present values along the rate paths) can be significantly higher.

SUMMARY AND CONCLUSIONS

This article has described a relatively simple model for incorporating random errors in projected prepayments into MBS valuation. The model involves specifying the correlation between month-to-month errors and the volatility of a noise term. In turn, these parameters determine the likely duration of deviations between actual and projected speeds, and the amplitude of the deviations. If the correlation between monthly errors is less than one, then the errors are mean reverting toward zero. Thus, over time, periods of underprediction balance periods of overprediction. As a result, while there is uncertainty about monthly speeds, this uncertainty is less for the average speed over a period, and in fact diminishes as the horizon period lengthens.

Random errors (that is, assuming that errors are likely to be negative or positive with equal probability) generally have little impact on OASs, even if we assume that the correlation between monthly errors is one and hence that the errors do not mean revert toward zero. This result suggests that when it comes to prepayment uncertainty, investors should really be more concerned about systematic rather than random errors.

---

[7] The fact that it has a fairly high OAS suggests that the market may be pricing in the prepayment risk.

CHAPTER 6

The Mortgage Origination Process

Lakhbir Hayre

As discussed in Chapter 4, many factors, such as demographics, borrower sentiment, and trends in the housing markets influence mortgage prepayment speeds. It is important to understand how these factors influence prepayments. It is also important, however, to understand the basic mortgage origination process, especially as the process has changes over time, leading to changes in prepayment patterns.

We review the basic steps of the refinancing process in the first section, **Anatomy of a Refinancing.** We then describe **Streamline Refinancing Programs** (SRPs), which simplify loan underwriting requirements. Recently, the GSEs began to offer **enhanced SRPs,** which further simplify the refinancing process. The key features of these programs, and the advantages they offer over a standard refinancing, are discussed. The final section describes **Automated underwriting** (AU) systems, which use computer programs to make underwriting decisions, and details how they affect the refinancing process. Appendix 6A at the end of this chapter summarizes the key requirements and restrictions of enhanced Streamline Refinancing Programs. A discussion of how the Internet is impacting the mortgage origination process is deferred to the next chapter.

6.1 ANATOMY OF A REFINANCING

We begin by giving an overview of the various steps involved in refinancing a mortgage. Despite improvements in the mortgage origination process, refinancing a mortgage loan can still be complicated, time consuming, and expensive. The time and effort spent in the refinancing process begin even before a refinance application is filed. At this preliminary stage, borrowers evaluate if "now is the best time to refinance"[1] by shopping around for the best rates, estimating the savings on their monthly payments if they were to refinance at current rates, deciding if they should wait for lower rates, and finally, considering if they want to restructure their debt either by borrowing on their equity or by altering the term on their mortgage.

The first formal step in a refinancing consists of filing an *application.* This step often involves assembling a comprehensive package of documents, which the lender uses to determine whether the borrower qualifies for mortgage credit. Borrowers who are self-employed or paid by commission, have a history of credit problems, or who own property are required to provide additional supporting documentation.

The heart of a refinancing consists of *loan approval* and *settlement (escrow).* The loan approval process is carried out or coordinated by the lender based on documents submitted by the borrower with the mortgage application, while the activities under the settlement process are orchestrated by a Title or Escrow company, or by a real estate attorney, depending on the state. The mechanics of each of these processes are as follows.

Loan Approval

The standard approval process involves:

- A *credit check,* which involves reviewing the applicant's mortgage payment history and obtaining their credit report.
- *Qualification,* or determination of the *ability to pay.* This involves (1) verifying income and financial assets by means of W2s, pay stubs, tax returns, and bank statements; (2) determining liabilities, typically through the credit report; and (3) calculating *qualifying ratios,* namely computing the ratios of monthly mortgage debt payment to monthly income and total monthly debt payments to monthly income.
- A determination of *property value,* typically by means of an *appraisal.*

When this process is complete, and the lender has approved the loan application, the result is a *mortgage commitment,* which is valid for a specified number of days (typically 60).

Settlement (Escrow)

The settlement process allows the lender to ensure that the borrower has legal title to the property, and complete other formalities related to funding the

---

[1] A catchphrase often used in advertisements by mortgage brokers and lenders.

mortgage loan. The various steps in the settlement process include ordering a *title search,* obtaining *title insurance, deed preparation* and *notarization,* obtaining a *survey,* procuring *loan documentation,* and completing the *closing* with the borrower, which entails paying off the existing loan and disbursing funds. Finally, lenders require the establishment of an escrow or impound account. Lenders use this account to ensure that borrowers pay off their real estate tax bills, hazard, and flood insurance premiums, and mortgage insurance premiums (if applicable) on a timely basis.

We can bracket the refinancing process into three stages: **application, approval,** and **escrow.** Each of these stages has a **time** and/or **cost** dimension associated with it. Enhancements to the refinancing process, such as those achieved by SRPs or AUs, reduce or even eliminate the time spent or the cost incurred in some or all of these stages. To begin with, however, it is most useful to consider the time and cost associated to the different stages of a standard mortgage refinancing. Exhibit 6.1 presents estimates of the typical fees charged, and typical amount of time spent in each stage of a representative refinancing. This information has been obtained by talking to lenders, and from the Web pages of major originators and other mortgage market participants.

The Time Dimension of a Refinancing

As Exhibit 6.1 suggests, the refinancing process can take one to two months, although most refinancings are completed in six weeks or less. A 1998 study by Transamerica Intellitech based on more than 1,000 Californians who refinanced their homes in the first quarter of 1998 provides some useful statistics on the time spent by borrowers on different parts of the refinancing process:[2]

- *Approval process.* 60% of all borrowers received their approval in one week, 18% received it in one to two weeks, and 18% took three or more weeks.
- *Closing period.* After the loan was approved, 25% of the borrowers closed within a week, 26% in one to two weeks, 12% in two to three weeks, and 38% of all borrowers closed in four weeks or longer.

---

[2] *Real Estate Studies: California Consumer Refinance,* 1998 edition, Transamerica Intellitech Market Insights. Transamerica Intellitech (www.ta-intellitech.com) creates software for title companies, lenders, agents, appraisers, and other real estate professionals. The company is a subsidiary of Transamerica Corporation.

EXHIBIT 6.1 Time and Cost Estimates for a Standard Mortgage Refinancing

Step in Refinancing Process	Typical Time Taken	Typical Fees Charged	Typical Fee Amount	Comments
Application	NA	Application	$225	Often waived or may consist of the fees for the appraisal and credit report.
Loan Approval	Few days to two weeks	Appraisal	$334	Paid to property appraiser.
		Credit Report	$50	For report summarizing borrower's credit history.
		Document Preparation	$175	Covers the costs to prepare final legal papers.
		Flood Certification	$25	Charged for certificate that informs lender of the flood zone classification of the property.
		Origination	One point	Charged by loan originator. If the mortgage broker charges an origination fee, the lender will typically also charge an underwriting fee.
		Survey	$125	Paid to surveying firm to verify that property lot has not been encroached upon by any structures since last survey.
		Tax Service	$75	Paid to entity that informs lender if borrower is delinquent on property taxes.
		Underwriting	$175	Paid to lender to underwrite and fund the loan, and to print documents. May be folded into origination fee.
Settlement (Escrow)	Two to four weeks	Attorney/Escrow Agent	$500	Paid to settlement agent for managing final paperwork and escrow funds.
		Notary	$75	Charged to notarize certain loan documents.
		Title Search/Insurance	$400	For title insurance policy.

NA: Not applicable.
Source: Salomon Smith Barney.

The Cost Dimension of a Refinancing

The total of the costs listed in Exhibit 6.1 may surprise some people, given the common perception about "painless" refinancings (in fact, people are often unpleasantly surprised by the magnitude of closing costs). Furthermore, in practice these fees do not cover all the "cash to close" needed by borrowers. In addition to these fees, every borrower is expected by the lender to prepay up to two months of their insurance and tax premiums to ensure that the lender has enough money to make payments when these are due. However, the following should be noted:

- Lenders sometimes waive some fees, particularly loan application fees.
- Borrowers often do not pay many of the costs (excluding prepaid escrow expenses) out of pocket. Instead, they either roll them into the

new loan balance or, in the case of a no-point/no-cost mortgage, pay them over time through a higher note rate.

It might be argued that the real change in the mortgage markets over the past ten years has not been a drastic reduction in closing costs but, through no-point/no-cost loans, the ability of borrowers to avoid paying these costs up front. Of course, the borrower pays these costs over time through higher monthly payments, but this is less onerous for most people than having to pay several thousand dollars at the outset.

6.2 STREAMLINE REFINANCING PROGRAMS

SRPs were one of the earliest attempts to simplify (or streamline) part of the standard refinancing process for select mortgagors by eliminating certain underwriting requirements, such as a full credit check or a new appraisal. These programs are directed toward borrowers whose loans are serviced by the original lender, who have a history of timely mortgage payments, and who wish simply to lower the monthly principal and interest payments on their current mortgage—that is, borrowers who do not wish to do a "cash-out" refinancing.

SRPs were first made available to lenders by the GSEs in the 1980s, and have been heavily used during refinancing waves by lenders in order to limit runoff from their servicing portfolios.[3] In an interesting recent trend, the GSEs have also made **Enhanced SRPs** available to selected originators. Based on information from half a dozen of these originators, we have compiled the common features offered by the various enhanced SRPs in Appendix A.[4] In Exhibit 6.2 we summarize the main differences between the requirements for a regular refinancing, a streamline refinancing, and an enhanced streamline refinancing.

As Exhibit 6.2 indicates, the most important differences between the standard refinancing programs and SRPs lie in the relaxed credit and documentation requirements for SRPs. The enhanced SRP loosens the requirements for documentation and credit checks even further. However, the agencies insist that variations on the standard SRP have existed on a

---

[3] See *Inside Mortgage Finance*, October 29, 1993.
[4] Based on the information we have received from various lenders, there seems to be little variation in the enhanced SRPs offered by different originators. A more detailed analysis of this issue is currently not possible since it is not known which lenders have enhanced SRPs.

EXHIBIT 6.2 GSE Refinance Programs—Typical Eligibility Requirements

	Standard or Cash-Out Refinance	Streamline Refinance Program	Enhanced Streamline Refinance Program
New Application	Required	Required	Required
New Appraisal	Required	Required only if lender determines property value has fallen	Required only if lender determines property value has fallen
Credit Check	New credit check required.	Review mortgage payment history. "In-file" credit report.	Review mortgage payment history.
Ability to Pay	Income/asset verification; qualifying ratios calculated.	Can verify income via paystub. Requalification not required in most cases.	Not required as long as borrower has a clean payment history and new P&I falls within guidelines
New Loan Amount	Based on new appraisal. Maximum LTV is 95% for no cash-out, 80% for cash-out.	Unpaid principal balance plus 5%.	Unpaid principal balance plus 2.5%.
Monthly Payment Increase	Based on new loan balance and requalification.	Up to 15%	Up to 20% allowed if loan term declines.

lender-by-lender negotiated basis since 1994. Thus, *the current enhanced SRPs do not seem to constitute a dramatic break with existing SRP programs.* Nevertheless, it is still informative to estimate how many borrowers qualify for an enhanced SRP and what refinancing cost savings these borrowers can realize relative to standard refinancing programs. These estimates should help to address the central question at hand: to what extent do enhanced SRPs affect refinancing rates?

How Many Borrowers Are Eligible for Enhanced SRPs?

It has been estimated (by Fannie Mae and Freddie Mac) that in 1998 enhanced SRPs were available to servicers that handle 20% to 30% of all agency loans. However, this program has two important restrictions (see Exhibit 6.2):

1. The lender must be the servicer of the existing loan; and
2. Cash-out refinancings are not permitted.[5]

The fraction of loans for which the lender is the current servicer of the loan varies significantly and depends on whether the lender focuses on retail or wholesale lending. The most important thing to keep in mind is that

---

[5] Defined here to be a refinancing that results in a loan with an unpaid balance at least 5% greater than the original loan.

as a result of this restriction, *third-party originations* (loans originated by mortgage brokers and loan correspondents) *are not eligible for the enhanced SRP.* This significantly diminishes the number of borrowers eligible for the enhanced SRP—*retail lending typically accounts for only about 40% of mortgage originations.*[6] In addition, by some estimates, mortgage brokers account for as much as 60% of originations in the important California mortgage market.[7]

The restriction against cash-out refinances is also significant. According to annual data published by Freddie Mac,[8] the percentage of refinance loans that represent cash-out transactions is often over 50% of all refinancings, and rarely drops below 30%.

Thus, the restrictions associated with enhanced SRPs suggest that these programs are not yet widely used. However, during periods of high refinance volume, lenders will use this program or the standard SRP to provide attractive financing for borrowers and, thus, limit the loss to their servicing portfolios. During such times, because the enhanced SRP does offer simplifications over the standard SRP, it will make refinancing easier for a small class of borrowers.

How Much Can Borrowers Save by Using an Enhanced SRP?

Do the savings from the enhanced SRP program provide a compelling and *previously unavailable* economic incentive for refinancers? The chief cost savings for enhanced SRPs arise from the following:

1. Waiving the appraisal (typical cost about $250–$350), and
2. Waiving the credit report (typical cost about $25–$50).

Other sources of savings may come from the lender charging less because of the reduced paperwork and lower hedging costs associated with enhanced SRPs. However, as Exhibit 6.2 makes clear, there do not appear to be substantial differences between a regular SRP and an enhanced SRP. In both cases an appraisal is only necessary if the lender feels that property values have fallen—an unlikely event given the robust housing economy of the past few years. Hence, *the typical borrower could save perhaps a maximum of about $500 in closing costs by using the enhanced SRP* over other programs.

---

[6] See note 3, May 15, 1998.
[7] See note 3, June 26, 1998.
[8] *Freddie Mac Annual Refinance Review.*

How SRPs Benefit Lenders

A crucial reason for the popularity for SRPs is that they offer significant benefits to lenders who service their loans by protecting their servicing portfolios from *runoff* and *adverse selection*. To guard against runoff (loss of servicing share), lenders will offer borrowers SRPs during periods of high refinance volume.

For a given pool of loans, the borrowers that refinance out of the pool typically are more credit-worthy than the borrowers who remain.[9] As the pool seasons, the servicer consequently tends to end up with a selection of borrowers with relatively high delinquency and default rates on their mortgages. This process is referred to as *adverse selection*. To guard against adverse selection, lenders try to retain borrowers who wish to refinance by offering them attractive rates, and a painless refinancing process through an SRP. SRPs can also therefore be thought of as *servicer-retention* programs.

6.3 AUTOMATED UNDERWRITING SYSTEMS

Underwriting refers to the process of estimating a borrower's ability and willingness to repay a loan. An *automated underwriting* (AU) system is a computer program that evaluates the likelihood that a borrower will repay their loan based on data summarizing how borrowers with similar loan, property, and credit characteristics had repaid their loans in the past. Our focus here is on the GSEs' AU systems first introduced in 1995 and refined steadily since then. Freddie Mac's AU system is called *Loan Prospector* (LP) and Fannie Mae's AU system is known as *Desktop Underwriter* (DU).[10]

As do SRPs, AU systems save time and money in a refinancing for some mortgage borrowers. The efficiencies are obtained by automating parts of the loan approval process that formerly involved a human underwriter. As we discussed in Section 6.1, in approving a loan, an underwriter decides whether to extend mortgage credit to an applicant based on the property value (Collateral), a credit check (Credit), and a determination of the borrower's ability to make the monthly mortgage payments (Capacity). Exhibit 6.3 provides a detailed breakdown of the "three Cs" of underwriting.

The current generation of automated underwriting technologies employ the factors presented in Exhibit 6.4 in two ways. One system implements

---

[9] To qualify for financing, a borrower will generally have had to experience some measure of income and equity growth and possess a solid credit history.

[10] LP was formally launched in February 1995 and DU in April 1995.

EXHIBIT 6.3 The Underwriting Decision: Key Factors

Collateral	Credit Reputation	Capacity
• House value	• History of repayments	• Income
• Down payment	• Current account balances	• Debt
	• Recent inquiries	• Cash reserves
	• New accounts	
	• Age of accounts	

Source: Adapted from Exhibit 3 of *Automated Underwriting: Making Mortgage Lending Simpler and Fairer for America's Families,* Freddie Mac, September 1996.

automated underwriting by creating rule-based expert systems that mimic the decision-making process of a skilled human underwriter. A second approach develops statistically-based, predictive models that correlate the underwriting data to credit performance. These models assign a loan to a risk category based on an estimate of the borrower's likelihood of default. Both GSEs currently use the second approach. Exhibit 6.4 depicts the flow of information through a GSE AU system.

The loan risk categories and the appraisal produced by the AU system form the basis for the lender's underwriting decision:[11]

■ An *Accept* (LP) or *Approve* (DU) designation denotes the lowest level of risk and indicates that the relevant GSE is willing to purchase the loan with minimal documentation.

EXHIBIT 6.4 The Automated Underwriting Process

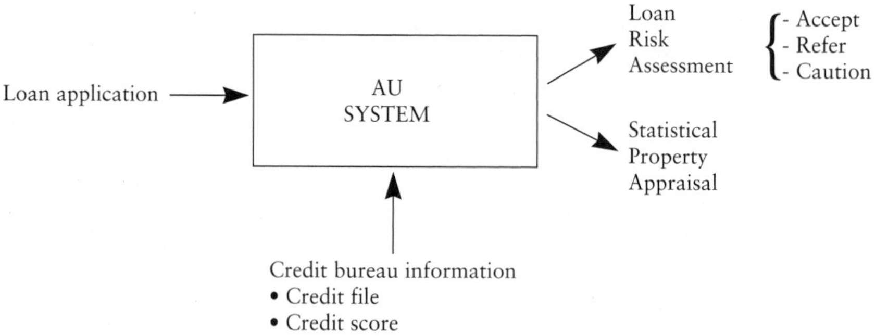

Sources: Freddie Mac and Salomon Smith Barney.

---

[11] These categories have been revised. As of November 8, Loan Prospector's **Refer** risk classification was eliminated, leaving only two classifications, **Accept** and **Caution.**

■ A *Refer* (LP and DU) designation indicates that the loan application needs to be referred to a human underwriter for further review. Based on additional information, the loan may still be acceptable to the agencies.

■ A *Caution* (LP) or *Refer with Caution* (DU) designation indicates that the application represents substantial risk and extenuating circumstances would have to be present for the loan to be acceptable for sale to the agencies.

■ For certain loans, the *statistical property appraisal* generated by the AU systems can be used in conjunction with an exterior property inspection in lieu of a full appraisal. This *streamlined appraisal* process can save from 50% to 75% of the costs associated with a standard appraisal.

Because the GSEs' AU systems are proprietary, the exact mechanism by which a loan is assigned a risk grade is not known. However, a review of publicly released AU documentation indicates that in deciding to which risk category a loan belongs, the current generation of AU systems relies most heavily on the borrower's credit information, followed by the property value and amount of down payment. The borrower's capacity is not given as much weight in the underwriting decision as previously.[12]

How Many Lenders Use AU Systems?

Automated underwriting has grown enormously in the past few years, with 1998 in particular marking an inflection point. Exhibit 6.5 illustrates this by charting the growth in the number of loans processed by Freddie Mac's Loan Prospector since its release in 1995 (estimate for 2000).

Some caveats apply to the data shown in Exhibit 6.5:

■ The loan counts may be inflated because of use of the AU system by the lender for portfolio evaluations, evaluations of nonconforming loans, and evaluations of loans that do not close;

■ A revealing statistic about AU usage is the percentage of applications approved by the typical AU system. Applications that are passed on to a human underwriter for further evaluation will not experience the same time and cost benefits as applications that are immediately accepted for purchase by the GSEs. Previously, the agencies' AU systems were only immediately approving 50% to 60% of all mortgage applications.

---

[12] "Automated Underwriting: Making Mortgage Lending Simpler and Fairer for America's Families," Freddie Mac, September 1996.

EXHIBIT 6.5 The Growth of Automated Underwriting: Loans Processed by Loan Prospector, 1995–2000

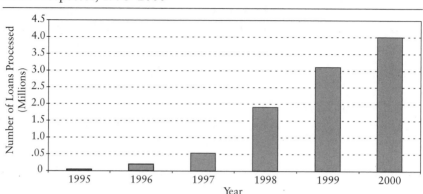

Source: Freddie Mac.

However, this number is expected to increase to as much as 80% to 90% in the newer versions of DU and LP.[13]

Regardless of the number of loans recently processed by AU systems, it seems clear that going forward, as AU systems are completely integrated into the internet (see Chapter 7), *most of the loans purchased by the GSEs will be processed through their AU systems.*

The Impact of Automated Underwriting on Loan Approval Times

AU systems significantly reduce the time spent on the loan approval process. In the sphere of underwriting decisions, these systems accept a streamlined data set of loan and borrower attributes, and can inform a lender in minutes whether the relevant GSE will accept the loan for purchase. Loans that qualify for a streamlined appraisal will experience even greater reductions in

---

[13] *The Fannie Mae Technology Review,* Fannie Mae, winter 1997; and *Freddie Mac Announces Major Enhancements to Loan Prospector,* LP/Outlook Press Release, Freddie Mac, October 13, 1998. The increase in acceptance rates arises from a better understanding by the agencies of the types of loans they are willing to purchase.

approval times. A case study done for Wells Fargo Bank by management consultant Grant Thornton LLP found the following:[14]

- The appraisal process accounts for up to 40% of the cycle time associated with loan origination; and
- The installation of an automated property valuation model can reduce the time spent on the appraisal process by as much as 60% to 80%.

It seems clear that as the use of AU systems continues to grow, a significant majority of conventional loans will be approved in a week or less.

The Impact of Automated Underwriting on Refinancing Costs

Industry sources estimate that the efficiencies introduced by automated underwriting lead to cost reductions ranging from about $300 to $1,000 per loan. These costs savings accumulate from the following sources:

- *Processing efficiencies.* AU systems streamline some of the paperwork inherent to the mortgage process, expediting underwriting decisions.
- *Reduction in personnel costs.* Decisions on most loan applications can be quickly made by the AU system, leaving human underwriters to focus on *Refer* and *Caution* applications.
- *Cost reductions in the loan approval process.* As detailed previously, AU systems save part of the costs of an appraisal and credit report.
- *Reductions in hedging costs.* Quick loan approvals reduce fallout risk and allow lenders to manage their pipelines more effectively.

At present, lenders probably do not pass all these cost savings through to borrowers. For example, lenders will probably keep the savings resulting from processing efficiencies and personnel reductions to defray the costs of their investments in technology. Thus, a savings of $300 to $500 (the typical costs associated with the appraisal and credit report, see Exhibit 6.1) from the loan approval process is probably the most a borrower can realize. As discussed, only borrowers with excellent credit who are immediately approved by AU systems will realize these savings.[15]

---

[14] *Reengineering the Loan Origination Process—An Automated Underwriting Case Study,* Dave Ross and Bruce Macurda, presentation at "Leveraging Technology to Enhance Mortgage Origination," Conference, May 18/19, 1998.

[15] For a comprehensive discussion, see *The Effect of Automated Underwriting on the Profitability of Mortgage Securitization,* Wayne Passmore and Roger Sparks, *Finance and Economics Discussion Series,* Federal Reserve Board, May 1997.

Automated Underwriting in the Government Mortgage Sector

Several AU systems underwrite government loans. They range from proprietary systems developed by individual lenders to pmiAURA, a system developed by PMI Mortgage Insurance Company, San Francisco. Only a small fraction of all government loans are underwritten using the GSEs' AU systems; recent estimates have Loan Prospector underwriting about 20% of all VA loans and about 10% of all FHA loans.[16] This lack of penetration stems from the agencies' having to customize their AU systems for FHA/VA loans and extensively test these systems with lenders. This situation will likely change rapidly in the future, mirroring the explosive growth of automated underwriting in the conventional sector. The benefits offered by AU systems in the government mortgage sector are familiar ones. Closings for government loans are quicker because of reduced paperwork and faster underwriting decisions. However, *government borrowers will not see immediate reductions in their refinancing costs*—most FHA/VA borrowers refinance through a SRP, for which an appraisal and credit report are typically not required.

---

[16] See note 3, October 23, 1998. Fannie Mae's Desktop Underwriter is being used in pilot projects with FHA lenders.

APPENDIX 6A
ENHANCED SRPs: REQUIREMENTS AND RESTRICTIONS

Eligibility Requirements	Loan Products	The loan must be a conforming FRM, ARM, or hybrid. (Balloons are allowed in some programs.)
	Borrowers	The borrowers on the new mortgage must be the same as on the original mortgage. No mortgagor may be deleted from the title. Some programs allow for the addition of a mortgagor.
	Qualifying Ratios	No qualifying ratios are required.
	Temporary Buydowns	No temporary buydowns allowed.
	P&I Increases	Increases in the borrower's monthly P&I are only allowed in the following cases: • Up to a 5% increase in P&I allowed if the borrower refinances from a 30-year ARM to a 30-year FRM. • Up to 20% increase in P&I allowed if the term decreases.
	Property Types	• One- to four-unit primary residence • One-unit second home • One- to two-unit investment property • Condominiums • PUDs • Cooperatives
Loan Size/LTV Restrictions	Maximum Loan Amount	The size of the new loan may not exceed **any** of the following: • Conventional conforming loan limits • The amount of the original loan • 105% of the unpaid balance of the existing loan (principal and interest only) if closing costs are financed. Incidental cash back to the borrower cannot exceed 1% of the new loan balance.
	Maximum LTV	The new LTV may not exceed the LTV of the original loan. (The new LTV is based on the original appraised value. If the property is a restricted type,[a] or located in a restricted market,[b] a new appraisal may be required.)
	Maximum CLTV	There is no maximum CLTV.
Documentation Requirements	Application	A new residential mortgage application (FNMA 1003/FHLMC 65) is required.
	Income/Employment	Verification of the borrower's income and employment is not required.
	Assets	Verification of the borrower's assets is not required.
	Credit Reports	A credit report is not required.
	Credit Score Policy	No credit score requirements.
	Mortgage History	A new mortgage payment history for the existing first mortgage is required. The mortgage payment history must show: • that the existing loan is current, and • no more than one 30-day late payment in the previous 12 months (or elapsed term of the mortgage if the mortgage is less than 12 months old).
	Appraisal	An appraisal is only required for: • restricted property types[a] • restricted markets • a borrower who requests cancellation of MI when the loan has amortized down to less than 80% LTV based upon the original property value.

[a] Restricted properties are three- to four-unit properties, Condominiums, and Cooperatives.
[b] Restricted markets are areas that have experienced housing price declines in prior years as determined by criteria established by the lender.
Source: Salomon Smith Barney.

CHAPTER 7

The Impact of the Internet on Prepayments

Lakhbir Hayre and Sergei Ivanov

There has been considerable speculation (and hype) about the impact that the Internet will have on the mortgage origination process, and about the resulting implications for prepayments. In this chapter we examine the current status of online mortgage originations (after defining exactly what we mean by this somewhat fuzzy term), discuss potential developments, and estimate the likely effect of online mortgage processing on prepayment behavior.

7.1 THE INTERNET IN EVERYDAY AMERICAN LIFE

Exhibit 7.1 demonstrates that over the last four years the Internet has entered the life of the vast majority of American adults. This penetration exceeds 80% for the age group most active in the real estate market (Exhibit 7.2).

The general penetration of the Internet into everyday life also applies to the mortgage sector. Exhibit 7.3 shows that the proportion of people considering using the Internet for getting a mortgage crossed the 50% mark over the past two years. Just over 50% of Americans believe that in 2005 most mortgages will be made over the Internet, and the same proportion believes that the Internet application process is easier and faster.

7.2 THE CURRENT STATUS OF ONLINE ORIGINATIONS

What can be done online now, in late 2000? Information about products and pricing is now widely available online. About 56% of home purchasers in the first half of 2000 stated that they got information about homes for

EXHIBIT 7.1   Americans Having Internet Access at Home or Work

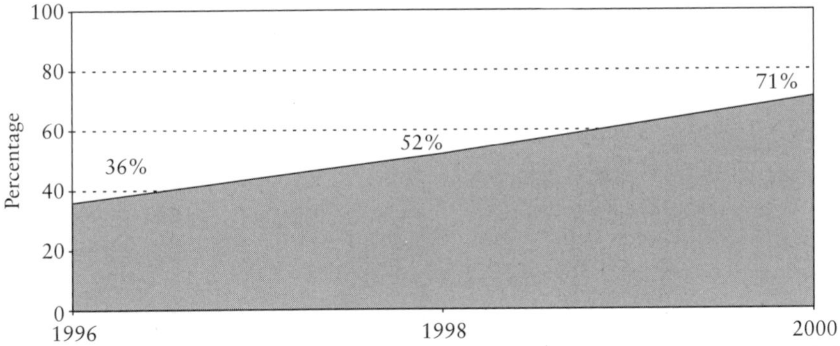

Source: Fannie Mae National Housing Survey.

sale over the Internet.[1] Prospective buyers save time and trips by learning about a neighborhood, checking available listings, looking through school reports and doing virtual tours. Sites like Realtor.com claim to have over 1.4 million listings. Although they are often incomplete, they do provide information about realtors and neighborhoods.

A significant proportion of home buyers use the Internet to educate themselves about mortgage products that are available in the market, to access mortgage calculators, and to find out more about the process. About 21% of recent purchasers said they shopped for a mortgage using the Internet, but only 4% reported that they applied for a mortgage over the Internet. Of all consumers, 77% agree that comparing rates, options, and fees is easier on the Web.

EXHIBIT 7.2   Proportion of American Adults Having Access to Internet in 2000

Age group	Access to Internet
18-24	84%
25-39	80%
40-54	81%

Source: 2000 Fannie Mae National Housing Survey.

---

[1] Data in this section is from the 2000 *Fannie Mae National Housing Survey.*

EXHIBIT 7.3 Comfort Level with Internet When Applying for a Mortgage

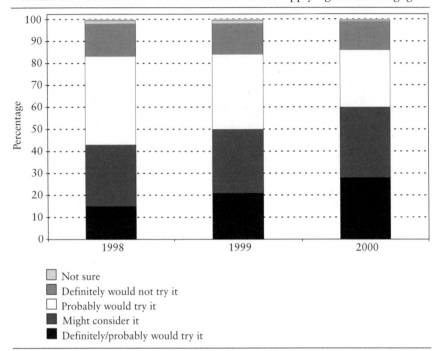

☐ Not sure
▨ Definitely would not try it
☐ Probably would try it
■ Might consider it
■ Definitely/probably would try it

Source: 2000 Fannie Mae National Housing Survey.

What Is Meant by an Online Mortgage Origination?

There is no single definition about what exactly constitutes an online mortgage origination. We will define an online mortgage as one that was processed electronically at all stages.[2] In fact, as we discuss next, this strict definition means that to date there have been almost no true online mortgage originations.

Application, Loan Approval and Settlement Stages

As described in Chapter 6, there are three stages in the mortgage origination process: *application, loan approval,* and *settlement.* The application process was relatively easy to move online, and the mortgage industry was

---

[2] Some sources define online mortgage as one for which only one stage—application—is online.

quick to start accepting online mortgage applications. This saves time for both the customer and the lender. Industry leaders like Countrywide follow up on an application with a telephone call shortly after the application submission. Others show flexibility in provisions. For instance, Priceline.com allows borrowers to design mortgage terms for purchase or refinancing and then decides within six hours whether such a loan is available.

At the time of application the lender will typically give a quote subject to verification of the application details. Some sites offer an opportunity to sign-up for automated e-mail reminders that will be sent once interest rates hit a certain trigger level (implying an enhancement of the *media effect* described in Chapter 4).

The other two stages in the mortgage origination process (loan approval and settlement) have proved more difficult to move online. Exhibit 7.4 reviews the different steps in each stage, with comments on the role of the Internet for each step.

We note that one part of the home purchase process, the home inspection, while not a mandatory part of GSE underwriting requirements, is done by many customers and lenders, but will be hard to move online. Currently, it may take up to two weeks to wait for the inspector.

As Exhibit 7.4 indicates, progress is being made on moving many parts of the process online, although some steps, such as title search and insurance, will be difficult to completely move online for many years, since the underlying information, in county recorders' offices, is often not available in electronic form. However, two developments—the recent passage of the "E-Sign" bill, and the increasing involvement of Fannie Mae and Freddie Mac—should help facilitate the move of mortgage originations online.

Electronic Signatures Become Legal

According to e-commerce experts the online mortgage industry is going to be the first to benefit from *The Electronic Signatures in Global and National Commerce Act,* signed on June 30, 2000, by President Clinton, and called the *E-Sign bill.* In general, starting October 1, 2000, the bill gave uniform nationwide legal recognition to digital signatures, and hence allowing executing transactions electronically. From March 1, 2001 (under some circumstances June 1, 2001) records of transactions may be stored electronically. Because insurance is state-regulated, the legislation made clear that it applies to title insurance as well.

This Act lifts an important legal barrier to the paperless mortgage origination future. It allows participants in the mortgage origination process to sign, exchange and store documents electronically. Once the technology is implemented it will significantly reduce time and increase the accuracy of

EXHIBIT 7.4 Likely Impact of the Internet on the Steps in a Mortgage Origination

Processing step		Likely impact of the Internet on the process
Application		One of the easiest parts of the origination to move online. Many lenders already have it on their websites. Electronic applications are likely to become the norm.
Loan Approval	Appraisal	GSEs already waive full appraisal in certain cases. Databases and automated or drive-by appraisals will be used more to verify that there is no major damage since previous appraisal. Hand-held devices, digital cameras, computer maps and e-mail reduce time and cost versus full appraisals.
	Credit Report + Information Verification	GSEs' automated underwriting (AU) systems have been linked to credit agencies. Credit check will be instant and at a lower cost.
	Document Preparation	Electronic processing will likely be used to streamline preparation of documents for closing (the mortgage, note, and truth-in-lending statement).
	Flood Certification	Many flood zone maps are already available electronically and most certifications are automatic now. Cost will gradually decrease.
	Origination	Origination costs and points should decrease as the process will be automated and connected to GSE systems
	Survey	Measurements of land will be put in electronic form, surveyors will only update records for improvements. Old references to known points and dimensions will be already on file.
	Tax Service	Fees for monitoring and timely payments of the borrower's property taxes and for preventing tax liens from occurring will decrease as services become further automated.
	Underwriting	As AU systems develop further these costs should fall
Settlement (escrow)	Attorney/Escrow Agent	"Closing" work of this third party[1] will change from handling paperwork to coordinating and securing the electronic process. Fees are likely to fall while accuracy and productivity should increase.
	Notary	Electronic attesting and certification of documents will cost less. New laws lift all paper stamp and seal requirements.
	Title Search and Title Insurance	Automation is proceeding along two paths. First, search bureaus are creating electronic databases for searches done in the past or duplicating official records; search from that time relies on new electronic records. Second, many county recorders' offices are converting paper and microfiche documents into digital form and use electronic records going forward. Once the information is available on-line (which in some parts of the US could be many years from now), the process will take from minutes to few hours, instead of the current 3-5 days.
	Recording Fees	As recorders' offices go online fees should go down as speed and accuracy increases
	Courier fee	Cost of an electronic transmission will be almost zero

[1] Can be either an escrow company, an attorney or a title company depending on state.
Source: Salomon Smith Barney.

mortgage processing. The signature is going to be either a password, a special card or a 3½ inch diskette that will have the digital signature on it.

Fannie Mae and Freddie Mac Internet Initiatives

Fannie Mae has launched a pilot project to buy 100 mortgages online, and Freddie Mac has recently started a similar program. Only a handful of transactions have been done so far.[3] "Online" in this case means the GSE gets the note in electronic, not paper, form.

---

[3] Four as of October 16, 2000, according to *National Mortgage News*.

As these pilot programs are not completed it is hard to guess when the process will be fully standardized, but the GSEs are taking the initiative. In October 2000, Fannie Mae released "Electronic Mortgage Guidelines," which selected XHTML (a combination of Extensible Markup and Hypertext Markup Languages) as the language for open data format for documents to be delivered to Fannie Mae. The GSE also required that an e-mortgage note contain clauses that the borrower has agreed to the electronic transaction and that requirements of the Electronic Signatures Act (discussed previously) are met. Fannie Mae stated it is developing its own platform that will have electronic databases for electronic appraisals, title insurance, flood insurance, and mortgage insurance.

Freddie Mac transferred its *Loan Prospector Automated Underwriting System* online in January 2000. All major credit repositories (Equifax, Experian, and Trans Union) agreed to exchange information electronically with the system. Loan Prospector on the Internet is affordable. Mortgage brokers pay only $20 to evaluate each conventional, FHA, or VA loan.[4] Lenders pay similar fees.

In a further move to help transfer the origination process online, Freddie Mac enhanced Loan Prospector with an option in certain cases to forego the time consuming appraisal process. Among the requirements are an LTV of 80% or less and the loan being a first-lien purchase mortgage. The cost of using the feature is $200, which is well below an estimated national average cost of $334 for an appraisal.[5]

The involvement of the GSEs will undoubtedly be a significant catalyst for moving online the steps of the origination process that involve the GSEs. However, it may be a while before borrowers see the benefits. For example, despite the low cost of using the automated systems, mortgage borrowers still typically pay several hundred dollars in underwriting fees.

Obstacles to Completely Online Mortgage Originations

As Exhibit 7.4 indicates, there are many independent participants involved in the various stages in originating a mortgage. Each one has its own priorities and strategies. The decentralized nature of the process means that there is no coordinated effort within the industry to move the whole origination process online. Challenges to moving the whole mortgage origination process online include the following:

---

[4] This initial loan evaluation fee includes up to 15 resubmissions and the assignment of loan data and feedback to one wholesaler.
[5] The estimate of $334 is from press release "Freddie Mac Enhances Loan Prospector Tools," October 25, 2000.

- Many borrowers are wary of using the Internet when hundreds of thousands of dollars are at stake. Some will just refuse to obtain a mortgage online.
- Electronic databases have to be created for title searches and records keeping.
- Income information such as tax-return copies and pay stubs is difficult to verify online.
- Many steps that involve physical contact with the property, such as appraisals or home inspections, will be difficult to completely move online (although, as discussed earlier, for borrowers with good credit the GSEs may waive an appraisal or use home price databases in place of, or as a supplement to, a full physical appraisal).

Perhaps the major challenge of online mortgage originations is the coordination and development of multiple pieces of compatible software for all parties in the mortgage processing. Any online software needs to be able to communicate with other parties in the process, and no standards exist at the moment. The Mortgage Bankers Association (MBA) did become involved to help standardize XML (extensible Markup Language), to allow easy information sharing within the mortgage industry. Freddie Mac got involved in developing the XML interface for its Loan Prospector Automatic Underwriting system. As noted above, Fannie Mae selected XHTML (combination of Extensible Markup and Hypertext Markup Languages) as the language for open data format for documents to be delivered to Fannie Mae. However, there is still no single coordinated effort on software development and standardization; such an effort would provide a tremendous boost to online mortgage originations.

First Completely Online Mortgage Origination   The hurdles described above explain why the first completely online mortgage origination took place only recently, on July 24, 2000, in Broward County, Florida. A $140,000 house was sold by Arvida Homebuilders to Mr. Jose Ignacio Arroyo who electronically executed the promissory note and mortgage. Mr. Arroyo's loan closing took less than three hours and he says he saved about $200.

The processing of the mortgage was paperless, used electronic documentation and a variety of proprietary technologies for its processing. Remarkably, title search and insurance was done electronically as well. Fannie Mae purchased this mortgage and the time to bring it to the secondary market was reduced to less than 5 hours versus the average of 45 days. However, this is only a pilot project for Fannie Mae and the electronic documentation was duplicated on paper. Potential cost savings may be several hundred dollars, but it is not clear how much of the savings will be passed on to consumers.

In summary, although the definitions of online mortgage used by many industry sources vary and it is difficult to give an accurate forecast, a Forrester Research estimate that was widely publicized projects 10% of mortgages to be online by 2003. This number gives some idea of where the industry is headed; namely, slow but gradual progress toward online mortgage originations.

7.3 IMPACT ON MORTGAGE ORIGINATION COSTS

The challenges of building the online mortgage-processing network imply that cost reductions are likely to occur in steps. What costs reductions can borrowers expect, and in what parts of the mortgage origination process?

An early estimate by a software vendor in the Freddie Mac publication *Secondary Mortgage Markets,* is shown in Exhibit 7.5. It was projected that the cost of obtaining a $100,000 mortgage may *eventually* go down 70% from $3,000 to $900. The key word here is eventually—apart from the application process, it is fair to say that most borrowers have not yet seen the benefits of the Web translated into lower closing costs. This may be partly because cost savings to the lender have not yet been passed onto the borrower. However, it is also probably true that, like other areas where the Internet is changing much how business is done, there was much hype and the immediate impact on consumers was greatly over-estimated.

In Exhibit 7.6, we show estimates, based on discussions with industry sources, of the cost to the lender of each part of the origination process once it has been moved online, along with an estimate of the cost to the borrower. Also shown are current estimated industry averages for a traditional origination, and quoted costs from a popular online mortgage web site.

It has to emphasized that the projected cost savings for completely online mortgage originations are very speculative, may take many years to realize, and may in many cases not be passed through to borrowers. Furthermore, these drops in cost and time are going to affect the customers with the best credit first (who would be the most likely to refinance anyway).

It is tempting to use current costs charged by some Internet services as a proxy of prices expected in the future. But this would be a mistake, for two reasons.

First, many Internet firms sell loans below their cost. This consideration, along with other market realities that equity investors seem to be finally

EXHIBIT 7.5 An Early Estimate for Reductions in Cost and Time

	Current Average	Final	Total Savings
Total cost	$3,000	$900	70%
Time required	4-5 weeks	1 week	78%

Source: Secondary Mortgage Markets, April 1999, Freddie Mac.

EXHIBIT 7.6   Estimates of Closing Costs for a $100,000 Mortgage

	Current Industry Estimates for Traditional Origination	Projected Eventual Cost to Lender if Completely Online	Projected Eventual Cost to Borrower if Completely Online	Current Quote from a Popular Mortgage Web Site
Application	$225 (*)	$25	$50	-
Appraisal	$334	$100	$200	$325
Credit Report	$50	$20	$25	-
Document preparation	$175	$0	$0	$30
Flood Certification	$25	$10	$15	-
Origination	$1,000 (One Point)	$175	$175	$892
Survey	$125 (*)	-	-	-
Tax service	$75	$30	$45	-
Underwriting	$175	$100	$150	-
Attorney/Escrow agent	$500	$225	$300	$325
Notary	$75	$35	$50	$75
Title search insurance	$400	$100	$300	$406
Recording fee		$15	$25	$65
Reconveyance fee	-	-	-	$50
Net fees excluding government fees	$2809[1]	$935	$1305	$2,153

*Often waived

[1]We assume that the application and survey fees have been waived.

Source: Salomon Smith Barney.

EXHIBIT 7.7   E-Loan Stock Price History

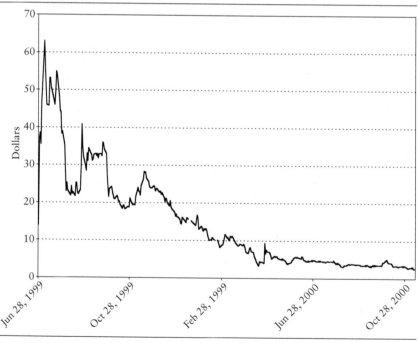

Source: Salomon Smith Barney.

taking into account likely explains most of the sharp drops in the stock prices of most online mortgage lenders. As Exhibit 7.7 indicates, many are trading at less than 10% of their highs in 1999.

Second, nobody operates a mass online mortgage processing operation yet. Therefore the costs (see Exhibit 7.6 for current pricing available on the Internet) in the current competitive environment are more reflective of the willingness to acquire an online customer rather than of the efficiencies of the online processing economics. The actual loss per such loan could be as much as several thousand dollars.[6]

7.4 THE POTENTIAL IMPACT ON PREPAYMENTS

For MBS investors, the bottom line question is what impact online mortgage originations will have on prepayments. Assuming that online mortgage lending lives up to its promise, and with the caveat that it will most likely be several years before we see the full impact, we foresee three major impacts:

- Lower closing costs, and a resulting "elbow shift";
- Reduction in friction and an enhanced media effect;
- A "Follow-On Effect," leading to more refinancings and greater negative convexity for pools with higher proportions of online mortgages.

Lower Closing Costs

While there is much uncertainty about the degree and timing of cost reductions for borrowers, it seems almost certain that the Internet will lead to lower closing costs for mortgage borrowers. This means an increase in the refinancing incentive, which can be thought of as a shift in the "refinancing elbow." For example, assuming that cost savings will be passed on to customers, total mortgage costs may decrease by 1% for a $100,000 mortgage over the next several years (see Exhibit 7.6). This saving is roughly equivalent to a 20bp to 25bp (basis points) reduction in the coupon rate, or shifting the elbow by 20bp to 25bp.

An Enhanced Media Effect

The media effect will be enhanced by the use of e-mail, with potential refinancers receiving e-mail notification when mortgage rates drop below a

---

[6] The August 2000 issue of *Mortgage Banking* estimates the cost to E-Loan to acquire a customer is $4,000 to $6,000.

specified trigger level. Lower transaction costs may stimulate more frequent refinancings, after smaller interest rate moves. However, some studies show that Internet users tend to be better educated than average, suggesting that the borrowers most affected are the ones most likely to refinance anyway. In other words, there may be a "preaching to the choir" effect, so that the actual impact on refinancing rates may be marginal.

The Follow-On Effect

Borrowers who obtained their mortgage online may be more likely to subsequently refinance their loan. They will have had experience of a faster and less document-intensive online process, and are likely to obtain future mortgages online as well. We will label this tendency to repeatedly refinance online, resulting from familiarity with the electronic process, the "Follow-On Effect." Thus pools where a significant proportion of the mortgages borrowed their loans online will be more negatively convex and hence less desirable from the investors point of view.

CONCLUSIONS

Although its impact has been overstated, there is no doubt that the Internet is having a profound effect on the mortgage origination process. The proportion of mortgages that are originated completely online is likely to remain small, but the Internet is leading to a gradual if slow decline in origination costs, some of which will be passed through to borrowers. In addition and perhaps just as important, the Internet has the potential to significantly reduce the friction, or the hassle factor, in the origination process. In this sense, the impact of the Internet will not be anything novel, but rather, it will sustain the trend towards lower costs and more efficient refinancing behavior seen in the mortgage market over the last decade.

Collateral Sectors

Ginnie Mae Prepayment Behavior

Lakhbir Hayre, Robert Young, and Vera Chen

What factors drive Ginnie Mae prepayment behavior? In this chapter, we discuss what we perceive to be the major influences on Ginnie Mae speeds: *regulatory changes,* the *streamline refinancing program,* the *demographics* of borrowers, *buyout activities,* and *geographical differences in market share and housing activity* for Ginnie Maes and conventionals.[1] This explanatory framework is then used to explain differences in Ginnie Mae and conventional prepayments, and to discern likely future trends in these differences.

Exhibit 8.1 shows ratios of recent Ginnie Mae to Fannie Mae CPRs for a range of coupons and origination years, and provides a focal point for our analysis. We can identify the following trends in these ratios:

- Brand new Ginnie Mae discounts generally prepay slower than corresponding conventionals as Ginnies tend to season slower than conventionals initially.
- Similarly, brand new Ginnie Mae premiums are also slower than corresponding conventionals.
- Slightly seasoned discounts tend to prepay at roughly the same rate as conventionals, but as seasoning increases, Ginnies generally become faster than conventionals, especially seasoned originations from around 1993.
- Cuspy (low premium) Ginnie Maes that are not brand new prepay on average faster than corresponding conventionals, but in a refinancing wave Ginnie premium speeds tend to be lower than conventionals.

---

[1] This chapter updates and expands an earlier paper *Ginnie Mae Prepayment Behavior,* Lakhbir Hayre and Sharad Chaudhary, September 1997, Salomon Brothers Inc.

EXHIBIT 8.1   Ratios of Ginnie Mae to Fannie Mae CPRs for Selected Coupons, October 2000

		1-YR.	6-MO	Jun	Jul	Aug	Sep	Oct
6.0	1999	0.83	0.86	0.83	0.87	0.78	0.94	0.91
6.0	1998	0.83	0.86	0.78	0.79	0.86	0.89	0.95
6.0	1993	1.13	1.13	0.99	1.02	1.27	1.17	1.21
6.5	1999	0.92	0.94	0.87	0.89	1.02	1.02	1.06
6.5	1998	0.91	0.94	0.93	0.92	0.95	0.96	1.00
6.5	1997	0.89	0.92	0.94	0.83	0.99	1.01	0.92
6.5	1996	1.07	1.12	1.08	1.16	1.13	1.14	1.10
6.5	1994	1.16	1.20	1.21	1.21	1.24	1.22	1.11
6.5	1993	1.15	1.16	1.05	1.10	1.15	1.23	1.18
7.0	2000	-	0.57	0.36	0.65	0.80	0.67	0.85
7.0	1999	1.07	1.05	1.00	1.06	1.08	1.03	1.05
7.0	1998	0.91	0.92	0.93	0.89	0.95	0.92	0.94
7.0	1997	0.96	0.97	1.02	0.99	0.93	0.93	0.98
7.0	1996	1.07	1.11	1.13	1.13	1.09	1.09	1.04
7.0	1995	0.98	1.02	0.97	1.02	1.12	1.00	0.97
7.0	1994	1.04	1.03	1.03	0.99	0.95	1.05	1.16
7.0	1993	1.12	1.14	1.14	1.08	1.13	1.18	1.12
7.0	1992	1.14	1.13	1.01	1.29	1.13	1.08	1.12
7.5	2000	-	0.66	0.56	0.72	0.72	0.65	0.64
7.5	1999	0.80	0.86	0.68	0.74	0.97	0.81	1.11
7.5	1998	0.98	0.96	1.17	0.78	0.99	0.92	1.11
7.5	1997	1.00	1.02	0.98	0.98	1.01	1.09	1.08
7.5	1996	1.01	1.01	0.99	0.99	1.03	1.04	1.03
7.5	1995	0.98	0.98	0.96	1.03	1.01	1.02	0.92
7.5	1994	1.08	1.06	1.07	1.04	1.12	0.99	1.09
7.5	1993	1.11	1.09	1.08	1.10	1.10	1.14	1.07
7.5	1992	1.14	1.14	1.05	1.11	1.16	1.36	1.12
7.5	1987	0.95	0.91	1.01	1.20	0.90	0.87	1.07
8.0	2000	-	0.60	0.42	0.44	0.61	0.66	0.78
8.0	1999	0.61	0.87	0.76	0.69	0.71	1.05	1.20
8.0	1998	1.02	1.36	0.94	0.92	1.14	1.40	3.22
8.0	1997	1.13	1.15	1.10	0.97	1.09	1.21	1.53
8.0	1996	1.12	1.13	1.06	1.08	1.15	1.22	1.32
8.0	1995	1.03	1.06	1.01	0.98	1.03	1.15	1.29
8.0	1994	1.03	1.10	0.94	1.05	1.19	1.18	1.30
8.0	1993	1.04	1.04	1.01	1.05	1.16	0.92	1.08
8.0	1992	1.13	1.18	0.96	1.14	1.22	1.31	1.36
8.0	1987	0.96	0.93	0.82	0.99	0.85	1.01	1.02
8.5	2000	-	0.46	0.35	0.44	0.46	0.59	0.64
8.5	1999	0.86	1.19	0.88	1.68	1.20	1.32	1.46
8.5	1997	1.24	1.21	1.34	1.48	1.20	1.16	1.34
8.5	1996	1.23	1.11	1.05	1.45	1.16	1.04	1.17
8.5	1995	1.04	1.05	0.99	1.38	1.27	0.80	1.17
8.5	1994	1.10	1.14	1.10	1.63	1.33	0.92	1.12
8.5	1992	1.17	1.13	1.12	1.40	1.11	1.04	1.17
8.5	1991	1.10	1.13	1.17	1.36	1.02	1.19	1.09
8.5	1987	1.08	1.15	1.24	1.42	1.34	0.91	1.04
9.0	2000	-	0.47	0.35	0.41	0.48	0.50	0.59
9.0	1995	1.04	1.02	1.07	0.95	1.09	1.12	0.98
9.0	1991	1.03	1.01	1.09	1.00	0.98	1.12	0.98
9.0	1989	0.97	0.98	1.14	1.09	1.07	0.88	0.90
9.0	1987	1.00	0.96	0.93	0.96	0.82	1.04	1.05
9.0	1986	1.02	1.08	1.07	1.09	1.15	1.13	1.02
9.5	1990	0.95	0.96	0.97	1.02	1.10	1.03	0.89
9.5	1987	0.94	0.97	1.08	1.07	0.99	0.90	0.95
9.5	1986	0.98	1.02	1.13	1.00	0.90	1.14	1.03
9.5	ALL	0.96	0.98	1.02	0.98	0.96	1.04	0.92
10.0	1988	1.01	1.09	0.99	1.24	0.98	1.21	1.23
10.0	ALL	0.96	0.97	0.93	1.06	0.95	0.98	0.87
10.5	ALL	0.96	0.97	1.06	1.15	0.83	0.91	0.75
11.0	ALL	0.89	0.98	0.89	0.84	1.15	1.01	0.98

Source: Salomon Smith Barney.

■ Higher premiums (which tend to be more seasoned) are prepaying at roughly the same rate as conventionals.

8.1 REGULATORY AND DEMOGRAPHIC FACTORS

Various changes in the FHA/VA programs over the years have had an impact on Ginnie Mae issuance and prepayments. Exhibit 8.2 lists the most significant

EXHIBIT 8.2 Selected FHA/VA Regulatory and Policy Changes and Estimated Effect

Date	Action	Estimated Effect
1/88	FHA loan ceiling increased from $90,000 to $101,250.	Increase in pool of potential borrowers.
3/88	VA requires (1) 50bp +$300 fee and (2) credit check for assumptions.	Reduce assumptions and hence increase speeds for discounts.
12/89	Investors barred from assuming an FHA loan and credit check required.	Reduce assumptions and hence increase speeds for discounts.
1/91	FHA loan ceiling increased from $101,250 to $124,875.	Increase in pool of potential borrowers.
7/91	(a) Percent of closing costs that can be financed limited to 57%. (b) MIP of 50bp for a period based on LTV. (c) Up-front premium to be gradually reduced from 3.8% to 2.25%.	Reduce FHA volume and reduce speeds on both discounts and premiums. Incentive for mortgagors paying the MIP to refinance.
5/92	Streamlined refinancings of mortgages closed before 7/91 not subject to 50bp annual premium.	Higher refinancings for pre-July 1991 premiums.
9/92	Effective on 9/30/1992, the FHA loan ceiling is the lesser of 75% of the FHLMC limit or 95% of the regional median home sale price. As a result, FHA loan ceiling increased to 151,725.	Increase in pool of potential borrowers.
10/92	57% limit on closing costs rescinded.	Increase in FHA volume and Ginnie Mae speeds.
1/94	a)FHA loan ceiling increased to $152,362. b)VA letter urging refinancings sent out.	Marginal increase in pool of potential borrowers. Increase in refinancings of premiums.
2/95	FHA underwriting guidelines revised to make more low- and moderate-income households eligible for the program.	Increase in pool of potential borrowers.
8/95	Reforms introduced to simplify and streamline processing for FHA lenders.	Increase number of FHA lenders and therefore pool of potential borrowers.
1/96	FHA loan ceiling increased to $155,250.	Marginal increase in pool of potential borrowers.
2/96	FHA mortgage insurance program streamlined for FHA lenders.	FHA lenders have greater flexibility leading to expanded home ownership opportunities.
6/96	FHA up-front MIP cut for first-time home buyers who receive housing counseling from 2.25% to 2%.	Increase in pool of potential borrowers.
1/97	FHA loan ceiling increased from $155,250 to $160,950.	Marginal increase in pool of potential borrowers.
6/97	a)FHA up-front MIP cut for first-time home buyers who receive housing counseling from 2% to 1.75%. b)Ginnie Mae urban lending incentives expanded.	Increase in pool of potential borrowers.
7/97	FHA up-front MIP cut for first-time buyers in central cities from 1.75% to 1.5%.	Increase in pool of potential borrowers.
1/98	FHA loan ceiling increased to $170,362.	Increase in pool of potential borrowers.
3/98	FHA approved Freddie Mac's Loan Prospector (LP) for use on FHA insured mortgages	Streamline the approval process, and potentially expand the pool of borrowers (especially among weaker credit borrowers).
10/98	a)Effective on 9/30/1998, the FHA loan ceiling is the lesser of 87% of the FHLMC limit or 95% of the regional median home sale price. b)Effective immediately, FHA loan ceiling increased to $197,621.	Increase in pool of potential borrowers.
1/99	FHA loan ceiling increased to $208,800.	Increase in pool of potential borrowers.
8/99	FHA approved Fannie Mae's Desktop Underwriter and PMI's pmiAURA Systems for use on FHA insured mortgages.	Streamline the approval process, and potentially expand the pool of borrowers (especially among weaker credit borrowers).
1/00	FHA loan ceiling increased to $219,849.	Increase in pool of potential borrowers.

MIP: Mortgage insurance premium.
Source: HUD, VA, and Salomon Smith Barney.

EXHIBIT 8.3 FHA Upfront and Annual MIP Rates[a]

	Mortgage Term More Than 15 Years		Mortgage Term 15 Years or Less	
LTV	Up-front MIP	Annual Premium/Term	Up-front MIP	Annual Premium/Term
89.99 and Under	2.25%	0.50%/7 Yrs.	2.00%	None
90.00-95.00	2.25	0.50%/12 Yrs	2.00	0.25%/4 Yrs.
95.00 and Over	2.25	0.50%/30 Yrs	2.00	0.25%/8 Yrs

[a] Streamline refinances of mortgages closed before July 1, 1991, are not subject to the 50bp annual premium but are subject to up-front MIPs of (i) 3.8% for mortgages with terms greater than 15 years, and (ii) 2.4% for mortgages with terms less than or equal to 15 years. Purchase money mortgages where the first-time home buyer received housing counseling are subject to an up-front premium of 1.75%. The MIP rates for streamline refinancers are the same as for the mortgages in this category.
Source: Salomon Smith Barney.

regulatory and policy changes in the Ginnie Mae sector along with an estimate of their likely impact.

Although some of the changes listed in Exhibit 8.2 explain past patterns seen in Ginnie Mae speeds,[2] the changes of the past few years have not had a significant effect on prepayment behavior. Two changes that occurred prior to 1992 continue to have some relevance for current speeds, however.

First, *the fees and qualification requirements imposed in 1988 and 1989 for assumptions reduce the value of the assumability option,* so that speeds on Ginnie Maes between 50bp (basis points) to 150bp below current coupon are faster relative to conventionals than in the past. Recent strong home appreciation rates have further reduced the value of the assumability option. Second, as we discuss next, mortgage insurance premium (MIP) fees may play a role in influencing refinancing behavior.

FHA MIP Fees

Exhibit 8.3 summarizes the two types of MIP fees that an FHA borrower paid on a loan closing prior to January 1, 2001 (the next section discusses new FHA MIP fees). The first is an up-front fee, equal to 2.25% of the loan amount for most borrowers (fees are lower for 15-year borrowers and first-time buyers, see Exhibit 8.3). The second is a 50bp per annum fee, which effectively increases the WAC by 50bp.

---

[2] For example, the July 1991 limitation of 57% on the percentage of closing costs that could be financed, the subsequent rescinding of the limitation in October 1992, and the May 1992 exemption of streamlined refinancings from the 50bp annual premium likely explain the slow GNMA speeds in the refinancing waves of 1991 and 1992, and their very fast speeds in 1993 and early 1994.

EXHIBIT 8.4 Refund of Up-Front MIP Fee

Number of months insurance has been in force	Percentage of up-front fee to be refunded
6	95%
12	90
24	80
36	60
48	39
60	22
72	8
84	0

Sources: HUD and Salomon Brothers Inc.

There are certain exemptions from the 50bp fee:

- Loans that were taken out prior to July 1, 1991 can be refinanced under the *Streamline Refinancing Program* without paying the 50bp fee.
- 15-year loans with a loan-to-value (LTV) ratio below 90% are exempt from the 50bp fee.

Note that 30-year loans are not exempt from the fee (unless they were originated before July 1, 1991) regardless of the LTV. If a loan is refinanced, the mortgagor is entitled to a refund of the "unused" portion of the up-front fee. HUD regulations state that the FHA Commissioner will determine the amount to refund after reviewing the annual audit of FHA's Mortgage Insurance Fund, but Exhibit 8.4 gives recent representative percentages that will be refunded.

We can assume that the up-front fee provides a *disincentive* to refinance into another FHA loan, since the fraction of the original fee that is refunded declines much faster than the mortgage amortizes, so that the refund will not cover the up-front fee that has to be paid on the new loan.[3]

The 50bp per annum fee, even though it effectively means a higher WAC, provides an *incentive* to refinance only if the new loan will not have the fee. This will be the case if the home price has increased to the point where the borrower can (and is willing to) refinance into a 15-year FHA loan, or into a conventional loan with an LTV below 80% (so that no private mortgage insurance is needed).

---

[3] In particular, this applies to first-time home buyers who paid a reduced up-front MIP, and will have to pay the full up-front fee when they refinance (see Exhibit 8.3).

EXHIBIT 8.5 FHA Up-Front and Annual MIP Rates for Mortgages Closed on or after January 1, 2001

LTV	Mortgage Term More Than 15 Years		Mortgage Term 15 Years or Less	
	Up-front MIP	Annual Premium[a]	Up-front MIP	Annual Premium[b]
89.99 and Under	1.50%	0.50%.	1.50%	None
90.00-95.00	1.50	0.50%	1.50	0.25%
95.00 and Over	1.50	0.50%	1.50	0.25%

[a] The annual MIP will be cancelled once the LTV reaches 78% (through amortization only) provided that it has been paid for at least 5 years.
[b] The annual MIP will be cancelled once the LTV reaches 78% (through amortization only).
Source: Salomon Smith Barney.

New FHA MIP Fees

A new fee structure for FHA loans was announced by HUD in October 2000. Exhibit 8.5 summarizes the new MIP rates that an FHA borrower will pay for loans closed on or after January 1, 2001. The up-front MIP fee is reduced to 1.50% of the loan amount from 2.25% on mortgages with terms of more than 15 years and 2.00% on those with terms equal to or less than 15 years. The annual MIP rates are unchanged, remaining at 50bp per annum on loans with terms longer than 15 years and 25bp on those with terms of 15 years or less. In the new policy, the annual MIP fee will be cancelled when the LTV reaches 78%, provided that it has been paid for at least 5 years on 30-year loans. However, this cancellation will occur through **amortization only** (including partial prepayments) as no new appraisal value is allowed. Also, the refund schedule in Exhibit 8.4 is being shortened from being over a period of seven years to five years.[4]

For a 30-year loan with an initial LTV of 95%, it will take more than 10 years for the LTV to drop below 78% through amortization alone (i.e., if we do not factor in increases in home prices). Hence the cancellation provision for the annual MIP fee will have little practical impact on Ginnie Mae prepayments. However, the lower up-front fee may provide a minor boost to Ginnie Mae prepayment speeds and issuance volume.

The FHA Streamline Refinancing Program

Almost all discussions of Ginnie Mae speeds nowadays sooner or later mention the streamline refinancing program (SRP). What is this program, and why is it important?

---

[4] The old, more generous 7-year refund schedule will continue to apply to loans closed prior to January 1, 2001.

The streamline program is important because the majority of Ginnie Mae refinancings in recent years have occurred through the SRP. The purpose of the SRP is "to lower monthly principal and interest payments on a current FHA-insured mortgage," and the main features of the program are the following:

- HUD does **not** require verification of income or employment, or a credit check.[5] However, the mortgage must be current.
- The lender is allowed to charge other typical closing costs, such as application fees, attorney's fees, points, and so on.
- The refinancing must involve no cash back to the borrower, except for minor adjustments at closing not exceeding $250.
- The refinancing may be done with or without an appraisal.
- **If there is no appraisal,** closing costs **cannot** be financed, and the balance on the new loan is limited to the unpaid principal balance, less any MIP refund, plus the new up-front MIP.
- Streamline refinancings **with an appraisal** allow the inclusion of closing costs (including *reasonable* points) into the new loan balance, subject to LTV limits. Although the calculation of the LTV limit is a little convoluted, in essence the goal is to ensure that the new LTV does not exceed the 95% to 97.75% range.
- *No-cost* refinancings, in which the lender charges a premium rate in return for paying the borrower's closing costs, **are permitted.** Hence, if rates have fallen by a sufficient amount, this provision allows a refinancing to be done without an appraisal, and without the mortgagor having to pay closing costs out-of-pocket.
- A 30-year loan on a principal residence can be refinanced into a shorter term mortgage provided the monthly payment does not increase by more than $50.
- An ARM may be refinanced into a fixed-rate loan provided that the note rate on the new loan is no greater than 200bp above the current rate on the ARM. Conversely, a fixed-rate loan can be refinanced into an ARM provided that the ARM rate is at least 200bp below that on the existing loan.

To sum up, the main benefit of the SRP is that it does not require some of the paperwork necessary with a standard refinancing, which may mean reduced closing costs. The rules governing the financing of closing costs and

---

[5] The lender may be required by law or banking regulations or its investors to obtain such checks. In such a case, the costs for these checks must be paid by the borrower out-of-pocket (i.e., not financed).

EXHIBIT 8.6 VA Loan Guaranty Entitlement

Loan Size	Guaranty Percent	Up to Maximum Amount*
< $45,000	50%	
$45,001 - $56,250	40-50%	$22,500
$56,251 - $144,000	40%	$36,000
$144,001	25%	$50,750
Manufactured Home or Lot	40%	$20,000

*For a loan between $56,251 and $144,000, the entitlement is 40% or $36,000, whichever is less.
Source: 2000 Federal Benefits for Veterans.

LTVs play a part in the refinancing patterns observed for new cuspy Ginnie Mae premiums, as we will discuss later in this chapter.

Features of the VA Home Loan Program

Veterans Administration (VA) loans comprise roughly 30% of the loans in Ginnie Mae pools, the remainder being FHA loans.[6] There are a number of differences in the procedures governing FHA and VA loan origination and refinancing, and we provide an overview of the salient features of the VA home loan program.

The purpose of the VA home loan program is to help veterans finance the purchase of their homes with favorable loan terms and at a competitive rate of interest. This is achieved by guaranteeing the lender against loss of a portion of the mortgage loan. The dollar amount of this guarantee (also termed an entitlement) depends on the size of the mortgage loan. Exhibit 8.6 summarizes the various entitlements.

Key features of the program include:

- Most lenders require that a combination of the guaranty entitlement and any cash down payment equal at least 25% of the value of the property. Given the current schedule of entitlements (Exhibit 8.6), no down payment is required in most cases, and the value of the loan can be 100% of the property value up to a maximum of $203,000. (This maximum is not an official limit and is usually imposed by lenders because of secondary market requirements.)
- VA mortgages are assumable, subject to VA approval of the assumer's credit.
- No annual MIP.

---

[6] Actually, there is a small third category of loans insured by the Rural Housing Service.

- "No-cost" and "no-point" loans are allowed.
- No commission or brokerage fees may be charged for obtaining a VA loan.
- No streamline refinance program exists for VAs, and loans are processed on a "prior approval" or "automatic" basis. The primary difference between the two methods is that "automatic" originations or refinancings are quicker because in this case the lender has the authority to make a credit decision on the loan without the VA's approval.
- A VA Funding Fee (VAFF), which depends on the LTV of the loan, is payable at the time of loan closing for purchase loans. VAFFs are also charged for refinancing a VA loan. Exhibit 8.7 lists typical funding fees for a variety of VA loans.
- Lenders can charge all the other typical costs associated with originating a loan. All funding fees may be added to the loan provided that the financing of the fee does not result in a loan amount above the maximum $203,000. Closing costs and origination charges may *not* be included in a purchase loan, only in a refinancing.

Refinancing a VA Loan   There are essentially two types of refinancing available under the VA loan program:

1. *Regular refinancing.* Refinancing a non-VA mortgage into a VA loan, or "cash-out" refinances of existing VA mortgages, are examples of such refinancings. In a regular refinance, existing mortgage loans can be refinanced into a VA loan with a maximum LTV of 90%. In addition, a VAFF of 2% of the loan amount may also be financed. As long as the LTV limit is not exceeded, the loan amount may also include closing

EXHIBIT 8.7 Funding Fee Table

Loan Type	Active Duty or Veteran	National Guard/ Reservists
Purchase/Construction		
LTV		
100%	2.00%	2.75%
90-95%	1.50	2.25
90% and Under	1.25	2.00
Regular Finance	2.00	2.75
Rate Reduction Finance	0.50	0.50
Assumptions	0.50	0.50

Source: 2000 Federal Benefits for Veterans.

costs, "reasonable" points, and so on. Regular refinances require a VA credit check and an appraisal.

2. *Interest-rate reduction* refinances are for the primary purpose of obtaining a lower rate and do not require a credit check or appraisal. The new loan amount can be at most the old loan amount plus closing costs (including points), a VAFF of 0.5%, and up to $6,000 in energy efficient improvements.

In general, the costs associated with originating and refinancing a VA loan seem a little lower than for a comparable FHA loan.

Demographics of Ginnie Mae and Conventional Borrowers

Exhibits 8.8 and 8.9 summarize some relevant demographic information for Ginnie Mae and conventional borrowers. Exhibit 8.8 shows that although average loan sizes have been increasing over the years, the ratio of FHA and VA to conventional loan sizes has remained relatively constant.

Exhibit 8.9 shows that in recent years lower income borrowers have come to comprise a more significant portion of Ginnie Mae borrowers. However, it is difficult to quantify the impact of this demographic shift on prepayments because of its gradual nature, and because of the variability of the numbers in the N/A category. In general, we should see larger numbers of "slow" refinancers in Ginnie Mae pools, but more data are needed to reach any further conclusions.

EXHIBIT 8.8 FHA, VA, and Conventional Average-Loan Sizes

Year	FHA Loan Size	VA Loan Size	Conv. Loan Size	FHA/ Conv. Ratio	VA/Conv. Ratio
83	$52,782	$62,884	$59,483	0.89	1.06
84	54,232	64,145	64,442	0.84	1.00
85	58,513	67,542	69,883	0.84	0.97
86	61,757	71,448	78,517	0.79	0.91
87	62,031	73,393	88,925	0.70	0.83
88	60,915	74,738	97,075	0.63	0.77
89	63,183	76,917	104,542	0.60	0.74
90	66.464	81,938	104,000	0.64	0.79
91	68,508	85,621	105,700	0.65	0.81
92	71,023	86,834	108,725	0.65	0.80
93	74,244	90,854	107,167	0.69	0.85
94	75,243	92,150	109,758	0.69	0.84
95	79,717	98,183	110,442	0.72	0.89
96	84,269	102,189	118,592	0.71	0.86
97	88,415	105,484	125,900	0.70	0.84
98	92,897	110,730	131,600	0.71	0.84
99	98,113	112,262	139,500	0.70	0.80

Sources: HUD, Freddie Mac, Fannie Mae, and Salomon Smith Barney.

EXHIBIT 8.9 Borrower Income Characteristics for Conventional and GNMA Loans

Borrower Income (% of Median)[a]	Conventional			Ginnie Mae		
	1991-1993	1994-1996	1997-1999	1991-1993	1994-1996	1997-1999
<80%	10.4%	15.8%	13.2%	13.5%	18.1%	19.3%
80-99%	9.4	11.3	11.3	8.1	10.6	11.6
100-120%	10.6	11.2	12.2	6.7	8.0	8.9
>120%	42.2	35.7	47.5	12.4	12.2	13.2
Income N/A	27.4	26.0	15.8	59.3	51.1	47.0

Income of Census Tract[b]	Conventional			Ginnie Mae		
	1991-1993	1994-1996	1997-1999	1991-1993	1994-1996	1997-1999
Low- or Moderate-Income	6.0%	7.6%	6.0%	11.1%	14.0%	13.3%
Middle Income	40.8	41.4	41.6	48.1	51.3	53.4
Upper Income	35.4	33.1	41.6	21.0	22.4	26.0
N/A	19.3	17.9	10.7	19.8	12.4	7.4

[a] MSA median is the median family income of the metropolitan statistical area (MSA) in which the property related to the loan is located.
[b] Low- or moderate-income census tracts are those in which median family income is less than 80% of the median family income of the MSA as a whole. In middle-income census tracts, median family income is 80% to 120% of the median MSA family income. In upper-income census tracts, median family income is more than 120% of the median MSA family income.
Sources: Home Mortgage Disclosure Act data and Salomon Smith Barney.

Loan-to-Value Ratios

Although the agencies do not provide LTV information for individual pools, aggregate information is available in annual reports from Fannie Mae and Freddie Mac, for example. The average LTV on conventional loans tends to be in the 70% to 80% range, while the majority of FHA and VA loans have LTVs exceeding 95%. As we discuss later in this chapter, differences in initial LTVs play a critical role in explaining differences in prepayment speeds between conventional and Ginnie Mae MBSs.

8.2 GEOGRAPHIC FACTORS[7]

There are differences in the geographical distributions of FHA/VA and conventional loans, and differences between regional economies can lead to differences between Ginnie Mae and conventional speeds. Steady increases in home prices are directly linked to strong regional economies, which in turn lead to higher prepayments because of greater turnover and enhanced refinancing opportunities (because of the homeowner's growth in equity, see Chapter 4). As an example, Exhibit 8.10 shows the cumulative home price appreciation experienced by the nine census regions over the period 1993 to 1996, and suggests one reason why Ginnie Mae prepayments were generally

---

[7] Rich Bohan and Gibbin Chung computed state level prepayment speeds.

EXHIBIT 8.10 FHA and Conventional Geographic Share and Cumulative House Price Appreciation, 1993–1996 by Census Division

	New Eng.	Mid Atl.	South Atl.	East South Central	West South Central	West North Central	East North Central	Mountain	Pacific
FHA Share	3%	8%	21%	5%	10%	8%	11%	13%	19%
Conventional Share	6	12	19	3	7	5	13	10	25
Cumulative Price Appr.	6	5	12	23	13	23	24	32	0

Sources: HUD, Freddie Mac, and Salomon Smith Barney.

faster than conventionals speeds in the mid-1990s. The census areas with the most pronounced differences in FHA and conventional geographical share during this period were the Pacific, Mid-Atlantic, Mountain, and New England areas, respectively. Among these regions, the ones with the greater conventional geographical share have the lowest overall home price appreciation during this period.[8] By contrast, the Mountain region, with a substantial number of Ginnie Mae borrowers, experienced the greatest cumulative home price increases of all the census areas over this period of time.[9]

Exhibit 8.11 shows more recent home price appreciation data by region, and indicates a move toward convergence between the different regions, both in terms of market share and home price appreciation.

The data in Exhibit 8.11 suggests that geographical factors may not be as important in explaining recent differences between Ginnie Mae and conventional speeds as they were in the past. Ginnie Mae recently started

EXHIBIT 8.11 FHA and Conventional Geographic Share and Cumulative House Price Appreciation, 1995–2000 by Census Division

	New Eng.	Mid Atl.	South Atl.	East South Central	West South Central	West North Central	East North Central	Mountain	Pacific
FHA Share	4%	10%	21%	4%	8%	5%	13%	11%	22%
Conventional Share	6	10	18	4	7	6	16	11	22
Cumulative Price Appr.	36	24	27	27	25	33	32	29	30

Sources: HUD, Freddie Mac, and Salomon Smith Barney.

---

[8] Geographical share is defined as the percentage of total U.S. originations that are from the given region.

[9] It should be noted that certain regions, such as the Pacific, and even certain states, such as California, contain quite diverse housing markets. In California, for example, conventionals are likely to be concentrated in regions such as Southern California, which have had weaker housing markets than the state as a whole.

providing geographic information on their pools. We use this information to more directly examine what role, if any, geography is playing in explaining Ginnie Mae versus conventional speed differentials.

Exhibit 8.12 shows geographical concentrations and speeds for 1993 6.5s. Also shown, in the last column, is the cumulative home price appreciation experienced by each region and state since the 1993 loans were originated, based on the repeat home sales price indices published by Fannie Mae and Freddie Mac.

The 1993 Ginnie Maes are prepaying about 13% faster than the 1993 Fannie Mae 6.5s. How can we determine what proportion of the difference in speeds is due to differences in geographical distributions, versus other factors? A simple approach to answering this question is:

Let G_{US} = Ginnie Mae U.S. prepayment speed (of a particular cohort like 1993 6.5s)

F_{US} = Fannie Mae U.S. prepayment speed (of corresponding cohort)

G_i = Ginnie Mae prepayment speed in state i

F_i = Fannie Mae prepayment speed in state i

w_i = percentage outstanding of Ginnie Mae cohort in state i

v_i = percentage outstanding of Fannie Mae cohort in state i

EXHIBIT 8.12   Geographic Concentrations for 1993 6.5s, June 2000

Census Region	Ginnie Mae		Fannie Mae		GN/FN	Cumulative Home Apprec. Since Orig.
	% of Loans	1-Yr. CPR	% of Loans	1-Yr. CPR	Ratio	
East North Central	6.6 %	11.7	11.4 %	9.6	1.22	44.8 %
East South Central	6.8	10.2	3.0	9.9	1.03	38.9
Middle Atlantic	4.8	8.1	12.9	7.9	1.03	23.8
New England	2.5	9.4	7.3	8.2	1.15	36.3
Mountain	11.1	11.8	6.4	10.7	1.10	49.9
Pacific	15.1	9.1	27.4	8.1	1.12	27.9
South Atlantic	34.2	9.4	20.4	9.2	1.02	30.7
West North Central	6.8	10.5	5.1	8.1	1.30	46.4
West South Central	12.0	9.8	6.0	9.9	0.99	31.5
US	100 %	9.9	100%	8.8	1.13	35.4
Major States						
California	9.8	8.2	18.7	7.7	1.06	25.0
Florida	6.7	9.7	4.9	10.5	0.92	30.4
Illinois	2.0	11.2	4.5	9.2	1.22	36.1
New York	1.2	5.9	4.1	7.2	0.82	27.0
Texas	8.2	10.1	4.6	9.9	1.02	32.2

Sources: Ginnie Mae, Fannie Mae, Freddie Mac, and Salomon Smith Barney.

Then we can decompose the ratio of the speeds as

$$
\frac{G_{US}}{F_{US}} = \frac{\displaystyle\sum_{i=1}^{50} w_i G_i}{\displaystyle\sum_{i=1}^{50} v_i F_i} = \left(\frac{\displaystyle\sum_{i=1}^{50} w_i G_i}{\displaystyle\sum_{i=1}^{50} v_i G_i}\right) \times \left(\frac{\displaystyle\sum_{i=1}^{50} v_i G_i}{\displaystyle\sum_{i=1}^{50} v_i F_i}\right) = \left(\frac{\displaystyle\sum_{i=1}^{50} w_i G_i}{\displaystyle\sum_{i=1}^{50} v_i G_i}\right) \times \left(\sum_{i=1}^{50} \left(v_i \frac{F_i}{F_{US}}\right) \frac{G_i}{F_i}\right)
$$

The first term to the right of the last equal sign is **the ratio of the Ginnie speed to the speed obtained by applying Fannie state distribution weights to Ginnie state speeds;** in other words, if, for each state, the Fannie Mae speed was equal to the Ginnie Mae speed, then the denominator in this term would be the U.S. Fannie Mae speed. Hence this term can be interpreted as the speed ratio due to differences in geographical dispersions between the Ginnie Mae and Fannie Mae coupons. The second term is the portion of the overall ratio due to other factors.[10]

For example, the Ginnie Mae 1993 6.5s are prepaying 13% faster than the corresponding Fannies Maes. Applying our equation shows that the first term is 1.02 while the second term is 1.11. Hence, roughly 2% out of the 13% is due to differing geographic concentrations while the remainder is due to other factors. (For example, the California Ginnie to Fannie ratio of 1.06 and the Illinois ratio of 1.22 indicate that there are significant differences in prepays within each state and that this accounts for most of the aggregate speed ratio being greater than one.)[11]

---

[10] The weights in this second term are $v_i(F_i/F_{us})$. If only the v_i were used as weights, then $\Sigma v_i(G_i/F_i)$ is a geographically weighted average of the individual Ginnie to Fannie state ratios. However, not only are the individual Ginnie to Fannie ratios important, but also important is how big each of the Ginnie and Fannie speeds in each ratio are. For example, suppose for some state, the Ginnie to Fannie ratio is 3. Whether that ratio resulted from (a) the Ginnie speed being 0.003 and the Fannie speed being 0.001 versus (b) the Ginnie speed being 30 and the Fannie speed being 10 makes a big difference, but would not be captured in $\Sigma v_i(G_i/F_i)$. (For case (a), the state has such small prepayment speeds that it would hardly impact the average Ginnie to Fannie ratio, but, for case (b), this state could have a substantial impact on the average Ginnie to Fannie ratio.) The additional (F_i/F_{us}) factor in the weight accounts for higher absolute prepayment speeds being more important in determining the average Ginnie to Fannie ratio.

[11] However, since we are using state-level data, intrastate geographic differences (for example, between the California coast and interior) would not show up in the geographic difference ratio, but rather in the other factors ratio.

EXHIBIT 8.13 Geographic Ratio Analysis—Ratios of 1-Yr CPRs, June 2000

Coupon		Overall Ratio	Ratio Due To Geographic Concentartions	Ratio Due To Other Factors
6.0	1999	0.78	0.92	0.84
6.0	1998	0.77	0.96	0.80
6.0	1993	1.11	0.98	1.13
6.5	1999	0.83	0.97	0.85
6.5	1998	0.83	0.98	0.85
6.5	1996	1.03	0.99	1.04
6.5	1993	1.13	1.02	1.11
7.0	1998	0.87	0.99	0.88
7.0	1997	0.91	0.98	0.93
7.0	1996	1.04	1.00	1.05
7.0	1993	1.09	1.02	1.07
7.5	1997	0.96	0.99	0.97
7.5	1996	0.98	0.99	0.99
7.5	1995	0.98	1.01	0.97
7.5	1993	1.10	1.01	1.08
7.5	1992	1.08	1.06	1.01
8.0	1997	1.05	0.99	1.06
8.0	1996	1.00	0.98	1.02
8.0	1994	0.94	1.00	0.94
8.0	1992	0.97	1.04	0.94
8.5	1995	1.01	0.99	1.03
8.5	1994	1.07	1.01	1.06

Sources: Ginnie Mae, Fannie Mae, and Salomon Smith Barney.

Exhibit 8.13, which applies our method to a number of coupons and vintages, indicates that differences in geographic concentrations account for only a relatively small amount of the recent difference in Ginnie and Fannie aggregate speeds in most cases. This is not surprising, since the uniformly strong housing markets of the last few years have diminished, at least for the time being, the impact of geographical differences. Other possible reasons for the relatively fast Ginnie Mae speeds of recent years are discussed in the rest of this chapter.

8.3 BUYOUT ACTIVITY

In July 1998, Ginnie Mae 9.5s and higher coupons experienced large increases in prepayment speeds. In fact, the overall increases were mostly owing to a doubling of speeds on pools from Midfirst Bank, an Oklahoma-based originator and servicer, which was one of the top 15 Ginnie Mae servicers as of 1997. In January 2000, a significant increase in speeds was observed on selected Ginnie Mae 8.5% and 9% pools. That increase again seemed to be mostly due to a large jump in speeds on the pools of one issuer, Norwest Mortgage in this case. For some cohorts, the pools serviced by Norwest experienced an average increase of 150% to 250% in prepayment speeds.

Erratic jumps in Ginnie Mae premium speeds continue to catch the attention of the market. While lender solicitation may be partly responsible, it seems clear that these jumps are mostly caused by *buyouts*, a term that refers to servicers buying out (that is, removing) delinquent loans from their pools. This explains why the jumps in speeds have largely occurred on moderately seasoned pools, such as 1996- and 1997-originated collateral, since delinquencies tend to be high when loans reach an age of roughly four to five years.

Ginnie Mae Policies on Delinquent Loans

Ginnie Mae has explicit rules governing the payoff of delinquent loans in Ginnie Mae pools by an issuer/servicer:

> *At its option and without Ginnie Mae's prior authorization, the issuer may purchase any pooled mortgage loan that comes into default, as defined by the mortgage insurance or guaranty agency, and continues in default for a period of 90 days or more (any loan in a delinquency status for three consecutive payments or more) for an amount equal to 100% of the remaining principal balance, less the principal payments advanced by the issuer on the loan.*[12]

As a complement to this regulation, issuers are required by Ginnie Mae to maintain delinquency rates on pools below specified threshold levels. For instance, not more than 5% of the loans in an issuer's Ginnie Mae portfolio can be in the foreclosure process or three or more months delinquent. The crux of the matter lies in how the issuer chooses to manage these delinquencies. Typically, delinquent loans are removed on a regular basis, hence there is no sudden spurt in prepayment speeds. On the other hand, an issuer who chooses to wait until delinquency rates reach some threshold level before liquidating loans can cause a dramatic jump in prepayment speeds.

---

[12] Ginnie Mae Guide I.

Currently, a servicer may buyout delinquent loans from a Ginnie Mae pool only if:

1. A monthly payment has not been received for three consecutive months; or
2. A borrower has failed to make up a monthly payment for four consecutive months.

Traditionally, most of the borrowers who were in category 1 eventually defaulted on their loans, and contributed to the typical default rate on Ginnie Mae pools. Borrowers who fell into category 2 were usually "cured" and were not typically bought out of Ginnie pools. This dynamic has changed recently, and an increasing investor appetite for reperforming FHA loans has altered business practices for several Ginnie Mae servicers. A number of such servicers are apparently involved in buying out category 2 loans from premium Ginnie Mae pools, and then selling them to private-label shelves.

These servicing practices have led to a steady increase in baseline Ginnie Mae premium speeds that was not really noticeable until recently because of high levels of refinancing activity from 1998 to early-1999.

Fannie Mae and Freddie Mac Policies on Delinquent Loans

The government-sponsored enterprises (GSEs) also have requirements that regulate the removal of delinquent mortgages from conventional pools. Though the acceptable delinquency rates and ratios are a little different than for Ginnie Mae, perhaps the key difference lies in the fact that the GSEs closely oversee the liquidation of delinquent mortgages by issuers, so liquidations happen as an ongoing and gradual process. In the government mortgage market, issuers/servicers appear to have a little more leeway in determining the timing of this liquidation process.

Investor Concerns

The issue of delinquency-related liquidations thus continues to be a source of concern for investors, particularly for those holding seasoned premiums. At issue perhaps is not the amount of the paydown in the case of bought out loans (presumably, these delinquent loans would eventually have been removed from the pool in any case), but the timing of it. In particular, prepayment models will be unable to predict sudden jumps in speeds caused by buyouts, since buyout activity is caused by the actions of particular issuers.

Although sudden large increases in premium speeds is jarring for investors, perhaps the key thing to keep in mind is that the negative impact of buyouts is somewhat diminished by the fact that these loans would have likely prepaid (i.e., would have been liquidated although perhaps at a later time) anyway with the principal returned to investors.

8.4 UNDERSTANDING GINNIE MAE SPEEDS

Summarizing the discussion so far in this chapter, there are a number of factors that are potentially responsible for differences in prepayment behavior between Ginnie Mae and conventional MBSs:

- Geographical differences;
- Buyout activity;
- Higher initial LTVs on FHA and VA loans;
- Differences in fees, primarily the 50bp Mortgage Insurance Premium paid by most FHA borrowers, which effectively raises the WAC by 50bp; and
- Demographic differences.

We have discussed geographical factors and buyout activity in the last two sections. We now discuss the impact of other factors.

Loan-to-Value Ratios and the 50bp MIP Fee

Higher initial LTVs on FHA and VA loans, relative to those on conventional loans, play a critical role in determining relative prepayment speeds on newer Ginnie Mae MBSs. A high initial LTV dampens prepayment speeds, as it severely limits mortgage choices, or makes getting a new mortgage expensive. It also makes it difficult to finance (i.e., roll into the new mortgage) closing costs. To clarify this last point, recall from Section 8.1 that new FHA and VA loans tend to have LTVs between 95% and 100%, and that there are limits on the allowed LTV under the FHA and VA refinancing programs. This means that unless there has been some noticeable appreciation in the price of the house, it will not be possible to finance closing costs, as the new loan balance may imply an LTV above the allowed upper limit.[13] This leaves the borrower with two choices:

---

[13] The new loan balance may equal the old loan balance plus closing costs (including points), less any up-front MIP refund. The new up-front MIP can also be financed but does not have to be included in the calculation of the new LTV.

1. Pay the closing costs out-of-pocket. Since closing costs (including points) on, say, a $100,000 loan can be several thousand dollars, paying them out-of-pocket may not be a feasible choice for many FHA/VA borrowers.

2. Have the lender pay the closing costs (this is called a *no-cost* refinancing). This means a higher note rate (often 100bp above the rate for a loan where the borrower pays closing costs and between one to two points), which means that refinancing is not worthwhile unless the coupon is well in the money.

These factors explain why the Ginnie Mae to conventional speed ratios in Exhibit 8.1 are low for new coupons, both for discounts and for cuspy (low premium) coupons. However, for higher premiums, which are well in the money, speeds on even newer Ginnie Maes can be high, as the borrower can do a no-cost refinancing, as described in point (2).

As loans season, assuming a reasonable housing market, the LTV will drop, and speeds on Ginnie Maes tend to rise relative to conventionals. This is quite noticeable in the speed ratios shown in Exhibit 8.1. In fact, the ratios are often higher than one for coupons seasoned more than a few years. Given that FHA/VA borrowers tend to be less affluent than conventional ones, why are the Ginnie Maes prepaying faster ? One reason may be buyouts. However, a key reason, we feel, is the *50bp Mortgage Insurance Premium (MIP)* paid by most FHA borrowers, which effectively raises the coupon on the underlying loans. As home prices appreciate, and the LTV falls below 80% (requiring cumulative home price appreciation of about 15% to 20% since the loan was originated), the borrower can refinance into a conventional loan, which will have no MIP. Because of the strong housing markets of recent years, most coupons originated prior to 1998 will have experienced at least 20% housing inflation, explaining the fast relative speeds on these coupons.[14]

Note that the speed ratios for 1980s origination coupons, where the Ginnies do not have the 50bp MIP fee, are generally 0.90 to 1, reflecting slightly slower speeds on the Ginnie Maes due to demographic differences.

---

[14] This does not explain the fast recent speeds on 1993 vintage Ginnie discounts. Our feeling is that it is not the Ginnies that are fast, but the conventionals that are slow, due residual problems from the weak coastal housing markets of the first half of the 1990s. Our view is that this aspect is not captured by the geographical analysis we outlined earlier, due to *adverse selection;* that is, the loans *remaining* in the pools have lower equity growth than the average.

Demographic Effects

Differences in demographics between conventional and Ginnie Mae borrowers are also apparent during periods of high refinancing activity, when conventional borrowers tend to prepay much faster. This is illustrated in Exhibit 8.14, which shows speeds on 1996 7.5s.

Prepayments were initially much slower on the Ginnies, reflecting their higher LTVs. Over time, as LTVs declined, the speeds on the Ginnie Maes increased relative to the Fannies. However, this trend reversed sharply as interest rates dropped and refinancings increased in late 1997 and 1998, when the Fannie Maes prepaid much faster, despite the 50bp MIP fee on the Ginnie Maes. Conventional borrowers, on average, react much faster to a sudden drop in rates and resulting refinancing opportunities. As the refinancing wave waned in 1999, speeds on the 1996 Fannie Mae 7.5s gradually declined relative to the corresponding Ginnie Maes.

In closing, we note that even though the demographics of conventional and Ginnie Mae borrowers may be quite distinct, the role these differences play in governing prepayment behavior has been diminishing in recent years due to an increasingly competitive and proactive group of mortgage lenders and a better educated consumer. Furthermore, market changes in recent years are also blurring some of the distinctions between Ginnie Mae and conventional borrowers; such changes include the growth of conventional agency high LTV lending, GSE affordable housing initiatives, which target lower income borrowers, and the Community Reinvestment Act, which makes originating loans of less affluent borrowers (who more closely fit the typical Ginnie borrower profile) more desirable for banks.

EXHIBIT 8.14 Prepayment Speeds and CPR Ratios for 1996 Ginnie Mae and Fannie Mae 7.5s

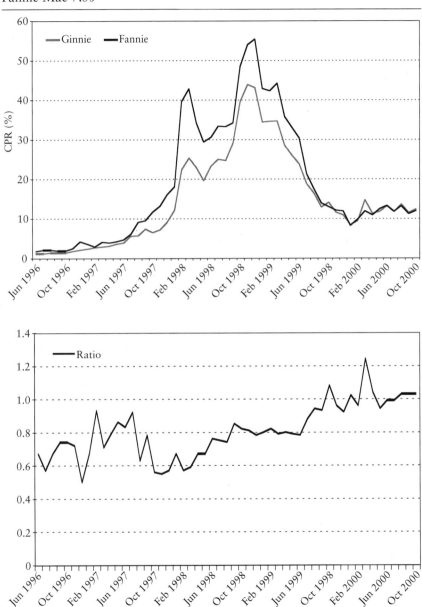

Sources: Ginnie Mae, Fannie Mae, and Salomon Smith Barney.

CHAPTER 9

Adjustable Rate Mortgages

Lakhbir Hayre and Debashis Bhattacharya

As discussed in Chapter 1, adjustable-rate mortgages (ARMs) have a coupon that is reset periodically (typically once a year) at a specified spread (or margin) over a specified index (typically the one-year Treasury yield). The floating nature of the coupon, and the self-selection of borrowers who choose an ARM rather than a traditional fixed-rate mortgage, lead to prepayment behavior distinctly different from that of fixed-rate loans. In this chapter we give a brief discussion on modeling ARM prepayments.[1] Exhibit 9.1 shows historical speeds on selected ARM cohorts.

There are some distinctive patterns to the speeds shown in Exhibit 9.1:

- Speeds rise rapidly after the first year, as the coupon starts resetting. The resets typically mean an increase in the coupon, as many ARMs are originated with below market coupons (or *teaser rates*) to attract borrowers, and this increase in the coupon leads many borrowers to refinance, often into another teasered ARM.
- Speeds increase much faster on average for more recent vintages, and are higher for conventional (Fannie Mae or Freddie Mac) than for Ginnie Mae ARMs.
- When ARMs are seasoned, they settle into speeds typically a little higher than for fixed-rate coupons.

In the rest of this chapter, we describe how these patterns can be captured in a prepayment model.

---

[1] In Chapter 10, we take a more detailed look at the rapidly growing hybrid ARMs sector.

EXHIBIT 9.1 Historical Prepayment Speeds on ARMs for Fannie Mae and Ginnie Mae by Origination Year and Net-Coupon at Origination

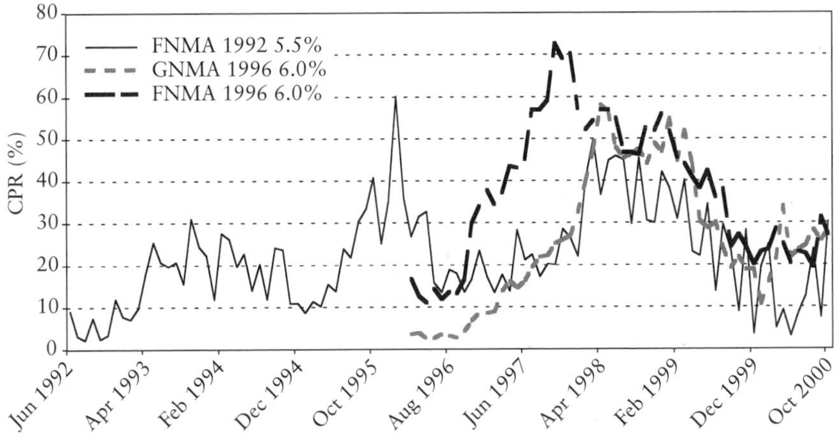

Source: Salomon Smith Barney.

9.1 MODELING SPEEDS ON ARMS

The basic structure of the SSB ARM prepayment model is similar to the fixed-rate model,[2] with one important change: the refinancing component is split up into two sub-models, one for ARM-to-fixed and one for ARM-to-ARM refinancings.

Structure of the Refinancing Model

We assume that ARM borrowers can be broadly categorized as being one of two types: (1) **risk-averse** borrowers who really prefer the certainty of a fixed long-term rate, but took out an ARM because fixed mortgage rates were unattractive at the time and/or they needed the lowest monthly payment possible, and (2) **opportunistic** borrowers who choose an ARM because of the below market *teaser rate,* and who plan to refinance into another teasered ARM when their coupons start resetting upward. There are two refinancing models corresponding to these two types of borrowers, with differing methods of calculating the refinancing incentive:

---

[2] See Chapter 4.

1. *ARM-to-Fixed Refinancings.* We first calculate an *effective WAC.* This is a weighted average of future WACs on an ARM, assuming unchanged rates (it can be thought of as a blend of the current WAC and the fully indexed rate to which the ARM will eventually reset). Exhibit 9.2 shows WACs and effective WACs for a Ginnie Mae ARM. The effective WAC is then compared with fixed mortgage rates (in the same way as for the fixed-rate model) to obtain the refinancing incentive. Some points to note:
   —Unlike the fixed-rate model, refinancings can occur even when the incentive is negative. If fixed rates have dropped sharply, and the borrower finds prevailing rates attractive, he or she may decide to lock them in regardless of the pure economics.
   —As indicated in the previous point, the level of rates now relative to the past (i.e., the *Media Effect*) plays a critical role. Sharp drops in fixed mortgage rates will lead to a pickup in ARM-to-fixed refinancings, regardless of the economic incentive, as borrowers try to lock in what are perceived to be attractive low rates.
2. *ARM-to-ARM Refinancings.* These are based on the estimated savings due to refinancing into a new teasered ARM. Estimates are obtained for three scenarios: unchanged rates, rates up 100bp (basis points), and rates down 100bp. Exhibit 9.3 illustrates the calculation for a GNMA ARM assuming unchanged rates. The current ARM has a WAC of 6.5%, while

EXHIBIT 9.2 WACs, Effective WACs, and Fully Indexed Rates for GNMA ARMS—1997 First Quarter Origination, 5% Net Coupon at Origination

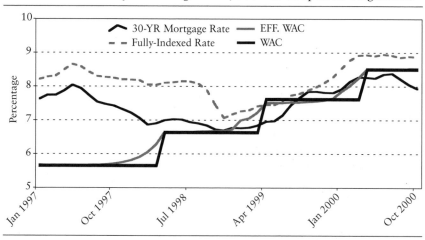

Source: Salomon Smith Barney.

EXHIBIT 9.3   Savings from Refinancing into a New ARM

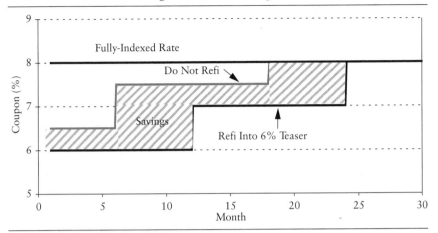

Source: Salomon Smith Barney.

a new teasered ARM is assumed to have an initial WAC of 6%. Assuming unchanged rates, the current ARM will reset to 7.5% in six months, and then to the fully indexed rate of 8% in 18 months, while the new ARM will reset to 7% in 12 months and then to the fully indexed rate of 8% in 24 months. We calculate the present value of the differences between the coupons until they both converge to the fully indexed rate. This is repeated for up 100bp and −100bp scenarios. *The refinancing incentive is the average of the three present values less refinancing costs.*

Changing Composition of ARM Borrowers

Speeds on newer ARMs have been substantially faster in recent years than in earlier periods, as shown in Exhibit 9.1. Our view, which is supported by much anecdotal evidence, is that the increase in speeds reflects a change in the mix of borrowers who take out ARMs. This view is embedded in the model:

- The borrower mix is assumed to have changed in recent years toward more opportunistic ARM-to-ARM refinancers, although ARM-to-fixed refinancings are still assumed to be more prevalent.
- Within each of the two types of refinancers, there are intrinsically slower and faster borrowers. We assume that due to more proactive originators, and higher gross margins on GNMAs (which allows more attractive

teasered rates to be offered), there are more "faster" refinancers in recent originations.

Convertible ARMs   Convertible ARMs allow the borrower to "convert" an ARM into a fixed-rate loan during a specified time window (typically from month 12 to month 60) for a nominal fee. This in effect means that the borrower can refinance with greatly reduced transaction costs, although the rate on the new loan is typically 25bp to 50bp above prevailing mortgage rates. As might be expected, prepayment rates on convertible ARMs are typically faster than those on nonconvertible ARMs during the convertibility window. A striking feature of conventional ARM speeds over the last few years has been the fact that nonconvertible ARMs have often been faster than convertibles, in the first two years or so. We feel that because of attractive teaser rates and hassle-free refinancings, some of the fastest refinancers, who in the past would have taken out a convertible ARM, now go into nonconvertibles. As a result, for new ARMs, speeds are initially faster for nonconvertibles, whereas for seasoned paper they are faster for convertibles.

CHAPTER 10

Hybrid ARMs

Debashis Bhattacharya and Lakhbir Hayre

As the name suggests, hybrid ARMs combine features of fixed-rate loans and adjustable rate mortgages (ARMs). The coupon on a hybrid is fixed for a specified period (typically 3, 5, 7, or 10 years), after which, like the coupon on an ARM, it resets annually at a specified spread to an index. The product appeals to borrowers who want an initial coupon lower than that on a 30-year fixed rate loan, but who are not completely comfortable with a standard ARM and the attendant risk of a sharp upward reset in the coupon after one year. Noticeable issuance of hybrids first occurred in the early 1990s, and hybrid ARMs have continued to grow as a percentage of the ARMs market since then; a recent report from FHLB indicates almost 50% of new conventional ARMs originated are hybrids. Roughly $24 billion in agency hybrid ARMs is outstanding at present.

This chapter provides a primer on hybrid ARMs. Section 10.1 describes key features of hybrid ARMs and profiles the market. Section 10.2 reviews historical hybrid ARM prepayment behavior, describing how hybrid speeds vary with the first reset period and how they compare with speeds on other MBS products, such as one-year ARMs, balloons, and fixed-rate MBSs. Section 10.3 describes how the historical patterns have been used to construct the Salomon Smith Barney Prepayment Model for hybrids, and Section 10.4 discusses investment characteristics of hybrid ARMs.

10.1 KEY STRUCTURAL FEATURES OF HYBRID ARMS

Hybrid ARMs are generally categorized by the length of the first reset period, typically 3, 5, 7, or 10 years. The term 5 × 1 **hybrid,** for example, is

259

used to denote a loan with a first reset after five years, with subsequent annual resets. Some other key features include the following:

■ *Index.* Most hybrids are indexed to the one-year constant-maturity Treasury (CMT), but some hybrids are indexed to the three-year and five-year CMT. For example, a 3 × 3 hybrid will be indexed to the three-year CMT and will reset every three years. All CMT rates are obtained from the Federal Reserve Board's weekly *H.15 Statistical Release.*

■ *Caps.* A hybrid pool can be characterized by three types of coupon caps: a *life* cap, a *periodic* cap, and an *initial reset* cap. For example, a 5-2-5 structure would indicate a life cap of 5% (i.e. 500bp [basis points]) above the initial coupon, a periodic cap of 2%, and an initial reset cap of 5%. Most periodic caps are 2%, most life caps are 5% (except for 3 × 1s, which have 6%), and most initial reset caps are 2% (except for 7 × 1s and 10 × 1s, which have 5%). However, it is not uncommon to see pools with a variety of mixed cap characteristics.

■ *Convertibility.* A convertibility option allows the borrower to convert into a fixed-rate mortgage during a specified period, called the *conversion window.* The conversion window is typically 60 months long and usually starts at month 1 or month 12. However, various other types of conversion periods are available (e.g. windows starting at month 60 or conversions allowed at the first three reset dates). The rate for the new loan is typically set between ³/₈% and ⁵/₈% above prevailing fixed 30-year mortgage rates. Convertible pools form about 13% of the current outstanding agency hybrids.

■ *Margins.* Typical *gross margins* (the amount added to the index to set the loan coupon) on the loans are around 275bp to 300bp and *net margins* (the difference between the MBS coupon and the index) are typically roughly 225bp. Minimum servicing spreads are set at 37.5bp for 3 × 1s and 5 × 1s, and 25bp for 7 × 1s and 10 × 1s. As with any other feature, margins and spreads can vary considerably among pools. The *lookback period* (the number of days between the coupon adjustment and the date the index level is determined) is typically 45 days.

Development of the Market

Exhibit 10.1 shows yearly issuance of hybrid ARMs. Issuance has grown steadily in recent years. Exhibit 10.2 describes major coupon vintages outstanding in the Fannie Mae hybrid ARM market and provides a snapshot of typical margins. Recent trends in the lending market suggest continuing growth in the hybrid sector. A recent Freddie Mac study finds 60% or more

EXHIBIT 10.1 Issuance of Hybrid ARMs (Fannie Mae and Freddie Mac), 1990–2000

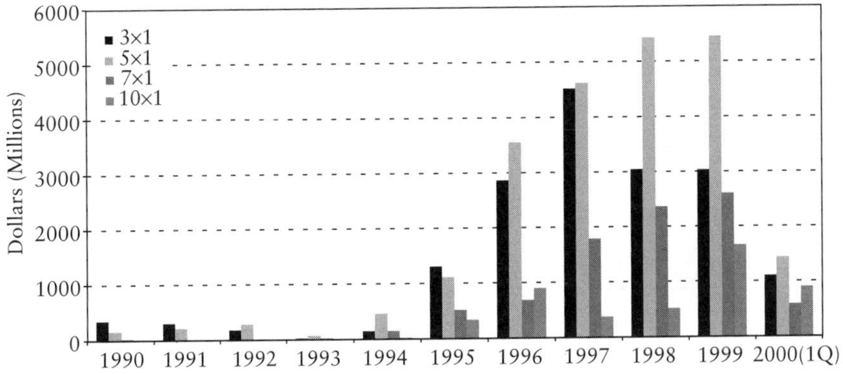

Source: Salomon Smith Barney.

of the lenders now offer all the hybrid products and the initial discount stands at a high of almost 80bp to 100bp for most hybrid products.

A Hybrid TBA Market Recently, the Bond Market Association proposed creating a TBA market for hybrid ARMs. The association recognizes that the security side of the market is rather static in contrast to the popularity of the product and the development of the origination market. TBAs are expected to create a liquid and active hybrid market. Consistent pricing, trading in forward months, creation of a roll market—typical features of a TBA market—would provide investors with a deeper market in which to transact hybrid securities. Details of securities to be specified for TBA delivery, such as index, net margin, months-to-roll, caps, and so on, are still being considered.

10.2 PREPAYMENT BEHAVIOR OF HYBRIDS

With seven to eight years of prepayment history and data on speeds around resets for 3 × 1s and 5 × 1s now available, it is possible to develop a good understanding of the prepayment characteristics of hybrids.

Traditionally, borrowers have chosen ARMs either to minimize initial monthly mortgage payments or because they do not expect to hold the mortgage for very long. The need for lower monthly payments may arise because

EXHIBIT 10.2   Profile of the FNMA Hybrid ARM Market as of March 2000

Orig Year	Orig Coupon (%)	Current Outstanding ($ Millions)	WAM (Mos.)	Net Margin	Gross Margin (bp)	Current Coupon (%)	Current WAC (%)
3x1 NON-CONV							
1997	6.0	408	333	2.194	2.835	6.06	6.70
1997	6.5	564	331	2.203	2.848	6.38	7.02
1997	7.0	44	329	2.296	2.935	6.86	7.50
1998	6.0	632	341	2.232	2.841	6.03	6.64
1998	6.5	58	340	2.341	2.956	6.30	6.91
1999	5.5	202.9	349	2.167	2.879	5.61	6.32
1999	6.0	395.6	350	2.175	2.885	5.99	6.69
1999	6.5	383.1	353	2.170	2.795	6.46	7.09
3x1 CONV							
1997	6.5	107	329	2.154	2.811	6.36	7.01
1998	6.0	65	340	2.275	2.900	5.96	6.59
5x1 NON-CONV							
1994	7.0	155	295	2.228	2.825	7.10	7.70
1995	6.5	105	308	2.196	2.820	6.52	7.15
1995	7.0	125	306	2.256	2.852	7.00	7.59
1996	6.5	139	318	2.283	2.883	6.54	7.14
1996	7.0	149	321	2.214	2.812	6.86	7.46
1997	6.0	162	332	2.150	2.777	6.05	6.68
1997	6.5	1335	331	2.260	2.838	6.46	7.04
1997	7.0	232	328	2.283	2.899	6.88	7.49
1998	6.0	808	342	2.202	2.791	6.04	6.62
1998	6.5	426	341	2.320	2.873	6.37	6.92
1999	6.0	433.2	349	2.154	2.805	5.98	6.63
1999	6.5	619.1	352	2.165	2.791	6.54	7.16
1999	7.0	313.9	353	2.231	2.800	6.93	7.50
5x1 CONV							
1998	6.5	120	340	2.256	2.758	6.27	6.78
7x1							
1997	6.5	249	333	2.220	2.835	6.51	7.12
1997	7.0	448	329	2.287	2.831	6.92	7.47
1998	6.0	417	344	2.189	2.777	6.05	6.63
1998	6.5	416	341	2.314	2.844	6.44	6.97
1999	6.0	476.2	348	2.145	2.772	5.97	6.59
1999	6.5	321.8	352	2.154	2.765	6.54	7.15
1999	7.0	189.4	354	2.184	2.768	6.89	7.47
10x1 NON-CONV							
1994	7.5	126	297	2.261	2.799	7.45	7.99
1997	6.5	143	327	2.366	2.880	6.91	7.43
1998	6.5	71	342	2.339	2.861	6.49	7.01
1999	6.0	121.7	348	2.131	2.774	6.02	6.66
1999	6.5	143.7	351	2.224	2.806	6.52	7.10
1999	7.0	204.4	354	2.126	2.780	6.98	7.63

Source: Salomon Smith Barney.

of the borrower's income situation or the size of the loan. A short horizon may be due to a planned move within a few years or because the borrower plans to refinance into a fixed-rate mortgage at the earliest opportunity. In recent years, ARMs have also become popular with opportunistic "teaser junkies," who refinance into a new, teasered ARM as soon as the coupon starts to reset upward.

A standard ARM exposes the borrower to the risk of a payment shock at coupon resets, the first of which is only 12 months away. A hybrid ARM diminishes this risk, because the first coupon reset is further away, while still providing a lower initial coupon rate than a 30-year fixed-rate loan. Thus, it seems likely that a hybrid borrower shares some of the characteristics of an ARM borrower and some of the more risk-averse traits of a fixed-rate borrower—the longer the first reset, the closer the hybrid borrower should be to a fixed-rate borrower. As we will show, empirical speeds support this conjecture. An analysis of hybrid speeds leads to several conclusions.

Hybrid ARMs Are Slower Than One-Year Conventionals ARMs

Exhibit 10.3 shows that standard one-year ARMs are significantly faster than hybrids, even in the first year, before the one-year ARM resets. This is presumably because one-year ARMs have higher proportions of opportunistic ARM-to-ARM borrowers as these borrowers would be most likely to select a product with the lowest rate. In addition, hybrid ARM borrowers likely have a longer horizon for holding on to the mortgage, implying slower speeds in the first few years. In fact, Exhibit 10.3 indicates that speeds on the one-year ARMs and 3×1 hybrids converge somewhat after two to three years (in the absence of rate shocks).

The Longer the Initial Reset Period, the Slower the Speed

The bottom frame of Exhibit 10.3 shows that, although 5×1 borrowers have marginally higher WACs (10bp–15bp), they prepay at a slower rate. Presumably, they have forgone the lower rates (or lower points) on 3×1s to protect themselves against rising payments for two more years. Hence, with the extra protection against reset and a longer horizon, they demonstrate a lower propensity to refinance or move.

The top frame of Exhibit 10.3 depicts similar differences in speeds between higher coupon hybrids (all have WACs around 7.5%). However, in this example, we see a temporary convergence in speeds during the 1998 refinancing waves. Hence, hybrid pools that are comfortably in the money during a period of exceptionally low rates are exposed to a significant amount of solicitation from lenders and show high speeds (irrespective of initial resets).

EXHIBIT 10.3 FNMA Hybrid Speeds for 1997

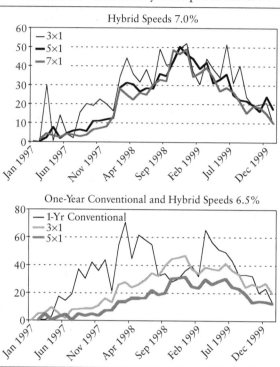

Source: Salomon Smith Barney.

Balloons Are Typically Faster Than Comparable Hybrids

The left frame of Exhibit 10.4 shows that hybrid speeds tend to be slower than those of balloon MBSs. This is probably because balloons have a higher concentration of fast movers and refinancers, the type of borrowers least worried about a balloon payment.

Longer Hybrids Are Faster Than Fixed-Rate MBSs

The right frame of Exhibit 10.4 compares speeds for 7×1 and 10×1 hybrids with those of fixed-rate MBSs. Speeds for 7×1s are consistently faster than those of 30-year fixed-rate MBSs. Likewise, speeds of 10×1s tend to be faster—but not as fast as 7×1 speeds—than those on 30-year fixed-rate MBSs. Among hybrids, a 10×1 borrower is most similar to a

EXHIBIT 10.4   FNMA Hybrid Speeds for 1995

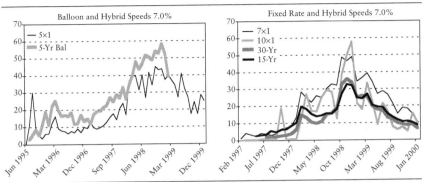

Source: Salomon Smith Barney.

fixed-rate borrower, being someone who has some aversion to variable coupons but, at the same time, is willing to take a bit of risk in return for a lower coupon rate. However, hybrids do exhibit a sharper response to low mortgage rates, as indicated by the sharp jumps in speeds on the 7×1s and 10×1s during the 1998 refinancing waves.

The responsiveness of hybrids to opportunities to lock in a low, long-term, fixed-rate mortgage rate is further illustrated in Exhibit 10.5, which shows a sharp rise in speeds for 1992 and 1997 origination 5×1s within

EXHIBIT 10.5   FNMA Hybrid Speeds

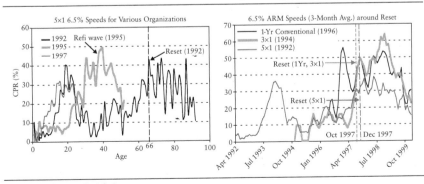

Source: Salomon Smith Barney.

the first two years, during the refinancing waves of 1993 and 1998, respectively. The 1995 origination 5 × 1s, on the other hand, seasoned less aggressively and peaked during the 1998 refinancing wave.

Prepayment Behavior Near the First Coupon Reset

With more data becoming available on resetting hybrids, it is easier to make inferences on prepayment speeds around resets. As the left frame of Exhibit 10.5 depicts, the 1992 origination 5 × 1s jumped from 20% CPR to about 40% CPR as the coupon reset from 7.25% to 8.5% in mid-1997, when 30-year mortgage rates were close to 7.5% (by comparison, 1992 FNMA 8s, with WACs around 8.50%, were prepaying at about 14% CPR during this time). The speeds trended down thereafter even though mortgage rates continued to fall, indicating that a coupon reset by itself can have a significant impact on hybrid speeds.

What about after the first reset? Will 3 × 1s and 5 × 1s behave like one-year ARMs after the first reset? As the right frame of Exhibit 10.5 indicates, speeds did converge somewhat after the reset between the 3 × 1 and the one-year ARM, but 5 × 1s remained distinctly lower. While the speeds of 3 × 1 and one-year ARMs in 1998 may have been driven by the refinancing waves, recent data suggest there is some convergence in their speeds.

Convertibility Makes a Difference

Exhibit 10.6 shows that convertible speeds in general are a little faster within the convertibility window. Moreover, the convertibility effect can be accentuated close to a reset or during a refinancing wave, as shown on the right frame for the 3 × 1.

These observations describe general patterns in hybrid ARM speeds. Investors should keep in mind that specific pools can depart from the average based on the geographical distribution of the loans, issuer profiles, WAC and margin dispersion, and so on.

10.3 PROJECTING SPEEDS ON HYBRIDS

The Salomon Smith Barney prepayment modeling framework assumes that speeds result from four causes, namely *housing turnover, refinancings, defaults,* and *curtailment/payoffs,* with separate models for each of

EXHIBIT 10.6   FNMA Hybrid Speeds for 1994 and 1995

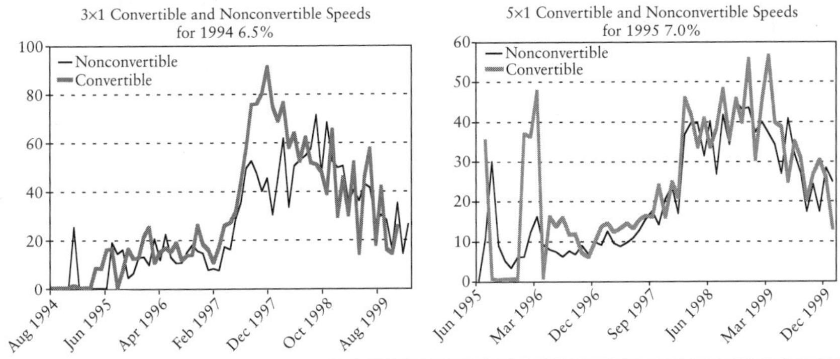

Source: Salomon Smith Barney.

these components.[1] ARMs are handled within this general framework. However, in the refinancing component, we make a distinction between *ARM-to-fixed refinancers* and *ARM-to-ARM refinancers*.[2] ARM-to-fixed refinancers are the traditional ARM borrowers, who choose an ARM to obtain the lowest monthly payments but who plan either to sell the house before too long (i.e., have a short tenure horizon) or to refinance eventually and lock in the security of a long-term fixed-rate loan. Hence, refinancing decisions are driven by the level of long-term fixed mortgage rates. The second group represents a more recent development: aggressive refinancers who take out a *teasered* ARM (i.e., one with an initial below-market coupon) and then refinance into another teasered ARM as soon as the coupon starts to reset upward. In this case, refinancing decisions are driven by the level of short-term rates. Thus, the refinancing incentive is based on different mortgage rates for the two types of borrowers.[3]

Hybrid ARM borrowers have characteristics of both ARM and fixed-rate borrowers, although one would expect most aggressive ARM-to-ARM refinancers (the so-called "teaser junkies") to opt for a one-year ARM. In

---

[1] A detailed discussion of the general approach and of each of the components can be found in Chapter 4.

[2] Each type has the usual mix of slow and fast refinancers.

[3] For a description of the general ARM prepayment model, see Chapter 9.

fact, as indicated by the analysis of hybrid speeds in the previous section, the longer the first reset, the closer the hybrid's prepayment behavior to a fixed-rate MBS.

Based on the empirical analysis discussed earlier, in the *housing turnover* component of the model, a *high relative mobility* and *fast seasoning* is assumed, reflecting the shorter tenure horizons of many ARM borrowers.[4] However, the longer the first reset, the lower the relative mobility factor.

Refinancing Model for Hybrids

This component has several distinctive features that we will discuss.

Effective WAC   Because the loan coupon is not fixed for the term of the security but will eventually reset until it is fully indexed, a weighted average of the coupon path going forward—the *effective WAC*—is calculated assuming unchanged rates (it can be thought of as a blend of the current WAC and the fully indexed rate to which the ARM will eventually reset). The effective WAC is then compared with mortgage rates (in the same way as for the fixed-rate model) to obtain the refinancing incentive for ARM-to-fixed refinancings.

Exhibit 10.7 shows examples of effective WACs for 3×1 and 5×1 hybrids with similar coupons and similar months-to-first roll. Because of our assumption that the shorter the initial reset, the greater the sensitivity to coupon resets, the effective WAC for the 3×1 rises more sharply near the coupon reset date.

ARM-to-ARM Refinancings   This component captures the part of refinancing attributed to **opportunistic** ARM borrowers who would refinance into another teasered ARM. The refinancing incentive is captured by the difference in WACs between the ARM in question and a new teasered ARM, until their WACs converge to the fully-indexed rate. (The analysis is done for the unchanged and the ±100bp shift scenarios and an average value is calculated.)

As indicated earlier, hybrids are assumed to have fewer opportunistic borrowers than one-year ARMs and, hence, to have a lower proportion of ARM-to-ARM refinancings. The proportion of ARM-to-ARM refinancing decreases with longer resets, because borrowers are assumed to become more risk-averse.

---

[4] In fact, many borrowers choose a hybrid as an alternative to a balloon mortgage, and the growth of the hybrid market has come at the expense of balloons.

EXHIBIT 10.7 3 × 1 and 5 × 1 Hybrid: Effective WACs, January 1997–April 2000 (Actual) and May 2000–March 2001 (Projected)

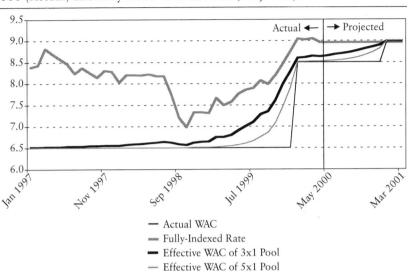

Note: For illustration, we have chosen a 3 × 1 pool (originated in January 2000) and a 5 × 1 pool (originated in January 1998), both with an original WAC of 6.5%.
Source: Salomon Smith Barney.

Projected Spike Around Coupon Resets

We assume a heightened sensitivity to refinancing opportunities into fixed-rate loans near coupon resets, because many borrowers will be anxious to lock in a fixed rate. In particular, at and around the first coupon reset, which may result in a sharp increase in the coupon because of the "teaser" nature of the initial coupon, there tends to be an extra spurt in refinancing activity.

Analogous to how the media effect captures the effect of sharp drops in interest rates,[5] the hybrid ARM model captures the effect of sharp changes in WACs around resets. This effect is most pronounced for the first reset (when most teaser ARMs reset up), for WACs that move from below the 30-year mortgage rate to above this rate, and for products with shorter initial resets. The longer the period to the first reset, the lower this spike, because of the

---

[5] See Chapter 4.

assumption that pools with longer first resets include fewer aggressive ARM refinancers. Exhibit 10.8 shows projected speeds around resets for different hybrid products. For 3 × 1 hybrids, for example, speeds are projected to increase to about 20% to 25% CPR by age 30 months and then spike to about 50% to 60% CPR after month 36, before declining back to about 20% CPR by about month 50. The spikes become less pronounced the longer the period to the first reset.

Exhibit 10.9 shows actual and projected speeds for 1992 6.5% 5 × 1 hybrids, which had their first reset in 1997. There was an initial burst of refinancing activity in late 1993 and early 1994, when mortgage rates fell to multiyear lows. Another burst in refinancings came in the middle of 1997, illustrating the impact of the first coupon reset. Even though mortgage rates were relatively high around this time, many borrowers still chose to refinance. The spikes in 1998 reflected the interest rate rallies that year. The model has tracked speeds quite well, both during the fixed coupon period (before the first reset) and after the first reset, when the loans became one-year ARMs.

Exhibit 10.10 shows more graphs of actual and projected speeds, illustrating that the model, on average, has tracked speeds reasonably well.

EXHIBIT 10.8 New Hybrid ARMS—Projected Speeds (Gross Coupon: 7.25%; Gross Margin: 300bp; Age: Four Months)

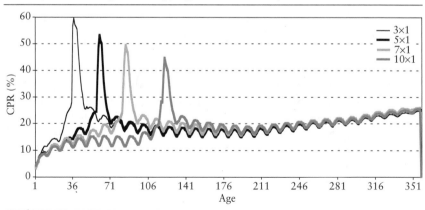

Source: Salomon Smith Barney.

EXHIBIT 10.9   Actual versus Projected Speeds for 1992 6.5% 5 × 1 Hybrids, February 1992–May 2000

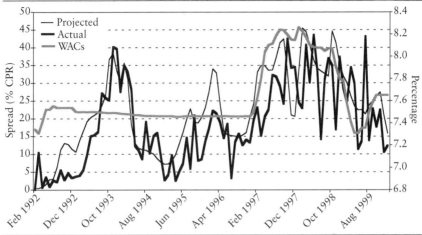

Source: Salomon Smith Barney.

10.4 INVESTMENT CHARACTERISTICS

Hybrid ARMs have traditionally been compared to balloon fixed-rate MBSs. For example, a 5 × 1 hybrid with an initial coupon of 7% would be compared to a 7% five-year balloon MBS, assuming some terminal exit price for the hybrid. This method is obviously simplistic, but provides a yardstick for investors when there are limited prepayment data and, hence, limited confidence in hybrid prepayment models. With hybrid prepayment modeling coming of age, we feel that OAS-based methods provide more accurate and meaningful valuation measures. We describe both methodologies.

Exit Price and Comparison to Balloons

The market convention has been to compare hybrid ARMs to balloons. To value the hybrid, a balloon payment is assumed at the first reset date, with a put price of 100 or 101. Exhibit 10.11 shows such a comparison, assuming

EXHIBIT 10.10 Selected Coupons and Vintages: Actual and Projected Speeds

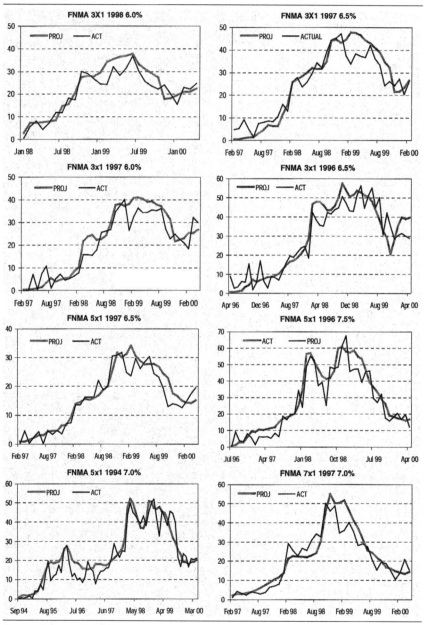

Source: Salomon Smith Barney.

EXHIBIT 10.11 5 × 1 Hybrid versus Gold Five-Year Balloon as of April 18, 2000

Pool	Coupon	WAC	Age	MTR (Balloon)	Current Price	Speed (CPR)	Exit Price	YTM
5x1 (N530552)	7.0	7.5	1	59	99-10	15 %	100	7.51
Balloon	7.0	7.5	1	59	99-28	15	—	7.05

Source: Salomon Smith Barney.

an exit price of par for the hybrid and a constant 15% CPR prepayment assumption for both securities.[6]

An exit price assumption of par (commonly known as par-to-put) was commonly used, but it is conservative and essentially equivalent to assuming that the entire hybrid pays down by the first reset. Over time, exit price assumptions have become more realistic, because it has become clear that hybrids do not completely pay down by the first reset. Exhibit 10.12 shows current factors for several hybrid vintages.

EXHIBIT 10.12 Factors for Selected Hybrid Vintages as of March 2000

Product	Origination Year	Factor
3x1 Nonconvertible	1997	0.47
	1996	0.27
3x1 Convertible	1997	0.49
	1996	0.26
5x1 Nonconvertible	1995	0.35
	1994	0.26
5x1 Convertible	1995	0.29
	1994	0.42

Source: Salomon Smith Barney.

---

[6] In an oversimplified sense, the hybrid price can be decomposed as follows: Hybrid = Cash flow for five years + Residual (Exit price × Factor at five years × Discount) and Balloon = Cash flow for five years + Par × Factor at five years × Discount. Therefore, Hybrid = Balloon + Factor × (Exit price − Par) × Discount, assuming the cash flows over the five years from the hybrid and the balloon (and hence, the factors) are similar. Consequently, the hybrid is worth at least as much as the balloon with either an assumption of Exit price = Par, or Factor = 0. For example, in this example at a factor of 0.44 and exit price of 101 the hybrid is approximately worth 99 − 28 + 0.44 × (101 − 100) × 0.70 = 100 − 06, whereas it is priced at 99 − 10.

Even though hybrid speeds can approach 60% CPR near the first-coupon reset date, in general a par price for a fully-indexed coupon is not justified unless the yield curve is unusually steep or discount margins are unusually wide. For example, the hybrid pool in Exhibit 10.11 would reset to a coupon of 8.14% [6.04% (Current one-year CMT) + 2.15% (Net margin)] for an unchanged one-year CMT rate. Even at a vector of 60% CPR for the first two years followed by a 15% CPR for the remaining term, the discount margin would have to be about 200bp, or 50bp wider than typical TBA hybrids and 40bp wider than fully-indexed hybrids or one-year conventional ARMs, to justify a par price.

Without a concrete understanding of possible exit prices and paydowns under various scenarios, it is difficult to judge the value of a hybrid. Given a reliable prepayment model, OAS analysis allows a more meaningful valuation.

OAS Analysis of Hybrid ARMs

Exhibit 10.13 shows an OAS analysis for a 5 × 1 hybrid pool. The OAS shown in Exhibit 10.13 is about 30bp to 40bp higher than that for a comparable balloon MBS. Is the hybrid really worth this much more than the balloon MBS? A simple way of justifying the OAS valuation is to relate it to the traditional exit price approach. At the first reset date, in 59 months, assuming unchanged rates, the hybrid will reset to a fully indexed coupon equal to the one-year Treasury rate plus the net margin 2.14%, or (6.04% + 2.14%), which is 8.18%. This implies that since the hybrid is priced at 99-10 now, it will be worth even more after its first reset (depending on prepayments). In contrast, a five-year balloon will return principal at par after five years and is expected to have faster speeds in the interim.

EXHIBIT 10.13 5 × 1 Hybrid FNMA Pool N530552: OAS Analysis as of April 18, 2000

Coupon	WAC	WAM	Price	Projected CPR		OAS	Opt. Cost	Eff. Dur.	Eff. Conv.
				1-Yr.	LT				
7.0%	7.50%	29-11	99-10	7.0%	16.0%	93	25	2.90	-0.72

Note: Pool has a net margin of 214bp, gross margin of 275bp, life cap of 13.00%, periodic caps of 2%, and 59 months to first reset. Index is 6.04%.
Source: Salomon Brothers Inc.

EXHIBIT 10.14 5×1 Hybrid FNMA Pool 530552: Prepayment Sensitivity as of April 18, 2000

	Projected CPR				Option	Eff.	Eff.
	Peak (%)	LT (%)	Price	OAS (bp)	Cost	Dur. (Yrs)	Conv.
Base Model	52.0	16.0	99-10	93	25	2.9	-0.72
Fast Model	60.5	18.8	99-10	84	27	2.7	-0.74
Faster Model	68.0	21.2	99-10	78	28	2.6	-0.76

Note: The peak speed refers to the maximum projected speed after the first reset date (59 months from now). The long-term speed is the WAL-equivalent CPR of the vector of projected speeds from now until maturity.
Source: Salomon Brothers Inc.

Sensitivity to Prepayment Assumptions

One possible reason for the cheapness of hybrids relative to balloons is prepayment uncertainty, especially around the first coupon reset date. Although there is now at least five years worth of meaningful prepayment data on hybrids and our prepayment model tracks hybrid speeds reasonably well (see Section 10.3, "Projecting Speeds on Hybrids"), it is still a useful exercise to stress test the results by using different prepayment assumptions.[7] Our model projects that speeds will spike to about 52% CPR around the first reset. Exhibit 10.14 shows the effect on the OAS of hybrid pool 530552 if speeds are assumed to spike much higher after the first reset than assumed by our base model. For the "fast" model, speeds spike to about 60.5% CPR after the first reset, while for the "faster" model speeds peak at about 68% CPR.

The pool loses OAS for faster projected speeds, but even under a fairly severe assumption of speeds close to 70% CPR around the first reset, the OAS is still 15bp to 20bp higher than those currently offered by balloons.

Returning to the exit price approach, we show in Exhibit 10.15 the price of the hybrid pool just after the first reset date (i.e., 59 months from now, when the ARM is seasoned five years), assuming unchanged interest rates and an unchanged OAS. We use the base model and the faster models defined earlier.

Even under fairly severe prepayment assumptions, the price of the hybrid ARM is still projected to be close to 102, higher than the 100 or 101 put prices typically assumed by market convention when valuing hybrids.

---

[7] In fact, this should be done for any MBS, regardless of how much data there are and how accurate the model has been in the past.

EXHIBIT 10.15 5 × 1 Hybrid Pool N530552: Exit Price After First Coupon Reset as of April 18, 2000

	Coupon (%)	WAC (%)	WAM	Projected Peak (%)	CPR 1-Year (%)	LT (%)	OAS (bp)	Price
Base Model	8.18	9.6	24-10	52.0	37.9	24.0	93	102.50
Fast Model	8.18	9.6	24-10	60.5	43.3	30.6	93	102.01
Faster Model	8.18	9.6	24-10	68.0	52.0	37.4	93	101.70

Note: Pool has 11 months to roll. Index value is 6.04%.
Source: Salomon Brothers Inc.

One caveat: The price of the hybrid is higher than what would be projected for a fixed-rate MBS with a comparable coupon. This is because the option cost of the hybrid ARM is much lower. While the hybrid is assumed to have speeds comparable to fixed-rate MBSs if rates decline, it is assumed to slow down less if rates rise, with long-term speeds still in double digits even if rates rise several 100bp. While this can be justified by the double-digit speeds on conventional ARMs in the late 1980s—when mortgage rates exceeded 10%—it is an assumption of which investors need to be aware.

CHAPTER 11

Jumbo Loans

Lakhbir Hayre and Robert Young

The term *jumbo loans* refers to loans with balances larger than the Fannie Mae and Freddie Mac conforming loan limits. At one time, the term *whole loans* was used interchangeably with jumbo loans. However, in recent years, the expansion in underwriting standards and hence in the types of nonconforming loans (such as subprime or alternative-A mortgages) means that many whole loans are not jumbo loans. In this brief chapter, we discuss how the prepayment behavior of jumbo loans differs from that of agency MBS, and how these differences are captured in the Salomon Smith Barney Prepayment Model.

11.1 DIFFERENCES IN LOAN CHARACTERISTICS

There are two main differences between jumbo and conforming loans:

1. *Geographical distribution.* Jumbo loans tend to have a higher California and Northeast concentration than conforming loans, due to higher housing costs in these regions. Hence regional housing market trends will have an impact on jumbo loan prepayments. For example, the weak coastal housing markets in the early to mid-1990s meant slow equity growth for jumbo loans originated during that period, and hence speeds were slow for both discount and premium jumbo loans. However, the recovery in both the California and Northeast housing markets over the last few years has led to a sharp increase in equity (and hence in the housing inflation indices used in the prepayment model and described in Chapter 4), leading to faster prepayment speeds.

2. *Loan balances.* As one would expect, average loan balances tend to be much higher for jumbo loans than for conforming loans. Recent average loan balances for jumbo loan MBSs have been around $300,000 to $350,000, almost three times the average balance in agency MBS pools. This implies that the costs of refinancing will be less of a hurdle for jumbo loan borrowers.

11.2 ASSUMED DIFFERENCES IN BORROWERS

In addition to the differences in *known* loan characteristics just described, which are captured through differences in data inputs into the prepayment model, we also *assume* a number of differences between conforming and jumbo loans:

■ We assume that jumbo loan borrowers have a *higher mobility rate* because of demographics and their high California concentration. We capture this effect by using a *higher relative mobility rate* in our turnover submodel for jumbo loan borrowers.

■ We assume that jumbo loan borrowers have a *greater propensity to refinance* because of demographics, and because of the economies of scale that can reduce the variable costs (as a percentage of loan size) associated with refinancing a high-balance loan relative to a low-balance loan. We model these effects by assuming whole loan borrowers have a greater proportion of "fast" refinancers, and have reduced variable costs when refinancing their loans.

■ We assume that the higher loan balances carried by jumbo borrowers imply a *lower degree of burnout;* that is, their reasons for not refinancing are more likely to be temporary. We capture this by assuming a higher "steady-state" level of refinancings (i.e., the slowest class of refinancers have a higher refinancing curve).

■ We assume jumbo borrowers to be somewhat *faster to react to refinancing opportunities* when interest rates fall. In addition to the likely greater financial sophistication of jumbo borrowers, the incentive of the originator can also reduce the lag between interest rate changes and prepayments.

Because most originators receive a percentage of the loan balance as an origination fee (typically around 1%), the fees collected by originators tend to be higher in absolute size for a jumbo loan, giving originators incentive to refinance their jumbo customers first (when inundated with business due to a refinancing wave, for example).

11.3 PREPAYMENT PROJECTIONS FOR JUMBO MBSs

Exhibits 11.1 and 11.2 compare projections for agency and Jumbo MBSs, and illustrate both the data and assumed borrower differences between the two types:

- A stronger *lock-in effect* (the disincentive to move due to currently holding a discount loan) for whole loans because of higher loan balances can result in out-of-the-money whole loan speeds converging to corresponding agency speeds. (While the stronger lock-in for jumbos tends to slow turnover projections, note that this is roughly balanced by the assumed higher mobility of jumbo borrowers discussed earlier.)
- If rates decline, whole loan speeds accelerate at a faster rate than agencies, due to the assumed differences noted above. Over time, burnout implies that speeds on both agencies and whole loans will decline, but a lower degree of burnout on the whole loans keeps the differentials from converging.

EXHIBIT 11.1 One-Year Prepayment Projections for New Production Current Coupon Agency and Jumbo MBSs

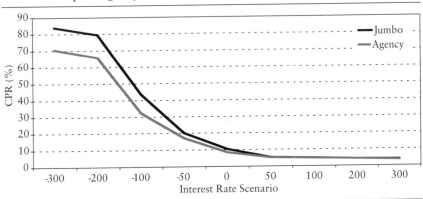

Source: Salomon Smith Barney.

EXHIBIT 11.2   Long-Term Prepayment Projections for New Production
Current Coupon Agency and Jumbo MBSs

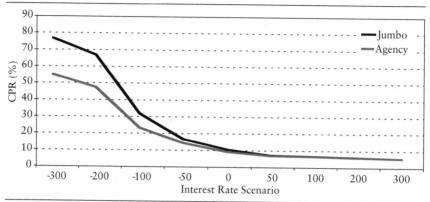

Source: Salomon Smith Barney.

CHAPTER 12

Alternative-A Loans

Peter A. DiMartino

Alternative-A (alt-A) mortgages have become an established niche within the private-label mortgage-backed securities (MBS) sector, developing rapidly in recent years. Alt-A lenders provide mortgage funding to borrowers whose qualifying characteristics fall just outside the margins of conforming underwriting guidelines established by the government-sponsored enterprises (GSEs). As a result, the alt-A sector stands apart from the more-established and relatively homogeneous agency and jumbo non-agency markets with respect to collateral performance and relative-value characteristics.

Alt-A collateral does not consist of a well-defined set of collateral characteristics, because alt-A lenders strive to serve borrowers that exist "outside the box." This lack of conformity carries with it much of the convexity advantage associated with this product. Alt-A loans are typically (but not exclusively) made to "A" quality credit borrowers whose mortgage characteristics encompass a wide range of loan balances, LTVs, documentation types, and so on. These borrowers pay a premium over conforming mortgage rates because their loan characteristics do not fit conforming underwriting guidelines. For instance, such borrowers may be unwilling or unable to provide the documentation required for the purposes of income verification, or their debt-to-income ratios may exceed conforming limits.

Initially, alt-A mortgages were typically held in portfolio by lenders, but the secondary markets have shown strong interest in securitizing these loans since the first alt-A securitization in mid-1994 by conduit Independent National Mortgage Corporation (Indy Mac). The sector has steadily gained sponsorship from investors who believe that alt-A collateral should exhibit favorable prepayment characteristics relative to agency and non-agency collateral, given the relatively low loan balances and high numbers of alternate-documentation borrowers in alt-A pools. Current sponsors for the sector include a wide range of fixed-income investors, including commercial banks, thrifts, insurance companies, mutual funds, and money managers.

We believe that substantial opportunities exist for investors in the alt-A subsector. To uncover these opportunities, Salomon Smith Barney introduced a suite of issuer-specific prepayment models in 1998. Our models have been constructed to fit the unique collateral attributes and prepayment histories for each issuer. These models strongly underscore our belief that alt-A issuers originate and securitize nonhomogeneous mortgage products. Consequently, our models offer investors a sound way to extract value in the alt-A subsector.

We have organized our review of the alt-A sector into eight main sections. First, we offer capsule descriptions of *Key Issuers in the Alt-A Sector.* Second, we chart the growth of the alt-A sector by discussing *Issuance and Production Volume* over the last few years. Third, we provide a detailed description of *Program and Collateral Characteristics* for the major alt-A issuers, thus illuminating the underwriting practices followed in this sector. Fourth, we discuss the *Credit Performance of Alt-A Collateral* by presenting cumulative loss snapshots. Fifth, we discuss the *Prepayment Characteristics of Alt-A Collateral* and characterize issuer-specific differences in prepayment speeds. Sixth, we discuss the *Prepayment Modeling of Alt-A Collateral* and the key features of our suite of issuer-specific prepayment models for the alt-A sector. Seventh, we examine *The Impact of the GSEs on the Alt-A sector.* In the final main section, we outline our *Conclusions.* An appendix to the report offers *A Loan-Level Snapshot of Alt-A Collateral.*

12.1 KEY ISSUERS IN THE ALT-A SECTOR

Since the inception of the first alt-A transaction in mid-1994, the number of alt-A lenders has expanded rapidly. The number of participants in the sector continued to grow in 1998—in addition to introducing alt-A securitizations by newcomers like Chase and Norwest (presently know as Wells Fargo), we also witnessed the entry of Fannie Mae and Freddie Mac into the sector. However, over the past few years, Headlands, ICIFC/IMPAC, RALI, and RAST have been the most prominent organizations in the origination, acquisition, and securitization of alt-A mortgages. Throughout this chapter, we focus on the lending patterns and collateral characteristics of these four lenders. Next, we provide a brief description of selected lenders and issuers in the alt-A sector. These organizations may issue alt-A under their own, or successor, company shelf registrations. In addition, instead of issuing MBS, they may sell whole loans.

■ *Chase Manhattan Mortgage Corporation (CMMC),* the nation's third-largest residential mortgage lender, is a subsidiary of The Chase Manhattan Corporation, a bank holding company with more than $365 billion in assets. CMMC has been originating alt-A collateral since September 1996, primarily through its *ChaseFlex* mortgage programs, and has delivered its fixed-rate alt-A collateral into both securitized and whole-loan transactions. Through August 1998, CMMC originated over $1 billion in alt-A mortgages. CMMC issued its first alt-A securitized transaction under its Chase Mortgage Finance Corp. shelf in July. The CMMC executive offices are located in Edison, New Jersey.

■ *Headlands Mortgage Securities, Incorporated (HMSI)*, a publicly owned mortgage company, has originated, acquired, sold, and serviced residential mortgage loans for over 10 years. HMSI's first securitization closed in February 1997. Prior to that, HMSI sold its alt-A production to other mortgage conduits. After completing six securities transactions in 1997 representing over $1.5 billion, HMSI has since sold its alt-A production as whole loans again. HMSI has 13 wholesale and nine retail locations in 13 states. HMSI is located in Larkspur, California. At the beginning of 1999, GreenPoint Financial acquired Headlands Mortgage.

■ *IMPAC Funding Corporation (ICIFC/IMPAC)*, formerly ICI Funding Corporation, is a mortgage REIT. IMPAC Mortgage Holdings, Incorporated (IMH), is the residential arm of IMPAC. IMH began acquiring niche residential mortgage loans nationwide in 1995 and, together with ICIFC/IMPAC, is one of the alt-A market's primary issuers. IMPAC is a subsidiary of Imperial Credit Industries Incorporated, also a publicly traded REIT. IMH's first securitization closed in March 1997 on the ICIFC shelf registration. Since then, ICIFC/IMPAC has securitized about $1.7 billion on its own shelf. Prior to that, ICIFC sold its mortgage production to other mortgage conduits. IMPAC's executive offices are located in Santa Ana Heights, California.

■ *Norwest Integrated Structured Assets, Incorporated (NISTAR)* is the alt-A shelf registration of Norwest Mortgage (a wholly owned subsidiary of Norwest Corp.), one of the nation's leading lenders and servicers of first-lien residential mortgages. Norwest Mortgage operates over 725 retail branches nationwide, the largest retail network in the country. As a major supplier of jumbo securities in the non-agency MBS market (on the NASCOR shelf), Norwest Mortgage marked its entry into the alt-A securities market by issuing NISTAR 1998-1 in the second quarter of 1998. In November 1998, Norwest Bank acquired Well Fargo Bank, but the organization continues to be known as Wells Fargo Bank. As of February 2000, however, alt-A issuance took place using the NISTAR shelf name.

■ *Residential Accredit Loan, Incorporated (RALI)* is one of four shelf registrations in the Residential Funding Corporation (RFC) family. RFC, a subsidiary of GMAC, is a mortgage conduit and a major issuer of traditional jumbo, alt-A, and home equity mortgage loans. Perennially the non-agency MBS market's top-ranked issuer by volume, RFC first securitized alt-A mortgages on the RALI shelf in September 1995. Since then, RFC has issued approximately $17 billion in RALI securities. RFC is located in Bloomington, Minnesota.

■ *Residential Asset Securitization Trust (RAST)* and INMC represent mortgage transactions by Independent National Mortgage Corporation (Indy Mac), a subsidiary of CWM Mortgage Holdings—a publicly traded REIT. Indy Mac, a mortgage conduit, is regarded as the first and largest issuer of alt-A niche mortgages. Indy Mac has issued nearly $20 billion in fixed-rate and adjustable-rate alt-A transactions since mid-1994 under the RAST and INMC labels. Indy Mac is headquartered in Pasadena, California.

12.2 ISSUANCE AND PRODUCTION VOLUME

Issuance data help underscore the vigorous growth of the alt-A sector over the past few years. Issuance in the sector has consistently comprised between 15% to 20% of the non-agency MBS market each quarter. Alt-A issuance has kept pace with the spectacular increase in non-agency MBS issuance this year. For example, in the first half of 1998, non-agency issuance neared $60

EXHIBIT 12.1   The Growth of the Alt-A sector, August 1998

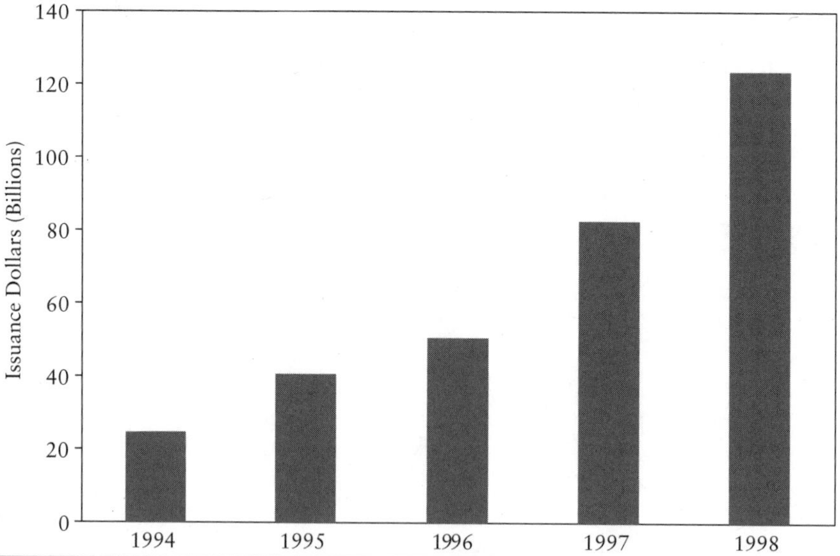

Source: Salomon Smith Barney.

EXHIBIT 12.2 Issuance and Production Volume for Alt-A Issuers, August 2000 (Dollars in Millions)

	CMMC	HMSI	ICIFC/ IMPAC	NISTAR	RALI	RAST
Issuance to Date	$1,000	$3,000	$1,750	$300	17,000	20,000
Date of First Securitization	July-98	Feb-97	Mar-97	May-98	Sep-95	Jun-94

[a] Retail only—does not include bulk acquisitions or wholesale originations.
[b] Alt-A product is held in portfolio.
Source: Salomon Smith Barney.

billion, while alt-As weighed in at about $10 billion. At this point, the relatively new alt-A sector represents about $28 billion in outstanding securities, about 11% of traditional non-agencies. Our estimates for issuance in the alt-A sector are based on securitizations by the major issuers in the alt-A market. Exhibit 12.1 aggregates the volume of these securitizations, and shows that the alt-A market has grown explosively since its inception in mid-1994. At the close of 1998, the volume of alt-A securitizations was about $22 billion for the year, about 2.5 times the volume for 1997.

Exhibit 12.2 summarizes issuance and production volume for the major alt-A issuers. Based on annual rates of production for the past two years, RALI and RAST have accounted for between 70% to 80% of all issuance in the alt-A sector.

12.3 PROGRAM AND COLLATERAL CHARACTERISTICS

Alternative-A mortgages often have conforming balances and are most often taken out by borrowers with an A–quality credit history. In addition, however, alt-A mortgages typically have some features that make them ineligible for sale to the agencies. These features vary from borrower to borrower and are not limited to but usually include the following borrower and loan characteristics:

- *A preference for expanded criteria underwriting.* Alt-A borrowers often utilize "Stated Income,"[1] "No-Ratio,"[2] and alternate forms of documentation for the purposes of establishing their eligibility for a mortgage.
- *Debt-to-income ratios that can exceed agency limits.* Alt-A borrowers' debt-to-income ratios can average 38% to 40% on the back end,

---

[1] Borrowers are required only to state their income and provide verbal verification of employment.
[2] Borrowers do not disclose their income, which means that debt ratios cannot be calculated.

EXHIBIT 12.3   Loan Purposes for Alt-A Collateral by Issuer, August 1998

	HMSI	ICIFC/IMPAC	RALI	RAST/INMC
Purchase	54%	65%	60%	48%
Refinance/Rate-term	18	14	17	26
Refinance/Cash-out	27	20	22	26
Construction	0	1	1	0

Source: Salomon Smith Barney.

whereas the maximum debt-to-income ratio permitted by Fannie Mae and Freddie Mac is 36% in most programs.

■ *LTV ratios that can exceed agency limits.* Alt-A programs permit LTV ratios that would exceed agency limits on certain types of loans. For example, alt-A programs are often a haven for *investor loans*[3] because of competitive rates and more liberal underwriting guidelines than those currently offered by the agencies. As another example, in return for paying an additional premium, alt-A borrowers may be permitted to take out a mortgage with an LTV exceeding 80% (but generally less than or equal to 95%) without paying private mortgage insurance (PMI).

While this summary provides us with a useful overview of the alt-A sector, the different alt-A issuers tend to specialize in specific combinations of borrower/loan/property characteristics. The result is that alt-A collateral may vary significantly from issuer to issuer. To clarify this issue, we provide a detailed summary of the differences and similarities in the collateral of major alt-A issuers with respect to certain characteristics. In the process, we also obtain a better grasp of the underwriting practices followed in this sector.

Loan Purpose

Broadly speaking, slightly more than half of all alt-A borrowers use their mortgage loans to purchase a house, while the remainder are refinancers (see Exhibit 12.3). More than half of all alt-A refinancers tap into the equity in their homes. The fact that these borrowers choose to do an equity-out refinance through an alt-A program suggests that they have nontraditional income and employment histories, often in combination with an LTV ratio that is higher than permitted in agency guidelines.

---

[3] An *investor loan* is a mortgage on a one- to four-family unit residential property that will be leased by the owner to others. If the owner lives in one unit and rents out the others, the property is called *owner-occupied;* otherwise it is called *nonowner-occupied.* An *investment property* is financed with an *investor* loan.

EXHIBIT 12.4   Documentation Type for Alt-A Collateral by Issuer, August 1998

	HMSI	ICIFC/IMPAC	RALI	RAST/INMC
Full Documentation	31%	17%	53%	37%

Source: Salomon Smith Barney.

Among the different issuers, ICIFC/IMPAC pools historically have the greatest fraction of purchase loans, while Headlands and RAST pools have the greatest fraction of refinance loans.

Documentation Type

A significant majority of alt-A borrowers prefer the convenience of reduced or alternate forms of documentation when qualifying for their mortgage loans (see Exhibit 12.4). As previously discussed, "Stated-Income," "No Income/No Asset," "No-Ratio," and other such programs are commonly used. *These programs usually focus on the borrower's credit score and the mortgage property to establish eligibility.* Furthermore, such programs are more restrictive in terms of the permitted minimum qualifying credit scores and the maximum loan-size/LTV combinations. ICIFC/IMPAC pools have the smallest fraction of Full Documentation (Full-Doc) loans, while RALI pools have the highest.

What type of borrower would take out an alternate/limited documentation loan? Given that lenders' full documentation programs often require borrowers to provide two years of W-2s and two to three months of bank statements, the typical alternate documentation borrower will usually not be able to, or not wish to, provide this type of detailed information. In particular, this would apply to self-employed borrowers who, *in addition to providing two years of tax returns, are also required to submit year-to-date profit-and-loss statements, balance sheets for the past two years,* and so on, in traditional lending programs.

Occupancy Type

Investor loans are popular in alt-A programs, since alt-A lenders typically offer a competitive rate compared to the agencies.[4] In addition, *underwriting guidelines for both purchase and refinance investor loans in alt-A*

---

[4]Conforming borrowers currently pay a premium of 1.5 points (about 37.5bp) on investor loans.

EXHIBIT 12.5   Occupancy Type for Alt-A Collateral by Issuer, August 1998

	HMSI	ICIFC/IMPAC	RALI	RAST/INMC
Primary Residence	80%	93%	69%	77%
Secondary	3	3	0	4
Investment	16	4	31	19

Source: Salomon Smith Barney.

programs are typically more relaxed with respect to maximum loan sizes/LTV ratios than for the agencies.[5] With regard to specific issuers, RALI pools have the greatest percentage of investor loans, while ICIFC/IMPAC pools have the least (see Exhibit 12.5).

Property Type

Single-family property types dominate alt-A collateral, though as Exhibit 12.6 shows, the pools also contain a fair number of loans on multifamily properties, condos, and planned unit developments (PUDs). *Most of the multifamily properties are investment properties.* Not surprisingly, given their relatively high percentages of investor loans, RALI pools have the largest proportion of loans on multifamily properties.

LOAN RATE

The notion of an alt-A mortgage rate is not particularly well-defined, because alt-A lenders offer a number of different financing programs, each of which will have a range of different premiums (depending upon the characteristics of the mortgage loan) associated with it.

EXHIBIT 12.6   Property Type for Alt-A Collateral by Issuer, August 1998

	HMSI	ICIFC/IMPAC	RALI	RAST/INMC
1 Family	72%	82%	62%	74%
2-4 Family	9	4	15	11
Condos	5	6	8	6
PUD	13	8	14	8

Source: Salomon Smith Barney.

---

[5] Agency guidelines for investor loans have recently been expanded (*see Bond Market Roundup: Strategy,* October 10, 1997). We return to this issue later in Section 12.7, "The Impact of the GSEs on the Alt-A Sector."

EXHIBIT 12.7   Loan Rate for Alt-A Collateral by Issuer, August 1998

		HMSI	ICIFC/IMPAC	RALI	RAST
WAC	1997	8.56%	9.00%	8.66%	8.58%
	1998	8.18	9.00	8.15	8.08

Source: Salomon Smith Barney.

Obviously, mortgage rates will also depend on the geographic location of borrowers. Keeping these uncertainties in mind, we can still obtain a rough estimate of an alt-A mortgage rate by computing the average spread between the WAC of alt-A transactions and prevailing conforming mortgage rates.[6] *This spread averaged between 100bp (basis points) and 150bp in early 1996 and has since narrowed to between 80bp and 100bp.*[7] Spread differences vary over time.

Exhibit 12.7 shows the loan coupon for the different alt-A issuers, averaged over all their outstanding loans from a specified origination year. *The WACs on ICIFC/IMPAC deals are higher, in our opinion, because of their very small proportion of Full-Doc borrowers and greater concentrations of loans originated with LTVs exceeding 80%.*

CREDIT SCORES

A credit score assesses a borrower's willingness and ability to repay the mortgage loan obligation. The most frequently cited credit score is the FICO score, developed by the Fair, Isaac Company, Incorporated. FICO scores can range from below 400 to a maximum of approximately 900. Higher scores imply a more favorable credit history. Therefore, a FICO score can be viewed as a measure of relative risk that a borrower represents to the holder/servicer of the mortgage. These scores may be used by the lender in the underwriting process, as well as by the rating agencies in the rating process.[8]

---

[6] The conforming mortgage rate is lagged by two months to coincide with the month the loans were originated in.

[7] Exhibit 12.1 has a graph of this spread. A topic of much interest is whether this spread has narrowed in the last year as a result of increased competition in the alternative-A sector because of the entry of the GSEs. The issue is addressed in Section 12.7, "The Impact of the GSEs on the Alt-A Sector."

[8] A detailed account of the factors considered in credit scoring may be found in our alt-A primer for 1997: *The "Alternative-A" Nonagency Subsector: A Primer,* Peter DiMartino, June 3, 1997.

EXHIBIT 12.8   Average FICO Score for Alt-A Collateral by Issuer, August 1998

	HMSI	ICIFC/IMPAC	RALI	RAST
1997	700	680	710	700
1998	700	690	710	710

Sources: Indy Mac, RFC, and Salomon Smith Barney.

About two-thirds of alt-A loans were scored last year, and credit scores are captured on virtually all new alt-A mortgage originations. Generally, the minimum FICO score in alt-A lending is 620. As seen in Exhibit 12.8, the weighted-average credit scores for these lenders' 1998 originations ranges from 690 to 710. For the sake of comparison, about 60% of all conventional borrowers (conforming as well as nonconforming) have FICO scores higher than 720, and only about 10% have FICO scores less than 620.[9] On the other hand, *less than 5% of alt-A borrowers have FICO scores less than 620.* The trend (see Exhibit 12.8) in the alt-A sector over the past year is toward higher FICO underwriting. Presently, RALI and RAST pools have the highest average FICO scores.

However, on a limited basis, and with significant compensating factors (like additional reserve requirements, maximum LTV, and loan amount restrictions), FICO scores below 620 may be included in some alt-A pools. For example, small percentages of borrowers in selected alt-A transactions have credit histories that are more commonly found in "B&C" pools. Clearly, these loans would not qualify under the standard agency underwriting guidelines, and bear higher interest rates than mortgage loans made to more creditworthy alt-A borrowers. *Small percentages of subprime loans in alt-A pools will likely enhance the convexity advantage of those pools without harming the credit performance of the entire pool.*

LOAN BALANCE

Exhibit 12.9 summarizes average loan balances for the various alt-A issuers. The average loan balances in alt-A transactions range from 1.3 to 1.7 times the average loan balances found in agency collateral of comparable characteristics. As Exhibit 12.9 also shows, alt-A collateral can contain a substantial number of nonconforming loans. Balances on nonconforming alt-A

---

[9] "The Contours of Default Risk," Dan Feshbach and Craig Focardi, *Mortgage Banking*, February 1998.

EXHIBIT 12.9 Original Loan Balances for Alt-A Collateral by Issuer, August 1998

	HMSI	ICIFC/IMPAC	RALI	RAST/INMC
Average Loan Balance	$156,000	$143,000	$118,000	$147,000
Loan Balance > $200,000	47%	38%	33%	47%

Source: Salomon Smith Barney.

loans average about $350,000, which is on the high end of the average loan balances occurring in non-agency transactions. As shown in Exhibit 12.9, *RALI transactions have the lowest overall average balances and the smallest percentage of loan balances greater than $200,000. Both these characteristics point toward RALI pools offering superior convexity.*

LOAN-TO-VALUE RATIOS

As Exhibit 12.10 shows, average loan-to-value ratios (LTVs) on alt-A pools range from a low of 72% for RAST to 78% for ICIFC/IMPAC. At the same time, HMSI has the fewest loans exceeding 80% LTV in its pools (5%), while ICIFC/IMPAC has 41%. In some recent transactions, ICIFC/IMPAC's LTVs averaged 80% with high LTV loans exceeding 50% of the pool. *ICIFC/IMPAC's convexity characteristics benefit from the high percentage of loans with LTVs exceeding 80%,* along with its low percentage of high balance loans (see previous section).

Geographic Concentration

Exhibit 12.11 shows that alt-A pools can have substantial California concentrations ranging from 20% to 65% of the pool. Typical California concentrations for comparable agency and non-agency collateral average about 15% and 30%, respectively. Recently originated alt-A pools are showing even heavier California concentrations than before, probably as a direct consequence of the resurgent mortgage origination industry in the state.

EXHIBIT 12.10 Original LTV Ratios for Alt-A Collateral by Issuer, August 1998

	HMSI	ICIFC/IMPAC	RALI	RAST/INMC
Average LTV	74%	78%	77%	72%
LTV > 80%	5	41	26	10

Source: Salomon Smith Barney.

EXHIBIT 12.11   Geographic Concentration for Alt-A Collateral by Issuer, August 1998

	HMSI		ICIFC/IMPAC		RALI		RAST/INMC	
Top 3 States	CA	65%	CA	33%	CA	20%	CA	49%
	OR	9	FL	17	FL	9	NY	6
	WA	8	NJ	9	TX	7	CO	3

Source: Salomon Smith Barney.

Apart from California, alt-A pools show a fair amount of geographic diversity, with typically no more than 10% of any pool's balance in a particular state. ICIFC/IMPAC is an exception as its pools appear to have high Florida concentrations too (see Exhibit 12.11). *Within California, loan concentration is dominant in the southern portion of the state* for each issuer's loan volume originated in 1998.

Loan Term

About 90% to 95% of all alt-A loans have a 30-year term, with the remainder consisting mostly of loans with a 15-year term. HMSI and ICIFC/IMPAC typically have a mixture of 30-year and 15-year collateral in their transactions, with about 10% to 20% of the collateral in any particular transaction having a 15-year term. On the other hand, RALI and RAST are currently issuing their 15-year collateral as a separate transaction. Based on the somewhat limited data available for 15-year alt-A transactions,[10] a comparison of 15-year and 30-year alt-A collateral shows that *15-year pools typically have smaller loan balances, a relatively larger number of refinance mortgages, and lower LTV ratios.* It is unclear whether 15-year alt-A collateral possesses an additional convexity advantage, given the net effect of its altered collateral characteristics.

A Loan-Level Snapshot of Alt-A Collateral

Although these descriptions provide a detailed picture of the characteristics of alt-A collateral, they give little idea of the interrelationships between these same characteristics. Exhibit 12.23 through Exhibit 12.29 at the end of the chapter summarize these interrelationships for RALI collateral in matrix form. Although the exact proportion of loans in various cells of the

---

[10] See MB766, available on the *Yield Book* or Salomon Direct.

matrix will vary from issuer to issuer, most of the general patterns will be the same. For instance, the data show that:

- A majority of investor loans are used for the purchase of a property. Investor loans are typically underwritten with full documentation, have conforming average loan balances, and have original LTV ratios that are a little higher than those on primary residence alt-A loans.
- Mortgage loans with original LTV ratios greater than 80% are principally purchase loans, and all such loans are underwritten using full documentation. A significant fraction of investor loans have original LTV ratios between 80% to 90%, but virtually none have original LTV ratios greater than 90%.

12.4 CREDIT PERFORMANCE OF ALT-A COLLATERAL

Cumulative Loss Snapshot

Given the prominence of RALI and RAST in the alt-A sector, the credit performance of these two issuers serves as a good proxy for the credit performance of the entire alt-A sector. Both RALI and RAST publish cumulative loss data monthly, and Exhibit 12.12 summarizes the loss data currently available by origination year as a percentage of original collateral balance.

Credit losses on alt-A transactions to date are not significant for investment-grade investors. As shown in Exhibit 12.12, cumulative losses for RAST's 1994 and 1995 production amount to 55bp and 25bp, respectively, as of June 1998. For RAST, these origination years are meaningful because they represent adequate seasoning and issuance. Cumulative losses on 1996 RALI (representing their first full year of issuance) and RAST pools are

EXHIBIT 12.12 Cumulative Losses for RALI and RAST by Origination Year,[a] June 1998

	Origination Year			
	1994	1995	1996	1997
RALI	NA	33 bp[b]	7 bp	<1 bp
RAST	55 bp[c]	25	9	<1

[a] Fixed-rate 30-year and 15-year collateral.
[b] Losses from RALI 1995-QS1.
[c] Transactions beginning with 1994-L, which is the first of Indy Mac's deals to close under the INMC banner.
Sources: Salomon Smith Barney, RFC, and Indy Mac.

presently lower (7bp and 9bp, respectively), yet within the realm of expectations for newer alt-A originations.

Cumulative losses in the alt-A sector occur sooner and reach higher peaks than those found in the traditional non-agency market for comparable origination years. For example, GE, Pru Home, and RFC transactions backed by 30-year fixed-rate mortgages issued in 1994 and 1995 experienced losses that average approximately 10bp presently. Losses sustained by 1996 traditional non-agency pools are about one-third of alt-A losses from the same year. Relative to traditional non-agencies, the alt-A loss curve appears steeper.

Loss distributions for alt-A vintages are unlike traditional non-agency vintages. For example, one year ago, cumulative losses on RAST's 1994 and 1995 fixed-rate loans were 23bp and 12bp, respectively.[11] Presently, losses from these vintages have doubled. For the lone RALI transaction issued in 1995 (RALI 1995-QS1), losses one year ago amounted to 7bp. In the past year, losses on that transaction increased almost five-fold to 33bp. During the same period, on the other hand, losses on traditional non-agency transactions issued in 1994 and 1995 increased by 25% to approximately 10bp on average.

Credit enhancement for alt-A triple-As exceeds traditional non-agency triple-As by more than 50%. Today, alt-A subordination levels average 6.5%, while the average credit enhancement level for fixed-rate, 30-year traditional non-agencies is about 4.00%. Since the first transactions in 1994 and 1995, alt-A credit enhancement requirements have decreased proportionately to traditional non-agencies. For example, the average subordination level for fixed-rate alt-A pools in 1995 was 10%, while traditional non-agencies averaged 6%.

We believe that current credit enhancement levels are justified given the following:

■ A better understanding of the alt-A borrower;
■ An improved focus on loss mitigation;
■ More clearly defined and consistently applied underwriting criteria; and
■ The use of credit scoring in the underwriting process since 1997.

With the advent of improved underwriting, we expect that recent originations will experience better credit performance than early alt-A origina-

---

[11] See "Fourth Annual Historical Loss Comparison of Major Nonagency Issuers," *Bond Market Roundup: Strategy,* October 24, 1997, Salomon Smith Barney.

tions. Also pointing toward improved credit performance for newer alt-A transactions is the accompanying stable real estate environment in the United States. Furthermore, faster baseline prepayment speeds experienced in alt-A pools creates the potential for faster deleveraging of the subordinate class (because of the five-year prepayment lockout typically structured into fixed-rate MBS transactions).

12.5 PREPAYMENT CHARACTERISTICS OF ALT-A COLLATERAL

The borrower and loan characteristics described in the previous sections interact to create a fairly distinctive profile for alt-A prepayment behavior. This section compares alt-A and agency prepayment behavior with respect to these distinctive patterns, and then maps out the issuer-specific characteristics of alt-A prepayments.

Interest-Rate Sensitivity Relative to Agency Collateral

With a majority of alt-A loans underwritten to "expanded criteria" guidelines, we would expect alt-A collateral to enjoy favorable convexity characteristics. This follows because the typical alt-A borrower will not, at least initially, have access to the same refinancing opportunities as an agency borrower. In general, historical prepayment speeds on alt-A collateral have supported this expectation. However, the February to March 1998 refinance wave constituted the first serious test of the interest-rate sensitivity of alt-A collateral.

To summarize alt-A prepayment behavior over this period, we created alt-A "generics" by aggregating loan level data from INMC, RALI, RAST, and HMSI transactions in WAC and origination year buckets. If we compare peak speeds on alt-A and Fannie Mae generics *with the same WAC*, we find that for premiums, March alt-A speeds were about 70% to 80% of those experienced by comparable Fannie Mae loans. Since the alt-A mortgage rate is typically 80bp to 100bp above prevailing conforming rates, a more telling comparison can be found in Exhibit 12.13 which compares alt-A and agency vintages *with the same refinance incentive*. Overall, the one-month, three-month, and one-year ratios in Exhibit 12.13 convincingly illustrate the diminished interest-rate sensitivity of alt-A collateral.

Also noteworthy in Exhibit 12.13 are the high speeds on alt-A vintages with WACs ranging from 7.5% to 8.5%. These lower WAC vintages tend to have a high concentration of nonconforming balance loans. We revisit the issue of prepayment speeds on nonconforming balance alt-A loans later in this section.

EXHIBIT 12.13 Historical Speeds on Fannie Maes and Alt-A Vintages as of March 1998

		Alternative-A						Fannie Mae					Ratio of Alt-A to FNMA Speeds for Last		
WAC	Orig	Amt Out				% CPR for Last						% CPR for Last			
Range	Year	($mm)	WAC	Age	1-Mo	3-Mo	12-Mo	Cpn	WAC	Age	1-Mo	3-Mo	12-Mo	1-Mo	3-Mo	12-Mo
7.50-7.99	1997	560	7.79%	6	17.0	18.1	6.3	6.5	7.26%	6	3.0	2.2	1.4	5.67	8.23	4.50
8.00-8.49	1997	1,832	8.22	8	26.7	23.6	14.3	7.0	7.66	8	13.1	11.4	4.5	2.04	2.07	3.18
	1996	383	8.25	21	43.8	40.4	21.6		7.64	23	18.7	14.9	8.2	2.34	2.71	2.63
8.50-8.99	1997	2,669	8.68	9	31.8	24.2	14.4	7.5	8.06	10	32.7	27.4	11.6	0.97	0.88	1.24
	1996	1,275	8.72	21	42.5	32.7	21.9		8.13	20	42.8	34.4	16.0	0.99	0.95	1.37
	1995	386	8.73	29	39.5	32.4	24.5		8.09	31	39.5	30.6	16.5	1.00	1.06	1.49
9.00-9.49	1997	938	9.13	10	33.5	26.1	19.4	8.0	8.47	10	42.9	34.4	17.8	0.78	0.76	1.09
	1996	983	9.18	20	45.1	37.6	26.2		8.53	20	52.3	41.7	21.6	0.86	0.90	1.21
	1995	474	9.19	30	32.5	29.7	25.2		8.59	33	52.7	41.5	24.3	0.62	0.72	1.04
9.50-9.99	1997	189	9.59	10	33.3	22.0	19.6	8.5	8.93	11	40.9	33.3	26.8	0.81	0.66	0.73
	1996	471	9.63	20	37.9	31.2	26.9		8.95	20	49.9	39.7	24.9	0.76	0.79	1.08
	1995	382	9.67	33	37.2	31.2	28.5		9.07	35	55.2	44.4	28.5	0.67	0.70	1.00

Source: Salomon Smith Barney.

Does alt-A collateral continue to retain its convexity advantages relative to agency collateral after a seasoning period of one to two years? Prepayment data that provide an answer to this question are still relatively sparse; the most seasoned alt-A collateral dates back to a handful of INMC deals issued in 1995. However, the available data do seem to suggest that alt-A speeds continue to be somewhat less reactive, *though only by a few CPR.* Exhibit 12.14 illustrates this by comparing speeds on two 1995 vintage INMC deals and Fannie Mae cohorts with comparable refinance incentive (as in Exhibit 12.13).

Seasoning of Prepayment Speeds

The prepayment data presented so far point toward fast baseline speeds for alt-A collateral. For example, despite the fact that the one-month ratios of alt-A to agency speeds in Exhibit 12.13 are mostly less than or equal to 1.0, the one-year speed ratios are typically greater than 1.0. Another piece of evidence comes from comparing INMC and Fannie Mae prepayment speeds in Exhibit 12.14 from mid-1996 to late-1997, when interest rates were fairly stable.

Exhibit 12.15 provides yet another perspective on this issue and shows how prepayment speeds on alt-A collateral season rapidly over the first year, and remain relatively stable after this point. In brief, in stable interest-rate environments baseline alt-A prepayment speeds seem as fast as, or a little faster than, agency speeds for comparable coupons. Over periods where

EXHIBIT 12.14 Historical Speeds on Fannie Maes and 1995 Vintage INMC Deals, August 1998*

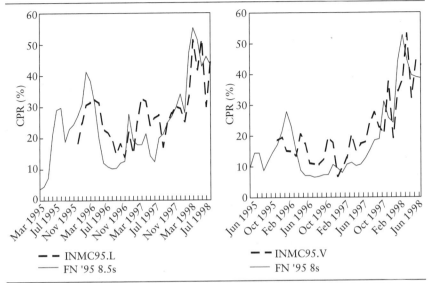

- - INMC95.L
— FN '95 8.5s

- - INMC95.V
— FN '95 8s

*WACs: INMC95.L 9.69%, INMC95.V 9.07%, FN '95 8s 8.58%, FN '95 8.5s 9.07%.
Source: Salomon Smith Barney.

interest rates decline sharply, speeds on alt-A pools will be slower than comparable agency pools.

Issuer-Specific Prepayment Differences

Overall prepayment levels on alt-A transactions with similar coupons and ages but originated by different issuers can vary quite significantly. For

EXHIBIT 12.15 Prepayment Rates in CPR (%) for Alt-A Collateral by Relative Coupon and Age, August 1998

	Age (months)					
Relative Coupon*	0-5	5-10	10-15	15-20	20-25	>25
0.25 - 0.35	13%	24%	31%	34%	34%	33%
0.15 - 0.25	15	18	26	21	23	28
0.05 - 0.15	11	11	13	14	11	13

*Relative coupon is calculated as $C/M - 1$, where C = WAC and M = FHLMC mortgage rate (lagged by two months).
Source: Salomon Smith Barney.

EXHIBIT 12.16   Issuer-Specific Differences in Prepayment Speeds,
August 1998*

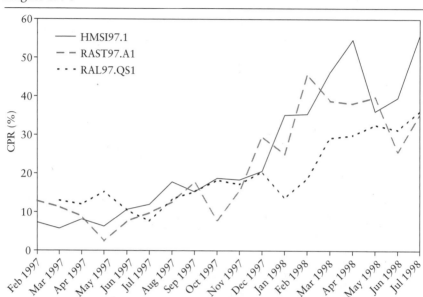

RAST97.A1: WAC = 8.62%, Age = 19 months, Average loan bal = $142K, CA% = 35.
RAL97.QS1: WAC = 8.77%, Age = 19 months, Average loan bal = $102K, CA% = 21.
Source: Salomon Smith Barney.

example, Exhibit 12.16 shows that HMSI97.1 has been prepaying about
10% CPR faster than RAST97.A1 over the past three months, and had a
peak speed that was 16% CPR higher during the 1998 refinance wave. Similarly, RAL97.QS1 has been prepaying 5% to 10% slower CPR than
RAST97.A1 over the past six months, despite having a WAC that is about
15bp higher.[12]

Exhibit 12.17 reveals one of the driving forces behind issuer-specific
differences in speeds. Here, we break down WAC and vintage year alt-A
"generics" by separating loans with conforming loan balances and nonconforming loan balances into separate buckets. We have chosen to highlight
RALI and RAST collateral in Exhibit 12.17, since these issuers constitute
the most consistent presence in the alt-A market.

Exhibit 12.17 shows that there is a dramatic difference in prepayment
speeds when loans are partitioned on this basis—on average, the noncon-

---

[12] The examples we have picked are quite representative. See MB766 for further
details.

EXHIBIT 12.17   RALI and RAST Prepayment Speeds: Conforming versus Nonconforming Balance Loans, August 1998*

Coupon Range	Orig. Year	Conf/ Nconf	WAC	WAM	Avg Ln Size ($k)	Avg LTV	Amt Iss ($m)	Amt Out ($m)	Factor	CPR (%) 1-Mo	3-Mo	6-Mo	12-Mo
RALI													
8.00 - 8.49	1996	Conf	8.27%	27.2	108	74%	53.0	43.1	0.81	25.2	27.1	24.4	16.6
	1996	Nconf	8.24	27.2	341	75	44.7	26.5	0.59	25.5	49.3	50.5	38.3
	1997	Conf	8.23	28.9	111	76	573.0	532.9	0.93	16.2	14.9	13.9	9.3
	1997	Nconf	8.22	29.0	329	76	260.3	229.1	0.88	31.4	27.5	24.3	16.8
8.50 - 8.99	1996	Conf	8.73	27.4	99	75	258.1	198.5	0.77	34.2	30.5	26.1	20.3
	1996	Nconf	8.73	27.6	336	76	125.1	75.4	0.60	46.7	51.7	43.1	34.6
	1997	Conf	8.69	28.7	94	78	1020.3	908.2	0.89	22.3	21.3	19.0	13.8
	1997	Nconf	8.66	28.8	324	76	287.7	227.4	0.79	35.1	31.8	32.7	25.4
RAST													
8.00 - 8.49	1996	Conf	8.27%	27.2	116	71%	90.3	67.6	0.75	34.4	35.5	32.4	22.9
	1996	Nconf	8.23	27.5	342	74	170.4	109.9	0.64	48.0	48.0	47.5	35.7
	1997	Conf	8.22	28.8	116	70	490.8	454.1	0.93	14.1	16.3	13.6	9.7
	1997	Nconf	8.19	28.8	341	70	509.0	380.0	0.75	38.3	37.4	40.2	34.4
8.50 - 8.99	1996	Conf	8.74	27.4	106	71	467.9	354.6	0.76	34.0	32.1	28.6	21.6
	1996	Nconf	8.70	27.7	339	74	422.8	234.8	0.56	39.0	51.0	46.9	40.3
	1997	Conf	8.68	28.6	103	72	859.0	759.2	0.88	23.4	22.3	19.5	14.1
	1997	Nconf	8.66	28.7	341	71	396.2	284.2	0.72	35.7	41.9	39.6	33.2

*Nonconforming (Nconf) balance loans have an original principal balance greater than $227,150.
Source: Salomon Smith Barney.

forming balance loans are prepaying almost twice as fast as the conforming balance loans. Furthermore, the speeds on conforming balance alt-A loans are significantly lower than for comparable agency loans. By contrast, nonconforming balance alt-A loans are prepaying at rates comparable to equivalent non-agency jumbo loans. This suggests that *average loan balance and the percentage of jumbo loans in an alt-A pool are the best indicators of convexity and value in alt-A securities.*

As Exhibit 12.16 shows, another current driver of prepayment speeds is the percentage of California collateral in alt-A transactions. Going forward, if the California region's housing markets continue to remain strong, transactions with higher California concentrations will likely have higher baseline speeds and show greater interest-rate sensitivity.

12.6 PREPAYMENT MODELING OF ALT-A COLLATERAL

Despite variations in the loan programs and collateral characteristics of alt-A issuers, the prepayment data in the previous section indicate that there is a fair amount of uniformity in the prepayment behavior of alt-A collateral. The central prepayment characteristics that seem to hold across the spectrum of alt-A issuers are: (1) reduced sensitivity to interest rates; (2) fast seasoning; and (3) for individual transactions, strong dependence of speeds on the average loan balance, the percentage of nonconforming balance loans, and the geographic dispersion of loans in the transaction. We describe how we model these prepayment characteristics, and conclude with a discussion of our model's projections in various interest-rate scenarios.

Differences between the Alt-A and Agency Prepayment Models

Since alt-A borrowers are typically A–quality borrowers, and since their mortgage loan characteristics are just outside the margins of agency guidelines, our starting point for the alt-A prepayment model is the agency prepayment model.[13] The distinctive prepayment characteristics of alt-A collateral are then captured by the following additional features:

- *Elbow shift.* The premium over prevailing conforming mortgage rates that alt-A borrowers pay reflects a number of factors (lack of proper documentation, reluctance to disclose income etc.) that were itemized in earlier sections. These factors also act to restrict the refinancing opportunities available to these borrowers. Consequently, for a given drop in rates, the refinancing incentive for an alt-A borrower is less than that for an agency borrower. In other words, we obtain the refinance S-curve of an alt-A borrower from the agency refinance S-curve by using an elbow shift.
- *Population mix.* The income/documentation issues that define the typical alt-A borrower also imply that, on average, alt-A pools contain a larger number of slower refinancers than a comparable agency or nonagency pool. Current prepayment data also seem to suggest that these borrowers continue to refinance somewhat more slowly than agency borrowers after a curing process (see Exhibit 12.14). We capture these characteristics of the alt-A borrower population by having a higher concentration of "slow" refinancers in the initial population mix for alt-A transactions relative to agency or whole-loan pools. As in our agency model, we assume that changes in personal circumstances over time will

---

[13] A detailed description of our agency prepayment model and the basic structure of all our prepayment models can be found on MB775, available in the Yield Book or Salomon Direct.details.

remove some of these problems, and this in turn is captured through an ongoing trickle of borrower migrations from slow to fast prepayment categories.

■ *Credit-driven refinancings.* Although the previous two features model why interest-rate driven refinancings are more muted for alt-A borrowers, they do not explain why baseline alt-A prepayment speeds are observed to be as fast as, or slightly faster than, agency speeds. Faster turnover seasoning for alt-A borrowers cannot be the explanation either. Given the presence in alt-A pools of a significant number of borrowers with income/documentation issues, high-LTV loans, and investment properties, it seems to us hard to argue that these borrowers would relocate at a quicker pace than agency borrowers. We believe that the fast seasoning of alt-A prepayment speeds is a result of credit curing, and the presence of borrowers with nonconforming loan balances.[14] Credit curing of alt-A borrowers is driven by improvements in borrower documentation and financial circumstances over a period of time. These credit-driven refinancings[15] are estimated to peak at between 4% to 6% CPR after a year, and then gradually decrease over the next few years.

■ *Pool-level loan balances and geographic distributions.* This data allows us to obtain precise estimates of the refinancing costs and equity buildup for the loans in a particular alt-A transaction.

Modeling Issuer-Specific Differences in Prepayments

Historical prepayment data show that prepayment levels on two alt-A transactions with similar WACs and ages, but originated by two different alt-A issuers can vary quite widely (see Exhibit 12.16). The previous section indicates that this difference seems to depend principally on the following three characteristics of the transactions: (1) the average loan balance, (2) the fraction of borrowers with nonconforming loan balances, and (3) the geographic distribution of the loans (particularly the California concentration). *The alt-A prepayment model uses pool-level information about the average loan balance and geographic concentration and therefore explicitly captures*

---

[14] Nonconforming balance borrowers are generally more sophisticated and have greater incentive to refinance because of their large loan balances.

[15] This term is somewhat of a misnomer in this context since the average alt-A borrower is an "A" credit from the FICO credit score perspective. However, from the *mortgage credit* perspective the borrower is clearly not "A" credit, since this is presumably why they are paying a premium rate and why credit enhancement levels are higher for alt-A pools than for traditional non-agency pools.

the differing prepayment characteristics of two transactions with dissimilar average loan sizes and geographic concentrations.

One problem is that these *issuer-specific differences in prepayment speeds cannot be completely explained by differences in average loan sizes and geographic concentrations.* For example, Exhibit 12.16 showed that speeds on HMSI97.1 had been much faster than speeds on RAST97.A1 over the last six to eight months. The two transactions are dissimilar in that HMSI97.1 has almost twice the California concentration of RAST97.A1, while RAST97.A1 has a WAC that is about 15bp higher. Now, the difference in equity buildup for borrowers in the two transactions after a year and a half of seasoning would not be expected to lead to such dramatic differences in prepayment rates, especially in light of the fact that the RAST transaction has a higher WAC. Some of the difference, in our opinion, can perhaps be attributed to aggressive wholesale mortgage originators.

The point is that loan balances and geographic concentrations for alt-A borrowers depend heavily upon the origination channels by which the alt-A lender acquires these loans. As such, these variables also signal information about the origination policies of the alt-A lender and the demographic characteristics of its borrowers. Therefore, *in order to fully capture issuer-specific characteristics of prepayment behavior, we separately estimate initial population mixes for each alt-A issuer. In other words, we have issuer-specific alt-A models for HMSI, ICIFC/IMPAC, RALI, and RAST transactions.* As one would expect from observed prepayment speeds, ICIFC/IMPAC and RALI transactions are assumed to have the largest proportion of slow refinancers.

Exhibit 12.18 provides an indication of the accuracy of our issuer-specific prepayment models by comparing actual and projected speeds for a representative selection of alt-A transactions. We feel the model has done an excellent job of capturing both the seasoning characteristics of alt-A prepayment speeds and issuer-specific differences in prepayment speeds. It should be kept in mind that prepayment speeds on alt-A transactions can be quite erratic, and investors in general should use a three-to-four-month horizon to gauge the accuracy of a prepayment model.

It is also possible that issuer-specific differences may be captured by using more pool-level information. For example, the percentage of investment properties in a pool, or the percentage of alternate documentation borrowers might reasonably be expected to have an impact on prepayment speeds. However, the precise impact of borrower and loan characteristics such as loan purpose, occupancy type, property type, and so on, on prepayments is still being clarified by us via loan-level analysis. Our insights from this analysis will be incorporated into future releases of the alt-A model. In the meantime, our current set of explanatory variables (as described previously) is doing a good job of modeling issuer-specific differences in prepayments.

EXHIBIT 12.18 Actual and Projected Speeds for Selected Alt-A Transactions, August 1998

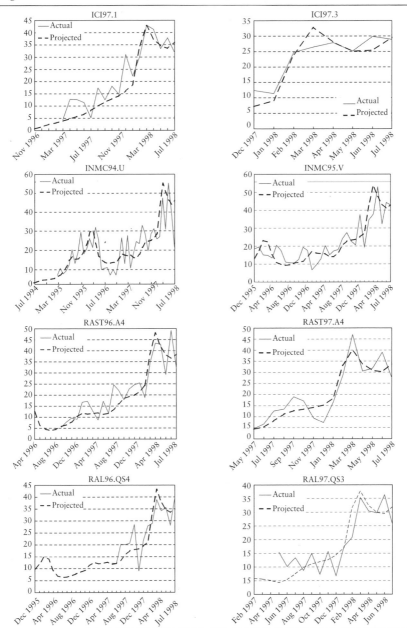

Source: Salomon Smith Barney.

Prepayment Model Projections

A comparison of the prepayment projections produced by the alt-A and agency models allows us to tie together some themes discussed in different sections of this paper. The differences in modeling assumptions are captured in the prepayment projections depicted in Exhibits 12.19 and 12.20. In summary:

- If rates decline, agency speeds accelerate at a faster rate than for alt-As because of the weaker refinance responsiveness of the alt-A borrower. Over time, burnout will cause speeds on both agency and alt-A to decline. However, alt-A speeds will decline faster because of the relatively larger number of slow refinancers in alt-A pools.
- If rates rise, alt-A speeds initially do not decrease by as much as agencies because of an ongoing stream of credit-driven refinances. Rates would have to increase by as much as 200bp for the RALI transaction to be at current coupon. At these rate levels, credit-driven refinancings would slow to a trickle, and alt-A and agency speeds would begin to converge.

EXHIBIT 12.19   One-Year Prepayment Projections for RAL 97.QS5 and Fannie Mae 97 8s, August 26, 1998

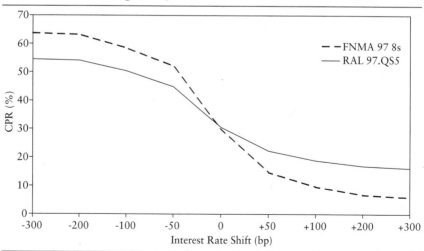

Source: Salomon Smith Barney.

EXHIBIT 12.20 Long-Term Prepayment Projections for RAL 97.QS5 and Fannie Mae 97 8s, August 26, 1998

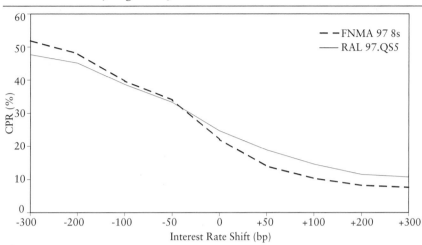

Source: Salomon Smith Barney.

12.7 THE IMPACT OF THE GSEs ON THE ALT-A SECTOR

A major concern in the alt-A sector has been the release of new versions of the government-sponsored enterprises' (GSEs) automated underwriting (AU) systems. The latest releases of these systems possess far more flexibility in the combination of borrower, loan, and property characteristics allowed, and clearly serve to increase the agencies' market share of the conforming balance loans originated in this sector. For instance, among the various enhancements available in one of the recent versions[16] of Fannie Mae's Desktop Underwriter, the following have direct bearing on the alt-A sector:

- *Limited documentation underwriting.* Loans with "low risk profiles" can now be underwritten using the borrower's stated income, and a verbal verification of employment.
- *80% Cash-out refinances.* The maximum LTV allowed for cash-out refinances is expanded from 75% to 80% on fixed-rate mortgages.
- *Expanded LTVs on investor loans.* The maximum LTV allowed for investor loans on single-unit properties is expanded from 70% to 80%.

---

[16] Desktop Underwiter (DU) 4.0, released September 1997.

Cash-out refinances are now permitted on investment properties up to a maximum of 65% LTV on single-unit properties, and 60% LTV on two-unit properties.

These initiatives could impact the alt-A sector in the following ways. First, increased competition for alt-A loans among lenders would eventually lower alt-A mortgage rates, thus increasing refinancing incentives for borrowers in current alt-A pools.[17] Next, an increasing fraction of conforming balance alt-A borrowers would find their way into agency pools with the net result that the average loan balances in new alt-A deals could increase substantially. Both these developments would erode the favorable convexity characteristics of alt-A collateral. In the year that has passed since these initiatives were first announced, Fannie Mae has been very active in the alt-A sector. Fannie Mae's purchases of alt-A product averaged about $500 million per month for the first half of the year, and has recently ramped up to approximately $900 million per month for the past two months.[18] Interestingly, Exhibit 12.21 shows that Fannie Mae's purchases have so far had little to no effect on alt-A mortgage rates, suggesting that the agency's current level of activity has been balanced by other factors.

Exhibit 12.22 provides perspective on what some of these factors might be by tracking the evolution of collateral compositions for RALI and RAST transactions. Viewed in this light, the entry of the GSEs clearly seems to have had an impact on loan balances in alt-A pools: Average loan balances have increased by about $15,000 over the past six months for both RALI and RAST transactions. There are other significant changes in alt-A collateral characteristics over the past year, but these may just reflect current trends in the housing markets. For example, geographic dispersion for RALI and RAST transactions seems to have shrunk as the proportion of California loans has increased by about 5% to 10%. Also, the proportion of investor loans in RALI deals has decreased from 33% to 28%.

However, a prognosis of increased prepayment reactivity for new RALI and RAST transactions based on these new collateral characteristics may be premature. New RALI and RAST transactions may in fact show equivalent (or even superior) diminished interest-rate sensitivity compared with the past. For example, although the new agency underwriting guidelines may siphon

---

[17] A previous analysis (see *Bond Market Roundup: Strategy,* October 10, 1997) showed that as many as 20% to 30% of the current borrowers in alt-A pools could qualify for an agency loan under these new criteria.
[18] Freddie Mac is currently working on an alt-A pilot with four lenders. They intend to aggressively expand their alt-A program later this year.

EXHIBIT 12.21   Spread between Conforming and Alt-A Mortgage Rates,
August 1998*

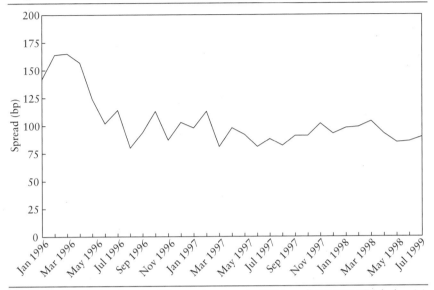

*The spread is calculated as the difference between the WAC on all INMC/RAST deals origi-
nated for a particular month, and the Freddie Mac Survey rate lagged by two months.
Source: Salomon Smith Barney.

off the alt-A borrowers with low loan balance/low LTV loan characteristics, it
is probably this set of borrowers who would have refinanced out of an alt-A
loan in any case after a short "curing" process. *Consequently, all other things
being equal, new alt-A pools may now experience a slower curing process
and have a greater proportion of slow refinancers than before.*

EXHIBIT 12.22   Evolution of Collateral Compositions in Alt-A Transactions,
August 1998

Issuer	Origination Year	Avg Loan Balance	Avg LTV	% CA	% Full Doc	% Investor	% Cash Out
RALI	1996	$114K	77%	23%	56%	34%	21%
	1997	$113K	78	19	52	33	19
	1998	$128K	77	24	51	28	26
RAST	1996	$139K	73%	36%	35%	19%	24%
	1997	$146K	71	40	38	19	25
	1998	$159K	72	52	35	19	31

Source: Salomon Smith Barney.

Given the uncertainties in what the future holds, our prepayment model simply assumes that refinancing costs will decrease at the same rate in the conforming and alt-A sectors[19] because of overall efficiencies introduced by automated underwriting. In other words, we do not make any special assumptions regarding the reduction of refinancing costs in the alt-A sector because of increased competition. Finally, *our prepayment projections will automatically capture changes in loan balances and geographic concentrations in the alt-A sector, since our prepayment model uses pool-level information with regard to these collateral attributes.*

CONCLUSIONS

In summary, the chief impact of the GSEs (most of which can be currently attributed to Fannie Mae) on the alt-A sector seems to have been to increase average loan balances on alt-A transactions by about $15,000 this year. Going forward, we should continue to expect evolution of collateral characteristics in this sector because: (1) the GSE's alt-A programs are directly linked to their AU systems, and these systems can be expected to enjoy an increase in usage in the future; (2) Fannie Mae will continue to revise and possibly expand its alt-A guidelines; and (3) Freddie Mac will expand its alt-A initiatives in the near future:

■ The alt-A sector was poised to enjoy strong growth for the remainder of 1998 and 1999 as borrowers continue to use a wide spectrum of mortgage financing options. RALI and RAST dominate issuance in this sector, and offer investors the best liquidity.

■ Overall assumptions regarding the diminished prepayment sensitivity and fast baseline speeds of alt-A collateral relative to comparable agency product have been justified by historical prepayment data.

■ Although reduced prepayment sensitivity and fast baseline speeds are displayed by almost all alt-A transactions, the extent to which these characteristics are present for a particular transaction depend heavily on the issuer of the transaction. *Consequently, investors should not rely on a "generic" alt-A prepayment model for prepayment estimates.* Our issuer-specific models are separately estimated using historical prepayment data corresponding to each individual issuer's transactions, and fully capture the issuer-specific characteristics of alt-A prepayment

---

[19] We estimate this reduction in refinancing costs to be about half a point over the next year or so.

behavior. We also find that RALI transactions exhibit the least negative convexity.

■ Thus far, the chief impact of GSE activity in the alt-A sector has been to increase average loan balances on new alt-A transactions. Our prepayment projections will automatically reflect changes in loan balances and geographic distributions in the alt-A sector, since our alt-A prepayment models use pool-level information with regard to these collateral attributes.

■ Contrary to popular opinion, going forward *the presence of the GSEs may actually make alt-A pools less negatively convex.* The GSEs will likely attract the more creditworthy borrowers (for example, those borrowers with high FICOs, low LTVs) that would most likely be among the first to refinance into a conforming loan.

■ Alt-A collateral appears to have a steeper loss curve than traditional jumbo collateral. Consequently, the additional credit enhancement required to achieve triple-A ratings in alt-A is warranted.

A LOAN-LEVEL SNAPSHOT OF ALT-A COLLATERAL

EXHIBIT 12.23   Mortgage Rates for RALI Collateral, August 1998

Mortgage Rates (%)	Percentage of Mortgage Pool	Average LTV	Average Loan Balance	Percent Purchase	Percent Full Doc	Percent Primary Residence	Percent Single Family
7.50 - 7.99	12%	75%	$163K	47%	44%	92%	72%
8.00 - 8.49	26	76	136K	55	44	81	67
8.50 - 8.99	36	78	112K	63	53	65	59
9.00 - 9.49	16	79	97K	68	61	50	55
9.50 - 9.99	7	80	87K	72	71	39	50

Source: Salomon Smith Barney.

EXHIBIT 12.24   Original Mortgage Loan Balances for RALI Collateral, August 1998

Original Mortgage Loan Balance	Percentage of Mortgage Pool	WAC	Average LTV	Percent Purchase	Percent Full Doc	Percent Primary Residence	Percent Single Family
$0 - 50,000	6%	8.96%	79%	78%	81%	23%	55%
50,001 – 100,000	26	8.72	78	69	65	44	59
100,001 – 150,000	24	8.57	79	66	54	63	58
150,001 – 200,000	14	8.42	77	58	41	80	61
>200,000	29	8.38	76	48	43	93	68

Source: Salomon Smith Barney.

EXHIBIT 12.25 Original Loan-to-Value Ratios for RALI Collateral, August 1998

Original Loan-to-Value Ratio (%)	Percentage of Mortgage Pool	WAC	Average Loan Balance	Percent Purchase	Percent Full Doc	Percent Primary Residence	Percent Single Family
0.01 - 50.00	4%	8.38%	$108K	23%	16%	83%	74%
50.01 - 60.00	5	8.50	127K	28	20	77	69
60.01 - 70.00	13	8.58	115K	33	36	67	64
70.01 - 80.00	51	8.41	142K	61	40	83	65
80.01 - 90.00	23	8.85	84K	85	100	26	53
90.01 - 100.00	4	8.57	157K	84	100	99	45

Source: Salomon Smith Barney.

EXHIBIT 12.26 Loan Purposes for RALI Collateral, August 1998

Loan Purpose	Percentage of Mortgage Pool	WAC	Average LTV	Average Loan Balance	Percent Full Doc	Percent Primary Residence	Percent Single Family
Purchase	62%	8.62%	81%	$107K	58%	61%	54%
Refinance	16	8.37	74	146K	44	76	70
Cash-out	21	8.45	70	138K	45	82	77

Source: Salomon Smith Barney.

EXHIBIT 12.27 Documentation Types for RALI Collateral, August 1998

Documentation Type	Percentage of Mortgage Pool	WAC	Average LTV	Average Loan Balance	Percent Purchase	Percent Primary Residence	Percent Single Family
Full Documentation	54%	8.63%	82%	$102K	67%	45%	54%
Limited/Alternative Documentation	46	8.44	72	144K	53	94	70

Source: Salomon Smith Barney.

EXHIBIT 12.28 Occupancy Types for RALI Collateral, August 1998

Occupancy	Percentage of Mortgage Pool	WAC	Average LTV	Average Loan Balance	Percent Purchase	Percent Full Doc	Percent Single Family
Primary	67%	8.39%	76%	$152K	54%	35%	68%
Investment	33	8.87	81	80K	74	92	49

Source: Salomon Smith Barney.

EXHIBIT 12.29 Property Types for RALI Collateral, August 1998

Property Type	Percentage of Mortgage Pool	WAC	Weighted Average LTV	Average Loan Balance	Percent Purchase	Percent Full Doc	Percent Primary Residence
1 Family	60%	8.47%	76%	$124K	52%	46%	75%
2-4 Family	16	8.89	82	f06K	74	83	32
Condo	8	8.64	78	84K	78	60	68
PUD	14	8.42	77	143K	69	44	80

Source: Salomon Smith Barney.

Option-Adjusted Spreads and Durations

CHAPTER 13

The SSB Two-Factor Term Structure Model

Y.K. Chan and Robert A. Russell

In view of the turbulent rate environments of the not too distant past, and given the increasing popularity of leveraged securities, it has become clear to investors that a good term structure model that properly accounts for the volatility of rates is important for the appraisal of fixed-income securities.

Salomon Smith Barney has developed such a model, which the firm and its customers have been using on a daily basis since 1994 for trading and hedging mortgage-backed securities. The same model has been implemented for corporate bonds and options, so that investors with access to the *Yield Book,* the Salomon analytics platform, can now manage portfolios of multiple sectors in a coherent system.

In this chapter, we present a detailed description of this model, a two-factor model that has randomness in both the rate level and yield curve slope. The chapter is intended also to serve as a tutorial on the basics of pricing. The presentation will be along the lines of logical evolution, starting without any consideration of rate volatility and ending with the implemented two-factor model.

13.1 VOLATILITY

Volatility and Option Cost

It is perhaps fair to say that the first important issue in the pricing of many fixed-income securities is the volatility of interest rates (i.e., the tendency for rates to fluctuate in an unpredictable manner). Unlike Treasury securities and plain vanilla interest-rate swaps, there is a large universe of fixed-income securities that have cash flows varying with the prevailing rates.

When rates drop, home owners and corporate borrowers exercise their refinancing options, and investors are forced to reinvest in a lower-rate environment. When rates rise, adjustable-rate mortgages have an increased coupon stream until the caps are reached. Collateralized mortgage obligations (CMOs) can have several embedded options, which can be further complicated by the structure of the deal. For example, a tranche in a CMO can be long an interest-rate floor and at the same time short a prepayment option. Such a CMO is effectively long an option on the yield curve slope.

If rates were perfectly predictable, such cash-flow uncertainty would not be an issue in pricing. To price a security, we would simply project the cash flow along the predicted rate path according to the indenture, and according to some cash-flow model if necessary. The yield to maturity would measure well the return on investment.

Future interest rates, however, are anything but predictable. The interest-rate-related option inherent in a security can substantially subtract from or add to its value. The more volatile the future rates, the more valuable the options. This calls for the proper modeling of volatility. The question is: Which volatility? Before proceeding, we will clarify several concepts of volatility.

Spot Volatility

Over a short period of time into the future, there are numerous possible rate changes. The mean of these possible changes can be called the *local drift* or *trend* of the rate. The short-term variability can be described by the variance of the changes. The variance is defined as the average of the squared deviations from the mean. The squaring is to get rid of the signs of the deviations, which are irrelevant, since we are measuring the unpredictable dispersion in both directions. Instead of variance, we can also use its square root, the standard deviation, which has the advantage of having the correct unit, since the squaring is balanced by a square root.

For example, suppose, in our assessment, the next possible rate moves in one day are +8bp (basis points) or −8bp with equal probabilities. Then the trend is 0, the variance is $64bp^2$, and the standard deviation is 8bp.

Over a period of time, a series of independent moves with the same variance would result in a cumulative variance that is the sum of the individual variances. Thus, the cumulative variance is proportional to the length of the time period. In the previous example, over a period of 365 days, the cumulative variance would be $365 \times 64bp^2$. The standard deviation, being the square root, would therefore be proportional to the square root of the time period. The annualized standard deviation in the example is

$$\sqrt{365} \times 8\text{bp}$$

It is customary to state the annualized standard deviation as a percentage multiple of the rate level. This is the definition of volatility.

To emphasize that this volatility refers to possible rate changes over a short period of time into the future (even though we may annualize it), we call it the *spot volatility*. If the starting rate level in the previous example is 6%, the spot volatility, designated by σ, is

$$\sigma = \sqrt{365} \times \frac{0.08}{6.00} = 25.5\%$$

In general,

$$\sigma = \frac{\text{Standard deviation of relative change in rate}}{\sqrt{\text{Time period}}}$$

Here, the time period is a short one, say one day or 1/365 year in the context of a 30-year security. Because a small relative change in a quantity is approximately the same as the absolute change in the logarithm of that quantity, the definition of the spot volatility can be restated as

$$\sigma = \frac{\text{Standard deviation of change in log(rate)}}{\sqrt{\text{Time period}}} \qquad (13.1)$$

The spot volatility σ can be estimated from historical data. For example, Exhibit 13.1 shows three-month and 10-year Treasury rates for the period from April 1, 1977, to 1997. The spot volatility for the three-month rate estimated from this series of data is 27.3%.

Spot volatilities for Treasury rates of other maturities are similarly estimated and displayed in Exhibit 13.2 It appears that longer-term rates have lower spot volatilities.

Effective Volatility

Spot volatility describes short-term fluctuations. Some securities, especially mortgage-backed securities, have uncertain cash flows up to 30 years. It is the volatility effective throughout the security's expected life that affects the

EXHIBIT 13.1 History of 3-Month and 10-Year Treasury Rates, 1977–1997

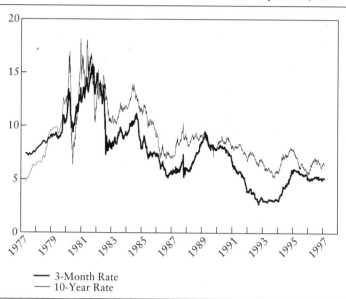

— 3-Month Rate
— 10-Year Rate

Source: Salomon Smith Barney.

cash flow and the security value. Equation 13.1 can be used to define the *effective volatility* for any time period. The effective volatility can also be estimated from historical data. In contrast to the spot volatility, in our 20-year time series there are only 20 non-overlapping samples of 1-year moves. The small sample size means that the estimate for effective volatility over longer time periods, unlike that for the spot volatility, is heuristic.

If the change in short rate over the time period is regarded as the cumulative result of a series of successive instantaneous changes that were independent, then, as alluded to previously, the standard deviation in the numerator of Equation 13.1 would be proportional to the square root of the time period, which happens also to be the denominator. Hence, the effective volatility σ would be the same regardless of the period length. In particular, it would be the same as the spot volatility. This, however, is not consistent with the historical data, which we will now examine.

Using the same series of three-month Treasury rates as in Exhibit 13.1, but using moves over monthly, quarterly, annual, and longer time periods, we estimate the respective volatilities. Those for horizon periods up to five years are displayed in Exhibit 13.3 on page 320. For the same rate, the effective volatility tends to decrease for longer horizons.

EXHIBIT 13.2 Empirical Spot Volatilities for Various Rates, 1977–1997

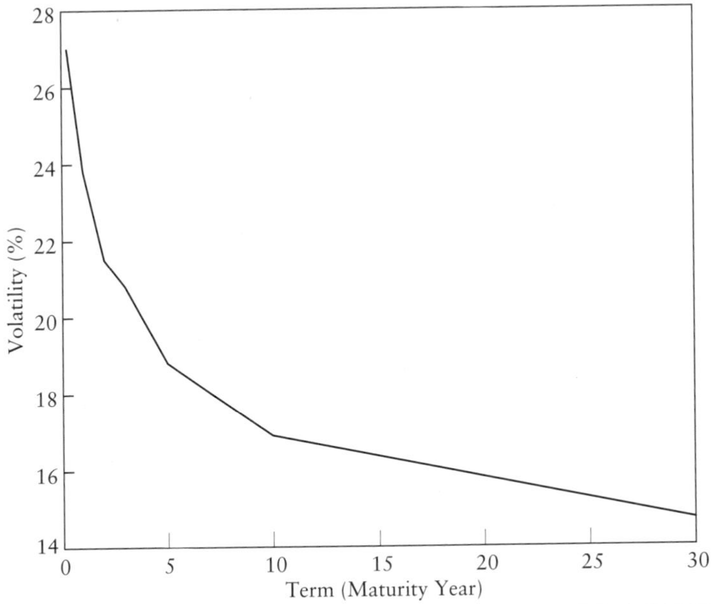

Source: Salomon Smith Barney.

It appears as though there is some mechanism that discourages extreme levels of rates—perhaps a mean reverting force, whether economical or political in nature, that brings rates down to levels with which we are familiar. It is not necessary for our purpose to investigate the cause of the mean reversion. However, mean reversion is a convenient and intuitive device with which to build a model that is consistent with the volatility market.

The Empirical Volatility Surface

Summing up, the effective volatility depends not only on the term of the rate, but also on the length of the time period over which it is measured. This surface of effective volatility from historical data is plotted in Exhibit 13.4 on page 321.

The Market Volatility Surface

Caps on three-month LIBOR are actively traded with a range of maturities up to 10 years. Typically, a cap pays quarterly the excess of LIBOR over the strike. The price of a cap maturing at year *n* embodies the market's opinion

EXHIBIT 13.3   Volatilities of 3-Month Rate for Various Horizons, 1977–1997

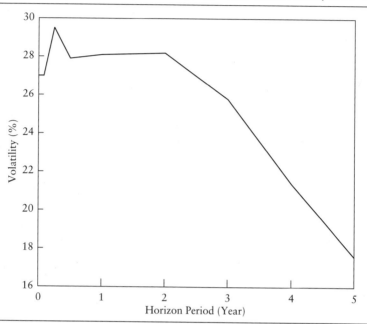

Source: Salomon Smith Barney.

of the effective LIBOR volatility for the next *n* years. The cap prices are usually quoted in terms of a volatility that is then translated to a dollar price according to a formula of Fischer Black.

For longer rates, there is an active market of options on swaps, or swaptions. The swap maturities at exercise can be up to 10 years, the option expirations up to five years. Longer swaptions are sometimes also traded. The prices of these swaptions indicate the market's opinion of the effective volatility of the swap rates of various terms for various time periods into the future. Again, the prices of swaptions are usually quoted in terms of a volatility that is translated to a dollar price via some simple, conventional model.

In short, there is a market volatility surface every trading day (see Exhibit 13.5 on page 322).

Modeling the Volatility Surface

There are several questions related to the volatility to be considered in pricing: Volatility of which rate? What is the effective period? From which sources—historical or market?

EXHIBIT 13.4   Empirical Volatility Surface, 1977–1997

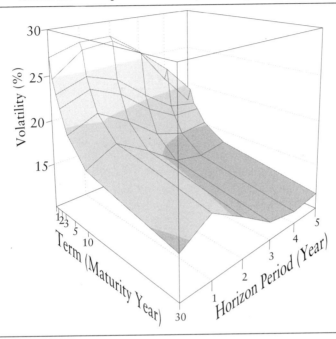

Source: Salomon Smith Barney.

The term of the relevant rate is obvious for mortgage pass-throughs. Prepayments are influenced by prevailing mortgage rates; when mortgage rates are low, the incentive to refinance is strong.[1] Since the mortgage rate moves approximately in tandem with the 10-year Treasury rate, the volatility of the latter is the main consideration. A less important, yet significant, factor that affects prepayment is the spread between the 10-year rate and shorter rates. For example, consider a FNMA pass-through with remaining maturity of 29 years, a net coupon of 7.5 (gross coupon of 8.12) in a flat 6% yield curve environment. The Salomon prepay model projects a long-term constant prepay rate (CPR) of 11.1%. If the yield curve steepens, so that the 10-year rate remains at 6% but the 1- to 3-year rates decline to 5%, then the prepay model projects the higher prepay rate of 13.6% CPR. This increase of 2.5% CPR is because the home owner's extra option of refinancing into shorter-term loans, such as 15-year, 7-year, or even ARMs, starts to look attractive. In the

---

[1] See Chapter 4 "Anatomy of Prepayments," Lakhbir Hayre, Sharad Chaudhary, and Robert Young, Salomon Smith Barney, April 2000.

EXHIBIT 13.5   Quoted Caplet/Swaption Volatilities, February 10, 1997

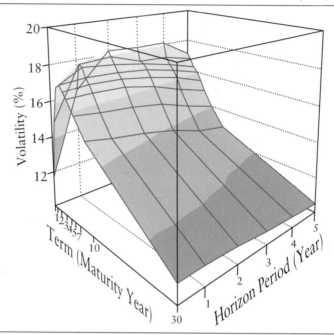

Source: Salomon Smith Barney.

other direction, if the yield curve inverts, so that the 1- to 3-year rates increase to 7% while the 10-year rate stays at 6%, the prepay model projects a 9.7% long-term CPR. This is a decrease of 1.4% CPR. Note that the decrease from the yield curve inversion is only about half of the increase from the steepening, since housing turnover and the fixed-rate to fixed-rate refinancing option provides a floor to the CPR. For a security that is negatively affected by prepayment, for example, one that receives interest only (IO) on the diminishing balance, ignoring the variability of yield curve steepness would overestimate the security value.

Thus, it is obvious that volatilities of both the 10-year and the 1-year rate need to be modeled. For a bond with a capped coupon that floats with 1-month LIBOR, it is equally obvious that the volatility of the 1-month rate is needed. With a CMO floater, it is necessary to model all three.

For a corporate bond with 30-year maturity but immediately callable, the relevant volatility is less clear. Is the volatility of the 30-year rate the essential consideration in view of the long maturity? Or should we use that of a shorter rate, since the call may be imminent and the expected remaining life of the bond, if not called today, is short?

Even when the term of the driving rate is clear, the choice of effective period for the determination of volatility is not necessarily so. Presumably, it should correspond to the expected life of the security. The expected life, however, varies from one security to another, changes with rate levels, and is itself dependent on the volatility assumption.

This suggests the need for a coherent pricing model that embodies the entire surface of volatility. That would obviate the need to examine the security beforehand to determine a volatility level.

The historical data suggest that a volatility surface is a plausible ingredient in pricing. The existence of caps and swaptions as benchmarks makes it essential. If a model is to price a CMO that is a cap in camouflage, we want it to produce the market price of the cap; similarly for swaptions. Otherwise, we could become victims of arbitrage.

13.2 TERM STRUCTURE MODELS

Principle of Derivative Pricing

Derivative pricing, along the lines of Merton and Black-Scholes, amounts to the principle of *playing Peter against Paul*. There is a market from which we can buy or sell unlimited amounts of certain traded benchmark securities. For our purpose, the benchmark securities are Treasuries, swaps, and related options. We want to value a derivative security, which may be a mortgage pass-through, a CMO, or any fixed-income security.

If we can replicate a derivative security with a portfolio of benchmark securities, guaranteed to produce identical cash flows under all circumstances, we will be happy to trade the derivative with any counterparty (*Paul*) at the market price of the portfolio, doing the opposite trade on the portfolio at the market (*Peter*), and charging a small risk-free profit spread on top for our trouble. We will do so regardless of what we expect the interest-rate trend to be, leaving the task of forecasting rate trends to the economists. For pricing derivatives, the forecasts of benchmarks are irrelevant. We also do not undertake *inside* the pricing model the job of discovering relative cheapness or richness among the benchmark securities. Once a pricing model is built, we will use it as a tool to predict price sensitivities to the changes in rate and volatility environments; then we will give the what-if scenarios whatever subjective probabilities we believe are appropriate.

When the derivative cannot be replicated in the manner mentioned previously, but, almost as good, can be matched in value by the portfolio under all possible rate moves over the next trading period, the same pricing method is still valid. However, since we do not yet know the present value of the derivative, let alone the possible values a short time period into the future, trying to match the possible values sounds like circular logic. The Merton and Black-Scholes method in effect breaks the circle by reasoning hypothetically backward from maturity, when the security value is indeed known, and going back one period at a time until the price at the present is obtained. They effectively proved that such a dynamic replication is possible, with cumulative error ignorable as the trading period becomes small, provided that the volatility assumption is right.

Technicality aside, a first test for a derivative pricing method is producing market prices of the benchmarks.

The Yield Curve Margin—The Zero-Factor Model

Suppose the benchmark securities consist of nothing other than one Treasury STRIP for each maturity. By a Treasury STRIP we mean a Treasury security with exactly one payment, its yield referred to as a *STRIP rate*. A very simple pricing model can be devised to be consistent with the market STRIP rates; this model ignores all rate uncertainties.

Consider time intervals at times $t = 0, 1, 2 \ldots$. We can define for the initial time period $[0, 1]$ a rate level $f(0)$ such that the STRIP maturing at $t = 1$, when discounted by $f(0)$ over this time period, has a present value exactly equal to its market price. Then we can define for the next time period $[1, 2]$ a rate level $f(1)$ such that the STRIP maturing at $t = 2$, when discounted successively over the first two time periods, first with $f(0)$ and then with $f(1)$, also has a present value matching its market price. Repeating this step, we find rate levels $f(t)$ for all the future time periods. Each security is priced by discounting its projected cash flows successively by the rates $f(t)$ over the respective periods. The rate $f(t)$ is called the *forward rate* at time t. It is the rate at time t that we can lock in now by selling a t-period STRIP and then buying an amount of $(t + 1)$ – period STRIP such that there is no net cash flow until time t.

A simplistic model can be defined that uses the forward rate $f(t)$ for the short rate at time t. If, for the purpose of cash flow projection, we need at time t a STRIP rate whose term is m periods, this can be obtained by (1) discounting 1 dollar payable at $t + m$ over the time periods $[t, t + 1]$, $\ldots$, $[t + m - 1, t + m]$ by the respective forward rates, and (2) translating the present value thus obtained back into a yield. Prices and rates of Treasury bonds with a nonzero coupon, if needed, can be synthesized from STRIP rates.

There are no uncertainty factors in this simple model, which can therefore be called a zero-factor model. Nevertheless, the benchmark Treasury STRIPS are priced correctly at the market level.

Other securities are not. There are unmodeled risks, interest-rate volatility among them. To compensate for these risks, a security would usually sell for a price different from the price obtained with this model. The market price is obtained only if a spread, the *yield curve margin,* is added to the forward rates $f(t)$ before any discounting. When the unmodeled risk is significant for a bond, its yield curve margin can be substantial.

At the risk of appearing pedantic, we have dwelled in great detail on this simple, and simplistic, model because it clarifies several basic concepts. Only some uncertainty factors remain to be introduced.

A SIMPLE LOGNORMAL MODEL—A ONE-FACTOR MODEL

Here, as in the simplistic model, the short rate follows a general rate path $f(t)$ except that it can wander haphazardly away from the path. Thus, the first six rates absent any randomness would be: $f(0)$; $f(1)$; $f(2)$; $f(3)$; $f(4)$; $f(5)$.

For illustration, consider one-year time periods. There is no uncertainty in the first period rate $f(0)$. Suppose the spot volatility is 20%. The uncertainty for the rate in the second period can be modeled by two possible levels: $f(1) \times 1.22$ and $f(1) \times 1.22^{-1}$ with equal probability. The multiplier 1.22 is chosen because $\log(1.22)$ and $\log(1.22^{-1})$ are approximately +0.20 and −0.20, respectively, and so the standard deviation of $\log(\text{rate})$ for the second time period is 20%. To simulate a rate for the third period, we generate a second random number that, independent of the first, can again be +1 or −1 with equal probability. The sum of these first two random steps can be +2, 0, or −2. For the third period rate, we accordingly use $f(2) \times 1.22^{+2}$, $f(2)$, or $f(2) \times 1.22^{-2}$. If the first five random numbers were −1, +1, +1, +1, −1, respectively, the cumulative random steps would be −1, 0, +1, +2, +1, and the first six simulated rates would be $f(0)$; $f(1) \times 1.22^{-1}$; $f(2) \times 1.22^{0}$; $f(3) \times 1.22^{+1}$; $f(4) \times 1.22^{+2}$; $f(5) \times 1.22^{+1}$.

Continuing this way, we get one simulation of a rate path. After a large number of random steps, the net number of positive steps follows the bell-shaped normal distribution, with probabilities for large positive or negative values tapering off to zero. The simulation can be made more realistic by using random steps that, instead of the two possible values, have a normal distribution of possible values. This is done in our implementation. Accordingly, this term structure model can be called a *lognormal model.* We will continue to use the +1 or −1 step in the discussion.

In the previous simulation, stepping above the general path $f(t)$ is as likely as stepping below. In other words, $f(t)$ is the median short rate in this model.

Just as in the simplistic model, we can calibrate the median rates $f(t)$ by adjusting them, one step at a time, to match the present values of the Treasury STRIPS with their respective market prices. The only difference is that now there are many possible paths of short rates, along each of which we have one present value. We need to average all of these into one expected present value.

If, in addition to the short rate, a STRIP rate of term T is needed at the time t, we can find the STRIP price as the average present value at time t of $1 payable at $t + T$ and translating this price to a yield; the average is to cover all simulated paths that start at the same given short rate level at time t. Thus, at any time t and at any given short rate level, there is a corresponding zero-coupon yield curve.

Because of the dispersion of rates in the model, the median path $f(t)$ calibrated to the Treasury STRIPS in this manner is somewhat different from the forward rates, that is, different from the rate path $f(t)$ calibrated in the simplistic model. Note that $f(t)$ is the future median rate path only according to this *pricing* model, and the pricing model is not intended for rate *forecasts*. Neither these median rates nor the forward rates imply any belief on our part as to the trend of rates in the future. That belief is irrelevant for derivative pricing, as noted earlier. The forward rate is real only in the sense that we can lock in this rate for the future period if *we commit to the borrowing now*.

The simple lognormal model above accounts for rate volatility. The spot volatility parameter σ can be chosen to produce the market price of one selected volatility instrument. Model volatility of all rates will come out close to σ. We will refer to this one-size-fits-all model as the *single-volatility model*.

As an example, a one-year cap may be priced correctly at $\sigma = 28\%$. However, the unrestrained evolution of rates is counterintuitive. If the short rate starts today, say, at the level of 6%, then the probability for it to exceed the level of 24% sometime in the next 30 years can be deduced from this model to be 36%.[2] That probability, more than one in three, seems high.

Much more importantly, other options, like caps of longer maturities, would tend to be overpriced compared to the market. Mean reversion is one intuitive device that can address this problem.

A One-Factor Model with Mean Reversion

Here, the short rate process is the same as in the simple lognormal model above, except that when the cumulative random step is above or below 0,

---

[2] See the section on reflection principle for Brownian Motions in *A First Course in Stochastic Processes*, S. Karlin, Academic Press, 1968.

EXHIBIT 13.6 An Illustrative Scenario of Rates Simulated with Mean Reversion

After time step	1	2	3	4	5
Random step without mean reversion	-1.00	+1.00	+1.00	+1.00	-1.00
Mean reversion step		+0.5000	-0.2500	-0.6250	-0.8125
Cumulative steps with mean reversion	-1.0000	+0.5000	+1.2500	+1.6250	+0.1875
Scenario rates	$f(1)1.22^{-1}$	$f(2)1.22^{+0.5}$	$f(3)1.22^{+1.25}$	$f(4)1.22^{+1.625}$	$f(5)1.22^{+0.1875}$

Source: Salomon Smith Barney.

the next random step is adjusted with a step that is proportional to the excess but opposite in sign. Exhibit 13.6 illustrates this process with a mean reversion coefficient of 0.50; a mean reverting step equal to half of the current cumulative step is subtracted from the next random step.[3]

The proportional coefficient, −0.50 in this example, limits the dispersion of the short rate over time. It can be varied as a function of time and adjusted until market cap prices are obtained. In other words, it can be calibrated to a range of caps. Alternatively, it can be calibrated to options on the 10-year rate with a range of expirations. The model still does not have the flexibility to do both. To model the volatility surface, we can introduce yet another uncertainty factor.

A Stochastic Yield Curve Slope—The Two-Factor Model

The mean reverting drift is closely related to the slope of the yield curve defined at the short end of the yield curve and restated in terms of a fraction of the short rate. For illustration, suppose the overnight rate is 8% and three-month rate is 8.1%. Then the slope of the curve at the short end is approximately $(8.1 - 8.0)/0.25 = 40bp$ per year. The restated slope is $0.40/8.00 = 5\%$ of the short rate per year. At the short end of this yield curve, as the term increases, the rate rises per year by 5% of its value. The same rise of 40bp per year would be considered more steep given a short rate of 4%, the slope being 10% of that level.

At any given time t and each rate level, the yield curve in the model has a slope. It turns out that the drift is the same as twice the excess of the slope over the median slope.[4] For example, if the median value of the slope is 5% of the short rate per year, then the yield curve corresponding to a drift of 1 would have slope equal to $5 + ½ = 5.5\%$ of the short rate per year, which is

---

[3] This mean reverting step is an example of the local drift defined in section 13.1.

[4] For a proof, see *Term Structure as a Second Order Dynamical System, and Pricing of Derivative Securities,* working paper, Y.K. Chan, Salomon Smith Barney, January 1993.

steeper than the median slope. Likewise, a drift of −20 would correspond to a yield curve inverted at the short end, with the rate decreasing by 5 − 20/2 = −5% of its value per year. Note that the slope refers to the very short end of the yield curve; even a curve very steep at the short end usually becomes flatter for longer terms.

It is observed empirically that the yield curve slope is not determined by the rate level. Given the level of the short rate, there remains uncertainty in the slope. This suggests the inclusion of another random factor in the drift, since the drift is equivalent to the slope. We therefore amend the model discussed in the previous section by adding yet another random deviation to the mean reverting drift itself. At each time interval, this random deviation takes a step that is proportional to a slope volatility σ_1, up or down as determined by another series of random numbers. This randomizes the yield curve slope independent of the rate level.

One final modification is needed. To prevent the slope from wandering off to extreme values, that is, to prevent unreasonably steep or unreasonably inverted yield curves, we subject also the random slope deviation factor to mean reversion.

This completes the model. The spot volatilities σ, σ_1, the median rate levels $f(t)$, and mean reversion coefficients for the rate and slope levels completely determine the ensemble of probable rate scenarios. So far, we have not mentioned the model rates for LIBOR. A simple way to include them is to model the short LIBOR by applying a deterministic multiplier $f_L(t)/f(t)$ to the Treasury short rate. Once the model parameters are determined, bonds can be priced.

Arbitrage-Free Bond Pricing

Conceptually, we can simulate a large number of interest-rate paths, project cash flows of the security along each path, discount and get one present value for each path, and average all these present values to be the bond price. As the number of simulated paths approaches infinity, the average is the *expectation* of the scenario present values.

The expected value pricing method is arbitrage free. If a cash-flow stream is equal to the sum of two others under any scenario, it is obvious that the average present value is the sum of the two averages of the component cash flows and so the price obtained from the expectation is the sum of the prices for the component securities. It is equally obvious that if each cash flow in one security is greater than or equal to the corresponding cash flow of a second security under any scenario, then the averaging process would produce a price for the first security that is greater than or equal to the price for the second.

Backward Induction

If a price is needed at time $t = n$, given the entire history of short rates and curve slope up to that time, we can use a similar expectation procedure. The averaging then covers the subset of all paths with the same given history up to time n.

Furthermore, we can segregate the paths in the average into subsets of paths that share the same history not just up to time n but up to time $n + 1$. For illustration, refer to Exhibit 13.7. Let the nine displayed paths represent schematically all equally likely scenarios with the given history leading up to time n.

Clearly, the average over these nine paths is equal to the average of three subaverages: (1) that over the upper three paths, (2) that over the middle three, and (3) that over the lower three. But each of these three sub-averages is equal to the respective price and cash flow at time $n + 1$ given the rate and slope levels at time $n + 1$, discounted for one period. Therefore,

EXHIBIT 13.7   Schematics for Bond Pricing

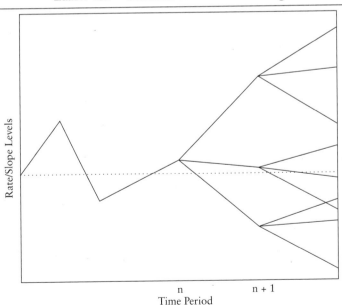

Source: Salomon Smith Barney.

$$\text{Price at time } n = \frac{\text{Expected price and cash flow at } n+1,}{\text{discounted by rate for period}} \qquad (13.2)$$

In short, if we know the price and cash flow at time $n + 1$ given any rate and slope level, then we know also the price at time n given any rate and slope level. This is certainly true if the cash flows are path independent, that is, if the cash flow at time n depends only on the rates at that time. In that case, we have a very fast method for calculating the model price, as follows. Set up at every time point n a grid of rate and slope levels. For example, we can have 10 rate levels spanning the probable short rates, and 10 slope levels spanning the probable slopes, for a total of 100 possible pairs of rate and slope levels. At maturity, there is no further cash flow and so the price is 0 for all 100 grid points. Suppose the price has been found at all the grid points at time $n + 1$. If a price is needed for some rate-slope pair *off* the grid points, it can be obtained by an interpolation. Now take any point on the grid at time n, the prices at time $n + 1$ are thus available for averaging; and the averaging can be done quickly because only a one-step average is involved. As for the cash-flow calculation, it requires only the knowledge of rates at time n. All the ingredients for the fast calculation of the price at each of the 100 grid points at time n are in place.

Summing up, from prices at the grid points at time $n + 1$ we can get prices at the grid points at time n. Repeating this process, step-by-step backward, we can fill the grid with the security's prices. In particular, we have the price at time 0.

One immediate application of the backward process is to fill the grid points with the prices of benchmark Treasury zero-coupon bonds. These prices in turn determine the par rates, that is, coupons of a Treasury bond that has a par price. In other words, at any time n we can have the yield curves, Treasury or LIBOR, stored at the grid points for use when needed.

If an option, say a call, is exercisable on the security at time n, then the backward induction process need only be modified by comparing the strike to the price at each time step and by modifying the price and cash flow accordingly. Thus, options or bonds with embedded options can be priced.

Monte Carlo Simulation

To project cash flows for a mortgage-backed security, we may need, at each step along the simulated path, rates other than the short rate. Fortunately, we already have a grid of rate-slope pairs populated with all the Treasury rates and LIBOR. As soon as we obtain a simulated pair of rate and slope levels, we can obtain any needed rates by interpolating across the grid.

The cash flow for a mortgage-backed security, in particular that of a CMO, is usually not path independent, and we are back to the expectation process by averaging present values over a large number of simulated paths. This is the Monte Carlo method. We note that both the Monte Carlo and the backward induction method are widely used and are two different practical schemes to solve the same expectation problem. There is no fundamental difference, and for a bond that can be treated by both methods, identical prices (except for numerical and sampling errors) should result.

13.3 CALIBRATION OF THE MODEL

Calibration to the Market

We set the spot volatility σ for rate and spot volatility σ_1 for slope to historical levels, and calibrate the median rate levels $f(t)$ and $f_L(t)$, and the mean-reversion coefficients for the rate and slope to the market prices of Treasury STRIPS, the swaps, the caps, and the swaptions.

As an illustration, we describe our current implementation and the choice of parameters. These are subject to change; for example, when more benchmark instruments become liquid, we may want to include them in the calibration and refine the model parametrization accordingly.

As mentioned previously in Section 13.1, the spot volatility estimated from the series of three-month T-bill rates from 1977 to 1997 is 27.3%. We use $\sigma = 28\%$ in our implementation, except for the first year, where the spot volatility starts at the level of the volatility of the six-month Eurodollar future and ramps up to 28% at the end of the first year. The initial level seems justified, since it can be argued that the market quotes of the short-term volatility of the short-term rate is the best indication of the likelihood of near-term surprises, that is, spot volatility. For example, the low level in the Eurodollar future volatility in April 1997 could be interpreted to mean that, given the history up to that time of action and pronouncements by the Fed, surprise is regarded as unlikely in the near future. It is difficult to feel this complacent about the probability of surprises beyond a year. Hence, the choice of the historical level of 28% beyond one year.

As for σ_1, it is the standard deviation of v which is twice the excess yield curve slope stated as a fraction of the short rate. From monthly data of the yield curve slopes at the short end obtained by a smooth fit to the curves, for the period December 1987 to May 1995, we estimate the standard deviation of the slope to be 10.7%. Accordingly, $\sigma_1 = 21.4\%$. We use $\sigma_1 = 20\%$ in the implementation.

The idea is that model parameters are calibrated to benchmark instruments when the latter are available, and set to historical levels when they are not. If and when benchmarks for σ and σ_1 become available and liquid, as for example periodic caps and yield curve spread options, they too could be used in place of the historical levels.

The benchmark Treasury STRIPS are obtained from the Salomon proprietary Treasury model curve, smoothed and adjusted so that par bond rates reconstituted from the STRIP rates agree with the Treasury par rates. The model median rates $f(t)$ are affected most by this input Treasury yield curve.

The swap curve is obtained from the Salomon derivatives analyst group, fitted to key swap rates, and translated to STRIP rates. The model median LIBOR $f_L(t)$ is affected most by this input swap curve.

We obtain volatility quotes on traded caps of three-month LIBOR maturing at 1, 2, 3, 4, 5, 7, and 10 years, respectively. To these, we add caps last resetting at one, three, and six months, respectively, each given the quoted volatility of a six-month Eurodollar future option, and we add a cap of maturity 15 years given a volatility equal to 92% of that for the 10-year cap. The 15-year caps are rarely traded, and the decay factor of 0.92 is a rough estimate. The volatility quotes are translated to price quotes for at-the-money caps using a conventional formula of Black. These price quotes, along with other inputs, will determine the mean reversion coefficients $a(t)$ for the yield curve rate level.[5]

We also obtain volatility quotes of 3-month, one-, three-, and 5-year European options on 10-year swaps, at-the-money forward. To these we add similar swaptions with 7-, 10-, and 20-year expirations, each given the volatility equal to that of the 5-year swaption diminished at a rate of 0.90 per five years expiration. The volatility quotes are translated to price quotes using a conventional method (a one-factor model applied to one swaption at a time). It does not matter what that conventional method is, as long as it is the same used by the traders who supply the quotes, that is, as long as the correct price quotes are used. These price quotes, along with other inputs, will determine the mean reversion coefficients $k(t)$ for the yield curve slope level.[6]

The previous pairing of the model parameters to the respective benchmark instruments (e.g., caps to rate mean reversion and swaptions to slope mean reversion), is not exact. For example, the cap volatilities can affect the

---

[5] In the current implementation, $a(t)$ is taken to be a step function with steps at the cap maturities.

[6] In our current implementation, k is parametrized as a continuous function that is linear on each of the time intervals [0.25, 1], [1, 3], [3, 5], [5, 7], [7, 10], and [10, 12], and constant outside them.

median rates $f(t)$, other benchmark prices being equal. So the several sets of parameters are not uncoupled in the calibration process. However, they are only weakly coupled. For example, when the slope mean reversion coefficients are held fixed, a cap of maturity t is affected only by those rate mean reversion coefficients $a(t)$ up to time T, so that the latter can be found recursively and quickly. The iterative scheme to find the model parameters from the benchmark prices is fast.[7]

We note that in this way, we fit *exactly* the model to 11 caps and 7 swaptions. We have modeled 18 points on the volatility surface. With these strategically chosen points well modeled, the other points on the surface are also approximately captured.

Every trading day, we obtain market quotes at closing, and calibrate the model for next day's use. As mentioned previously, recalibration, whether for a significant change in the market or for volatility scenario analysis, can be done quickly.

Exhibit 13.8 shows some of the quoted and model prices of caplets and swaptions for February 10, 1997. Some of the targeted prices are marked with an asterisk. The model prices are reasonably close to the quoted prices even for those not targeted in the calibration.

Exhibit 13.9 shows the quoted volatility surface versus the model. Note that the quoted volatilities are just that. They do not come from a single coherent model. There is no reason to expect the model volatility surface to be the same as the quoted surface. The prices are what count, and they are plotted in Exhibit 13.10.

Exhibit 13.11 shows the one-month correlations between the 2-year rate and the other rates. Both the model correlations and the empirical correlations are displayed, as are those implied by two traded yield curve spread options. Yield curve spread futures and options were recently traded on the Chicago Board of Trade. In particular, futures and options on the spread of 2-year to 10-year rates were traded, as were those for the 2-to-30 spread. From the quotes on these options, we can calculate the market-implied correlation between the 2- and the 10-year rates, and that between the 2- and the 30-year rates. (See the Appendix in this chapter for the calculation.)

Even though we had made no effort to match these market-implied correlations, the agreement between these and the model seems reasonable. (We note, however, that as the option nears expiration, the quoted price volatility of the spread futures increase dramatically, and the implied

---

[7] The current implementation takes approximately one hundred seconds for the calibration on the *Yield Book*.

EXHIBIT 13.8 Quoted and Model Caplet/Swaption Prices, February 10, 1997

Expiration.	Term	Quoted	Model	Market Price	Model Price
0.25 Yr.	0.25 Yr.	11.7	11.7	0.03*	0.03
0.25	1.00	14.9	11.7	0.17	0.13
0.25	2.00	16.9	14.1	0.38	0.32
0.25	3.00	17.1	15.8	0.58	0.53
0.25	4.00	16.8	16.5	0.74	0.72
0.25	5.00	16.5	16.7	0.89	0.88
0.25	7.00	15.8	16.3	1.15	1.15
0.25	10.00	14.8	15.3	1.43*	1.43
0.25	30.00	11.0	11.3	1.91	1.87
1.00	0.25	16.3	15.4	0.09*	0.09
1.00	1.00	17.8	15.7	0.40	0.35
1.00	2.00	17.7	16.8	0.79	0.75
1.00	3.00	17.2	17.1	1.13	1.13
1.00	4.00	16.9	17.0	1.45	1.46
1.00	5.00	16.5	16.7	1.73	1.75
1.00	7.00	15.6	16.0	2.21	2.22
1.00	10.00	14.5	14.8	2.70*	2.69
1.00	30.00	11.0	10.9	3.64	3.48
2.00	0.25	18.2	19.9	0.14*	0.15
2.00	1.00	17.9	18.7	0.56	0.58
2.00	2.00	17.5	18.0	1.07	1.09
2.00	3.00	17.1	17.5	1.52	1.57
2.00	4.00	16.8	17.1	1.95	1.99
2.00	5.00	16.4	16.6	2.33	2.35
2.00	7.00	15.4	15.8	2.91	2.95
2.00	10.00	14.2	14.5	3.56	3.55
2.00	30.00	10.9	10.8	4.77	4.57
3.00	0.25	18.1	18.4	0.17*	0.17
3.00	1.00	17.3	17.7	0.63	0.65
3.00	2.00	17.2	17.3	1.22	1.23
3.00	3.00	16.9	16.9	1.75	1.76
3.00	4.00	16.5	16.6	2.22	2.24
3.00	5.00	16.0	16.2	2.64	2.66
3.00	7.00	15.1	15.4	3.30	3.32
3.00	10.00	13.8	14.1	3.97*	3.97
3.00	30.00	10.7	10.7	5.38	5.14
4.00	0.25	18.1	18.1	0.18*	0.18
4.00	1.00	17.2	17.3	0.69	0.69
4.00	2.00	16.8	16.8	1.31	1.31
4.00	3.00	16.5	16.5	1.88	1.88
4.00	4.00	16.1	16.1	2.38	2.38
4.00	5.00	15.4	15.8	2.77	2.82
4.00	7.00	14.5	14.9	3.45	3.49
4.00	10.00	13.2	13.7	4.14	4.17
4.00	30.00	10.6	10.5	5.72	5.43
5.00	0.25	17.1	17.1	0.19*	0.18
5.00	1.00	16.8	16.6	0.71	0.71
5.00	2.00	16.3	16.3	1.35	1.35
5.00	3.00	16.0	16.0	1.93	1.93
5.00	4.00	15.5	15.7	2.42	2.44
5.00	5.00	14.9	15.3	2.83	2.87
5.00	7.00	14.0	14.4	3.51	3.55
5.00	10.00	12.9	13.3	4.22*	4.21
5.00	30.00	10.5	10.3	5.90	5.54

*Used to fit the model.
Source: Salomon Smith Barney.

EXHIBIT 13.9   Quoted and Model Caplet/Swaption Volatilties,
February 10, 1997

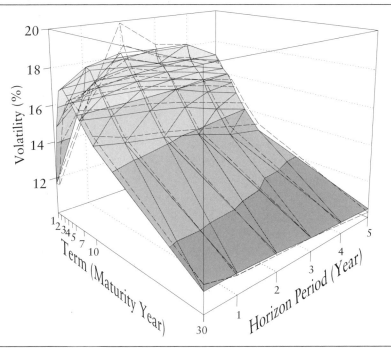

Source: Salomon Smith Barney.

correlation is much lower, to the 80s range. We also note that as of the time
of this printing, the spread futures and options market has dried up.)

Calibration to Fixed Volatilities

To accommodate investors who wish to have a fixed set of model parameters, we can also calibrate the model to a simplified and fixed set of volatilities. For example, we can select model parameters such that the
three-month rate has effective volatilities of 19.6% over a six-month horizon and 10% over a 30-year horizon, and such that the 10-year rate has effective volatility of 10% over a six-month horizon. The slope volatility σ_1 is
chosen so that the correlation between the one- and 10-year rates is approximately 82%. These parameters have been estimated from the series of
monthly average rates from January 1981 to May 1995.

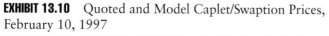

EXHIBIT 13.10   Quoted and Model Caplet/Swaption Prices, February 10, 1997

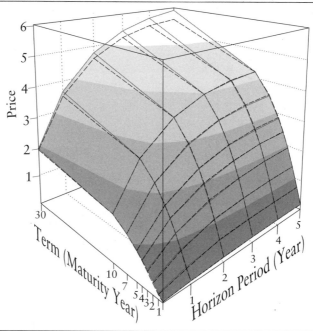

Source: Salomon Smith Barney.

So, for the pricing of MBSs and derivatives, we have the alternatives of using the single-volatility model, the two-factor fixed-volatility model, and the two-factor market-volatility model. In the remainder of this chapter, unless otherwise stated, the two-factor model will mean the one calibrated to the market volatilities, and the single-factor model will be the one with 13% volatility for the short rate.

We present some look-and-feel characteristics of the models.

Exhibit 13.12 shows five yield curve scenarios in the single-volatility model one month out corresponding to 0, ±1, ±2 standard deviations in the rate level. It is seen that as one rate moves up, so do all others.

Exhibit 13.13 shows 13 yield curve scenarios in the market-volatility two-factor model, one month out. These correspond to (0, 0), (0, ±1, (±1, 0), (±1, ±1), (0, ±2), and (±2, 0) standard deviations of (rate, slope). We see that the immediate changes in rate level and in slope level are independent of each other. We also see that the standard deviation of the 30-year rate is

EXHIBIT 13.11 Correlation between the 2-Year Rate and Others, February 10, 1997

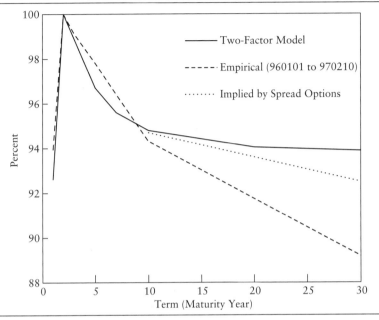

Source: Salomon Smith Barney.

smaller than that for the five-year rate—an illustration of the term structure of volatilities.

Exhibit 13.14 displays a scenario of three-month and 10-year rates for the next 30 years from the one-factor model. Typically, the rates move in tandem and the three-month rate remains below the 10-year rate; because today's forward curves are not inverted, no scenarios are inverted. In contrast, in Exhibit 13.15 the scenario yield curve from the two-factor model inverts from time to time (i.e., when the three-month rate is higher than the 10-year). The short-term variations are more pronounced, but the long-term dispersion of rates is lower, thanks to mean reversion. Compared to the historical graph in Exhibit 13.1, the sample in Exhibit 13.15 has more frequent and longer lasting inversions. This is a consequence of the given market term structure of rates and volatilities. We know that on the example date (1) the forward curve two or more years out is relatively flat, (2) the three-month rate has bigger dispersions from the forward level than does

EXHIBIT 13.12   Four Sample Yield Curves One Month Out (One-Factor Model), February 10, 1997

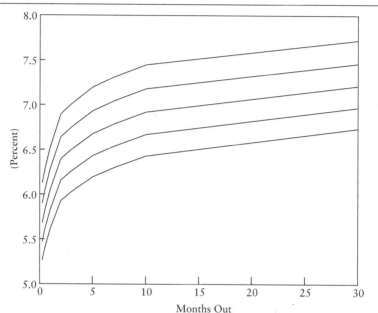

Source: Salomon Smith Barney.

the 10-year, and so (3) there is a substantial probability for the three-month rate to exceed the 10-year. In the risk-adjusted rate process where the forward curves serve more or less as the center line, inversions are necessarily more frequent than the empirical data indicate. By the same token, bonds are priced using the forward curves even when the latter are typically flatter than historical curves.

Exhibits 13.16 and 13.17 give the sample distributions of three-month rates from the one-factor model and the two-factor model, respectively, in terms of percentiles. The latter shows higher near-term dispersion and lower long-term dispersion. Exhibits 13.18 and 13.19 are similar percentile plots for the 10-year rate.

These sample statistics show that our model not only conforms to benchmark market prices but also produces rate scenarios that are intuitively plausible.

EXHIBIT 13.13 Thirteen Sample Yield Curves One Month Out (Two-Factor Model), February 10, 1997

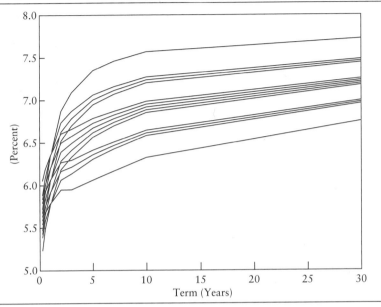

Source: Salomon Smith Barney.

SUMMARY AND CONCLUSION

For the management of fixed-income securities with option features, it is necessary to consider the effect of a surface of volatilities and the volatility of yield curve slopes. The Salomon Smith Barney two-factor term structure model provides an intuitive, consistent, robust, and fast method to price securities with reference to the market surface of volatilities.

APPENDIX

Equations for the Models

A zero-factor model

$$r = f(t) \tag{13.3}$$

EXHIBIT 13.14 A Sample of Future Rates (One-Factor Model), February 10, 1997

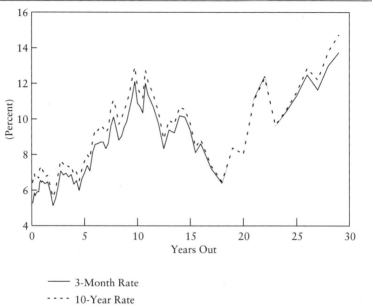

Source: Salomon Smith Barney.

A one-factor lognormal model

$$r = f(t)e^x \tag{13.4a}$$

$$dx = \sigma dz \tag{13.4b}$$

A one-factor model with mean reversion

$$r = f(t)e^x \tag{13.5a}$$

$$dx = vdt + \sigma dz \tag{13.5b}$$

$$v = -a(t)x \tag{13.5c}$$

EXHIBIT 13.15   A Sample of Future Rates (Two-Factor Model), February 10, 1997

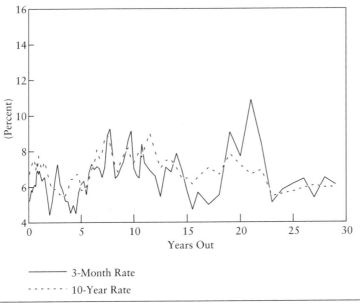

——— 3-Month Rate

- - - - - - 10-Year Rate

Source: Salomon Smith Barney.

A two-factor model

$$r = f(t)e^x \tag{13.6a}$$

$$dx = v\, dt + \sigma\, dz \tag{13.6b}$$

$$v = -a(t)x + u \tag{13.6c}$$

$$du = -k(t)u\, dt + \sigma_1 dz_1 \tag{13.6d}$$

Price of security as expected present values of cash flows in the risk-adjusted process

$$P_0 = E_0\left\{\frac{c_1}{1+r_0} + \frac{c_2}{(1+r_0)(1+r_1)} + \frac{c_3}{(1+r_0)(1+r_1)(1+r_2)} + \ldots\right\} \tag{13.7a}$$

EXHIBIT 13.16   Distribution of 3-Month Rate (200 Samples, One-Factor Model), February 10, 1997

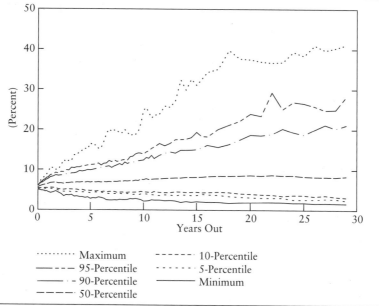

Source: Salomon Smith Barney.

Model price at a future time as a conditional expectation given history up to time n

$$P_n = E_n \left\{ \frac{c_{n+1}}{1+r_n} + \frac{c_{n+2}}{(1+r_n)(1+r_{n+1})} + \frac{c_{n+3}}{(1+r_n)(1+r_{n+1})(1+r_{n+2})} + \ldots \right\} \quad (13.7b)$$

Price at time n as conditional expectation of prices one period later—the backward equation

$$P_n = E_n \left\{ \frac{c_{n+1}}{1+r_n} + \frac{c_{n+2}}{(1+r_n)(1+r_{n+1})} + \frac{c_{n+3}}{(1+r_n)(1+r_{n+1})(1+r_{n+2})} + \ldots \right\}$$

$$= \frac{c_{n+1}}{1+r_n} + \frac{1}{(1+r_n)} E_n \left\{ E_{n+1} \left[\frac{c_{n+2}}{1+r_{n+1}} + \frac{c_{n+3}}{(1+r_{n+1})(1+r_{n+2})} + \ldots \right] \right\} \quad (13.7c)$$

$$= \frac{c_{n+1}}{1+r_n} + \frac{E_n P_{n+1}}{1+r_n} = \frac{c_{n+1} + E_n P_{n+1}}{1+r_n}$$

EXHIBIT 13.17   Distribution of 3-Month Rates (200 Samples, Two-Factor Model), February 10, 1997

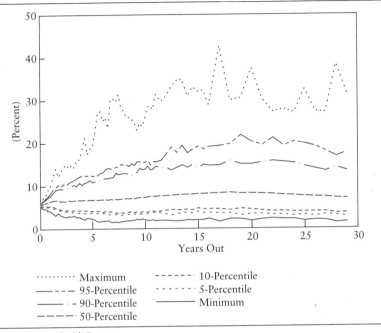

· · · · · · · · · Maximum   - - - - - - 10-Percentile
——— - - - 95-Percentile   - · · - · · · 5-Percentile
——— · - 90-Percentile   ——— Minimum
- - - - 50-Percentile

Source: Salomon Smith Barney.

In case callable

$$P_n = \min\left\{ strike, \frac{c_{n+1} + E_n P_{n+1}}{1 + r_n} \right\} \qquad (13.7d)$$

Definition of OAS

$$P_0 = E_0 \left\{ \frac{c_1}{1 + r_0 + s} + \frac{c_2}{(1 + r_0 + s)(1 + r_1 + s)} + \frac{c_3}{(1 + r_0 + s)(1 + r_1 + s)(1 + r_2 + s)} + \ldots \right\} \qquad (13.8)$$

EXHIBIT 13.18   Distribution of 10-Year Rates (200 Samples, One-Factor Model), February 10, 1997

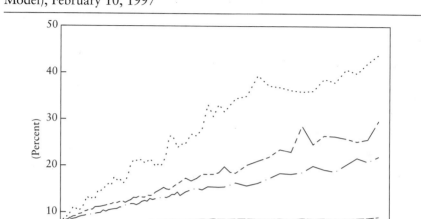

.... Maximum   - - - - - - 10-Percentile
— - - - - 95-Percentile   - - - - - - 5-Percentile
——— · - 90-Percentile   ——— Minimum
— — — · 50-Percentile

Source: Salomon Smith Barney.

Backward equation with OAS

$$P_n = \frac{c_{n+1} + E_n P_{n+1}}{1 + r_n + s} \qquad (13.9)$$

Rate Correlation Implied by Yield Curve Spread Options

The future contract on the two- and 10-year rates, expiring on March 31, 1997, and designated ZCH7, was quoted on February 10, 1997, at the price of 10047.50. That means that the forward spread $(y_{10} - y_2)$ between the two-year and the 10-year rate for March 31 is quoted as 47.50bp, and for

EXHIBIT 13.19   Distribution of 10-Year Rates (200 Samples, Two-Factor Model), February 10, 1997

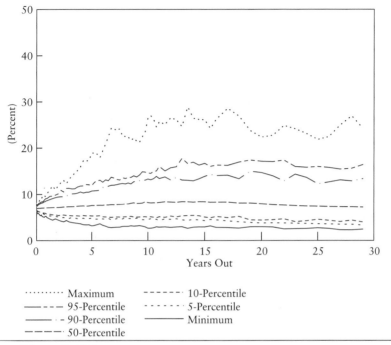

every basis point increase in the spread, the future price increases by 1. On February 10, the option on the future, was quoted at 0.32% price volatility. That means that the annualized standard deviation of the spread $(y_{10} - y_2)$ is $0.0032 \times 10047.50 = 32.152$bp.

$$\mathrm{std}(y_{10} - y_2) = 0.0032 \times 10047.50 = 32.152\mathrm{bp}$$

On February 10, we have $y_{10} = 6.41$ and $y_2 = 5.90$. From Exhibit 13.8 we see that the short-term volatility of the 10-year rate is 14.8%, meaning that the annualized standard deviation of y_{10} is

$$\mathrm{std}(y_{10}) = .148y_{10} = .148 \times 6.41\% = 94.9\mathrm{bp}$$

Similarly for y_2

$$\text{std}(y_2) = .169y_2 = .169 \times 5.90\% = 99.7\text{bp}$$

The correlation between two random variables y_{10} and y_2 is related to their standard deviations by

$$\text{std}(y_{10} - y_2) = \text{std}(y_{10})^2 + \text{std}(y_2)^2 - 2\text{cor}(y_{10}, y_2)\text{std}(y_{10})\text{std}(y_2)$$

Solving for the market correlation we get

$$\text{cor}(y_{30}, y_2) = 94.7\%$$

The quoted price volatility of the 2-to-30 spread option on February 10 is 0.38%. A sequence of calculations similar to the above shows that

$$\text{cor}(y_{30}, y_2) = 92.5\%$$

CHAPTER 14

Mortgage Durations and Price Moves

Lakhbir Hayre

Understanding the durations of mortgage-backed securities (MBSs) is critical for all participants in this market. Mortgage durations were discussed briefly in Chapter 1. In this chapter, we present a more detailed analysis of both model- and market-based durations.

The first part of this chapter discusses model-based durations, which are derived from option-adjusted spread (OAS) models.[1] We describe the various assumptions that are part of standard *effective duration* calculations, and which typically lead to deviations between actual price moves and those predicted by effective durations; an expression for this deviation is derived in terms of the various *risk factors* that impact MBS prices and the *partial durations* of the MBS with respect to these risk factors.

The second part of this chapter discusses *empirical durations,* which are obtained by comparing actual MBS and Treasury price moves.[2] Empirical durations are popular as sanity checks on model-based durations, but it is necessary to understand the characteristics and biases of these statistical estimators. Appendix 14B derives the statistical properties of standard empirical duration estimators, and this in turn leads to a relationship between empirical and effective durations. This relationship can be used to intelligently combine the relevant information provided by empirical and effective durations, and leads to the concept of an *updated empirical duration.*

---

[1] See Chapter 1.

[2] For illustrative simplicity, we will assume that MBS price moves are being compared to Treasuries. Obviously, the concepts and results still hold if the benchmark is not Treasuries, but some other, such as swaps.

14.1 EFFECTIVE AND PARTIAL DURATIONS

Recall from Chapter 1 that the effective duration is calculated as follows:

1. For a given price P, calculate the OAS.
2. Shift the yield curve upward in parallel by Δy and reprice the MBS at the original OAS. Call this price P^+.
3. Shift the yield curve downward by Δy in parallel and reprice the MBS at the original OAS. Call this price P^-.
4. Effective duration is then given by[3]

$$100 \times \frac{\left(P^- - P^+\right)}{P \times 2 \times \Delta y} \tag{14.1}$$

An effective duration of 4.5, say, is often interpreted to mean that if, for example, rates decline by 100bp (basis points), the price of the MBS is projected to increase by approximately 4.5%. Price movements for other shifts are obtained through linear interpolation or extrapolation; for example, if rates increase by 20bp, the price of the MBS is projected to decrease by 0.2 × 4.5%, or 0.90%.

However, an examination of the effective duration calculation shows that a number of assumptions are embedded in the measure, notably the following:

- The yield curve moves in parallel.
- Volatilities remain unchanged as interest rates change.
- Mortgage rates change in parallel with Treasuries—in other words, current coupon mortgage spreads to Treasuries remain unchanged.
- The convexity of MBS prices is ignored.
- The OAS remains unchanged as interest rates change.

The price of an MBS depends on the whole yield curve, and many other variables (or *risk factors*), such as mortgage to Treasury spreads, volatilities, the OAS, and so on. The effective duration projects price moves *assuming a parallel yield curve shift and no change in other risk factors*; hence it can be interpreted as a measure of the price sensitivity of a MBS to a single risk factor, namely a parallel yield curve change. We can similarly calculate the MBS's

---

[3] Equation 14.1 is a numerical approximation to the exact formula $(-1/P) \times (dP/dy)$.

price sensitivity to other risk factors. We define the *partial duration*[4] with respect to risk factor k as:

$$D_k = 100 \times \frac{P(-\Delta k) - P(\Delta k)}{P \times 2 \times \Delta k} \qquad (14.2)$$

where $P(\Delta k)$ is the price of the MBS if risk factor k is changed by Δk and everything else is unchanged.

In Appendix 14A, we derive an expression for the change in price in terms of partial durations and changes in risk factors. Given the widespread use of effective duration to estimate likely MBS price changes, we will use the difference between the actual price move and the one projected by effective duration to discuss the various risk factors that influence mortgage price movements. Equation 14.1 gives a general formula for the difference between the actual price change and that projected by effective duration:[5]

$$
\begin{aligned}
\text{Actual} - \text{Projected price change} &= \Delta P - \Delta \hat{P} \\
&\cong P\left[-D_s \Delta s - D_v \Delta v - D_c \Delta c + \tfrac{1}{2} C_y \Delta y^2 - \sum_j D_{y_j} (\Delta y_j - \Delta y) \right]
\end{aligned}
\qquad (14.3)
$$

where D_k and C_k represent duration and convexity, respectively, with respect to risk factor k, and s = OAS, v = Volatility, c = Current coupon spread, y = Chosen Treasury yield (the 10-year) and y_j = Key yield curve rates. For each risk factor that affects the MBS price, the contribution to the price discrepancy is in essence the change in the factor times the partial duration of the MBS with respect to that factor.

Although the impact of departures from the effective duration assumption of a parallel yield curve assumption may be minor in many periods and, in fact, may average out over longer periods (unless there is a systematic dependence of model OASs on the level of rates), in a volatile market, with wide swings in Treasury yields, OASs, and so on, caution needs to be exercised in using standard effective durations. We illustrate this latter point, and discuss the risk factors in Equation 14.3 with an example from a particularly volatile period, the Fall of 1998.

---

[4] Partial Durations are also called *Key Rate Durations*. See *Beyond Duration: Risk Dimensions of Mortgage Securities*, Salomon Brothers, July 1992, and *Strategic Fixed-Income Investments*, Thomas Ho, Dow Jones-Irwin, 1990.

[5] Appendix 14A gives a derivation.

EXHIBIT 14.1 Partial Durations (September 14, 1998) and Changes in Risk Factors for Fannie Mae 6.5s

	Treasury			
	2 Yr	5 Yr	10 Yr	30 Yr
Partial Durations	.8	1.1	.9	.5
Change in Treasury Yield (Sep 14 –Oct 14)	-65 Bp	-44 Bp	-29 Bp	-24 Bp

Source: Salomon Smith Barney.

Deconstructing Mortgage Price Moves: A Case Study

On September 14, 1998, TBA Fannie Mae 6.5s were priced at 100-24, and had an effective duration of 3.1, while the 10-year Treasury yield was 4.86%. A month later (October 14, 1998, close), the 10-year yield had dropped 29bp. The effective duration would hence have implied a price move for the Fannie Mae 6.5s of

$$-(3.1) \times (-.29) \times (100\text{-}24) = 0.90$$

or about 29 ticks. The actual price increase was 3 ticks, a discrepancy of 26 ticks. What led to this significant discrepancy? We decompose the price move using Equation 14.3 to calculate the contribution of the various risk factors.

Treasury Curve Reshaping When using effective duration to predict price changes, the 10-year Treasury was used as a proxy for the whole curve; that is, in calculating the projected price move of 0.90, we implicitly assumed that the whole yield curve declined in parallel by 29bp.[6] In fact, as shown in Exhibit 14.1, the curve did not move in parallel, but steepened over the month. The exhibit also shows the partial durations of the Fannie Mae 6.5% with respect to different parts of the Treasury Curve. We use four points to represent the whole curve. Note that the sum of the partial durations is approximately equal to the effective duration. This is by design; in shifting the yield curve round each of the four points, we ensure that the sum of the four shifts is a parallel shift.

Using Equation 14.3, the contribution of each maturity to the price discrepancy was:

---

[6] In the notation used in Equation 14.3, the y is the 10-year yield.

2-yr:	$-(0.8)[-65bp-(-29bp)](100-24) =$	9 Ticks
5-yr:	$-(1.1)[-44bp-(-29bp)](100-24) =$	5
10-yr:	$-(0.9)[-29bp-(-29bp)](100-24) =$	0
30-yr:	$-(0.5)[-24bp-(-29bp)](100-24) =$	-1
		13 Ticks

Hence, *other things being equal,* the yield curve steepening would have led to an extra 13 ticks increase in the price of the 6.5%, versus what is implied by the effective duration and the change in the 10-year yield.

Current-Coupon Spread The effective duration calculation assumes that the mortgage rates that are used to obtain prepayment projections move in parallel with Treasuries; in other words, that the spread between MBS current-coupon yields and Treasuries remains unchanged. In fact, the crisis in the financial markets in the fall of 1998 led to a dramatic widening in spread products, including MBSs, and current coupon spreads widened 30bp over the month.

The current-coupon spread duration measures the impact on the MBS price of a change in this spread; in our calculations, it is calculated for a 10bp change in the spread. For the Fannie Mae 6.5%, the current spread duration was −0.13 at the beginning of the period,[7] which, from Equation 14.3, means that the contribution to the discrepancy was

$$-(-0.13)\left(\frac{30bp}{10bp}\right)(100-24) = 12 \text{ ticks}$$

The widening in current coupon spreads helps the MBS, as it implies higher mortgage rates and hence a lower degree of refinancing risk.

Volatilities Volatilities increased over the period, with, for example, the 1×10 swaption volatility going up 3.63% and the 5×10 swaption volatility going up 0.63%. For simplicity, we will use just these two instruments to capture the impact of volatility changes, since in our model they contribute a large fraction to the total volatility impact on the 6.5s.

The *vol duration* of the 6.5% is 0.08 with respect to the 1×10 swaption, and 0.12 with respect to the 5×1 swaption (the positive durations

---

[7] A widening in current-coupon spreads raises mortgage rates, which reduces refinancings and hence helps MBSs, giving a negative partial duration. As indicated in the text, this duration is calculated assuming a 10bp change in the current-coupon spread.

reflect the adverse impact of an increase in volatility on MBS prices). Hence, from Equation 14.3, the contributions of the higher volatilities to the price change are

$$1\times10: \quad -(.08)(3.63\%)(100\text{-}24) = -9.5 \text{ ticks}$$
$$5\times10: \quad -(0.12)(0.63\%)(100\text{-}24) = -2.5 \text{ ticks}$$

or -12 ticks in total. Thus the increase in vols means a 12-tick drop in the price of the Fannie Mae 6.5%, other things being equal.[8]

Convexity or Asymmetric Price Movements Effective duration is in essence obtained by averaging projected price changes when rates move up and down. If price changes are assymetric, then effective duration will tend to overproject or underproject the changes. In many cases, MBSs have negative convexity,[9] which means that, other things being equal, effective duration will over-project price increases when rates move down and underproject price declines when rates move up.

If we define D^+ and D^- to be the durations when rates move up and when rates move down, respectively, then

$$\text{Effective duration} = 0.5\times\left(D^- + D^+\right)$$

Hence, if with the benefit of hindsight we knew that rates were going to move down, we would use D^- for projecting the price move. The difference versus using effective duration is

$$D^- - 0.5\times\left(D^- \text{ and } D^+\right) = 0.5\times\left(D^- + D^+\right)$$
$$\cong 0.5\times\Delta y\times\text{Convexity}$$

Hence, the difference in projected prices is approximately

$$\text{Price}\times\Delta y\times\left(0.5\times\Delta y\times\text{Convexity}\right) = \text{Price}\times0.5\times\left(\Delta y\right)^2\times\text{Convexity}$$

as given in Equation 14.3.

---

[8] Note that the vols are making an explicit contribution to the price change, since we are using market vols. If we were using fixed vols, the impact of vols would show up as part of the change in OAS.
[9] For a discussion of MBS convexity and how it is calculated, see Chapter 1.

The Fannie Mae 6.5% had a convexity of −3.2 at the beginning of the period, which implies a negative impact on the price appreciation as rates rallied, equal to

$$0.5 \times (-3.2)(-29\text{bp})^2 (100\text{-}24) = -4 \text{ ticks}$$

OAS Changes in the OAS reflect changes in risk factors other than the ones (discussed previously) which are explicitly accounted for in the OAS calculations; for example, concerns about supply, hedge fund liquidations, changes in prepayment views, and so on as well as any general widening in spread product (assuming we are calculating OASs to Treasuries). This last point has been especially relevant over the last two years, as the correlation between movements in spread products and in Treasuries has weakened, leading to increased volatility in OASs calculated to the Treasury curve (MBS OASs to swaps have been much more stable).

The OAS of the Fannie Mae 6.5% widened 27bp over the period (to market vols). The *spread duration* of the 6.5s was 4.1 at the beginning of the period, so the price impact of the OAS widening was

$$-(4.1)(27\text{bp})(100\text{-}24) = -35 \text{ ticks}$$

Net Impact on Price Change Summarizing the analysis above, the various risk factors had the following impact on the price of the Fannie 6.5%:

Treasury Yield Curve Reshaping	+13 Ticks
Increase in Current Coupon Spread	+12 Ticks
Increase in Volatilities	−12 Ticks
Convexity	−4 Ticks
Widening in OAS	−35 Ticks

The sum of these price changes comes to [13 + 12 − 12 − 4 − 35], or −26 ticks, about the same as the difference between the actual price change and the change implied by effective duration. Thus the risk factors discussed here explain almost all the deviation between actual and projected price changes.

Time Value, or the Cost of Carry

One risk factor that is not included in the above discussion, but that can sometimes explain part of the discrepancy between actual and duration-projected price moves, is the difference in *carry adjustments* between the two dates. This term refers to the change in prices that occurs as we move closer to the settlement date, reflecting the difference between the yield on the bond and short-term money market rates. For example, MBS trading is typically for forward settlement, and prices tend to increase as the settlement date approaches (and hence the higher yield of the MBS, versus cash, will be obtained sooner). This increase in price will not be reflected in effective durations, and hence in the price change projections based on these measures.

For periods of a few days or less, the time factor will usually not be important. Even for longer periods, the impact of time typically depends typically not on the difference between the two dates but on the time from each date to the next settlement date. Because of these considerations, we have not explicitly included time as one of the risk factors in Appendix 14A, but it is something investors should keep in mind. Using carry-adjusted prices will typically remove most of the effect of time.

14.2 EMPIRICAL DURATIONS

Empirical durations refer to estimates of MBS price elasticity, typically with respect to Treasury rates, obtained from market data. While there are many possible ways of obtaining such measures, the standard approach involves regressing percentage MBS price changes against corresponding Treasury yield changes. We describe this method in more detail below, discuss what information it provides, and derive a relationship between empirical and effective durations. This relationship is used to derive an "updated" empirical duration, which combines the effective duration with the pertinent information provided by the empirical duration. Also discussed are alternative methods of calculating empirical durations, including those based on a fixed relative coupon (or constant dollar price); however, as we show, these other measures have their own limitations.[10]

---

[10] Earlier work on empirical durations includes papers by Pinkus and Chandoha, *Journal of Portfolio Management,* summer 1986; DeRosa, Goodman and Zazzarino, *Journal of Portfolio Management,* winter 1993; and Breeden *Journal of Fixed Income,* September, 1991, and December, 1994. The focus of these papers is measuring market durations and (in the Breeden papers) on their hedging effectiveness, whereas ours is on exploring the theoretical relationships between empirical and effective durations.

Standard Empirical Duration Estimates

The usual method for calculating empirical durations is to regress daily MBS percentage price changes against corresponding yield changes for a benchmark Treasury (typically the 10-year). If P denotes MBS price and y the Treasury yield, then by definition,

$$\frac{dP}{P} = -\text{Duration} \times dy \qquad (14.4)$$

If $\Delta P/P$ and Δy are the actual price and yield changes on a given day, then based on Equation 14.4 we assume that

$$\frac{\Delta P}{P} = \alpha - \beta \times \Delta y + \text{Noise term} \qquad (14.5)$$

where β is the "true" duration, and α is a constant term. Given data $(\Delta P/P, \Delta y)$ for a number of days, standard regression methods can be used to obtain an estimate for β (see Equation 14.B2 in Appendix 14B); this estimate, $\hat{\beta}$, say, is taken to be the empirical duration for the period.[11]

The Relationship between Empirical and Effective Durations

Earlier in this chapter, we noted that the price of an MBS will depend on a number of factors: various points on the yield curve, volatilities, the OAS, and so on. Appendix 14B derives an expression for the empirical duration estimate β obtained using Equation 14.19 in terms of the true duration β and these various risk factors. If s denotes OAS, v denotes volatility,[12] and so on, then as shown in Appendix 14.B,

---

[11] Why is an intercept term used in Equation 14.5? In other words, why not use $\Delta P/P$ $= -\beta \times \Delta y + \text{Noise term}$ to estimate the duration? The reason is that having an intercept term "detrends" the data, so that the estimate for β is not distorted through having to incorporate price changes unrelated to yield changes. In practical terms, it typically makes little difference as to whether an intercept term is used or not.

[12] For ease of notation, we will assume just one volatility, although our formulation allows us to include as many volatilities (and other risk factors) as desired.

$$\hat{\beta} \cong \beta + \mu + D_s \times Corr(\Delta s, \Delta y) \times \frac{Vol(\Delta s)}{Vol(\Delta y)}$$

$$+ D_v \times Corr(\Delta v, \Delta y) \times \frac{Vol(\Delta v)}{Vol(\Delta y)} + \ldots \qquad (14.6)$$

where
$\hat{\beta}$ = Empirical duration estimate
β = Current effective duration
μ = Average difference between current effective duration and the effective durations over time period used for the data
D_k = Duration of MBS with respect to risk factor k
$Corr(\Delta k, \Delta y)$ = Sample correlation between changes in risk factor k and changes in y over the sample time period
$Vol(U)$ = Sample standard deviation (or volatility) of daily changes in variable U over the sample time period

In practice, the most important factor is a change in OAS. If we ignore other risk factors, ignore the effect of noise *and assume that the duration is fairly stable over the time period used,* then, approximately,

$$\begin{matrix} \text{Empirical} \\ \text{duration estimate} \end{matrix} = \hat{\beta} \cong \beta + D_s \times Corr(\Delta s, \Delta y) \times \frac{Vol(\Delta s)}{Vol(\Delta y)} \qquad (14.7)$$

where D_s is the OAS duration of the MBS, Corr $(\Delta s, \Delta y)$ is the correlation between OAS and yield changes over the time period used, and Vol (Δs) and Vol (Δy) denotes the standard deviation of Δs and Δy respectively, over the sample time period.

Why Effective Durations Are Often Longer Than Empiricals   Equation (14.7) shows why empirical durations are often shorter than effective durations. If there is significant directionality between daily OAS and yield changes, with a negative correlation between them (so that a drop in yield leads to widening in OAS), then the empirical duration will be shorter than the effective duration. *This will be true even if there is no net change in OAS over the period, and the cumulative price change is in line with that predicted by effective duration.*

Empirical and effective durations will tend to diverge when there is a high correlation between OAS and yield changes, which tends to occur during periods when there is a high degree of prepayment fear.

Combining Empirical and Effective Durations Investors who lean toward empirical durations should instead use an adjusted version derived from Equation 14.6. We define this as

$$\begin{matrix} \text{Update empirical} \\ \text{duration} \end{matrix} = \begin{matrix} \text{Empirical} \\ \text{duration} \end{matrix} - \mu \cong \beta + D_s \times \text{Corr}(\Delta s, \Delta y)$$
$$\times \frac{\text{Vol}(\Delta s)}{\text{Vol}(\Delta y)} + D_v \times \text{Corr}(\Delta v, \Delta y) \times \frac{\text{Vol}(\Delta v)}{\text{Vol}(\Delta y)} + \dots \quad (14.8)$$

This is in effect equivalent to the empirical duration adjusted for duration changes over the sample time period. In other words, the updated empirical duration incorporates the information provided by empirical duration and also uses current market information, as captured by the effective duration. *It can alternatively be thought of as the effective duration adjusted for the correlations between changes in the yield and changes in risk factors displayed by recent market data.*

The updated empirical duration is generally very close to the empirical; any differences between the two reflect the effect of recent market moves that can make the empirical durations out of date. For example, in the spring of 1995, when rates were falling, the updated empirical duration declined faster; similarly, a year later, when rates were rising, the updated empirical duration rose faster.

Constant Relative Coupon (or Constant Price) Durations MBS durations change with interest rates, so that if rates have moved substantially, the empirical duration for a given coupon can be a poor indicator of the likely duration going forward. This had led to the development of empirical durations for a fixed relative coupon (or, more or less equivalently, for a fixed dollar price), where we estimate the empirical duration not for a fixed coupon (say 7.5s), but a fixed relative coupon (for example, the current coupon). Thus the price moves used in the calculation may not (and typically will not) be for the same MBS over the whole time period; for example, if we are calculating the empirical duration for the current coupon, then for each day, the price move will be for the MBS that was the current coupon on that particular day.

Though empirical durations by relative coupon can provide valuable information, there can be problems with this solution to a real problem (durations changing over the time). The first and obvious one is that different MBSs may differ in key features such as WAMs, previous prepayment history, and so on, and hence will not display the same durations even when they are the same relative coupon. Second, as the last several years have made clear, prepayments, and hence durations, depend not just on the relative coupon but also on the absolute level of rates. Thus, even for the same relative coupon, durations can change substantially over time.

Even for discount relative coupons, the duration can change by more than half a year in a single month, and for a cuspy coupon (such as current coupon plus 200bp), the duration has sometimes changed by a factor of two or more in a single month.

A practical problem with relative coupon durations is that available data may be suspect or may not even exist. For example in the spring of 1995, after rates started falling sharply, the "+200bp" durations were based on price moves of 10s and higher coupons, which tend to be illiquid.

Empirical Durations Based on Price Levels, Not Price Changes

An implicit assumption in empirical duration calculations is that the Treasury yield change on a given day impacts the MBS price that same day; this is what is expressed, for example, by Equation 14.5. While this is a reasonable assumption for liquid actively traded securities, it may not be true in other cases.

An example is provided by high premium pass-throughs. The float on these MBSs is small, much of the trading is on a specified pool basis, and hence there is not much of a TBA market. As a result, prices for high premium TBAs often react with a lag, responding cumulatively to several days worth of Treasury curve changes. Hence, comparing daily price changes with corresponding Treasury yield changes suggests very little relationship, leading to a low estimate for empirical duration.

An alternative approach[13] is to compare price levels with yield levels that is, rather than regressing $\Delta P/P$ versus Δy, we can, for example, regress log P versus y.[14] The negative of the slope will be the empirical duration estimate.

It is important to be clear as to what this empirical duration estimate measures. It describes the relationship between MBS price and Treasury yield *levels* over a period of time, rather than the relationship between day-to-day *changes*; hence it may lead to a poor hedge against daily yield curve fluctuations. Even for it to be useful in deriving a long-term hedge, it has to be assumed that changes in OAS, and so on, that occurred during the historical period would be repeated over the time period for the hedge.

---

[13] See *Bond Mortgage Roundup: Strategy*, November 3, 1995, Salomon Brothers Inc.
[14] Log P versus y is preferable to P versus y, since, if log $P = a + by$, then $[dP/dy]/P = -\text{Duration} = b$.

Partial Empirical Durations   Partial durations can be used to hedge against yield curve reshaping. We can estimate empirical partial durations by using a multiple regression version of Equation 14.5:

$$\frac{\Delta P}{P} = \beta_0 - \beta_1 \times \Delta y_1 - \ldots - \beta_j \Delta y_j + \text{Noise term}$$

for selected Treasury yields $y_1, \ldots, y_j$. However, Treasury yields of different maturities tend to be highly correlated, leading to regression estimates for the betas that can be unstable. As a result, partial empirical durations do not seem to be widely used in the market.

14.3 DURATIONS AND HEDGING

Traditionally, either effective or empirical duration has been used to calculate hedge ratios for MBSs, typically with respect to the 10-year Treasury. As we have discussed in this chapter, the choice between using empirical or effective durations for hedging involves making fundamentally different assumptions about the relationship between past and future price movements. To reiterate (note that Equation 14.7 in Appendix 14A gives the difference between predicted and actual price changes if we use effective duration, while Equation 14.24 in Appendix 14B gives the corresponding difference if we use empirical duration):

Effective duration hedges against a parallel yield curve shift, and assumes that other risk factors are unchanged. If effective duration is used, the prediction error will be due to changes in risk factors such as yield curve reshaping, volatilities, current-coupon spreads, OASs, and due to second order (convexity) effects.

Empirical duration assumes that past relationships (such as correlations) between changes in the 10-year Treasury yield[15] and changes in risk factors such as OASs, volatilities, and so on will hold going forward; in other words, for a given yield change, the OAS and other factors will change by amounts implied by past patterns (where past means the time period over which the empirical duration is calculated). Hence hedging errors will be due to OASs, and so on changing by amounts different than those implied by past data. In addition, hedging errors may arise due to the duration changing over the sample time period and due to noise.

Thus, effective duration is preferable to empirical duration if we believe that, for example, correlations between OAS and yield changes do not gen-

---

[15] Or, more generally, in the benchmark rate against which empirical durations are calculated.

erally show any systematic pattern (i.e., our OAS model does not on average display any rate dependence) and hence that we should not try to predict such correlations. Even if daily OAS and yield changes do show a correlation, changes over a week or a month may not, and hence effective duration may still be better unless reducing day-to-day fluctuations in our position is of critical importance. Conversely, the empirical durations will be preferable if we believe that past correlations between Treasury yield changes and the various risk factors will repeat themselves going forward (for example, if the OASs from our model show a systematic and predictable rate dependence). However, in this latter case, it is preferable to use the updated empirical duration defined next, to take account of substantial market moves over the time period used for empirical duration calculations, and to eliminate the effect of noise.

Note that neither effective nor empirical durations will lead to a hedge against price moves that are *uncorrelated* with yield moves. For example, if the OAS widens or tightens in a way unrelated to Treasury yield changes—due to, for example, general spread movements of spread products versus Treasuries—then Treasuries will not provide a hedge for the MBS price change resulting from the OAS move.

Hedging Implications

It is self-evident that we cannot predict changes in the various risk factors that influence MBS prices. Hence, if we want to minimize short-term fluctuations in a hedged position, then we should use multiple instruments to hedge MBSs against movements in the various risk factors, using partial durations to compute hedge ratios. Although some of this is straightforward (such as using several Treasuries to hedge against yield curve reshaping, or using options to hedge volatility changes), the difficulty is likely to lie in hedging the residual risk, as incorporated in OAS changes. OAS changes can be decomposed into those due to general widening in spread product, and those specific to MBSs, such as prepayment or supply concerns or other technicals.

We can attempt to hedge the first component by, for example, using **swaps** rather than Treasuries; for example, in the case study of the Fannie Mae 6.5s analyzed earlier in this chapter, over the month, the OAS of the 6.5% versus swaps widened only 9bp, versus the 27bp against on-the-run Treasuries.[16] Hedging against the second component is more difficult and specific to the security, although the IO market does provide a means of hedging against changes in market expectations of prepayments.

---

[16] Off-the-runs Treasuries would have also been better than the on-the-runs—the OAS to off-the-run Treasuries widened 14bp versus the 27bp for the on-the-runs.

If short-term fluctuations are not a major concern, and we have a long-term horizon, then using the effective duration may suffice. The basic assumption is that changes in risk factors will average out over time. Some evidence that this will occur is provided the fact that OASs have not shown a systematic downward or upward trend over time, implying that changes in the various risk factors generally reverse themselves over time.

APPENDIX 14A
PRICE CHANGES AND EFFECTIVE DURATIONS

Actual Price Move

Let k_1 through k_N be risk factors such as OAS, volatilities, yield curve rates, et cetera. For given changes $\Delta k_1 \ldots , \Delta k_N$ in these risk factors, using a Taylor Series expansion, a mortgage security's price change can be expressed as

$$\Delta P = \sum_{j=1}^{N} \left[\frac{\partial P}{\partial k_j} \Delta k_j + \frac{1}{2} \frac{\partial^2 P}{\partial k_j^2} \Delta k_j^2 \right] + \text{Cross / higher order terms}$$

Dividing by the original price P, the percentage change in price is given by

$$\frac{\Delta P}{P} = \frac{1}{P} \sum_{j=1}^{N} \left[\frac{\partial P}{\partial k_j} \Delta k_j \frac{1}{2} + \frac{\partial^2 P}{\partial k_j^2} \Delta k_j^2 \right] + \text{Cross / higher order terms} \quad (14.9)$$

Defining partial duration with respect to k as $D_k = D_k = -\frac{1}{P} \frac{\partial P}{\partial k}$, and partial convexity with respect to k as

$$C_k = \frac{1}{P} \frac{\partial^2 P}{\partial k^2}, \text{ then (14.9) becomes}$$

$$\frac{\Delta P}{P} = \sum_{j=1}^{N} \left[-D_{k_j} \Delta k_j + \frac{1}{2} C_{k_j} \Delta k_j^2 \right] + \text{Cross / higher order terms}$$

Limiting risks to OAS, a single volatility, current coupon spread, and yield curve risks,[17] and neglecting all higher-order terms except yield curve convexity gives

---

[17] This is by no means a complete set of risk factors or durations; among others could be prepayment and time durations. The risk factors cited are generally the most important for typical MBSs, and in addition (apart from OAS) are observable.

$$\frac{\Delta P}{P} = -D_s \Delta s - D_v \Delta v - D_c \Delta c - \sum D_{y_j} \Delta y_j + \frac{1}{2} \sum C_{y_j} (\Delta y_j)^2 \quad (14.10)$$

where s = OAS, v = volatility, c = current coupon spread, and y_j = key yield curve rates.

For a given yield curve rate, y, say let D_y and C_y be the effective duration and convexity. Note that, neglecting higher order terms, $D_y = \sum D_{y_j}$ and $C_y = \sum C_{y_j}$. We can now rewrite (14.10) as

$$\frac{\Delta P}{P} = -D_s \Delta s - D_v \Delta v - D_c \Delta c - D_y \Delta y$$
$$+ \frac{1}{2} C_y \Delta y^2 - \sum D_{y_j} (\Delta y_j - \Delta y) \quad (14.11)$$

where we have ignored terms involving $(\Delta y_j^2 - \Delta y^2)$. Note that the $(\Delta y_j - \Delta y) = \Delta(y_j - y)$ terms measures yield curve reshaping.

Effective Duration

Effective duration assumes that the yield curve shifts in parallel and other risk factors are unchanged. That is, $\Delta y_j \equiv \Delta y$, $\Delta s = 0$, $\Delta c = 0$, and $\Delta v = 0$. Equation 14.11 then becomes (ignoring higher order terms)

$$\frac{\Delta P}{P} \cong -D_y \Delta y + \frac{1}{2} C_y \Delta y^2 \quad (14.12)$$

Assume that $\Delta y > 0$. Then if rates backup by Δy, Equation 14.12 gives

$$\frac{P^+ - P}{P} \cong -D_y \Delta y + \frac{1}{2} C_y \Delta y^2 \quad (14.13)$$

Similarly, if rates rally by Δy, Equation 14.12 gives

$$\frac{P^- - P}{P} \cong D_y \Delta y + \frac{1}{2} C_y \Delta y^2 \quad (14.14)$$

Equation 14.14 – Equation 14.13 gives

$$\frac{P^- - P^+}{P} \cong 2D_y \Delta y$$

Effective duration is then given by

$$\left[\frac{P - P^+}{P}\right]\left[\frac{1}{2\Delta y}\right] \cong D_y = -\frac{1}{P}\frac{dP}{dy} \qquad (14.15)$$

Hence, for a given yield change Δy, the projected percentage change in price using effective duration is given by

$$\frac{\Delta\hat{P}}{P} = -(\text{Effective duration})\Delta y \cong D_y\Delta y \qquad (14.16)$$

Difference between Actual and Projected Price Changes

The difference between the actual percentage price change and that projected by effective duration is given approximately by subtracting Equation 4.11 from Equation 4.16.

$$\frac{\Delta P}{P} - \frac{\Delta\hat{P}}{P} \cong -D_s\Delta s - D_v Dv - D_c\Delta c + \tfrac{1}{2}C_y\Delta y^2 - \sum D_{yj}\left(\Delta y_j - \Delta y\right) \quad (14.17)$$

APPENDIX 14B
LINEAR REGRESSION ESTIMATES OF DURATION

Linear Regression

Empirical durations are typically calculated using a linear regression model given by

$$Y_t = \alpha - \beta X_t + \varepsilon_t \qquad (14.18)$$

where

$$Y_t = \frac{\Delta P}{P} = \frac{P_t - P_{t-1}}{P_{t-1}}$$

or the proportional change in price, and $X_t = \Delta y_t = y_t - y_{t-1}$, or the daily yield change, for example, for the 10-year treasury.[18]

---

[18] Note a change in notation: in Appendix 14A, Δy_k denoted the change in the kth yield curve rate, whereas here Δy_t represents the change in a given yield curve rate between times t and $(t-1)$.

Least squares minimization leads to a slope estimator of

$$\hat{\beta} = -\frac{\sum Y_t X_t - \frac{1}{N}\sum Y_t \sum X_t}{\sum X_t^2 - \frac{1}{N}\left(\sum X_t\right)^2} \tag{14.19}$$

where N = number of observations. The empirical duration is then taken to be $\hat{\beta}$.

What Does Empirical Duration Measure?

Equation 14.18 assumes that α and β are constant. In fact, referring to Equation 14.11 in Appendix 14A and neglecting higher order terms,

$$\frac{\Delta P}{P} \cong \left[-D_s \Delta s - D_v \Delta v - D_c \Delta c + \frac{1}{2}C_y \Delta y^2 - \sum D_{yj}\left(\Delta y_j - \Delta y\right) \right] \tag{14.20}$$
$$-D_y \Delta y$$

For day t, let α_t be the value of the term in brackets, and let $\beta_t = D_y$. Hence, the true relationship is

$$Y_t = \alpha_t - \beta_t X_t + \varepsilon_t$$

where ε_t captures influences on $\Delta P/P$ other than those shown in Equation 14.20. Substituting this Y_t into Equation 14.19, the numerator becomes

$$\sum Y_t X_t - \frac{1}{N}\sum Y_t \sum X_t$$
$$= \sum \left(\alpha_t - \beta_t \Delta y_t + \varepsilon_t\right)\Delta y_t - \frac{1}{N}\sum \left(\alpha_t - \beta_t \Delta y_t + \varepsilon_t\right)\sum \Delta_{yt}$$
$$= \sum \alpha_t \Delta y_t - \sum \beta_t \left(\Delta y_t\right)^2 + \sum \varepsilon_t \Delta y_t - \frac{1}{N}\sum \alpha_t \sum \Delta y_t$$
$$+ \frac{1}{N}\sum \beta_t \Delta y_t - \frac{1}{N}\sum \varepsilon_t \sum \Delta y_t$$

Let β denote the current value of β_t (i.e., of $-1/P\, dP/dy$), and define $\mu_t = \beta_t - \beta$.

Without loss of generality, we can assume that the ε_t term is noise. We further assume that μ_t and Δy_t have a very low correlation.

In addition, if we define

$$\text{Sample covariance} = \text{cov}(A, B) = \tfrac{1}{N}\left[\sum (A_i B_i) - \tfrac{1}{N}\sum A_i \sum B_i\right]$$
$$\text{Sample variance} = \text{var}(A) = \tfrac{1}{N}\left[\sum A_i^2 - \tfrac{1}{N}\left(\sum A_i\right)^2\right]$$

then straightforward algebra shows that, approximately

$$\hat{\beta} = \beta + \mu - \frac{\text{cov}(\alpha, \Delta y)}{\text{var}(\Delta y)} + \text{Noise} \qquad (14.21)$$

where μ is the average of μ_t over the sample period (that is, it is the average difference between the current effective duration and the ones from the data period), and *Noise* refers to the terms involving ε_t.

From Equation 14.20,

$$\alpha_t = -D_s \Delta s_t - D_v v_t - D_c \Delta c_t + \tfrac{1}{2} C_y (\Delta y_t)^2 + \dots$$

Now, for any variables U and V,

$$\frac{\text{cov}(U, V)}{\text{var}(V)} = \rho_{uv} \frac{\sigma_u}{\sigma_v}$$

where ρ_{UV} = Correlation between U and V
σ_U = Standard deviation of U
σ_V = Standard deviation of V

Equation 14.21 can now be written as

$$\hat{\beta} \cong \beta + \mu + D_s \rho_{\Delta s \Delta y} \frac{\sigma_{\Delta s}}{\sigma_{\Delta y}} + D_v \rho_{\Delta v \Delta y} \frac{\sigma_{\Delta v}}{\sigma_{\Delta y}} + \dots + \text{Noise} \qquad (14.22)$$

where $\rho_{\Delta s \Delta y}$, and so on are sample correlations.[19]

---

[19] For simplicity, we have assumed that D_s, D_v, ... are relatively constant over the sample period. In general, under fairly reasonable assumptions, Equation 14.22 will hold with D_s, ... replaced by sample averages.

Prediction Error Using Empirical Duration

Equation 14.17 in Appendix 14A gave the difference between actual and projected prices using effective duration. The corresponding error using empirical duration is

$$\frac{\Delta P}{P} - \left(-\hat{\beta}\Delta y\right) \cong \mu\Delta y + D_s\left[\rho_{\Delta s\Delta y}\frac{\sigma_{\Delta s}}{\sigma\Delta_y}\Delta y - \Delta s\right] + D_v\left[\rho_{\Delta v\Delta y}\frac{\sigma_{\Delta v}}{\sigma_{\Delta y}}\Delta y - \Delta v\right] + \dots \quad (14.23)$$

Interpretation of Prediction Error

Equation 14.23 is easier to interpret if we first note that the linear regression predicted value for, say, Δs based on the sample data is

$$\rho_{\Delta s\Delta y}\frac{\sigma_{\Delta s}}{\sigma_{\Delta y}}\Delta y$$

In other words, if we had to predict the change in Δs given Δy, then historical data would give the linear regression predictor as

$$\hat{\Delta s} = \rho_{\Delta s\Delta y}\frac{\sigma_{\Delta s}}{\sigma_{\Delta y}}\Delta y$$

Hence the prediction (or hedging) error shown in Equation 14.23 can be rewritten as

$$\text{Error} \cong \mu\Delta y + D_s\left(\hat{\Delta s} - \Delta s\right) + D_v\left(\hat{\Delta v} - \Delta v\right) + \dots \quad (14.24)$$

Equation 14.24 states that if we use empirical duration, then hedging errors will be due to changes in OAS, and other risk factors displaying correlations with changes in y and relative volatilities that differ from those displayed in the past. In contrast, Equation 14.17 in Appendix 14A states that if we use effective duration, then any differences between actual and projected prices will be due to *changes* in OAS, volatilities, and other risk factors.

Agency Collateralized Mortgage Obligations (CMOs)

Structuring Mortgage Cash Flows

Bob Kulason

Since the first CMO was issued in June 1983, many CMO cash-flow structures have been developed. The earliest structure was the sequential pay CMO. As the name suggests, CMO tranches in a sequential pay structure are amortized in sequence. The sequential pay structure partitions the underlying mortgage collateral into bonds of varying maturities and durations, but does not allow the optionality of the bonds to be tailored directly. The development of accrual or Z-bonds in October 1983 extended the structuring envelope modestly, allowing the creation of bonds with longer durations and greater negative convexities than was possible in a standard current-pay sequential structure. However, it was not until 1986 that structuring techniques became available to more directly tailor both the effective duration and effective convexity of a tranche. These techniques included principal payment scheduling and prioritization (e.g., PACs and TACs), variable coupons (e.g., floaters and inverse floaters), and coupon stripping (e.g., IOs and POs). In this chapter we introduce these techniques by analyzing a selection of cash-flow structures. Our focus is on how the risk characteristics of a CMO are affected by the interaction between the prepayment sensitivity of its underlying collateral and the structure's principal and coupon payment rules.

15.1 STRUCTURING PRINCIPAL PAYMENTS

Sequential Structures

Exhibit 15.1 depicts how the bonds in a hypothetical four-tranche sequential pay CMO backed by current-coupon collateral are projected to amortize assuming three different collateral prepayment rates. The sequential

EXHIBIT 15.1 Four-Tranche Sequential Pay CMO—Projected Principal Payments at Selected PSAs

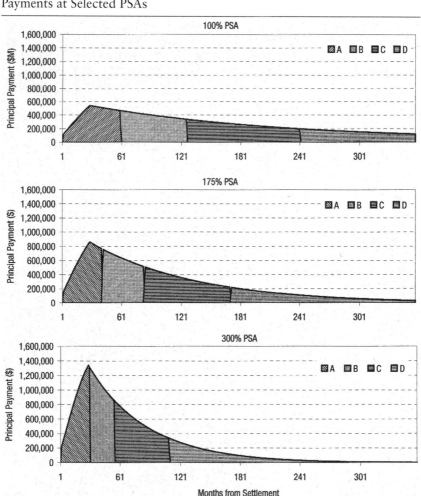

Source: Salomon Smith Barney.

structure segments the widely dispersed principal payments of the underlying mortgage collateral into a series of short-, intermediate-, and long-maturity bonds. However, although the maturities of the bonds have been targeted to an extent, they are all still subject to uncertainty stemming from the prepayment risk of the underlying pass-throughs. If realized prepayments are faster than anticipated, all of the bonds will shorten; if realized prepayments are slower than anticipated, all of the bonds will extend.

EXHIBIT 15.2   Option-Adjusted Characteristics of a Four-Tranche, Sequential-Pay CMO Backed by Current-Coupon Collateral—Market-Implied Vols, LIBOR-Treasury Swap Curve, October 5, 2000

Class	Principal Amount ($MM)	Coupon	Tranche Type	Price	Yield	WAL	Mkt Vol OAS	Opt Cost	Eff Dur	Eff Cnvx
A	$24.85	7.5 %	Seq	$100.48	7.14 %	1.8 Yrs.	0 bp	35 bp	0.9	-1.4
B	26.57	7.5	Seq	100.16	7.51	5.0	0	66	2.9	-2.0
C	30.16	7.5	Seq	98.91	7.74	10.2	0	73	4.9	-2.0
D	18.42	7.5	Seq	99.22	7.67	20.0	0	59	7.0	-0.9
P-T*	$100.00	7.5 %	P-T	$99.66	7.63 %	8.6 Yrs.	0 bp	64 bp	3.8	-1.6

*Underlying current-coupon pass-throughs.
Source: Salomon Smith Barney.

While Exhibit 15.1 makes it clear that the prepayment risk of the underlying collateral is passed through to the CMOs, it is not obvious how this risk is apportioned among the tranches. This is the primary reason that OAS models—which allow the embedded optionality of each bond to be quantified—have become key analytical tools used in the valuation and hedging of CMOs. In Exhibit 15.2, using the SSB OAS model, we calculate the option-adjusted characteristics of these CMOs and compare them to those of the underlying mortgage collateral.[1] We see that the collateral has indeed been parsed into a series of bonds with short, intermediate, and long durations. However, we also see that the option cost of the underlying collateral has been unequally distributed across the tranches. The shortest and longest bonds have lower option costs and better convexities than the underlying pass-throughs, while the intermediate bonds have higher option costs and more negative convexities.

Collateral Matters

Although CMO structures can redistribute prepayment risk among their tranches, the total prepayment risk of their underlying collateral cannot be changed. Consequently, the optionality of CMOs will depend on both their structure and their underlying collateral. This fact becomes evident when the characteristics of the current-coupon-backed sequentials analyzed in Exhibit 15.2 are compared to identically structured bonds backed by collateral with a coupon 1% below the current coupon, shown in Exhibit 15.3. The discount-backed bonds are longer and less negatively convex than are

---

[1] For illustrative purposes, all of the CMOs analyzed in this chapter were priced at a 0bp OAS over the LIBOR-Treasury swap curve of October 5, 2000. Consequently, the option costs shown were also the bonds' zero-volatility OASs over that curve.

EXHIBIT 15.3   Option-Adjusted Characteristics of a Four-Tranche,
Sequential-Pay CMO Backed by Discount Collateral—Market-Implied
Vols, LIBOR-Treasury Swap Curve, October 5, 2000

Class	Principal Amount ($MM)	Coupon	Tranche Type	Price	Yield	WAL	Mkt Vol OAS	Opt Cost	Eff Dur	Eff Cnvx
A	$24.85	6.5 %	Seq	$99.36	6.87 %	1.5 Yrs.	0 bp	9 bp	1.3	-0.4
B	26.57	6.5	Seq	97.58	7.14	4.8	0	30	3.7	-1.1
C	30.16	6.5	Seq	94.21	7.39	10.2	0	38	6.3	-0.8
D	18.42	6.5	Seq	91.90	7.37	19.4	0	29	8.5	-0.1
P-T*	$100.00	6.5 %	P-T	$95.97	7.29 %	8.4 Yrs.	0 bp	31 bp	4.7	-0.7

*Underlying discount-coupon pass-throughs.
Source: Salomon Smith Barney.

their current-coupon-backed counterparts, because their collateral is longer
and less negatively convex—and the collateral's characteristics are passed
through to the CMO bonds.

Accrual or Z Bonds

An accrual or Z bond has two phases. First, an accrual phase, during which
interest is not paid currently, but is instead added to the outstanding principal balance of the bond. Second, a payment phase, when the Z is paid interest and its principal is amortized (during this phase the Z is equivalent to
a standard, current-pay bond). During the accrual phase, the deferred interest (referred to as Z accretion) can be used to accelerate the amortization of
shorter maturity tranches. Accordingly, increasing the size of a Z bond in a
structure will increase the degree to which earlier maturity bonds are shortened. Consequently, introducing a Z into a structure will affect the characteristics of other bonds in the structure.

For example, in Exhibit 15.4 we compare (at 175% PSA) the principal
amortization diagram of the four-tranche sequential pay CMO depicted in
Exhibit 15.1 to that of an identical structure, except that the final tranche
has been changed from a current-pay to a Z bond. Several differences are
immediately obvious. First, the maturities of the first three bonds in the Z
structure are shorter than are those in the current-pay structure. Second,
there is a discontinuity in the Z structure's principal payments just as the Z
starts to amortize. Third, the size of the Z is larger than the size of its corresponding current-pay bond. All of these effects stem from the Z's accretion.
Although the Z and its current-pay counterpart were structured to have the
same size principal balances at issue, as the Z accretes its size increases as
its interest payments are used to accelerate the principal payments on the
shorter tranches. The discontinuity in the Z structure's principal payments

EXHIBIT 15.4 Comparison of Two Four-Tranche Sequential Pay CMOs: Current-Pay versus Z Structure—Projected Principal Payments at 175% PSA

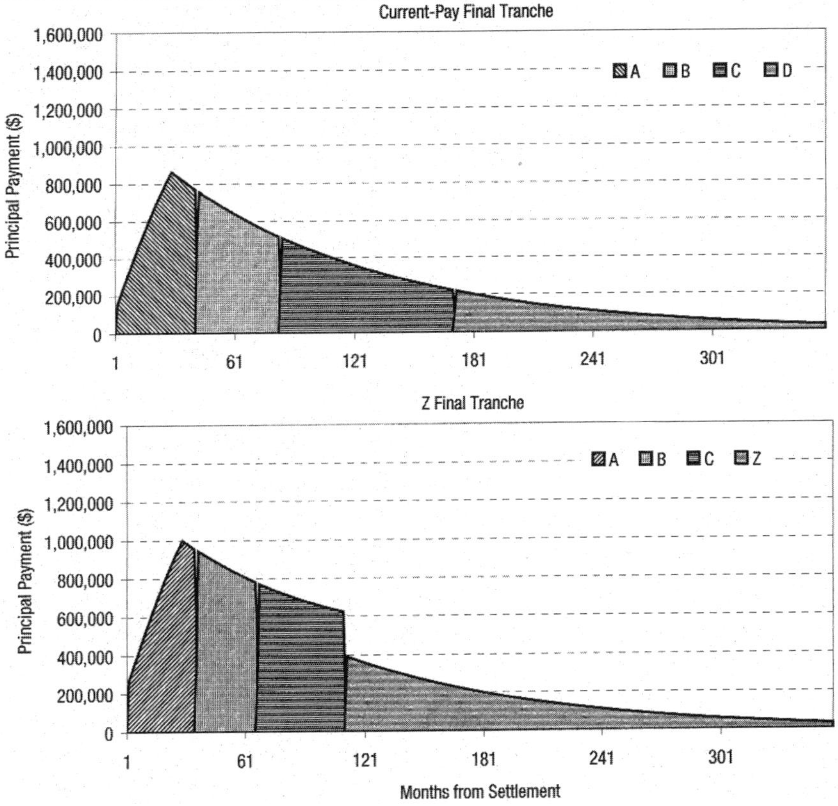

Source: Salomon Smith Barney.

occurs when all of the shorter tranches in the structure have matured and the Z's coupon is no longer used to accelerate the amortization of other bonds, but is instead paid out currently as the coupon on the Z.

In Exhibit 15.5 we show the option-adjusted characteristics of the bonds in the Z structure, which contrast with those of its current-pay counterpart shown in Exhibit 15.2. As expected, the effective durations of the first three bonds in the Z structure are shorter, and that of the Z is longer, than the corresponding bonds in the standard sequential pay structure. Also evident from Exhibit 15.5 is that the addition of the Z improved the convexities of the other tranches in its structure. In contrast,

EXHIBIT 15.5   Option-Adjusted Characteristics of a Four-Tranche, Sequential-Pay CMO Structure Backed by Current-Coupon Collateral with Final Tranche Converted to a Z—Market-Implied Vols, LIBOR-Treasury Swap Curve, October 5, 2000

Class	Principal Amount ($MM)	Coupon	Tranche Type	Price	Yield	WAL	Mkt Vol OAS	Opt Cost	Eff Dur	Eff Cnvx
A	$24.85	7.5 %	Seq	$100.49	7.06 %	1.5 Yrs.	0 bp	26 bp	0.8	-1.2
B	26.57	7.5	Seq	100.62	7.35	4.1	0	54	2.3	-1.8
C	30.16	7.5	Seq	100.08	7.55	7.3	0	63	3.9	-1.9
Z	18.42	7.5	Z	96.65	7.85	15.9	0	74	10.0	-1.8

Source: Salomon Smith Barney.

the convexity of the Z itself is worse than that of its corresponding current-pay bond. These effects occur because the Z accretion that is directed to the earlier maturity tranches not only shortens them, it reduces their extension risk in rising interest rate (falling prepayment rate) environments—and reduced extension risk results in improved convexity. The reduction in extension risk arises from the Z's accretion, which is independent of prepayment rates—the Z's accretion continues to build over time (compounding at the Z's coupon rate) regardless of how slowly the collateral underlying the CMO prepays.

Accretion-Direct Bonds

We have just seen how the addition of a Z to a standard sequential pay CMO can shorten and stabilize the other tranches in the structure. Because of their greater stability, tranches benefiting from Z accretion have better convexity and smaller option costs than comparable bonds in a standard current-pay structure and, consequently, should theoretically trade at tighter nominal yield spreads over Treasuries (or any other benchmark curve).

However, prior to the early 1990s (when the use of OAS models became widespread), the market was often reluctant to pay a significant premium for this additional stability—probably because the magnitude of the improvement was usually modest and, without an OAS model, difficult to value. This situation changed in the late 1980s, when the first accretion-directed bonds were issued. In the first Z structures with accretion-directed tranches, the Z's accretion was not used to accelerate the amortization of all shorter tranches, but was instead "directed" to a new category of bonds—the "accretion-directed" tranches. The beauty of the accretion-directed structure was that a very stable cash flow—the Z accretion—was focused in a small group of bonds (instead of being diffused over the entire structure). Because their additional stability was obvious, the market was willing to pay a significant yield premium for the accretion-directed tranches.

Exhibit 15.6 depicts how the tranches in the Z structure shown in Exhibit 15.4 (modified to include a group of accretion-directed tranches) will amortize at three different prepayment rates.[2] At the slowest prepayment rate shown (100% PSA), the accretion-directed tranches do not exhibit any extension because all of the cash flows to amortize the accretion-directed tranches come from the coupon accretion of the Z, which, in turn, comes from the coupon on the underlying collateral. In fact, because they do not rely on principal payments from the underlying collateral for amortization, even at 0% PSA these accretion-directed bonds would not extend. Consequently, accretion-directed tranches provide absolute extension protection. However, they still have call risk, because they must be amortized prior to the paydown of their corresponding Z bond. (A group of accretion-directed tranches must mature prior to the start of amortization of their corresponding Z, because as soon as the Z starts to amortize—and becomes a current-pay bond—the Z accretion is no longer available to amortize the accretion-directed bonds.)

In Exhibit 15.7 we compare the projected weighted-average lives of three bonds: tranche B from the standard Z structure[3] and tranches B and VB from its accretion-directed counterpart. We see that tranche B from the accretion-directed structure, which is a standard sequential, has the most volatile weighted-average life. Tranche B from the standard Z structure is marginally more stable because it is stabilized, to an extent, by its Z's accretion. In contrast, tranche VB, which is amortized entirely from Z accretion, is significantly more stable.

In Exhibit 15.8 we compare the option-adjusted characteristics of the bonds in the standard Z structure to those in its accretion-directed counterpart. Given our prior discussion, the results are not surprising. The accretion-directed tranches have the lowest option costs and best convexities, followed, in order, by the sequentials in the standard Z structure and the sequentials in the accretion-directed structure.

---

[2] The size of the Z was reduced to match the weighted-average lives of tranches A, B, and C to those of the standard sequential-pay structure discussed earlier. This was done to improve the comparability of the weighted-average life profiles shown in Exhibit 15.7 and the option-adjusted characteristics shown in Exhibit 15.8.

[3] With Z resized as discussed in note 2.

EXHIBIT 15.6   Sequential-Pay Z Structure with Accretion-Directed Tranches—
Projected Principal Payments at Selected PSAs

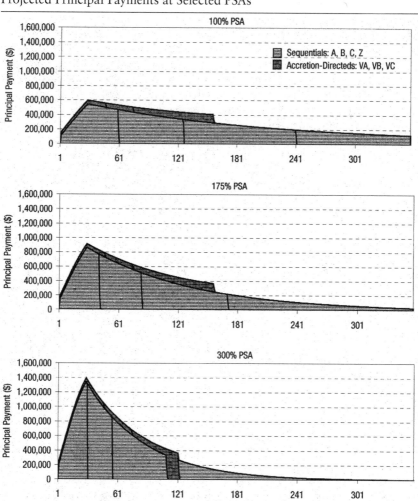

Source: Salomon Smith Barney.

PAC Structures

PAC structures are designed to create a stable set of bonds by directing the prepayment risk of the underlying collateral to other bonds in the structure. Conceptually, PAC structures are very simple. One set of bonds (the PACs) is assigned a principal redemption schedule, which is given priority

EXHIBIT 15.7 Weighted-Average Life Profile Comparison: Tranche B from Standard Z Structure versus Tranches B and VB from Its Accretion-Directed Counterpart

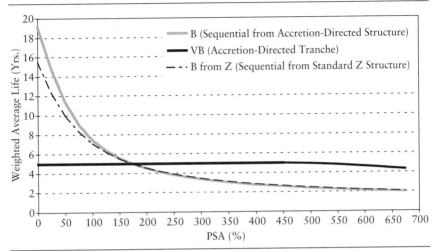

Source: Salomon Smith Barney.

EXHIBIT 15.8 Option-Adjusted Characteristics of a Standard Z Structure Backed by Current-Coupon Collateral Versus Its Accretion-Directed Counterpart—Market-Implied Vols, LIBOR-Treasury Swap Curve, October 5, 2000

Class	Principal Amount ($MM)	Coupon	Tranche Type	Price	Yield	WAL	Mkt Vol OAS	Opt Cost	Eff Dur	Eff Cnvx
Standard Z Structure										
A	27.20	7.5 %	Seq	$100.50	7.13 %	1.8 Yrs.	0 bp	34 bp	0.9	-1.4
B	28.32	7.5	Seq	100.30	7.47	5.0	0	63	2.8	-2.0
C	37.48	7.5	Seq	99.39	7.66	10.1	0	66	4.9	-1.8
Z	7.00	7.5	Z	95.66	7.85	19.6	0	72	12.9	-1.0
Accretion-Directed Structure										
A	$24.84	7.5 %	Seq	$100.48	7.14 %	1.8 Yrs.	0 bp	35 bp	0.9	-1.4
B	26.58	7.5	Seq	100.16	7.51	5.0	0	66	2.9	-2.0
C	30.15	7.5	Seq	98.91	7.74	10.2	0	73	4.9	-2.0
Z	7.00	7.5	Z	95.96	7.84	20.0	0	70	12.5	-0.9
VA	2.30	7.5	AD	101.16	6.80	2.0	0	2	1.7	-0.1
VB	1.76	7.5	AD	102.25	6.99	5.0	0	16	3.2	-0.9
VC	7.37	7.5	AD	101.01	7.42	9.8	0	43	4.6	-1.2

Source: Salomon Smith Barney.

over principal payments to the remaining bonds (the supports) in the structure. PAC redemption schedules are typically created by taking the minimum of two schedules. The two schedules correspond to the principal cash flows available from the underlying collateral when the collateral is amortized at the upper and lower bounds of the desired PAC range. If the collateral prepays at any single speed within this range, the PAC redemption schedule will be met. However, this approach does not guarantee that the PAC redemption schedule will be met for prepayment rates that vary over time, even if they remain within the protected range.

Exhibit 15.9 illustrates the creation of a PAC redemption schedule with a protected range of 100% to 275% PSA. First, the collateral cash flows available to make principal payments on the PACs assuming the collateral prepays at 100% PSA are plotted. Second, the cash flows available at 275% PSA are superimposed on the first curve. The PAC redemption schedule is defined as the minimum of these two curves, as shown by the height of the shaded region. The area of the shaded region to the right of any point on the time axis represents the face amount of PACs then outstanding, assuming departures from the PAC schedule have not occurred. After the overall PAC schedule has been determined, it can be partitioned to produce bonds with the desired weighted-average lives and principal amortization windows.

Generally, the upper and lower bounds of a PAC redemption schedule's protected range are significantly above and below the prepayment

EXHIBIT 15.9   Creating a PAC Redemption Schedule with a Protected Range of 100%–275% PSA

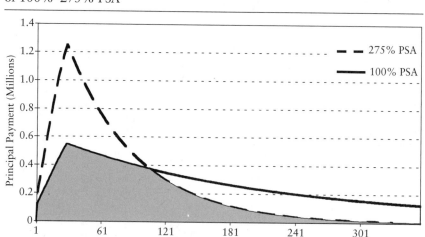

Source: Salomon Smith Barney.

rate that is anticipated on its underlying collateral when the CMO is issued. This provides the PACs with a degree of both call and extension protection at issuance, which is illustrated in Exhibit 15.10. The middle panel of the exhibit shows the allocation of principal cash flows between the PAC and PAC-support bonds of a typical PAC structure assuming that its collateral prepays at 175% PSA (a reasonable long-term prepayment projection for a newly issued CMO backed by current-coupon collateral). At this speed, the PAC-support bonds amortize simultaneously with the PACs. The top panel illustrates the allocation of principal cash flows assuming a prepayment rate of 125% PSA. In this case, the PAC redemption schedule is still met; the effects of the reduction in available cash flows are transferred entirely to the PAC-support bonds, which undergo a significant amount of extension. The bottom panel of Exhibit 15.10 depicts the allocation of principal cash flows assuming the collateral prepays at 250% PSA. Again, the PAC redemption schedule is met—by shifting the effects of the accelerated collateral payments to the PAC-support bonds.

As previously discussed, PAC redemption schedules are usually structured using a single range (e.g., 100%–275% PSA). However, once the overall redemption schedule is partitioned into a series of short-, intermediate-, and long-maturity PACs, the individual PACs—with the exception of the longest PAC—will likely have protected ranges that are wider than the range used to structure the schedule. This occurs because at fast prepayment rates the PAC-support bonds may still be outstanding during the amortization phase of a short average life PAC, yet may pay down completely prior to the maturity of a longer PAC. In this case, schedule departures would occur only for the longer PACs, as illustrated in Exhibit 15.11.

A further complication is that the protected range of each PAC in a structure will drift over time. For example, in Exhibit 15.12 we show how the effective ranges of the PACs analyzed above are projected to drift at three different prepayment rates. At prepayment rates within the bounds of the current PAC range, both the lower and upper bounds of the range drift upward over time. In contrast, at prepayment rates above the current upper bound, the lower bound still drifts upward, but the upper bound declines, that is, the PAC range collapses. If a high prepayment rate is sustained long enough, a PAC's protected range can vanish. When this occurs, the PAC is referred to as a "broken" or "busted" PAC. We can see why this occurs in Exhibit 15.13. At fast prepayment rates, the support bonds in the PAC structure are quickly amortized. When all of the supports have matured, the protected ranges of the remaining PACs vanish. Exhibit 15.13 also makes clear that once all of the supports in a structure mature, the remaining PACs—now busted—are simply sequentials.

In Exhibit 15.14 we compare the projected weighted-average lives of three bonds: tranche B from the standard sequential pay structure and

EXHIBIT 15.10   PAC CMO Structure—Projected Principal Payments at Selected PSAs

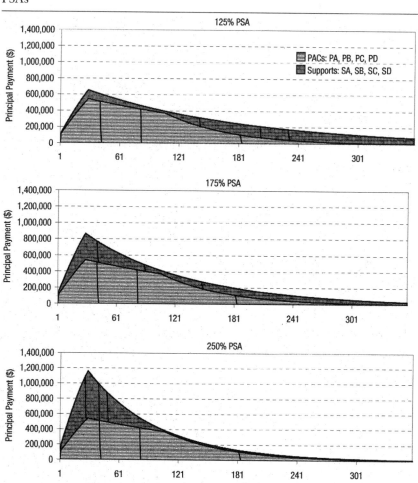

Source: Salomon Smith Barney.

tranches PB (a PAC) and SB (a support) from the PAC structure. Because the PAC structure is designed to direct prepayment risk away from the PACs and into the supports, it is not surprising that the PAC is more stable, and the support less stable, than the sequential.

In Exhibit 15.15 we show the option-adjusted characteristics of the bonds in the PAC structure, which contrast with those shown in Exhibit 15.2

EXHIBIT 15.11 Departure from Schedule of Longer PACs—Projected Principal
Payments of a PAC CMO Structure at 350% PSA

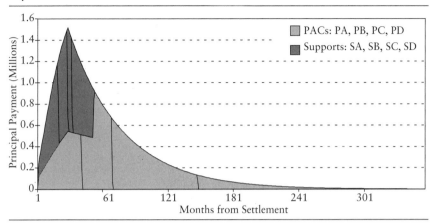

Source: Salomon Smith Barney.

EXHIBIT 15.12 PAC Range Drift—Projected PAC Ranges (% PSA) over Time
at Selected Prepayment Rates

		125% PSA For Stated Number of Years					
Class	WAL	0 Years	1 Year	2 Years	3 Years	4 Years	5 Years
PA	2Yrs	100-415	105-450	105-580	105-1280	Matured	Matured
PB	5Yrs	100-285	105-290	105-315	110-360	110-440	110-600
PC	10Yrs	100-275	105-275	105-285	110-295	110-310	115-325
PD	19Yrs	80-275	80-275	80-280	80-285	80-290	80-295

		250% PSA For Stated Number of Years					
Class	WAL	0 Years	1 Year	2 Years	3 Years	4 Years	5 Years
PA	2Yrs	100-415	105-435	115-515	125-1045	Matured	Matured
PB	5Yrs	100-285	110-285	120-290	140-300	160-320	170-365
PC	10Yrs	100-275	110-275	135-275	170-275	205-280	220-280
PD	19Yrs	80-275	85-275	95-275	115-275	135-275	155-275

		500% PSA For Stated Number of Years					
Class	WAL	0 Years	1 Year	2 Years	3 Years	4 Years	5 Years
PA	2Yrs	100-415	110-405	140-360	Matured	Matured	Matured
PB	5Yrs	100-285	120-275	175-240	None	None	Matured
PC	10Yrs	100-275	130-245	None	None	None	None
PD	19Yrs	80-275	90-260	140-210	None	None	None

Source: Salomon Smith Barney.

EXHIBIT 15.13   At High Prepayment Rates the Support Tranches Are Rapidly Amortized and the PACs "Break"—Projected Principal Payments of a PAC CMO Structure at 500% PSA

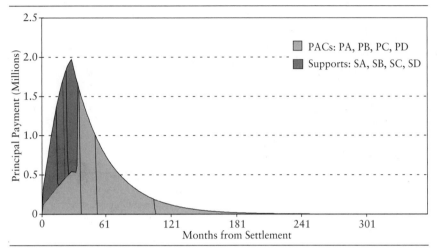

Source: Salomon Smith Barney.

EXHIBIT 15.14 Weighted-Average Life Profile Comparison: Five-Year Sequential versus Comparable PAC and Support

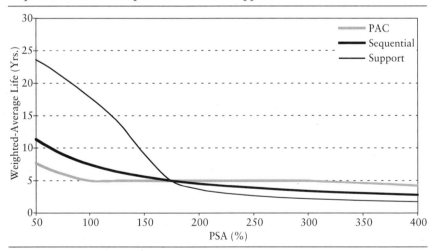

Source: Salomon Smith Barney.

for the sequential structure. Consistent with our prior discussion, we see that the PACs have the smallest option costs and the supports the largest option costs.

TAC Structures

In a pure TAC structure, the TAC bonds, like PACs, are shielded to an extent from the prepayment risk of the underlying collateral by assigning them a redemption schedule that has priority over principal payments to the remaining bonds (the supports) in the structure. TACs differ from PACs because their prepayment protection is asymmetric. At prepayment rates faster than the pricing speed, the weighted-average life of a TAC contracts less than that of a comparable sequential. If prepayment rates fall below the pricing speed, however, TACs will extend like sequential CMOs. TAC CMO structures afford TACs a degree of call protection, but do not shield these bonds from extension risk.

To understand why PACs are protected from extension, but TACs are not, it is necessary to know how TAC redemption schedules are devised. In contrast to PAC redemption schedules, TAC redemption schedules are devised by amortizing the underlying collateral at a single prepayment rate—usually the pricing speed. Once the collateral principal cash flows are determined, they are partitioned into the TAC and TAC-support bonds. The way this is accomplished differentiates TACs from PACs. TAC redemption schedules are sized so that, at the pricing speed, the TACs always amortize first; the TAC-supports amortize only after the TACs have completely paid down. By comparison, PAC and PAC-support bonds amortize simultaneously at the pricing

EXHIBIT 15.15 Option-Adjusted Characteristics of a PAC CMO Structure Backed by Current-Coupon Collateral—Market-Implied Vols, LIBOR-Treasury Swap Curve, October 5, 2000

Class	Principal Amount ($MM)	Coupon	Tranche Type	Price	Yield	WAL	Mkt Vol OAS	Opt Cost	Eff Dur	Eff Cnvx
PA	$16.01	7.5 %	PAC	$101.01	6.88 %	2.0 Yrs.	0 bp	11 bp	1.4	-0.7
PB	18.84	7.5	PAC	101.35	7.21	5.0	0	37	2.5	-2.0
PC	25.97	7.5	PAC	100.41	7.51	10.0	0	52	4.3	-1.6
PD	6.01	7.5	PAC	101.36	7.45	19.1	0	37	7.5	-0.4
SA	8.83	7.5	Supp	99.11	8.06	1.5	0	133	2.7	-3.0
SB	7.65	7.5	Supp	97.32	8.21	5.2	0	125	5.0	-2.5
SC	3.76	7.5	Supp	96.57	8.05	11.4	0	97	5.3	-1.3
SD	12.93	7.5	Supp	96.10	7.99	20.2	0	92	5.6	-1.9

Source: Salomon Smith Barney.

prepayment rate. A hypothetical pure TAC structure is illustrated at its pricing speed in Exhibit 15.16, and contrasts with the PAC structure shown at its pricing speed in the middle panel of Exhibit 15.10.

Although TAC redemption schedules are structured differently than are those of PACs, TAC structures can still display a protected range effect similar to that of their PAC counterparts. A protected range generally will not exist for the entire TAC redemption schedule, but protected ranges will usually apply to each of the individual TAC bonds except the longest one.

If the collateral prepays at a rate below the pricing speed, there are no cash flows available to be diverted from the TAC-support bonds to the TACs. Consequently, the lower bound of a TAC-protected range will be equal to the pricing speed. This is the reason for the asymmetry of TAC prepayment protection. The upper bound of the TAC prepayment range is highest for the shortest average life TAC because it is scheduled to be redeemed first. At a fast prepayment rate, the TAC-support bonds might still be outstanding during the scheduled amortization period of a short TAC, but could be exhausted before the maturity of a long TAC.

Exhibit 15.17 depicts the principal payments on our hypothetical TAC structure at three different prepayment rates. The top panel demonstrates that, at prepayment rates below the pricing speed (175% PSA), all of the bonds in a TAC structure extend like standard sequential CMOs. The bottom panel shows that, at prepayment rates above the pricing speed, a short

EXHIBIT 15.16   TAC CMO Structure—Projected Principal Payments at 175% PSA

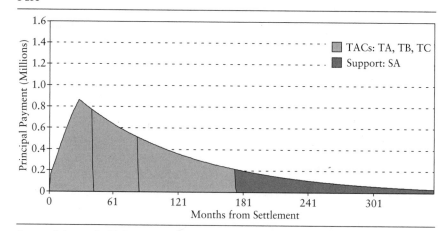

Source: Salomon Smith Barney.

EXHIBIT 15.17 TAC CMO Structure—Projected Principal Payments at Selected PSAs

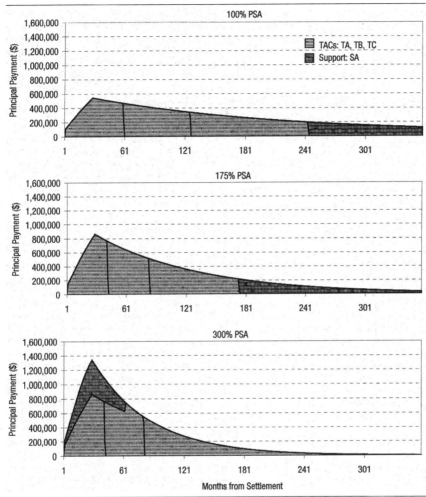

Source: Salomon Smith Barney.

TAC may meet its payment schedule even when departures from a long TAC's redemption schedule occur.

The longest maturity TAC is an exception: Typically it will only meet its schedule if the collateral prepays at the pricing speed. The longest TAC does not normally have a protected range. At prepayment rates moderately above the pricing speed, the weighted-average life of the longest TAC will actually extend. At prepayment rates well above the pricing speed, the weighted-average life of the longest TAC will contract, but less than that of a comparable sequential.

The extension of the longest TAC at prepayment rates moderately in excess of the pricing speed is caused by the amortization of the TAC-support classes. In this case, when the longest TAC starts to pay down, less collateral is outstanding than had the collateral prepaid at the pricing speed. Consequently, although prepayments continue to occur at a rate in excess of the pricing speed, the principal payments generated by the reduced collateral balance are less than those specified in the TAC schedule. If prepayment rates are fast enough, however, the effect of the reduced collateral balance is overcome and the TAC's weighted-average life will contract. The extension of the longest TAC at prepayment rates moderately in excess of the pricing speed can be seen in the bottom panel of Exhibit 15.17.

In Exhibit 15.18 we compare the projected weighted-average lives of three bonds: tranche B from the standard sequential pay structure, tranche PB (a PAC) from the PAC structure, and tranche TB (a TAC) from the TAC structure. The asymmetry of the TAC's prepayment protection is obvious: Its weighted-average life extends like that of the sequential at slow prepayment rates, but it is to an extent protected from contraction—like the PAC—at fast prepayment rates.

EXHIBIT 15.18 Weighted-Average Life Profile Comparison: Five-Year Sequential versus Comparable PAC and TAC

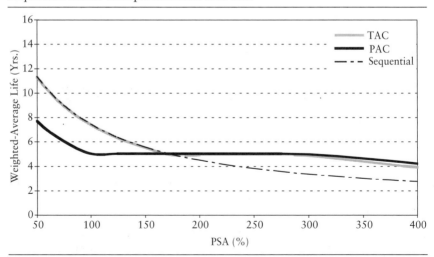

Source: Salomon Smith Barney.

EXHIBIT 15.19 Weighted-Average Life Profile Comparison: Long Sequential versus Comparable PAC Support and TAC Support

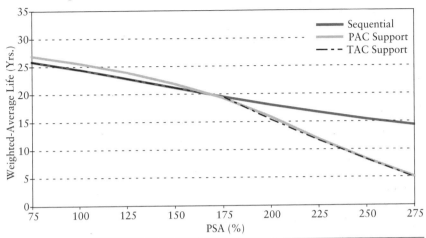

Source: Salomon Smith Barney.

A similar comparison is shown in Exhibit 15.19 for the long sequential, the long PAC-support, and the long TAC-support. The asymmetry of the TAC's prepayment protection just demonstrated is reflected as a corresponding asymmetry in the increase in the prepayment risk of its support bonds: The TAC-support bond extends like a sequential, but contracts like a PAC support.

In Exhibit 15.20, we show the option-adjusted characteristics of the bonds in the TAC structure, which contrast with those shown in Exhibits 15.2 and 15.15 for the sequential and PAC structures, respectively. Not surprisingly, the rank order of the bonds' option costs is consistent with the rank order of the stability of their weighted-average lives.

EXHIBIT 15.20 Option-Adjusted Characteristics of a TAC CMO Structure Backed by Current-Coupon Collateral—Market-Implied Vols, LIBOR-Treasury Swap Curve, October 5, 2000

Class	Principal Amount ($MM)	Coupon	Type	Price	Yield	WAL	Mkt Vol OAS	Opt Cost	Eff Dur	Eff Cnvx
TA	24.85	7.5 %	TAC	$100.82	7.01 %	2.1 Yrs.	0 bp	23 bp	1.4	-1.0
TB	26.55	7.5	TAC	100.50	7.43	5.3	0	58	3.0	-2.2
TC	30.75	7.5	TAC	99.91	7.59	10.9	0	57	5.4	-1.5
SA	17.85	7.5	Supp	96.50	7.99	18.4	0	92	5.5	-2.2

Source: Salomon Smith Barney.

Structures with Multiple Redemption Schedules

In the hypothetical PAC and TAC CMOs illustrated above, we included only a single redemption schedule in each structure. This was done for two reasons. First, it simplified the explanations of these structuring techniques. Second, it was faithful to the historical evolution of the market—the first PAC and TAC CMOs issued in the late 1980s were structured with single redemption schedules. However, since the early 1990s, many PAC CMOs have contained multiple levels of PACs, and most TACs have been issued out of structures that contained PACs. This occurred because the use of multiple redemption schedules allowed greater flexibility in allocating the prepayment risk in the underlying collateral among the CMO bonds.

Many structures are possible, but the key to the behavior of the bonds in all of these CMOs is the relative priorities of their schedules. In Exhibit 15.21 we illustrate a relatively simple one containing three redemption schedules: PAC Is, PAC IIs, and TACs. The PAC Is were structured with a protected range of 100% to 275% PSA; the PAC IIs were structured with a protected range of 125% to 225% PSA; and the TACs were "TACed" at 175% PSA. The rules for allocating available principal payments in this structure are as follows: (1) scheduled payments on the PAC Is; (2) scheduled payments on the PAC IIs; (3) scheduled payments on the TACs. If, after making all scheduled principal payments, principal is still available, make excess principal payments in the following order: (1) supports; (2) TACs; (3) PAC IIs; (4) PAC Is.

EXHIBIT 15.21   CMO Structure with Multiple Redemption Schedules (PAC I, PAC II, and TAC)—Projected Principal Payments at 175% PSA

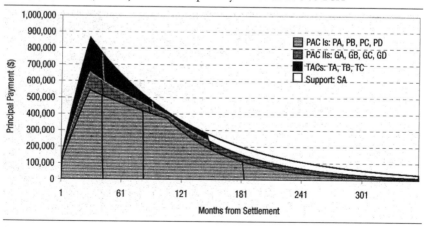

Source: Salomon Smith Barney.

Given these structuring ranges and paydown rules, it is clear that the PAC Is in this structure are identical to the PACs in the simple PAC structure analyzed in Exhibits 15.9 through 15.15. The changes relative to the earlier structure have all occurred in the support bonds. After the PAC I schedule was determined, the PAC II schedule was carved out of the support bonds by calculating its redemption schedule using a narrower (125%–225% PSA) protected range than that used to size the PAC Is. After the PAC II schedule was determined, a portion of the remaining supports were then TACed at 175% PSA. The resulting schedules are represented in Exhibit 15.21, which shows the structure's projected principal paydowns at 175% PSA.

The effects of these schedules and paydown rules are illustrated in Exhibits 15.22 and 15.23. At slow prepayment rates (Exhibit 15.22), the TACs and support extend first (see 125% PSA panel); then the PAC IIs extend (see 100% PSA panel); finally the PAC Is extend (see 75% PSA panel). At fast prepayment rates (Exhibit 15.23), the support shortens first (see 200% PSA panel); then the TACs shorten (see 225% PSA panel); followed by the PAC IIs (see 275% PSA panel); and ultimately by the PAC Is (see 400% PSA panel).

In Exhibit 15.24, we show the option-adjusted characteristics of the bonds in this structure. Not surprisingly, the rank order of the bonds' option costs is generally consistent with the rank order of the stability of their weighted-average lives.

15.2 STRUCTURING COUPON PAYMENTS

So far we have focused almost exclusively on the effects of principal payment schedules and paydown rules—with a brief aside about the role of underlying collateral—on CMO bond characteristics. Implicit in our discussions of CMO bond optionality was the assumption that all of the CMOs had fixed coupons and were priced near par. This assumption allowed us to establish an intuitive correspondence between greater weighted-average life variability and increased option cost. However, the optionality of CMOs can also be changed by varying their coupons. Examples of this approach are illustrated in the following two sections.

Floaters and Inverse Floaters

A floating-rate CMO is a bond structured so that its coupon resets periodically (typically monthly) at a rate equal to that of an index (usually one-month LIBOR) plus a spread (the reset margin) subject to a lifetime cap and floor (and potentially subject to interim caps and floors as well). In contrast,

EXHIBIT 15.22 CMO Structure with Multiple Redemption Schedules—Projected Principal Payments at Selected Prepayment Rates Below the Pricing Speed of 175% PSA

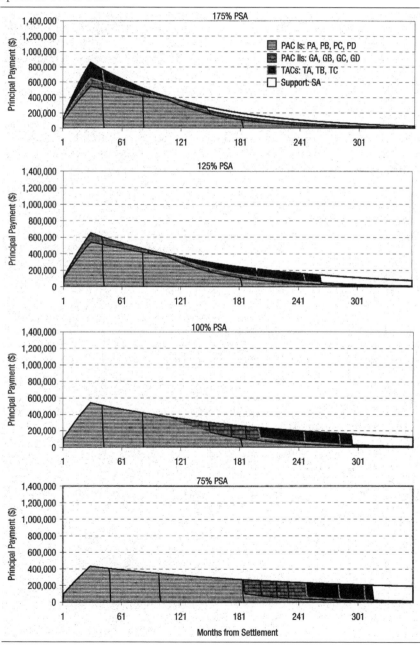

Source: Salomon Smith Barney.

EXHIBIT 15.23 CMO Structure with Multiple Redemption Schedules—Projected Principal Payments at Selected Prepayment Rates Above the Pricing Speed of 175% PSA

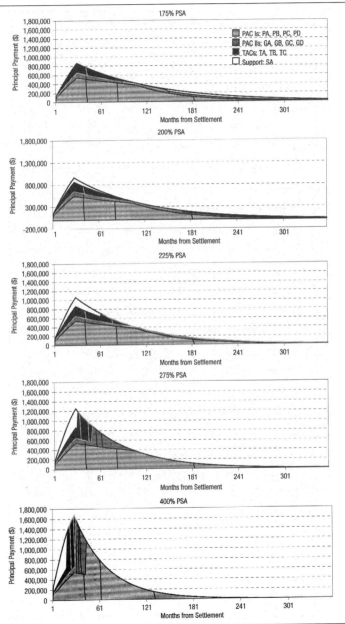

Source: Salomon Smith Barney.

EXHIBIT 15.24   Option-Adjusted Characteristics of a CMO Structure with Multiple Redemption Schedules Backed by Current-Coupon Collateral— Market-Implied Vols, LIBOR-Treasury Swap Curve, October 5, 2000

Class	Principal Amount ($MM)	Coupon	Type	Price	Yield	WAL	Mkt Vol OAS	Opt Cost	Eff Dur	Eff Cnvx
PA	$16.01	7.5 %	PAC I	$101.01	6.88 %	2.0 Yrs.	0 bp	11 bp	1.4	-0.7
PB	18.84	7.5	PAC I	101.35	7.21	5.0	0	37	2.5	-2.0
PC	25.97	7.5	PAC I	100.41	7.51	10.0	0	52	4.3	-1.6
PD	6.01	7.5	PAC I	101.36	7.45	19.1	0	37	7.5	-0.4
GA	2.97	7.5	PAC II	99.57	7.70	2.0	0	92	2.2	-2.1
GB	2.94	7.5	PAC II	98.11	8.02	5.0	0	118	3.5	-2.0
GC	2.23	7.5	PAC II	97.41	7.96	10.0	0	96	4.1	-1.9
GD	5.27	7.5	PAC II	96.65	7.95	18.7	0	88	4.9	-2.3
TA	5.85	7.5	TAC	97.68	8.53	2.7	0	169	4.0	-2.1
TB	4.71	7.5	TAC	96.25	8.15	10.4	0	97	5.3	-1.4
TC	1.55	7.5	TAC	96.02	8.02	17.6	0	93	5.5	-1.9
SA	7.65	7.5	Supp	96.83	8.00	16.4	0	98	5.9	-3.2

Source: Salomon Smith Barney.

an inverse floater has a coupon that resets in a direction opposite to that of its index, also subject to caps and floors.

Splitting a fixed-rate CMO into two pieces, which amortize simultaneously, is how floaters and inverse floaters are typically created. The face amounts, coupon reset equations, and caps and floors of the floater and inverse must be selected so that the weighted-average coupon of the pair is always equal to that of the underlying fixed-rate bond. For example, in Exhibit 15.25 we illustrate splitting the PB PAC I shown in Exhibits 15.21 to 15.24 into a floater (class FB) and an inverse floater (class IB). The ratios of the face amounts of the bonds are 3:1. Consequently, the reset equation of the inverse must have a multiplier of negative three, in order for the weighted-average coupon of the bonds to equal that of the underlying fixed-rate PAC for all levels of LIBOR. In addition, the cap on the floater must be aligned with the floor on the inverse (and vice versa). For example, when LIBOR equals 9.75%, the floater's coupon hits its 10% cap; simultaneously, the inverse floater's coupon hits its 0% floor.

In Exhibit 15.26, we compare the option-adjusted characteristics of the underlying fixed-rate PAC to those of the floater and inverse floater. If the floater did not have a cap, its effective duration would be negligible and its effective convexity neutral. The presence of the 10% coupon cap adds

EXHIBIT 15.25 Schematic Representation: Splitting a Fixed-Rate PAC into a Floater and an Inverse Floater

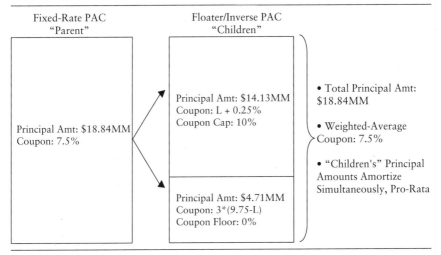

Fixed-Rate PAC
"Parent"

Floater/Inverse PAC
"Children"

Principal Amt: $18.84MM
Coupon: 7.5%

Principal Amt: $14.13MM
Coupon: L + 0.25%
Coupon Cap: 10%

Principal Amt: $4.71MM
Coupon: 3*(9.75-L)
Coupon Floor: 0%

- Total Principal Amt: $18.84MM

- Weighted-Average Coupon: 7.5%

- "Children's" Principal Amounts Amortize Simultaneously, Pro-Rata

Source: Salomon Smith Barney.

some duration and negative convexity to the floater. However, even accounting for its cap, the floater is still shorter and less negatively convex than the fixed-rate PAC. Because the floater and inverse floater add up to the fixed-rate PAC, the inverse floater must therefore be longer and more negatively convex than the underlying PAC. Another way of thinking about this relationship is that the inverse floater is a leveraged position in the underlying fixed-rate PAC. That is, an investor in the inverse floater is, in effect, buying the fixed-rate PAC and financing it with the floater.

EXHIBIT 15.26 Option-Adjusted Characteristics of a Floater and Inverse Floater versus Their Underlying Fixed-Rate PAC—Market-Implied Vols, LIBOR-Treasury Swap Curve, October 5, 2000

Class	Principal Amount ($MM)	Coupon	Type	Price	Yield	WAL	Mkt Vol OAS	Opt Cost	Eff Dur	Eff Cnvx
FB	$14.13	L+0.25 %	PAC I	$99.89	6.93 %	5.0 Yrs.	0 bp	11 bp	0.4	-0.5
IB	4.71	3*(9.75-L)	PAC I	105.70	8.03	5.0	0	112	8.3	-6.3
PB	$18.84	7.5 %	PAC I	$101.35	7.21 %	5.0 Yrs.	0 bp	37 bp	2.5	-2.0

Source: Salomon Smith Barney.

IOs and POs

IOs and POs are typically created by dividing the cash flows from an underlying mortgage security into two pieces: the IO, which receives 100% of the interest payments; and the PO, which receives 100% of the principal payments. The largest and most liquid segment of the IO/PO sector is comprised of STRIP IOs and POs. STRIP IOs and POs mimic (add up to) the cash flows of the underlying mortgage pass-throughs. Consequently, the cash flows of STRIP IOs and POs are sometimes referred to as being "unstructured." Most STRIP IOs and POs have been issued out of dedicated trusts—that is, the only bonds produced from the underlying pass-throughs were STRIP IOs and POs. However, any CMO bond can be divided into an IO and PO during the structuring process. IOs and POs produced by splitting the interest and principal payments of bonds with "structure" (bonds with cash flows that differ from those of the underlying pass-throughs) are referred to as structured IOs and POs.

IOs and POs have investment characteristics that differ markedly from those of most other mortgage securities. These characteristics are best illustrated by examining their price movements under moving interest rates. In the top panel of Exhibit 15.27, we use the SSB OAS model to project the price paths of a STRIP IO and PO backed by current-coupon pass-throughs. When interest rates rise, the projected IO prices increase rapidly while the projected PO prices fall sharply—that is, the IO displays large negative effective durations and the PO displays large positive effective durations. These price movement characteristics can be explained by the prepayment response of the underlying collateral to movements in interest rates, which is shown in the bottom panel of Exhibit 15.27.

For an IO, the amount of interest received varies directly with the principal balance outstanding, which in turn depends on the prepayment rate of the underlying pass-throughs. Faster prepayments reduce the principal balance more quickly, leading to smaller interest payments in future periods. Slower prepayments diminish the outstanding balance more slowly and result in larger interest payments. Because prepayments accelerate when interest rates fall, and vice versa, the size of the payments from an IO will vary in the same direction as interest rates. Thus, the value of this IO falls when interest rates fall and rises when interest rates rise, that is, the IO's effective duration is negative.

The PO is also sensitive to prepayments, but its price response is opposite that of the IO. Because a PO only receives principal payments, it is priced at a discount to par and, consequently, its value will increase when principal is returned (at par) at a faster rate. This occurs when interest rates fall and prepayments accelerate. When interest rates rise and prepayments slow the value of the PO decreases. Thus, the PO's effective duration is positive.

EXHIBIT 15.27 Projected Price Paths: IO and PO versus Underlying Current-Coupon Pass-Throughs, October 5, 2000

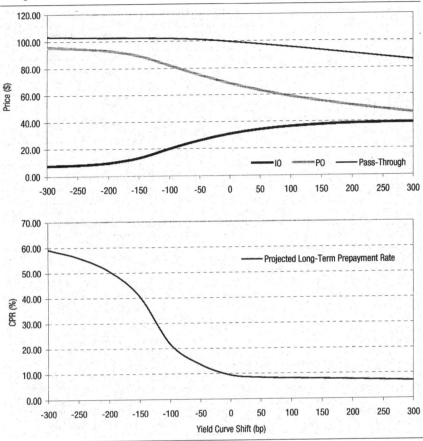

Source: Salomon Smith Barney.

Another way to interpret the price behavior of the IO and PO is by viewing their underlying pass-throughs as the sum of the IO and PO. Thus, if all three instruments were priced at the same OAS, the prices of the IO and PO would add up to the price of the pass-throughs and the effective duration of the pass-throughs would equal the weighted average of the effective durations of the IO and PO.

The price patterns in Exhibit 15.27 illustrate an additional feature of IOs and POs backed by current-coupon collateral. For a region around the current market price, the PO path is curved in the investor's favor. That is for interest rate movements of similar magnitude, the prices rise more rapidly under market rallies than they fall when the market declines. This represents positive convexity. The IO, in contrast, is negatively convex—its prices fall more rapidly than they rise.

These properties can also be explained in terms of the response of prepayments to interest rate movements. The projected long-term average prepayment rate for the underlying pass-throughs for various market levels is displayed in the bottom panel of Exhibit 15.27. The prepayment rate is projected to rise substantially under a market rally, but to fall only moderately under a market decline. Consequently, the price gain on the PO in a rally will be greater than the price loss in a decline, given comparable movements in interest rates. Similarly, the price loss on the IO in a rally will be greater than the price gain in a decline.

This pattern holds until interest rates rally about 100bp (basis points) to 150bp; then, the relationship reverses. The price levels of the IO and PO explain the reversal of this relationship. If interest rates were to rally more than about 100bp, the expected rapid prepayment rate of the underlying mortgages reduces the value of the IO and raises the value of the PO, so that these issues trade at relatively low and high price levels, respectively. At these levels, the IO price has much more room to expand than to decline further. In contrast, the value of the PO has much more room to fall than to rise. These characteristics are illustrated explicitly in Exhibit 15.28, which shows the projected duration and convexity paths that correspond to the projected price paths of Exhibit 15.27.

CMO Bond Characteristics Change as Interest Rates Move

Exhibits 15.27 and 15.28 make clear that the investment characteristics of IOs, POs, and pass-throughs are not static. In fact, they can change dramatically as interest rates move. The same is true for any CMO tranche, although the magnitudes of the changes for most tranches are much smaller than those shown for the IO and PO. To illustrate the magnitudes of changes that are more typical, in Exhibit 15.29 we compare the projected price, duration, and convexity paths (versus interest-rate move) of the 10-year PAC and sequential CMOs discussed in this chapter to those of a comparable duration Treasury.

Vast Range of Possibilities

In this chapter, we provided an introduction to CMO bond types and structuring techniques by analyzing a selection of structures. However, we have only glimpsed the tip of the iceberg. A vast range of bond types (with widely differing investment characteristics) have been produced, largely by using

EXHIBIT 15.28   Projected Effective Duration and Convexity Paths: IO and PO versus Underlying Current-Coupon Pass-Throughs, October 5, 2000

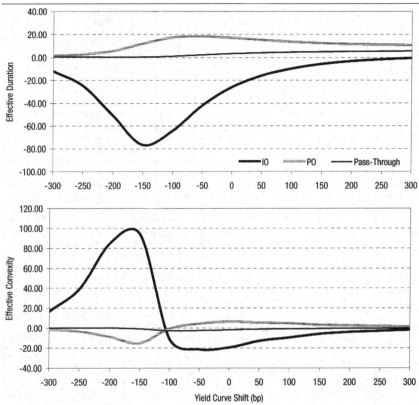

Source: Salomon Smith Barney.

combinations of the techniques we have outlined. For example, coupon stripping has been combined with principal payment scheduling and prioritization to produce PAC IOs and POs, TAC IOs and POs, and support IOs and POs. Similarly, fixed-rate PACs, TACs, and supports have been divided into floating-rate and inverse-floating-rate PACs, TACs, and supports. The end result has been the production of a range of bonds, selections of which can be used to express virtually any view on interest-rates or prepayment-rates. A brief description of most major CMO bond types can be found in Appendix B of this book.

EXHIBIT 15.29   Projected Price, Effective Duration, and Effective Convexity Paths: 10-Year PAC and Sequential versus Comparable Duration Treasury, October 5, 2000

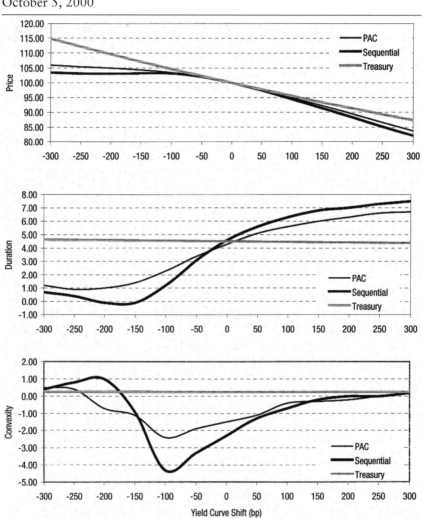

Source: Salomon Smith Barney.

Commercial Mortgage-Backed Securities (CMBSs)

CHAPTER 16

A Guide to Commercial
Mortgage-Backed Securities

Darrell Wheeler

Commercial mortgage-backed securities (CMBSs) have emerged as an important market sector since 1996. With more than $250 billion of outstanding issuance the CMBS sector has developed a broad investor base and a liquid secondary market.

This chapter provides a description of commercial mortgage-backed securities, discusses the credit analysis and rating methods of the rating agencies, discusses CMBS relative value, and provides investors with some suggested analysis techniques. Salient points include the following:

- **Pooled commercial mortgage security payments to investors depend primarily on the cash flow generated from the underlying commercial properties, rather than on the credit of an issuer or borrower.** The current credit strength of this security is best reflected through the debt service coverage ratio (DSCR). Strong commercial property fundamentals and long amortization terms of many commercial mortgages (typically 25 to 30 years) have made near-term loan defaults infrequent. To analyze final repayment risk, investors and rating agencies focus on the expected balloon mortgage balances at maturity and possible refinance market conditions at that time using the property's loan-to-value ratio (LTV).

- **The rating agencies' credit enhancement models appear to provide excess credit protection relative to the default and loss experience of the last real estate recession.** The rating agencies have developed methods for measuring the likelihood that a particular commercial transaction will meet its scheduled payments to investors under various economic scenarios. These methods focus on financial leverage statistics, as well as on underwriting standards, for different property types, and property tenancy.

During the past four years, rating agencies have adjusted the commercial models to compensate for the strong collateral performance and more realistically reflect the commercial property default probability. We expect commercial credit enhancement levels will continue to decline as the CMBS market experiences an economic slowdown and gains maturity.

■ A relatively low level of construction funding in combination with the economic expansion of the past few years has created the currently strong commercial real estate fundamentals. *Seasoned CMBS transactions offer significant relative value as the underlying collateral has experienced significant appreciation since the loans were securitized and yet the loans remain precluded from prepayment by strong prepayment penalties.*

■ *Relative value analysis comparison with other spread products suggests CMBSs offer significant excess return.* Considering the CMBS markets' improved liquidity during 1999 and 2000 and given the credit risk similar to other rated structured debt products, CMBS would seem to have collateral structure and market characteristics that justify a tighter overall spread. (This is especially true for the triple-A rated classes including IO.)

16.1 A DESCRIPTION OF THE SECURITY

A commercial mortgage security is backed primarily by the cash flows of a mortgage or pool of mortgages on commercial real estate and may take a variety of different structural and legal forms. We focus on those securities that are backed by pools of performing commercial mortgages.

The structure of a commercial mortgage security is quite similar to that of its single-family, residential counterpart. Principal and interest payments on underlying loans, after the deduction of servicing expenses, are passed through directly to the certificate holders. Similar to residential securities excess interest payments are bundled and sold as IO certificates. However, the cash flow of a CMBS IO certificate is more certain than residential IOs as the underlying commercial mortgages are usually locked out from prepayment and then usually have a high prepayment penalty or a defeasance mechanism. Unlike the agency residential mortgage security, there is no built-in implied government guarantee for the payment of principal and interest to the investor, making CMBS more similar to a non-agency residential mortgage security. *The bond's payments stream depends on the cash flows produced by the mortgage pool and the refinancability of the mortgages at their balloon maturity.* Exhibit 16.1 summarizes the major differences between commercial and residential mortgage bonds.

EXHIBIT 16.1 Commercial Mortgage Loan versus Single-Family
Loan Characteristics

Loan Characteristics	Commercial	Residential
Recourse	Nonrecourse to the borrower.	Recourse to the borrower.
Call Feature	Usually noncallable for the life. Loan prepayments usually permitted via defeasance.	Prepayable at par without penalty.
Security	Secured by income-producing assets (office building, retail property, hotel or multifamily).	Secured by single-family residential properties.
Structure	Bullet structure—typically ten-year balloon payment based on a 25- to 30-year amortizing schedule.	Fully amortizing—typically 15 or 30 years.

Source: Salomon Smith Barney.

The commercial mortgage security is generally structured with credit enhancement to protect against potential cash-flow delays and shortfalls. This credit enhancement usually takes the form of internal support via allocation of loan losses in reverse sequential order. Loan prepayments are usually applied to the senior rated classes first. Exhibit 16.2 presents a typical CMBS sequential pay structure. Some floating rate CMBS structures may allocate principal prepayments based on a pro rata class allocation to allow for a higher likelihood of prepayment on a less diverse mortgage pool or the possibility that most of the high quality loans prepay first.

Exhibit 16.2 also highlights the typical credit enhancement level to protect investors in a fixed CMBS conduit transaction. Early 1996 and 1997 CMBS transactions featured credit enhancement levels of 30% at the triple-A level (70% of the transaction was rated triple-A), while recent 2000 transactions have had triple-A subordination levels below 24%.[1] (Exhibit 16.3 presents historic CMBS credit enhancement levels.) Recent commercial transactions have featured credit enhancement as much as two to three times greater than residential mortgage securities.

Later in this chapter, once we have fully reviewed credit enhancement, we discuss the adequacy of the credit protection contained in current CMBS transactions.

---

[1] See "CMBS Subordination Levels—Whatever Happened to 30%, 20%, 10%?" Darrell Wheeler, October 12, 1999.

EXHIBIT 16.2   CMBS Certificate Structure with Typical Subordination Levels

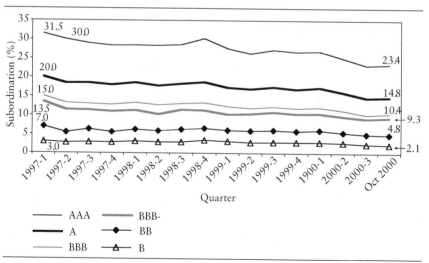

$850MM IG CMBS	Sub Level
Aaa/AAA	20%-32%
Aa/AA	18%-24%
A/A	14%-19%
Baa2/BBB	10%-14%
Baa3/BBB-	7%-12%

$1 Billion Pool of Mortgages

$30-$100MM Non-Inv Grade CMBS	
Ba/BB	4%-7%
B/B	2%-4%

$20-$40MM Unrated CMBS

Last Loss — Lowest Risk

Loss Position — Credit Risk

First Loss — Highest Risk

Source: Salomon Smith Barney.

EXHIBIT 16.3   Historic Fixed Rate CMBS Conduit Credit Enhancement Levels

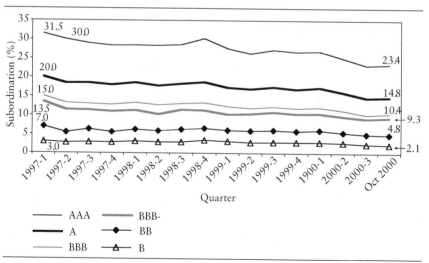

Source: Salomon Smith Barney.

16.2 LOAN SERVICING AND ADVANCING

Monthly mortgage debt service payments are collected and aggregated by a "master servicer." On a set monthly date this master servicer remits the payments to the trustee, which makes the monthly payments to the certificate holders. If a loan defaults, certificate holders are insulated from possible short-term cash-flow shortfall by the master servicer, which is obligated to make bond principal and interest advances to the trustee and pay property taxes and insurance payments to the extent that such advances are recoverable from the underlying mortgage obligation.

The "special servicer" is a separate entity from the master servicer and is responsible for loan collections on defaulted loans. Any loan that has been in default for more than 60 days is usually transferred to the special servicer, which has an obligation to work out the loan with the objective of maximizing "the net present value of the proceeds realized from the loan." The special servicer is often an entity related to the subordinate certificate investor, providing an additional motivation to minimize the loan's losses. The special servicer usually has extensive commercial real estate expertise, enabling it to evaluate whether to foreclose and liquidate the loan or to restructure the loan to enable it to be returned to the master servicer. During the loan workout, certain trigger events require the special servicer to obtain a new appraisal for the property. Usually, if the appraisal suggests that the property is worth less than 90% of the outstanding loan balance and service advances, the special servicer must reset the principal loan amount to the new appraisal value. This is referred to as an appraisal reduction. This appraisal reduction is meant to preserve capital for the senior-rated certificates, as it no longer makes sense to continue advances to the junior classes that have lost their economic interest in the loan.

The agreement and mechanics of how each CMBS transaction's cash flows are handled are outlined in a pooling and servicing agreement between the issuer, servicer, special servicer, and trustee. This agreement is intended to make every element of converting the mortgage's cash flow to bond cash flow very mechanical and is summarized in the prospectus.

16.3 A DESCRIPTION OF THE TYPICAL COMMERCIAL MORTGAGE

Commercial mortgages differ from single-family residential loans in several ways. Commercial mortgages are all backed by income producing properties, such as office buildings, retail shopping centers, multifamily apartments, industrial/warehouse properties, and hotels. In 2000, the average fixed-rate conduit had the following property composition: 29.76% multifamily loans; 14.3% anchored retail; 10.1% other retail; 18.5% office; 6.6% industrial; 8.0% hotels; 2.1% health care; and 2.4% manufactured housing. The mortgages on such properties tend to have a shorter maturity than their residential counterparts. Moreover, many of the commercial mortgages are either non-amortizing or partially amortizing and, hence, mature with an outstanding principal balance, or "balloon." In addition, commercial mortgages are larger sized loans ranging in size from $300,000 up to several hundred million. Finally, commercial mortgages, particularly industrial/warehouse properties, may be subject to environmental risk at higher levels than single-family properties.

The typical commercial mortgage is a balloon loan, with a 30-year amortization schedule and a balloon payment due after 10 years. Unlike residential mortgages, most commercial loans have a complete prohibition (or *lock-out*) on prepayments for several years, and then a prepayment penalty for several more years. The mortgage loan may be structured to offer prepayment flexibility via three mechanisms that are designed to maintain the collateral pool's cash flow or compensate the investors for lost payment:

1. *Yield maintenance.* Making the lender whole for the loss of an above market coupon on a net present value basis (so that in effect there is generally no economic incentive for the borrower to refinance).
2. *Defeasance.* Involves the borrower pledging to the holder of the mortgage U.S. Treasury securities whose cash flows equal or exceed that of the mortgage.
3. *Fee or percentage of balance.* Rarely, it might be a declining fee proportional to the remaining balance, for example, a 5-4-3-2-1 schedule means that the penalty is equal to 5% of the outstanding loan balance in the first year of the penalty period, 4% during the second year, and so on.

An owner may make voluntary prepayment and incur the yield maintenance or defeasance cost if they have a compelling necessity to sell. In that case, the fee is usually distributed via a formula that will maintain each certificate's return and usually enhances the IO return. In many instances the early repayment may actually increase the IO holder's yield. In the case of defeasance, the U.S. Treasury collateral remains in the trust and the bondholders receive their regular monthly mortgage payments. Certificates from pools that have had a significant number of loans defease are good candidates for rating agency upgrades as the underlying loan collateral has been replaced with triple-A-rated U.S. Treasuries.

The intent of these prepayment restrictions create securities with very certain loan prepayment expectations. A typical CMBS transaction would be MCFI 1998-3, a $908mm deal priced by Salomon Smith Barney in December 1998. Virtually all (over 99%) of the loans are balloons, the majority having the balloon payment due after 10 years. All the loans have restrictions on prepayments: about 98% have a lock-out period followed by either yield maintenance (about 78% of the loans), defeasance (19% of the loans), or a declining fee schedule (just under 1% of the loans). The remaining 2% of the loans have a prepayment penalty equal to the greater of yield maintenance or 1% of the loan balance; for some loans, this is followed by a declining fee penalty schedule.

Restrictions on prepayments usually end about three to six months before the balloon date. The objective is to allow the borrower time to refinance the loan and, hence, make the balloon payment. Later in the chapter when we describe pricing scenarios, we discuss CMBS mortgage prepayment experience and useful scenarios.

The borrower on larger mortgages (over $1 million) is usually structured as a special purpose entity (SPE) to insulate the property's cash flow from the parent company. The SPE is usually restricted via covenants to only owning and operating the property and prevented from incurring further liabilities. Many times on larger loans, the SPE will have a special legal opinion that says it is separate from its parent's operating activities (bankruptcy remote) and have an independent director in an effort to prevent the loan from being involved in any bankruptcy proceeding that might evolve from a future troubled parent company. The loan may also have an independent director as an additional safeguard to prevent fraudulent bankruptcy filings by the SPE.

The commercial mortgages usually require the borrower to fund an escrow account with one month's payment of debt service, taxes, and insurance. On many commercial tenanted mortgage loans, there may also be an escrow reserve amount for future re-leasing costs such as tenant inducement payments or leasing commissions. The borrower will also likely be required to provide annual financial statements and tenant rent rolls to enable the servicer to monitor property performance. The servicer usually uses these statements to recalculate the loan's debt service and makes that information available to certificate holders, via the servicer's Web site.

16.4 MARKET DEVELOPMENT

Prior to the early 1980s, a market for trading commercial mortgages existed, but it was limited and the loans were not sold in security form. Instead, financial institutions would trade such loans among themselves either as whole loans or as commercial mortgage participations.

In the mid-1980s, however, commercial mortgage originators began utilizing the securities market, albeit at a slow pace. A few insurance companies turned to the Eurobond market, where they issued securities that carried S&P ratings based on the credit of the respective insurance company. The primary benefit that they received from issuing in the Eurobond market was that they faced no Securities and Exchange Commission (SEC) registration requirements. Securitization in the domestic market also began in the mid-1980s, helped partly by the development of the collateralized mortgage obligation (CMO), the introduction of the rating criteria for certain commercial mortgage transactions and the Tax Reform Act of 1986, which authorized a new mortgage securities vehicle known as a Real Estate Mortgage Investment Conduit (REMIC).

The first pooled commercial mortgage security was issued in 1984—a $205-million CMO issued by Penn Mutual Life Insurance Company. In 1985, estimated issuance of pooled commercial mortgage securities totaled a healthy $2.7 billion. Issuance slowed thereafter, however, totaling approximately $10.5 billion in cumulative issuance by year-end 1991 (see Exhibit 16.4). Compared with the single-family market—where roughly 50% of outstanding mortgages are securitized (representing about 1.3 trillion)—the proportion of securitized commercial mortgages initially was quite small.

EXHIBIT 16.4   Estimated Issuance of Pooled Commercial Mortgage Pass-Throughs and CMBS, 1984–2000 (Dollars in Billions)

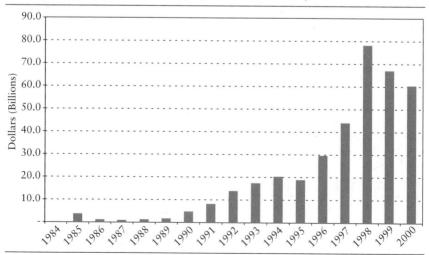

Sources: Salomon Smith Barney, Financial World Publications, Commercial Mortgage Alert.

It wasn't until the real estate recession of the early 1990s that CMBS issuance increased. The Financial Institutions Reform, Recovery and Enforcement Act (FIRREA) of 1989, was the catalyst for the CMBS market, as it chartered the Resolution Trust Corporation to manage and resolve insolvent thrifts formerly insured by the Federal Saving and Loan Insurance Corporation (FSLIC) and placed in receivership. FIRREA also included new regulations, making it more onerous for savings institutions to hold certain amounts of commercial real estate loans. The new capital standards required savings institutions to maintain total regulatory capital equal to 7.2% of their total risk-weighted assets in 1992 and at least 8% thereafter. Under FIRREA, commercial real estate loans held by commercial banks and thrifts had a 100% risk-weighting classification.

In addition, the 1989 Act imposed categorical asset restrictions on savings institutions, limiting secured nonresidential real property loans to 400% of capital. The new requirements were onerous for many thrifts, which were forced either to liquidate commercial mortgages or, at a minimum, to curtail originating them. Exhibit 16.4, which shows CMBS issuance since 1984, demonstrates the large increase in CMBS issuance that took place after 1990.

Early issuance was driven by weak real estate markets, rising loan losses and the RTC's need for an efficient loan exit strategy. Over the years, sourcing of CMBS issuance collateral has moved from RTC distressed loans to commercial mortgages specifically originated and warehoused for securitization. Early annual issuance levels were low. *It was not until 1997 and 1998 that there was sufficient outstanding issuance to justify third-party reporting services and dealer secondary trading efforts, which have since increased liquidity and enabled relative value comparison with other debt products.* Today's CMBS market has evolved to the point where there are a variety of different CMBS pool types. Exhibit 16.5 summarizes the various CMBS classifications that are based on the pool diversity.

Exhibit 16.6 presents recent historic issuance by these different product types. The most notable change is the decline in fixed-rate transaction size, which has dropped by 16% for conduit transactions and 23% for fusion transactions. We expect that fixed-rate issuance size will remain above $750 million in the future because smaller transactions hurt issuance economics.

Today's CMBSs market is supported by a broad array of institutional investors that hold CMBSs to diversify their bond portfolios. New institutional investors continue to recognize the benefit of the underlying asset diversity and credit enhancement structure. *This increased investor base combined with strong underlying collateral fundamentals to create an asset class that has become a capital safe haven in times of economic distress. The market has evolved to the point where several hundred million CMBS*

EXHIBIT 16.5   Major CMBS Pool Types

Transaction Type	Market Size (MM)	Description
Regular Conduit	$96,300	Pool containing more than 80 loans usually with no on loan representing more than 10% of the total balance.
Fusion	$49,236	Pool containing more than 80 loans with one loan representing more than more than 10% of the pool.
Large Loan	$11,913	Pool containing less than 30 loans with several loans each being more than 10% of the total pool balance.
Single Asset/ Single Issuer	$21,023	Pool collateralized by a single asset or a pool of assets all owned by the same entity. Usually a low leverage loan that the rating agencies can give an investment grade rating on a stand-alone basis.
Floating Rate Conduit	$25,100	Pool collateralized by any number of loans with mortgages paying based on a floating rate benchmark.

Source: Salomon Smith Barney.

certificates can be bought and sold in minutes at bid/asked spreads of 1 or 2bp (basis points) for the triple-A certificates. The liquidity in triple-A CMBSs (75% of the issuance) is similar to Agencies and less like many of the other structured debt products. Much of the liquidity has been driven by the rating agency's diversity guidelines and B-piece investor reviews, which have formed homogeneous pools and attracted more investors to CMBSs. *If the secondary CMBS market continues to experience the strong secondary*

EXHIBIT 16.6   CMBS Issuance Statistics, 1999 and 2000 (U.S. Dollars in Millions)

Type	1999				2000			
	Total	Pct. of Total	No. of Deals	Average Size ($MM)	Total	Pct. of Total	No. of Deals	Average Size ($MM)
Conduit	$29,319	43.7%	33	$887	$22,995.4	38.3%	30	$766.51
Fusion	7,765	11.6	6	1,294	5,256.9	8.8	5	1,051.38
Floating Rate	5,510	8.2	8	662	10,940.7	18.2	18	607.81
Single Borrower	7,078	10.6	17	413	5,238.8	8.7	22	238.13
Other	6,236	9.3	18	338	2,689.9	4.5	5	537.98
Lease Backed	1,262	1.9	6	228	109.7	0.2	1	109.69
Large Loan	—	0.0	—	—	949.9	1.6	4	237.48
International	9,847	14.7	31	308	11,890.1	19.8	32	371.57
Total	$67,018	100.0%	119	$557	$60,071.3	100.0%	117	$513.43

Source: Commercial Mortgage Alert and Salomon Smith Barney.

*market that has existed since 1999, we feel CMBS spreads can tighten fur-
ther relative to the liquid agency debt product.*

16.5 COMMERCIAL LOAN EVALUATION AND THE RATING PROCESS

The rating agencies have developed analysis models that take much of the
investigative onus off the investor. Following extensive analysis, the agencies
provide investors with an consistent measurement of the likelihood that
cash flow from the underlying mortgages will be sufficient to meet scheduled payments of principal and interest on the security at each certificate
rating. At higher rating levels, mortgage cash flows will be expected to hold
up under increasingly severe economic conditions. Thus, for a given pool,
progressively greater credit support is needed at higher rating levels. *When
the rating agencies initially developed their models, the commercial mortgage market suffered from a lack of standardization, and a shortage of historical delinquency and foreclosure data, which caused the rating agencies
to develop subordination models based on very conservative default and
loss assumptions.*

The process used for rating commercial mortgage securities is, in some
respects, similar to the residential mortgage rating process—the primary
focus of the analysis in each case is on the credit quality of the underlying
collateral; however, significant differences exist.

First, commercial mortgages are nonrecourse loans, so securities are
backed by income-producing properties whose profit-oriented owners' motivation depend on different factors than those affecting a residential home
owner. Of primary concern in analyzing a commercial mortgage is the property's underlying net operating income (NOI) and net cash flow (NCF), and
all factors that influence them. An analysis of the credit quality of a commercial loan therefore requires a careful review of underlying tenants' creditworthiness, the structure and term of underlying leases, the historical level
of vacancies and rents on the property and on other properties in the region,
and the economic climate in the local markets. All of this analysis feeds into
a review of the mortgage's loan to value (LTV) and debt service coverage
ratio (DSCR).

In reviewing a property's cash flow, a rating agency will typically reduce the property cash flow to the lower of market rent or lease contractual
rent. A higher contractual rent may be accepted as cash flow if the underlying tenant is publicly rated and the term of the lease extends beyond the
term of the mortgage loan. The property's occupancy may also be adjusted
downward to reflect surrounding market conditions on the assumption that
even a fully occupied building will eventually lose tenants and stabilize at

EXHIBIT 16.7   Typical Cash Flow Underwriting Adjustments for a Commercial Property

Revenue	Mark to sustainable market (may be trailing 12 months or current annualized rent roll or current rent roll with above-market rents marked to recent market rates). May allow for above-market rents for rated credit tenants that expire beyond term. Rent roll and similar market lease comparables are analyzed to determine appropriate subject rental rate.
Vacancy	Market vacancy (subject to agency minimums of 5%–10% for various property types). In the case of lodging properties, the historic occupancy is assessed as a base.
Management Fees	Marked to market based on third-party independent cost to manage property.
Operating Costs	Historic figures inflated (review 3 years historic figures).
Net Operating Income	**Revenue less vacancy, management fees, and operating costs.**
Tenant Allowance	Stabilized amount based on average turnover and recent concessions (subject to agencies' minimum standards). May exclude investment-grade tenants expiring beyond the loan term. Usually requires a separate reserve for any large single-tenant expiry.
Commissions	Average turnover times standard amounts (i.e. 2.5% for renewals, 5% for new).
Capital Expenditures	A structural reserve for items not recoverable from tenants. Usually based on the greater of engineer's report or agencies' standardized allowances (usually $0.15–$0.40 psf for retail and office and $200–$250 per unit for apartments).
Net Cash Flow	**Net operating income less tenant allowance, commissions and capital expenditure reserves.**

psf: Per square foot.
Source: Salomon Smith Barney.

the market occupancy rate. The property's operating costs are assessed at historic levels adjusted for inflation with any lower than market costs increased to reflect a third party's cost in anticipation of the possibility the mortgagee may have to foreclose and operate the property. The net operating income, which is derived from revenues less the operating expenses, is then further adjusted by an estimated annual market re-leasing commission cost and tenant inducement that reflect the lease expires and releasing costs for similar buildings. Finally, the agency subtracts a capital expenditure allowance in anticipation of ongoing property structural repair costs that will not be recoverable from tenants. The rating agencies' resulting net operating cash flow is usually 3% to 5% less than the underwriter figure, but reflects an objective opinion of the property's likely ongoing cash flow in a stressed environment. Exhibit 16.7 illustrates typical property costs and comments on rating agency adjustments.

Property Underwriting and Assessment Variables

Before reviewing specific rating agency methodology, we briefly discuss loan underwriting variables considered in an analysis of commercial mortgage securities, including:

- Debt service coverage ratio;
- Loan-to-value ratio;
- Mortgage payment structure;
- Mortgage amortization/term;
- Tenancy; and
- Property location.

DSCR is calculated as follows:

1. The current NOI on a property divided by the actual mortgage debt service obligation. This is the NOI DSCR, which is usually provided by the underwriter and reported on an ongoing basis by the servicer.
2. The *estimated cash flow (after leasing costs and capital expenditures not recoverable from the tenants)* divided by the actual mortgage debt service obligation.
3. The cash flow after leasing cost and capital expenditures not recoverable from the tenants divided by a *stressed refinance constant (a debt constant that is higher than the actual rate to account for potential unfavorable refinance conditions when the balloon comes due)*. This is referred to as a "stressed DSCR" and is used by rating agencies to perform their analysis.

LTV refers to the ratio of the outstanding loan balance on a property to the estimated valuation of that property. *LTV is assessed as an important indicator of potential loss severity, because the analysis of how much will be lost upon default relies heavily on the property value relative to the outstanding debt on that property.* Loss severity can also be affected by state foreclosure laws. If a state's foreclosure laws could potentially delay the mortgage servicer's property liquidation, the agency may toughen the LTV parameters for that state. In summary, the rating agencies treat DSCR as the best indicator of default probability, while LTV is the best indicator of loss severity.

Similar to the residential market, floating-rate structures in the commercial market are viewed as inherently more risky than fixed-rate structures. *The potential inability to meet an increase in debt service payments in the future increases the risk that the borrower may default.* The presence of a floating rate also lessens somewhat the reliance of the analysis on a DSCR. To compensate rating agencies usually assess the loan's DSCR ratio at a higher debt constant, which creates a lower coverage ratio and requires higher credit enhancement levels. If the borrower has the benefit of an interest rate cap agreement, the rating agency may recognize the contract's benefit by using the cap contract rate to calculate DSCR. *Overall, floating-rate mortgages are viewed as more risky by the agencies and carry significant extra credit enhancement.*

Whereas, most residential mortgages fully amortize over a 15- or 30-year life, many commercial mortgage structures either are partially amortizing or do not amortize at all (interest only). Many carry shorter terms than residential mortgages, and a large majority mature with an outstanding balloon payment. From a credit perspective, fully amortizing mortgages are the least risky. As a loan amortizes, principal is paid down, thus reducing the indebtedness of the borrower and reducing the risk of default (equity buildup is an important protector against default in the commercial market, as well as minimizing loss severity). A partially amortizing loan will have paid down only part of its principal by maturity, and a non-amortizing loan will have paid only interest and no principal by maturity, translating into little or no equity buildup. Partial or no amortization loans will mature with a remaining principal balance—a balloon payment—that must be made. For example, after 10 years of amortization a loan has usually only paid 15% of the principal, if the loan is on a 30-year amortization schedule. Typically, the borrower will try to refinance that balance into a new mortgage, creating refinancing risk into the credit equation.

Various factors may impair the borrower's ability to refinance the remaining principal at maturity, including:

- An increase in interest rates;
- A decline in property values;
- More restrictive underwriting criteria;
- A relatively large number of vacancies; and
- Tight credit conditions.

All or any of these factors may inhibit lenders in the primary market from providing refinancing on the mortgage. Given this potential risk, the rating agencies focus on the coupon rate on the mortgage and analyze the ability of property to support a new mortgage in the amount of the balloon at a potentially higher rate level. *Moody's and Fitch use a maximum refinance interest constant for the collateral, typically 9.25% for Moody's and 8.88% to 11.33% for Fitch, depending on the property type and loan amortization to the balloon.* These refinance constants are based on historic rates and reflect a worst case DSCR. The resulting stressed DSCR is usually 0.10 to 0.15 lower than the underwriter's DSCR. For reference, a typical CMBS transaction may have a NOI DSCR of 1.35 to 1.45, a CF DCSR of 1.20 to 1.40, and a "stressed DSCR" by an agency such as Fitch of 1.05 to 1.20. The rating agencies also look at the expiration dates for major leases on the property relative to the maturity date of the mortgages to help determine vacancy potential and, thus, the releasing risk exposure that will be evident on the balloon date. If many leases expire close to maturity, the loan will usually be structured to accrue a sufficient releasing reserve to mitigate the risk. To the extent the rating agencies perceive lease rollover risk, they will increase their probability of default assessment and potentially decrease their specific estimated loan recovery leading to higher subordination levels.

The rating agencies also take into account the structure of the security to evaluate the level of credit support necessary to protect against balloon risk. In many cases, the loans may have an early permitted repayment date of 10 years, after which the rate steps up and all cash flow is captured to amortize principal (an ARD loan). The ARD loan structure provides a built-in loan restructuring as the lender pays down the loan without having to foreclose.

The rating agencies also evaluate the flexibility of the servicer in situations where refinancing risk is present. The question of whether or not a workout will be attempted is an important one—both in terms of whether a default will, in fact, occur and if it does, what the loss severity will be. Traditionally, commercial lenders have maximized recoveries when afforded flexibility in these loan workout situations. In some cases, they have extended the term of the mortgage; in other cases, they have reduced the monthly payments on the mortgage. While the servicer's ability to extend loans may lead to a maximum loan recover, it also impacts the certificate's average life and has an impact on the investor's yield if they paid a premium or discount for their bonds.

Sometimes in a forced foreclosure and cash sale of property will result in much higher losses than a workout negotiation whereby the current borrower is allowed to continue under new terms. In addition to a potentially low sales price, the expenses incurred in a foreclosure are generally higher than those associated with a loan workout, particularly if the borrower uses bankruptcy as a delay method. Even in cases where the underlying property does not support the outstanding loan balance, a reduction of the debt claim and avoidance of the above mentioned expenses may result in higher recovery levels. Therefore, the ability of the servicer to manage a workout is a critical factor in minimizing potential loan losses. Such ability will be a function of servicer experience, knowledge of the local markets and of the pertinent property type, and finally, workout volume capacity. *As previously mentioned, most recent CMBS transactions give the special servicer the ability to modify loans subject to a standard of care to maximize expected loan net present value. Therefore rating agencies assess the special servicer's abilities and may adjust the credit enhancement levels by 0.5% to account for the special services ability.*

The viability of an income producing property depends on its tenants. The loss of a major tenant can cause insolvency. Most recent commercial mortgage defaults have been caused by either lease expires or leases not being affirmed by a bankrupt entity. Leases rolling over to lower market rents can create lower DSCR and lead to defaults. Thus, rating agency models favor multitenanted buildings and, in addition, will look to the creditworthiness of the individual tenants, particularly the anchor tenant in a transaction backed by mortgages on shopping centers. Single tenanted buildings are usually penalized with higher subordination levels to ensure there is sufficient loss recovery should the individual tenant vacate causing a default and loan liquidation. Tenant concentrations may be somewhat offset by a strong property location and the resulting ability to attract new replacement tenants at low retenanting costs.

16.6 RATING AGENCY MODEL MECHANICS

The number of mortgages in the pool and the relative size of the larger loans as a percentage of the pool are a major determinant of agency subordination, which is the major reason CMBS pools are classified by loan size. Smaller pools and pools with loan or borrower concentration merit closer scrutiny as they represent greater risk and, thus, require greater credit support.

The agencies' loan size analysis can create an add-on to subordination of 0% to 4% for a diverse pool, 3% to 10% for a fusion pool, and anywhere from 10 to 20% for a large loan pool or single asset transaction. The increase in credit enhancement generally steps up to ensure the default of a single loan concentration cannot affect the rating of the pool. This lumpiness requires a subordination approach, ensures that in the event of a random default of a large loan, the loan recovery will be sufficient to paydown the upper rated classes and maintain the original relative subordination and credit rating. On more diverse pools, the rating agencies rely less on the pool's ability to withstand an individual loan's default and focus more on the pool's anticipated cumulative lifetime defaults being similar to the experience in the early 1990s default studies.[2]

Thus, the loan pool's size diversity decides whether the agencies use a property specific approach (with ratings based on each single-property characteristics) or an actuarial analysis. **The actuarial approach relies on an evaluation of credit characteristics from a sample of the overall pool.** The degree of individual loan analysis depends on the pool's diversity. An analysis of pool credit quality through aggregate loan characteristics generally

---

[2] "Update to Commercial Mortgage Defaults," Mark P. Snyderman, *The Real Estate Finance Journal*, Vol. 10, No. 1, summer 1994.

will be sufficient if the pool was originated with uniform underwriting standards, contains a sufficiently large number of loans, and the distribution of the loan balance is not widely skewed. To the extent any of these conditions is lacking, the agency may rely more on a loan-by-loan analysis.

To determine the loss coverage required on a commercial mortgage pool, each agency reviews a large sample (40% to 60%) of the individual loans to assess the pool's cash-flow underwriting and asset valuation by property type. This assessment of cash-flow underwriting by property type is extrapolated to the entire pool to determine the DSCR and loan to value leverage characteristics. This leverage analysis is the core of the agencies' assessment as they feed the DSCR and loan to values into a *base pool* loss matrix that produces a foreclosure frequency and loss potential of the loans at various rating levels. Thus, for a given LTV, DSCR, and rating, the agency's base matrix provides a foreclosure frequency and principal loss value.

The rating agencies view LTV as the key determinant of loss severity following loan default. To estimate collateral values used in the calculation of LTV, the agencies capitalize[3] their estimated cash flow at yields that reflect property type, property-specific characteristics, and local market conditions. The rating agencies assess both fixed and variable liquidation/workout expenses in the loss severity calculation. For smaller loans, fixed expenses can have a significant impact on loss severity. State foreclosure laws also affect loss severity. Accrued interest and deteriorating property performance will increase losses; the longer it takes for the mortgage servicer to gain control over the property and to liquidate it, the higher those losses will be.

In Exhibit 16.8 we present a generic example of how an agency matrix might translate debt service to an actual subordination level. For simplicity the example is based on an early Fitch default and loss table, which has evolved considerably over the years.

Fitch has a matrix of different refinance constants based on historic loan interest rates for different property types, which it adjusts for loan amortization and other structural recovery features. All of the agencies supplement the DCSR analysis with a loan-to-value loss matrix, which accounts for the differences in property types by valuing the properties using property-specific capitalization rates.

The loan in the Exhibit 16.8 has a 1.15 × debt service coverage ratio based on the rating agencies' assessment of cash flow and a higher than actual property specific debt refinance constant. Fitch has a matrix of different

---

[3] One of the simpler commercial real estate valuation methods is to divide the property's expected cash flow by a required property yield. The required property yield is commonly referred to as a "cap rate."

EXHIBIT 16.8 Loan Subordination, Using Default and Loss Matrix and Loan with 1.15 times Coverage

Loan DSCR	Default Prod.	x Loss Prob. =	A Level Loss	Class	A Level Enhance	Class Gearing	Initial Subord.=	+ Add-on Subord.=	Final Level
0.10	80%	40%	32.00%	Class	Enhance	Gearing	Subord.=	Subord.=	Level
0.50	65%	40%	26.00%	AAA		AAx1.25	22.4%	6.3%	28.7%
0.80	55%	40%	22.00%	AA		A x1.28	17.9%	5.0%	22.9%
0.90	45%	40%	18.00%	A	14.00%	Ax1	14.0%	3.9%	17.9%
1.00	40%	40%	16.00%	BBB		A/1.39	10.1%	2.8%	12.9%
1.15	35%	40%	14.00%	BBB-		BBB/1.125	9.0%	2.5%	11.5%
1.25	32%	40%	12.80%	BB		BBB/ 1.9	5.3%	1.5%	6.8%
1.34	28%	40%	11.20%	B		BBB/ 4.2	2.4%	0.7%	3.1%
1.50	25%	40%	10.00%						
1.75	20%	40%	8.00%						

Source: Illustration using Salomon Smith Barney Assumptions and Fitch DSCR Default and Loss Matrix.

refinance constants based on historic loan interest rates for different property types, which they adjust for loan amortization and other structural recovery features. All the agencies supplement the DSCR analysis with a loan to value/default and loss matrix, which accounts for the differences in property types by valuing the properties using property specific capitalization rates. Exhibit 16.8 assigns the 1.15 × coverage ratio a 35% probability of default with an expected loss of 40%.

Although the above example assumes each loan has a 40% loss severity, the agency would actually adjust the loss severity for loan to value, loan amortization, and state foreclosure laws. Typical loan loss expectations range from 30% to 50% depending mostly upon LTV. The Fitch default and loss variables were based on the last recession, which Fitch considered to be an A-level recession (meaning any loan rated less than A leverage was expected to have defaulted). Thus, its matrix creates credit enhancement at the A credit level. **Therefore, the loan in the example that has a 35% chance of default times a 40% expected loss requires a 14% credit enhancement at the single-A credit level.** Fitch then gears that 14% credit enhancement up and down the credit classes based on gearing multiples that they estimate reflects an appropriate level of relative credit risk of each level.

To create their base default and loss matrixes, the rating agencies have had to make some generic assumptions about the underlying mortgage pool. **To the extent the pool varies from the generic assumptions (or concentrations based on the grouping analysis) then the subordination levels are increased or decreased by an additional subordination "add-on."** In the previous example the add-ons are added to the initial loan's leverage credit enhancement to create the final loan's credit enhancement level. The subordination add-ons can be pool or loan specific features that differ from the characteristics considered in the default and loss matrix. If a loan deviates from the base pool characteristics, the rating agencies adjust levels by changing the loan's foreclosure frequency and/or principal loss. In Appendix 16A, we review the full list of pool characteristics that would cause each agency to adjust its overall credit enhancement levels (such as geographic concentration, underwriter quality, special servicer quality, property type, loan amortization, property quality, leasehold mortgages, secondary debt, environmental issues, and operating history).

16.7 RATING AGENCY CREDIT ENHANCEMENT LEVELS PROVIDE EXCESS PROTECTION

Exhibit 16.3 demonstrated that CMBS credit enhancement levels have declined from 30% in the second quarter of 1997 to 23.4% in October of 2000. Our original report titled "CMBS Subordination Levels—Whatever Happened to 30%, 20%, 10%"[4] attributed two-thirds of the decline in subordination to improved underwriting, decreased leverage, and a declining proportion of volatile property types being underwritten in recent years. With most of the decline in triple-A subordination levels occurring in the last year, many investors are asking whether current subordination levels provide sufficient credit protection.

Since October of 1999, we have made only a couple of adjustments to Salomon Smith Barney's subordination model. One model adjustment accounted for the amortization of the loan balance, a major change from determining the loss factors based on the loan balance at origination. We feel that adjusting for loan balance amortization is reasonable, given that loan defaults usually take place only after the mortgage has had time to amortize to some extent. The rest of the subordination level decline can still be accounted for by further improvements in the composition of loan pool property types and decreased leverage. *Overall, our original model, with the couple of adjustments, continues to match the rating agencies' levels, suggesting that there have been few other agency modifications caused by "agency competition."*

So, what has caused underwriters to drastically improve their underwriting standards over the past year, creating the improved subordination

---

[4] "CMBS Subordination Levels—Whatever Happened to 30%, 20%, 10%?" Darrell Wheeler, October 28, 1999

levels? The answer lies in the 1998 bond market crisis, during which many subordinate CMBS buyers were eliminated from the market, leaving a group of five or six buyers for the double-B, single-B, and unrated CMBS classes. With limited competition, these B-piece buyers have had tremendous buying clout and have been able to remove high leverage loans from CMBS pools and request that certain property types (such as limited service hotel) not be included. This has shaped underwriting standards and the pools' property composition. The B-piece buyer clout is demonstrated in Exhibit 16.9 by the wider CMBS spreads that subordinate buyers have been able to achieve in recent years.

Exhibit 16.9 highlights the 67%-plus CMBS spread widening during the 1998 bond market crisis and the relatively small contraction in non-investment-grade spreads since the crisis. This steepening of the credit slope between triple-A and unrated classes also developed in the investment-grade CMBS classes, with the credit spread between triple-B and triple-A CMBS classes still significantly higher than precrisis levels.

Issuers now report that as much as 5% to 10% of a pool may be removed ("kicked out") from a transaction, usually based on leverage and property type. **This B-piece buyer screening is the major factor in improving underwritten pool quality, which has driven the decline in subordination levels.**

Evolving Rating Agency Models Reflect a Maturing Market

We classify the CMBS market as just at the end of its development phase, with the rating agencies frequently adjusting their models to account for

EXHIBIT 16.9   Ten-Year CMBSs—Spreads, May 28, 1998, October 8, 1998, and December 29, 2000

	Precrisis	Crisis	Percentage	Year-End	Percentage
	28 May 98	8 Oct 98	Increase*	29 Dec 00	Decrease*
AAA	77 bp	205 bp	166%	143 bp	30%
A	110	300	173	178	41
BBB	145	350	141	231	34
BB	265	550	108	535	3
B	460-540	840-900	74	840-900	0
Unrated Yield	15%-18%	25%-30%	67	25%-30%	0
Credit Curve					
BBB-AAA	68 bp	145 bp		88	
BB-AAA	188	345		383	

*Percentage change based on the midpoints.
Source: Salomon Smith Barney.

improved loan structural features, the benefits of pool diversification, the strong real estate market, and additional data from CMBS transactions. The original rating agency models were based on the study of early 1990 life insurance company mortgage default and loan recovery rates. These underlying life insurance loans were significantly different from the structured mortgages currently placed in CMBS pools, leaving the rating agencies to estimate subordination measures for the new structural features. Given the untested nature of the CMBS market, the rating agencies tended to use conservative default and loss assumptions when creating their first CMBS models. However with today's fundamentally strong commercial mortgage market, many investors and rating agencies now expect that the next economic slowdown will create a less severe real estate downturn. Considering the strong real estate market and conduit pool performance, it is not surprising that the agencies decided to make small adjustments to their models.

We should caution that not all rating agencies may have changed their models, and yet, they may be able to match other rating agencies' lower levels on current 2000 transactions. From this perspective, their models may not have changed mathematically, but rather their analysts may be interpreting the mortgage loan data with an eye to the strong markets and improving property values. *Overall, we believe that the contraction in rating agency subordination models reflects flexibility and the realization that their initial models may have been too conservative in assessing some pool characteristics.* But what are the implications of the declining levels for investors?

Investor Implications

But what are the implications of declining levels for investors? Even with the 6% decline in triple-A CMBS subordination levels, CMBS pools can still withstand a high frequency of defaults and loss severity prior to experiencing a loss. The credit support built into 2000 CMBS transactions is well in excess of that found in high-risk mortgage security products (subprime or home equity loans).

To illustrate this point, in Exhibit 16.10, we analyze average 2000 CMBS subordination levels and the implied default rate at each credit enhancement level. To back out the implied default rate, we divided each subordination level by a 40% expected loan loss. As previously discussed, rating agencies use different expected loss rates, typically ranging from 30% to 50%, depending on their actual assessment of the underlying real estate. We felt the 40% loss rate was conservative given the structural features of 2000 conduit mortgages and current, stable real estate market conditions. Specifically, we believe that the currently strong real estate market will make it less likely that

EXHIBIT 16.10   CMBSs—Implied Default Rates at 40% Loan Loss

Class	2000 CMBS Class Credit Enhancement		Divide Level by Expected Loan Loss	=	Loan Defaults Required for Loss
AAA	24.61 %	/	40.0 %	=	**61.5** %
AA	20.10	/	40.0	=	**50.2**
A	15.65	/	40.0	=	**39.1**
BBB	10.99	/	40.0	=	**27.5**
BBB-	9.61	/	40.0	=	**24.0**
BB	5.33	/	40.0	=	**13.3**
B	2.60	/	40.0	=	**6.5**

Source: Salomon Smith Barney.

borrowers will default, while professional servicing and the cash management structure of current conduit loans should limit future foreclosure loan losses.

In Exhibit 16.10, we take the average 2000 CMBS conduit subordination levels and calculate that a mortgage pool experiencing a 40% loan loss (on every default) would require 39% of the loans to default before the single-A rated class lost any of its principal (a 24% loan default is required for a triple-B-minus loss and a 61.5% loan defaults is required for a triple-A class loss).

It is helpful to compare the implied default rates in Exhibit 16.10 to those in the 1994 Snyderman commercial default study.[5] This study tracked 10,955 commercial mortgage loans, originated by eight insurance companies. The study observed a 13.8% default rate over a five-year period and projected an 18.3% lifetime default rate for the entire pool. The study provided further expected lifetime default rates that ranged from 7.6% to 21.5%, depending on the period studied, the originator, and the lifetime projection method. The investment-grade implied default rates in Exhibit 16.10 have a more than sufficient buffer when compared with the study's worst lifetime default rate of 21.5%.

If we accept that a 40% expected loss is reasonable, then the projected default rates for triple-A through triple-B seem very conservative relative to historical default data and projections for the next real estate recession. The realization that early credit enhancement models were tougher than current subordination calculations helps explain why most CMBS spreads have tightened significantly after only a couple years of seasoning. Investors looking at 2000 transactions should also take comfort from the fact that

---

[5] "Update to Commercial Mortgage Defaults," Mark P. Snyderman, *The Real Estate Finance Journal*, Vol. 10, No. 1, summer 1994.

rating agencies have room to contract subordination levels further, possibly creating typical conduit CMBS levels with 20% subordination in the triple-A class. **Therefore, we expect 2000 issuance will become another vintage subordination level year and quickly season to tighter spreads.** In contrast, we feel that double-B, single-B, and unrated subordination levels have declined as far as they can, but double-B and single-B CMBS investors buy at a discount to par and receive a full return of their capital in the first few years of their investment.

16.8 COLLATERAL FUNDAMENTALS—COMMERCIAL REAL ESTATE

Banks, real estate investors, and developers continue to watch for a real estate recession, mindful of the last real estate market meltdown in 1991. This cautionary approach to the real estate market has created a market in which speculative development is rare. U.S. construction starts in office and industrial properties have not returned to the levels of the late 1980s because bank financing has been largely unavailable without significant preleasing.[6] Although 1999 retail, multifamily, and hotel construction levels approached late-1980s levels, CMBS investors have demonstrated good market awareness and avoided CMBS transactions with large exposures to hotel, unanchored retail, and power centers.

We cannot project when another real estate recession will occur, but we believe that whenever it is, it will be less severe than the previous one. Exhibit 16.11 presents vacancy figures for various real estate segments, and

EXHIBIT 16.11   U.S. Vacancy Rates by Product Type: Early 1990s versus Early 2000s

	1991	1999	2000
Office	18.9%	9.5%	9.0%
Retail	11.6	7.4	8.0
Warehouse	7.9	7.0	6.8
Multifamily	8.9	7.7	7.1

Source: Salomon Smith Barney.

---

[6] Preleasing is a real estate development term used to refer to the percentage of the development that has contractual lease agreements signed before the construction lender advances funding to a developer to build.

they are currently better than they were just before the previous recession. These vacancy rates suggest that if an economic slowdown were to occur in 2001, it would affect occupancies and rents somewhat. However, it would have to be a severe recession to have a significant impact on the current market, which is currently at relatively low vacancy levels. These low vacancy levels are a direct outcome of the market's experience during the last recession. At this stage in the economic cycle, we expect to see construction starts for office properties—which are in short supply—rise, but starts for other property segments should decline or level off. A good indicator to monitor potential office market supply is to calculate inventory under construction as a percentage of each market's total inventory. Any market that has a total vacancy rate and potential supply figure greater than 12% bears watching.

Another feature that is different about the current real estate market is that the cap rates[7] used to value real estate are 3% to 4% higher than Treasury rates. In contrast, during the 1980s real estate boom, cap rates equaled Treasury rates, leaving very little room for interest rates to increase without denting values. In Exhibit 16.12, we calculate the spread between cap rates and Treasury rates.

Given current high cap rates and low vacancy rates, we do not expect the next real estate recession to be as severe as the last. We would be concerned if construction starts were to increase or the cap rate-Treasury rate differential were to decrease. However, investors' cautious approach to retail and hotel exposures in CMBS transactions is prudent. Retail construction starts never declined significantly from late-1980 levels. Rather, retail development moved from regional shopping centers to power centers. This retail construction has been supported by strong consumer spending (including at times a negative savings rate), which means the pace of retail sales may be unsustainable in an economic slowdown. Investors should actively monitor retail loans as slowing retail spending will likely increase retail delinquencies. Because it is impossible to avoid retail loans altogether, investors should consider employing a retail tenant concentration review such as the one that we outline later in this chapter in "CMBS Collateral Credit Review: A Loan-by-Loan Approach for Real Estate Novices." It is also important to realize that while retail loans may experience a high level of delinquency, retail loan recoveries are usually higher than recoveries for other commercial property types because the property space can have many alternative retail uses.

---

[7] A common method to value commercial real estate is to divide the property net operating income by a capitalization percentage. The interest rate used is referred to as a "cap rate."

EXHIBIT 16.12 Cap Rate Spreads Differential with Ten-Year Treasury Yield, 1983–1999

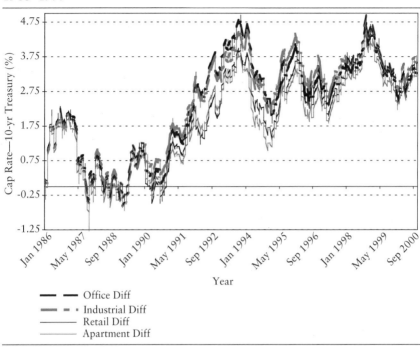

Office Diff
Industrial Diff
Retail Diff
Apartment Diff

Source: Salomon Smith Barney.

16.9 CMBS RELATIVE VALUE AND PRICING METHODOLOGY

Traditionally commercial mortgage investment has been considered to be a high-risk activity requiring specific market expertise. Therefore when CMBS was introduced, only accounts with specific real estate experience took to the new product and were able to command significant spread differentials. Exhibit 16.13 presents historic CMBS investment-grade spreads.

As the market grew and more investors began to follow the CMBS asset class, CMBS spreads tightened. CMBS spreads reached their tightest point in mid-1997, when even mezzanine investment grade classes were very tight to the higher rated classes. The October 1998 bond market crisis surprised the developing CMBS market, as many commercial mortgage originators and issuers had been carrying large mortgage inventories, enabling them to assemble optimal CMBSs and enjoy he excess mortgage spread return while the mortgages where on their books. When all debt spreads suddenly

EXHIBIT 16.13   CMBSs—Historic Investment-Grade Spread to Treasury Notes, January 1996 to December 2000

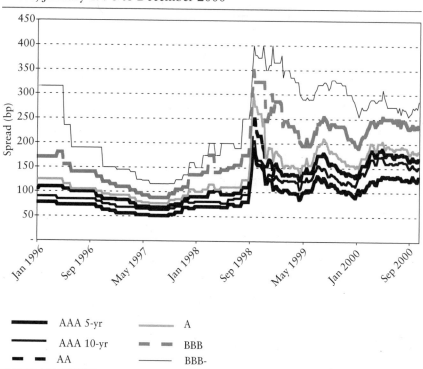

Source: Salomon Smith Barney.

widened, these issuers suffered significant inventory losses as many had only partially hedged their positions. The bond market crisis' impact on the CMBS market was compounded by the repurchase positions many issuers held from selling bonds to subordinate investment-grade investors. These positions experienced large margin calls and culminated in CRIIMI MAE being unable to meet its margin requirements and filing for bankruptcy protection. At that point, the market issuers that had made an active secondary market had as much exposure to CMBS as their credit mechanisms would permit, which causing bid/offer spreads to widen in the secondary market.

During late 1998 and the first quarter of 1999, issuers cleared their inventories and have since diligently worked to clear their mortgage inventory on a quarterly basis. Repurchase financing leverage levels have been significantly scaled back. Today the market makers carry smaller CMBS primary, secondary, or financing exposures. These positions are also being more actively hedged using combinations of treasuries, swaps, and single family mortgages.

Since 1997 the relationship between swaps and CMBS spreads has been very strong. Exhibit 16.14 presents the 10-year CMBS triple-A spread versus the 10-year swap.

Over the past five-years the 10-year triple-A CMBS and 10-year swap differential has averaged 42bp. However the differential has varied from the average on several occasions. From January 1997 to September 1998, the differential averaged 29bp, and increased to a 117% differential during the bond market crisis. Since late 1999 the differential has moved in a 38bp to 42bp range, demonstrating a very stable CMBS secondary market. Exhibit 16.14 does not reflect the CMBS market convention of actually quoting the CMBS spread to the on the run interpolated swap, which would be 5.7 years for most 5-year class and 9.5 years for most 10-year classes. Therefore the actual spread differential may be 1 or 2bp wider than the stated differential as the treasury swap curve is downward sloping.

The other CMBS classes have well established trading ranges relative to the 10-year triple-A classes: Exhibit 16.15 summarizes these various class trading ranges and averages.

EXHIBIT 16.14 Historical 10-year CMBS Triple-A Spread versus the 10-year Swap, January 1995 to December 2000

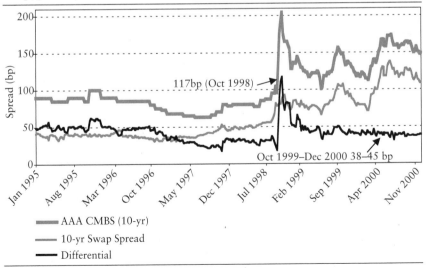

Source: Salomon Smith Barney.

EXHIBIT 16.15   Generic Tier 2 CMBS Spread Interrelationships for Relative Value Judgment, December 29, 2000

	Ten-Year AAA to Five-Year AAA	AA to AAA	AA to A	BBB to AAA	BBB– to BBB
29 Dec 00	20.7	17.0	15.0	85.0	50.0
One-Year Average	30.2	16.0	15.8	83.8	48.5
Two-Year Average	25.3	17.9	18.6	95.3	69.3
Three-Year Average	20.9	18.2	18.5	90.5	60.1
Five-Year Average	17.3	15.7	15.2	74.3	60.2
Five-Year Low	8.0	5.0	4.0	25.0	15.0
Five-Year High	45.0	50.0	65.0	170.0	145.0

Source: Salomon Smith Barney.

We show the differential between triple-A 5- and 10-year CMBSs for reference only. Because of the differing maturity these two classes should really be assessed based on their long-term relationship with their related swap. The generic tier, 5-year triple-A CMBS has a 3-year average differential of 32bp with the 5-year swap. And as previously illustrated, the 10-year triple-A has a 5-year differential of 42bp with the 10-year swap.

If we look at the 5-year average spread step up for going down one class, Exhibit 16.15 demonstrates investors should expect to pick up 15.7bp for investing in double-A versus triple-A and 15.2bp for investing in single-A versus double-A. In addition, the 5-year differential between triple-B and triple-A is 74.3 but has been much wider in recent years. While the recent strong Collateralized Bond offering bid makes the opposite true for triple-B minus spreads which are currently trading well inside their 5-year average differential with triple-B.

We have given the above CMBS interrelationship ranges and averages as a reference point only. The high and low spread differentials have varied significantly from their averages over different periods of time. The key to successful relative value investing is to spot the collateral feature, or trend that will attract investors to one of the various certificate classes and cause one of the relationships to move away from its established average range.

CMBS spreads have demonstrated significant value relative to corporate bond spreads. In the fall of 2000, corporate bond spreads widened significantly leaving many investors wondering if CMBS spreads would follow. While investors should keep an eye on the entire market, we have never strongly highlighted the differential between corporate bond spreads and CMBS spreads. Due to the credit protection provide by the senior/subordinate structure and the strong underlying collateral performance, we believe CMBS rated credit to be as good or better than similarly rated corporate credits. Specifically, the CMBS structure means that any CMBS downgrade usually only downgrades a certificate one notch from single-A to single-A minus (incrementally) due to the subordinate credit enhancement built into each transaction. By contrast, corporate downgrades have demonstrated that they can move through multiple classes (single-A corporate ratings can become double-B or single-B in a short time frame). Of course, to perform a full relative-value analysis investors should still review alternative investment opportunities.

In addition, the CMBS market continues to demonstrate strong liquidity that should persist in an economic stress scenario as long as the underlying collateral fundamentals remain strong. In an economic slowdown we would expect that cash flow deterioration would be slow and, as Fitch highlighted in a recent study,[8] partially offset by the loan diversification in the CMBS pools. **However, as CMBSs are a relatively new product, the market needs tangible evidence of how CMBS collateral delinquencies and losses perform versus other debt products in an economic stress scenario.** Once CMBS have demonstrated the credit benefit of their subordinate structure, then their strong liquidity should ensure they trade on par with similarly rated corporate classes.

16.10 CMBS PREPAYMENT VARIABLES IMPACT TOTAL RETURN

Restrictions on prepayments, along with the time and cost (typically 3% to 5% of the loan balance) involved in refinancing a commercial loan, means that CMBS investors are unlikely to experience the sudden refinancings that afflict investors in MBSs backed by residential loans. **However, defaults and resulting liquidations of loans can prepay principal to the upper rated classes and create losses to the most subordinate class.** Therefore, many investors also supplement their spread analysis with analysis that takes into consideration the potential of early bond prepayment from voluntary or involuntary loan prepayments. Alternatively, if the loan defaults occur at loan maturity, then the CMBS certificate holder can find the mortgages being extended, increasing their average life.

Because of their potential cash flow volatility many CMBS investors use collateral cash flow services to evaluate the bonds under different prepayment, default, and loss scenarios. The three major CMBS cash-flow-modeling services are Charter Research, Intex Solutions, and TREPP. Any

---

[8] _Comparing CMBS and Corporate Bond Defaults,_ Diane Lans and Janet Price, Fitch, November 17, 2000.

one of these services enables an investor to model the different prepayment speeds, delinquencies, and losses to evaluate CMBS pricing and yield sensitivity. Because defaults have been random and unpredictable, many investors feel that general overall default and prepayment rates, while unrealistic, at least provide some stress analysis. Below we list four common pricing scenarios that are used by investors:

1. *0% CDR[9] and 0% CPY.[10]* Zero defaults, no prepayments during the loan lock-out and yield maintenance periods, followed by no prepayments after the loan's yield maintenance periods (0%CPY). Although unrealistic this measure is the most common starting point for referencing CMBS pricing.

2. *0% CDR and 100% CPY.* Zero defaults, no prepayments during the lock-out and yield maintenance periods, followed by a prepayment in full (an assumption usually labeled 100% CPY). This is also a common scenario and used by investors as a baseline.

3. *0% CDR for 2 years, 1% CDR thereafter and 100% CPY.* Zero defaults for the first 2 years, followed a 1% constant default rate (1% CDR) at a 40% loss severity over a 12-month recovery period with no prepayments during the lock-out and yield maintenance periods, followed by a prepayment in full. A default rate of 1% per year (or a Constant Default rate (CDR) of 1%) implies a cumulative default rate of 9.5% after 10 years, which we view as a likely scenario. Investors usually also vary the loss rate from 30% to 50%.

4. *0% CDR for 2 years, 2% CDR thereafter and 100% CPY.* Zero defaults for the first 2 years, followed a 2% constant default rate (2% CDR) at a 40% loss severity over a 12-month recovery period with no prepayments during the lock-out and yield maintenance periods, followed by a prepayment in full. A 2% CDR (cumulative default rate of 18% after 10 years represents a possible delinquency scenario).

The various property scenarios outlined above can have a different impact on each of the various certificates within a CMBS structure. In Exhibit 16.16 we present the WAL and yield of a 5-year triple-A, 10-year triple-A, and triple-B and IO certificates in a recently issued, tier two CMBS transaction.

---

[9] CDR refers to a Constant Default Rate that is applied annually to the outstanding pool balance.

[10] CPY refers to Constant Prepayment rate following the Yield Maintenance Period.

EXHIBIT 16.16   CMBS WAL and Price for Generic Tier 2 CMBS Issue Under Multiple Scenarios

	Five-Year Triple-A		Ten-Year Triple-A		Ten-Year Single-A		Ten-Year Triple-B		Ten-Year IO
Scenario	WAL (Yrs)	Yield (%)	WAL (Yrs)	Yield (%)	WAL (Yrs)	Yield (%)	WAL (Yrs)	Yield (%)	Yield (%)
I. 0% CDR, 0% CPY	5.87	6.38	9.71	6.52	9.90	6.85	9.90	7.42	9.17
II. 0% CDR and 100% CPY	5.74	6.38	9.51	6.52	9.82	6.85	9.90	7.42	8.83
III. 0% CDR for 24 Mos., 1% CDR, 100% CPY	5.58	6.38	9.48	6.52	9.82	6.85	9.97	7.42	8.38
IV. 0% CDR for 24 Mos., 2% CDR, 100% CPY	5.46	6.37	9.44	6.52	9.86	6.85	9.98	7.42	7.93

Source: Salomon Smith Barney.

Exhibit 16.16 highlights many pricing characteristics of the various CMBS classes:

1. The early prepayments shortened the certificate's average life, but only slightly decreased the yield on the 5-year triple-A class. If the certificates had been selling at a premium or discount the yield would have been more sensitive to the prepayment speed. The IO class was the only class that was significantly affected by the faster prepayment as its yield decreased 34bp.

2. Increasing the delinquency rate also didn't have a significant impact on any of the regular certificates as no principal was lost at even the triple-B level. The transaction's triple-B minus certificates do not lose any principal until the CDR rate is increased to 3%, which we have not shown, as it would result in a 30% overall pool default rate, which is unrealistic for the underlying pool. The IO however is impacted with increases in default rate as the IO is prepaid earlier with no collection of prepayment penalty. At the 2% CDR the IO yield decreases more than 90bp to yield 7.93%. However, we view 2% CDR as a high pool stress given that it results in a cumulative pool default rate of approximately 18%, which is higher than the expected pool default rate estimated in life insurance loan analysis. Nonetheless the IO return at 2% CDR of 7.93% is still significantly higher than an initial in-going yield on the 10-year triple-A class demonstrating the strong relative value of CMBS IO. This analysis ignored the possibility of loan extensions, which also should have resulted from loan defaults and increased the yield on the IO certificates. CMBS IO is a complex investment area that we explain further in Chapter 17.

This analysis was intended to highlight that the 10-year investment grade classes are fairly insensitive to reasonable prepayment and default scenarios. While a premium or discount priced 5-year triple-A class and the IO are most sensitive to changes in the prepayment speed and defaults. The scenarios should be considered simplistic as they treat every CMBS pool as having the same probability of default and expected prepayment speeds. A more sophisticated analysis would involve basing prepayments on expected underlying equity refinance "cash-out" objectives and defaults on expected the future loan-to-values. All three of the major cash flow modeling companies provide data on the underlying properties' most recent reported NOI that enables investors to adjust the future expected property cash flow based on property or region specific NOI growth assumptions. There are also other third-party services that can be tied into the three cash-flow models providing cash-flow growth and valuation parameters based on analysis of each of the various regions' property market conditions.

16.11 CMBS DEFAULT DATA

As discussed earlier, a good starting place for reviewing CMBS defaults is the 1994 Snyderman commercial default study[11] and our recent performance report of the public universe of CMBS data.[12] The Snyderman study tracked 10,955 commercial mortgage loans, originated by eight insurance companies. The study observed a 13.8% default rate over a 5-year period (equivalent to an annual rate of 2.6% CDR[13]) and projected an 18.3% lifetime default rate for the entire pool (1.7% CDR). The study provided further expected lifetime default rates that ranged from 7.6% (1% CDR) to 21.5% (2% CDR), depending on the period studied, the originator, and the lifetime projection method. Salomon Smith Barney Delinquency Performance data shows that post-1993 CMBS collateral has accrued a 0.28% delinquency after two years, a 0.55% delinquency after three years, and a 1.05% rate after four years. We feel that a reasonable range of default rates for scenario analysis is from 1% to 2% CDR.

The assumption for the severity of loss from a resulting liquidation following default is also critical to the analysis of CMBS cash flow. In Exhibit 16.17 we reviewed each occurrence of loss in the outstanding public CMBS universe as at September 30, 2000. These loss rates typically range from

---

[11] "Update to Commercial Mortgage Defaults," Mark P. Snyderman, *The Real Estate Finance Journal*, Vol. 10, No. 1, Summer 1994.
[12] "SSB Issuer Performance Report," Darrell Wheeler and Jeffrey S. Berenbaum, October 18, 2000.
[13] CDR—Constant default rate

EXHIBIT 16.17 Outstanding Public CMBS Universe—Loss Severity of Defaulted Loans, as of September 30, 2000

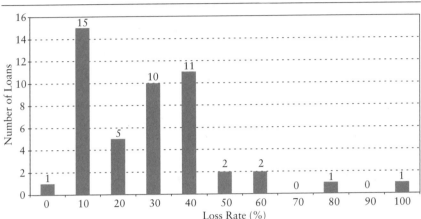

Source: Salomon Smith Barney.

10% to just over 50%, which puts the 40% in fair prospective. In a recession that caused loan defaults to increase, we would expect the loan loss to be more severe, likely shifting to around the 40% loan loss used by many investors.

The time until default and the recovery period following the default will also effect the CMBS cash flow. Typical default curves show that default rates rise between years 2 and 7. Thus using analysis based on an immediate default is extreme, we would suggest analysis should allow for a 12-months to 24-months delay before defaults occur. The defaulted loan's recovery period can also impact the underlying cash flows. Recent experience suggests a careful special servicer can take anywhere from 12 months to 36 months to foreclose, workout, and liquidate a loan after a delinquency. In many instances, it is not uncommon for the special servicer to spend the first 3 months to 6 months just assessing whether the delinquent borrower is acting in good faith to determine if foreclosure is necessary or whether a restructured loan might create the highest loan workout value.

This discussion was intended to highlight that there is no specific expected default and loss scenario for analyzing CMBS. **Which is why the CMBS structure was developed as a sequential pay form that insulates the longer term investment grade classes from default prepayments, while exposing only the short triple-A class, the IO and the non-investment grade classes to significant default prepayment risk.**

16.12 EXPECTED DEFAULT RATES AND CREDIT TIERING OF ISSUERS

The impact defaults can have on a transaction has caused investors to develop the concept of different CMBS pricing based on perceived underwriter quality and transaction liquidity. Tiering CMBS transactions for liquidity made sense because the events of 1998 removed some issuers from the market, creating orphan issues with no broker specifically committed to providing a market. While the second factor of underwriter quality is meant to account for the concept of "credit culture," which the market suggests is stronger in bank-based originators. Credit culture is the idea that some institutions have underwriting checks by third parties whose compensation is in no way tied to issuance volume. However, as discussed in the Appendix of this chapter, the rating agencies review the underwriter's credit origination process and adjust credit enhancement levels to account for their analysis. Agencies' opinions on an underwriter are contained in the presale report and, in our experience, can cause a subordination variance of up to 2% between transactions. *The extra subordination built into some transactions may mean investors are overcompensating for issuer quality with the additional spread premium.* We have analyzed CMBS default rates by issuer but, given the current strong real estate environment, are unable to detect a meaningful relationship between issuer and loan performance.

To date loan defaults could be best described as random events. In general, defaults are higher in floating-rate transactions and on retail properties. The retail defaults have occurred usually when an asset is highly dependent on a specific, single tenant for cash flow. Our database of losses showed a $27 million loss on an entire CMBS pool of $233 billion, which appears impressive relative to other asset-backed securities. However, the current economic environment is not a good recession test of the CMBS credit-enhancement structure, and none of these pools has aged to the typical 10-year balloon test date. We expect that when we go through the next recession, a default pattern will develop based on origination year, underwriting quality, and property type.

Delinquency rates are important, as any large delinquency immediately affects a CMBS transaction's liquidity and price. This spread widening is well acknowledged as illogical, given that some defaults were originally projected for all CMBS transactions and are unlikely to create an investment-grade principal loss. *However, given that spreads quickly widen on any bad, deal-specific news, investors have actively bid for transactions with low expected default rates, creating a small pricing difference between some issuers.*

Although highly subordinated transactions may experience more defaults, they are unlikely to remain on credit watch for long periods because the extra credit enhancement usually enables the rating agency to affirm levels quickly. In 1999, a good example of the benefits of high subordination came from three credit tenant lease (CTL) transactions that contained a large amount of Rite Aid exposure.[14] In November, Moody's downgraded Rite Aid to B1, putting three CTL transactions on credit watch. Although MLMI 1998 CTL had more than 20% Rite Aid exposure and the other two transactions had less than 10% exposure, MLMI also contained almost twice the credit enhancement of the other CTL transactions. This enabled Moody's to quickly affirm MLMI, while the other transactions remained on credit watch.

Transactions vary and this simple example may not always apply. *However, in general, transactions with high credit subordination levels have extra default and loss protection and may weather a recession better than a lower leverage low deal that has better subordination levels.* Specifically, a transaction with 1% extra subordination at the AAA level can withstand 2.5% more loan defaults than a pool with lesser subordination (assuming a 40% loan loss rate).

Long-term CMBS investors will find value in the lower-tier CMBS categories, which have greater subordination and wider spreads, while short-term CMBS investors that mark to market should stick with the tier 1 and 2 categories to avoid defaults and the resulting immediate spread widening caused by headline risk. *In 1999, the market actively bid tier 1 and 2 issues, while tier 3 transactions had limited liquidity. In 2000, the tiering price differential declined as investors realized there was more relative value in tier 2 and 3 transactions.* Over time, as the CMBS market experiences more defaults, investors should grow more comfortable with defaults, reducing any underwriter tiering differentiation currently in the market.

16.13 CMBS COLLATERAL CREDIT REVIEW—A LOAN-BY LOAN APPROACH FOR NON-REAL ESTATE EXPERTS

Even though CMBS transactions have significant credit enhancement, it is still useful to review the underlying collateral to gain familiarity with transactions and be able to compare one transaction to the next. The best way to do this is by stratifying the property information provided via a spreadsheet using the property file provided in the issuer's schedule A. Given the

---

[14] We presented a full analysis of this transaction in our article, "Pricing Tenant Concentration Risk into Credit Tenant Lease Transactions," *Bond Market Roundup: Strategy,* November 12, 1999.

information in schedule A, even a real estate novice can summarize and review the properties' key loan data in a consistent format to spot loan leverage or tenant irregularities.

We suggest that investors develop a format that takes schedule A and first shows the property type, loan name, address, balance, building area, loan per that area, and the top two tenants' names with their square footage and lease expiry dates. Once in this format, an investor can quickly scan all the properties in a transaction and determine who the major tenants are, how much of the area they occupy, and when their leases expire. Some property classifications, such as anchored retail lets investors get a sense of what the underwriter considered to be "anchored" and how far the issuer felt he or she needed to stretch the definition. This tenant analysis does not require significant real estate or retail expertise, just a general knowledge of the nation's major retailers and corporations and an eye to question when one tenant may account for too much of a loan's square footage. Exhibit 16.18 shows a typical loan stratification format we would suggest.

We gain comfort when we see that the two largest tenants are less than 6,000 square feet of any larger property, because it is easier to replace that smaller tenant from the larger pool of potential replacement tenants. In addition, having more, smaller tenants means that the property's revenues are more widely distributed than a property with fewer, larger tenants.

This loan stratification technique is especially helpful in reviewing retail properties. In a retail mall in which one or two large tenants represent more than 60% of the loan's rentable area, they likely provide the draw to the center that enables the smaller tenants to pay high rents. Anchor tenants usually undercontribute to the mall's revenues (paying $2–$12 per square foot (psf), while the smaller tenants usually provide the bulk of the property's income (paying rents of $15–$30 psf or more). **The real risk of anchored retail is that the loss of the anchor tenant can leave the other smaller tenants without the necessary traffic to generate their higher rent payments.** In the current strong economy an anchor tenant loss has not presented a huge issue to borrowers, as in most cases a replacement tenant has been available. This section raises the issue and cautions that in a slower economy the loss of a large tenant may have a severe impact.

This analysis also enables investors to get used to a range of loan per square foot or per unit in the case of apartments or hotels and determine when the loan per unit varies from the normal loan range. The loan stratification approach will enable even a non-real estate expert to recognize when the loan amount is higher than normal requiring an underwriter explanation. We suggest the amounts in Exhibit 16.19 provide a rough loan per square unit guide only. Strong properties can certainly carry higher loan per unit, but using a guide will enable an investor to ask the underwriter why

EXHIBIT 16.18 Suggested Loan Stratification Worksheet to Review Annex A

Property Type:	Total/ Ave. Pool	Anchored Retail	Office	Hotel / limited service	Outlet Center
ID #		1	3	4	5
Property Name		Arizona Mall, 100 Arizona Circle	19 Roadway Building, 19 Roadway	Motel 4 Suites Portfolio	21 East Center, 21 East St
City / State		Tempe, Arizona	, Colorado	various, FL,AZ,OH,NJ	New York, New York
Year Built / Renovated		1997,	1985,	1967, 1998	1999/2000,
Cut-off Bal	$ 950,457,000	140,000,000	49,966,246	31,200,000	29,978,826
Category % of Pool:	100%	14.73%	5.26%	3.28%	3.15%
Area/Units		1,100,500	621,577	891	94
$/AreaUnit		$ 127.21	$ 80.39	$ 35,017	$ 318,924
Occupancy		97%	96%	76%	100%
Major Tenants		1. Sears 103,000 sf, 11/30/03 & 2. Lord & Taylor 88,000 sf, 05/31/09	1. Column Systems, Inc. 100,420 sf, 12/31/08 & 2. AT&T, 55,000 sf, 09/31/02	N/A	1. Bed Bath & Beyond 60,522 sf, 08/31/10 & 2. Marshalls 33,450 sf, 05/31/08
Sponsor		ABC Real Estate Company	ZYX Company	FGX LTD.	ZYX Company
Leasehold		Fee Simple	-	-	Fee Simple
Lockbox		Hard	Hard	None	None
Required Reserves		184,500.00	127,147.00	-	30,288.00
TI/LC Reserve		1,300,000.00	840,575.00	-	-
Appraisal	$1,335,365,000	$ 250,000,000	$ 79,000,000	$ 70,800,000	$ 45,900,000
App LTV	71.18%	56%	63%	44%	65%
Balloon LTV	61.11%	52%	57%	37%	58%
Loan Rate:	8.11%	7.90%	7.97%	8.44%	7.75%
Loan Cash Flow:	$ 139,070,228	$ 20,097,142	$ 6,499,426	$ 6,175,617	$ 3,786,951
Actual Maturity:	122.2	120	120	120	120
Actual Amortization:	354.7	360	360	300	360
U/W DSCR:	1.44	1.58	1.48	1.93	1.47

Source: Salomon Smith Barney.

EXHIBIT 16.19 Typical Conduit Loan Lending Amounts

Property Type	Typical Loan Range ($/unit)
Multifamily (high quality)	$30,000 to $80,000/unit
Multifamily	$10,000 to $30,000/unit
Office (downtown)	$80 to $150 psf
Office (suburban)	$60 to $125 psf
Retail (anchored)	$40 to $125 psf
Retail (unanchored)	$40 to $130 psf
Industrial (warehouse)	$30 to $80 psf
Hotel (full service)	$40,000 to $80,000/suite
Hotel (limited service)	$20,000 to $45,000/suite

Source: Salomon Smith Barney.

the loan has the higher loan per unit and may lead to important transaction screening information.

The ranges in Exhibit 16.19 vary by geographic region and local market conditions. In many areas where alternative development sites are plentiful and the economy is weak the figures will be too high and in other areas where there is limited infill development sites and strong economies the figures will be too low. We have discussed the loan stratification method as a means for investors to get to know the underlying real estate information and to develop a comfort with those assets. *For investors that only buy the senior rated classes of CMBS transactions there is a strong argument that current subordination levels provide sufficient credit protection and that they never need to know the underlying real estate of a diverse pool.* But for investors who wish to scratch below the transaction surface a loan stratification table is a good start.

16.14 LIQUIDATION AND PAYDOWN—AN ANALYSIS FRAMEWORK FOR DISTRESSED CMBS TRANSACTIONS

Many CMBS investors are sophisticated real estate investors and find value in reviewing the few distressed CMBS situations currently available in the market. In the last section of this chapter, we review a simple methodology for reviewing distressed CMBS certificates.

Given the strong economy of the past few years no CMBS conduit transactions have experienced significant defaults. Therefore to get an idea of how CMBS will perform in a distressed scenario, we are forced to review lumpier Fusion or CTL transactions. Among these lumpier CMBS transactions, a major collateral event can cause a significant widening in spreads and loss of value. This section describes an SSB collateral disaster methodology which investors can use to independently evaluate a bond's collateral risk.

This methodology assumes a worst case liquidation value for the affected collateral and then removes the distressed loans from the pool using the recovery to pay down the triple-A classes and reduce the subordinate classes by the amount of the loss.

Although analysis is simplistic and ignores potential loan amortization that may take place before a default event, it enables investors to quickly estimate if distressed loans represent principal or even rating agency downgrade risk. In the majority of cases using reasonable liquidation assumptions, the subordination to the triple-A class actually improves after liquidating the affected loans. The analysis suggests the triple-A classes of CMBS transactions that have experienced a collateral event can offer excellent relative value. Investors in the lower rated classes can use the same methodology to assess investment opportunities but must carefully calculate the loans' estimated liquidation value.

To illustrate how to analyze the liquidation distressed loans, we review two transactions that have experienced a major decrease in collateral quality.

Case 1 Rite Aid Exposure in MLMI 1998-C1-CTL

The first CMBS transaction we review is Merrill Lynch Mortgage Investors, Inc, Series 1998-C1-CTL. This transaction is a credit tenant lease (CTL) transaction[15] with a 20.6% concentration of loans supported by bondable leases with Rite Aid Corporation. On October 18, 1999, Rite Aid announced that it would restate its financial statements for each of its fiscal years ended 1999, 1998, and 1997 by as much as $500 million. After the announcement the market became illiquid with the MLMI triple-A classes trading at triple-B spreads.

Even 18 months after the company's original disclosure the market was uncertain as to whether the company could service its corporate debt on an ongoing basis. We reviewed this transaction in the fall of 1999, when Rite Aid's corporate rating was downgraded form BBB-/Baa3 to BB/Ba2. At that time we said that we expected the triple-A classes to continue to be rated triple-A even if Rite Aid were to file for bankruptcy. Since that report, S&P and Moody's have downgraded Rite Aid's corporate rating to single B with no impact on the investment-grade rating of the transaction. Below, in Exhibit 16.20, we review the liquidation analysis that enabled us to have confidence in the triple-A classes of the transaction.

To analyze Rite Aid's potential impact on the transaction, we determine the liquidation value for the related loans and then remove them from the pool, realizing the liquidation value as a prepayment to the triple-A class. Any shortfall between the liquidation value and the outstanding loan balance is treated as a loss to the subordinate classes. After the entire loan balance has been removed from the pool with the proceeds prepaying the triple-A class, we recalculate the resulting subordination levels based on the smaller loan pool. We focus on the triple-A class because the majority of the CMBS universe is triple-A rated, and this class directly receives the benefit

---

[15] Credit tenant lease transactions contain commercial mortgages loans secured by one or more properties leased to tenants that have a rating agency credit rating. The credit tenant is usually responsible for all of the costs associated with operating the property and makes loan payments to fully amortize the loan. A fully structured credit tenant's obligation enables the rating agencies to analyze a high leverage mortgage loan as though it carried the rating of the underlying tenant.

EXHIBIT 16.20   Subordination Levels Without Rite Aid with Expected Paydown from Rating Agency Value

Rating	Current Credit Enhancement	Class Size	Current Class Size (MM)	Less Paydown/ Loss (MM)	Class Size Without Rite Aid (MM)	Subord % After Loss
AAA/Aaa	31.3%	68.7%	$425.09	$91.11	$337.48	32.0%
AA and A Class	19.8	11.5	71.07		71.07	17.6%
BBB and BBB- Class	12.0	7.8	48.46		48.46	7.7%
Noninvestment Grade		12.0	74.30	36.44	37.85	
Total With and Without Rite Aid:			618.90	127.56	491.35	

Expected Loss on Rite Aid Stores		**Comment**
Rite Aid Loan Balance (MM)	$127.56	
Loan to Dark Value	140%	A ratio based on the liquidation value of the empty stores calculated by capitalizing the market rent and deducting new tenant inducement, commissions, loss revenue, and new investor profit.
Underlying Dark Value MM)	$91.11	Equals paydown to triple-A and is greater than difference between the old triple-A class size and the new required triple-A class size.
Expected Loss (MM)	36.44	Loss to Noninvestment Grade classes

Conclusion: Resulting 32% Triple-A subordination remains above initial 30% subordination. No downgrade.

Source: Salomon Smith Barney.

of the liquidation prepayment. The mezzanine investment-grade classes also receive a benefit from the triple-A prepayment, being next in line for prepayment; however, the subordination loss from the reduction in the lower classes usually overshadows the prepayment benefit.

In a CTL transaction such as MLMI, the rating agencies have developed the concept of *dark property value* to refer to the alternative use value of a property that would be realized if the tenant were to default and the property redeveloped for another tenant. This dark valuation technique typically calculates value based on the area's market rent for similar retail space capitalized at a stabilized cap rate or yield. The final dark value is derived from the alternative use value by deducting the cost of re-leasing the space, the lost rental revenue during the building's foreclosure and redevelopment, and a profit for the developer who buys and redevelops the asset.[16] This dark value is effectively the liquidation value needed to remove the Rite Aid loan from the transaction. In Exhibit 16.20 we calculate the liquidation value for the Rite Aid Stores' loan and deduct the proceeds from the MLMI transaction. The result is that the triple-A subordination level increases to 32%.

---

[16] *DCR's Large Pool Credit Lease Rating Methodology,* Duff and Phelps, May 1998, gives a detailed explanation of property dark value.

However, the downgrade risk in MLMI increases in the investment-grade classes as one goes down the credit classes. In the example in Exhibit 16.20, a rating agency committee would likely not downgrade the double-A or single-A classes based on 2.2% less subordination after liquidating the Rite Aid loans. However, investors in the double-A or single-A class of a transaction that has already experienced significant losses should undertake independent liquidation analysis to ensure they are comfortable with the classes' downgrade potential. We do not see any principal loss risk in the double-A and single-A rated classes. In this liquidation scenario the triple-B and triple-B minus classes could likely be downgraded a notch because they lose a larger portion of subordinate protection (12% subordination before the liquidations becomes 7.7% after).

This example assumes Rite Aid defaults on all the locations. A more likely scenario might involve Rite Aid's filing for bankruptcy and then affirming only the leases on the better retail locations on which the company has achieved its best sales. This type of scenario would leave the special servicer with a smaller number of below-average store locations to liquidate. We used this methodology to default and liquidate different combinations of Rite Aid and other tenants at higher loan to dark values ranging from 140% to 200%, and we feel comfortable that the triple-A class of the transaction is unlikely to be downgraded. In our worst-case liquidation scenario, the triple-A subordination decreased to 25.5%, which we think would be a borderline point for the rating agencies to consider downgrading the triple-A class.

Investors who bought the triple-A paper at a discount should actually want a tenant default and liquidation, because the early principal paydown will increase their yield to maturity without triggering a downgrade to their security. The liquidation analysis suggests that the triple-A class of the transaction is an excellent long-term value given its current triple B spread premium.

Case 2 Asset Securitization Corporation, 1997 MD VII (Limited Service Hotel Exposure)

ASC 1997 MD VII is a large loan transaction containing seven mortgages on 71 properties. The loans range in size from 5% to 33% of the pool. All four of the rating agencies originally rated various classes of the transaction, determining that the loans were well-structured low-leverage loans. On August 31, 1999, the largest loan's borrower, Fairfield Inns by Marriott LP, requested possible loan modifications, causing the loan to be transferred to the special servicer. Since the initial inquiry, no formal request was received from the borrower, so the loan was transferred back to the master servicer.

However, the request caused the four agencies to review the loan and adjust their opinion of the collateral.

On September 2, 1999, Fitch IBCA downgraded the A-5 and A-6 classes, originally rated BBB–, to BB and B, respectively. On November 17, Moody's downgraded the A-3 and A-4 classes from A2 to A3 and from Baa2 to Baa3, respectively. On November 24, 1999, S&P affirmed the triple-A class and downgraded the B-1 and B-1H classed from double-B to single-B. DCR followed on December 14, when it downgraded the A-4 class from triple-B to triple-B minus and the A-5 class from triple-B minus to double-B. All of this rating agency activity was a direct result of a decline in the Fairfield Hotel portfolio's performance.

At the time of our review, the Fairfield Inns' loan, had an outstanding balance of $153.5 million, and constituted 32.6% of the transaction total pool balance. The loan was structured as a first-priority, cross-collateralized, and cross-defaulted mortgage on 50 Fairfield Inns' limited service hotels spread across 16 states (6,673 rooms). All of the rating agencies determined that the underlying properties had experienced a significant increase in operating expenses and a decline in room revenue owing to increased competition in the various submarkets. This operating performance translated into a significant declined in debt service coverage since the original rating agency reviews (see Exhibit 16.21).

Using the liquidation methodology to evaluate this situation requires a worst-case estimate of the underlying value of the limited-service hotel portfolio. The rating agency values represent a value based on a sustainable cash flow and cap rate. These rating agency values suggest a liquidation value

EXHIBIT 16.21   Fairfield Loan—Rating Agency Assessment of Performance

Agency	Original DSCR[a]	Original Value/ LTV (MM)*	Recent DCSR	Comment
UW	1.62x	$270/61%		As per the offering materials.
Fitch IBCA	1.57x	NA	1.16x 9/2/99	Recent DSCR based on TTM cashflow and actual debt service for period ending 30 Jun 99.
Moody's	1.53x	$239/69%	1.19x 11/17/99	Recent DSCR based on servicer report ending 30 Jun 99.
S&P	1.59x	$221.3/74.5%	1.34x 11/24/99	Recent DSCR based on 25% cash flow reduction and actual debt service.
DCR	1.53x	$252.5/65.6%	1.15x 12/14/99	Recent DSCR based on 12 months results ending 30 Sep 99.

*Original DSCR and values based on the offering documents or each rating agencies' presale report.

Sources: Rating presale reports and rating actions.

EXHIBIT 16.22 ASC 1997-MD VII Subordination Levels after Fairfield Loan Liquidation

Class / Rating	Current Credit Enhancement	Class Size	Current Class Size (MM)	Less Paydown/ Loss (MM)	Class Size without Fairfield (MM)	Subord % After Loss
AAA	36.1%	63.9%	$300.21	$100.10	$200.12	36.8%
AA and A	18.6	17.5	82.43		82.43	10.7
BBB and BBB-	2.7	15.9	74.94	(40.90)	34.03	
Noninvestment Grade		2.7	12.49	(12.49)	—	
Total With and Without Fairfield Loan			470.07	153.49	316.58	

Expected Loss on Fairfield Loan		Comment
Fairfield Loan Bal. (MM)	$153.49	
Recovery/Suite	15,000	Based on worst case liquidation value.
Total Recovery (MM)	100.10	
Expected Loss (MM)	53.39	Loss to noninvestment-grade classes.

Conclusion: Resulting 36.8% Triple-A subordination remains above initial 33% subordination. No downgrade to triple-A classes.

Source: Salomon Smith Barney.

range of $33,000 to $38,000 per room. However, our experience from the early 1990s compels us to calculate a lower distressed value for limited-service hotels. If the hotels' occupancy rate were to drop from the original underwritten 70% range to below 50% it is possible to envision only a marginal portfolio cash flow, leaving value to be determined by a minimum value per room benchmark. We called several hotel industry experts and were given recent unflagged limited-service hotel comparable sales figures of $20,000 to $30,000 (we assume that the liquidated portfolio would no longer benefit from the Fairfield hotel flag). However, most of the experts agreed that at $15,000 per room, a buyer would purchase the portfolio no matter what the economic circumstances. Therefore, for our liquidation scenario we will use an extreme $15,000 per room value figure (see Exhibit 16.22). Alternatively, investors who do not have access to real estate expertise may have used a 40% loan loss rate[17] on the original loan of $25,000 per room and achieved the same estimated liquidation proceed of $15,000 per room provided by our experts.

Just as in the Rite Aid analysis the liquidation of the Fairfield loan actually improves the triple-A subordination levels, as the paydown to the

---

[17] The 40% loan loss severity is a common loan loss rated used to estimate potential loan losses. Commercial mortgage portfolio studies from the early 1990s suggest that a commercial mortgage will typically experience a 35% loan loss when liquidated.

triple-A class is greater in proportion than the original transaction's triple-A credit enhancement. The loss on the lower levels, however, significantly decreases the protection to all the mezzanine investment-grade classes, leaving even the double-A class exposed to a potential downgrade. We should caution that a scenario in which only $15,000 per room is realized is an extremely tough stress test. A more realistic asset liquidation figure of $20,000 to $30,000 would likely only expose the triple-B and triple-B minus classes to potential downgrades.

Liquidation/Paydown Test Conclusions

The liquidation and paydown stress test is a simple calculation that any investor with a spreadsheet can perform to make a judgment on collateral safety in CMBS transactions that have experienced poor collateral performance. The test does not account for the amortization that will take place during any loan liquidation and is only as good as the liquidation assumptions that are fed into the calculation. *However, a liquidation and paydown test usually demonstrates that the triple-A classes maintain their original credit enhancement levels even under the most severe liquidation assumptions. This suggests that the triple-A classes of CMBS transactions that have experienced collateral distress represent significant relative value for investors that can ride out headline risk.*

The analysis can also be used to investigate the principal safety of the lower rated classes of CMBS transactions to the extent these lower classes are not eliminated by the estimated loss reduction at the bottom of the transaction. However, using the tool to estimate downgrade potential in the mezzanine investment-grade classes is more uncertain, because firm rules are not established as to how much subordination can be lost before a rating agency credit committee deems a class downgrade necessary.

Finally, investors in distressed transactions should consider using one of the cash flow modeling programs that are available to phase in expected losses and allow for amortization of the loans during workouts. In our examples, cash flow analysis demonstrated a reduction in loan loss and a significant yield pickup in the triple-A classes, which currently sell at a discount and therefore benefit from the early default prepayment.

16.25 CONCLUSION

Investors reviewing CMBSs should understand the following points:

- The rating agencies have developed methods for measuring the likelihood that a particular commercial transaction will meet its scheduled payments to investors under various economic scenarios. These methods focus on financial leverage statistics, as well as on underwriting standards, property types, and property tenancy. Overall the rating agencies' credit enhancement models appear to provide excess credit protection relative to the default and loss experience of the last real estate recession. During the past four years, rating agencies have adjusted the commercial models to compensate for the strong collateral performance and more realistically reflect the commercial property default probability. We expect commercial credit enhancement levels will continue to decline even as the CMBS market experiences an economic slowdown and gains maturity.

■ Current CMBS collateral fundamentals are strong because of the relatively low level of construction funding. Seasoned CMBS transactions have benefited the most from the strong real estate market as the underlying properties have experienced significant appreciation since the loans were securitized and yet the loans are precluded from prepayment by strong prepayment penalties. These conditions mean it could take several years of low economic activity to significantly affect the credit quality of existing CMBSs.

■ Relative value analysis comparison with other spread products suggests CMBSs offer significant excess return. Considering the CMBS market's improved liquidity during the past 24 months and given the credit risk similar to other rated structured debt products, CMBSs would seem to have collateral structure and market characteristics that justify a tighter overall spread (this is especially true for the triple-A rated classes including IO). If during the next few years CMBS collateral performs well during a slowing economy, we expect strong investor demand and a potential tightening of CMBS credit spreads.

APPENDIX
RATING AGENCY SUBORDINATION ADD-ONS

In this Appendix we describe the potential subordination add-on to CMBS pools to assist investors with reading an agency presale report. If a pool characteristic is highlighted as a negative in an agency presale, investors shouldn't be overly concerned, rather the concentration discussion means the rating agency caught a specific item and increased subordination levels to account for the feature. This extra credit subordination in transactions that have specific concentration issues may cause them to price behind the standard generic CMBS transactions offering extra relative value.

Most of the adjustments described below reflect specific characteristic concentrations, which are a direct function of the overall pool size. **Generally,** the more diversified and less dependent on any one entity a pool is, the less concentrated the credit exposure and the better the subordination levels. The various pool concentration or individual loan factors that can cause a rating agency to increase or decrease credit support levels are discussed next.

Diversity

A measure of the loan concentration or "lumpiness" of the pool, diversity can impact subordination from 0 to 20%. Moody's uses a Herfindahl Index to measure the pool's loan concentration and then scales their add-on accordingly. The Herfindahl score is calculated by taking the inverse of the sum of the squares of each mortgage loan as a percentage of the overall pool.

$$\text{Herfindahl Index} = \frac{1}{\Sigma\left(\dfrac{\text{Loan}}{\text{Loan Pool}}\right)^2}$$

Most recent fixed rate conduit transactions have had a Herfindahl score of 75 to 85, while a Herfindahl score of 100 is considered to be diverse requiring no add-on. Pools with a Herfindahl score below 60 should be considered lumpy requiring significant extra credit enhancement. Investors in these lumpy pools are protected by the extra credit enhancement, but should make an effort to understand the larger underlying loans.

In the past, Fitch has looked at the three largest loans as a percentage of the pool and assumed that they default to create an add-on factor, thus the larger the percentage represented by the three loans the larger the add-on. Similar to Moody's, Fitch is now adjusting its model to go beyond the largest three loans by also using a statistical measure of the pool's loan diversity. Fitch then applies a scale to its diversity score to reflect a pool add-on of 0% to 15% depending on the lumpiness of the mortgage pool.

Geographic Concentrations

Similar to property type, a commercial mortgage pool diversified by geographic location will reduce risk and, thus, required loss coverage. The agencies have developed a variety of methodologies to increase or decrease a CMBS transaction's subordination levels to account for geographic diversity. In most cases once a pool is located more than 20% in one state there will be a subordination penalty scaled to the concentration (California is divided into a North and South state to account for its economic diversity and population size). In addition, within the past year both Moody's and Fitch have introduced pool scoring methodologies to account for the pool's diversity by property type and industry concentration, which they use to adjust their geographic diversity scores and the pool's overall subordination levels. Moody's has taken this logic one step further with their measure of economic diversity that also looks at the pool's exposure to specific industries within each geographic region.[18]

Underwriting Quality

This evaluation reviews whether the underwriter carefully reviewed the underlying property and its market and requires appropriate loan structural features. For example a loan with significant lease expires may require a releasing reserve to be escrowed or even a hard lock box and cash trap in cases where loan default is considered highly probable.

Underwriter review also requires analysis of the underwriting criteria, approval process, appraisal standards, special hazard policies, and workout policies of the originator and servicer. The agencies will focus closely on the following areas in their evaluation:

1. Property appraisal standards and procedures.
2. Originator quality—based on historical portfolio performance.
3. Originator's area of expertise—by mortgage purpose (for example, refinance versus new construction), property type, and property location.
4. Servicing standards and policies—including those regarding balloon mortgages.
5. Approval procedure—approval procedures that require third-party nonbusiness line credit review are seen as objective and receive subordination credit.
6. Documentation procedures and loan tracking systems.

In cases in which all or some of these data are unavailable, increased credit levels protect investors from potentially increased credit exposure. The rating agencies carefully review the underwriters and may adjust subordination levels by plus or minus 2% to reflect their opinion of the underwriter's credit and loan structuring skills.

---

[18] See Moody's report titled: CMBS: Conduit Economic Diversity Update for 2000, by Sally Gordon, John Chen and Natasa Agathocleous, September 29, 2000.

Special Servicing

The transactions' master servicer is usually required to transfer servicing to the special servicer after a loan has been in default for 60 days. The special servicer is responsible for dealing with the defaulted loans to restructure the loan or recover the loan proceeds based on its assessment of the best method to maximize the net present value of loan proceeds. The workout negotiation of a defaulted commercial loan is a complex analysis and negotiation that benefits from the special servicer's previous experience and ability to focus resources on the loan file. One person can handle 5 to 20 defaulted files at any one time depending on the complexity of the loan files. Therefore, the rating agencies review each special servicer's human resources and experience and may adjust subordination levels by 0 to 0.75% to reflect their opinion of the special servicer. The issuers realize that their issuance levels can suffer from having a poorly assessed special servicer and since 1997 have only used special servicers that the agencies have evaluated favorably and that have the resources to handle the next real estate recession.

Environment Risk

When the issuer's underwriter reviews a loan for approval, part of the loan due diligence requires that the property undergo a Phase 1 Environmental Assessment. A Phase I Assessment usually involves a physical inspection of the property by an engineer to detect common signs of potential environmental contamination. The engineer will usually determine a history of the property's past uses and investigate related potential environmental contamination. Typical Phase I investigation may involve soil sampling, paint inspection, and a sampling of other building materials such as tiles or insulation. If the Phase I testing determines that there are potential environmental issues with the property then a full scale Phase II Environmental Assessment would be undertaken during which any test needed to determine the extent of contamination would be undertaken and a site cleanup assessment would be preformed.

Any environmental cleanup costs determined in the Phase II would have to be reserved 125% (to ensure a contingency buffer) before a mortgage loan can be approved. This environmental assessment procedure has become standard mortgage loan due diligence for CMBS conduits and regular portfolio lenders, as many state environmental laws now have site clean-up standards that can create costs in excess of the mortgage value or even the property value. Some times small balance commercial loans may be approved without a Phase I environmental review in this case the rating agency may adjust the loan's subordination levels up by 5% to 10% depending on their assessment of likely contamination in the loan. However, most times when an issuer secures a loan or group of loans that have not had an environmental assessment, the issuer will obtain an environmental insurance policy that provides protection from preexisting, but undetected contamination, and any liabilities that may result from the contamination.

Property Type (Loan Specific)

The agencies believe that the optimal credit consists of a pool perfectly diversified by property type (multifamily, office, retail, and industrial). Given a less than perfectly diversified pool, the agencies make a credit assessment based on assumptions regarding the credit risk of each property category. To do this, the rating agencies assign the different property types different default probabilities or loss severity based on property specific valuation property yields or DSCR. Generally, the property types listed from least risky to most volatile would be: multifamily, mobile home, anchored retail, industrial, office, unanchored retail, full service hotel, self storage, nursing home or health care and then limited service hotels. The agencies may also penalize the more volatile property types with higher probability of defaults in addition to the tougher valuation parameters to reflect their less stable cash flows.

Recently, Moody's and Fitch have taken this property type analysis further to reflect the individual MSA property market vacancy and expected rental growth projections. S&P is on the record as stating individual property inspections is the best property assessment method. S&P's property review methodology is valid to the extent an agency is able to sample a large enough sample of the property pool being reviewed. As the market matures, the agencies have been sampling smaller portions of the overall pools, which Moody's and Fitch's MSA methodology is meant to address.

Loan Amortization (Loan Specific)

Most fixed rate conduit commercial mortgages are 10-year balloon loans with 30-amortization schedules. Sometimes the underwriter may create a loan with a shorter amortization period (20 or 25 years) to reduce the balloon refinance risk for one of the more volatile property types. Or at a borrower's request the underwriter may grant an interest only loan with no amortization. The rating agencies adjust their loan credit enhancement levels to account for the extra or less amortization by changing their assessment of loss potential or default risk at expiry. For instance, Fitch may assess a regular 10-year term, 30-year amortization, a 36% loss severity, and an interest only loan at full 40% loss severity. These assessments may change the specific loan's credit support by 2% to 4%.

Leasehold Interests (Loan Specific)

When the mortgaged property is encumbered by a ground lease the rating agency carefully reviews the terms and rights of the ground tenant and the landlord. Specifically, the rating agency will look to see if the ground owner's rights are subordinated to the leasehold mortgage. If the ground lease is not subordinated to the mortgage the mortgagee should have the right of notice of borrower's default and the ability to cure that default. In addition most mortgage loans will not have a balloon mortgage maturity within 10 years of a ground lease expiry as that would limit the borrower's economic interest in managing the property and put the mortgagee's principal at risk. To the extent the rating agency believes a land lease hinders mortgage security, the agency may increase subordination on a loan by 5% to 20% to account for the detrimental ground lease. If a ground lease is fully subordinate to the mortgage, there may be no subordination penalty, while penalties greater than 10% are rare as underwriter standards prevent mortgages with no notice and cure rights.

Property Quality Assessment (Loan Specific)

The agencies will visit and assign a property quality score based on their assessment of the property's location, competition, physical condition, tenancy, and market position. S&P and Moody's use a scale of 1 to 5 with 1 being good and 5 being worse. While Fitch assesses a property grade A through C– with most high quality pools being assessed as B+ and typical conduit pools being B– and poor properties being C or worse. This property score can affect the overall subordination levels by 1% to 3%, but usually only accounts for 0.5% to 1% difference between pools as most recent conduit transactions are of similar quality.

Secondary Financing (Loan Specific)

Many borrowers use secondary financing to leverage their property beyond the limits imposed by the rating agency's first mortgage guidelines. These secondary loans can take the following forms:

- *Mezzanine debt or Preferred Equity:* The most common form of additional financing used by borrowers. A mezzanine loan is a loan secured by the equity interests of the first mortgage borrower, so they can only foreclose on the equity in the mortgage borrower leaving the first mortgage unaffected. Another version of mezzanine financing is a preferred equity interest whereby the borrower issues preferred equity that earns a fixed interest rate and converts to equity in the borrower SPE if interest payments are deferred.

- *A/B note structures:* One loan is divided into a senior participation interest which is deposited in the securitization vehicle while the junior participation interest is privately placed outside of the securitization vehicle. In recent years, A/B notes have been used by issuers to de-leverage larger loans which permit the large loan to be shadow rated investment grade and improves the CMBS transaction's overall credit levels attracting a broader investor base. Investors further interested in the implications of A/B notes should read A/B Note Structures in CMBS Transactions.[19]

- *Second mortgage loans:* A subordinate mortgage is secured by a lien on the property that is subordinate in priority to the first-mortgage lien. If a second mortgage exists on a property, the rating agencies usually require an intercreditor agreement that subordinates the second mortgage lender's rights to the first mortgage lender.

Any form of additional property leverage increases the property's obligations which reduces the cash flow available to improve the property and therefore increases the first mortgage's probability of default. To reflect this increased default risk the agencies generally increase the first mortgage's required subordination. Each of the rating agencies has published materials that detail the subordination add-ons created by subordinate financing.

Operating History (Loan Specific)

There can be a significant difference in the cash flow stability of a new property relative to a property that has been in operation for a number of years. Newly developed properties may have all of their leases expire in the same year leaving significant lease rollover risk if the tenants find they originally signed leases that are uneconomic. While a property that has been operating for a number of years generally has stabilized tenant rental levels and diversified tenancy leases expire over a longer time frame. The rating agencies usually require three years of property statements to review the property's cash flow stability and adjust their underwritten cash flow based on the property's operating history. Any property that has been newly built and has no operating statement is penalized. While properties that have no statements due to recently being purchased are penalized to a lesser extent.

---

[19] "A/B Note Structures in CMBS Transactions," Darrell Wheeler, *Bond Market Roundup*, February 18, 2000.

CHAPTER 17

A Guide to CMBS IO

Darrell Wheeler and Jeffrey Berenbaum

The CMBS market has seen strong growth over the past few years with issuance levels of $78.3 billion in 1998, $67.0 billion in 1999, and $60.1 billion in 2000. As the market has developed and liquidity has improved, the triple-A CMBS sector has become more closely linked with other fixed income debt instruments and has increased its investor base while the lower rated, unrated, and IO sectors have remained primarily with those investors willing to do more fundamental real estate analysis. CMBS IO segregation with the lower rated credit classes has limited the investor universe and potentially created a relative value opportunity.

Most investors view CMBS IO as a specialized credit sensitive product requiring detailed default analysis. This is in contrast to the single-family, residential IO market where most investors' analysis revolves around the high interest-rate sensitivity of prepayments. The strong fundamentals of the current commercial mortgage market, however, suggest several reasons to expect CMBS IO to have a fairly stable return:

- We expect strong underlying commercial real estate fundamentals to moderately slow down during the next 24 months. During this time CMBS transactions should experience a low level of prepayments from defaults making their IO classes good relative value.
- Conservative default and prepayment assumptions suggest CMBS IO could provide a 200bp (basis points) to 250bp spread over treasuries.
- Relative value analysis comparison with other spread products suggests CMBS IO offers significant excess return. Considering the CMBS market's improved liquidity in 1999 and 2000, CMBS IO characteristics justify a tighter overall spread.

The purpose of this chapter[1] is, firstly, to provide a brief description of CMBS IO; and secondly, to present a table that addresses the cash flow uncertainty of 78 CMBS IOs with a ranking by mean yield change under 82 different stressed scenarios. We have created the summary table to highlight IO relative value and take some of the unknown qualities out of the IO investment. The table will hopefully expand the investment class opportunity to a broader base of investors.

17.1 WHAT IS A CMBS IO?

The typical commercial mortgage security structure is sequential pay: principal and interest payments on the underlying loans, after the deduction of servicing expenses, are passed through directly to the certificate holders. Excess interest payments beyond what is required to pay bond coupons are stripped class by class and sold as triple-A rated IO certificates. Hence, the CMBS IO strips cash flow from multiple, different rated bond classes.

The structure of the bond classes is determined based on the shape of the treasury yield curve and on the competing constraints of various participants in the transaction. Triple-A investors may require par dollar-priced bonds, whereas B-piece buyers may require a minimum coupon. Meanwhile, the issuer is interested in achieving the best execution for the entire structure and will try to maximize proceeds where possible. These factors will determine how the IO is structured and the quality of its cash flows.

As an example, we show the bond classes from a hypothetical CMBS deal in Exhibit 17.1 and the structure of this deal in Exhibit 17.2. The X class represents the IO, which has an initial notional balance of $1.0 billion and an initial weighted average coupon (WAC) of 1.5%. Excess interest for this hypothetical IO is stripped off classes A-1, A-2, B, C, F, and G. The example assumes that the collateral has a net WAC of 8.5%.

In this example, the IO is stripped off of the front classes (A-1 through C) and off of the rear classes (F and G), but not off of the middle classes (D and E). The front two classes are dollar-price constrained (i.e., A-1s at 100, A-2s at 100½) by the investment grade buyer, and, therefore, are structured with fixed coupons to achieve this (in this case, 6.75%). The IO will initially earn an excess coupon of 1.75% (8.5% − 6.75%) off of these senior classes. The next two classes are also dollar-price constrained (close to par) but are structured as WAC bonds with the coupon capped at 7.5%. The IO initially earns

---

[1] This chapter supplements the article "An Introduction to CMBS IOs," Lakhbir Hayre and Ronald E. Thompson, Jr., *Bond Market Roundup*, March 19, 1999.

EXHIBIT 17.1   Bond Classes of a Hypothetical CMBS Transaction

Class	Initial Rating	Face Amount ($MM)	Initial Credit Support (%)	Pass-Through Rate (%)	Coupon Type	Weighted Avg Life (years)
A-1	Aaa/AAA	200.0	30.0	6.75	Fixed	5.70
A-2	Aaa/AAA	500.0	30.0	6.75	Fixed	9.25
B	Aa2/AA	90.0	21.0	7.50	Fixed/WAC	9.70
C	A2/A	70.0	14.0	7.50	Fixed/WAC	9.75
D	Baa2/BBB	40.0	10.0	8.50	WAC	9.80
E	Ba2/BB	40.0	6.0	8.50	WAC	9.80
F	B2/B	40.0	2.0	6.75	Fixed	9.80
G	NR/NR	20.0	0.0	6.75	Fixed	9.80
X*	Aaa/AAA	1,000.0	NA	1.50	WAC	NA
	Total Offered	1,000.0		8.50		

*Notional amount.
NA: Not applicable.
Source: Salomon Smith Barney.

1.0% off of these two classes. The D and E classes are pure WAC bonds and are sold at a discount. These bonds do not contribute to the IO cash flow, and are structured in this manner to improve the overall execution for the issuer (i.e., these discount bonds sell better in whole than if a portion had been stripped off and sold as IO). It is customary, however, to include the principal of these classes in the stated notional amount of the IO. The F and G classes have fixed coupons that are specified by purchasers (typically, these coupons will range from 6.5% to 7.0%, or 100bp over the 10-year treasury). The IO initially earns 1.75% over these junior classes. *Thus, the amount of IO stripped off the front end versus the back end of the structure will be a key factor in determining the credit sensitivity of the IO. The pricing spread of the IO will be strongly related to this structural allocation.*

EXHIBIT 17.2   Structure of a Hypothetical CMBS Transaction

X-IO Aaa/AAA $1,000 MM Notional Amount		B Aa2/AA $90 MM	C A2/A $70 MM	D Baa2/BBB $40MM	E Ba2/BB $40 MM		
A-1 Aaa/AAA $200 MM	A-2 Aaa/AAA $500 MM					F B2/B $40 MM	G NR/NR $20 MM

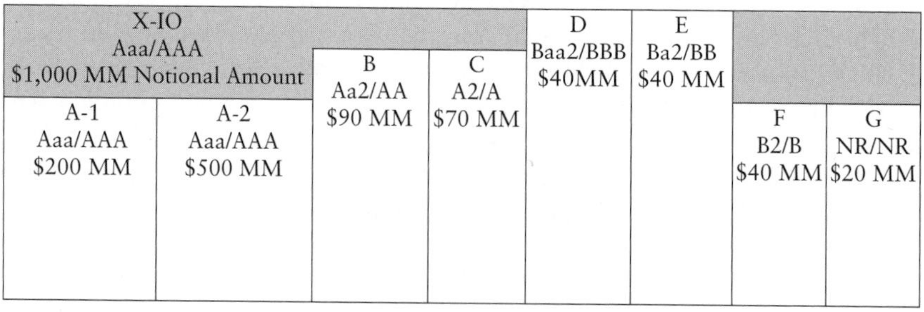

Note: Classes not shown to scale.
Source: Salomon Smith Barney.

Sources of Cash Flow Uncertainty

Once the IO is structured, the amount and duration of cash flows from the underlying pool of mortgage loans and various structural features of the transaction will determine the yield of the security. The IO's complex nature can be analyzed by first understanding the sources of cash flow uncertainty which could impact its expected yield. Three primary sources of uncertainty in the expected cash flows will affect the yield of the IO: voluntary borrower prepayments, defaults from the underlying mortgages, and mortgage extensions.

Prepayments   Restrictions on prepayments, along with the time and cost (typically 3% to 5% of the loan balance) involved in refinancing a commercial real estate loan, means that prepayment risk on CMBS IOs is smaller than that of IOs backed by single-family, residential loans. A CMBS IO certificate's cash flow is more certain than that of a residential IO since, whereas the typical residential mortgage has no restriction to prepayment, the typical commercial mortgage is either locked out from prepayment for a set period and then has a prepayment penalty, or is fully locked with a defeasance mechanism to permit borrower prepayment with no impact on the bond cash flow (refer to Appendix 17A for a further discussion of commercial mortgage prepayment provisions). A borrower may make a voluntary prepayment and incur the yield maintenance, fixed-point, or defeasance cost if they have a compelling necessity to sell. In that case, the IO holder typically gets a share of the penalty and the prepayment may actually enhance the IO holder's yield. The difference in the market's perception of prepayment risk between CMBS IO and residential IO can be ascertained in Exhibit 17.3 where representative spreads of these two products are shown along with 10-year treasury yields. The exhibit also demonstrates that CMBS IO spreads have been very stable, while residential IO spreads change significantly with interest rates. Overall, CMBS IO have had very stable pricing characteristics.

Defaults   Because of the strong prepayment lockout, default risk is the critical element to evaluate in understanding expected IO cash flows. The level and timing of defaults within a CMBS transaction heavily determine the realized yield of an IO investment (refer to Appendix 17A for a further discussion of commercial mortgage defaults). Defaults, and the resulting liquidation of loans, can mean an early return of notional principal and loss of IO cash flow. Commercial transactions typically have credit support for the triple-A sequential classes in the form of subordination. Defaults are first absorbed by the lower-rated classes of the structure, protecting the senior classes. However, since many CMBS IOs are stripped off of the entire

EXHIBIT 17.3 CMBS IO versus Residential IO Spreads (March 1998 through October 2000)

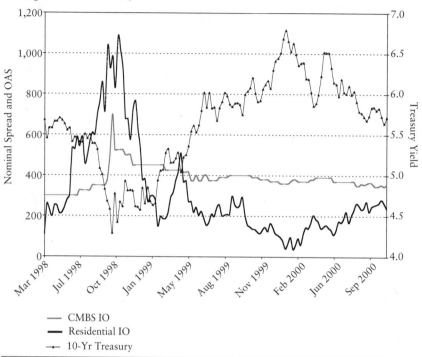

Nominal Spread of Generic Conduit CMBS IO, OAS of FNMA Trust 277 (7.5% Coupon).
Source: Salomon Smith Barney.

structure, any resulting loss of principal will negatively affect the future IO cash flow as the loss means there is less principal balance on which to earn the excess interest.

In addition to the level and timing of defaults, the recovery rate and timing of the resulting liquidations will greatly impact the realized yield of the IO. For an IO certificate, the longer principal is outstanding, the better its return. Therefore, once a default has occurred, the longer it takes to resolve the liquidation or restructuring, the better for the IO. This, however, is true only as long as the servicer is advancing interest payments on the outstanding principal. The recovery rate (or inversely, severity rate) that minimizes the reduction in return for the IO, however, depends upon the structure of the particular transaction. Since recovered principal will be treated as prepayments (without penalty) and used to pay down senior classes, and liquidated principal will be written off of junior classes, the net effect on the IO will depend upon the relative coupons and balances of these classes and on how much they were contributing to the IO. Overall, any loan prepayment caused by a liquidation reduces the IO's return.

Refinancing at Balloon   Another source of uncertainty to the IO holder is the commercial borrower's potential inability to refinance the loan at maturity (on the balloon date). In this case, the special servicer could choose to extend the loan while working with the borrower to maximize the proceeds realized from the mortgage. The IO holder would benefit from the loan's extension in this situation. Estimating commercial mortgage extension risk is entirely dependent upon prevailing mortgage refinance rates at the loan's balloon maturity and the unamortized loan balance at that time. The future mortgage refinance market is unpredictable as is the likelihood of loan extensions. Thus, the market attributes very little value to possible loan extensions.

Structural Issues

The impact of these sources of cash flow uncertainty on an IO's yield will vary depending on certain structural elements of a CMBS transaction. Three of these elements are the effect that the WAC dispersion of the collateral pool will have on the composition of the deal structure over time, the allocation of any prepayment penalties to the IO, and the deal's optional call provision.

WAC Dispersion   The amount of excess spread the IO receives will change over time as the deal structure evolves based on the blend of prepayments and defaults, as well as on normal amortization. As mortgage loans with coupons higher (lower) than average leave the pool, the amount of excess spread available to the IO will decrease (increase). The wider the distribution of loan coupons in the pool, the more uncertain is the early prepayment effect on the WAC of the IO.

The WAC of an IO will also vary month-to-month because of a collateral/bond basis mismatch. Since commercial loans accrue on an actual/360 basis but CMBS bonds, including IOs, accrue on a 30/360 basis, the actual interest payable to an IO certificate holder will vary based on the number of days in a month. This variation will be reflected each month in the reported WAC of the IO.

Allocation of Prepayment Penalties   In the event a voluntary loan prepayment occurs during a yield maintenance or fixed-point penalty period, the borrower is obligated to pay a premium to compensate the holder of the mortgage. CMBS transactions have various methods for allocating the premium among the regular classes and the IO including the discount rate fraction method (DRF), the PV yield loss amount method (PVYLA), and the straight percentage method. First, we define the formulas for the **discount rate fraction method.** Let B equal the coupon of a regular bond class in percent (for example, 7%); M equal the coupon of a prepaid mortgage loan in percent (for example, 9%); and D equal the discount rate in percent as defined in each transaction's prospectus (for example, 6%). This rate is typically equal to the yield of the constant maturity treasury that has a maturity date closest to the assumed final distribution date of the prepaid mortgage loan.

Then, the prepayment premium allocated to the regular bond class will equal

$$\text{Bond allocation percentage} = \frac{(B - D)}{(M - D)}$$

For example,

$$\frac{(7\% - 6\%)}{(9\% - 6\%)} = 33\frac{1}{3}\%$$

leaving the IO to receive any remaining excess premium (for example, 66 ⅔%). This percentage, by definition, will fall between 0% and 100%.

Under the DRF method, the fixed-point and yield maintenance penalties are distributed first to the holders of the regular bond classes (based on the preceding formula) and then to the IO class. The IO would receive any remaining penalty amount after the regular class payments had been satisfied. In general, the IO receives a greater share relative to the regular classes as discount rates rise.

For the **PV yield loss amount (PVYLA) method,** let B equal the coupon of a regular bond class in percent (for example, 7%); X equal the coupon of the IO class in percent (for example, 1.5%); D equal the discount rate (see definition under DRF method) in percent (for example, 6%); P equal the prepayment amount in dollars (for example, $1,000,000); N equal the number of years between prepayment date and assumed final payment date (for example, 3.5 years); and A equal the annuity factor.

Then, let

$$A = \frac{1 - (1 + D)^{-N}}{D}$$

For example,

$$\frac{1-(1+0.06)^{-3.5}}{0.06} = 3.075$$

Lost coupon amount $(LC) = P \times (B - D)$ for the regular bond class;
$P \times X$ for the IO class

For example,

$$\$1,000,000 \times (7\% - 6\%) = \$10,000 \text{ for the regular bond}$$
$$\$1,000,000 \times 1.5\% = \$15,000 \text{ for the IO}$$

Then, the prepayment premium allocated to each class will equal

$$\text{Premium allocation amount} = LC \times A$$

For example,

$$\$10,000 \times 3.075 = \$30,748 \text{ for the regular bond}$$
$$\$15,000 \times 3.075 = \$46,122 \text{ for the IO}$$

Under PVYLA allocation, the IO class and the regular classes receive pro rata a portion of the penalties calculated as shown in the preceding formula. Any prepayment penalty amount remaining after the pro rata payments have been satisfied is paid to the IO class.

Under the third method, the **straight percentage method,** the prepayment premiums are allocated among the regular classes and the IO class on a simple, predefined fixed percentage. For example, the regular classes may receive 25% of the prepayment penalty premiums while the IO receives 75%.

Most deals utilize the DRF method. However, many deals use a blend of these three methods for allocating the different types of penalties. For example, in the KEY 2000-C1 deal, 75% of the fixed-point penalties are distributed to the IO class with the remainder going to the sequential classes. The yield maintenance penalties, however, are distributed to the IO class after the sequential classes are satisfied under the DRF method.

Optional Redemption   One other structural feature that affects the value of the IO is the percentage of outstanding principal relative to the original balance at which the deal can be called by the issuer. For most deals, this percentage is equal to 1% of the original balance, but can be as high as 5% for some transactions. The earlier the issuer has the right to call (i.e., the higher the percentage), the sooner the IO can be terminated, decreasing the IO certificate holder's yield. This factor usually does not affect IO yield calculations, but we highlight the point to make investors aware to watch out for any deal that has an earlier call percentage.

17.2 SCENARIO ANALYSIS TO QUANTIFY IO CASH FLOW UNCERTAINTY

Because of their potential cash flow volatility, CMBS IO investors use a variety of different prepayment and default assumptions to price IOs. As the CMBS market is a relatively new market, there is a lack of historical data, which makes it difficult to settle on precise expectations for these assumptions. We examined the historical data available to us to help define a range of reasonable assumptions under which to produce IO cash flows for a selected set of 78 CMBS IOs and to quantify their volatility (refer to Appendix 17B for details of the selection of the scenario assumptions). We settled on 81 scenarios consisting of various combinations of prepayments (0% CPR,[2] 50% CPY,[3] 100% CPY), defaults (1% CDR,[4] 2% CDR, 3% CDR), loss severity (20%, 35%, 50%), and timing of loss (immediate, 12 months, 24 months) in addition to a zero loss, zero prepayment case and the base-case pricing scenario. Exhibit 17.4 summarizes these parameter values while Exhibit 17.5 describes in more detail six scenarios commonly used by investors.

A criticism of this analysis is that under a particular scenario, all loans within a deal are treated equally in the application of the assumptions, without taking into account loan-specific information or overall pool leverage. A more robust scenario analysis would take current loan and property characteristics such as loan age, coupon, debt service coverage, and local real estate market conditions into account when applying assumptions.

The set of CMBS IOs selected for analysis in this chapter include WAC IOs from public conduit, seasoned loan, and lease-backed CMBS transactions issued from January 1997 through August 2000. The IOs are listed in

---

[2] CPR refers to a constant prepayment rate that is applied annually to the outstanding pool balance.
[3] CPY refers to a constant prepayment rate following the yield maintenance period.
[4] CDR refers to a constant default rate that is applied annually to the outstanding pool balance.

EXHIBIT 17.4 Parameters of CMBS IO Scenario Analysis

Parameters	Values
Prepayment Speed	0% CPR, 50% CPY, 100% CPY
Default Rate	0%, 1%, 2%, 3% CDR
Loss Severity	20%, 35%, 50%
Lockout Before Loss	0, 12, 24 months
Loss Recovery Period	12 months
Balloon Extension	None
Call Exercised	Yes
Total Combinations	83 (including base case)

Source: Salomon Smith Barney.

EXHIBIT 17.5 Commonly Used Investor Pricing Scenarios

Scenario	Description	Comments
(Base) 0% CDR and 100% CPY	Zero defaults, no prepayments during the lock-out and yield maintenance period, followed by a prepayment in full.	Used by investors as a base line case and as the pricing scenario within this report.
(A) 0% CDR and 0% CPR	Zero defaults and zero prepayments	Although unrealistic, this scenario provides a counterbalance to the 100% CPY case with **many investors using the difference between the two as a prepayment exposure measure referred to as slope.**
(B) 0% CDR for 24 months, 2% CDR thereafter and 100% CPY	Zero defaults for the first 2 years, followed by a 2% constant default rate at a 35% loss severity over a 12 month recovery period with no prepayments during the lock-out and yield maintenance periods, followed by a prepayment in full.	A constant default rate of 2% per year (2% CDR) implies a cumulative default rate of over 20% after 10 years, which we view as a possible scenario.
(C) 0% CDR for 24 months, 3% CDR thereafter and 100% CPY	Zero defaults for the first 2 years, followed by a 3% constant default rate at a 35% loss severity over a 12 month recovery period with no prepayments during the lock-out and yield maintenance periods, followed by a prepayment in full.	A constant default rate of 3% per year (3% CDR) implies a cumulative default rate of over 30% after 10 years, which we view as a less likely, but possible, scenario.
(D) 0% CDR for 24 months, 3% CDR thereafter and 50% CPY	Zero defaults for the first 2 years, followed by a 3% constant default rate at a 35% loss severity over a 12 month recovery period with no prepayments during the lock-out and yield maintenance periods, followed by a prepayment rate of 50% CPR.	This scenario provides a prepayment counterbalance to case C, and helps with assessing the underlying structural features of the IO.
(E) 0% CDR for 24 months, 3% CDR thereafter and 0% CPR	Zero defaults for the first 2 years, followed by a 3% constant default rate at a 35% loss severity over a 12 month recovery period with zero prepayments.	This scenario provides a prepayment counterbalance to cases C and D, and helps with assessing the underlying structural features of the IO.

CDR: Constant default rate, CPR: Constant prepayment rate, CPY: Constant prepayment rate following yield maintenance period.
Source: Salomon Smith Barney.

Exhibit 17.6 with relevant structural information and the original pricing spread, if known. We excluded single asset/issuer IOs as these deals are very event sensitive (i.e., they either receive all of the collateral cash flow or there is a single default). Also, because single asset/issuer transactions are usually backed by higher quality real estate at a low leverage, they have a very low probability of early prepayment. Typically, the IO and the lower-rated classes will price very tight to regular triple-A CMBS. The triple-A classes from these transactions, however, still price wide of other triple-A CMBS.

A review of the basic CMBS IO characteristics highlights several interesting trends. First, the contribution from senior classes to the IO has been steadily decreasing since 1998. This infers that more recently issued IOs may have more volatility than earlier issued ones. Secondly, while pool WAC has varied with interest rates, IO WAC has steadily declined. This indicates that issuers are trying to minimize IO spread because of its high cost.

Analysis of the CMBS IOs under the 82 Scenarios

In our analysis, we computed the yield loss (give-up) or gain (pick-up) for each IO under each of the 82 scenarios relative to a base case-pricing scenario of 100% CPY, and then determined the mean and standard deviation yield change across the scenarios. First, we priced the CMBS IOs as of October 31, 2000, under the base case scenario (100% CPY, 0% CDR) using each bond's original pricing spread. If the original pricing spread was not known, we used the average spread for the bond's issuance year (1997—215bp, 1998—340bp, 1999—389bp, 2000—374bp). We then used the resulting base case price to determine each IO's yields and spreads under each of the 82 scenarios described previously. Then we computed the difference between each scenario yield and the base case yield and calculated a mean and standard deviation for each IO.

Exhibit 17.7 is a plot of the mean versus standard deviation of the yield differences. The points further along the x-axis represent IOs with greater cash flow uncertainty (higher x-values have higher volatility). The points in the positive portion of the y-axis are IOs that, on average across the 82 scenarios, have gained yield relative to the base case while those in the negative portion of the y-axis have lost yield.

From Exhibit 17.7, we note three groups of IOs. The majority is clustered together where each averages a loss of approximately 150bp of yield, with a standard deviation of 100bp. The second group includes those that, on average, gain yield relative to the base case, although with greater cash flow volatility than the first group. The third group includes those that lose more yield, on average, than the first group, and additionally, have greater cash flow uncertainty.

EXHIBIT 17.6 Basic CMBS IO Characteristics Sorted by Transaction Issuance Date (as of October 31, 2000)

		IO Notional		Collateral					Percentage Contribution to IO Cashflow[a]			Current	IO Portion of Prepay Penalties[b]		Optional	Original Pricing
		Amt ($MM)	DSCR	WAM	WALA	GWAC	NWAC	Senior (%)	Mezzanine (%)	Junior (%)	Coupon	Fixed Pts	Yld Maint	Call (%)	Spread
2000 Average								**65.9**	**5.9**	**28.2**	**0.553**				**374**
GMACC 2000-C2	X	772.9	1.34	113	7	8.325	8.248	80.7	6.2	13.1	0.810	DRF	DRF	1	355
SBM7 2000-C2	X	780.4	1.33	114	10	8.295	8.234	73.0	6.7	20.2	0.847	DRF	DRF	1	370
DLJCM 2000-CF1	S	884.4	1.32	114	7	8.401	8.347	75.3	7.1	17.7	0.746			1	376
KEY 2000-C1	X	814.0	1.30	112	12	8.190	8.123	66.0	7.3	26.7	0.470	75%	DRF	1	384
PNC 2000-C1	X	798.4	1.35	110	14	8.103	8.001	66.0	7.9	26.0	0.477	DRF	DRF	1	400
CCMSC 2000-C2	X	737.2	1.45	113	6	8.339	8.272	71.9	6.5	21.6	0.697			1	366
SBM7 2000-C1	X	711.0	1.34	115	14	8.191	8.058	66.9	13.6	19.4	0.613	DRF	DRF	1	345
FUNB 2000-C1	IO	774.3	1.27	122	9	8.299	8.240	58.3	4.0	37.7	0.530	75%	DRF	1	400
CCMSC 2000-C1	X	694.4	1.35	106	10	8.357	8.292	65.2	8.6	26.2	0.629			1	380
GMACC 2000-C1	X	876.4	1.36	108	11	8.333	8.248	73.2	5.7	21.1	0.564	DRF	DRF	1	390
BSCMS 2000-WF1	X	881.7	1.59	108	12	7.959	7.903	57.2	2.1	40.7	0.243	DRF	DRF	1	349
HMAC 2000-PH1	X	951.8	1.37	111	14	8.022	7.961	53.8	1.6	44.5	0.298	75%	DRF	1	350
JPMC 2000-C9	X	808.9	1.42	103	14	8.074	7.976	52.1	1.7	46.2	0.376	100%	DRF	NA	395
1999 Average								**71.8**	**5.3**	**22.9**	**0.618**				**389**
FUNB 1999-C4	IO	880.7	1.29	105	14	8.005	7.948	72.9	3.9	23.2	0.636	75%	DRF	1	
PNC 1999-CM1	S	754.9	1.36	106	15	7.983	7.898	77.3	5.5	17.2	0.579	DRF	DRF	1	370
NLFC 1999-2	X	1,068.0	1.62	83	39	7.775	7.634	61.8	3.7	34.5	0.699	DRF	DRF	1	
CCMSC 1999-C2	X	777.0	1.43	111	12	8.135	8.071	73.0	9.6	17.5	0.907	100%		1	360
CSFB 1999-C1	AX	1,159.1	1.67	106	19	8.036	7.975	78.7	5.5	15.8	0.664	75%	DRF	1	390
MLMI 1999-C1	IO	587.8	1.47	103	16	7.990	7.925	69.3	4.7	26.0	0.429	75%	DRF	1	
CMAT 1999-C2	X[c]	767.4	1.54	130	25	7.893	7.839	49.7	3.6	46.7	0.418			1	
DLJCM 1999-CG3	S	891.8	1.47	108	15	8.042	7.988	78.3	4.5	17.3	0.652	DRF	DRF	1	375
GMACC 1999-C3	X	1,141.8	1.40	104	17	7.896	7.786	81.7	2.1	16.2	0.532	DRF	DRF	1	410
BSCMS 1999-CLF1	X	312.0	1.04	227	22	7.307	7.189	92.5	6.7	0.8	0.124	DRF[d]	DRF[d]		
CMFUN 1999-1	X	1,384.3	1.34	113	17	7.684	7.625	58.1	0.9	41.0	0.311	75%	DRF	1	
SBM7 1999-C1	X	722.6	1.51	109	25	7.255	7.157	58.3	0.1	41.5	0.036	DRF	DRF	1	
JPMC 1999-C8	X	721.6	1.55	103	20	7.542	7.447	23.4	0.0	76.6	0.215	DRF	DRF	1	400

[a] The percentage contribution to IO cash flow is computed by multiplying a bond's current face amount by the difference between its passthrough rate and the net WAC of the collateral. This dollar-coupon amount is totaled and the percentages for the senior classes (AAA), mezzanine classes (AA through BBB–), and junior classes (below BBB–) are calculated.

[b] Under the IO portion of prepay penalties columns, DRF refers to the Discount Rate Fraction method where the IO receives penalties remaining after the sequential classes are satisfied, and PVYLA refers to the PV Yield Loss Amount method where the IO receives penalties pro-rata with the sequential classes.

[c] Strip of all classes less $48mm of A1.

[d] IO receives 40% of penalties after sequential classes.

(continued)

EXHIBIT 17.6 (Continued)

		IO Notional	Collateral					Percentage Contribution to IO Cashflow[a]			Current	IO Portion of Prepay Penalties[b]		Optional	Original Pricing
		Amt ($MM)	DSCR	WAM	WALA	GWAC	NWAC	Senior (%)	Mezzanine (%)	Junior (%)	Coupon	Fixed Pts	Yld Maint	Call (%)	Spread
PSSF 1999-C2	AEC1	853.6	1.62	109	21	7.606	7.540	75.1	3.0	21.9	0.347	75%[c]	DRF[c]	1	
CMAC 1999-C1	X	723.8	1.58	105	19	7.737	7.637	79.3	6.7	14.0	0.615	75%	DRF	1	365
MSC 1999-CAM1	X	778.9	1.49	113	37	7.671	7.477	84.0	2.8	13.3	0.586	75%	DRF	1	400
BSCMS 1999-WF2	X	1,061.3	1.97	112	20	7.236	7.183	63.9	1.3	34.8	0.260	75%	DRF	1	345
DLJCM 1999-CG2	S	1,531.3	1.46	108	19	7.661	7.658	63.5	3.1	33.4	0.455	DRF	DRF	1	385
PMAC 1999-C1	X	689.2	1.57	111	23	7.402	7.296	71.7	3.3	25.1	0.595	75%	DRF	1	390
HFCMC 1999-PH1	X	991.1	1.48	102	24	7.174	7.106	78.8	1.6	19.6	0.331	75%	DRF	1	350
FUNCM 1999-C2	IO	1,162.7	1.43	111	22	7.360	7.286	73.7	6.5	19.8	0.706	75%	DRF	1	
JPMC 1999-C7	X	785.8	1.72	95	27	7.221	7.131	74.6	6.3	19.2	0.693	DRF	DRF	1	420
MSC 1999-FNV1	X	621.8	1.59	101	24	7.628	7.499	74.4	8.9	16.8	0.979	DRF	DRF	1	
DLJCM 1999-CG1	S	1,219.8	1.59	103	22	7.321	7.271	73.2	12.5	14.3	0.889	DRF	DRF	1	435
PSSF 1999-NRF1	AEC	896.2	1.62	103	25	7.360	7.298	75.8	7.9	16.3	0.859	75%	DRF	1	425
COMM 1999-1	X	1,289.1	1.54	95	26	7.145	7.104	67.4	7.7	24.9	0.716	DRF	DRF	1	415
NLFC 1999-L1	X	474.4	0.87	206	35	7.484	7.341	71.1	11.8	17.1	0.534	DRF	DRF	1	
MSC 1999-RM1	X	831.6	1.57	104	26	7.179	7.071	75.7	5.3	19.0	0.420	DRF	DRF	1	
NLFC 1999-1	X	1,198.4	1.66	97	25	7.268	7.105	80.4	8.8	10.8	0.733	DRF	DRF	1	
MSC 1999-WF1	X	943.2	1.88	101	27	7.065	7.007	82.2	7.4	10.5	0.835	DRF	DRF	1	
BSCMS 1999-C1	X	467.2	1.85	114	23	7.139	7.082	79.4	9.4	11.2	1.053	DRF	DRF	1	
FUNCM 1999-C1	IO1	1,138.5	1.43	123	26	7.047	7.002	73.8	7.1	19.1	0.948	DRF	DRF	1	375
GSMS 1999-C1	X	869.5	1.53	103	26	7.202	7.118	76.9	5.5	17.6	0.961	DRF	DRF	1	
1998 Average			**1.55**	**101**	**32**	**7.449**	**7.335**	**76.1**	**9.6**	**14.3**	**0.893**	**DRF**	**DRF**	**1**	**340**
MCF 1998-MC3	X	872.6	1.59	89	30	7.468	7.317	76.0	6.4	17.5	0.971	DRF	DRF	1	
MLMI 1998-C3	IO	621.8	1.50	113	26	7.085	6.978	80.2	8.1	11.7	1.001	DRF	DRF	1	
DLJCM 1998-CF2	S	1,081.4	1.69	104	25	7.117	7.067	77.5	6.6	15.9	0.853	100%	DRF	1	435
NLFC 1998-2	X	1,529.9	1.59	96	29	7.247	7.107	78.5	2.9	18.6	0.704	PVYLA	PVYLA	1	
MSC 1998-HF2	X	1,031.4	1.51	102	30	7.231	7.172	77.4	3.8	18.7	0.733	DRF	DRF	1	
MSC 1998-CF1	X	1,064.5	1.52	108	31	7.600	7.488	81.5	7.5	10.9	0.828	DRF[f]	DRF[f]	1	475

		IO Notional	Collateral					Percentage Contribution to IO Cashflow[a]			Current	IO Portion of Prepay Penalties[e]		Optional	Original Pricing
		Amt ($MM)	DSCR	WAM	WALA	GWAC	NWAC	Senior (%)	Mezzanine (%)	Junior (%)	Coupon	Fixed Pts	Yld Maint	Call (%)	Spread
PSSF 1998-C1	AEC	1,099.2	1.61	106	31	7.413	7.340	71.8	8.6	19.6	0.792	75%	DRF	1	325
CMAC 1998-C1	X	1,119.9	1.70	104	32	7.410	7.386	74.8	10.1	15.1	0.830	DRF	DRF	1	
BSCMS 1998-C1	X	694.3	1.78	106	30	7.280	7.222	76.3	10.7	13.0	0.797	DRF	DRF	1	
DLJCM 1998-CG1	S	1,521.2	1.66	104	31	7.210	7.150	85.0	8.5	6.6	0.699	DRF	DRF	1	275
MSC 1998-WF2	X	1,028.2	1.72	108	31	7.258	7.201	77.6	9.8	12.6	0.671	DRF	DRF	1	245
MCF 1998-MC1	X	1,256.0	1.58	85	34	7.487	7.360	70.5	11.0	18.4	0.713	DRF	DRF	1	
MLMI 1998-C1	IO	615.9	NA	215	37	7.468	7.423	68.9	14.9	16.2	0.875	DRF	DRF	1	
MLMI 1998-C2	IO	1,038.0	1.48	95	36	7.959	7.854	74.3	13.0	12.7	1.440	DRF	DRF	1	
MSC 1998-HF1	X	1,198.9	1.65	92	35	7.655	7.569	76.9	12.8	10.3	1.003	DRF	DRF	1	350
NLFC 1998-1	X1	679.9	1.65	78	35	7.697	7.539	100.0	0.0	0.0	1.119	PVYLA[g]	PVYLA[g]	1	
NLFC 1998-1	X2	305.6	1.65	78	35	7.697	7.539	0.0	42.5	57.5	1.166	PVYLA[g]	PVYLA[g]	1	275
LBCMT 1998-C1	IO	1,664.2	1.47	99	35	7.600	7.477	72.6	12.5	15.0	0.999	DRF	DRF	1	
MSC 1998-WF1	X1	1,326.1	1.69	87	35	7.758	7.700	76.9	12.7	10.3	0.606	DRF	DRF	1	
1997 Average			**1.53**	**94**	**44**	**8.563**	**8.449**	**68.4**	**17.2**	**14.4**	**1.465**				**215**
MSC 1997-ALIC	IO	558.2	1.46	87	99	9.296	9.242	41.9	30.1	28.0	2.723	DRF	DRF	5	
MLMI 1997-C2	IO	663.1	1.65	107	36	7.866	7.774	72.1	13.5	14.4	1.232	DRF	DRF	1	
CCMSC 1997-C2	X	744.3	1.54	84	38	8.142	8.044	70.2	18.3	11.5	1.474	75%	DRF	4	
MCF 1997-MC2	X	843.1	1.68	81	38	8.232	8.047	71.4	15.4	13.2	1.364	PVYLA	PVYLA	1	
FULB 1997-C2	IO	2,110.3	1.38	116	38	8.208	8.092	75.3	14.1	10.6	1.380	DRF	DRF	1	
GMACC 1997-C1	X	1,531.9	1.55	102	44	8.617	8.518	70.1	17.6	12.3	1.617	DRF	DRF	1	220
JPMC 1997-C5	X	951.0	1.67	92	42	8.760	8.676	65.8	15.7	18.5	1.530	100%	DRF	1	
AMR 1997-C1	X	439.1	1.63	71	45	8.745	8.620	68.6	17.5	13.9	1.461	75%	DRF	1	
CCMSC 1997-C1	X	469.6	1.58	83	45	8.900	8.796	68.4	19.8	11.9	1.434	75%	DRF	4	210
MCF 1997-MC1	X	618.9	1.45	73	44	8.782	8.569	67.1	16.2	16.7	1.327	80%	80%	1	
MLMI 1997-C1	IO	1,043.3	1.50	90	45	8.897	8.856	68.8	19.0	12.2	1.317	80%	DRF	1	
FULB 1997-C1	IO	1,219.1	1.42	90	44	8.711	8.560	67.5	17.1	15.4	1.248	PVYLA	PVYLA	1	
MSC 1997-C1	IO1	539.8	1.70	80	48	8.973	8.830	59.7	19.3	21.1	1.337	75%	75%	3	

e Penalties are split between the two IO classes with 85% going to AEC1.

f IO receives penalties from loan group one only.

g Penalties are split between X1 and X2 based on outstanding balances.

Source: Salomon Smith Barney and Intex Solutions.

EXHIBIT 17.7   CMBS IO Yield Volatility

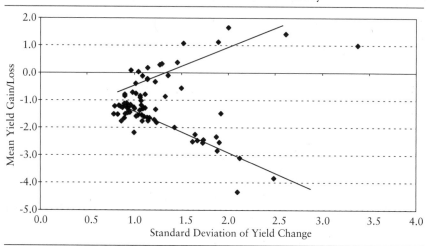

Source: Salomon Smith Barney and Intex Solutions.

We examine one IO from each of these three groups in Exhibit 17.8. This figure includes results of the pricing scenario; spreads for the other five commonly used investor scenarios as discussed in Exhibit 17.5; the mean, standard deviation and maximum yield loss from the 82 scenarios; and each IO's yield slope.[5]

FULB 1997-C1 is an IO that exhibits a better than average cash flow characteristic. It gains, on average, 0.4% in yield. This IO benefits greatly from slower prepayments (for example, scenarios A and E). With zero prepayments and zero defaults (scenario A), the spread to treasury is 527bp, an increase from 215bp in the base case for a yield slope of 312bp. The gain is expected since the average life extends with no prepayments from 5.5 to 6.5 years, but the magnitude of over 300bp is quite large. Even under the extreme 3% CDR case with no prepayments (scenario E is one sample), the spread increases to 401bp. We note that at a reasonably severe 2% CDR and 100% CPY (scenario B), the yield is still a respectable 7.207%, a spread of 140bp above treasuries and a drop of 75bp from the base case. The maximum yield loss experienced by this IO under any one scenario is 290bp (100% CPY, 3% CDR, 50% loss, immediate).

---

[5] Yield slope refers to the change in yield between the 0% CPR and the 100% CPY scenarios.

EXHIBIT 17.8 Example of 3 IOs with Different Cash Flow Characteristics (as of October 31, 2000)

		Base Scenario - 100% CPY, 0% CDR				Selected Scenarios[a]					Yield Change Across Scenarios			
		Price[b]	WAL	Yield	Spread	A	B	C	D	E	Mean	Std Dev	Max[c]	Slope
Moderate Yield Gain and High Volatility														
FULB 1997-C1	IO	5.565	5.48	7.958	215	Spread 527	140	102	267	401	0.4	1.5	-2.9	3.1
						WAL 6.51	5.34	5.28	5.68	6.15				
Average Yield Loss and Average Volatility														
SBM7 2000-C2	X	5.644	8.64	9.474	370	Spread 390	265	203	220	222	-1.5	0.9	-4.0	0.2
						WAL 8.77	8.31	8.15	8.24	8.25				
High Yield Loss and High Volatility														
CMAT 1999-C2	X	3.479	9.60	9.654	389	Spread 399	181	62	67	68	-2.8	1.9	-8.5	0.1
						WAL 9.69	9.08	8.84	8.90	8.91				

[a] Scenario A: 0% CDR, 0% CPY; B: 2% CDR, 100% CPY, 35% Loss, 24-Month Lag; C: 3% CDR, 100% CPY, 35% Loss, 24-Month Lag; D: 3% CDR, 50% CPY, 35% Loss, 24-Month Lag; E: 3% CDR, 0% CPY, 35% Loss, 24-Month Lag.
[b] Pricing as of October 31, 2000.
[c] Maximum yield loss.
Source: Salomon Smith Barney and Intex Solutions.

SBM7 2000-C2 is an IO that falls with the majority, losing 1.5% in yield on average with a standard deviation of 0.9%. This IO has a yield slope of only 20bp, and loses yield relative to the base case with no prepayments when defaults are included. The maximum yield loss is 396bp, which occurs in the scenario with 100% CPY, a CDR of 3% starting immediately, and a loss severity of 50%, which is very unlikely. Yet, even at these unlikely levels, the IO still earns a yield of 5.519%. The yield differences occur in a relatively narrow range leading to a low standard deviation, or expected volatility. At a more reasonable 2% CDR with a 35% loss severity, this typical IO still earns 265bp over treasuries. This 265bp spread seems very high given that triple-A 10-year CMBS sells at a 145bp spread.

CMAT 1999-C2 is an IO that loses more yield than the average group and, additionally, has greater volatility. It loses 2.8%, on average, and has a standard deviation of 1.9%. It has a yield slope of only 10bp, and loses 852bp under the worst scenario. This IO is extremely sensitive to the default assumptions an investor chooses to analyze. This transaction had an initial subordination level of 28.5% which is lower than that of the first example (30.0%). This suggests the rating agencies viewed the underlying collateral pool as more stable. Therefore, an investor in this type of collateral should maybe use a lower CDR or loan specific default analysis that accounts for the stronger collateral. This should be taken into account when making an investment in this type of volatile IO.

Yield Volatility

Investors may view Exhibit 17.9 as an IO investment guide. Investments in the moderate yield gain, high volatility category should be viewed as a strong IO investment with potential for some yield increase if certain events transpire. Since there is little certainty that events will kick up the IO yield, we expect that these IOs only price a little tighter than standard IO and represent good value (this premise is supported by how these IOs priced at origination relative to other transactions).

Investors in the average yield loss, average volatility IO classes should consider their yield safe as long as a real estate recession does not transpire in the near term. Review of the expected economic scenarios suggests these IO classes will provide significant excess yield (150bp to 250bp) relative to other triple-A investments even at a 2% CDR and a 100% CPY. It is only under the 3% CDR stress that any of the IO classes really show a significant yield loss. Even so, in most cases, they still have a positive spread to treasuries and investors never had any principal at risk. Given an expected cumulative default rate of approximately 1.8%, these "average" IOs would appear to have extraordinary value.

IOs with above average yield loss and high volatility should price usually with 20bp to 50bp of excess yield. Investors in these classes should do careful cash flow analysis that considers likely possible default scenarios. Investors in these securities are likely sophisticated investors that have sized up the underlying pool as strong credit and consider a real estate recession as unlikely in the near term. Many of the "low leverage" conduits fall into this category, as they are likely to have less defaults and limited loss severity. A more appropriate analysis for the low leverage conduits would use a lower default probability to reflect their higher credit quality. None the less, we would recommend that investors in these pools evaluate the collateral as a few unexpected defaults could significantly cut into the IO yield.

17.3 SUMMARY

IOs from CMBS deals have radically different investment characteristics from single-family residential MBS IOs. They have little of the negative convexity associated with standard IOs, due to severe prepayment restrictions, and can actually benefit from speeds as a result of receiving a share of prepayment penalties. The major risk for CMBS IOs is from a severe recession and a high level of defaults, which could cause IO yields to fall. However, it would require a severe recession to cause IO yields to decrease to the spread yield of short-term fixed rate triple-A CMBS certificates.

EXHIBIT 17.9 Public CMBS IO Scenario Analysis—Pricing Scenario, Spreads under 5 Common Evaluation Scenarios, and Statistics across 82 Scenarios (as of October 31, 2000)

		Base Scenario – 100% CPY, 0% CDR			Spread Under Selected Scenarios [a]					Yield Change Across Scenarios			
		Price[b]	WAL	Yield Spread	A	B	C	D	E	Mean	Std Dev	Max[c]	Slope
Moderate Yield Gain and High Volatility														
AMR 1997-C1	X	5.488	4.26	7.990	215	687	177	158	445	608	1.6	2.0	-2.2	4.7
MSC 1997-C1	IO1	5.122	4.27	7.989	215	809	138	100	312	691	1.4	2.6	-3.1	5.9
MCF 1997-MC1	X	5.625	4.34	7.987	215	625	161	133	409	531	1.1	1.9	-3.3	4.1
NLFC 1998-1	X1	4.804	5.02	9.213	340	678	298	277	496	608	1.1	1.5	-2.6	3.4
BSCMS 1999-CLF1	X	0.616	10.58	9.651	389	1084	231	143	341	887	1.0	3.4	-5.3	6.9
FULB 1997-C1	IO	5.565	5.48	7.958	215	527	140	102	267	401	0.4	1.5	-2.9	3.1
MLMI 1997-C1	IO	5.695	4.56	7.979	215	496	144	109	246	387	0.3	1.3	-2.3	2.8
MCF 1997-MC2	X	6.544	5.63	7.956	215	467	156	128	298	368	0.3	1.3	-2.8	2.5
CCMSC 1997-C2	X	6.792	5.86	7.954	215	450	156	123	238	358	0.2	1.1	-2.3	2.3
CCMSC 1997-C1	X	6.411	5.71	7.906	210	393	154	127	256	309	0.1	1.0	-2.2	1.8
JPMC 1997-C5	X	6.794	5.59	7.957	215	418	147	112	241	312	0.0	1.0	-2.4	2.0
Average Yield Loss and Average Volatility														
MSC 1998-WF1	X1	4.138	6.01	9.202	340	590	260	217	357	460	-0.1	1.4	-3.7	2.5
MLMI 1998-C2	IO	6.768	6.19	9.201	340	549	269	232	340	428	-0.1	1.1	-2.8	2.1
GMACC 1997-C1	X	7.627	6.43	7.998	220	430	134	89	204	294	-0.2	1.1	-3.1	2.1
LBCMT 1998-C1	IO	4.979	6.56	9.197	340	548	250	205	326	409	-0.2	1.1	-3.1	2.1
MCF 1998-MC1	X	3.469	6.15	9.201	340	540	258	218	352	413	-0.3	1.2	-3.7	2.0
MSC 1997-ALIC	IO	11.774	5.19	7.961	215	390	116	79	171	270	-0.4	1.0	-2.6	1.7
FULB 1997-C2	IO	7.053	6.77	7.944	215	482	70	-9	128	260	-0.6	1.5	-4.0	2.7
GSMS 1999-C1	X	5.127	7.08	9.681	389	519	298	251	338	376	-0.7	1.0	-3.4	1.3
PSSF 1999-C2	AEC1	1.938	7.48	9.677	389	528	289	240	330	375	-0.8	1.0	-3.3	1.4
MSC 1998-HF1	X	4.940	6.31	9.299	350	508	255	202	277	346	-0.8	1.1	-3.7	1.6
MLMI 1997-C2	IO	6.521	7.03	7.942	215	332	120	71	132	183	-0.8	0.9	-3.2	1.2
NLFC 1999-1	X	4.086	7.12	9.681	389	525	297	247	322	371	-0.8	1.1	-3.6	1.4
MLMI 1998-C3	IO	5.339	7.79	9.184	340	447	242	191	263	294	-0.8	0.9	-3.1	1.1
MSC 1998-CF1	X	4.201	7.06	10.541	475	666	355	287	390	472	-0.9	1.3	-4.5	1.9
JPMC 1999-C7	X	3.481	6.84	9.994	420	539	322	273	357	381	-0.9	1.1	-3.9	1.2
MCF 1998-MC3	X	4.832	6.62	9.196	340	445	242	191	272	291	-1.0	1.1	-4.0	1.0
CMAC 1999-C1	X	3.729	7.69	9.435	365	433	267	218	270	282	-1.1	0.9	-3.8	0.7
DLJCM 1999-CG3	S	4.094	8.08	9.530	375	444	273	222	276	288	-1.1	0.9	-3.6	0.7
SBM7 2000-C1	X	4.219	8.37	9.227	345	401	249	189	230	244	-1.2	0.9	-3.8	0.6
CMAC 1998-C1	X	4.587	7.18	9.190	340	418	231	173	229	244	-1.2	1.0	-3.9	0.8
PNC 1999-CM1	S	3.787	7.93	9.482	370	442	262	204	260	270	-1.2	0.9	-3.6	0.7
MSC 1998-HF2	X	3.938	7.27	9.189	340	436	236	179	229	272	-1.2	1.1	-4.3	1.0
MSC 1999-FNV1	X	5.572	7.51	9.677	389	439	294	247	283	291	-1.2	0.8	-3.4	0.5
GMACC 2000-C2	X	5.195	8.61	9.325	355	399	253	202	234	241	-1.2	0.8	-3.2	0.4
GMACC 1999-C3	X	3.417	7.95	9.882	410	452	310	260	296	302	-1.2	0.9	-3.7	0.4
MSC 1999-WF1	X	4.359	7.05	9.681	389	484	271	205	269	298	-1.3	1.1	-4.2	1.0
CSFB 1999-C1	AX	4.040	7.93	9.682	390	455	283	229	278	287	-1.3	0.9	-3.6	0.6
DLJCM 2000-CF1	S	5.057	8.69	9.534	376	436	265	209	256	264	-1.3	0.9	-3.8	0.6
NLFC 1999-2	X	2.834	6.13	9.691	389	416	310	277	296	300	-1.3	1.0	-4.7	0.3
CCMSC 1999-C2	X	5.790	8.39	9.377	360	404	256	203	239	244	-1.3	0.9	-3.7	0.4
DLJCM 1998-CF2	S	4.603	7.31	10.139	435	548	301	243	321	357	-1.3	1.1	-4.4	1.1
DLJCM 1999-CG1	S	5.028	7.58	10.136	435	498	326	268	316	327	-1.3	1.0	-4.2	0.6
MSC 1998-WF2	X	3.923	7.37	8.238	245	333	118	53	114	138	-1.3	1.1	-4.6	0.9
MSC 1999-RM1	X	2.417	7.44	9.677	389	506	267	202	253	316	-1.3	1.2	-4.9	1.2
DLJCM 1998-CG1	S	3.919	7.14	8.540	275	368	138	52	125	141	-1.4	1.1	-4.1	0.9
COMM 1999-1	X	3.806	7.15	9.940	415	460	307	258	299	304	-1.4	0.9	-3.9	0.5
GMACC 2000-C1	X	3.791	8.35	9.678	390	432	275	217	251	255	-1.4	1.0	-4.0	0.4
SBM7 2000-C2	X	5.644	8.64	9.474	370	390	265	203	220	222	-1.5	0.9	-4.0	0.2

(continued)

EXHIBIT 17.9 (Continued)

		Base Scenario - 100% CPY, 0% CDR				Spread Under Selected Scenarios [a]					Yield Change Across Scenarios			
		Price[b]	WAL	Yield	Spread	A	B	C	D	E	Mean	Std Dev	Max[c]	Slope
NLFC 1998-1	X2	6.458	6.82	8.544	275	408	152	93	203	203	-1.5	1.9	-8.1	1.3
MLMI 1999-C1	IO	3.068	7.90	9.672	389	381	295	237	248	227	-1.5	0.9	-4.0	-0.1
BSCMS 1999-C1	X	6.259	8.38	9.667	389	390	281	227	228	228	-1.5	0.8	-3.2	0.0
BSCMS 1998-C1	X	4.810	8.03	9.181	340	345	231	176	180	181	-1.5	0.8	-3.4	0.1
FUNCM 1999-C1	IO1	5.483	8.16	9.530	375	434	246	180	214	229	-1.5	1.1	-4.7	0.6
CCMSC 2000-C1	X	4.239	8.27	9.578	380	422	257	193	227	232	-1.6	1.0	-4.5	0.4
CCMSC 2000-C2	X	4.756	8.78	9.433	366	402	244	173	201	204	-1.6	1.0	-4.3	0.4
PNC 2000-C1	X	3.508	8.10	9.780	400	449	271	204	241	249	-1.6	1.1	-4.8	0.5
FUNCM 1999-C2	IO	4.291	7.92	9.672	389	439	260	190	225	237	-1.6	1.1	-5.0	0.5
FUNB 1999-C4	IO	3.899	8.00	9.671	389	437	261	189	224	233	-1.7	1.2	-5.0	0.5
PSSF 1999-NRF1	AEC	4.703	6.88	10.043	425	411	320	268	268	242	-1.7	0.9	-4.1	-0.2
HFCMC 1999-PH1	X	2.004	7.54	9.286	350	398	226	159	198	202	-1.7	1.2	-5.3	0.5
PMAC 1999-C1	X	3.732	7.75	9.684	390	420	259	191	216	217	-1.8	1.1	-5.2	0.4
MLMI 1998-C1	IO	5.592	11.66	9.162	340	340	201	130	130	129	-1.8	0.9	-3.7	0.0
KEY 2000-C1	X	3.200	8.48	9.616	384	403	256	188	204	203	-1.8	1.1	-4.8	0.2
MSC 1999-CAM1	X	2.486	6.84	9.794	400	427	264	192	238	216	-1.8	1.2	-5.5	0.3
High Yield Loss and High Volatility														
DLJCM 1999-CG2	S	3.036	8.02	9.631	385	429	242	166	199	205	-2.0	1.4	-6.6	0.4
PSSF 1998-C1	AEC	4.118	6.66	9.046	325	267	190	117	97	30	-2.2	1.0	-4.6	-0.6
JPMC 2000-C9	X	2.544	7.76	9.734	395	427	237	155	190	178	-2.2	1.6	-7.8	0.3
JPMC 1999-C8	X	1.636	7.46	9.787	400	474	223	133	171	199	-2.3	1.9	-8.6	0.7
SBM7 1999-C1	X	0.525	7.71	9.674	389	458	194	88	143	149	-2.4	1.7	-7.8	0.7
FUNB 2000-C1	IO	3.964	9.07	9.770	400	439	217	103	123	133	-2.5	1.7	-7.2	0.4
HMAC 2000-PH1	X	2.342	8.33	9.278	350	377	159	68	94	89	-2.5	1.6	-7.5	0.3
NLFC 1998-2	X	3.913	6.91	9.193	340	449	122	-1	79	107	-2.5	1.9	-7.6	1.1
CMFUN 1999-1	X	2.300	8.34	9.668	389	419	211	113	127	129	-2.6	1.7	-7.8	0.3
CMAT 1999-C2	X	3.479	9.60	9.654	389	399	181	62	67	68	-2.8	1.9	-8.5	0.1
BSCMS 2000-WF1	X	1.934	7.87	9.273	349	371	146	7	17	18	-3.1	2.1	-8.6	0.2
BSCMS 1999-WF2	X	1.975	7.59	9.236	345	310	103	-44	-51	-103	-3.8	2.5	-10.8	-0.4
NLFC 1999-L1	X	3.291	11.02	9.651	389	391	19	-130	-128	-128	-4.3	2.1	-8.9	0.0

[a] Scenario A: 0% CDR, 0% CPY; B: 2% CDR, 100% CPY, 35% Loss, 24 Month-Lag; C: 3% CDR, 100% CPY, 35% Loss, 24 Month-Lag; D: 3% CDR, 50% CPY, 35% Loss, 24-Month Lag; E: 3% CDR, 0% CPY, 35% Loss, 24-Month Lag.
[b] Pricing as of October 31, 2000.
[c] Maximum yield loss.
Source: Salomon Smith Barney and Intex Solutions.

Given the currently strong real estate fundamentals, we do not anticipate a severe real estate recession in the next downturn. This suggests that
triple-A IO provides triple-B like spreads with no loan principal at risk as
the yield is supported by excess cash flow that has only moderate expected
variability. Overall, while CMBS IO spreads are currently wide on a historic
basis, this sector represents significant relative value for investors willing to
invest in this nonconventional spread product.

APPENDIX 17A
COMMERCIAL MORTGAGES

Voluntary Prepayment Provisions

Commercial mortgages are usually balloon loans, having a 30-year amortization schedule with the balance due after 10 years. Most commercial loans have a complete prohibition (or *lock-out*) on prepayments for several years, and then a penalty period which can consist of one or more mechanisms for deterring early payoff. Following the lock-out and penalty periods, the borrower typically has six months, referred to as the open period, in which to refinance prior to the balloon. The mortgage loan may be structured to offer prepayment flexibility via three mechanisms that are designed to maintain the collateral pool's cash flow or compensate the investor for lost payment:

1. *Fixed-point schedule,* which can be a declining fee proportional to the remaining balance, for example, a "5-4-3-2-1" schedule means that the penalty is equal to 5% of the outstanding loan balance in the first year of the penalty period, is equal to 4% during the second year, and so on.
2. *Yield maintenance,* which means making the lender whole for the loss of an above market coupon on a net present value basis (so that in effect there is generally no economic incentive for the borrower to refinance).
3. *Defeasance,* which means the loan can be prepaid early, but the borrower must replace the property cash flow by pledging to the holder of the mortgage U.S. Treasury securities whose cash flows are equal to or exceed that of the mortgage.

Fixed-point schedules and yield maintenance were commonly used up until 1998. After 1998 most commercial mortgages were structured with defeasance as it maintained the mortgages' original anticipated cash flow and provided certainty to investors. To avoid prepayment costs, some commercial borrowers have defaulted as an exit strategy.

Defaults

The economics of a commercial borrower are driven both by the equity contained in the property and the expected net cash flow of the underlying property. A property that has experienced a decline in revenue or an increase in operating costs will reflect a decreased debt service coverage ratio (DSCR). At some point the borrower may determine that it is advantageous to default on the loan payments if there is negligible equity in the property and significant future cash flow requirements. Alternatively, a property's value may fall because of a change in the economic environment of the surrounding area or because of deferred maintenance issues. This condition may also lead a borrower to default.

Following a payment default, the master servicer of the transaction transfers servicing to a special servicer after 60 days of delinquency. The special servicer must assess the loan/borrower situation with an eye to maximize the loan's net present value. This can involve restructuring the loan with lower interest payments that the property can support or, more typically, liquidation via power of sale or foreclosure and sale. During the workout, the special servicer is required to continue loan advances to the trust subject to the anticipation that loan payment advances will be fully recovered after the loan's liquidation and full repayment of loan proceeds. The proceeds from that liquidation and the timing of the disbursement to the trust are critical to the bondholders.

APPENDIX 17B
SELECTION OF SCENARIO ASSUMPTIONS

Prepayment Assumptions

Commercial loan prepayment speeds are almost impossible to predict. Existing data for loans is inconsistent as early commercial loans allowed prepayment based on points or yield maintenance and only recently (1998) evolved to fully locked out with prepayment via defeasance. The data available to us for analysis reflected only limited data for each prepayment mechanism. In addition, prepayments of commercial mortgages are influenced by a variety of external economic factors such as property value, interest rates, and other economic conditions. Exhibit 17.10 presents quarterly prepayment speeds by

EXHIBIT 17.10   Quarterly Prepayment Speeds by Loan Origination Year

Origination Year	CPR (%) By Quarter								
	Q4 98	Q1 99	Q2 99	Q3 99	Q4 99	Q1 00	Q2 00	Q3 00	Q4 00
1993	22.3	24.8	7.9	16.5	11.1	7.0	6.0	31.7	0.4
1994	13.1	15.8	15.9	12.0	14.6	8.7	8.6	10.0	2.3
1995	0.9	3.8	9.6	5.6	5.2	2.8	3.8	5.8	3.7
1996	0.3	0.8	0.7	2.0	2.8	1.9	2.3	2.6	2.2
1997	0.1	0.1	0.5	0.9	0.7	0.7	0.7	0.8	1.0
1998	0.1	0.0	0.1	0.0	0.6	0.2	0.2	0.2	0.3
1999			0.0	0.0	0.0	0.0	0.0	0.0	0.0

Source: Salomon Smith Barney and Intex Solutions.

loan origination year. Exhibit 17.11 focuses on the more seasoned loans and graphically shows during which stage of prepayment provision the prepayments have occurred. Prepayment speeds appear to be below 3% CPR until loans reach approximately their fifth year, then begin to rise to levels from 5% CPR to over 30% CPR depending on age and loan-specific prepayment provision. Prepayments tend to occur either during the open period or during the fixed-point penalty period. However, in some cases, prepayments have occurred during the yield maintenance period. At this stage of analysis, the few years of defeasance based loans suggest a CPR of less than 2%.

Since the data let us only make a few general comments about prepayments, two extreme assumptions of 0% CPR and 100% CPY, as well as one intermediate value of 50% CPY, seems like a valid starting point. The difference between the yield under the two extreme cases is termed the prepayment slope. We expect analysts will develop a variable CPR rate that changes over time based on research of how the current mortgages respond to various variables.

EXHIBIT 17.11 Prepayment Speeds for Loans Originated from 1993 through 1995

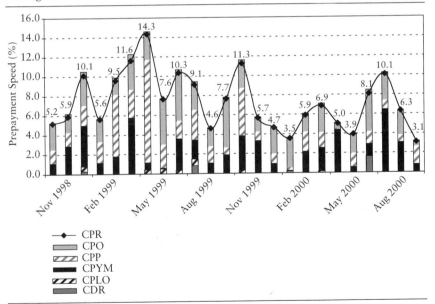

CDR: Prepayment due to default, CPLO: Prepayment during lockout period, CPYM: Prepayment during yield maintenance period, CPP: Prepayment during fixed-point penalty period, CPO: Prepayment during open period, CPR: Total prepayment rate.
Source: Salomon Smith Barney and Intex Solutions.

EXHIBIT 17.12   Loss Severity of Defaulted Loans

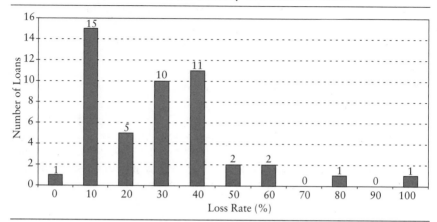

Source: Salomon Smith Barney and Intex Solutions.

Default Assumptions

For establishing a range of default rate assumptions, we reviewed the 1994 Snyderman commercial default study[6] and our recent performance report of the public universe of CMBS data.[7] The Snyderman study tracked 10,955 commercial mortgage loans, originated by eight insurance companies. The study observed a 13.8% default rate over a 5-year period (equivalent to an annual rate of 2.6% CDR[8]) and projected an 18.3% lifetime default rate for the entire pool (1.7% CDR). The study provided further expected lifetime default rates that ranged from 7.6% (1% CDR) to 21.5% (2% CDR), depending on the period studied, the originator, and the lifetime projection method. Our performance report shows that post-1993 CMBS collateral have accrued a 0.6% delinquency after two years, a 1.3% delinquency after three years, and a 1.7% rate after four years. We feel that a reasonable range of default rates for scenario analysis is from 1% to 2% CDR, but we add in 0% and 3% to demonstrate the extreme cases.

---

[6] "Update to Commercial Mortgage Defaults," Mark P. Snyderman, *The Real Estate Finance Journal,* Vol. 10, No. 1, summer 1994.

[7] "SSB Issuer Performance Report," Darrell Wheeler and Jeffrey S. Berenbaum, October 18, 2000.

[8] CDR—Constant default rate.

The assumption for the severity of loss from a resulting liquidation following default is also critical to the analysis of the expected IO cash flow. We reviewed each occurrence of loss in our data set (see Exhibit 17.12). These loss rates typically range from less than 20% to just over 50%. Given this data, we felt that 20%, 35%, and 50% were reasonable values for severity of loss.

The time until default and the recovery period following the default will also effect the IO cash flow. It is beneficial for the IO to have any default put off as long as possible and to have a slow liquidation, as long as the special servicer is advancing payments. Typical default curves show that default rates rise between years 2 and 7. We settled on using immediately allowable defaults as an extreme case as well as delays of 12 months and 24 months before defaults occur. In each of the scenarios we assume a 12-month recovery period for the special servicer to liquidate the underlying properties.

Finally, two other parameters that affect the yield of an IO are the percentage of balloon extensions that may occur and whether or not a deal's optional redemption call is exercised. We used a conservative assumption for each of the scenarios, assuming that there are no balloon extensions, and that the optional redemption call is exercised.

CHAPTER 18

A Guide to Fannie Mae DUS MBSs

Darrell Wheeler

Securitized multifamily Delegated Underwritings and Servicings loans (DUS) have strong prepayment protection and carry the creditworthiness of Fannie Mae. This versatile sector can be used in fixed-income portfolios as (1) Substitutes for convex alternatives, such as corporates, agencies, or Treasuries; (2) higher quality substitutes for non-agency multifamily or commercial MBSs; or (3) alternatives to asset-backed or PACs. To help broaden the understanding of this unique asset class, we have prepared this guide to DUS MBSs, divided into the following sections:

18.1   What Is DUS?
18.2   DUS Loan Characteristics
18.3   The New Alternative DUS REMIC
18.4   Prepayments and Convexity of the MBS
18.5   DUS Relative Value
18.6   Where to Find Information

Fannie Mae's DUS program has been one of the more successful origination programs in the commercial/multifamily arena. Although the program was launched in 1988, securitization of DUS multifamily loans did not begin until 1994. Since then, Fannie Mae DUS securities have gained in popularity with investors, tightening spreads and, in turn, lowering mortgage rates for prospective borrowers. As a result, the DUS MBS niche has grown rapidly and now represents over $27 billion outstanding—small by the standards of the capital markets, but large enough to support good liquidity. With recent DUS/MBS issuance running at annual pace of approximately $5 billion, the sector could grow to a $40 to $50 billion market by 2004.

18.1 WHAT IS DUS?

As implied by the name, Delegated Underwriting and Servicing, Fannie Mae delegates to selected lenders the responsibility for underwriting, closing, and delivering multifamily mortgages *without* Fannie Mae's prior review.[1] In exchange for granting the DUS lender greater autonomy in both underwriting and servicing, Fannie Mae requires: (1) the DUS lender meet strict eligibility requirements, and (2) the DUS lender share in risk of default.

Besides expertise in multifamily lending, DUS lender eligibility requirements include a minimum net worth of $7.5 million, with at least $500,000 in liquid assets. Furthermore, DUS lenders have to maintain a loss reserve as a percentage of their DUS servicing portfolio.

In the event of a default-related loss, the risk sharing arrangement puts the DUS lender at risk with Fannie Mae. The DUS lender bears the first 5% of loss and then shares in the loss up to a cap, set by Fannie Mae, but dependent on lender performance. The most typical cap limits lender losses to 20% of the original loan balance.

DUS servicing compensation varies from 25bp (basis points) to 45bp which appears relatively attractive versus standard conduit servicing fees that range from 4bp to 10bp. However the high servicing fees are also intended to compensate the DUS lender for assuming their loan loss risk. In addition, DUS lenders earn up-front fees at the time of origination. Therefore, originating and servicing DUS mortgages can be highly profitable—if losses are kept to a minimum. Thus, the DUS lenders have a compelling, economic incentive to underwrite prudently and service aggressively. Currently, Fannie Mae has 24 approved DUS lenders (see Exhibit 18.1).

EXHIBIT 18.1 Fannie Mae Approved DUS Loan Originators

Allfirst Mortgage Corporation	Green Park Financial LP
American Property Financing, Inc.	Greystone Servicing Corporation, Inc.
AMI Capital, Inc.	Homestreet Capital
Arbor National Commercial Mortgage LLC	Investment Property Mortgage, LLC
ARCS Commercial Mortgage Co., LP	Key Corp Real Estate Capital Market, Inc.
Berkshire Mortgage Finance LP	Lend Lease Mortgage Capital LP
Capri Capital DUS, LLC	Mercantile Mortgage Corporation
Collateral Mortgage, Ltd.	Midland Mortgage Investment
Continental Wingate Associates, Inc.	PW Funding, Inc.
EF&A Funding, L.L.C.	Reily Mortgage Capital Corporation
Glasser Financial Group, Inc.	Prudential Mortgage Capital Company
GMAC Commercial Mortgage Corp.	Red Capital Markets

Source: Fannie Mae.

---

[1] See *Delegated Underwriting and Servicing/Mortgage Backed Securities (MBS/DUS),* February 1999, Fannie Mae.

EXHIBIT 18.2   Fannie Mae DUS/MBS Issuance (Dollars in Billions)

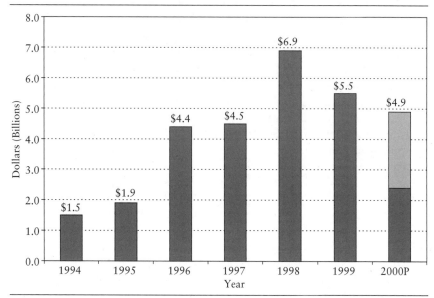

Source: Salomon Smith Barney.

Fannie Mae instituted the DUS program in 1988, initially as a cash program for its own portfolio. Since inception, Fannie Mae has purchased or guaranteed more than $40 billion of multifamily mortgages under the DUS program. DUS securitization did not begin until 1994, when a $1.5 billion of DUS MBSs were issued. Since 1996, securitization has been $4 to $6 billion per year. Exhibit 18.2 shows DUS/MBS annual issuance since 1996. Recent monthly issuance has typically ranged between $250 and $350 million, with heavy issuance activity in December and January. In September of 2000 the current outstanding amount of DUS MBSs was just over $27 billion (which includes DUS on Fannie Mae's balance sheet).

18.2 DUS LOAN AND POOL CHARACTERISTICS

To be eligible for the DUS program, loans must be first liens collateralized by multifamily, cooperatives, or manufactured housing with five or more units. Loans can be to refinance or to purchase a new existing property. They can have either balloon maturity or be fully amortizing (over 25 or 30 years) and must have been closed no more than six months prior to being securitized by Fannie Mae. In most cases, there is one loan per pool, and loan sizes can range between $1 million and $50 million. Generally the loans underlying the DUS/MBS are of a higher quality than regular conduit multifamily loans as Fannie Mae usually has superior mortgage pricing to attract the higher quality multifamily properties. If a group of DUS/MBS have coupons within 100 basis points, Fannie Mae may pool the transactions into one large Fannie Mega pool to lessen administrative costs of managing multiple pools. Among outstanding MBSs, the average loan size is approximately $5.3 million.

DUS loans can vary substantially in terms of their maturities and "lockout" provisions. The different DUS features are:

- *Balloon maturities* are usually 5, 7, 10, 15, or 18 years.
- Most loans have *yield maintenance provision* designed to make the investor whole in the event that a borrower voluntarily prepays. For example, a 10/7 DUS has a 10-year balloon maturity and yield maintenance for the first seven years. After the yield maintenance period expires, the borrower still has to pay a 1% prepayment fee[2] until 90 days prior to maturity, when the loan may be prepaid without penalty.
- Recently, Fannie Mae has also offered borrowers a *defeasance provision* on loan terms less than 10.5 years. Defeasance loan pools achieve better pricing in the securitization market enabling Fannie Mae to offer borrower's a lower cost mortgage if they select this option over the standard yield maintenance prepayment provision.
- *Partial prepayments (curtailments)* are not permitted in the DUS program.
- DUS loans are generally *assumable* with payment of a 1% assumption fee shared equally by the lender and Fannie Mae.

There is approximately $16 billion of 10-year DUS/MBS outstanding making the 10-year loan the most common bond tenure. Most DUS loans have 25- or 30-year amortization schedules. The 10-year mortgages are usually prepayable with yield maintenance until year 9.5 or as with the recent defeasance loans locked out for three or four years with defeasance until year 9.75. Other loan terms account for almost $9 billion in outstanding issuance (e.g., 5-, 15-, and 20-year balloons and 25- and 30-year fully amortizing loans. While Mega pools of grouped DUS mortgages grouped by coupon account for almost $4.5 billion in outstanding issuance. *Overall,*

---

[2] This 1% prepayment penalty is not passed through to the investor and, from the investor's perspective, merely serves as a prepayment deterrent.

the common 10-year loan maturity has created a very homogeneous DUS investment universe, with few pool variables to complicate analysis.

Fannie Mae also offers borrower floating rate loans with a 7- or 10-year term based on either 1 or 3 month LIBOR. These loans usually have a similar yield to the fixed rate mortgages, but give borrowers the option to prepay after a one-year lockout for only a nominal fee. As the mortgage coupon is similar to the fixed mortgage rate, origination of this DUS ARM product is mostly dependant upon borrowers' expectations of future interest rates. With the low interest rates of previous years origination of DUS loans has been low, but the interest rate increase in early 2000 has enabled Fannie Mae to originate more than $400 million in ARM DUS in the first nine months of 2000.

18.3 FANNIE MAE'S NEW ALTERNATIVE DEFEASANCE MULTIFAMILY DUS

As an alternative to traditional DUS mortgages, Fannie Mae has developed a DUS program that gives borrowers the option of opting for defeasance for the life of the loan. The borrower's incentive is a slightly lower coupon than the traditional rate on a "10/9.5" DUS loan.

The new defeasance structure of the loans allows Fannie Mae to guarantee the interest and principal payment on the bonds through to the bond's scheduled maturity regardless of whether a borrower defaults or prepays. This is achieved through the following:

- Voluntary borrower prepayments via defeasance only;
- Fannie Mae's guarantee of defaulted mortgage cash flows as opposed to traditional DUS bonds that could prepay at par in the event of default; and
- Fannie Mae's obligation to replace involuntarily prepaid mortgage cash flows with a new Fannie Mae debt obligation.

In September, Fannie Mae aggregated its first pool of defeasance loans and successfully issued a $510 million noncallable DUS/MBS transaction (FNGT 2000 T5).

Fannie Mae's Underwriting Standards

For underwriting and pricing Fannie Mae ranks loans into one of four leverage tiers based on their debt service coverage ratio (DSCR) and loan to value (LTV). Exhibit 18.3 shows the DSCRs and LTVs in each tier. Tier 1 represents

EXHIBIT 18.3 Credit Tiers in the Fannie Mae DUS Program

Tier	Minimum DSCR	Maximum LTV
I	1.15	80%
II	1.25	80
III	1.35	65
IV	1.55	55

DSCR: Debt service coverage ratio, LTV: Loan to value.
Source: Fannie Mae.

the highest borrower leverage with a DSCR of 1.15X and maximum LTV of 80%, while Tier IV corresponds to the lowest borrower leverage with a minimum DSCR of 1.65X and maximum LTV of 55%. Fannie Mae charges lower guaranty fees for higher Tiers. To date, most loans have been in Tier II. The credit tier is reviewed annually by FNMA and is subject to change.

18.4 PREPAYMENTS AND CONVEXITY OF THE MBS

Traditional DUS have used yield maintenance,[3] prepayment penalties, and lock out periods to discourage prepayment. While the new defeasance based DUS/MBS ensures an early voluntary mortgage prepayment has no impact on the investors cash flows.

Borrower that chooses to voluntarily prepay a DUS loan during the yield maintenance period are assessed a prepayment fee that is the greater of: (1) 1% of the unpaid principal balance; or (2) the unpaid principal balance times the present value of the difference between the mortgage note rate and the yield on a prespecified Treasury. The present value is calculated[4] over the remaining term of the yield maintenance period (not the remaining term of the loan) and uses the current yield of a prespecified Treasury as the discount rate. The reference Treasury issue is set at the time

---

[3] Conceptually, the term "Treasury yield maintenance" implies that an investor should receive in proceeds (from a prepayment) enough to invest in Treasuries and maintain the same yield he would have received had the mortgage not been paid off. It is similar to "Treasury make whole" provisions found in the corporate market.

[4] Present value is calculated using the following formula:

$$\frac{\left(1 - \left(1 + \text{Treasury Yield}\right)^{-n}\right)}{\text{Treasury Yield}}$$

where n is the number of years remaining in the yield maintenance period.

EXHIBIT 18.4   Yield Maintenance Values versus Month of Prepay

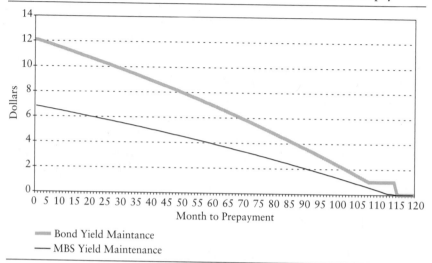

Bond Yield Maintance
MBS Yield Maintenance

Source: Salomon Smith Barney.

of commitment by Fannie Mae and is chosen to be the Treasury with the nearest maturity date to the maturity date of the DUS loan. The reference Treasury for each pool can be found in Schedule A (available with the prospectus supplement).

The DUS MBS investor receives the portion of the yield maintenance calculated by using the pass-through rate of the security rather than the mortgage note rate. While the 1% penalty imposed after the yield maintenance period is not shared with the MBS investor. In essence, the DUS investor is being compensated for the spread over Treasuries that would have been earned had the loan not paid off before the end of the yield maintenance period. Exhibit 18.4 shows the yield maintenance payment (as a percentage of par) versus age for a newly originated 10-year DUS MBS with 9.5 years of yield maintenance[5] (interest rates unchanged). Exhibit 18.4 presents both the total yield maintenance paid by the borrower and the yield maintenance payable to the holder of the DUS MBS. (The difference is shared by FNMA and the lender.)

If the loan prepaid immediately after issue, (zero "Month of Prepay" in Exhibit 18.4), then the yield maintenance owed the MBS investor is equal to about 7 points—at a point when the price of the security is just over par.

---

[5] The DUS MBS in Exhibits 18.4 and 18.5 has the following characteristics: Mortgage note rate 8.26%, pass-through rate 7.49%, reference Treasury yield 6.50%.

The yield maintenance decays over time, but does not go below 0.5 points until after the eighth year. This feature gives DUS MBS excellent convexity.

Voluntary prepayments usually enhance the return of the DUS MBS, because the DUS MBS investor is "called out" at a price above the market price of the MBS, regardless of the level of interest rates. Exhibit 18.5 plots the yield maintenance (as a percentage of par) versus changes in interest rates (up-and-down 100bp) for a 1-year seasoned, 10-year DUS with 9.5 years of original yield maintenance.

The yield maintenance penalty increases as interest rates decline, consistent with the duration of the reference treasury issue. In Exhibit 18.5, the yield maintenance premium to the MBS investor is increased $6.5 for every 100bp decline in the reference treasury. However because DUS MBS trade with modest negative convexity the MBS/Bond will have a price slightly lower than the bond's implied nonconvexity price. So any early yield maintenance prepayment should enhance the investor's overall return.

When interest rates rise, the MBS yield maintenance payment declines, reaching zero near the +100bp scenario (Exhibit 18.5). As interest rates rise further, the DUS MBS investor receives par if the loan prepays, increasing the premium over market. Therefore, if interest rates were to rise more than 100bp, the DUS MBS would require prepayment at par, which

EXHIBIT 18.5   Yield Maintenance Values versus Changes in Interest Rates, April 1997

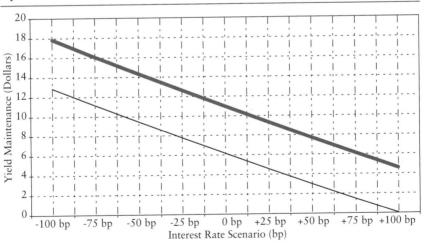

Total Yield Maintenance

- - - - MBS Yield Maintenance

Source: Salomon Smith Barney.

would also enhance the investor's return as the bond would be trading at a discount to par.

Because DUS prepayments have been low, DUS investors usually attribute little value to the potential prepayment penalty collection. In addition some investor's doubt the enforceability and collection of the prepayment penalty. This doubt of the enforceability of the yield maintenance penalty arises from the commercial MBS market in which we have seen borrowers dispute yield maintenance clauses with mixed results. While, Fannie Mae does not have the right to waive the yield maintenance penalty, Fannie Mae *does not guarantee* the yield maintenance. However, we believe the yield maintenance provisions are fairly enforceable for several reasons. First, yield maintenance is an obligation written into the mortgage note. Consequently, if a borrower refuses to pay yield maintenance, the lien on the property will not be released. Second, if a borrower tries to "manufacture" a default, to avoid yield maintenance, Fannie Mae and the DUS servicer have the right to foreclose and take the property. Third, both Fannie Mae and the DUS servicer receive a substantial portion of the penalty, giving them a tangible economic incentive to collect.

As can be seen in both Exhibit 18.4 and 18.5, the total yield maintenance paid by the borrower is a substantial deterrent to prepayment. For example, in the unchanged interest-rate scenario (0bp) in Exhibit 18.5, total yield maintenance paid by the borrower is almost 11 points. If interest rates decline 100bp, the total yield maintenance payment rises above 17 points (Exhibit 18.4).

To date yield maintenance has been an effective prepayment deterrent. Anecdotal evidence suggests that most of these payoffs are from refinancings of existing loans. *When a loan pool does prepay the bond investors have been compensated for the early bond call.* Overall the yield maintenance structure has ensured a fair yield to DUS investors. However, the new defeasance DUS/MBS just adds an additional level of cash flow certainly, which has enabled them to attract investors and price slightly tighter than the traditional yield maintenance pools.

Involuntary Prepayments from Defaults

Only a borrower default is likely to negatively impact a traditional DUS/MBS's cash flow as the investor will not be compensated for the early prepayment. Default-related prepayments are minimized by careful underwriting and the risk sharing arrangement between Fannie Mae and the DUS lenders. As described previously, underwriting criteria require borrowers to have 20% to 45% equity (LTVs of 55% to 80%). More importantly, risk sharing puts the DUS lender's own capital at risk. The delinquency rate on outstanding DUS MBS was 0% on June 30, 2000, which compares favorably with the 0.55% delinquency rate on the $42 billion of multifamily loans contained within public universe of regular CMBS transactions.[6]

Because Fannie Mae guarantees the principal balance of the MBS, a default-related prepayment results in a par payoff to the MBS DUS investor. Similar to other non-DUS MBSs, these prepayments hurt return when the MBS is at a premium and enhance return when the MBS is at a discount. Although defaults are likely to be minimal, investors can reduce the likelihood even further by purchasing MBSs backed by higher tier loans; for example, Tiers III or IV. (Although, as a practical matter, most DUS are Tier II.)

Because most DUS MBS pools consist of a single loan, a loan prepayment of one loan retires the entire principal balance of the security. Hence, investors are more exposed to potential defaults, because of this all-or-none nature of prepayments. To diversify default-related prepayment risk, investors can either build a portfolio of DUS or buy Mega pools. Mega pools were introduced in July 1996 and allow the combination of individual DUS pools into one large pool. Individual fixed-rate DUS pools with coupons within a 100bp range may be pooled into a Mega pool.

18.5 THE NEW NONCALLABLE DUS/MBS OFFER COMPLETE PREPAYMENT PROTECTION

The new noncallable DUS/MBS, such as FNGT 2000 T5, overcomes involuntary prepayment risk as Fannie Mae has agreed to repay any defaulted loan with a new loan thus negating the impact of an early loan default. While voluntary prepayment is prevented via the 10-year term lockout provided by the defeasance only loan feature.

To create additional cash flow certainty the mortgages underlying the new noncallable bonds all mature in the same month, enabling the structure to provide an absolute bullet bond maturity. The new noncallable bond structure consists of a short-term class created from the mortgage pool's scheduled amortization, a 10-year monthly pay bullet class from the balloon payment and an IO to account for any excess interest. With this structure, each of the bond component cash flows is established with absolute certainty. Exhibit 18.6 summarizes the major differences between the traditional DUS and the new multifamily noncall bonds.

---

[6] Salomon Smith Barney Third Quarter 2000 Issuer Performance Report, Darrell Wheeler & Jeff Berenbaum.

EXHIBIT 18.6   Traditional MBS/DUS versus New Multifamily Noncall
Bonds—Structure Summary

Characteristic	Traditional MBS/DUS (FNMA POOL)	Multifamily Noncall Bonds (REMIC or FASIT)
Structure	Ten-year term with 30-year amortization; 9.5 years of call protection with last six months open at par.	Trust comprising amortizing class, Ten-year bullet and residual.
Size	One loan per pool, small average size approximately $5.3 million. Can be larger with a mega pool.	Dealer warehouses until issuance pool is $250-$750 million.
Loan & Bond Prepayment Lockout	9.5 years of call protection as yield maintenance.	Ten-year bond as borrower is only permitted to defease.
Bond Call Protection if Loan Defaults	FNMA can repurchase after making four months of principal and interest payments (i.e. bond premium is at risk).	Structure ensures the coupon through maturity regardless of mortgage pool performance, (i.e. cash flow guarantee of Fannie Mae).

Source: Salmon Smith Barney.

18.6 DUS BOND RELATIVE VALUE

Traditional Fannie Mae DUS bonds have traded at a slight spread premium
to swaps because of the single loan structure, which limits liquidity and
increases the risk of an involuntary prepayment or a planned prepayment
from the mortgage default. Over the past year MBS/DUS bonds have usually
traded at a 14bp to 25bp premium to 10-year swaps, having established a
14bp average differential during the past year (Exhibit 18.7 presents the 10-
year DUS/MBS differential to the 10-year swap).

The first new noncall DUS/MBS priced September 19, 2000 at ¾ of 1bp
inside the 10-year swap. This pricing premium to traditional DUS bonds is
based on the extra value investors attribute to:

- *The removal of the six-month early prepayment risk.* The extra six
  months of lock-out through to 120 months has value to investors;
- *The removal of default par prepayment risk,* creates bullet maturity certainty;
- *Improved liquidity from the larger issuance size.* The new noncall securities are backed by multiple loans, creating larger pools that should be
  more widely held and, therefore, more liquid. The first issue contained
  37 individual loans for a total pool size of $510 million.

Going forward, we expect that the noncallable DUS/MBS will maintain
their premium to the regular DUS/MBS which should enable Fannie Mae to
aggregate more noncallable DUS loans which should eventually increase issuance and create a more liquid market.

DUS Bonds are unique in that both the traditional DUS and the new
noncallable DUS provides the credit backing of the agency guarantee

EXHIBIT 18.7 Regular 10-year Fannie Mae DUS/MBS Differential with the 10-year Swap

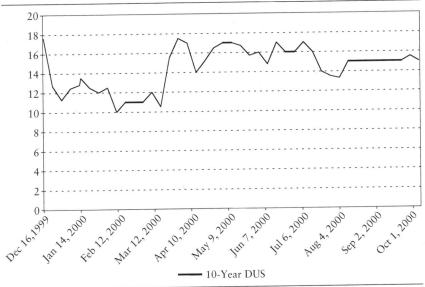

Source: Salomon Smith Barney.

combined with the additional credit support of an underlying multifamily mortgage pool, which would likely shadow rate 70% to 80% triple-A as a stand-alone CMBS pool. Investors that are comfortable with default prepayment risk should buy the traditional DUS bonds while investors that want absolute cash flow guarantee regardless of the defaults, should buy the new noncallable DUS bonds.

18.6 WHERE TO FIND INFORMATION

Fannie Mae provides information on DUS MBSs in a number of formats:

- *www.Fanniemae.com.* Fannie Mae Web site provides a DUS collateral performance data, and general DUS bond descriptive reports.
- *Bloomberg.* Coupon, WAC, and maturity information are available by accessing the DUS pool number. Schedule A information, such as yield maintenance period, amortization schedule, reference Treasury, and credit quality is accessible within the DES page by typing "FN," and the

pool number, followed by the "Mortgage" and "Go" keys. All Schedule A information reflects the MBS as of issuance.

■ *Schedule A/Prospectus Supplement.* A copy of the Schedule A is attached to the MBS DUS Prospectus Supplement. These are available directly from Fannie Mae by calling (800) BESTMBS.

■ *Pool Talk.* A voice response phone system (800-BESTMBS) provides factors, CUSIPs, issue and maturity dates, MBS coupon rates and updated WACs and WAMs.

Mortgage-Related Asset-Backed Securities

Home Equity Loan (HEL) Securities

Ivan Gjaja and Lakhbir Hayre

Home equity debt has grown dramatically during the last decade. According to estimates by SMR Research Corporation, aggregate outstandings of open- and closed-end home equity loans more than tripled between the end of 1986 and the end of 1997,[1] reaching $445 billion at the end of 1997. At that level, the home equity debt outstanding was comparable to the total consumer revolving credit, as reported by the Federal Reserve. Between 1994 and 1998, closed-end receivables alone increased by more than 100%. Closed- and open-end loans constituted approximately 65% and 35% of total outstandings in 1998, respectively.

The home equity loan ABS market has developed rapidly, even exceeding the growth of the home equity loan outstandings. Although the market almost doubled in size between 1990 and 1991, the majority of the growth has occurred since 1994. Since then, annual new-issue volumes have increased nearly eight-fold. Most of this explosion in supply has been fueled by closed-end loans, including both fixed- and adjustable-rate products and, more recently, hybrid loans. Exhibit 19.1 shows public U.S.-dollar home equity loan ABS new-issue volume since the first transaction in 1989.

Until 1998 the largest securitizers of HEL product have been the specialty finance companies. These companies would typically obtain short-term lines of credit to fund the origination or purchase of loans, sell the loans on a quarterly basis into a securitization, compute a gain on the sale of the loans based on the present value of projected residual cash flows, and book the gain as one component of earnings for the quarter. However, the liquidity

---

[1] *Home Equity Loans, 1998,* SMR Research Corporation.

EXHIBIT 19.1   Public U.S.-Dollar Home Equity Loan ABS New-Issue Volume, 1989–2000*

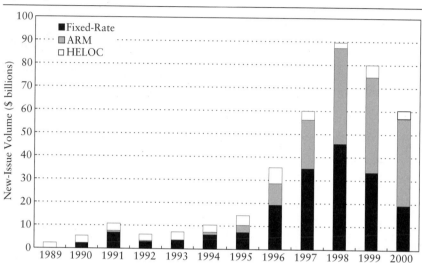

*Through the first nine months of 2000.

Source: MCM Corporate Watch and Salomon Smith Barney.

crisis of 1998 and rising defaults on HEL portfolios grown aggressively over the preceding years have brought into question the business model of specialty finance companies. Their place in the ranks of the largest securitizers has been now filled by well-capitalized companies that are much less dependent on rapid volume increases and gain-on-sale assumptions for their revenue growth. Consequently, the rapid growth of HEL issuance has slowed down over the past two years, while at the same time the profile of HEL collateral has shifted slightly toward higher-credit borrowers.

Home equity loans are essentially a segment of an increasingly well rounded residential mortgage spectrum offering products to a wide borrower base. From this perspective, home equity loans may be differentiated—but only somewhat ambiguously—from nonconforming alt-A, or A–, loans. As a result, in the context of prepayment modeling, the same theoretical foundation should apply to a wide variety of mortgage products. After providing an overview of home equity loan speeds in the next section, we discuss various aspects of this theoretical foundation and present the Salomon Smith Barney Home Equity Loan Prepayment Model. Finally, we discuss the inherent limitations and assumptions in the modeling process.

19.1 CHARACTERISTICS OF HOME EQUITY LOANS

In the context of the ABS market, home equity lending generally refers to the extension of mortgage loans to credit-impaired borrowers. Originators are frequently referred to as *subprime* or B and C lenders, reflecting an industry convention grading borrowers from A (lowest risk) to D (highest risk) by credit quality. Interestingly, a recent study suggests that the demographic and economic attributes of home equity borrowers are not dramatically different from those of the population of all homeowners.[2] Home equity borrowers tend to be somewhat younger with tighter income distribution concentrated around the median, but that median itself is close to the median income for all homeowners ($34,000 for home equity borrowers versus $37,000 for all homeowners), and about the same as the median income for all U.S. households.

The characteristics of home equity loan pools can vary significantly by vintage and originator. In this chapter, we focus on the fixed-rate home equity originations of the lenders for whom we have developed prepayment models. Although there are clear similarities among the pools of these originators, there is enough variation to defy generalization. The following is a brief review of some of the major loan characteristics.

Loan Purpose

Borrowers take out home equity loans for many reasons. The three most common reasons include (1) refinancing an existing mortgage, combined with an equity take-out; (2) refinancing an existing mortgage without equity take-out, and, to a lesser degree; (3) home purchase. Refinancing has generally been motivated by the opportunity to lower monthly payments, either by taking advantage of falling interest rates or by trading into a higher credit-category mortgage after performing on an existing subprime loan for at least several months. Competition in the industry has created more opportunities during the last couple of years for borrowers to trade up in credit quality.

In most equity take-out (or cash-out) refinancings, borrowers appear to be using the available equity in their homes to refinance higher-cost, nontax-deductible consumer debt at more affordable rates by consolidating all of their debt (including existing mortgages) into a single, larger

---

[2] John C. Weicher, *The Home Equity Lending Industry,* Hudson Institute, 1997, p. 52.

first-lien mortgage. In other cases, borrowers may take equity out of their homes to finance home improvements, the purchase of an automobile, vacations, medical expenses, and childrens' educations. As a result, borrowers may find incentives to prepay existing mortgages in the absence of any obvious interest rate-related refinancing opportunities as long as they believe that the overall monthly payment on a new, single consolidated loan is lower than that of alternatives. Equity take-outs are enhanced by rising home prices and improvement in borrower credit. Higher prices directly increase the equity available in the property, while an improvement in borrower's credit often allows the borrower to obtain a loan with a higher loan-to-value (LTV) ratio, again increasing the amount of equity that can be taken out.

The precise breakdown of loan purposes differs significantly from issuer to issuer. New-home purchases, for example, generally account for 30% to 35% of RFC deals, for less than 20% of Countrywide deals and for less than 10% of EquiCredit and Conseco Finance deals. Cash-out refinancings typically account for 50% or more of all the loans in a deal, but the fraction can be 75% for some issuers, such as Conti, and even reach 100% for the 1999 EquiCredit deals. Other issuers, such as Advanta, for example, do not report the breakdown of loan purposes for the collateral in their deals.

Loan Coupon

On average, home equity loan coupons tend to be 300bp (basis points) to 400bp higher than the FHLMC primary mortgage market survey rate, a benchmark measure of the interest rate on conforming mortgages. Our earlier loan-level study of EquiCredit's home equity portfolio suggested that the coupon differentials between A and C credits and A and D credits were 200bp to 300bp and 400bp to 500bp, respectively[3]—roughly consistent with averages reported by Weicher in his study of the home equity lending industry.[4]

Credit Grades

The distribution of credit grades within a portfolio varies by issuer and vintage. Lenders frequently focus on a specific niche within the industry and therefore may be weighted more heavily among lower- or higher-risk

---

[3] Arvind Rajan et al., *Home Equity Loan Prepayments: A Study of EquiCredit Corporation,* Salomon Brothers Inc., April 1996.
[4] John C. Weicher, *The Home Equity Lending Industry,* Hudson Institute, 1997, p. 65.

borrowers. Mortgage Information Corporation recently reported that, as of March 1998, A–, B, C, and D risk grades accounted for first-lien market shares of 45.6%, 23.0%, 16.9%, and 4.5%, respectively.[5] However, these figures must be viewed somewhat fluidly, since there is no standard classification system. Although it is usually reasonable to assume that a specific originator's A loans are on average less likely to default than the same originator's B, C, and D loans, it is not always reasonable to assume that the A loans of one originator carry a similar likelihood of default as those of another originator.

Loan Balance

Typical loan balances for HELs range from $50,000 to $80,000. Conseco, EquiCredit and Advanta originations have generally remained at the lower end of this range and Long Beach, RFC, New Century and Countrywide at the higher end. Some originators, such as Saxon may offer a greater percentage of higher-balance loans, with average balances that exceed $90,000.

Lien Position

Home equity loans are predominantly a first-lien product. Generally, 75% to 100% of the loans in a pool will be first-lien mortgages. This distribution is consistent with the large percentage of originations that are equity takeout refinancings, including consumer-debt consolidations.

Loan Term

Typical loan terms range from 15 to 30 years. Since the early 1990s, loan maturities have gradually extended from the lower end of this range to the higher end, at least in part due to competitive pressure. For most issuers the average initial loan term currently equals or exceeds 20 years. An exception are deals issued by EquiCredit, for which the initial weighted average maturity is at or below 180 months.

By offering longer amortization schedules, originators can lower borrowers' monthly payments. For example, the monthly payment on a $50,000 loan with an 11% coupon and a 180-month maturity declines by $52 when the maturity is extended to 240 months. This improvement is equivalent to the change in monthly payment that would result from reducing the loan coupon by 170bp (while keeping the maturity constant at 180 months).

---

[5] *The Market Pulse,* Mortgage Information Corporation, summer 1998, p. 6.

Thus, maturity extension can provide some borrowers with an incentive to refinance that is virtually as strong as that of a significant interest-rate rally or the opportunity to trade up a notch in credit quality.

In addition to level-pay loans, most originators offer balloon products, which can account for as much as half the balance of a given pool. Balloon loans generally carry a 30-year amortization schedule with an actual maturity date of 5, 7, 10, or 15 years after origination.

Combined Loan-to-Value Ratio

Average LTVs for most HEL issuers range from 70% to 80%. Originators usually require lower credit-quality borrowers to have lower LTVs to help protect against the higher risk of default and to mitigate the loss if a default occurs. For example, our loan-level study of EquiCredit suggested that typical LTV limits for A, B, and C borrowers were 90%, 80%, and 75%, respectively.[6] Citing unpublished data from Mortgage Information Corporation, Weicher reports that 23% of subprime loans have LTVs below 60%, 67% have LTVs of 60% to 80%, and 10% have LTVs over 80%.[7] Our recent loan-level study of RFC indicates that loans to A–credit borrowers carry an average LTV of 77%, loans to B-credit borrowers an LTV of 75%, and loans to C- and D-credit borrowers carry an average LTV of 66%.

Prepayment Penalties

The proportion of loans protected with prepayment penalties has increased dramatically in the past several years. While very few loans originated in 1996 and earlier years carried prepayment penalties,[8] the majority of fixed-rate HELs that are securitized today are subject to some form of prepayment penalty. Typically, loans with penalties comprise between 50% and 95% of recent fixed-rate deals. The most common penalty amount is six-months' interest on the prepayment amount that exceeds 20% of original principal balance in any given year, although there are variations between issuers. Many loans originated by Advanta, for example, are subject to penalties of 12-months' interest on the prepayment amount that exceeds 20% of original principal balance. Less frequently the penalties are a fixed

---

[6] Arvind Rajan et al., *Home Equity Loan Prepayments: A Study of EquiCredit Corporation,* Salomon Brothers Inc., April 1996, p. 14.

[7] John C. Weicher, *The Home Equity Lending Industry,* Hudson Institute, 1997, p. 61.

[8] There are exceptions. For example, about 60% of fixed-rate HELs originated by Long Beach in 1996 carried prepayment penalties.

percentage of the outstanding balance (e.g., 2%). The most common penalty terms are three years and five years.

19.2 OVERVIEW OF HEL PAYMENT BEHAVIOR

In this section, we review the basic characteristics of HEL speeds and discuss some of the differences relative to agency MBS prepayments. In the next section, we describe how HEL speeds are modeled within the general framework of the Salomon Smith Barney Prepayment Model.

Comparison of HEL and Agency Speeds

Prepayments on HELs differ sharply from those on conforming loans. Their most distinguishing features include the following:

■ *Higher baseline speeds.* Speeds on seasoned HELs that are not subject to an interest rate incentive, or disincentive, typically tend to be in the 20% to 30% CPR range, or about three times the typical average speeds on 30-year current-coupon agency MBSs. Exhibit 19.2 illustrates the difference. Both prepayment vectors show an increase of

EXHIBIT 19.2   HEL and Agency Baseline Prepayment Speeds

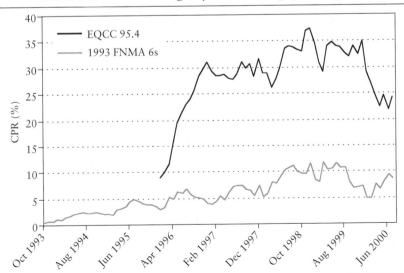

Source: Salomon Smith Barney.

EXHIBIT 19.3   Refinancing Response in 1993 and 1994 of HEL and Conforming Loans Originated in 1991

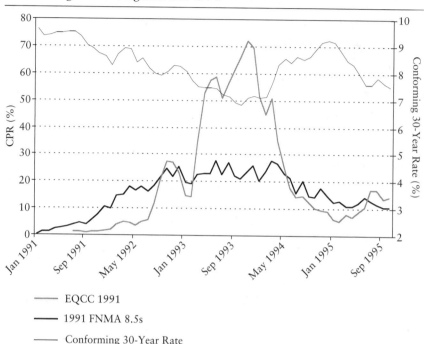

——— EQCC 1991

——— 1991 FNMA 8.5s

——— Conforming 30-Year Rate

Source: Salomon Smith Barney.

speeds in 1998. Recently, with the uptick in interest rates, changes in the HEL lending industry and the increasing prevalence of loans with prepayment penalties, the HEL speeds have been coming in at the lower end of the 20% to 30% CPR range.

■ *Lower sensitivity to interest rates.* Whether the refinancing incentive is measured by the difference between the prevailing mortgage rate and the coupon on the loan by relative coupon[9] or by some other measure,[10] prepayments on HELs are less affected by rate movements than prepayments on conforming loans. Exhibits 19.3 and 19.4 offer two examples.

---

[9] Relative coupon is defined as the ratio of the weighted-average coupon of the pool (or original coupon if referring to a single loan) and the current prevailing mortgage rate for that type of loan, minus one. Therefore, a positive value of the relative coupon implies the existence of an incentive to refinance.

[10] Such as percent savings.

EXHIBIT 19.4 Aggregate HEL and Conforming Loan Prepayments during the 1998 Refinancing Period

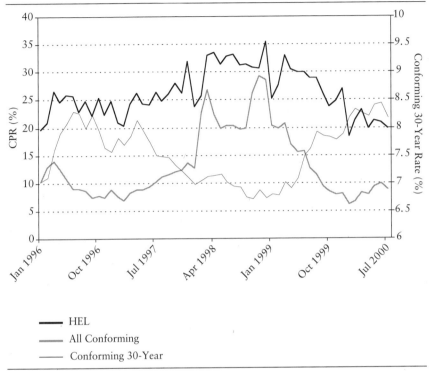

— HEL
— All Conforming
— Conforming 30-Year

Note: To remove the effect of the seasoning ramp on HEL prepayments, only transactions backed by collateral with loan ages 13 months and higher were included in the calculation.
Source: Salomon Smith Barney.

Exhibit 19.3 is taken from the refinancing wave of 1993,[11] and Exhibit 19.4 shows the data from 1996 to the present. Included is the refinancing wave of 1998.

■ *Faster seasoning.* HELs typically season in 12 to 15 months, compared with about 30 months for conforming loans (see Exhibit 19.2). The seasoning ramp for the most recent deals appears to be at the upper end of this range.

---

[11] The baseline prepayment levels on EquiCredit 1992 originations are lower than those on later originations by EquiCredit or by other issuers we model.

Key Determinants of HEL Speeds

The differences between HEL and conforming loan prepayments can be accounted for by the characteristics of HEL borrowers and loans discussed in the previous section. Based on our loan-level studies,[12] we have found that, in addition to *loan age* and the level of interest rates, some of the most important variables for determining prepayments are *the amount and term of prepayment penalties, borrowers' credit, average loan size, LTV, loan term,* including the presence of balloons, *geographical distribution, loan purpose,* and borrowers' *debt-to-income ratio.* To these we can add the costs of refinancing, which depend on the credit status of the borrower as well as the competitive conditions in the industry, and the *amount paid in points at origination* (rarely available on a pool level).

Our pool-level HEL prepayment models include some of these variables explicitly, such as interest rates, loan size, the evolution of initial LTV and costs of refinancing.[13] Prepayment penalties are sometimes included explicitly, when the detailed breakdown of penalty terms and amounts is available, but more often they are included implicitly through direct fitting of model parameters. *Borrowers' credit,* on the other hand, *is proxied by the difference between the WAC of a deal and the prevailing* conforming mortgage rate at the time of loan origination (WAC-original current coupon, or WAC-OCC spread in the rest of this chapter). The effect of WAC-OCC spread is allowed to depend on the issuer. Still other variables are taken into account only implicitly, through model parameters that may depend on the issuer and on calendar time.

The identification of WAC-OCC spread with borrowers' credit is a matter of convenience, not necessity. By direct fitting, we have found this variable to be a reliable numerical measure of prepayment behavior. Although it is most directly related to credit, as discussed next, it also reflects other collateral characteristics that affect the spread, such as lien position or the changing competitive environment in the industry.[14]

By allowing for a dependence of model parameters on the issuer, we avoid dealing with incomplete information, arrest the proliferation of explanatory variables, and account for differences that cannot be captured by a profile of loans or borrowers (such as loan servicing). We have found that only a small variation in models can successfully account for the observed

---

[12] Arvind Rajan et al., *Home Equity Loan Prepayments: A Study of EquiCredit Corporation,* Salomon Brothers Inc., April 1996, Chapter 20 of this volume and unpublished studies.

[13] In contrast to pool-level prepayment models, our *loan-level* models, such as the RFC model, explicitly include nearly all relevant collateral characteristics.

[14] Competition also has an impact on other factors, such as costs.

prepayments for several issuers for which we have developed models—across origination times from 1992 to the present.

19.3 SALOMON SMITH BARNEY FIXED-RATE HEL PREPAYMENT MODEL

Our fixed-rate HEL prepayment model is a member of a family of Salomon Smith Barney prepayment models for various mortgage instruments. These models have the same general structure, with prepayments assumed to result from four sources: *housing turnover, refinancings, curtailments* (including *full payoffs*), and *defaults*. For HELs, we further divide the refinancing component into refinancings that result from declines in *interest rates* and refinancings that are driven by changes in the borrower's *credit*. Therefore, the basic structure of the HEL prepayment model is

Total speed = Housing turnover + Credit-driven refinancings

+Rate-driven refinancings + Defaults + Curtailments and payoffs

In practice, we observe only the total prepayment, and hence cannot directly estimate each component. Nevertheless, having separate components provides a conceptual framework for modeling prepayments and, as we illustrate in the rest of this section, allows loan or borrower characteristics (whether known or assumed) to be incorporated in a logical manner. We next discuss each of these components.

Housing Turnover

We assume that the turnover component is the product of four factors: an overall *turnover rate,* a *relative mobility factor,* a *seasoning curve,* and a *lock-in effect.*

The *overall turnover rate* is the percentage of existing homes sold each year, and is estimated by dividing total existing home sales by the total stock of single-family homes. Historically, it has averaged between 5% to 7%, and is currently at the upper end of this range. Data on existing home sales (and monthly seasonal factors) are reported each month by the National Association of Realtors. We also assume a weak dependence of turnover on interest rates.[15]

---

[15] For a description of the agency turnover model see Chapter 4, "Anatomy of Prepayments."

The *relative mobility factor* captures demographic or socioeconomic differences between borrowers in different types of loans. HEL borrowers generally have lower credits compared to their conforming loan counterparts and many have taken equity out of their home in order to consolidate debt or finance home improvements. This suggests that their ability or desire to move is suppressed. We therefore assume that the relative mobility factor is lower than for conforming loans, with the fitting process suggesting that it is approximately 20% less than that for conforming 15-year loans. Also consistent with these assumptions, the seasoning ramp extends to 10 years, much longer than for conforming loans, though the increase after the second year is much smaller than in years 1 and 2. When loan-level data is available, the mobility factor becomes an explicit function of loan characteristics.

The *lock-in effect* refers to the disincentive to move because of rising interest rates. It is modeled in the same way as for agencies, by comparing the cost of higher rates with the likely amount of a new loan. (Hence, because of inflation, the lock-in effect diminishes over time.)

In our pool-level models *the turnover component of prepayments is assumed to be the same for all issuers.* For current coupon HEL loans seasoned about 30 months, prepayments from turnover average about 6% CPR.

Credit-Driven Refinancings

Our loan-level studies of HEL prepayments show that many refinancings occur because borrowers take advantage of lower rates made possible by an improvement in their credit standing. The incentive to refinance can be considerable. The interest charged to subprime-A-credit borrowers for a 30-year first lien HEL is typically 150bp to 250bp above the prevailing conforming rate, and increases by 100bp to 150bp for a second lien. It is only weakly dependent on the term of the loan. Moving to lower credits, the B to A credit spread is about 100bp; C to A about 250bp; and D to A between 350bp and 450bp. In addition, a borrower whose credit improves can often obtain a loan with a larger LTV ratio. For a representative HEL issuer, such as Centex, the LTV limits are 90% for A-credit borrowers, 85% for B-credit borrowers, 75% for C-credit borrowers, and 70% for D-credit borrowers. (The *actual* LTVs are significantly lower than these limits, as we described in the previous section.)

Although a borrower may be able to find a lender who will refinance the loan into a higher credit category with as little as six months of adequate financial performance, more typically, credit improvement requires about one year of satisfactory performance. In addition, over the past year, the refinancing standards have tightened further for lowest-credit borrowers.

EXHIBIT 19.5   Average CPR versus Rate Change-Related Incentive by
Credit Class

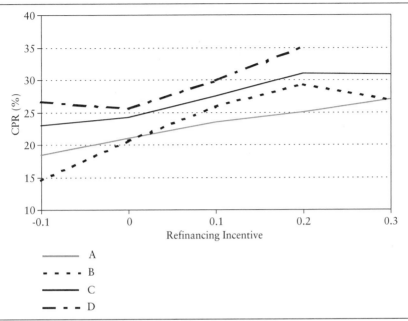

Note: Incentive = Original note rate/current note rate – 1.
Source: Salomon Smith Barney.

Therefore, most fixed-rate HEL pools exhibit a pick-up in prepayments at
the loan age of 12 to 15 months. After this period, the rate of credit-driven
refinancings depends on the rate at which borrowers improve their credit
and the availability of refinancing opportunities.[16] Exhibit 19.5 shows prepayment rates by credit and relative coupon.

As illustrated in the exhibit, prepayments on lower-credit loans tend to
be faster than prepayments on higher-credit loans, even in the presence of a
refinancing incentive. This illustrates the dominant role played by credit-
driven refinancings, compared to refinancings that result from drops in interest rates. In addition, it is generally easier to upgrade credit status from
one subprime category to a higher one than from the subprime A category to
the standards for conforming loans. Because of their lower overall financial

---

[16] The availability of refinancing opportunities, in turn, depends on the conditions in
the HEL lending industry and the state of the economy.

strength, lower credit borrowers are also more likely to be able to use additional financing to consolidate installment debt that was acquired since the origination of the first mortgage, or to extend the term of the mortgage (even without overall savings), in order to decrease the monthly payments, as we discussed in the previous section.

Direct fits of the seasoning ramp for credit-driven refinancings on the deal level suggest that for most issuers the ramp peaks at between 12 and 15 months, declines very gradually until loan age of 5 to 6 years, after which it declines more steeply at about 2% CPR per year. While we fit the seasoning ramp independently for each issuer, the differences are small, arising primarily in the steepness of the ramp in the first 15 months of loan life. These differences account for, among other things, variations in underwriting policies between issuers (for example, the number of points charged). The overall level of the ramp for credit-driven refinancings is determined largely by the credit composition of the pool and by the refinancing incentive (how far in or out of the money a pool is). In our model, the credit composition is taken into account through the WAC-OCC spread.

Exhibit 19.6 shows a typical baseline curve. Prepayment penalties can significantly modify both the level and the shape of the seasoning ramp. We discuss the impact of penalties in detail in Chapter 20.

EXHIBIT 19.6   Model Seasoning Ramp for Credit-Driven Refinancings

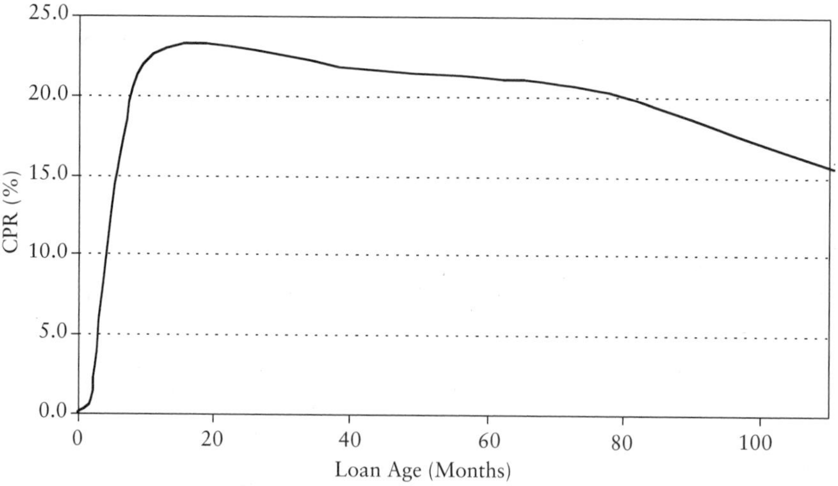

Source: Salomon Smith Barney.

The decrease in credit-driven refinancings for loans aged more than 5 or 6 years is the result of the decreasing likelihood of a borrower curing his credit in a given year after an appreciable time has elapsed. It is supported by data on pools originated in the 1980s. Exhibit 19.7 provides an example.

To allow for the variation of the borrowers' credit composition from deal to deal for a given issuer, we make credit-driven refinancings depend on the WAC-OCC spread in the prepayment model. For EquiCredit this spread has remained approximately constant since 1993 at about 300bp, but for other issuers, such as The Money Store and Conti, there has been a clear trend toward increasing spread over some periods in the past. Exhibit 19.8 shows the values of the WAC-OCC spread for the five HEL issuers, at the origination time of each deal.

Based on our interpretation of the WAC-OCC spread, and the dependence of prepayments on credit as illustrated in Exhibit 19.5 we would expect that this quantity impacts prepayment speeds directly. This is indeed what we find. Exhibit 19.9 provides an illustration.

EXHIBIT 19.7   Prepayment Speeds on EquiCredit Loans Originated in 1985 and 1986

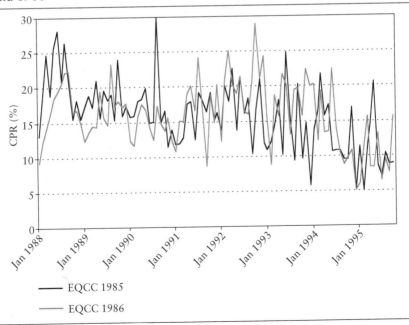

Source: Salomon Smith Barney.

EXHIBIT 19.8   The WAC-OCC Spread for Five HEL Issuers

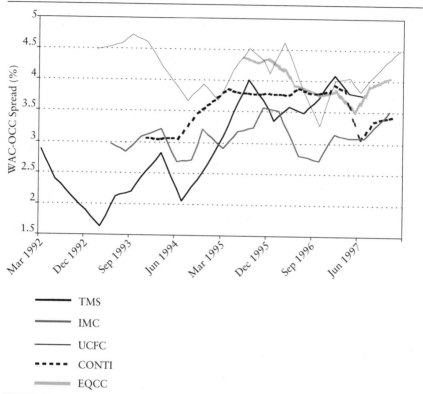

——— TMS

——— IMC

——— UCFC

- - - - CONTI

▬▬▬▬ EQCC

Source: Salomon Smith Barney.

Even though TMS92.C and TMS95.C have comparable original WACs (11.13% versus 11.27%), their baseline prepayment speeds are quite different. The WAC-OCC spread is one of the contributing factors. The two deals differ also in the original WAMs (160 months versus 280 months), mean loan amounts ($30,000 versus $45,000), and original LTVs (61% versus 71%). Some of these factors, such as the original WAM and the original LTV, have an effect on the WAC-OCC spread.

We assume that credit-driven refinancings also depend on interest rates (although in an interest-rate rally the increase in credit-driven refinancings is empirically hard to distinguish from rate-driven refinancings). In the model, we allow for an increase in credit-driven refinancings over approximately the first 50bp of the rally. In this regime the economic incentive is insufficient to trigger pure interest rate-driven refinancings, but it is assumed

EXHIBIT 19.9 The Effect of WAC-OCC Spread on Prepayment Speeds (The Money Store 92.C and 95.C)

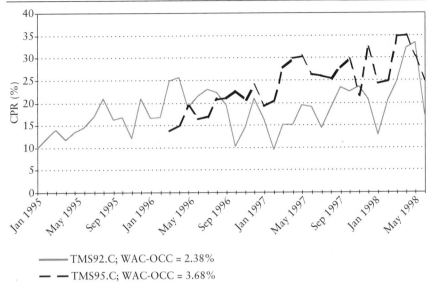

——— TMS92.C; WAC-OCC = 2.38%
— — TMS95.C; WAC-OCC = 3.68%

Source: Salomon Smith Barney.

to increase credit-driven refinancings by a modest amount. Increases in interest rates, on the other hand, suppress credit-driven refinancings. In particular, in extreme scenarios where the rate increase is comparable to the differences in coupons between credit classes, it is logical to expect credit-driven refinancings to slow to a trickle.

Interest Rate-Driven Refinancings

As discussed earlier, HELs are less sensitive to refinancing opportunities presented by declining interest rates than conforming loans. Their prepayment patterns over three recent refinancing waves illustrates this point. Exhibit 19.10 shows the typical prepayments of HEL loans during the 1993 refinancing wave, separated by credit type. Even though the loans carried an average coupon of 11.60%, the prepayment speeds generally remained below 40% CPR throughout the refinancing wave. (In contrast, agency speeds in some cases reached 70% CPR during the same period.) Exhibit 19.10 also demonstrates the different sensitivities of credit classes to refinancings. While the

EXHIBIT 19.10　Prepayments on Loans Originated in 1992 by Borrower's Credit

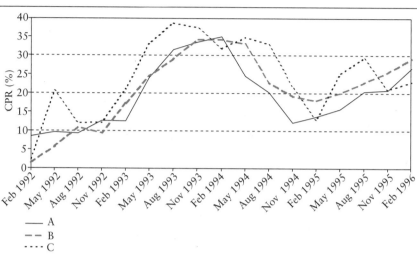

Source: Salomon Smith Barney.

baseline levels are lowest for the highest credit grade, the increase in prepayment speeds is inversely related to the credit grade. This is expected, since higher credit borrowers experience a proportionally larger increase in the refinancing incentive—compared to the incentive available from credit improvements alone—than the lower credit ones. In addition, the relatively greater financial resources and sophistication of higher credit borrowers make them more likely to take advantage of declines in interest rates.

Refinancings of HELs picked up speed again during the 1995 interest rate rally, when mortgage rates declined by about 220bp between early 1995 and early 1996. Exhibit 19.11 shows the behavior of a typical HEL deal during this period. Again the increase in speed was moderate, registering about 15% CPR.

The most recent refinancing wave occurred in 1998. Mortgage rates for 30-year conforming loans dropped to well below 7%, equaling the lows in 1993. From April of 1997 this represented a decrease of about 120bp. Exhibit 19.12 shows the prepayment on a typical seasoned HEL deals that were, on average, originated at rates comparable to the ones prevailing in the first half of 1997. Increases in HEL speeds typically appear to be about 6% CPR or slightly less for a 100bp decline in mortgage rates.

EXHIBIT 19.11 Typical Increase in HEL Prepayment Speeds during the 1995–1996 Rate Rally (UCFC 93.B1)

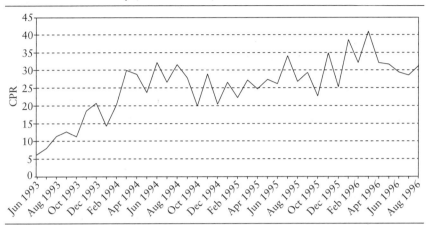

Source: Salomon Smith Barney.

EXHIBIT 19.12 Prepayments on Seasoned Advanta Deals during the 1997–1998 Refinancing Wave

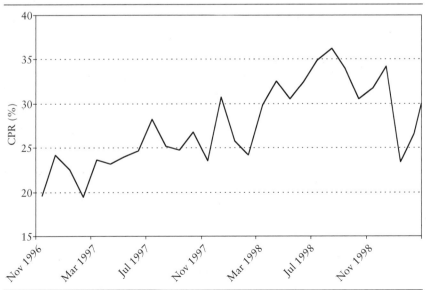

Source: Salomon Smith Barney.

Although historical data indicates that the pickup in speeds due to a coupon becoming about 100bp in-the-money seems to be less than about 6% CPR, further drops in rates can lead to larger pickups in speeds. Prepayment speeds also seem to level off after the refinancing incentive exceeds about 300bp. Thus, the interest rate refinancing pattern of HELs exhibits the well-known S-curve.

Our interest-rate refinancing model follows the approach of other prepayment models in the Salomon Smith Barney family. To allow for burnout and differences in the composition of deals, the total refinancing prepayment is a sum of prepayments for different populations, each of which has its own refinancing curve and refinancing costs.[17] The refinancing incentive is represented by the relative coupon, where the current coupon is computed from the FHLMC survey rate and the WAC-OCC spread. The relative coupon is then adjusted for refinancing costs, which are divided into *fixed* and *variable* costs. Fixed costs do not depend on the size of the loan and represent items such as application fee, title search, legal fees, and so on. For HELs, which typically have loan balances in the $50,000 to $80,000 range, fixed costs can represent a significant obstacle to refinancing. Variable costs depend on the loan amount and cover items such as origination fees and points. These costs can also significantly dampen prepayments, since the number of points can be as high as 8 for some lenders. Overall, for a typical HEL loan the costs of refinancing are in the range of 4% to 8%[18] of the loan balance, considerably higher than for conforming loans.

Initial Population Mix   The initial population distribution (which represents the initial proportions of borrowers in each class, ranging from very slow to very fast refinancers) is assumed to differ from issuer to issuer. The estimated credit distribution of borrowers, as determined by the WAC-OCC spread, is used to estimate the initial mix. The initial mix can also vary by the origination date of a deal, to account for possible changes in underwriting practices of a particular issuer over time.

The Media Effect   The SSB prepayment models assume that the refinancing response to a drop in interest rates is also influenced by the perception of the level of rates compared to their "historical levels."[19] We refer to this

---

[17] See Chapter 4, "Anatomy of Prepayments."

[18] John C. Weicher, *The Home Equity Lending Industry,* Hudson Institute, 1997.

[19] As can be measured by the ratio of current rates to their historical average and the number of months since the rates have been at their current level.

phenomenon as the media effect. While the data for HELs is more limited, a comparison of the magnitudes of refinancing waves in 1993 and 1996 suggests that the 30bp difference in the level of mortgage rates does not fully explain the appreciably greater degree of refinancings in 1993. Similarly, the refinancings in early 1998 displayed substantially higher speeds on many seasoned deals than in 1996, even though the difference in the lowest rates was again only about 30bp. Our model therefore incorporates the media effect for interest rate-driven refinancings. Its implementation is the same as in the prepayment model for conforming mortgages.[20]

Cash-Out Refinancings Even when a borrower cannot realize savings from refinancing his loan, he may still choose to refinance in order to take advantage of the equity available in his home. We refer to this type of prepayment as cash-out refinancing. Its effect is most pronounced when interest rates are at historically low levels, the coupon on the loan is not far out of the money and following a period of sustained increases in home prices. Therefore, we assume that cash-out refinancings are a function of the media effect, the ratio of the WAC to the current coupon, and of the *current* LTV. The last one is a function of amortization and home-price appreciation. Our model of cash-out refinancings is issuer-specific.

One reason for this refinement is the need to account for the different geographical distributions of the issuers, which leads to home appreciations that deviate from the national average, and therefore to different levels of cash-out refinancings.

Compared to agency mortgages, HELs are susceptible to cash-out refinancings at lower levels of the media effect and smaller declines in LTV. Not surprisingly, lower-credit borrowers, many of whom have already taken equity out of their home to repay installment debt or to finance other purchases, are more likely to face financial circumstances that would prompt them to seek additional liquid assets through HEL borrowing.

Defaults

Defaults on HELs depend on loan age, current LTV, borrower credit, and other collateral and macroeconomic variables. Exhibit 19.13 displays a typical default curve. The probability of default is highest about three years after origination, when the cumulative probability of adverse price movement is large, yet the amortization of the loan has not decreased the LTV

---

[20] See Chapter 4, "Anatomy of Prepayments."

EXHIBIT 19.13   Typical Seasoning Curve for HEL Defaults

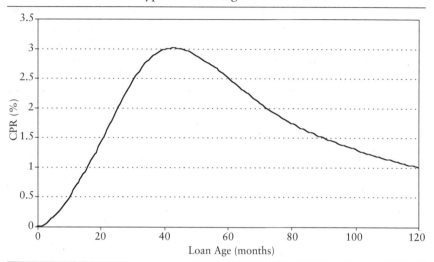

Source: Salomon Smith Barney.

ratio enough to avoid the possibility of negative equity. Our model assumes that defaults peak at the age of 42 months at about 3.5% CPR and decline afterwards.

Curtailments and Full Payoffs

For conventional loans, partial prepayments (curtailments) form a minor component of prepayments, contributing about 0.5% CPR to the prepayment speed. They tend to increase slowly as loans become more seasoned. Since HEL borrowers are generally in a weaker financial position than agency borrowers, we estimate that curtailments do not exceed those of conventional loans. Such conclusion is also supported by loan-level studies on a variety of mortgage products. Full prepayments, on the other hand, are negligible early in the life of the loan, but can become a significant source of prepayments in the last few years of the term, adding upward of 10% CPR to the total speed. For HELs, however, such considerations are of limited importance. Given the high level of credit-driven refinancings, the balances remaining in a deal close to the expiration of the term are likely to be extremely small.

Fits and Projections

The HEL prepayment models described above track historical speeds well for all issuers for which we have issuer-specific models, for all deals originated since 1992.[21] Exhibit 19.14 shows a sample of the fits.

In addition to the generally good agreement between the actual speeds and the model projections, both for baseline levels and when the refinancings pick up in response to interest rates, several specific features are apparent from the graphs in Exhibit 19.14:

■ The model successfully accounts for differences in baseline speeds between different vintages for the same issuer. For example, at the time of origination of the two Money Store deals displayed, late 1993 and late 1996, the conforming mortgage rates were about 80bp apart. Yet the difference in coupons between the two deals is much higher (original WAC is 9.30% for 94.A and 11.92% for 96.D), which could correspond, in part, to differences in credit composition of the deals. The baseline speeds for the two deals are also different, as is successfully captured by our model.

■ Even though the low of mortgage rates in early-1996 is within 20bp of the low in January 1998, the prepayment data show considerably stronger refinancing activity in 1998. This is successfully accounted for by our prepayment projections. Much of this difference is a result of a stronger media effect in 1998 compared with 1996.

Exhibit 19.15 shows the one-year and long-term averages (life of the deal) of projected speeds for a number of HEL deals for the representative issuers. Three deals are shown for four representative HEL issuers. With the recent runup in conforming mortgage rates, none of the deals shown are significantly in the money. The collateral for all but three of them, Advanta 2000.1, EquiCredit 1998.2, and The Money Store 1998.C, was originated when the conforming rates were within 30bp of the present level.

Although there is significant variation between issuers, the broad outline of HEL prepayment behavior is clear from Exhibit 19.15:

■ Projections for long-term baseline speeds for all issuers range from 20% to 26% CPR. Projections are generally lower for the most recent deals, in accordance with the increasing proportion of prepayment penalties and lower loan age.

---

[21] Comparisons are made for deals available on Bloomberg.

EXHIBIT 19.14 Actual and Projected Speeds on Selected Money Store, Conti, EquiCredit, and Advanta

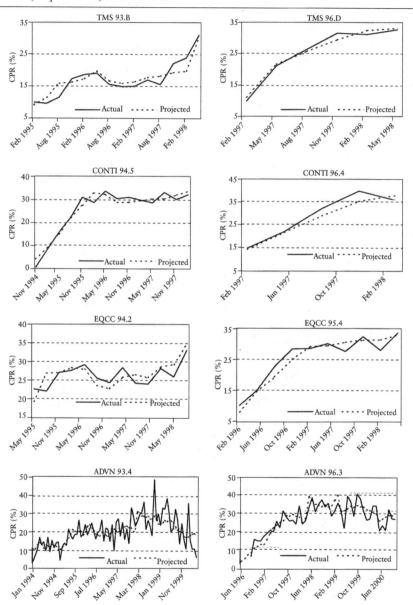

Source: Salomon Smith Barney.

EXHIBIT 19.15   Prepayment Speeds under Various Interest-Rate Scenarios

Deal	Issue Date	Original WAC WAM WALA	Historical Speeds (% CPR) 1-Mo.	3-Mo.	12-Mo.	-300 1-Yr.	LT	-200 1-Yr.	LT	-100 1-Yr.	LT	0 1-Yr.	LT	+100 1-Yr.	LT	+200 1-Yr.	LT	+300 1-Yr.	LT
RASC 1997.KS3	8/97	10.84% 23-04	41	18.9 29.1	24.2	55.4	50.2	45.2	41.8	32.3	31.1	26.0	24.1	22.5	19.8	20.6	17.5	18.3	14.9
RASC 1999.KS2	6/99	9.98% 24-10	17	20.1 19.8	16.9	47.9	45.3	38.2	37.9	24.8	26.5	20.4	21.5	17.6	18.1	14.9	14.6	13.5	13.1
RASC 2000.KS2	3/00	10.57% 24-08	8	10.1 10.8	-	48.2	45.3	37.2	37.9	25.1	29.4	19.7	23.0	16.1	18.7	14.2	16.5	11.7	13.5
ADVN 1997.2	5/97	10.85% 20-08	41	20.4 20.7	23.9	47.4	42.3	39.8	36.5	29.4	28.0	27.4	25.4	23.2	20.4	20.0	16.5	18.2	14.5
ADVN 1999.1	2/99	10.39% 21-02	21	18.2 18.4	17.3	38.5	36.7	27.5	28.3	24.6	25.2	20.0	19.8	16.5	15.6	14.7	13.7	14.1	13.2
ADVN 2000.1	5/00	10.48% 21-00	9	12.1 -	-	42.1	36.6	29.6	29.8	21.3	24.4	17.8	19.9	15.7	17.3	12.7	13.7	11.0	11.8
EQCC 1996.4	12/96	10.85% 14-04	48	19.6 20.8	24.7	48.7	42.5	39.6	35.0	28.6	27.0	25.0	23.0	22.7	20.4	19.9	17.4	17.2	14.6
EQCC 1998.2	6/98	10.31% 15-10	31	18.0 18.3	20.9	45.1	39.5	36.4	32.7	26.0	24.5	23.1	21.3	20.2	18.2	17.2	14.9	15.2	13.1
EQCC 1999.3/g1	8/99	10.35% 18-00	16	19.7 19.4	15.6	40.3	37.4	32.7	32.0	24.8	25.0	22.1	21.8	19.3	18.5	16.3	15.0	14.3	12.9
TMS 1996.A	3/96	10.56% 25-04	56	17.1 17.7	21.9	44.9	40.4	38.7	34.9	28.7	26.2	23.9	21.9	19.7	17.4	17.3	14.8	15.7	13.2
TMS 1997.B/g1	6/97	11.52% 21-03	41	22.4 26.2	27.0	49.1	43.6	41.9	37.7	32.9	30.8	28.0	25.8	24.4	21.5	21.0	17.5	18.7	15.0
TMS 1998.C	9/98	10.65% 23-04	27	20.7 21.9	21.3	45.2	39.8	38.1	33.9	27.5	25.3	23.6	21.5	19.1	16.8	16.7	14.2	14.9	12.5

Yield curve of October 16, 2000; Ten-year Treasury: 5.745%; Conforming mortgage rate: 7.83%.
Source: Salomon Smith Barney.

■ Prepayment sensitivity of long-term speeds to a 100bp interest rate rally is 3% to 6% CPR while the sensitivity to interest rate selloffs is slightly lower, 3% to 5% CPR. For a given issuer, deals that are already out of the money display a slightly greater sensitivity to rate increases. (For example, TMS 1998.C compared to the other two TMS deals.)

■ The *second* 100bp decrease in interest rates brings about a higher increase in speed, ranging from 6% CPR to 11% CPR. (An exception is Advanta 1999.1 which is about 100bp out of the money.) Two reasons are mainly responsible: the steepening of the refinancing curve and the appearance of the media effect. A 200bp drop in interest rates would bring the conforming mortgage rate to less than 6%. This level, not seen in several decades, would trigger a strong media effect.

■ For seasoned deals the one-year projection is higher than the long-term projection. In interest rate rallies this difference is a result of burnout. In selloffs, the difference is a result of the slowdown of credit-driven refinancings with loan age (a form of burnout for credit-driven refinancings). Under slow speeds brought on by a sharp increase in rates, the WAL extends sufficiently so that long-term projections feel the slowdown in credit-driven refinancings (shown in Exhibit 19.15).

■ In significant rate rallies burnout becomes more important than seasoning, and the one-year speed projection is always higher than the long-term speed projection.

19.4 LIMITATIONS AND ASSUMPTIONS IN MODELING: A USER'S GUIDE

While prepayment models are an essential tool for analyzing HELs, they incorporate a host of assumptions, and users should be aware of their limitations.

Projections Are for a Specified Scenario of Interest Rates

Thus, to the extent that prepayments vary with interest rates, actual speeds going forward will differ from projections for any static scenario. While projections over a variety of interest rate scenarios will give an indication of the likely range of speeds, actual speeds going forward will depend on future interest rates, which we cannot project.

The same comments apply to any other economic variable that influences speeds and that is explicitly or implicitly included in the model. Examples include *home price appreciation and volatility, the level of housing turnover,* and, most significantly, *the underwriting policies of lenders.*

In addition to coupon rates, the underwriting policies are most directly reflected in the costs of refinancing, such as points charged, application fees, and so on. While our model includes the costs explicitly, their future values are a matter of conjecture. In an industry that is undergoing dynamic growth, along with a wave of consolidations, it is likely that market forces will alter the refinancing costs in the future.

Projections Are Conditional on Historical Relationships Holding into the Future

Like any econometric model, a prepayment model is based on observed relationships over a given period in the past. There is no guarantee that relationships in the future will resemble those in the past, and significant changes could make the models obsolete (even if the input variables, such as costs, are correctly predicted).[22] For example, competitive forces could lead to increasing refinancing efficiency in the HEL market, so that the refinancing levels in a few years could be higher than predicted by current models.

---

[22] This can be viewed, of course, as a failure of the model to *explicitly* include all the relevant variables. The distinction is academic, however. No realistic model can include *all* potentially significant variables, and then *predict their future values.*

Fitting Limitations

Most of the parameters in our pool-level models were estimated by direct fitting on pool-level data. As with any statistical procedure, the values obtained are subject to uncertainty (the confidence interval). Therefore, the projected speeds should be viewed as the most likely speeds under a given scenario, *not as the only possible* projections consistent with historical experience. The uncertainties are particularly large for issuers where relatively little historical data is available.

Random Error (or Noise) in Monthly Speeds

A projected speed represents an *expected* value for the speed. Even if the model is perfectly accurate, and the interest rates and other variables are known with certainty, the presence of statistical sampling error, or noise, implies that actual speeds will fluctuate randomly around projected speeds from month to month.[23] To illustrate the magnitude of fluctuations we consider a hypothetical pool consisting of 6,000 loans that prepay on average according to the ramp: 6% CPR at month 0, increasing uniformly to 30% CPR in month 12. Initially, the 95% confidence interval for the one-month speed is 3.9% to 8.1% CPR, which grows to the 24.9% to 34.8% CPR range in month 24. The width of the confidence interval is approximately inversely proportional to the square root of the number of loans. Pools with few loans exhibit more fluctuation in month-to-month speed than pools with a large number of loans.

19.5 SUMMARY

The HEL sector is the largest single-sector of the ABS market, with issuance volume of over $70b in 1999. However, the meaning of the term HEL has evolved over time. At one time, HELs meant second mortgages, being vehicles by which homeowners could tap the equity in their homes. In recent years, though, the majority of loans backing HEL deals have typically been first liens. These loans tend to be of lower credit quality than those backing agency MBSs, and are typically the result of refinancings used to consolidate existing consumer debt.

The credit characteristics of HEL collateral lead to distinctive prepayment patterns. Base case speeds tend to be much faster than on current

---

[23] See Chapter 5, "Random Error in Prepayment Projections."

coupon agency MBSs, due to lower credit HEL borrowers improving in credit and hence being able to refinance into a new loan with a lower rate. On the other hand, lower credit and loan balances (relative to agency collateral) also imply lower prepayment sensitivity to changes in interest rates, and indeed HEL speeds do not surge as much as those on agencies in a sharp rally; while agency speeds can sometimes reach 70% CPR, HELs rarely prepay above 40% CPR.

There also tend to be differences in the prepayment patterns of HELs from different issuers, because of differences in underwriting policies, targeted borrower demographics, geographic concentrations, and so on. We have developed a series of issuer-specific models for HEL prepayments. Despite the differences between HEL and agency collateral, the general framework of the Salomon Smith Barney prepayment model can also be used to model HEL prepayments. The one change that has been made is to split up the refinancing component into two parts: one to model refinancings driven by changes in borrower credit and equity take-outs, and the second to model refinancings due to declines in interest rates. By using issuer and time dependent measures of borrower credit, as well as variables such as loan balances, the model successfully captures differences not just between issuers, but also for the same issuer across time. Since reliable prepayment projections are obviously critical in the evaluation of HELs, the model should prove to be a very useful tool for participants in the HEL market.[24]

---

[24] The model can be accessed through SSB's analytic system, *The Yield Book*.

CHAPTER 20

Prepayments on RFC Fixed-Rate Subprime/HELs

Ivan Gjaja

Residential Funding Corporation (RFC) is a leading issuer of mortgage-backed securities across the full spectrum of collateral types. Loans backing their transactions include jumbo A-credit mortgages, conforming loans, alt-A loans, subprime/home equity loans (HEL) and high-LTV loans. Through its association with General Motors Acceptance Corporation, of which it is an independent, wholly owned subsidiary, RFC derives considerable financial strength. Its corporate parent is a single-A rated company with a large borrowing capacity, unregulated capital, and a wealth of strong banking relationships.

Securities backed by subprime/HEL loans are a dynamic growth area for RFC. From its first, modestly sized, subprime securitization in 1995, the company has grown to claim top-issuer ranking in 1998 and 1999. With the financial backing of its parent, RFC enhanced its market leadership in the wake of the liquidity crisis of 1998, increasing the volume securitized in 1999 by 22% over the previous year, and reaching $8.8 billion in issuance. During the same period, the total volume of new subprime/HEL deals brought to market declined by $7 billion, a factor that contributed to RFC's increase in market share from 9% in 1998 to 13% in 1999. Most of the subprime/HEL volume issued by RFC has appeared on the HEL RASC shelf.

In this chapter, we provide an overview of the RASC collateral, outline the main determinants of prepayments and defaults, and introduce our new RFC HEL loan-level prepayment model. The model fully accounts for major determinants of prepayments, including prepayment penalties.

Our results follow from a loan-level analysis of over 137,000 HEL loans purchased by RFC since 1995. About 77,000 of the loans are fixed-rate loans. Each loan is described by about 20 attributes, which include loan characteristics such as loan balance, loan purpose (purchase vs. refinance vs. equity takeout), WAC, term, margin, LTV, prepayment penalty term and level of documentation, and borrower's characteristics such as the credit grade, the FICO score, and debt-to-income ratio. Each loan record includes a full history of payment activity, including delinquencies, foreclosures, and REOs. This feature allows a straightforward calculation of prepayments on floating-rate loans, as well as partial prepayments.

20.1 COLLATERAL CHARACTERISTICS

Almost all HEL loans securitized on the RASC shelf were originated in 1995 and subsequent years. In the beginning, the production consisted primarily of floating-rate loans, but the proportion of fixed-rate loans has grown in the past two and a half years. In 1999, the volume of fixed-rate mortgages was about $2.6 billion, which is 15% lower than the volume of floating-rate mortgages, but the number of fixed-rate loans exceeded the number of floating-rate loans by 10% (fixed-rate loans have lower average balances). In 2000 year-to-date,[1] floating-rate loans have outnumbered fixed-rate loans by about 10%.

About 32% of the fixed-rate volume originated in 1999 and 34% of the volume originated in 2000 had amortization terms of 15 years or less, with the remainder predominantly in 30-year loans. Of the 15-year loans, about 60% of the current production are balloons.[2] Exhibit 20.1 shows historical loan originations along with the average loan balances for fixed- and floating-rate loans.[3] Since 1995, the loan balances for both types of product have declined to match industry norms, although RFC HEL balances still remain at the upper end of the HEL spectrum.

Collateral Summary by Deal

Other loan characteristics indicate that RFC is a mainstream HEL issuer, with a slight bias toward higher-balance, longer-term loans issued to better-credit borrowers. In the fixed-rate sector, to which we now turn,

---

[1] Our analysis includes loans securitized through RASC 2000-KS3.

[2] The number of 15-year balloons and 15-year level-pay mortgages is nearly the same, but balloons generally carry higher balances. Balloons typically amortize according to the 30-year schedule.

[3] Loan balances are adjusted for CPI inflation to December 1999 dollars. Over 98% of the floating-rate loans currently originated are hybrids. The most common types are 2/28 and 3/27 hybrids.

EXHIBIT 20.1 RFC HEL Originations: Loan Types and Average Balances by Origination Year, 1995–2000*

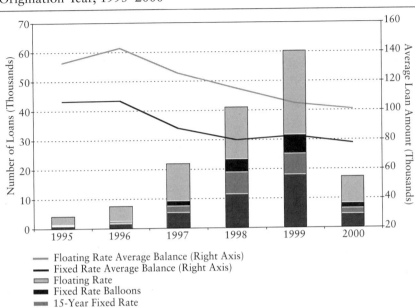

Floating Rate Average Balance (Right Axis)
Fixed Rate Average Balance (Right Axis)
Floating Rate
Fixed Rate Balloons
15-Year Fixed Rate
30-Year Fixed Rate

*Through RASC 2000-KS3.
Source: Salomon Smith Barney.

average initial loan terms are in the 25-year range, somewhat longer than for many other HEL issuers. At the same time, the spread between the deal WACs and the conforming mortgage rate is in the 250bp (basis points) to 300bp range for recent deals, which is at the lower end of the HEL spectrum, indicating a stronger borrower credit profile. Exhibit 20.2 provides a collateral cross section of fixed-rate RFC HEL deals, along with some key performance measures.

In addition to the mean LTV, the distribution of LTVs is also significant since the effects of high and low LTVs on credit performance and prepayments do not offset each other. (See Sections 20.2 and 20.3.) For 1998 to 2000 originations, the average original LTVs (OLTVs) were clustered around 77%, with about 50% of the loans falling between 75% and 86%. Fifteen percent of the loans carried OLTVs of 55% or less and 13% had OLTVs of 90% or greater. There were no loans with OLTVs in excess of 95%. Over the same period, over 90% of the loans were collateralized by single-family detached homes, and more than 92% of the loans were taken out for owner-occupied properties. First liens constituted over 96% of originations.

EXHIBIT 20.2 RFC Fixed-Rate HEL Collateral and Performance

Deal	Issue Date	Original Amount	Original WAM	WAC	WAM	WALA	Avg Loan Bal ($000)	Coll. Curr Type 30 yr/BLN	Avg LTV	90+ Days Delinq*	REO	6-mo Avg Loss Rate	12 mo	3 mo	1 mo
													(% CPR)		
RASC 96.KS2	May-96	100.5	24-09	9.75	20-07	54	92	70/20	69%	6.91%	1.65%	0.59%	23.8	29.2	25.0
RASC 96.KS4	Sep-96	94.9	25-10	10.36	21-11	48	87	75/15	73	7.86	1.11	2.51	25.2	21.3	16.5
RASC 97.KS1	Mar-97	121.7	23-02	10.35	20-05	43	78	60/24	72	7.32	1.10	0.65	28.5	13.3	20.8
RASC 97.KS3	Aug-97	200.0	23-04	10.31	21-04	38	75	65/22	72	9.57	2.07	1.72	25.4	18.6	18.1
RASC 97.KS4	Nov-97	200.1	24-04	10.14	22-03	35	78	70/18	74	5.45	1.56	1.92	26.0	22.8	26.2
RASC 98.KS1	Mar-98	380.5	24-11	9.86	22-11	31	80	72/14	74	4.78	1.91	1.73	24.9	21.0	23.0
RASC 98.KS2	Jun-98	401.8	22-11	10.02	21-02	27	72	56/23	74	7.34	2.13	1.13	22.2	18.5	15.6
RASC 98.KS3	Sep-98	450.1	22-10	9.95	21-03	24	71	54/20	76	8.10	1.92	0.80	22.3	19.1	18.1
RASC 98.KS4	Dec-98	350.1	23-08	10.00	22-01	21	66	58/22	77	7.82	1.55	0.66	20.3	17.2	19.5
RASC 99.KS1	Mar-99	650.0	24-11	9.98	23-06	18	75	66/17	76	6.27	0.87	0.43	18.0	20.2	20.8
RASC.99KS2	Jun-99	650.0	24-10	9.93	23-10	14	78	66/20	77	5.71	0.45	0.18	14.6	18.2	19.9
RASC 99.KS3	Sep-99	700.0	25-01	10.18	24-02	12	74	67/19	77	4.51	0.35	0.08	-	16.0	16.4
RASC 99-KS4	Nov-99	350.0	24-10	10.45	24-02	9	77	66/21	79	3.57	0.07	0	-	11.1	12.9
RASC 2000-KS1	Feb-00	650.0	24-11	10.44	24-07	7	75	67/20	77	1.86	0.01	0	-	9.2	11.4
RASC 2000-KS2	Mar-00	300.0	24-08	10.57	24-04	5	73	64/22	77	0.36	0	0	-	5.3	6.4
RASC 2000-KS3	Jun-00	500.0	24-07	10.82	24-07	2	73	64/21	76	0	0	-	-	5.3	6.4

*90-plus day delinquencies include foreclosures, but not REOs.
Source: Salomon Smith Barney.

Loan Purpose

The majority of HEL loans originated by RFC since 1995 were refinancings of existing loans. Of the refinancings, in more than 80% of the cases the new loan had a larger balance than the original loan, indicating a borrower's interest in taking additional equity out of the house, rather than just lowering the monthly payments. Exhibit 20.3 shows the loan purpose by origination year. Equity takeout/debt consolidation loans have recently accounted for about 50% of the loans, home purchases for 30% to 35% and pure interest rate/term refinancings for the remainder. Exhibit 20.3 also shows the fraction of loan originations where the borrower has provided full documentation. After varying between 69% and 80% between 1995 and 1998, the fraction of loans with full documentation has held steady in 1999 and 2000 at about 75%.

Borrowers generally financed home purchases and rate/term refinancings by 30-year loans. Equity takeouts, on the other hand, were financed by a mixture of 30-year loans, 15-year level-pay loans and 15-year balloons that amortize according to the 30-year schedule. Exhibit 20.4 shows the breakdowns.

Borrower Credit

Our loan-level analysis has found that the strongest predictor of defaults is the letter credit grade assigned to each borrower by RFC. *The majority of loans originated by RFC are in the two highest subprime credit grades, A*

EXHIBIT 20.3   RFC HEL Originations: Loan Purpose and Documentation by Origination Year, 1995–2000*

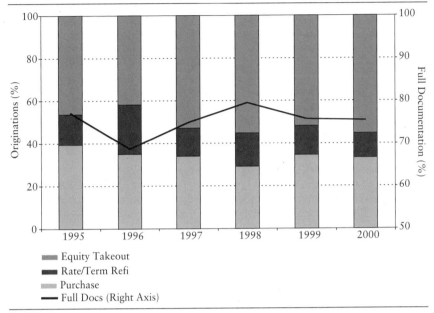

*Through RASC 2000-KS3.
Source: Salomon Smith Barney.

and A–. The A credit grade has accounted for 45% to 49% of originations since 1997, while the proportion of A– credit borrowers has stayed in the 23% to 29% range. Less than 8% of the borrowers are in the lowest C/D credit grades. The debt-to-income ratio, which is another significant credit variable, has improved in the past three years for RFC originations. After exceeding 40% in 1996, it has declined gradually to 38% in 1999 and has

EXHIBIT 20.4   Distribution of Loan Terms for Different Loan Purposes, 1995–2000*

Loan Term	Loan Purpose		
	Purchase	Refinancing	Equity Takeout
30-Year	77.2 %	69.5 %	56.5 %
15-Year	4.3	13.0	23.1
15-Year Balloon	18.5	17.5	20.4

*Through RASC 2000-KS3.
Source: Salomon Smith Barney.

stayed at that level in 2000. Exhibit 20.5 provides a historical summary of credit and debt-to-income ratio.

   Differences in credit grades imply differences in other collateral characteristics, as shown in Exhibit 20.6. Not surprisingly, loan balances, loan terms, and FICO scores decrease with decreasing credit standing of the borrower. On the other hand, the proportion of loans that are equity takeout/debt consolidation loans, the percent of loans that are balloons and the percent of loans with prepayment penalties are all inversely related to borrower credit. Lower-credit borrowers evidently have a greater need to tap the equity in their house. Often the most cost-effective way to do this is through loans with balloon payments and prepayment penalties.

How Comparable Are Credit Grades from Different Vintages?

Although credit grades are an excellent predictor of defaults, their definition as well as their use in underwriting may change from time to time as RFC

EXHIBIT 20.5   RFC HEL Originations: Credit Grade and Debt-to-Income Ratio by Origination Year, 1995–2000*

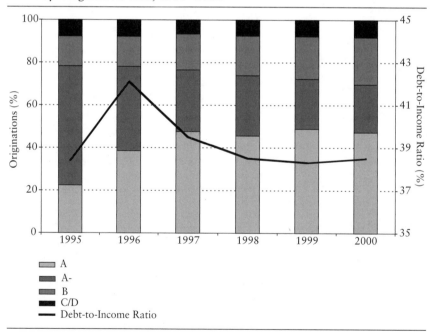

*Through RASC 2000-KS3.
Source: Salomon Smith Barney.

EXHIBIT 20.6 RFC HEL Originations Collateral Cross Section by Credit Grade, 1995–2000*

Credit Grade	Loan Balance (000's)	OLTV	Loan Term (Months)	DTI	Prepayment Penalty Pct.	Prepayment Penalty Term (Months)	Percent Balloons	Percent Equity Take out	FICO scores
A	96	77 %	312	38 %	44 %	37	13 %	47 %	640
A-	84	78	291	40	56	37	22	53	595
B	70	75	283	38	65	38	28	60	566
C/D	58	66	278	37	62	38	28	67	550

*Through RASC 2000-KS3.
Source: Salomon Smith Barney.

refines its underwriting practices or responds to competitive conditions in the HEL lending industry. In addition, the credit grades of A and C/D consists of several subcategories, whose changing proportion over time may contribute to changes in loan profiles. We examine the trends of collateral composition within each credit grade by tracking the FICO score, debt-to-income ratio and OLTV across different origination years. The FICO score and debt-to-income ratio are measures of borrower's creditworthiness, while OLTV is a measure of the riskiness of the loan. Results are displayed in Exhibit 20.7. The FICO scores are not shown for the first two origination years, as they became widely available only in 1997.

EXHIBIT 20.7 RFC HEL Originations: Debt-to-Income, FICO Score and OLTV by Credit Grade and Vintage

Debt-to-Income / FICO / OLTV Credit Grade	Origination Year					
	1995	1996	1997	1998	1999	2000*
A	36 %	46	40	38	38	38
			645	640	639	640
	72 %	76	76	77	78	78
A-	38	40	39	40	39	41
			602	600	590	587
	73	75	76	77	79	78
B	45	38	39	38	38	38
			575	567	563	563
	70	72	74	74	76	75
C/D	51	41	39	38	37	36
			555	552	547	546
	65	66	64	66	67	66

*Through RASC 2000-KS3.
Source: Salomon Smith Barney.

Three trends are identifiable in Exhibit 20.7:

1. Decrease in the debt-to-income ratio for C/D-credit borrowers;
2. Modest downward drift of FICO scores for borrowers rated below A; and
3. Small uptick in average LTVs for A-minus and B-credit borrowers.

In parallel with a decline in average loan balances shown in Exhibit 20.1 the changes shown in Exhibit 20.7 demonstrate a development of RFC's HEL business model to reflect the industry standards. The FICO scores, for example, have moved closer to being representative of the HEL lending industry, although they still remain at the upper end of the spectrum. As RFC perfects its use of FICO scores in underwriting and settles on a mixture of borrowers, given the improving competitive environment, we expect that this drift of FICO scores will end. An indication of stabilization is already evident in the small changes in FICO scores between 1999 and 2000 originations. The debt-to-income ratio and OLTV, which have been used in underwriting since 1995, have stabilized earlier, showing few changes over the past three years.

Prepayment Penalties

With regard to collateral prepayment characteristics, the most important development in the HEL industry over the past several years has been a dramatic increase in the proportion of loans with prepayment penalties. RFC's collateral has reflected this trend. Starting with less than 10% of loans with prepayment penalties in 1995, the production has evolved so that more than 55% of loans made in 1999 and 2000 carry prepayment penalties. Currently, the most common penalty terms are three years and five years, with the proportion of five-year penalties growing steadily over the past five years. For the loans originated in 2000 the three-year penalty accounted for 28% of originations and the five-year penalty for 21% of originations.[4] Exhibit 20.8 shows the prepayment penalty profile of RFC loans.

Geographical Concentration   *RFC originates loans in all 50 states, with the largest contribution coming from the southern states, at 40% of the total*

---

[4] We do not have information on prepayment penalty amount. The maximum allowed penalty term and amount are regulated on the state level. Most states cap the penalties at six-months' interest on 80% of original principal balance for up to five years.

EXHIBIT 20.8 RFC HEL Originations: Prepayment Penalty Term by Origination Year, 1995–2000*

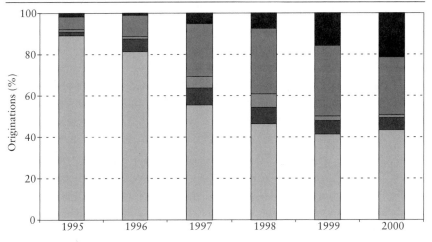

No Penalty
1-Year
2-Year
3-Year
5-Year

*Through RASC 2000-KS3.
Source: Salomon Smith Barney.

volume.[5] The top seven states in terms of loan production are California (8.6% of the total volume), Florida (8.4%), Michigan (7.2%), Georgia (7.1%), Texas (6.9%), New York (5.8%) and North Carolina (4.0%). These account for 48% of all originations.

Although regional economic trends may be useful in explaining prepayment history and offering guidance on short-term prepayment outlook, we prefer to stay away from them when making long-term prepayment projections. The cyclical nature of local economies, coupled with the inherent difficulty of forecasting regional developments, favor a consideration of the economic environment on the national, rather than the regional level. For an investor, the best hedge against local economic fluctuations is geographic diversity of the underlying collateral. RFC's HEL portfolio easily fulfills that requirement.

---

[5] We include Virginia and Florida in this count.

20.2 VOLUNTARY PREPAYMENTS

Voluntary prepayments on RFC HEL loans follow a prepayment pattern typical of subprime residential mortgages. Compared to agency prepayments, it is characterized by:

- *Higher baseline speeds.* In the absence of interest rate incentives, agency prepayments typically level off at about 9% CPR, driven primarily by sales of homes. By contrast, in the absence of interest rate incentives, voluntary prepayments on RFC HEL loans reach between 20% and 30% CPR, depending on the loan characteristics.
- *Lower sensitivity to interest rates when the collateral is in the money, but significantly higher extension risk when the collateral is out of the money.* This situation is illustrated in part in Exhibit 20.9.
- *Faster seasoning.* In the absence of interest rate incentive, agency collateral seasons in about four years. Prepayments on RFC HEL loans typically season in about 15 months.
- *Greater variability of prepayments across different pools and issuers.* Loan characteristics with a material impact on prepayments can vary significantly from HEL pool to HEL pool and from issuer to issuer, in contrast to a relative uniformity of agency collateral. Examples of such loan characteristics include prepayment penalties and borrower's credit profile.

The history of RFC HEL voluntary prepayments is shown in Exhibit 20.9 along with the conforming mortgage rate and aggregate prepayments on FNMA 30-year loans. To remove the effect of the seasoning ramp, we exclude loans that in a given month were less than 13 months seasoned. Exhibit 20.9 clearly points to interest rate sensitivity of HEL prepayments, although the effect is more muted than for conforming loans.

Interest rates do not tell the whole story, however. For example, as conforming rates reached their multiyear lows at the end of 1998, RFC HEL prepayments responded only with a slight uptick. In addition, the interest rates at the beginning of 2000 were comparable to the rates in the middle of 1996, yet the prepayment speeds were lower in 2000 by 3% to 4% CPR. In what follows we discuss in detail the interest rate sensitivity of RFC HEL loans and review loan characteristics and other macroeconomic variables that impact voluntary prepayments.

The Seasoning Process and Benchmark Speeds

Voluntary prepayments on HELs generally exhibit strong dependence on loan age, leading to a definition of various seasoning ramps for the purposes of

EXHIBIT 20.9 Voluntary Prepayments on RFC HEL Loans and Prepayments on Conforming Loans

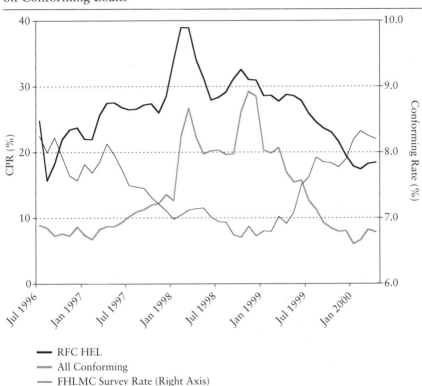

- ▬ RFC HEL
- ▬ All Conforming
- — FHLMC Survey Rate (Right Axis)

Source: Salomon Smith Barney. The Seasoning Process and Benchmark Speeds.

pricing HEL securities. Generally the ramp consists of a seasoning period of 12 months, followed by a period of constant prepayments until the deal pays off. For the most recent RASC deal, RASC 2000-KS3, the ramp was assumed to level off at 23% CPR, for older transactions at 25% CPR.

While convenient for pricing, a flat seasoning ramp does not coincide with actual HEL prepayments even for homogeneous pools with simple loan features. For pools with a significant portion of the loans subject to prepayment penalties, the difference between the flat seasoning ramp and actual prepayments is even larger. Therefore, the first aim of our analysis is to find a suitable benchmark prepayment ramp, or a collection of ramps distinguished by prepayment penalty terms.

The explicit inclusion of prepayment penalties in specifying benchmark speeds is indicated by three reasons:

1. In statistical terms, prepayment penalties are the most important predictor of voluntary prepayments, implying that differences in prepayment behavior between loans with different penalty terms are sharply defined.
2. The magnitude of the slowdown caused by prepayment penalties is large, exceeding 10% CPR in many cases.
3. The rapid increase in the proportion of prepay penalty-protected loans in the RFC HEL pool implies that historical prepayments on older deals cannot be used as reliable indicators of the likely prepayment behavior of recent deals.

Exhibit 20.10 shows the seasoning ramps by prepayment penalty term. In all cases, prepayments on penalty-protected loans are significantly lower than prepayments on no-penalty loans, until the expiration of the penalty.

EXHIBIT 20.10 Seasoning Curves for Voluntary Prepayments by Prepayment Penalty

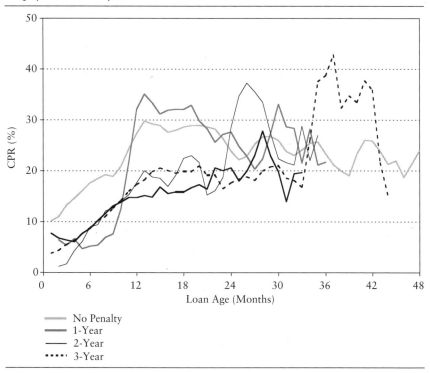

Source: Salomon Smith Barney.

The difference between the prepayment rates is not constant, however. *After about 20 months of seasoning, speeds on no-penalty loans start declining, while repayments on penalty-protected loans remain relatively flat.* They decline sharply a few months prior to penalty expiration, as the borrower postpones prepayments until the penalty has expired.

The end of the penalty period is followed by a relatively short-lived surge of prepayments, reaching over 37% CPR for the two-year penalty and over 40% CPR for the three-year penalty.[6] Such a surge can be explained by economic modeling that equates the prepayment penalty with an effective increase in the refinancing rate available to the borrower. Expiration of the penalty then corresponds to an *anticipated* sharp rate rally, enhancing the refinancing behavior. During the period shown, and well before the expiration of the penalty, no significant difference is evident in the prepayment behavior of loans with penalties of two years or more.[7]

Although essential, *loan age and prepayment penalty term are not sufficient to account fully for the observed differences in prepayment behavior between different RASC deals.* An example is provided in Exhibit 20.11, which shows voluntary prepayments by loan age for loans that carry no prepayment penalty but are of different vintages. Loans originated in 1996 and 1997 clearly had much higher prepayment rates for loans ages between 10 months and 20 months than loans originated in 1995, 1998, and 1999. Next we examine some of the collateral characteristics and external factors that contribute to such differences.

Main Determinants of Voluntary Prepayments

The wealth of loan-level information available to us for RFC HEL collateral can be efficiently taken into account by using Proportional Hazards Analysis. This established statistical procedure provides reliable estimates of the relative influence of both collateral characteristics and external variables on prepayments, and allows for a calculation of the baseline scenario using all available loans.[8] The output of the analysis is a set of risk multipliers that specifies the adjustments to the baseline prepayment curve for any other, nonbaseline, type of loan. When implementing the results of the analysis

---

[6] The prepayment rates shown are three-month averages of actual prepayment rates, with the prepayment shown in the middle of the three-month period. The averaging reduces random patterns in the data, but for rapidly increasing prepayments it also shows to an uptick in speeds one month before it actually occurs.

[7] We do not control for prepayment penalty type. See note 4.

[8] Rather than a subset of loans that possess some defined characteristics.

EXHIBIT 20.11   Seasoning Curves for No-Penalty Loans by Origination Year

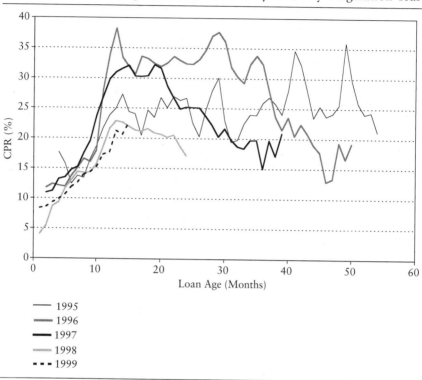

1995
1996
1997
1998
1999

Source: Salomon Smith Barney.

into our prepayment model, we refine the baseline curves by comparing them closely with the empirical curves of the type given in Exhibit 20.10.

In addition to *loan age* and *prepayment penalty term*, the most important collateral determinants of voluntary prepayments are *OLTV, borrower's credit grade, balloon versus level pay loan, loan balance,* and *loan purpose*. Together with the external inputs of the *refinancing incentive, or disincentive, caused by movements in HEL rates* and the national *level of household debt service burden*, these seven variables account for 88% of the fit.[9] Loan age and prepayment penalties are included in the definition of baseline curves and are not fitted.

---

[9] The fit is measured by the change in the log-likelihood function. The household debt service burden is a quarterly statistic compiled by the Federal Reserve Board. It represents an estimate of the ratio of debt payments to disposable personal income.

EXHIBIT 20.12 Risk Multipliers for Voluntary Prepayments

Variable		Multiplier	90% Confidence Interval	Contribution to the Fit
Refinancing Incentive (%)				34%
	Less than -13.0	0.55	0.49 – 0.61	
	-13.0 to -9.4	0.75	0.71 – 0.79	
	-9.5 to -6.4	0.96	0.92 – 1.00	
	-6.5 to -3.5	**1**		
	-3.4 to 1.0	1.22	1.17 – 1.27	
	1.0 to 4.5	1.34	1.23 – 1.44	
	Greater than 4.5	no data		
OLTV (%)				13
	Less than 70	1.21	1.16 – 1.26	
	70 - 79	**1**		
	80 - 84	0.89	0.85 – 0.92	
	Greater than 84	0.90	0.87 – 0.94	
Credit Grade				12
	A	0.93	0.90 – 0.96	
	A-	**1**		
	B	1.12	1.07 – 1.16	
	C/D	1.28	1.22 – 1.35	
Balloon vs. Nonballoon				11
	30-year, Nonballoon	**1**		
	Balloon	1.14	1.09 – 1.20	
Loan Balance ($000's)				10
	Less than 47.5	0.89	0.85 – 0.93	
	47.5 – 68.3	0.94	0.90 – 0.98	
	68.4 – 95.3	**1**		
	95.4 – 138.2	1.07	1.02 – 1.12	
	Greater than 138.2	1.23	1.17 – 1.28	
Loan Purpose				4
	Purchase	0.96	0.93 – 0.99	
	Rate/Term Refi	0.87	0.83 – 0.91	
	Equity Takeout	**1**		
Debt Service Burden (%)				4
	12.5 - 13.1	0.73	0.69 – 0.78	
	13.2 – 13.8	**1**		
	13.9 – 14.5	1.32	1.25 – 1.39	

Source: Salomon Smith Barney.

Exhibit 20.12 gives the overall risk multipliers for these variables arranged in the order of decreasing importance for the fit. The baseline case for each variable is indicated in bold. We also include the 90% confidence interval for each multiplier as an indicator of the statistical reliability of the estimators. Some points to note:

■ An independent calculation of the correlations between the collateral characteristics listed above shows that no two of them are correlated by more than 20%, justifying the inclusion of all of them in the model.[10]

■ Values of some continuous variables, such as the refinancing incentive, OLTV and loan balance, are divided into ranges and a risk multiplier is determined for each range. With interpolation between the midpoints of the ranges shown, the multiplier becomes a piecewise linear function of the underlying characteristic. For other variables, such as the debt service burden, the ranges are displayed for convenience.

■ Because the refinancing incentive is defined net of refinancing costs, the unchanged interest rate scenario, which we take to be the baseline case, corresponds to a *negative* refinancing incentive of 5%.

Interest Rate Effects

Changes in the level of interest rates are the most important determinant of voluntary prepayments. In contrast to conforming loans, where this sensitivity is primarily in effect for loans that are in the money, RFC HEL loans retain strong sensitivity to interest rates even when the collateral is out of the money. The extension risk in this case is due to the decline in equity takeouts and credit-driven refinancings as interest rates increase. In a sufficiently strong rate selloff, a borrower who has improved his credit standing may still face a higher loan rate than the one he is holding, diminishing his incentive to refinance. (Although the effect is always mitigated by the possibility of obtaining a higher OLTV loan in a higher credit grade.)

A simple illustration of interest rate sensitivity of RASC loans is provided in Exhibit 20.13 which shows an average of actual historical prepayments for seasoned deals as a function of interest rate incentive.[11] In this case the rate incentive is simply measured by the difference between the conforming mortgage rate at the time of loan origination and at the time of prepayment. *The indicated sensitivity to rate shifts is about 7% CPR for the first 100bp of rate rally,* continuing approximately along a straight line for stronger rate rallies. Prepayments continue to decline with rising interest rates even when the loans are out of the money. *The first 100bp of a rate selloff reduces speeds by about 5% to 6% CPR.*

---

[10] Nevertheless, it is essential the fits of the various explanatory variables be performed simultaneously. Otherwise the results can become grossly skewed.

[11] To remove the effect of the seasoning ramp, only loans aged 13 months or more are included in the calculation. Each point in the figure is the average of realized speeds over a 5bp bucket of rate incentive.

EXHIBIT 20.13   Average Response of RFC HEL Prepayments to Interest
Rate Shifts

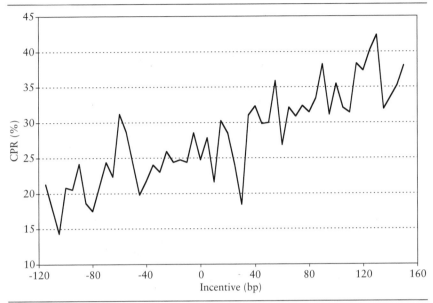

Source: Salomon Smith Barney.

Following the proportional hazards framework, the refinancing incentive risk multipliers shown in Exhibit 20.12 are applied to baseline curves specified by loan age and prepayment penalty term. In a formula,

$$\text{SMM (incentive, penalty term)} = f\,(\text{incentive})\,\text{SMM}(0,\ \text{penalty term})$$

where the function f is given in Exhibit 20.12 and SMM is single-month mortality. Therefore, prior to the expiration of the penalty, when penalty-protected loans prepay at lower speeds, this approach implies that the interest rate sensitivity for penalty-protected loans is lower than for no-penalty loans.

A direct empirical test of this proposition is provided in Exhibit 20.14. The refinancing incentive used in the calculation is the same as the one used in the proportional hazards analysis and in our prepayment model. It is defined as the percent savings that can be realized over the life of the loan by

EXHIBIT 20.14　RFC HEL Collateral: Voluntary Prepayments by Refinancing Incentive and Prepayment Penalty

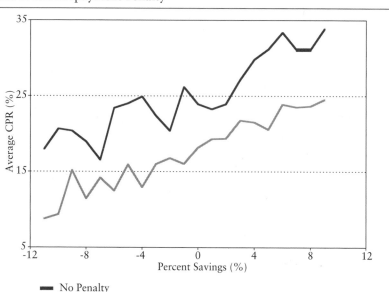

Source: Salomon Smith Barney.

refinancing the loan at *the prevailing rates for the given type of loan, net of loan origination costs.*[12] The savings is therefore approximately given by

$$\frac{1-\left(\text{Prevailing rate for given type of loan}\right)}{\left(\text{Original coupon of the loan}\right)}\times\left(1+\text{Cost}\right)$$

The prevailing rate for each loan is taken to be the benchmark HEL rate at that time, adjusted for the spread between the loan WAC and benchmark HEL rate at loan origination time. The conforming rates do not enter into

---

[12] See Chapter 4, "Anatomy of Prepayments." We do not have information on the loan origination costs for RASC loans (points and fees paid). We therefore assume that the cost is 5% of the loan balance. The precise cost is not essential for our prepayment model, because the response to interest rate changes is obtained by direct fitting from historical data.

the calculations performed for Exhibit 20.14. We discuss the benchmark HEL rates in detail in Section 20.4.

Although the historical data is limited, the assumption of lower sensitivity of penalty-protected loans to interest rate movements appears justified when the loans are in the money. When the loans are out of the money, however, which corresponds to the left half of the figure, speeds on three-year penalty loans appear to slow down faster than speeds on no-penalty loans. *For the refinancing incentive of –8%, for example, speeds on three-year penalty loans are about 7% CPR lower than when the incentive is zero. For no-penalty loans the difference is 4% to 5% CPR.* This result can be expected if the prepayment penalty is viewed as an effective increase in the refinancing rate available to the borrower. It is also included in our prepayment model. But this difference between the results of proportional hazards analysis and empirical evidence is a useful reminder that a prepayment model should always be checked against actual data.[13]

OLTV

OLTV is the most important collateral determinant of voluntary prepayments. According to Exhibit 20.12, a loan with an OLTV of less than 70% prepays on average 21% faster than a loan with an OLTV in the range 70% to 79%, *holding all other variables fixed.* By contrast, loans with an OLTV of 80% or greater prepay at about 90% of the level of loans with intermediate OLTVs. (The 90% confidence intervals imply that the difference between the 80% to 84% OLTV range and the greater than 84% OLTV range is not significant.) The difference in prepayment speeds is especially noteworthy as borrowers with lower-OLTV loans generally pay lower loan rates. Since the beginning of 1998, for example, A and A-minus credit borrowers paid a rate that was on average 32bp lower for 55% OLTV loans compared to 74% OLTV loans, and 52bp higher for 88% OLTV loans compared to 74% OLTV loans.

When a borrower is refinancing a loan to take equity out of the house, which is a dominant source of new loans, as shown in Exhibit 20.3, the OLTV is a powerful determinant of the refinancing incentive: *The amount of equity that can be taken out of the property, following an improvement in borrower's credit or an increase in the value of the property, for example, is directly related to OLTV.* Exhibit 20.15 shows historical prepayments on

---

[13] In this case the assumption of proportional hazards does not hold. The proportional hazards analysis can still be carried out if the risk multipliers for the refinancing incentive are allowed to depend on the prepayment penalty.

EXHIBIT 20.15 Impact of OLTV on Voluntary Prepayments

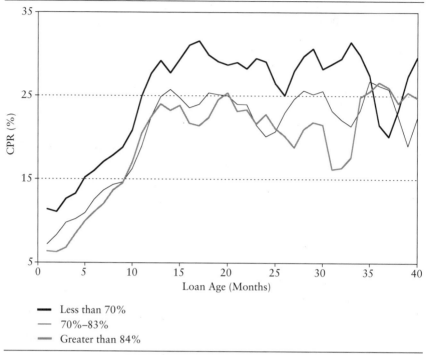

Less than 70%
70%–83%
Greater than 84%

Source: Salomon Smith Barney.

loans in three different OLTV categories, aggregated by loan age. As implied by the risk multipliers in Exhibit 20.12, the most significant difference in prepayments is between loans with very low OLTVs (below 70%) and all the other loans. Loans with OLTVs in excess of 70% do not display large differences in speeds.

Borrower Credit

Borrowers of lower credit have a stronger incentive to improve their credit history and refinance a loan than borrowers in a higher credit grade. Such a transaction allows lower credit borrowers to reduce their loan rate significantly, while at the same time taking out a bigger loan, because the maximum allowed OLTV increases with credit. An indication of the range of possible interest rates available to RFC HEL borrowers is provided in Exhibit 20.16. The figure shows the 5th, 25th, 50th (median), 75th, and 95th percentiles of

EXHIBIT 20.16   WAC Dispersion by Origination Year

| Origination | WAC Percentiles | | | | |
Year	5 %	25 %	50 %	75 %	95 %
1995	8.88 %	9.75 %	10.38 %	11.49 %	14.13 %
1996	8.95	9.88	10.63	11.38	12.75
1997	8.65	9.63	10.38	11.38	13.45
1998	8.50	9.49	10.25	11.25	13.48
1999	8.63	9.65	10.50	11.38	13.05
2000	9.17	10.13	10.99	11.99	13.85

Source: Salomon Smith Barney.

the distribution of loan rates for each origination year. The dispersion of WACs within a given vintage is an indicator of the range of refinancing opportunities that borrowers can tap by improving their credit. As the figure suggests, these opportunities generally exceed the change in WACs from year to year, which are due to the overall movements of interest rates.

The results in Exhibit 20.12 imply that, *holding all other relevant variables fixed,* A-credit borrowers prepay about 7% more slowly than A– credit borrowers, B-credit borrowers prepay about 12% faster than A– credit borrowers, and C/D-credit borrowers prepay about 22% faster than A– credit borrowers. Exhibit 20.17 displays voluntary prepayments for different credit grades. (To keep the graph easily readable we do not display the prepayment vector for A– credit borrowers. It lies between the vectors for A- and B-credit borrowers.)

Somewhat unexpectedly, the FICO scores, which are the most widely used measure of consumer credit, are not among the top determinants of voluntary prepayments. One contributing factor is the high correlation between FICO scores and credit grades (over 60%). Since credit grades hold more explanatory power by themselves, and are therefore entered into the fit, the remaining relevance of FICO scores is decreased. Another factor is the relatively short history of loans with FICO scores—their inclusion in mortgage records started only in 1997. Going forward, then, it may be expected that their significance in predicting voluntary prepayments will increase.

Balloons versus Level-Pay Loans

It may be expected that *balloons prepay faster than nonballoon loans,* as the requirement of a large balloon payment motivates the borrower to seek refinancing opportunities throughout the life of the loan. The risk multiplier shown in Exhibit 20.12 refers to the expected speed of a balloon loan relative to a reference 30-year loan. Relative to nonballoon 15-year loans the

EXHIBIT 20.17   Impact of Credit on Voluntary Prepayments

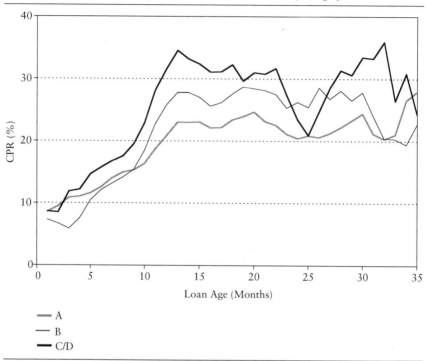

Source: Salomon Smith Barney.

pickup in speed of balloons appears somewhat greater, although the difference in prepayments between nonballoon 15- and 30-year loans is poorly isolated.[14] Exhibit 20.18 shows historical prepayments on level-pay 30-year loans and balloons. (As mentioned in the previous section, balloons amortize according to the 30-year schedule.)

Other Loan Characteristics

High-balance loans prepay faster than low-balance loans, holding all other variables fixed, although the difference is not large until balances exceed

---

[14] For level-pay loans the fits indicate that 15-year loans prepay on average about 10% more slowly than 30-year loans. However, the statistical significance of the fit is small, as historical prepayment vectors cannot be clearly separated.

EXHIBIT 20.18 Voluntary Prepayments on Balloon and Nonballoon Loans

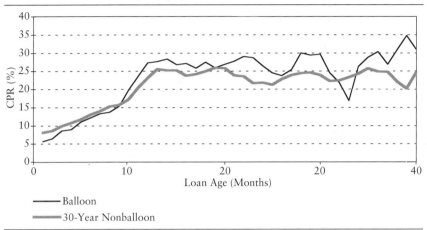

Source: Salomon Smith Barney.

$138,000. Greater financial sophistication of borrowers with high loan balances and the smaller fraction of loan balance taken by refinancing fees contribute to the pattern.

Of other explanatory variables, *the external input of household debt service burden provides a link between the economic environment and voluntary prepayments.* The relationship is not surprising, keeping in mind that the majority of RFC HEL loans are equity takeout/debt consolidation loans. As consumers' outlays for debt grow, so does the incentive to refinance an existing HEL loan and use the equity in the property to consolidate all other debt, reducing monthly payments. (Many of the consolidated loans are likely to be high-interest installment loans, such as credit cards.) We will review debt service burden in greater detail in the next section.

20.3 DEFAULTS

After a borrower has missed two or more scheduled monthly payments, RFC may act to liquidate the loan in order to recover the principal and delinquent interest payments. The liquidated loan is termed a default. Liquidation may take place through legal proceedings, in which RFC acquires title to the property and subsequently sells it, or through a negotiated work-out. In the latter case RFC agrees to close the loan in exchange for the proceeds of a sale of the property that covers only a portion of the loan

EXHIBIT 20.19   RFC HEL Originations: Aggregate Default Rate

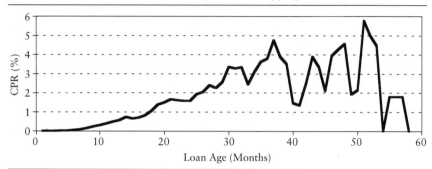

Source: Salomon Smith Barney.

balance and delinquent interest payments. In the absence of transfer of title to RFC, then, a default is primarily identified as a resolution of a loan that entails a loss.[15]

Our loan-level data enables us to determine on a monthly basis which loans exit the pool and what their status is prior to the exit. Therefore, a loan that exits the pool from the real-estate-owned status (REO, ownership of property by RFC) is clearly a default. However, a loan that exits the pool while seriously delinquent or while in foreclosure proceedings may be either a default or a voluntary prepayment. (Refinancings are common among delinquent borrowers.) We decide which one is the case based on our extensive database of recovery rates across a number of subprime lenders. Of loans that exit the pool while in foreclosure, about 33% are defaults and 67% are voluntary prepayments. Of loans that exit from serious delinquencies about 25% are defaults and 75% voluntary prepayments. (The majority of loans in serious delinquency or in foreclosure do not exit the pool, but proceed to REO.)

Baseline Curve and Main Determinants of Defaults

Because the RFC HEL collateral is of high subprime credit grade, and the seasoning of most loans is relatively short, only 570 defaults have been observed to date. Their history aggregated by loan age is shown in Exhibit 20.19. *The defaults appear to increase to about 3.5% CPR over*

---

[15] The main reason for closing a loan in exchange for an incomplete payment is the avoidance of lengthy foreclosure proceedings. A delay in recovery generally increases loss severities.

EXHIBIT 20.20   RFC HEL Originations: Historical Cumulative Defaults

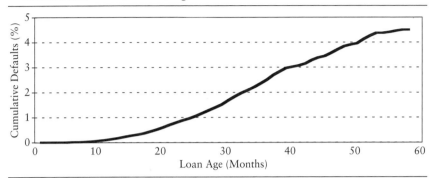

Source: Salomon Smith Barney.

36 months after which no further increase is evident. Exhibit 20.20 gives the cumulative defaults for the RFC HEL collateral, computed using the historical prepayment vector for each loan.[16] Based on historical default rates, *after 20 months cumulative defaults reach about 0.6% of the original pool balance, after 30 months about 1.7% and after three years about 2.5% of the original pool balance.*

Default Risk Multipliers

Based on the proportional hazards analysis, defaults are best predicted by *credit grade, original loan term* (30-year nonballoon vs. 15-year nonballoon vs. 15-year balloon loan), *OLTV* and *owner occupancy. These four variables account for about 84% of the fit, with the credit grade contributing more than half of that amount.* Among macroeconomic variables, we have identified the effect of the national level of household debt service burden, although the statistical significance of the variable is relatively low. Over the time period examined, which includes 1995 to the present, we did not find any meaningful relationship between the default rates and other macroeconomic factors such as unemployment and home price appreciation.[17]

The default risk multipliers are shown in Exhibit 20.21. As with voluntary prepayments, the baseline case is indicated in bold. The high uncertainty of the estimates is indicated in part by the wide ranges of the 90% confidence intervals.

---

[16] In addition to the default rate, the calculation of cumulative defaults requires the total prepayment rate for the loan pool.

[17] We used only national averages of all macroeconomic variables. The small number of defaults would likely make the results of any regional analysis unreliable.

EXHIBIT 20.21   Risk Multipliers for Defaults

Variable		Multiplier	90% Confidence Interval	Contribution to the Fit
Credit Grade				48%
	A	0.77	0.63 – 0.95	
	A-	1		
	B	1.81	1.49 – 2.19	
	C/D	3.09	2.47 – 3.87	
Payment Schedule				17
	30-year, Nonballoon	1		
	15-year, Nonballoon	0.67	0.55 – 0.82	
	15-year, Balloon	1.30	1.05 – 1.63	
OLTV (%)				12
	Less than 70	0.72	0.60 – 0.86	
	70 - 84	1		
	Greater than 84	1.52	1.27 – 1.81	
Occupancy				7
	Owner	1		
	Nonowner	1.67	1.34 – 2.08	

Source: Salomon Smith Barney.

EXHIBIT 20.22   RFC HEL Originations: Default Rates by Credit Grade

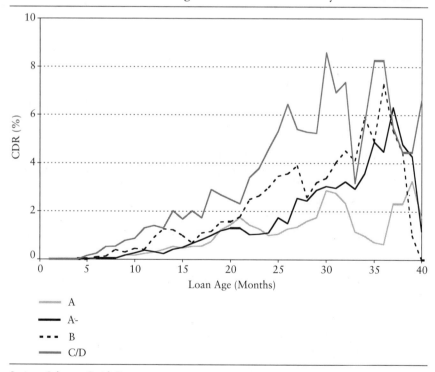

Source: Salomon Smith Barney.

Borrower Credit

The main determinant of default propensity is, not surprisingly, the credit grade of the loan. Its predictive power for defaults is illustrated in Exhibit 20.22 and Exhibit 20.23. Since the proportion of A-credit loans has increased since 1996, as shown in Exhibit 20.5, the more recent vintages may exhibit lower peak default rates than the 1995–1996 vintages. A balancing factor is a modest increase in B-credit borrowers over the same period, at the expense of A– credit borrowers.

A more surprising result of the default analysis is the *absence of strong correlation between FICO scores and defaults.* While our approach did establish a relevance of FICO scores, their contribution to the fit was low (about 3%) and the uncertainties of the parameter estimates large. As in the case of voluntary prepayments, this result may be due to the short seasoning of loans with FICO scores and to a strong correlation between FICO scores and credit

EXHIBIT 20.23   RFC HEL Originations: Cumulative Defaults by Credit Grade

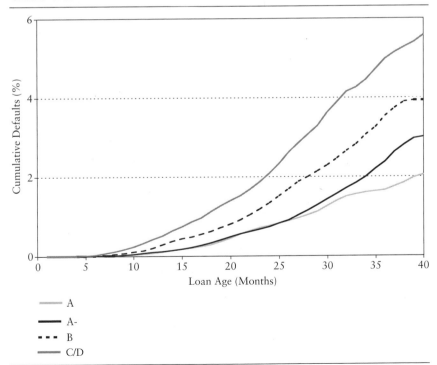

grades (over 60%). However, the absence of FICO scores may also indicate their weak predictive power for mortgage loans. The credit performance of the RASC collateral over the next year, as loans originated in 1997 enter their peak default period, should help clarify the role of FICO scores.

Original Loan Term

Fifteen-year loans default at only 67% of the rate of 30-year loans, all other things being equal. A short-term loan generally indicates a borrower who has accepted higher monthly payments in order to pay off the loan as quickly as possible, thereby indicating a stronger financial determination and ability, implying lower defaults. Independent of the borrower's mindset, on the other hand, rapid equity buildup resulting from fast amortization shortens the risk period over which the LTV ratio can exceed 100%, leading to defaults.

The situation is radically different for a 15-year balloon loan, which normally requires a borrower to refinance his loan prior making the

EXHIBIT 20.24 RFC HEL Originations: Cumulative Defaults for Different Payment Schedules

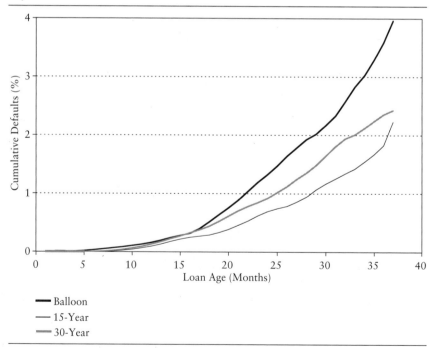

- Balloon
- 15-Year
- 30-Year

EXHIBIT 20.25 RFC HEL Originations: Cumulative Defaults by Original LTV

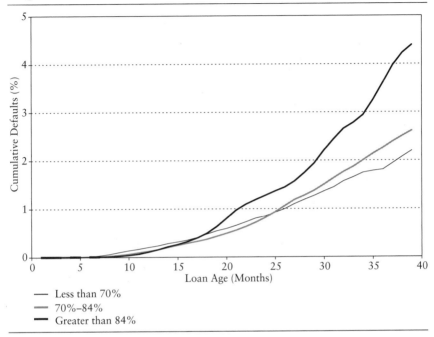

Source: Salomon Smith Barney.

balloon payment. The refinancing process puts significant requirements on the borrower, such as maintaining his creditworthiness, holding a steady job, paying the refinancing fees, preparing the paperwork, and so on. A difficulty in satisfying these requirements may serve as a springboard for defaults. Exhibit 20.24 illustrates the dependence of defaults on payment schedule.

OLTV

A strong dependence of defaults on OLTVs is a standard feature of all mortgage loans. In case of an adverse movement in the price of a home, a loan with a higher OLTV has a higher probability of leading to negative equity in the property and triggering a default.[18] The dependence of defaults on OLTV is illustrated in Exhibit 20.25. *The cumulative defaults are not very different*

---

[18] See Chapter 21, "Manufactured Housing (MH) Loan Securities."

for the middle and low LTV ranges, but increase sharply when OLTV exceeds 84%. This behavior stands in contrast to the impact of OLTVs on voluntary prepayments, where only the very low OLTVs prepay at a significantly different rate (Exhibit 20.15).

Role of the Economic Environment

In periods of economic and housing distress, such as the Oil Patch depression of the mid-1980s or the plunge in California's real estate prices in 1991, conforming loans have experienced significant increases in default rates. It is therefore reasonable to assume that the default rates on RFC HELs would also rise in a strong economic downturn. However, the modern HEL product, such as the loans on the RASC shelf, came into widespread existence only in the mid-1990s and has continued to season under the conditions of declining unemployment and strong home price appreciation across the country. At first sight, it would appear then that the RFC HEL default history has not been subject to any unfavorable external macroeconomic forces.

Less widely followed than the growth in the GDP or the decline in unemployment, however, the economic indicators of consumer finances have been showing growing strain in the consumer sector. *Credit card chargeoffs and personal bankruptcies are near their multiyear lows, and the household debt service burden is at its highest level since 1990.*[19]

Our analysis has established a connection between debt service burden lagged by 12 months and default rates on RFC HELs.[20] *Although the uncertainty in the estimated parameters is large, the magnitude of the effect is significant:*[21] An increase in the debt service burden from the current value of 13.6% to 14.1%, may be expected to increase defaults by 60%. In parallel, a decrease in the debt service burden from 13.6% to 13.1% may be expected to decrease defaults by 38%. Exhibit 20.26 shows the default rates of RFC HELs aged between 20 and 40 months as a function of calendar time, together with the debt service burden.[22]

---

[19] Historical data is available for household debt service burden from the first quarter of 1980 to the present. Over that period the debt service burden has ranged from 14.0% in the middle of 1987 to 11.6% at the end of 1993.

[20] The lag implies that today's value of debt service burden affects defaults one year from now.

[21] In approximate terms, both the mean and the standard deviation of the parameter estimate are large. The mean refers to the magnitude of the effect, the standard deviation to the uncertainty of the estimate.

[22] We choose the interval of 20 to 40 months to remove most of the effects of the default seasoning ramp.

EXHIBIT 20.26   Defaults on Seasoned RFC HEL Loans and Debt
Service Burden

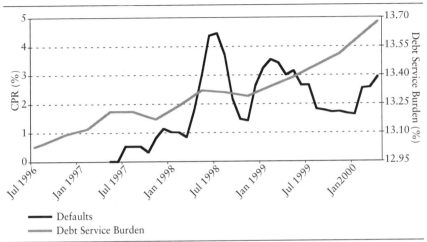

Although the relationship between these two variables does not appear
unassailable, both have registered secular increases over the period shown.
A consideration of consumer's cash flows also would imply a link between
the two. Given the potential impact of a continuing rise in debt service burden on RFC HEL defaults, we believe that this relationship merits close attention in the coming months.

20.4 PREPAYMENT MODEL

The Salomon Smith Barney RFC HEL fixed-rate prepayment model fits
within the framework of all Salomon Smith Barney prepayment models, but
relies on monthly updates of loan-level data to account for prepayment
penalties and other collateral characteristics. **It is a fully loan-level prepayment model.** The model was released on Salomon Smith Barney's proprietary analytic system *The Yield Book* in August 2000.

Application of the RFC HEL prepayment model proceeds through a sequence of steps. First, the loans in a deal are distributed into 20 to 30 groups
according to key collateral characteristics, such as prepayment penalties, the
WAC, loan age, and so on. For each collateral group average values are computed for relevant loan-level variables including the *credit grade, LTV, loan
balance, loan purpose, loan term* (including balloon/level-pay split), and *level*

of documentation. The prepayment model is then applied independently to each collateral group to generate cash flows. Prepayment projection for a deal follows from a combination of the cash flows for each collateral group. This approach has several desirable features:

- The refinement of collateral breakdown is sufficiently fine to represent a realistic distribution of various loan characteristics, but it avoids getting bogged down with the calculation of cash flows for each loan.
- *Burnout is naturally taken into account* through differences in prepayment projections for each collateral group.
- The composition of collateral groups is updated monthly using loan-level data.

At the level of individual groups, RFC prepayment projections consist of four separate components: *sale of a home* (turnover), *refinancings* (which include refinancings due to credit improvement, interest-rate declines, and cash-out refinancings), *defaults,* and *partial prepayments.* While in practice we observe only the split between voluntary prepayments and defaults, and therefore have to rely on indirect methods to estimate each component of voluntary prepayments, the separation of total speed into distinct components provides a useful conceptual framework for modeling.[23] Our loan-level approach impacts each component independently. Compared to our pool-level models for other HEL issuers, the new RFC HEL model includes:

1. Explicit modeling of prepayment penalties in credit-driven refinancings, consistent with past prepayments.
2. An accounting for the weakening of the refinancing incentive due to prepayment penalties. In interest-rate rallies, this change implies lower sensitivity to rate shifts for penalty-protected loans, consistent with Exhibit 20.14.
3. An explicit calculation of the effect of various collateral characteristics on both voluntary prepayments and defaults, using the grouping of loans described above and the results of our loan-level analysis.

---

[23] One of the applications of the separation of components, for example, is in accounting for the impact of the economic environment on prepayments. Some economic variables, such as home sales, have a significant effect on one component but not on the others. A separation of components is then likely to yield more reliable estimates of future prepayments in a given economic scenario.

EXHIBIT 20.27 RFC HEL and Conforming Mortgage Rates

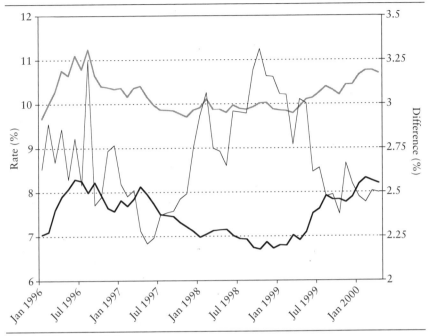

Source: Salomon Smith Barney.

4. Calculation of the media effect based on historical values of HEL rates, rather than conforming mortgage rates.[24] In our prepayment model, the most important role of the media effect is to stimulate cash-out refinancings when interest rates reach their multiyear lows. Direct fitting of the model has shown that under such conditions, cash-out refinancings of HEL borrowers are affected more strongly than cash-out refinancings of conforming-rate borrowers.

Use of HEL rates rather than conforming rates in estimating the refinancing incentive faced by an RFC HEL borrower and in computing the media effect, is essential to explain historical prepayment patterns and to generate reliable prepayment projections. Exhibit 20.27 shows historical

---

[24] The current implementation of all HEL models uses HEL rates to calculate the refinancing incentive. However, the media effect parameters, such as the number of months since rates have been at the current level and the ratio of current rates to their historical averages, are based on conforming rates.

EXHIBIT 20.28   Voluntary Prepayments on RFC HEL Loans and
Prepayments on Conforming Loans

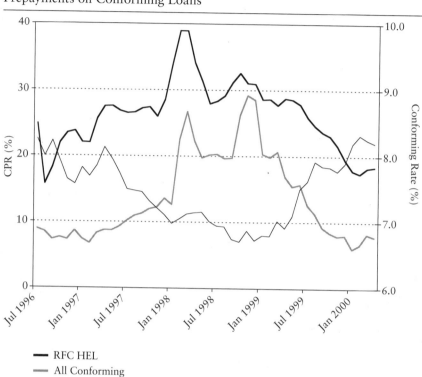

— RFC HEL
— All Conforming
— FHLMC Survey Rate (Right Axis)

Source: Salomon Smith Barney.

values of the conforming rate together with the HEL rate charged on loans
originated by RFC for an LTV in the 70% to 83% range. Also shown is the
difference between the rates, which has varied considerably over the past
three years.

*The variation of the HEL-conforming rate spread accounts for some
of the observed differences in prepayment patterns between HEL loans
and conforming loans.* For example, as the liquidity crisis took hold in the
middle of 1998, the HEL rates failed to follow the conforming rates lower,
and RFC HEL prepayments declined. The divergence of the rates is shown
in Exhibit 20.27 by a sharp increase in the difference between the two.
Differences in prepayments in the October through December 1998 period

are evident in Exhibit 20.28.[25] (This is Exhibit 20.9, reproduced here for convenience.) Subsequently, as conforming rates started to increase at the beginning of 1999, HEL rates declined, bottoming out in March 1999. The result was an uptick of HEL prepayments, that is absent in the prepayment pattern of conforming loans.

Model Fits

Our implementation of the RFC HEL prepayment model assumes that the current spread between HEL rates and conforming rates will stay constant into the future.[26] In addition, we assume that loan origination costs will stay the same. Both of these propositions may be open to question, as the GSEs enter the subprime market, and as new regulations affect the rate and fee structure of the industry. We are monitoring these developments closely and expect to adjust the parameters as the conditions change. Other variables that affect prepayment model projections include the *HEL ARM rates* (assumed to stay at a constant spread to conforming ARM rates), *household debt service burden* (assumed to remain at current level), *existing home sales, home price appreciation,* and the *strength of the media effect* (one measure of competitive conditions).

The Salomon Smith Barney RFC HEL prepayment model accurately tracks historical prepayments of RFC HEL collateral over the past few years. However, the relatively short history of RFC HEL prepayments, as well as the small size of older deals, implies that the estimates of model parameters are subject to sizeable uncertainty. Some of this uncertainty is exhibited through the 90% confidence intervals in Exhibits 20.12 and 20.21.

Exhibit 20.29 shows six examples of model fits for voluntary prepayments. The collateral in each deal has been grouped by prepayment penalty term, and the fits are displayed for a specific collateral group. Three fits are for groups of loans with no prepayment penalty and three are for three-year penalty loans. (The three-year penalty is the most common penalty type. See Exhibit 20.8.) In addition to the level and steepness of the seasoning curves for different penalty types, the model captures the continued high speeds of

---

[25] A modest pickup in aggregate RFC HEL prepayments shown in Exhibit 20.7 is likely due to the presence of nearly conforming borrowers in RFC HEL pools.

[26] Salomon Smith Barney is currently developing a new method for projecting conforming rates from simulated future values of Treasury and swap rates. When that method is implemented, we will also implement an update to the calculation of HEL rates from the conforming rates.

EXHIBIT 20.29 Actual and Projected Speeds for Different RASC Deals and Prepayment Penalties

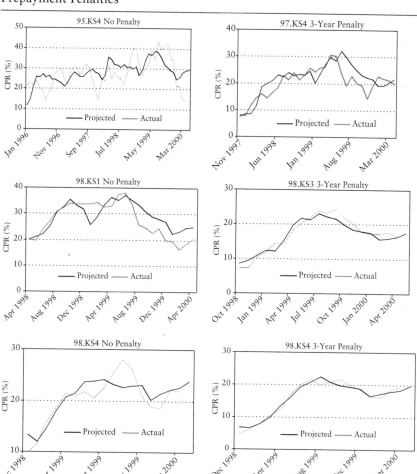

RFC HEL prepayments in the first half of 1999 and the subsequent decline of speeds in the second half of 1999 and the beginning of 2000.

Model Errors Are Unbiased

Differences between model projections and actual speeds do not depend on either the loan age or the refinancing incentive over the full range of loan ages and refinancing incentives observed. This lack of bias indicates that the

EXHIBIT 20.30 Prepayment Model Error by Refinancing Incentive

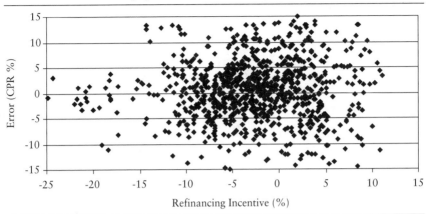

Source: Salomon Smith Barney

model, on average, correctly takes into account the dependence of prepayments on loan ages and interest rates. Therefore, it can be used as a reliable tool to estimate the option cost of RFC HEL securities associated with interest-rate volatility. Exhibit 20.30 shows the model error as a function of the refinancing incentive (defined as percent savings), and Exhibit 20.31 shows the error as a function of loan age.[27] Errors are shown for all loan groups created by controlling for the prepayment penalty term within each deal.

Projections

Model projections for five RASC deals are given in Exhibit 20.32. Several key features are apparent from the results:

- Baseline projections for long-term speeds are in the 21% to 23% CPR range, in line with the recent pricing speed of 23% HEP.
- The sensitivity of long-term speeds to rate selloffs is about 4% CPR for the first 100bp rate shift, while the sensitivity of speeds to rate rallies is 5% to 6% CPR.[28] Both numbers show appreciable variation from deal

---

[27] Error = Projected speed − Actual speed.

[28] This increase in prepayment speed in an interest rate rally is lower than that implied by Exhibit 20.13. The main reason is that at the current level of interest rates, a 100bp rally would not trigger a sizeable media effect. By contrast, many prepayments that are included in Exhibit 20.13 occurred under strong media effect in 1998 and early 1999.

EXHIBIT 20.31 Prepayment Model Error by Loan Age

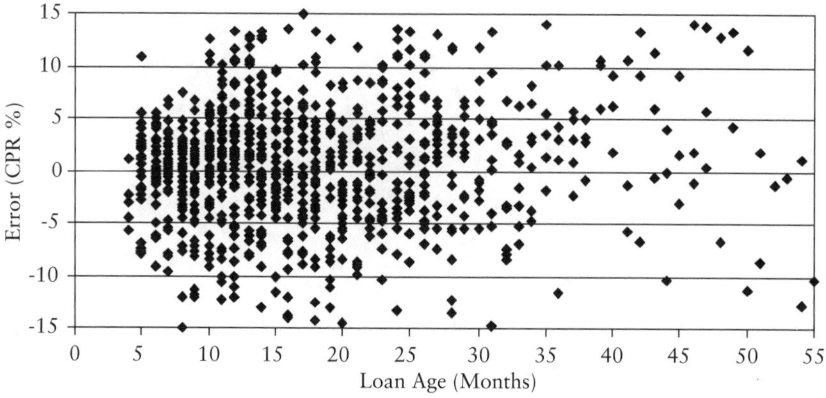

Source: Salomon Smith Barney

to deal, corresponding to different collateral characteristics and how far in or out of the money a deal is.

- The projected increase in speed for the second 100bp rally is much greater, exceeding 10% CPR for seasoned deals. In addition to bringing the deals to a steeper part of the refinancing curve, a 200bp rate rally would trigger a strong media effect.
- For seasoned deals, one-year projections are generally higher than long-term projections. In the absence of interest-rate incentives or in a rate

EXHIBIT 20.32 Typical RASC Deals: Scenario Projections

	Issue				Historical Speeds (% CPR)				Projected Speed (% CPR) For an Interest Rate Change of						
	Date	WAC	WAM	WALA	1-Mo	3-Mo	1-Yr		-300bp	-200bp	-100bp	0bp	100bp	200bp	300bp
RASC 00-KS3	Jun 00	10.82	294	3	4.9	-	-	LT	44.4	37.2	30.5	23.5	19.1	16.0	13.6
								1-Yr	43.8	32.5	21.2	17.1	14.3	12.2	10.6
RASC 99-KS4	Nov 99	10.44	289	10	9.9	9.6	-	LT	44.1	36.9	26.7	22.2	17.4	15.1	12.5
								1-Yr	44.9	35.0	22.8	19.6	15.9	14.2	12.1
RASC 99-KS1	Mar 99	9.98	281	19	16.6	19.3	18.0	LT	45.3	37.6	26.1	21.1	17.2	14.6	12.8
								1-Yr	46.8	36.9	24.4	20.7	17.8	15.8	14.3
RASC 98-KS3	Sep 98	9.94	254	25	24.2	19.9	22.0	LT	46.3	38.4	26.5	21.4	17.5	14.9	13.2
								1-Yr	48.4	38.7	26.1	22.2	19.2	17.2	15.7
RASC 97-KS3	Aug 97	10.29	256	39	38.9	26.4	25.8	LT	47.8	39.5	27.9	22.9	18.4	16.2	13.8
								1-Yr	51.0	41.2	28.9	25.3	21.8	20.2	18.4
RASC 96-KS4	Sep 96	10.35	262	49	5.3	8.1	22.8	LT	45.9	37.8	27.3	22.0	18.1	15.9	13.8
								1-Yr	49.6	40.5	29.1	25.1	21.7	19.9	18.1

LT: Long-term speed, 1-Yr: 1-year speed.
Note: 10-year Treasury = 6.23%.
Source: Salomon Smith Barney.

EXHIBIT 20.33 Securities Valuation under the New and Old Models

RASC 2000-KS3 Security	Pricing WAL (Yr)	Price	WAL (Yr) New	Old	Diff	OAS (bp) New	Old	Diff.	Yield Curve Margin (bp) New	Old	Diff.	Eff. Dur. (Yr) New	Old	Diff.	Eff. Convexity New	Old	Diff
A2	2.0	$100.35	1.9	1.8	0.1	21	22	-1	33	31	2	1.69	1.56	0.13	-0.91	-0.74	-0.17
A3	3.0	100.58	2.7	2.6	0.1	13	16	-3	40	38	2	2.45	2.31	0.14	-1.16	-1.08	-0.08
A4	5.0	101.04	4.3	4.1	0.2	13	17	-4	63	62	0	3.67	3.47	0.20	-1.65	-1.60	-0.05
A5	8.5	102.23	7.4	7.3	0.1	38	38	0	83	83	0	4.34	4.28	0.06	0.32	0.56	-0.24
A6 (NAS)	6.5	100.98	6.1	6.1	0.0	17	18	-1	49	49	0	4.31	4.28	0.03	-0.61	-0.64	0.03

Note: OASs computed to the swap curve of August 3, 2000. All securities priced to call.
Source: Salomon Smith Barney.

selloff, two reasons are principally responsible for the difference: (1) the expiration of prepayment penalties, which leads to brief but powerful refinancing activity; and (2) a general slowdown of credit-driven refinancings and defaults for collateral that is more than about four years seasoned.[29] In rate rallies, the slowdown of prepayments is primarily the result of burnout and the attenuation of the media effect.

Valuation Implications of Loan-Level Updates to the Model

The new RFC HEL prepayment model is a second generation RFC HEL prepayment model. The model that it is replacing includes an explicit accounting of prepayment penalties and several basic collateral characteristics, such as the WAC, the WAM, loan age, and so on, but does not include explicit loan-level modeling of most collateral characteristics we have found to be significant for prepayments. These additional collateral characteristics, such as OLTV and credit grades, are included in the old model only implicitly, through fitted parameters. A comparison of valuations provided by the two models for all bonds with WALs of two years or more from RASC 00.KS3 is given in Exhibit 20.33.

The new model has slightly lower baseline speeds, leading to longer WALs for all bonds and to slightly higher (or unchanged) yield curve margins. The OASs under the new model are lower, however. Therefore, the option costs in the new model are higher by 0bp to 5bp, and similarly the effective convexities of all bonds are lower (more negative). For this particular deal, the collateral characteristics combine to give slightly higher sensitivity to interest rates than may be expected by assuming that loan properties do not vary from deal to deal. This observation is in agreement with the slightly

---

[29] Since the history of RFC HEL prepayments is relatively short, we rely on experience with other HEL lenders to provide projections for very seasoned collateral.

higher sensitivity of RASC 2000.KS3 to movements in interest rates of 100bp compared to other RASC deals, as shown in Exhibit 20.32.

All of the differences between the two models displayed in Exhibit 20.33 are significantly smaller than the differences that arise when comparing models with and without prepayment penalties. Inclusion of prepayment penalties, without any additional collateral features, can lead to changes of OASs of up to 9bp, compared with the maximum difference of 4bp in Exhibit 20.33. Therefore, *for RASC deals, prepayment penalties are more significant for the valuation of HEL securities, than the detailed accounting for collateral differences between deals.*

CHAPTER 21

Manufactured Housing Loan Securities

Ivan Gjaja, Lakhbir Hayre, and Arvind Rajan

The manufactured housing (MH) asset-backed securities (ABS) market has grown from $1 billion in new origination volume in 1990 to almost $14 billion in 1998, with total current outstandings of approximately $41 billion. The market is actively traded and consists of a broad spectrum of fixed-rate, investment-grade investors drawn primarily from the core ABS, corporate, and mortgage markets. As enough historical experience accumulated to increase the comfort level of this diverse group of market participants, valuations have become increasingly driven by detailed forecasts of prepayments and defaults on the underlying loan portfolios.

Conseco Financial has been the largest player in this sector, accounting for about 40% of MH securitizations in 1998 (see Exhibit 21.1). Incorporated in 1975, as Green Tree Financial Corporation, the company was acquired by Conseco, Inc. in 1998 and renamed Conseco Financial. Conseco,

EXHIBIT 21.1 MH Issuers: Securitization Market Share, 1998

Originator	Share of Total New-Issue Volume
Conseco	40 %
Merit	11
BankAmerica	11
Oakwood	8
Vanderbilt	7
GreenPoint	5
Bombardier	5
Top Seven Share of Industry	87 %

Source: Salomon Smith Barney.

Inc. is now a diversified financial services company whose retail lending operations include MH, home equity loans, home improvement loans, and consumer loans. Conseco's involvement in the MH market goes back to the company's origins, when it started purchasing and servicing MH loans. In recent years, its MH securitization volume has grown steadily, from $4.0 billion in 1995, to $5.0 billion in 1996, $5.4 billion in 1997, and $5.6 billion in 1998.

In this chapter, we present the results of our analysis of 940,000 loans originated by Conseco from the mid-1980s onward. We discuss in detail how demographic attributes, credit characteristics, and interest rates affect voluntary prepayments and defaults, and formally introduce the Salomon Smith Barney Manufactured Housing Prepayment and Default models.

21.1 MANUFACTURED HOUSING INDUSTRY AND CONSECO

In contrast to a traditional site-built single-family home, a *manufactured house* is a dwelling constructed at a factory and transported in one or more sections to a land site for attachment. Since June 1976, all MH units have been required to meet design, material, and construction quality standards set by the Department of Housing and Urban Development. The combination of quality and affordability have helped improve the popularity of MH during this decade. In fact, by 1998, about one out of three new single-family homes sold was an MH unit, compared with one out of five in 1990.

MH comes in two forms: (1) single-section units, which are built on one chassis and have an average living area of 1,125 square feet and (2) multisection units, which are built on multiple chassis connected at the site and have an average living area of 1,615 square feet. In 1997, the percentages of single and multisection MH unit shipments were approximately 41% and 59%, respectively.

A relatively small number of manufacturers dominate MH production. In 1998, for example, the top five accounted for 60.5% of total units shipped (see Exhibit 21.2). Since 1990, the MH market has experienced a 9% compound annual growth rate, with annual unit shipments reaching 372,843 in 1998. More recently, however, with the maturing of the market the annual growth rates have declined.

Securitization is a well-established funding vehicle for MH loans. Assuming that every new unit shipped was sold and financed with an 87% loan advance rate at the average sales price of $42,300, we estimate that 1998 new loan volume was approximately $13.7 billion, about the same as the total 1998 securitized volume of $13.9 billion. (Securitized transactions include loans for used units and sometimes for the land on which units are

EXHIBIT 21.2   Top Five MH Builders, 1998

Manufacturer	Units Shipped
Champion Enterprises	68,264
Fleetwood Enterprises	66,222
Oakwood Homes	38,237
Clayton Homes	28,429
Cavalier Homes	24,387
Total	225,539
Industry Total	372,843
Top Five Share of Industry	60.5 %

Sources: MH Institute and *Manufactured Home Merchandiser Magazine,* June 1999.

located.) Several large players dominate issuance of securities. Their 1998 market shares are shown in Exhibit 21.1.[1]

For a purchaser, the main benefit of an MH unit over a site-built residence is cost savings. In 1997 (the latest year for which full data are available), the average sales prices of single- and multiunit MH homes were roughly $29,000 and $49,500, respectively, compared with $132,150 (excluding land) for a site-built home. Similarly, the cost per square foot of an MH unit in 1997 was about half that of a site-built home. According to the MH Institute, purchasers of MH units span a wide range of ages, with the largest groups the 30- to 40-year bracket and the over-70-year bracket. The median household income is in the $25,000 to $35,000 range. MH growth has been concentrated in the South and Southeast, where the top seven states received about 47% of all shipments (see Exhibit 21.3).

The average Conseco borrower is 40 years old, has a household income of nearly $35,000, and finances 88% of the purchase price.[2] As Exhibit 21.3 shows, Conseco's 1998 originations were geographically concentrated in much the same way as the industry's.[3]

Historically, MH units have been financed as either personal property, when a unit is sold without land, or as real estate, when land is included in the transaction and is treated as a single real estate entity under state law. Personal property generally is financed with an installment sales contract, which combines a loan and a security interest in the unit in a single instrument and allows repossession and sale of the unit to remedy default. A real

---

[1] Because of changes in their business orientation, some of the issuers listed in Exhibit 21.1 are not expected to be regular participants in the market in 1999 and subsequent years.

[2] Data from 1996 to 1998.

[3] For a more detailed analysis of the demographic characteristics of Green Tree's historical originations, see Sections 21.2 and 21.3.

EXHIBIT 21.3 MH Industry and Conseco: Geographic Concentration of Unit Shipments and Financing

State	Industry* Percentage of Total Units Shipped	State	Conseco* Percentage of Total Units Shipped
Texas	12.1 %	North Carolina	9.9 %
North Carolina	8.9	Texas	8.1
Georgia	6.0	Florida	6.8
Florida	5.4	Michigan	6.0
South Carolina	5.4	Georgia	5.9
Alabama	5.2	Alabama	5.6
Tennessee	3.9	South Carolina	4.4
Share of Total	46.9 %	Share of Total	46.7 %

*1998 data.
Source: National Conference of States on Building Codes and Standards, Conseco.

estate loan, in contrast, requires a separate note and mortgage. Default is remedied through a foreclosure process, which typically is more expensive and lengthier than a repossession. Historical experience suggests that the existence of private land in an MH loan portfolio reduces both defaults and voluntary prepayments (see Section 21.2, "Prepayment Behavior"and Section 21.3, "Defaults").

21.2 PREPAYMENT BEHAVIOR

Salomon Brothers developed Wall Street's first prepayment models for MBSs in the mid-1980s,[4] and other major firms subsequently developed similar models. These "first-generation" models were basically statistical fits, with prepayment rates regressed in terms of known variables such as interest rates and the WAC of the MBS. Although they may provide good "within sample" fits, these models generally fail to accurately take into account the relationships between variables. Consequently, they work over time only if all the variables reproduce very closely the historical conditions over which the fit was performed. Changes in the mortgage finance industry, with increasing refinancing efficiency and greater borrower awareness of refinancing opportunities, meant that existing prepayment models generally failed to predict the high speeds observed in 1991 through 1993. In

---

[4] See *The Salomon Brothers Prepayment Model: Impact of the Market Rally on Mortgage Prepayments and Yields,* Salomon Brothers Inc., September 1985.

response, Salomon Smith Barney developed a more fundamental approach to modeling prepayments.

A General Framework for Modeling Prepayments

Regardless of the type of mortgage or of economic conditions, prepayments arise from the following distinct sources:

- *Housing turnover.* The sale of a home generally triggers a prepayment, unless the loan is assumable *and* is assumed by the buyer, or unless the home does not have a mortgage.
- *Refinancings.* Mortgagors refinance an existing loan on the home.
- *Curtailments and payoffs.* Curtailments occur when mortgagors send in more than the scheduled monthly payment, while payoffs occur when the whole loan is paid off (a significant source of prepayments for very seasoned loans in the case of site-built homes).
- *Defaults.* Liquidation of a loan after a foreclosure on the property results in a prepayment.

Based on our experience with the prepayment and default behavior of a broad variety of mortgage instruments, we have developed a comprehensive mathematical framework to model the economic underpinnings of housing turnover, refinancing, curtailments, and default behavior.[5] Our approach allows us to naturally capture the impact of the mix of borrower, loan, and collateral characteristics and interest rates on prepayments. As a result, we can compare the prepayment and default behavior of MH loans, home equity loans, conventional mortgages, non-agency jumbo, and nontraditional loans within a common framework of models. Most important, Salomon Smith Barney's prepayment models are attached to a uniform OAS valuation framework that allows apples-to-apples comparison with other ABS or mortgage products.

Central to this unified modeling approach is the requirement that prepayment and default models possess two characteristics. First, they should be based on fundamental relationships that are likely to persist over time, rather than just on a statistical fit to the data. Second, the model and its assumptions should be easily understandable to users and testable by empirical data. The key features of the resulting model are the following:

---

[5] The approach is described in detail in "A Simple Statistical Framework for Modeling Burnout and Refinancing Behavior," Lakhbir Hayre, *Journal of Fixed Income,* December 1994, and Chapter 4, "Anatomy of Prepayments."

- The prepayment and default behavior of a given loan is determined by the changing levels and relationships of certain key variables such as interest rates, loan size, loan-to-value ratio, and home prices over the life of the loan. The role of each variable depends in a logical manner on its likely influence on mortgagor behavior or response.

- Borrowers have different propensities to voluntarily prepay or default on their loans based on characteristics such as the credit score, income, the nature of the collateral, and other factors. These differences may be captured by a statistical distribution of the borrower population. In general, those segments of the borrower population most likely to voluntarily prepay their loans are also the least likely to default on them.

- Because the population of loans is selectively depleted by prepayments and defaults that occur earlier in the life of the pool, both prepayment and default rates depend on the history of the pool.

- Differential rates of prepayment and default alter the shape of the distribution, leading to changes in the behavior of a pool of loans.[6] External events, such as large changes in interest rates, may also cause shifts in the distribution over time.

- Within each component of the model, relationships among the fundamental variables may be easily modified, to explore the effects of unanticipated demographic or market changes on prepayments and, hence, on values.

In the rest of this section we describe the implementation of this approach for voluntary prepayments on MH loans. In Section 21.3 we discuss defaults.

Application to Manufactured Housing Loans

The main difference between modeling prepayments on agency MBSs backed by site-built homes and on Conseco MH loans is the *wealth of loan level information that is available in the latter case*. With agency MBSs, the available information typically consists of the loan type and the WAC, WAM, and WALA of the loans in a pool. In contrast, with Conseco, information is available on many other characteristics, such as the original LTV (OLTV), borrower's credit and employment status, age of the borrower, size and location of the MH unit, whether the loan was used to purchase a home or refinance,

---

[6] For example, during a period of refinancing, the most financially capable borrowers will refinance at higher rates, leading to a higher proportion of "slow refinancers" in the remaining pool.

and so on. To take advantage of the availability of loan-level information, while simultaneously taking into account significant external variables such as interest rate levels and MH shipments, we use Proportional Hazards Analysis (PHA). This powerful statistical tool provides reliable estimates of the relative influence of all the variables on the different components of speeds, as well as a numerical determination of the baseline scenario. The results of PHA are combined with direct empirical and, in the case of defaults, also theoretical calculation of the baseline scenario. Together with a procedure for calculating the dynamical evolution of a pool of loans, this approach leads to a complete understanding of prepayment and default behavior.

What are some of the issues that need to be addressed? Starting with *housing turnover,* which is typically the most important component of MH prepayments, key elements include:

- An **overall turnover rate,** which is the proportion of homes that will be sold in a given period. This variable captures the effects of affordability and general economic conditions on turnover-related prepayments. For site-built homes, the turnover rate can be obtained by taking the volume of existing single-family homes sold (provided by the National Association of Realtors) and dividing it by the total stock of single-family homes in the United States (based on U.S. Census Bureau data).[7] For MH, however, no reliable information is available on the number of used units sold. We therefore use shipments of new MH units as a proxy for the strength of the MH sector. Projections can be modified for any assumed changes in interest rates or industry trends.

  Exhibit 21.4 shows the historical shipments of new MH units along with site-built home resales. Clearly, the two time series are not related by a simple multiplicative transformation, suggesting that the economics underlying the two processes are different. For example, MH shipments steadily increased over the 1992 through 1995 period, while sales of site-built homes changed little. By contrast, the steep declines in overall interest rates in 1998 led to a surge in sales of existing homes, while MH shipments stayed mostly flat.

- A **seasoning process,** which captures the rate at which home sales increase for the first few years, before leveling off. The seasoning process tends to vary by the type of loan and unit, and by the demographics of the borrowers.

---

[7] Sales of existing homes recently were about four million per year, while the total single-family housing stock is about 65 million units, giving a turnover rate of just over 6% per year.

EXHIBIT 21.4   MH Shipments and Site-Built Home Resales (In Thousands Per Month)

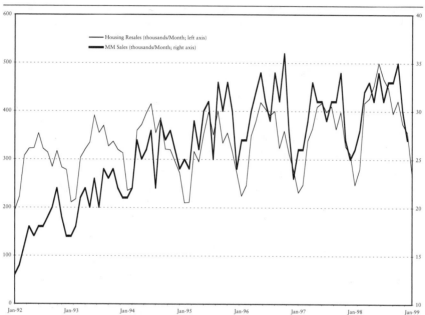

Sources: Manufactured Housing Institute and Salomon Smith Barney.

- **Relative mobility,** which captures how turnover rates vary by loan type, unit characteristics, and the demographics of the borrowers. The extensive loan-level information allows us to take into account a large number of loan-specific factors to distinguish precisely between likely speeds on different groups of loans. Furthermore, as prepayments change the mix of the pool, we can update the overall multiplier for the remaining loans, capturing the dynamics of the evolution of a loan pool.
- The **lock-in effect,** which refers to the disincentive to move resulting from rising interest rates.

The second major component of voluntary prepayments is *refinancings.* Although refinancings are not as important for MH loans as for site-built homes, there is evidence that the refinancing levels have increased over the past few years. In contrast to turnover, burnout plays a more significant role here. In the loan-level model, we capture burnout through the dependence of each loan's refinancing propensity on its characteristics. As

EXHIBIT 21.5 Mortgage Rates on MH Loans

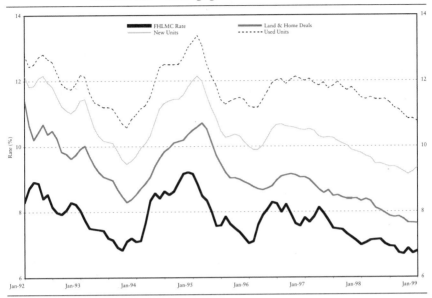

Sources: Salomon Smith Barney.

the pool experiences refinancings, the faster prepayers become depleted at faster rates, leading to a higher proportion of slower refinancers among the remaining borrowers. Hence, even if interest rates stay constant, the pool's refinancing rate slows down over time. This feature of refinancing is essential for any realistic modeling of refinancings, whether the calculations are done at the loan-level or on aggregated groups of loans.

A key variable in modeling refinancings (and for estimating the lock-in effect for turnover) is the prevailing mortgage rate for each loan. *For MH loans, it is important to use the appropriate rate for each loan, because rates vary by loan type* (new versus used versus land/home and others), *unit size,* and *OLTV.*[8] We have constructed historical MH rates for different loan categories based on the coupons on Conseco loans originated at those times. These are shown in Exhibit 21.5, along with the FHLMC weekly survey 30-year conforming mortgage rate. Although the spread between

---

[8] Loan characteristics can change over time, so that a class of rate appropriate at origination may not be the same as the one used for refinancings. We discuss this question in more detail later in this section.

the land-and-home loans and the conforming rate has decreased over the past several years, reflecting a convergence of products and an increased efficiency of this segment of the MH market, the spread between the rates on conforming loans and new or used MH units (without land) has actually increased over the same period. This is likely a result of more conservative pricing of risk associated with defaults and recoveries.

The final component of voluntary speeds is *curtailments and full payoffs*. For site-built homes, curtailments (or partial prepayments) are relatively minor (less than 0.5% CPR) for new or moderately seasoned loans, but increase as the loans become more seasoned. For MH loans, the Conseco data indicate that curtailments are quite low. *By comparing actual and amortized remaining loan balances, we estimate that curtailments amount to less than 0.25% CPR.*

The Seasoning Process and Benchmark Speeds

The starting point of our analysis is the seasoning process, a topic that has led to disagreements among researchers. The industry standard, the *MH Prepayment (MHP) Model*, which includes both voluntary speeds and defaults, assumes that loans are fully seasoned by age 24 months, with 100% MHP implying an initial speed of 3.7% CPR in month one, followed by an increase of 0.1% CPR in each subsequent month, until the speed levels out at 6% CPR in month 24. In fact, most MH deals have prepaid considerably faster than 100% MHP, leading to suggestions for a faster benchmark speed.

Exhibit 21.6 shows the realized *voluntary* prepayments of Conseco loans as a function of loan age. The loans are stratified into two classes, those originated prior to 1992 and those originated in 1992 and later.

Although the exact shape of the seasoning curve is not simple for either class, showing several levels of steepness early in the life of the loan and a peak around the age of five or six years, it appears that voluntary prepayments stop increasing after about six years. Because defaults enter a systematic decline after the age of about four years (as discussed in Section 21.3), it is not plausible to assume that the *total* speed remains constant after the initial seasoning period, as required by the MHP convention.

The impact of declining defaults on total speeds is illustrated in Exhibit 21.7, which shows speeds on loans originated in 1989.[9] After sharp run-ups in 1993 because of a refinancing wave, the total speed leveled out in 1996, even though voluntary prepayments increased in 1997 and 1998 in response

---

[9] To reduce the sampling error, the speed for each month is replaced by a three-month average over the adjacent months.

EXHIBIT 21.6 Origination Loans, 1988–1991 and 1992–1999: Voluntary Speeds versus Loan Age

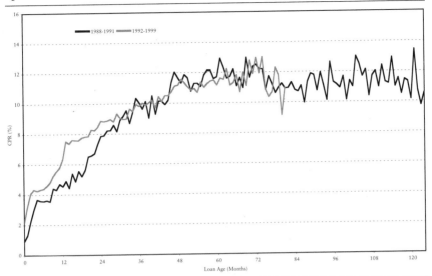

Source: Salomon Smith Barney.

EXHIBIT 21.7 Origination Loans, 1989: Voluntary Speeds and Defaults

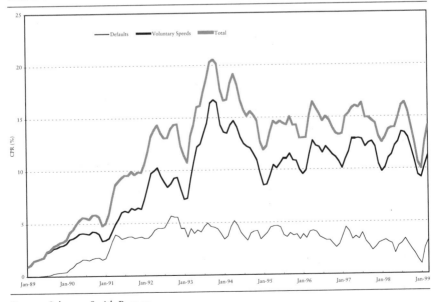

Source: Salomon Smith Barney.

to interest rate incentives. The reason is the decline in defaults, which is evident starting in 1993.

Exhibits 21.6 and 21.7 hint at some of the challenges encountered in estimating seasoning curves and benchmark speeds, including:

- **Interest rates.** Most of the loans originated prior to 1991 have been premiums in the 1990s, so that their speeds display the effect of interest rates as well as seasoning. Similarly, loans originated in late 1994, early 1995, late 1996, and early 1997 have experienced significant interest rate incentives from late 1997 onward.
- **MH shipments.** As Exhibit 21.4 shows, MH shipments have not been constant over the years. Higher shipments imply higher turnover and, thus, higher speeds.
- **Other external factors** that may be relevant for prepayments, such as MH depreciation and inflation rates, unemployment, and the level of personal bankruptcies, have undergone significant changes in the past 10 years. The steep decline in unemployment since 1992 and an equally steep rise in personal bankruptcies since 1994 are two examples.
- The **loan mix** has changed significantly since the early 1990s, for example, toward longer loan terms, often issued for a land/home combination, making older data of questionable relevance and suggesting a need to account for key collateral characteristics.

The last point indicates a more fundamental problem, namely, that a single seasoning curve will not work for different types of MH loans. For example, as we discuss later, it is reasonable to expect refinance loans to season faster than purchase loans and for loans on used units to season faster than those on new units. **Thus, just as loan, borrower, or unit characteristics affect the seasoned level of speeds, they also determine the time until the loans are fully seasoned.** Our approach is to first obtain prepayment curves for a **baseline** set of characteristics and then use the **loan-age** and **interest-rate dependent multipliers** obtained from PHA to adjust the curves for different cases. The baseline curve is defined to be the prepayment rate on a loan with a **20-year original term,** with a coupon that would provide **no more than 5% of refinancing savings** in that particular month, for the **purchase of a new single-wide unit** located on **private land,** with an OLTV between 87% and 93%.[10]

---

[10] Other variables that determine the baseline include loan size, points paid at origination, borrower's credit score and age. See Exhibit 21.9 for baseline values of these variables. Voluntary prepayments in Exhibit 21.8 are adjusted for the level of MH shipments.

EXHIBIT 21.8   Originations, 1992–1999: Baseline Prepayment Curves for Voluntary Prepayments and Defaults

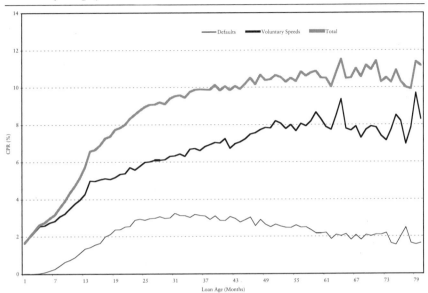

Source: Salomon Smith Barney.

Exhibit 21.8 shows historical speeds versus loan age for loans satisfying the baseline definitions. Only loans originated in 1992 and later are used in the calculation of the multipliers and the first six and a half years of the baseline curves. Beyond this period the curves are extended using earlier originations and, in the case of defaults, also theoretical arguments.

Compared with the aggregate voluntary prepayments shown in Exhibit 21.6, the baseline curve for voluntary prepayments is substantially lower, reaching only about 9% CPR. One of the key reasons is the absence of refinancing prepayments from the baseline curve. Another is the absence of loans for used units and units located in MH parks, both of which tend to turn over faster (see Section 21.3).

Projections for a specific deal will differ appreciably from the baseline curve, depending on the differences between the deal collateral and the baseline collateral. However, several general, qualitative statements can be made from Exhibit 21.8,[11] including:

---

[11] In Section 21.4 we provide prepayment projections for various Green Tree deals that incorporate the seasoning curves with all the adjustments.

- The seasoning curve is substantially longer than the 24 months assumed by MHP.
- The level at which total speeds plateau is much higher than implied by 100% MHP, which will not surprise anybody who has examined recent speeds. (Our projections for recent deals suggest speeds of about 190% MHP).
- Total prepayments decline for very seasoned loans in the absence of interest rate incentive, unlike the assumption of constant MHP.

The first adjustment to be made to the baseline curves is *seasonal variation*. Just like the seasonal variation of site-built home sales in the United States, due to factors such as the school year calendar and the weather, MH sales follow a seasonal pattern. Exhibit 21.4 shows the yearly variation of shipments of new MH units. Conseco prepayment data indicate that similar factors hold for voluntary prepayments. The estimated seasonal curve for MH prepayments is given in Exhibit 21.9.

EXHIBIT 21.9   MH Home Sales: Estimated Seasonal Factors

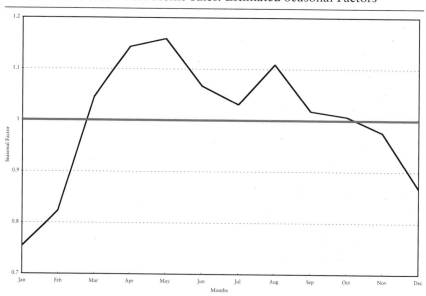

Source: Salomon Smith Barney.

The seasonal adjustments shown in Exhibit 21.9 are applied only to the housing turnover component of voluntary speeds.[12] For example, if the seasonal factor from Exhibit 21.9 is 1.1, then the projected turnover speed will be multiplied by 1.1.

Other adjustments to the baseline curve depend on the differences between the baseline case and the actual loans, and the levels of external factors that influence prepayments.

Major Determinants of Voluntary Prepayments

PHA provides an established statistical methodology for using loan-level data to identify major determinants of voluntary prepayments. The output of the analysis is a set of multipliers that allows us to adjust the baseline prepayment curve for any other type of loan. In addition to static variables, describing loan, borrower, and unit characteristics, we explicitly incorporate the dependence of voluntary prepayments on the level of MH shipments and the economic incentive to refinance (which in turn depends on interest rates and refinancing costs). The refinancing incentive (or, rather, the degree to which the loan is in or out of the money) enables us to clearly identify refinancing behavior, as well as the dependence of MH turnover on interest rates (the *lock-in effect*, for example).

Our analysis indicates that the most important collateral determinants of voluntary prepayments are *loan type* (new versus used versus land/home), *OLTV, location of unit* (MH park versus private land), *term of the loan, Salomon Smith Barney's credit score, size of the unit, loan purpose* (purchase versus refinance), and *loan size*, in that order. Together with the external inputs of the *level of MH shipments* and *interest rates*, these eight variables account for 94% of the fit.[13]

Other variables that have a statistically significant effect on voluntary prepayments are *borrower's age* and *employment status, disposable income,* and the *debt-to-income ratio.* In contrast to default behavior, for which borrower's characteristics are the most important predictors of default, here loan characteristics hold the largest explanatory power.

---

[12] Seasonal variation for refinancings is considerably less pronounced. It does not coincide with the seasonal variation of home sales.

[13] The fit is measured by the change in the log-likelihood function. When using PHA, it is essential that the fits for various explanatory variables be performed simultaneously; otherwise the effects of individual variables are poorly isolated and the resulting predictions for the combined effect can become grossly skewed.

EXHIBIT 21.10   Multipliers for Voluntary Prepayments: Maximum Likelihood Estimates

Variable		Multiplier	90% Confidence Interval
Loan Type	New	1	
	Used	1.377	1.340-1.414
	Land/Home	1.157	1.108-1.209
	Other	1	
OLTV (%)	≤80	1.295	1.266-1.325
	≥81	1	
Location of Unit	MH Park	1.233	1.205-1.262
	Private Land	1	
	Leased Land	0.848	0.822-0.875
Original Term (Months)	≤139	1.455	1.404-1.508
	140-169	1.170	1.115-1.228
	170-229	1.066	1.036-1.096
	≥230	1	
Credit	≤0.21	0.808	0.780-0.837
	0.22-0.48	0.825	0.799-0.852
	0.49-0.71	0.900	0.873-0.928
	0.72-1.21	1	
	1.22-1.57	1.133	1.101-1.166
	≥1.58	1.182	1.147-1.218
Unit Size	**Single**	1	
	Double	1.249	1.219-1.280
Loan is a Refinancing	Yes	1.318	1.270-1.368
	No	1	
Loan Size ($)	≤17,600	1.120	1.085-1.156
	17,601-46,400	1	
	46,401-54,000	1.072	1.027-1.119
	≥54,001	1.163	1.114-1.213
MH Shipments (000s/Month)	23-28	0.859	0.849-0.870
	28-33	1	
	33-38	1.183	1.168-1.198

Sources: Salomon Smith Barney.

Summary of Multipliers

Exhibit 21.10 gives overall multipliers for the key characteristics just discussed.[14] We also include the 90% confidence interval for each multiplier, as an indicator of the statistical reliability of the estimators. Some points to note:

■ The multipliers are averages across age and refinancing incentive. In many cases the multipliers vary by loan age and by refinancing incentive—in other words, a particular characteristic may have a different impact on new versus seasoned loans or on turnover versus refinancings.

---

[14] Except for refinancing savings whose impact is shown in Exhibit 21.11.

■ Values of some continuous variables (such as OLTV, loan term, and the credit score) are divided into ranges, and a multiplier is determined for each range. With interpolation between the midpoints of the ranges shown, the multiplier becomes a piecewise linear function of the underlying characteristic, removing restrictions of linearity inherent in PHA.[15] For other continuous variables (such as MH shipments) the ranges are displayed for convenience. Projected speeds are obtained by applying the multipliers to the exact value of the continuous variable.

Baseline values of the characteristics are indicated in bold. Projections for a particular group of loans would be obtained by adjusting the baseline voluntary prepayment curve shown in Exhibit 21.8 by the multipliers corresponding to the particular characteristics of the group.

In the rest of this section we discuss the effect of the key characteristics on overall speeds, on refinancing, and on seasoning.

Interest-Rate Effects and Refinancings

In addition to enhancing home sales, interest rate rallies can give rise to refinancings, which is the second major component of voluntary prepayments. Exhibit 21.7 shows a clear jump in voluntary speeds on 1989 loans in 1992 and 1993, when interest rates fell to their lowest levels in many years, indicating that refinancings are a factor in MH speeds. Further evidence is provided in Exhibit 21.11, which shows voluntary speeds for 1988 and 1992 origination loans along with the spread between the loan rates and prevailing MH rates.

The dependence of voluntary prepayments on interest rates is quite clear. Speeds increased in 1993, in 1996, and then again in the 1997 to 1998 refinancing period, although the refinancing levels on MH loans remained at only a fraction of the 60% CPR seen on many agency coupons in 1992, 1993, and 1998. Exhibit 21.11 also shows many additional features of rate sensitivity of MH loans. First, even though the 1988 origination loans experienced a higher rate incentive in 1998 than in 1993, the prepayment rate was lower. This is an example of *burnout*. Similarly, the prepayment speeds of 1992 loans in 1998 were not significantly higher than they were in 1996, again suggesting burnout. Second, the speeds of 1992 and 1988 loans were similar during the 1996 to 1998 period, even though the rate incentives differed by nearly 200bp (basis points). This suggests that the *collateral composition of each origination year should be taken into account*. It may also

---

[15] Linearity of the logarithm of prepayments, more precisely.

EXHIBIT 21.11 Loans Originated in 1988 and 1992: Voluntary Speeds and Spread to Prevailing Rates

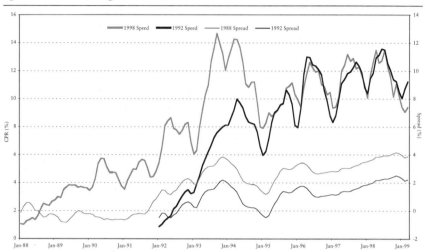

Source: Salomon Smith Barney.

imply that the simple difference in rates may not be the most effective way to measure the prepayment response to rate movements. Third, the dampening effect of higher rates on speeds, due to lower affordability and the lock-in effect, is also evident in Exhibits 21.7 and 21.11 (for example, in early 1995).

We measure the amount a loan is in or out of the money by the relative (percentage) savings (in present value terms) that can be realized if the loan were refinanced today into the currently available rate. The savings are given approximately by:

$$1 - \frac{(\text{Prevailing rate for given type of loan})}{(\text{Original coupon of the loan})} \times (1 + \text{Cost})$$

The cost estimate is obtained directly from Conseco, and it depends on the type of loan. It includes points charged, legal fees, processing fees, and appraisal fees. Typical values range from 3% to 5% of the loan amount.

Determination of the appropriate refinancing rate and costs for a given loan is not straightforward, however. Specifically, if a borrower is considering refinancing a unit which he or she purchased as new, should he expect to pay the prevailing rate and refinancing costs for a new unit or a used unit? We answered this question by identifying all pairs of Conseco loans in which the second one is a refinancing of the first.[16] Virtually all refinanced loans were identified as used units.[17] However, borrowers who originally purchased new units refinanced into a rate that was generally *between the rates available for purchases of new and used units.* In fact, the rate was about 50bp higher than the prevailing rate for the purchase of new units, but the variation over time was considerable.

The historical data, however, is too sparse to construct a reliable time series of a refinancing rate for new units (or for land/home loans), and in addition, the refinancing of a Conseco loan by another Conseco loan may not be fully indicative of the range of choices the borrower has. We therefore calculate the relative savings using the prevailing rate and costs *without change in loan type,* and then rely on direct fitting of historical prepayments to arrive at the correct refinancing curve.

Exhibit 21.12 shows the multipliers for the relative savings obtained from PHA. The multiplier in this case provides a measure of sensitivity of prepayments of baseline loans to interest-rate movements. The graph displays the multiplier for the relative savings versus the value of this variable (solid line) along with the 90% confidence interval (broken lines). The wide confidence interval for very high values of relative savings is an indication of a paucity of data in this regime. For easy comparison, the horizontal line representing the value of the refinancing multiplier at savings of −0.04 is highlighted. This multiplier corresponds to the scenario of unchanged interest rates, assuming a refinancing cost of 4%.

MH loans have much lower refinancing levels than site-built homes. Typically low loan balances (the mean is $33,000 in 1997 dollars), low equity, and relatively weaker credit borrowers explain part of the difference. Another part are the significantly higher refinancing costs and the new unit/used unit rate adjustment. Refinancings seem to pick up at relative savings of about 12% and accelerate sharply when the savings exceed 20%. Because the average coupon for Conseco's originations between 1992 and 1999 is about 10.2%, refinancing behavior becomes evident with a decrease in MH rates of about 160bp, and the trend accelerates rapidly when the rates fall by about 230bp. This is consistent with the patterns seen on agency MBSs, although the levels are much lower for MH loans; at a rate

---

[16] We matched the borrower's social security number, last payment on the first loan and origination date on the second loan, model year of the unit, and we required that the second loan be identified as a refinancing.

[17] Of all the refinanced loans, about 12% of all refinancings are identified as new units. In almost all of these cases, however, it was not possible to identify the loan that was refinanced, suggesting that other issuers originated the refinanced loans.

EXHIBIT 21.12   Effect of Relative Savings on Voluntary Prepayments

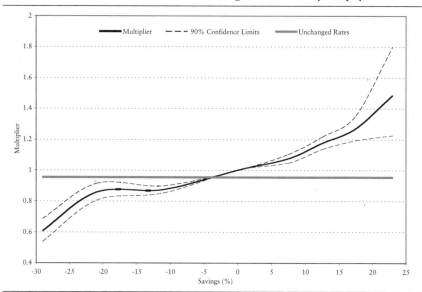

Source: Salomon Smith Barney.

incentive of about 200bp, agency MBSs are likely to have speeds in excess of 50% CPR (assuming little burnout), whereas the same rate change in Exhibit 21.12 implies a multiplier of about 1.4 and, hence, a voluntary speed of less than 12% CPR.

Over the past few years Conseco originations have included an increasing proportion of higher credit borrowers who purchase double-wide units, typically in a land-and-home deal and take out larger loans that amortize over 30 years. The response of such loans to rate incentives can be much stronger than that of a typical MH loan. We review later the prepayments speeds of such loans during the refinancing wave of 1998.

In addition to their impact on refinancings, interest-rate changes also have an effect on sales of existing MH units, with increasing interest rates leading to a drop in discount speeds. The suppression is the well-known *lock-in effect,* which results from the higher required payment that a move would entail. The decline in speeds is dramatic for savings of –20% and lower, suggesting that affordability of a new home plays a significant role in the decision of MH borrowers to relocate. It also appears that lower mortgage rates lead to an increase in home sales. Although it is difficult to separate turnover from refinancings, the modest increase in speeds for savings of less than about 10% and a multiplier of 1.1 is most likely due to increased home sales. A decrease in interest rates leads to greater housing affordability and, therefore, to increased turnover.

Loan Characteristics

Loans taken for the purchase of used units prepay on average about 38% faster than those on new units, holding all other variables fixed. The faster speeds on used units are apparent in Exhibit 21.13, which shows voluntary prepayments on 1993 origination loans for new and used units. Also displayed is the spread between the loan rates and the prevailing MH rates.

One explanation for faster speeds on used units is the slowdown of unit depreciation with age, as shown in Exhibit 21.24. This means that the loss resulting from the sale of a used unit is less severe than that for a new unit. In addition, the lower price of a used manufactured home, and a lower initial down payment, suggests a borrower who is more likely to have a temporary dwelling place in mind. This "self-selection" toward borrowers with shorter time horizons implies faster seasoning as well as faster speeds, and indeed, the data bear this out. Exhibit 21.14 shows the multipliers for used

EXHIBIT 21.13 1993 Loans for New and Used Units: Voluntary Speeds and Spread to Prevailing Rates

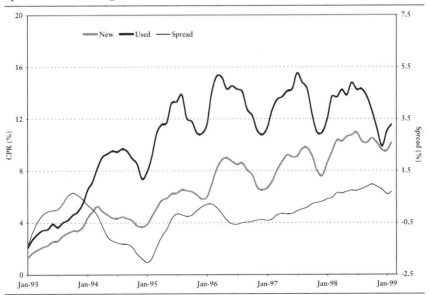

Source: Salomon Smith Barney.

EXHIBIT 21.14   Multipliers for Loans on Used Units

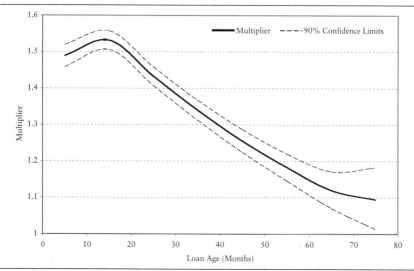

Source: Salomon Smith Barney.

units as a function of loan age, along with the 90% confidence interval. Following a small uptick between the ages of six and 15 months, the multipliers decline with age, although they remain above one even for seasoned loans. This indicates that after the first 15 months, loans on used units season faster than loans on new units, as indicated by the declining multiplier, but continue to prepay at a higher rate, as indicated by the fact that the multiplier remains greater than one. After several years, the prepayment rates for new and used units converge, as may be expected. This convergence is also evident for loans originated in 1993 (see Exhibit 21.13).

We expect most of the increased prepayment for used units to result from turnover. Lower loan balances, shorter time horizons (as demonstrated by significant negative correlations), and weaker financial strength of these borrowers lead to a diminished impetus to refinance. PHA supports this thesis, because *the multipliers are higher when the relative savings are negative* (when speeds would all be from housing turnover) *than when the relative savings are positive* (when a portion of the speeds is likely to derive from refinancings).

Exhibit 21.15 shows the mix of loan types in Conseco originations since 1988. The proportion of loans backed by used units has been relatively stable since 1992, ranging from 16% to 25%. We therefore do not expect a significant change in their impact on future prepayments. The situation is different

EXHIBIT 21.15   Conseco Originations: Distribution of Loan Types by
Origination Year, 1988–1998

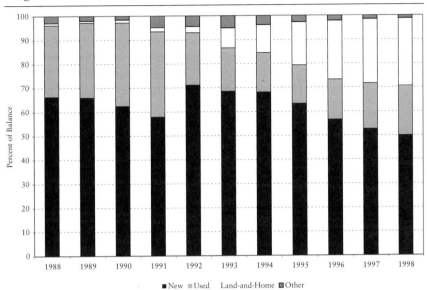

Source: Salomon Smith Barney.

with *land-and-home loans* whose proportion has grown rapidly in the collateral mix. Weighted by balance, they account for about 30% of loans originated in 1998 and 1999.

Compared with other MH loans, land-and-home loans have higher balances ($68,000 versus the average of $33,000 in 1997 dollars), longer loan terms (336 months versus the average of 264 months), lower OLTV (84% versus the average of 87%), and are taken for larger units (90% double-wide versus the average 62%) by borrowers of higher credit standing.[18] Not surprisingly, they refinance more readily than loans for homes without land, as the experience of 1998 has shown. Exhibit 21.16 displays the voluntary prepayments of land-and-home loans originated in 1994 through 1997, together with the interest-rate incentive as measured by differences between the origination rates and the prevailing coupon. The sharp spikes in speeds in 1998 show clear refinancing activity, which is roughly coincident with

---

[18] In contrast to loans for MH units alone, which are legally considered installment contracts, land-and-home loans are true mortgages.

the refinancing wave for agency mortgages (although the speeds are lower). PHA analysis takes the sensitivity of land-and-home loans to rate movements into account by delivering a *multiplier that increases with increasing relative savings.*

The steep prepayment peaks in March 1998 illustrate the role of the *media effect*[19] in MH refinancings. In early 1998 mortgage rates across a wide spectrum of products, including MH, reached multiyear lows, generating publicity that increased borrower awareness of refinancing opportunities and lender activity—the media effect. The result was an increase in refinancing speeds that was *greater than implied by refinancing savings.* Although muted compared with agency collateral, the effect was still significant for land-and-home MH loans (see Exhibit 21.16).

The prepayment pattern shown in the exhibit also points to the importance of conforming rates for the media effect relevant for MH prepayments. Even though land-and-home MH rates continued to decline after March 1998, the prepayment speeds slowed down. Apart from burnout, the explanation for the slowdown lies in the level of conforming rates. As shown in Exhibit 21.5, conforming rates increased slightly in the spring of 1998, leading to a rapid attenuation of the media effect and a slowdown in prepayments.[20]

Statistical identification of the media effect is not easy in loan-level analysis. We incorporate it into the prepayment model at the last stage, by direct fitting. For some deals, the sharp spikes in speeds triggered by the media effect correspond to prepayments of loans that are marginally in the money. This can be taken as evidence that, in addition to enhancing in the money refinancings, the media effect can also enhance turnover or generate cash-out refinancings.

OLTV

Borrowers with low OLTVs exhibit higher voluntary prepayment rates, but the effect levels off for OLTVs greater than about 85% (Exhibit 21.17). Our analysis suggests that loans with OLTVs lower than 81% prepay about 30% faster than those with OLTVs greater than 81%, other things being equal. One reason for this is that an adverse event (such as a divorce or loss of job) that could trigger a default in a more leveraged borrower here tends to lead

---

[19] See Chapter 4, "Anatomy of Prepayments."

[20] By the time conforming mortgage rates reached new multiyear lows in the fall of 1998, triggering a still stronger refinancing wave for agency collateral, the MH lending industry was experiencing a liquidity crisis that led to a suppression of refinancing opportunities for borrowers.

EXHIBIT 21.16 Land-and-Home Loans for Different Origination Years: Voluntary Speeds and Interest Rate Spreads

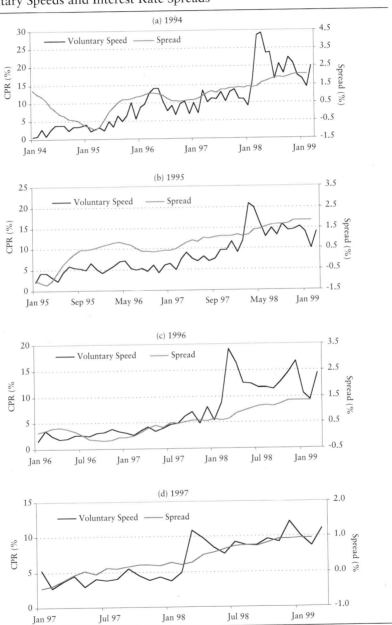

Source: Salomon Smith Barney.

EXHIBIT 21.17 Loans Originated in 1993: Voluntary Speeds by OLTV

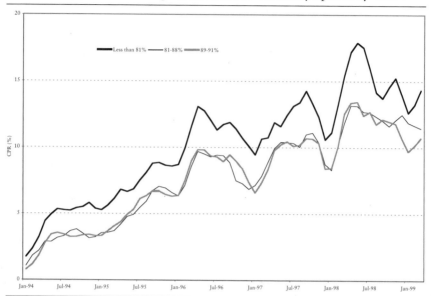

Source: Salomon Smith Barney.

to a sale, because the borrower's equity is less likely to become negative even if prices fall significantly. Another reason is that higher equity in the property enhances the borrower's ability to trade up (turnover) or to take equity out of the property through a refinancing.

The multipliers for OLTV decline with age, although remaining greater than one; for OLTVs less than 81%, for example, the multiplier for new loans is about 1.42, about 10% higher than the multiplier for loans that are 30 months seasoned. This indicates that *loans with lower OLTVs season faster;* over time, as might be expected, the effect of the initial LTV diminishes.

The multipliers also increase with relative savings, although the change is small until the savings reach about 15%. For larger savings, the multiplier increases significantly. At 20% relative savings, for example, loans with OLTVs less than 81% prepay 1.87 times faster than loans with higher OLTVs, indicating *a greater impact of OLTV on refinancings than on turnover.* Equity take-out refinancings are probably the major reason, although low OLTV borrowers are also likely to have higher awareness of refinancing opportunities, as a larger downpayment generally suggests greater financial resources and sophistication.

Exhibit 21.18 shows the distribution of OLTVs in Conseco originations over time. The fraction of loans with OLTV of less than 81% has decreased only modestly in the 1988 to 1999 period, from a high of 24% in 1991 to about 17% for recent originations. Correspondingly, we do not expect a significant shift in the relative importance of these loans in future voluntary prepayments. The significant increase of high-OLTV loans starting in 1993, however, does have a significant impact on default rates (see Section 21.3).

Original Loan Term

The effect of term is complicated, depending on whether the loan is a discount or a premium. Short-term loans (terms less than or equal to 15 years) have higher speeds than the baseline 20-year loans in the absence of a rate rally, but prepay *more slowly* when the relative savings exceed 13%. (The multiplier is about 0.9 for relative savings of 13% and decreases with increasing savings.) This indicates *faster turnover on shorter loans, but lower refinancings.* By taking a short-term loan the borrower indicates the expectation of a shorter stay in the property. In addition, the refinancing savings

EXHIBIT 21.18 Conseco Originations: Distribution of OLTV by Origination Year, 1988–1998

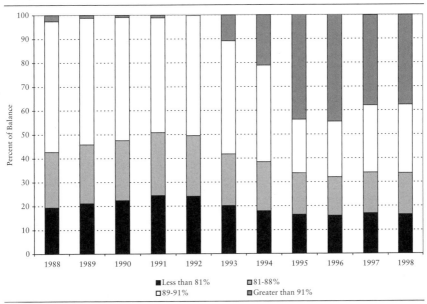

Source: Salomon Smith Barney.

that can be realized over the life of the loan are lower for short-term loans than for longer-term ones. At the other end of the spectrum, prepayments on 30-year loans are indistinguishable from prepayments on 20-year loans in the absence of refinancing opportunities, but longer loans prepay slightly faster for high values of relative savings (of about 20%).

Shorter borrowers' time horizon for short-term loans would also indicate *faster seasoning*. This is indeed the case, as is revealed in PHA through a multiplier that declines with loan age for the first several years. However, the multiplier *increases* for fully seasoned loans, suggesting the rapid amortization leads to a fast buildup of equity in the manufactured home, which in turn enhances the borrowers' ability to trade the property for a different one (and in some cases, perhaps to pay off the remaining balance). An example of some of the dependence of voluntary speeds on loan term is displayed in Exhibit 21.19, which shows the prepayments on 1996 origination loans with the original terms of 10, 20, and 30 years. Also displayed is the spread between the origination rate of the loans and the prevailing MH rate.

Exhibit 21.20 shows the mix of loan terms in Conseco originations in recent years.

The most significant trend in Exhibit 21.20 is the dramatic increase in 30-year loans since 1995, at the expense of all other loan terms. This change

EXHIBIT 21.19   Loans Originated in 1996 with Terms of 10, 20, and 30 Years: Voluntary Prepayments

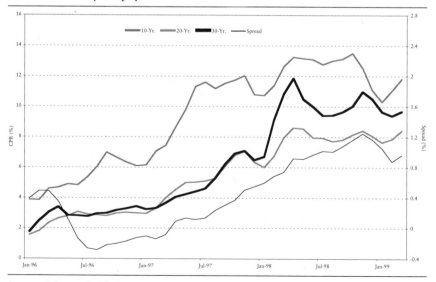

Source: Salomon Smith Barney.

EXHIBIT 21.20 Conseco Originations: Distribution of Loan Terms by
Origination Year, 1988–1998

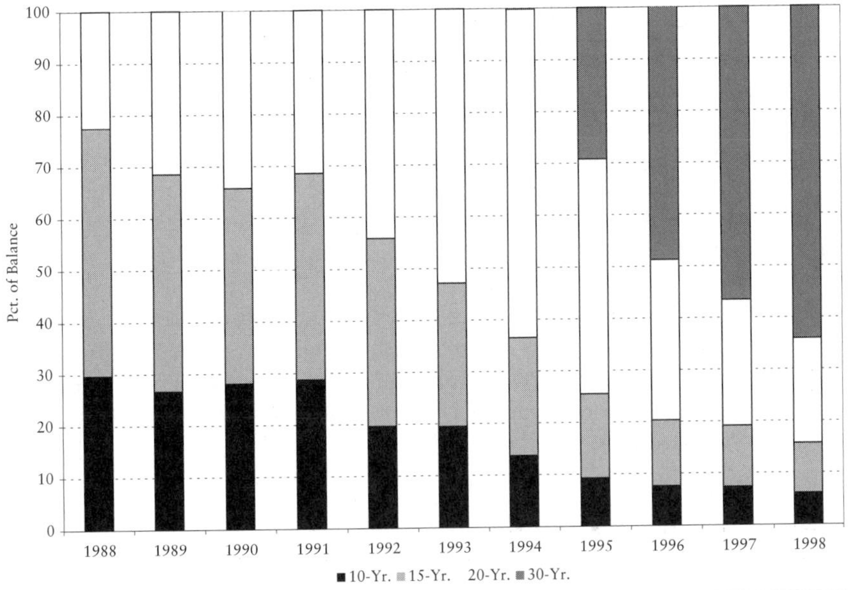

Source: Salomon Smith Barney.

suggests that the recent deals may be expected to have *lower baseline voluntary prepayment speeds, but higher sensitivity to interest rates.* This is consistent with the expected trend based on other collateral characteristics, such as
loan type.

Other Loan Characteristics

Refinancing loans prepay about 30% faster than purchase loans. This is not
surprising: A borrower who has refinanced a loan has already demonstrated
characteristics indicating faster speeds, such as equity in the property and
the financial knowledge to go through the refinancing process. The same
characteristics protect the borrower against defaults, triggering a sale of the
property instead. The multiplier declines with age, being about 1.40 for
loans age 0 to 18 months, and about 1.26 for loan ages greater than 18
months. *This indicates faster seasoning for refinanced loans,* which again is
in line with intuition; some of the factors that contribute to seasoning, such
as a growing family or increasing income, may already be in place when a
loan is refinanced.

Exhibit 21.21 displays the proportion of Conseco's originations that have been refinancings, along with the current coupon series for the baseline collateral and the average FHLMC coupon series. The exhibit shows that MH refinancings increased sharply in 1993 and 1998 when rates reached historical lows. Although MH refinancing activity did subsequently decline as rates rose in 1994 and then again at the end of 1996, it did not disappear. Our analysis of Conseco loans that were also refinanced by Conseco (described earlier) suggests a reason. In a significant portion of refinancings, ranging from 7% in 1994 to 21% in 1996 and nearly 60% in 1998, the new coupon was less than 50bp lower than the old coupon. In many cases it was actually higher. Yet, the borrowers typically benefited from refinancings by extending the loan terms and, therefore, reducing their monthly payments even without a significant decline in coupon, or by taking equity out of the property.

Loan balances are also a statistically significant determinant of prepayments. Both lower-balance and higher-balance loans prepay faster than baseline loans. The former benefit mostly from higher turnover (similar to short-term loans), while for the latter the enhancement of voluntary

EXHIBIT 21.21   Conseco Originations: Proportion of Loans That Are Refinancings and Interest Rates, 1992–1998

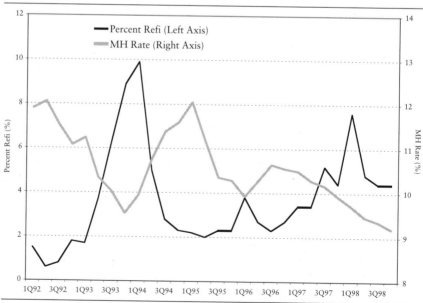

Source: Salomon Smith Barney.

speeds results mostly from higher prepayments in the presence of interest-rate incentives.

Unit Characteristics

A MH unit can be located in a MH park, on land the borrower owns (almost all land-and-home loans are in this category),[21] or on leased land. The presence of private land is a significant determinant of voluntary prepayments. Borrowers who own land have a larger financial stake in a (nonmovable) property and are naturally inclined to consider a longer time horizon, which implies slower turnover. PHA estimates that borrowers in a MH park are about 23% more likely to prepay than borrowers who own the land (which we take to be the baseline case). Leasing land, in contrast, suggests a borrower of weaker economic means who is able to afford the land but is unwilling or unable to afford to live in a MH park. Economics and long leases that likely result in such cases are suggestive reasons for the low turnover of such borrowers. They prepay 15% more slowly that those who own the land, and 31% more slowly than MH residents. All multipliers are relatively flat with age, *indicating uniformly slower speeds, rather than a seasoning effect.* Exhibit 21.22 shows voluntary prepayments for loans originated in 1994, separated according to the presence of private land, along with the spread between the loan rates and the prevailing MH rates.

One of the most striking features of Exhibit 21.22 is the sharp acceleration of prepayments for owners of land during the refinancing wave of 1998. (The 1998 pattern closely follows the prepayments on land-and-home loans shown in Exhibit 21.16.) PHA recognizes this enhanced sensitivity to rate movements. At relative savings of 18%, the multiplier for an MH park is about 0.67, which represents a 45% decrease compared with the base case of no refinancing incentive. More limited financial resources of park residents relative to owners of land, coupled with a lower incentive to refinance (presence of land is positively correlated with loan size and loan term), lead to a lower refinancing propensity. Relative to owners of land, the prepayments land lessees are also inversely related to the relative savings, although the decrease is only about half of that for MH park loans.

Since 1988 the proportion of loans financing units in MH parks has declined gradually, from about 48% in 1990 to 31% in 1998. The difference has been evenly divided between loans in which the borrower owns and those in which he leases the land (in 1998 the breakdown was 54% for land

---

[21] The borrower can either own the land outright or have purchased it through a financing arrangement.

EXHIBIT 21.22   Loans Originated in 1994: Impact of Land on
Voluntary Prepayments

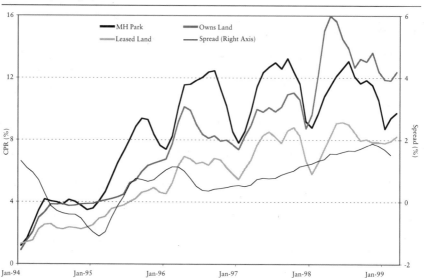

Source: Salomon Smith Barney.

ownership versus 15% for land leasing). This trend implies that newer deals
may exhibit *lower baseline speeds, but higher refinancing propensity in rate
rallies.*

Unit size also affects voluntary prepayments, with loans on double-
wide (and multiple-wide) units prepaying about 25% faster than loans on
single-wides, all other things being equal. The multiplier for double-wide
units increases slowly with relative savings, indicating slightly higher refinancing propensity, and decreases with loan age, suggesting a longer seasoning ramp.

Borrower Characteristics

Salomon Smith Barney's credit score is the most significant borrower characteristic for voluntary prepayments (as it is for defaults—it is by far the
strongest predictor of default behavior). Not surprisingly, lower credits prepay more slowly than higher ones. (Trading up in credit, which is so prominent for home equity loans, does not play a significant role here.) There
seems to be little dependence on relative savings, suggesting that credit

EXHIBIT 21.23 Loans Originated in 1994: Voluntary Speeds by Borrower Credit

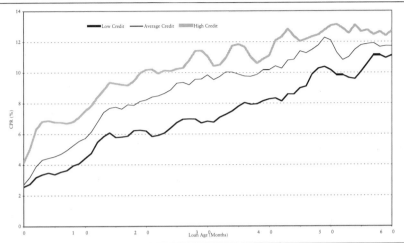

Source: Salomon Smith Barney.

impairment (or enhancement) has similar effects of turnover and refinancings.[22] After the loan age exceeds five years, the explanatory power of credit wanes. Reasons for this decline fall into three broad categories. First, the behavior of borrowers with different credit scores may converge as other variables become more significant after an appreciable amount of time has passed. Second, the value of the credit score itself may age, so that it fails to accurately represent a borrower's credit profile after five or more years have elapsed. And third, the gaps in reported information are larger for older originations, making the separation of borrowers according to credit score less reliable. Exhibit 21.23 illustrates the effect of credit scores on prepayments, as a function of loan age. Loans originated since 1992 are divided into six credit groups, and the first, fourth, and sixth group in the order of increasing score are displayed. We discuss the credit score in more detail in Section 21.3.

Of the remaining variables, disposable income and borrower's age exhibit a non-negligible correlation with credit, which diminishes their explanatory power. The multipliers for both of these variables, as well as the

---

[22] The statistical uncertainty of credit dependence on relative savings is large, however.

debt-to-income ratio follow expectations. Younger borrowers with higher disposable incomes and lower debt-to-income ratios prepay faster than average.

21.3 DEFAULTS

Our analysis and modeling of defaults is a synthesis of two distinct approaches. The first one is a mathematical model, which provides a *baseline curve* for default rates as a function of loan age. The second one is PHA, which is used to derive *risk multipliers* for nonbaseline values of loan, unit, borrower, and macroeconomic characteristics.

As with our analysis of voluntary prepayments, we rely primarily on 820,000 loans originated between 1992 and March 1999 to determine the impact of various variables on defaults. When evaluating long-term historical trends, however, such as MH inflation and depreciation, we make use of older loans as well.

Our key conclusions are as follows:

- The most important drivers of defaults are Salomon Smith Barney's proprietary credit score, the presence of private land, loan type, OLTV, and the national level of personal bankruptcies.
- The top three variables account for more than 81% of the fit and the top five variables account for more than 92% of the fit.[23]
- The model developed explains *quantitatively* the full range of observed default rates.

Theoretical Modeling of Defaults

To model defaults (for any type of loan), we first use a mathematical formulation to derive a theoretical baseline default curve as a function of loan age. The approach is described in detail in Appendix 21A, but the key features are the following:

- Home prices are assumed to fluctuate randomly around some price trend. For example, if the price trend is 3% per year, then for a particular pool of loans, home prices will on average increase 3% per year, but will display some volatility around this average increase.

---

[23] As measured by the log-likelihood estimate.

- For MH loans, the average trend will be a combination of general increases in the price of MH units of fixed age (i.e., housing inflation rate
  for MH) and the depreciation of used units.
- Defaults are assumed to occur if (1) there is negative equity in the home,
  and (2) there is some external trigger event, such as loss of job or divorce,
  that diminishes the borrower's ability to make monthly payments.

Net Changes in MH Prices   As noted, changes in MH unit prices depend on
depreciation as well as inflation. We evaluate both quantities directly from
Conseco data.

Exhibit 21.24 shows the average depreciation rate as a function of unit
age for single-wide units manufactured since 1980 (which form the baseline
case for defaults), with loans originated between January 1992 and March
1999. The exhibit was obtained by first calculating the depreciation curve
for each loan origination year, weighing the annual depreciation rate for
each unit age by the original balance, and then averaging the depreciation
curves over the origination years. *The annual depreciation rate declines with
unit age,* starting from more than 7% in year one and reaching the level of
1% to 2% in years 16 and greater. For the model we take the depreciation

EXHIBIT 21.24   Annual MH Depreciation Rate by Unit Age

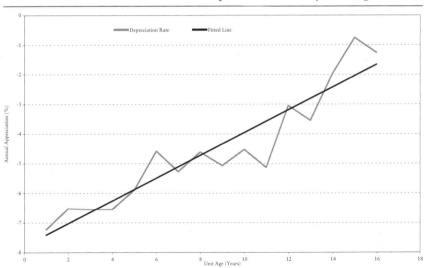

Source: Salomon Smith Barney

EXHIBIT 21.25   Annual MH Inflation Rate by Year

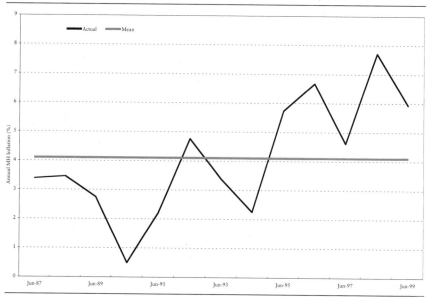

Source: Salomon Smith Barney

curve to be given by the straight line shown in the exhibit, leveling off at −1% for loan ages greater than 16 years.[24]

Exhibit 21.25 displays the annual MH inflation rate for used single-wide units for the period of January 1987 through March 1999.[25] Although an increasing trend of MH inflation with time is discernible, we do not take it into account for the modeling of the baseline curve. In the absence of an econometric model of MH inflation, a long-term average is likely to have the most relevance for long-term projections. We therefore take the MH inflation rate to be constant, at just over 4%. This number is higher than the overall inflation rate as measured by the Consumer Price Index (CPI). (Over the same period, CPI increased at an annual rate of about 3%.) The difference is mostly due to increased demand for manufactured homes and improving quality of the units. (The latter does not have an impact on defaults,

---

[24] The depreciation rate may depend on the presence of land. Although the data are very limited, the combined price of land and a MH unit appears to decrease with age at a slightly slower rate than the price of a MH unit alone.

[25] We computed the inflation rate separately for each year of unit age and then averaged the results. Each calendar year is represented by one point on the graph.

but we do not attempt to distinguish the contributions of the two factors to the MH inflation rate.)

According to Conseco data, then, the average price trend[26] for a used single-wide unit is a function of unit age, starting at age one with a *decrease* of 3.1%. That is, *in current dollars,* the price of a unit that is one year old diminishes by 3.1% per year, with the rate of price decrease slowing over time. For older units, inflation may become the dominant factor, leading to a net *increase* in price.

What Is the Appropriate Volatility of MH Prices?

There are three main sources of volatility:

1. Volatility of general MH inflation (as measured, for example, by changes in prices of new MH units);
2. Volatility in depreciation rates of used MH units; and
3. Volatility owing to the condition, upkeep, location, and so on, of a particular unit.

Although direct empirical estimation is difficult for (2) and (3), we can use our model and observed Conseco default rates to estimate an *implied volatility.* Using direct fitting, we obtain an implied annual volatility of approximately 12% for loans originated since 1992.

Default Lags

The lag between the time a borrower stops making payments and when the repossessed unit is sold (thus terminating the loan) is often substantial, and needs to be taken into account when modeling defaults. Exhibit 21.26 shows a distribution of these lag times based on Conseco data.

Because our approach to defaults deals with economic conditions that trigger the response of a borrower, the distribution of lag times shown in Exhibit 21.26 is used to determine when a default would actually be registered. For example, if a borrower stops making payments in month 36, then the actual default would occur in months 37, 38, or thereafter according to the probability weights shown in Exhibit 21.26. The average lag time for Conseco is about 8.9 months.

As an example of the usefulness of the approach described so far in explaining MH defaults, we apply this model without any refinements to the

---

[26] Price trend = Inflation – Depreciation.

EXHIBIT 21.26 Distribution of Lag Times between Last Payment and Loan Termination

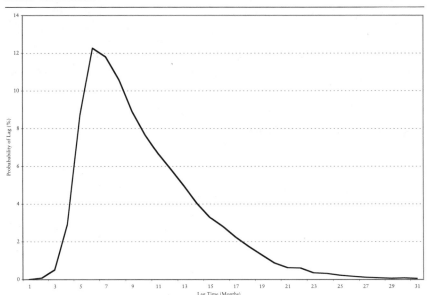

Source: Salomon Smith Barney.

actual default rates of loans originated in the 1988 to 1991 period. Exhibit 21.27 shows the actual and projected default rates as a function of loan age. Model projections were obtained using a WAC of 13.86%, an original loan term of 192 months, an OLTV of 86%, an initial average unit age of 46 months (these are averages of loans in the sample), and an inflation rate of 4.1%. The implied volatility was calculated to be about 14% and the constant likelihood of an external trigger event (the scaling factor Q in Equation 21.3, Appendix 21A) was estimated to be 0.0116 per month.

The projected curve matches the actual curve quite well. This is particularly noteworthy, given the many simplifying assumptions that were made in computing the projected curve: we used a single OLTV, loan term, and WAC (rather than several, and then averaging the projected defaults), and we completely neglected the variation in collateral characteristics and macroeconomic factors.

Nevertheless this simple approach has limitations. For example, the WAM, WAC, OLTV, and so on, of loans originated since 1992 are sufficiently different from those of the loans originated prior to that time, so

EXHIBIT 21.27   MH Loans Originated from 1988 to 1991: Actual and
Projected Seasoning Curves for Defaults

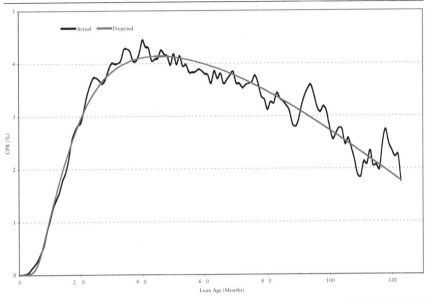

Source: Salomon Smith Barney.

that a single curve cannot offer a satisfactory fit of defaults of all Conseco
MH loans. Moreover, and more significantly, the fit presented in Exhibit
21.27 does not offer a prescription for the variation of the level of defaults
(the scaling factor Q) with collateral characteristics and economic conditions, thus precluding a meaningful comparison across deals or vintages.
Next we remove some of these restrictions by showing how loan characteristics and the economic environment can be taken into account through risk
multipliers, which can then be used to improve deal-level fits and obtain reliable projections.

Which Characteristics Best Predict Defaults?

Based on PHA, the most important determinants of defaults are *Salomon
Smith Barney's credit score, location of unit* (MH park versus private land),
OLTV, the *national level of personal bankruptcies* (number of quarterly fil-
ings for personal bankruptcies per 1,000 population), *loan type* (new versus

used versus land/home), and *original loan term*.[27] These six variables account for more than 91% of the fit, indicating a greater concentration of explanatory power than for voluntary prepayments. The credit variable alone explains more than 54% of the fit, making it by far the best predictor of default propensity. In addition to these six determinants of defaults, other variables whose impact can be identified include *borrower's employment status, debt-to-income ratio, loan amount, unit size* (single versus double), *borrower's age, presence of cosigner,* and marginally, *the level of unemployment.*

The definition of the baseline case, indicated in bold, and the risk multipliers are given in Exhibit 21.28. As for voluntary prepayments, the multiplier for some continuous variables, such as the credit score, OLTV, and loan term, is a piecewise linear function of the underlying characteristic, obtained by interpolation between the midpoints of the ranges shown.

Credit

As we noted, Salomon Smith Barney's credit score is by far the most important determinant of defaults. The score is constructed from the information reported by the borrower on the loan application and from credit bureau reports. It is designed to simplify the measurement of various credit-related characteristics on defaults, while maintaining the predictive power of all of the components. The definition of the credit score is independent of origination year, enabling a uniform comparison of collateral of varying vintage. For loans originated between January 1992 and March 1999, the credit score ranges from about −2.0 to 4.4 and has a mean and standard deviation of 0.91 and 0.62, respectively. Exhibit 21.29 shows the actual default rates for loans originated since 1992, as a function of loan age for five different groups of borrowers, separated by credit score (the approximate mean value of the credit score for each group is given in the legend). The clear separation of curves demonstrates the predictive power of the variable.

In addition to *faster seasoning* and *higher peak default rates,* loans with low credit scores in the exhibit also display a *much faster decline* of defaults with age relative to loans with average credit. A similar conclusion follows by comparing Exhibits 21.29 and 21.27. This may be taken as evidence of positive selection among the lowest-credit borrowers. The ones most likely to default exit the pool at a higher rate, whereas the remaining ones likely improve their credit standing, reverting their default propensity toward the mean.

---

[27] As for voluntary prepayments, the fit is measured by the change in the log-likelihood function.

EXHIBIT 21.28 Multipliers for Defaults: Maximum Likelihood Estimates

Variable		Multiplier	90% Confidence Interval
Credit	≤0.21	2.493	2.429-2.558
	0.22-0.48	1.715	1.671-1.761
	0.49-0.71	1.279	1.244-1.315
	0.72-0.94	**1**	
	0.95-1.21	0.799	0.775-0.825
	1.22-1.57	0.613	0.591-0.635
	≥1.58	0.439	0.420-0.458
Location of Unit	MH Park	1.648	1.617-1.681
	Private Land	**1**	
	Leased Land	1.230	1.202-1.259
OLTV (%)	≤80	0.733	0.714-0.752
	81-90	**1**	
	91-94	1.252	1.213-1.292
	≥95	1.261	1.237-1.284
Personal Bankruptcies	0.81-0.91	0.705	0.676-0.735
	1.00-1.10	0.844	0.826-0.861
	1.18-1.28	**1**	
	1.36-1.46	1.185	1.161-1.210
	1.55-1.65	1.418	1.360-1.480
Loan Type	**New**	**1**	
	Used	1.617	1.582-1.653
	Land/Home	0.432	0.410-0.455
	Land-in-Lieu	0.374	0.334-0.419
Original Term (Months)	≤139	0.593	0.573-0.614
	140-169	0.673	0.644-0.702
	170-229	0.759	0.742-0.776
	230-309	**1**	
	≥310	1.082	1.054-1.111
Employment	**Employed**	**1**	
	Retired	1.272	1.231-1.315
	Not Employed with Income	1.656	1.596-1.719
Debt-to-Income Ratio (%)	≤ 23	0.879	0.823-0.939
	24-30	0.920	0.870-0.973
	≥ 31	**1**	
Loan Size ($)	≤ 17,600	0.663	0.638-0.689
	17,601-25,400	0.721	0.700-0.743
	25,401-33,200	0.855	0.833-0.876
	33,201-46,400	**1**	
	46,401-54,000	1.216	1.173-1.260
	≥ 54,001	1.358	1.306-1.411
Unit Size	**Single**	**1**	
	Double	0.683	0.668-0.699

Source: Salomon Smith Barney.

EXHIBIT 21.29 Loans Originated Since 1992: Impact of Credit on Defaults

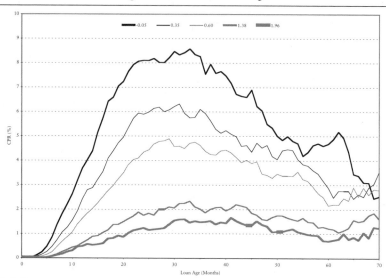

Note: −0.05 denotes a SSB credit score of less than 0.22, 0.35 denotes a SSB credit score of 0.22 to 0.48, and so on.
Source: Salomon Smith Barney.

The credit categories below the baseline as defined in Exhibit 21.28 contribute to the fit much more significantly than the ones above. Therefore the default behavior of low-credit borrowers is more predictable, implying that the most useful application of the SSB credit score is in identifying borrowers likely to exhibit defaults significantly above the mean.

Two views of the historical distribution of credit scores are provided in Exhibits 21.30 and 21.31. Exhibit 21.30 shows the mean and the standard deviation of credit scores by quarter of origination, whereas Exhibit 21.31 shows the distribution of scores by origination year.

Following a significant uptick in credit in 1993, registered by a rise in the mean score, an increase in the proportion of highest credit borrowers and a decrease in the proportion of lowest-credit borrowers, the mean credit score has declined since that time, stabilizing at about 0.9. Its standard deviation has increased, however, indicating that the spectrum of borrowers has widened. Significantly for defaults, the proportion of lowest-credit borrowers has increased since 1993, reaching about 16% in

EXHIBIT 21.30 Conseco Originations: Mean and Standard Deviation of SSB Credit Score by Quarter of Origination, 1992–1999

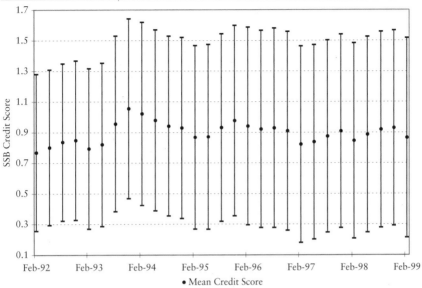

Note: The circle in the center of each line is the mean, and the line represents two standard deviations.
Source: Salomon Smith Barney.

1997 and 15% in 1998.[28] Therefore, based on credit alone we would not expect that the recent vintages would have a significantly better performance than those of the early to mid-1990s. But credit is only part of the story, of course.

Location of Unit

Ownership of land strongly suppresses the default rate. One of the reasons is the time evolution of the value of land. In contrast to a MH unit, the price of land generally increases with time, decreasing the likelihood of negative equity that could trigger a default. Another reason is the longer time horizon that land, either purchased or leased, implies. As we noted in

---

[28] The distribution of borrowers in early 1999 originations does not appear significantly different from that in 1998 originations.

EXHIBIT 21.31   Conseco Originations: Distribution of SSB Credit Score by Origination Year, 1988–1998

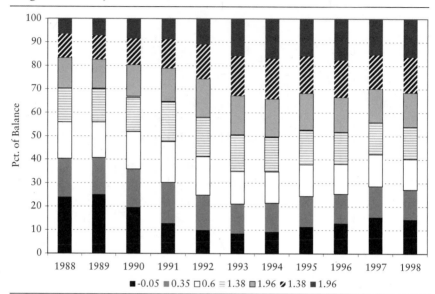

Source: Salomon Smith Barney.

the section on voluntary prepayments, a borrower located in a MH park has a higher likelihood to sell the property than a borrower who owns or leases land. If the equity in the property is very small, such a borrower may simply decide to default and move, becoming, in effect, a convenience defaulter. A third reason is the greater financial and credit strength of borrowers who own or lease the land. For example, owners of land have higher credit scores than park residents (0.98 versus 0.84), higher disposable incomes ($1,500 versus $1,300 per month), and lower debt-to-income ratios (36% versus 37.5%).[29] Those who lease the land generally fall between the two categories. Exhibit 21.32 shows the actual default rates for three groups of borrowers based on the location of unit, for loans originated since 1992.

As we pointed out in the section on voluntary prepayments, as a fraction of the overall loan production, the ownership of land has increased over time,

---

[29] Because unit location is such an important determinant of default, the correlation with these other variables can account only for part of its significance.

EXHIBIT 21.32   Loans Originated Since 1992: Impact of Land Ownership on Defaults

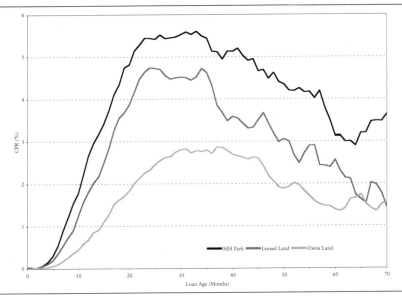

Source: Salomon Smith Barney.

from 43% in 1990 to 54% in 1998, while leasing of land has risen from 9% to 15%. These trends clearly have a *beneficial effect on default rates*.

OLTV

The role of OLTV in defaults is clear from our description of the default process at the beginning of this section and in Appendix 21A. Higher initial LTV increases the likelihood that equity in the property will become negative at some point, opening a door for a default. PHA confirms this intuition by assigning increasing multipliers to higher OLTVs. (Although the difference between a low 80%s OLTV and a high 80%s OLTV is not statistically significant.) Exhibit 21.33 shows actual defaults on loans with different OLTVs, as a function of loan age.[30] The exhibits in the legend give the approximate mean OLTV for each group.

---

[30] Because there were few high-OLTV loans originated prior to 1994, the maximum loan age is smaller than that in Exhibits 21.26 and 21.30.

EXHIBIT 21.33   Loans Originated Since 1992: Impact of OLTV on Defaults

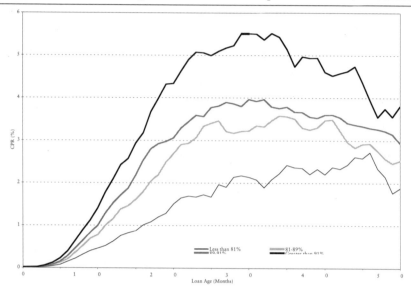

Source: Salomon Smith Barney.

As we discussed in the section on voluntary prepayments (see Exhibit 21.18), the proportion of loans with OLTV's greater than 91% has increased significantly since 1992.[31] It peaked in 1996 at 45% of balance-weighted originations and declined subsequently to about 38% in 1998. Taken by itself, this fact suggests higher default rates for pools originated in 1995 and later, compared with 1992 to 1994 originations.

Loan Type

Loans for used units are about 60% more likely to default than loans for new units, whereas land-and-home loans are nearly 60% *less* likely to default than loans for new units, all other things being equal.[32] The reasons are

---

[31] An OLTV of 95% appears to be a practical cutoff, because the number of loans with higher OLTVs is small, amounting to less than 3% of originations since 1992.

[32] Land-in-lieu refers to loans where land that is not financed is pledged as collateral. Even though their default behavior is significantly better than that of other groups, these loans are of limited importance because they form a very small fraction of new originations (about 0.5% in 1997 and 1998).

similar as the ones for the location of the unit: presence of land for land-and-home loans, longer time horizons for either new units or land-and-home loans compared with used units, as demonstrated by higher turnover rate on used units, and stronger financial profiles of land-and-home borrowers compared with purchasers of new and used units. As Exhibit 21.15 shows, land-and-home loans have formed an increasing part of recent origination, accounting for about 30% of the volume in 1998 and 1999. At the same time, the proportion of loans for used units has remained relatively steady since 1992, between 16% and 25%. Based on this characteristic, then, more recent vintages should have significantly better default performance.

Loan Term

Compared with long-term loans, shorter-term loans default at significantly lower rates, all other things being equal. Although the difference between 20- and 30-year loans is small, 10-year loans default at only 60% of the rate for 20-year loans. A short-term loan generally indicates a borrower who has the determination and financial ability to pay off the loan as soon as possible. He or she does not seek to maximize the amount of loan by extending the term to keep the monthly payments manageable. Rather, the rapid buildup of equity is probably the motivation. Independent of the financial condition of the borrower, rapid equity buildup resulting from fast amortization also shortens the risk period over which the LTV ratio can exceed one, leading to lower defaults.

This reasoning also suggests an explanation for two additional features. First, the difference in default rates between 20- and 30-year loans is small, as would be expected based on amortization rates. Over the first few years of the life of the loan, the difference in the amount of principal paid off between these two loan terms is small. And second, for all loan terms the default rates over the first 15 months are very similar. Referring to Exhibit 21.26, which shows the distribution of lag times between last payment and default, the defaults registered over the first 15 months of loan age result from borrower action that takes place prior to the first anniversary of loan origination. Over such a short amortization period the differences in equity buildup between different loan terms are negligible. Exhibit 21.34 illustrates the dependence of defaults on loan term for loans originated since 1992.[33] The historical distribution of loan terms is shown in Exhibit 21.20.

---

[33] The default history of 30-year loans is too limited to cover the full range of loan ages displayed.

EXHIBIT 21.34   Loans Originated Since 1992: Impact of Loan Term on Defaults

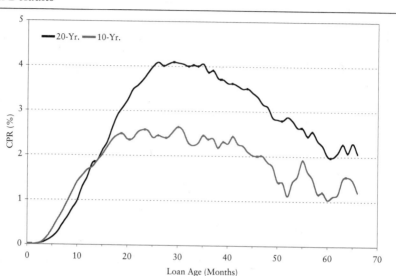

Source: Salomon Smith Barney.

Macroeconomic Factors

The national level of personal bankruptcies is an important predictor of the default rate on MH loans, both in terms of the magnitude of the effect and its statistical significance. As Exhibit 21.28 indicates, an increase in the bankruptcy rate of 0.12 per 1,000 population (a 10% rise from the baseline level of about 1.23[34]) increases the default rate by 12%, whereas a rise of 0.24 (a 20% increase relative to the baseline level) increases the defaults by 26%. Such changes in personal bankruptcies are fully within the range of recent historical experience. For example, between the first quarter of 1994 and the second quarter of 1998 the level of personal bankruptcies increased by 0.60 per 1,000 population, representing an increase of nearly 80%. Exhibit 21.35 shows historical prepayments on loans taken out for units on private land and originated since 1988. Also shown is the level of personal bankruptcies. The correspondence between the two time series is clear.[35]

---

[34] The level indicates the number of personal bankruptcy filings in the preceding three months, divided by the size of the population in thousands.

[35] The relative change in defaults from 1994 to 1998 becomes even more pronounced if, in addition to the location of the unit, borrower's credit score and original loan

EXHIBIT 21.35   Defaults on Loans Originated Since 1988 and
Personal Bankruptcies

Source: Salomon Smith Barney.

A detailed discussion of personal bankruptcies is outside the scope of this chapter. However, over the 1990 to 1994 period, the level of bankruptcies was closely correlated with unemployment, mirroring the state of the economy. Subsequent to this period, personal bankruptcies started to increase sharply, as shown in Exhibit 21.35. The increase was in line with the deteriorating credit performance of the consumer loan industry, such as credit card receivables, and can be attributed to a number of factors. These include the development of technology-driven, economy-of-scale players, intense competition for market share, high consumer debt leverage levels, demographic shifts in the population, and rising disposable income. The dependence of MH default rates on personal bankruptcies is therefore a reflection of broader trends in the consumer lending industry.

---

term are also controlled for. Such a refinement, however, leads to a relatively small sample size and noisy defaults, especially for the period prior to 1993.

Default Projections

As we pointed out, the mix of originated loans has changed substantially since the late 1980s and early 1990s in ways that unambiguously affect defaults. Some noteworthy changes with a potentially favorable impact on default rates include:

- The proportion of land-and-home loans has increased dramatically since 1992, as shown in Exhibit 21.15. At the same time, the proportion of used units has decreased since the late 1980s and early 1990s, from the high of 36% in 1991 to the current level of 16% to 19%.
- The proportion of loans for units located on private or leased land has increased modestly at the expense of units located in MH parks.
- Double- and multiple-wide units form a larger fraction of current originations, increasing from 46% in 1988 and 47% in 1989 to 65% in 1997 and 69% in 1998.

Changes with a potentially negative impact on defaults partially offset these trends:

- The proportion of lowest credit borrowers has increased since 1993 (see Exhibit 21.31).
- Loans originated recently carry substantially longer terms (see Exhibit 21.20). For example, until 1993 the majority of loans had terms of 15 years or less, whereas today such loans represent less than 26% of originations. Part, though not all, of the increase is due to land-and-home loans.
- Newer loans have higher OLTV ratios (see Exhibit 21.18). Significantly for defaults, the increases came from loans with OLTV greater than 90%.
- The debt-to-income ratio has increased modestly, from the low of 32% in 1992 to 37% in 1997 and 36% in 1998. Most of the increase came from the growing ranks of borrowers for whom the debt-to-income ratio exceeds 45%. According to the data in Exhibit 21.28, however, the impact of such borrowers on defaults is not significant, as long as other relevant variables are controlled for.
- Inflation-adjusted average loan size has increased, from $25,000 in 1988 and $26,000 in 1992 to $39,000 in 1998 (in constant 1997 dollars).

To estimate the net effect of these collateral trends on default propensity, we use the results of PHA together with the composition of pools originated at different points in time to arrive at the *average risk multiplier* as a

EXHIBIT 21.36 Originations, 1992–1999: Estimated Collateral Default Risk by Loan Origination Time

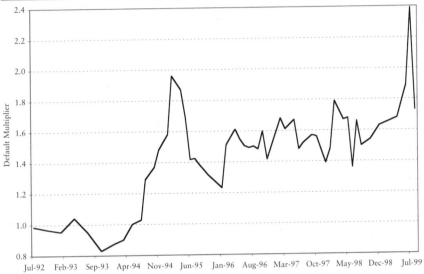

Source: Salomon Smith Barney.

function of loan origination date. The default vector of a pool is then given approximately by the multiplication of the corresponding risk factor and an appropriate baseline curve.[36] The initial values of multipliers are displayed in Exhibit 21.36. Because the results take only collateral composition into account, personal bankruptcies do not affect the curve shown.

After more than doubling between 1993 and early 1995, the default risk multiplier stabilized in the subsequent period, remaining in the 1.5 to 1.7 range since 1996. This suggests that the various competing collateral trends have been nearly balanced over the past few origination years. Nevertheless, these vintages may still be expected to register default rates that are 50% to 70% higher than those on loans originated in 1992, under the same level of personal bankruptcies. Nevertheless, one of the most prominent features of Exhibit 21.36 is the sharp spike in the default risk for the collateral originated in the second half of 1999. The runup in default propensity is primarily a function of borrower credit (as measured by Salomon Smith Barney's

---

[36] The average multiplier may change over time, as borrowers who default or prepay voluntarily exit the pool.

credit score), indicating a different underwriting standard. Since the peak is very narrow, and is followed by a steep decline of default propensity, it is likely that the loans responsible for it were not originated under the usual Conseco underwriting guidelines. These loans may represent a one-time inclusion into Conseco MH deals of collateral purchased from another originator targeting lower-credit MH borrowers.

Increases in default rates should not be automatically assumed to lead to identical increases in realized losses. Recovery rates themselves may depend on collateral characteristics and market conditions, requiring additional adjustments to project losses.

How Well Are the Observed Defaults Explained?

Exhibit 21.37 shows the actual default rates for loans originated in the second quarters of 1993, 1995, and 1996. The three origination quarters were chosen so that the observed default rates span the full spectrum of historical performance of Conseco MH loans. Loans originated in the second quarter of 1995 had some of the highest default rates of all originations since 1992, whereas loans originated in the second quarter of 1993 had some of the lowest. As the exhibit shows, 1996 originations had intermediate rates.

EXHIBIT 21.37   Selected Origination Periods: Actual Default Rates

Source: Salomon Smith Barney.

EXHIBIT 21.38 Selected Origination Periods: Normalized Default Rates

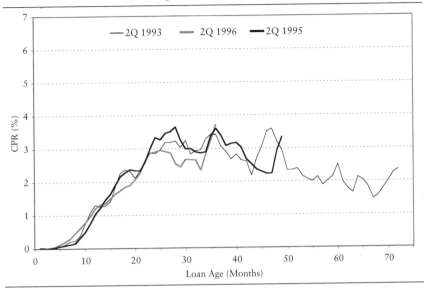

Source: Salomon Smith Barney.

Based on the collateral composition shown in Exhibits 21.31, 21.19, 21.15, and 21.30, the default rates for the 1996 vintage may be expected to be representative of more recent originations as well.

To test the usefulness of results obtained from PHA, we factor out from the curves given in Exhibit 21.37 the risk multipliers based on the collateral composition and the level of personal bankruptcies. This procedure effectively transforms each pool into a set of baseline loans, defaulting in an environment where the level of personal bankruptcies stays fixed.[37] The collateral multipliers are obtained using the risk factors given in Exhibit 21.28 and the actual composition of each loan group. The results are shown in Exhibit 21.38.

The normalized default curves lie very close to each other, implying that *the differences in default rates between different vintages can be almost completely accounted for by the risk multipliers based on the collateral composition and the economic environment.* A comparison of Exhibits 21.37 and

---

[37] The constant level of personal bankruptcies is taken to be 1.23. Baseline values for other variables are given in Exhibit 21.24.

21.38, therefore, validates our approach. The remaining differences between the normalized default rates are likely due to different MH inflation rates to which the pools were exposed (see Exhibit 21.25), as well as the differences in OLTVs, WACs, and original loan terms that affect the baseline curve (see Appendix 21A).[38]

21.4 PUTTING IT ALL TOGETHER: THE PREPAYMENT MODEL

Based on the results presented in the previous two sections, we developed a loan-level model of Conseco MH prepayments. The model was cast into the Salomon Smith Barney prepayment framework described in Section 21.2 and has been implemented on Salomon Smith Barney's proprietary analytic system, *The Yield Book*.

Construction of the model proceeds in two steps. In the first step, we apply the baseline curves and multipliers described in the previous sections to *each loan* in a given pool to arrive at the conditional probability of voluntary prepayment and default for each loan. By construction, these probabilities depend on the full set of loan attributes and external factors. To project speeds for the actual components of prepayments described in Section 21.2, voluntary prepayments are decomposed into turnover and refinancing components, based on the assumption that past a certain point in relative savings gains in prepayments come from refinancings and not the turnover. In the second step, we aggregate the loans in the pool into a small number of groups *based on the overall calculated prepayment response of each loan under a given set of conditions.*[39] The groups are therefore chosen according to all the characteristics relevant for prepayments, rather than some arbitrary subset of characteristics. The results of the loan-level calculation provide the parameters for the prepayment behavior of each group, such as the refinancing curves. As we discuss at the end of this section, we find our method of aggregation preferable to the tracking of each loan individually for every month of the remaining term (which we have also explored). With little loss in accuracy, the amount of required computation is greatly reduced.

---

[38] If additional small discrepancies remain even after accounting for the different baseline curves, they generally do not warrant a further refinement of the model. A careful monitoring of ongoing default performance, coupled with a small adjustment, if necessary, is likely the most efficient approach.

[39] For defaults we use only one group.

Fits

In Exhibit 21.39 we compare actual and projected voluntary speeds and defaults for eight selected Conseco deals originated between 1992 and 1998.

As the exhibit indicates, the model tracks the historical speeds well. We have found this to be the case for almost all Conseco deals originated since 1992. The results are especially noteworthy given the *wide range of interest rates experienced during the period shown and the significant changes in the collateral.* As given in Exhibit 21.5, between early 1992 and November 1993 the MH rates declined by more than 250bp. They subsequently retraced nearly all of the gains by February 1995, only to enter a sustained rally that led to a nearly 300bp decline and historical lows at the end of 1998. These rate movements are reflected to some extent in the WACs of the deals shown. For example, the WACs on GT92.2 and GT95.1 are 11.23% and 11.85%, respectively, while the WACs on GT96.1 and GT98.3 are 9.82% and 9.61%, respectively. Comparisons of collateral characteristics illustrate additional differences. For example, the inflation-adjusted average balance for GT92.2 is $26,600 compared with $35,300 for GT97.2. The respective fraction of land-and-home loans is 3% versus 29%, and the original term is 201 months versus 297 months.

Projections

Forward-looking projections obtained from the Conseco MH prepayment model depend on the assumed future values of several key variables. In addition to the *level of various Treasury rates,* these include the *spread between Treasuries and MH rates, shipments of new MH units, MH price depreciation and inflation, MH loan origination costs,* and *the strength of the media effect* (two measures of competitive conditions in the industry), and the *national level of personal bankruptcies.* Apart from the Treasury yield curve, which is always modeled explicitly either through a static scenario or through a dynamic simulation, and the MH depreciation rate, whose loan-age dependence is described in "Defaults," the other variables are projected to remain at their recent averages. Their inclusion in the model, however, allows a direct manipulation of the assumptions, with the accompanying impact on prepayment projections.

Prepayment projections under different interest rate scenarios are shown in Exhibits 21.40 and 21.41. Exhibit 21.40 includes the month-by-month projections for four representative deals under the scenarios of unchanged interest rates and parallel shifts of the yield curve by plus and minus 100bp. Exhibit 21.41 shows one-year and long-term projected speeds under seven

EXHIBIT 21.39   Selected Conseco MH Deals: Actual and Projected Speeds

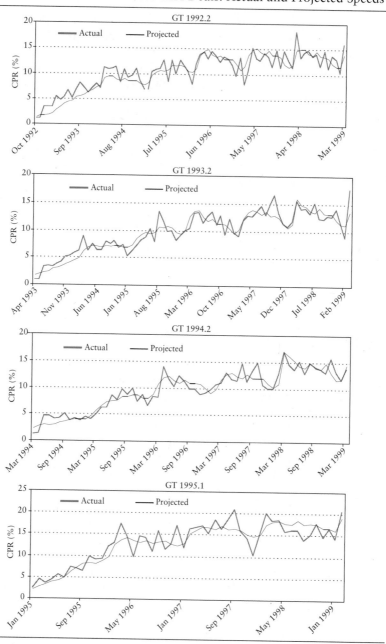

Source: Salomon Smith Barney.

EXHIBIT 21.40   Selected Conseco MH Deals: Scenario Projections

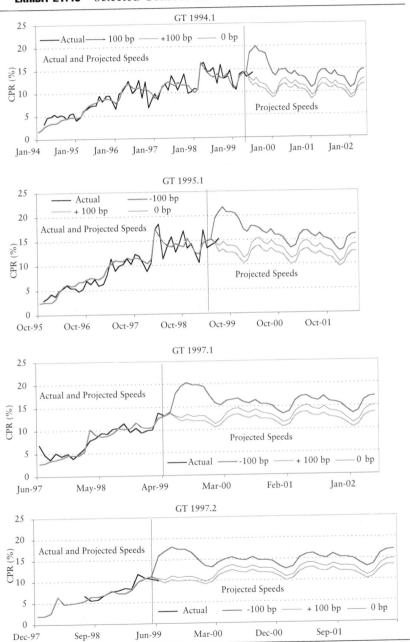

Source: Salomon Smith Barney.

EXHIBIT 21.41   Conseco MH Deals Originated Since 1992: Collateral Cross Section and Prepayment Projections

Deal	Current WAC (%)	WAM (Mos.)	WALA (Mos.)	Original Avg. Loan Balance*	Land/Home (%)	Used (%)	Historical Speeds (% MHP) 1-Mo	3-Mo	12-Mo		Projected Speed (% MHP) for an Interest Rate Change of -300bp	-200bp	-100bp	0bp	+100bp	+200bp	+300bp
92-1	11.82	126	82	25,800	2	22	216	244	242	LT	326	300	245	220	198	185	175
										1-Year	326	313	245	229	217	211	205
92-2	11.17	133	79	26,600	3	21	193	223	224	LT	326	283	227	202	186	174	170
										1-Year	319	296	227	212	203	197	194
93-1	11.28	140	76	27,200	7	19	211	232	233	LT	331	288	228	202	185	173	168
										1-Year	321	301	228	213	203	197	194
93-2	10.67	143	73	27,300	6	18	186	226	218	LT	343	287	225	197	181	170	166
										1-Year	327	300	226	209	200	195	192
93-3	10.27	149	70	28,400	8	18	244	241	225	LT	331	259	203	181	169	165	157
											313	273	205	191	184	182	176
93-4	9.70	151	67	29,200	9	18	218	237	233	LT	324	255	199	181	172	167	157
										1-Year	308	270	203	191	186	183	175
94-1	9.73	160	64	29,800	13	19	223	231	227	LT	320	254	198	181	174	168	155
										1-Year	307	273	206	194	189	185	177
94-2	10.23	155	62	28,500	9	18	190	224	233	LT	342	269	211	189	178	173	162
										1-Year	326	287	220	204	197	194	186
94-3	10.59	160	60	28,600	8	19	271	248	243	LT	361	286	226	196	181	176	167
										1-Year	344	304	236	216	207	204	198
94-4	10.97	162	60	29,300	9	17	281	271	249	LT	361	285	226	196	181	176	167
										1-Year	344	304	236	216	207	204	198
94-5	11.13	169	58	31,200	17	14	262	286	272	LT	376	328	252	216	193	180	175
										1-Year	363	341	264	239	227	220	217
94-6	11.40	165	57	29,200	9	16	218	272	251	LT	375	332	255	218	194	180	175
										1-Year	363	345	267	241	228	221	218
94-7	11.39	171	55	30,500	13	15	248	260	252	LT	365	326	256	225	203	190	184
										1-Year	361	346	270	248	236	229	226
94-8	11.49	175	54	31,000	14	15	217	269	259	LT	366	328	258	227	205	191	186
										1-Year	363	349	273	251	239	232	228
95-1	11.81	190	52	32,100	18	14	208	276	266	LT	366	342	281	249	221	206	196
										1-Year	376	364	293	274	260	252	247
95-2	11.99	197	51	30,300	15	18	191	216	285	LT	360	344	293	258	232	214	202
										1-Year	379	362	305	285	271	262	256
95-3	11.56	206	49	30,000	10	19	288	276	263	LT	374	351	291	259	232	217	206
										1-Year	385	375	305	286	273	265	259
95-4	11.08	212	48	30,900	9	17	134	218	271	LT	375	341	275	245	220	208	201
										1-Year	379	364	289	272	260	253	249
95-5	10.06	224	47	33,900	20	15	206	240	242	LT	370	314	252	221	202	191	187
										1-Year	367	341	268	250	240	234	231
95-6	10.19	229	46	33,700	20	15	181	199	209	LT	363	297	239	208	192	185	179
										1-Year	358	325	255	236	228	223	219
95-7	10.07	230	45	34,400	20	15	171	226	228	LT	356	284	230	202	187	182	173
										1-Year	349	311	245	227	219	215	210
95-8	10.06	236	44	34,700	23	16	219	256	228	LT	356	284	229	202	186	181	172
										1-Year	347	309	243	225	216	213	208
95-9	10.09	238	43	35,200	24	16	230	246	235	LT	360	288	233	203	187	182	174
										1-Year	350	312	246	226	217	214	209
95-10	9.99	244	42	36,200	26	15	232	245	231	LT	359	286	231	201	185	180	170
										1-Year	348	310	245	223	215	211	206
96-1	9.71	252	41	38,000	32	13	238	238	230	LT	354	279	223	197	182	177	164
										1-Year	341	301	237	216	208	205	198
96-2	9.80	240	39	32,900	17	18	216	202	190	LT	341	269	215	191	180	174	158
										1-Year	327	289	227	207	201	197	189
96-3	9.88	243	38	32,400	16	20	191	219	199	LT	316	248	198	180	171	165	151
										1-Year	308	271	206	195	190	186	179

EXHIBIT 21.41 Continued

Deal	Current WAC (%)	WAM (Mos.)	WALA (Mos.)	Original Avg. Loan Balance*	Land/Home (%)	Used (%)	Historical Speeds (% MHP) 1-Mo	3-Mo	12-Mo		Projected Speed (% MHP) for an Interest Rate Change of -300bp	-200bp	-100bp	0bp	+100bp	+200bp	+300bp
96-4	10.01	250	37	33,900	19	18	129	202	208	LT	337	268	220	199	188	182	168
										1-Year	328	289	226	215	209	205	198
96-5	10.22	254	35	34,500	21	17	129	216	213	LT	353	282	231	206	191	186	173
										1-Year	341	301	236	223	215	212	206
96-6	10.31	262	34	35,600	26	16	139	213	222	LT	361	292	240	209	193	186	177
										1-Year	348	310	243	227	219	216	211
96-7	10.40	263	33	35,200	25	17	122	194	221	LT	363	295	241	209	193	186	177
										1-Year	349	313	245	227	219	216	211
96-8	10.31	267	32	36,100	29	17	138	212	232	LT	367	298	243	211	194	188	178
										1-Year	351	315	247	228	220	217	212
96-9	10.45	266	31	34,700	21	19	128	208	231	LT	367	295	240	210	193	187	176
										1-Year	349	311	245	226	217	214	209
96-10	10.18	273	30	37,200	32	14	179	222	229	LT	367	295	239	207	190	185	173
										1-Year	348	309	247	222	214	211	206
97-1	10.37	270	28	34,300	23	19	157	218	222	LT	363	292	238	210	193	188	174
										1-Year	345	307	244	223	215	213	206
97-2	10.20	273	27	35,300	29	17	258	239	226	LT	360	290	237	210	194	189	175
										1-Year	344	306	242	223	216	213	206
97-3	10.21	271	25	34,100	19	19	233	236	209	LT	347	278	226	203	190	183	166
										1-Year	328	291	225	211	205	202	194
97-4	10.02	276	24	35,900	26	16	242	216	207	LT	348	279	228	204	190	184	167
										1-Year	329	291	225	212	205	202	194
97-5	9.95	273	23	36,700	25	26	225	231	224	LT	348	278	226	202	188	181	164
										1-Year	326	288	221	208	201	198	190
97-6	9.82	281	21	38,000	31	18	234	220	212	LT	354	282	229	205	191	182	165
										1-Year	327	287	219	206	200	195	187
97-7	9.81	281	19	36,800	26	20	217	225	194	LT	350	279	227	203	190	181	163
										1-Year	323	283	215	202	196	191	184
97-8	9.79	261	19	39,400	31	18	247	244	192	LT	346	275	224	199	187	174	160
										1-Year	317	277	208	195	190	184	177
98-1	9.68	279	18	36,200	27	21	178	210	196	LT	342	271	221	196	185	170	158
										1-Year	316	276	206	193	188	182	175
98-2	9.77	277	18	35,300	21	23	204	213	162	LT	346	277	227	203	192	175	168
										1-Year	323	283	213	200	195	188	183
98-3	9.61	288	14	36,500	20	22	180	168	135	LT	337	272	223	200	190	170	166
										1-Year	301	272	200	189	184	176	173
98-4	9.57	289	13	36,500	20	23	170	145	131	LT	327	265	217	194	186	164	163
										1-Year	302	265	192	181	177	168	167
98-5	9.09	304	12	43,000	39	14	171	167	—	LT	323	262	214	192	183	163	162
										1-Year	298	261	187	176	172	163	162
98-6	9.53	292	11	36,600	19	23	158	153	—	LT	318	255	206	186	174	154	153
										1-Year	290	252	175	164	160	150	150
98-7	9.20	301	11	40,300	34	19	138	130	—	LT	323	262	214	192	182	163	162
										1-Year	301	263	185	175	170	161	160
98-8	9.11	304	8	40,200	28	20	119	117	—	LT	320	258	209	187	176	158	157
										1-Year	290	250	167	157	151	143	142
99-1	9.14	306	6	40,200	26	26	100	106	—	LT	312	252	206	188	171	159	159
										1-Year	271	230	148	139	132	125	125
99-2	9.45	297	7	—	—	—	113	—	—	LT	332	266	214	193	181	162	162
										1-Year	346	289	172	156	148	135	134

*Balance is adjusted for inflation to 1997 dollars.

LT: Long term.

Note: Projections as of July 12, 1999. Ten-year Treasury = 5.732%.

Source: Salomon Smith Barney.

different interest rate scenarios for all Conseco MH deals originated since 1992, along with three-month, six-month, and one-year historical speeds and selected collateral characteristics for each deal. All speeds are expressed as percent MHP.

The projected speeds illustrate several key features of the model:

- Long-term projections on new current-coupon deals, such as GT99.2, are typically around 190% MHP, slightly faster than the recent pricing speed.

- One-year projections for such deals are *lower* than long-term projections, even when stated in MHP. The reason is that our seasoning ramp, as shown in Exhibit 21.8, is about three and a half years long, compared with the 24 months assumed by the MHP ramp. This is also the reason why the one-year projected speeds are higher than recent actual speeds for newer deals.

- The WAC is clearly an important determinant of speed, with higher-WAC deals having higher speeds relative to lower-WAC deals originated around the same time. However, additional collateral characteristics also play a central role. For example, some deals originated in late 1994 and 1995 have lower WACs than deals originated in 1992 and early 1993, yet their historical and projected speeds are higher. This is the result of the collateral characteristics (higher balances, longer loan terms, etc.) discussed in Sections 21.2 and 21.3.

- As rates rally, for the first 200bp of rate shift the increase in long-term speeds is generally less than 50% MHP per 100bp rate move. This pattern reflects, in part, the steepening of the refinancing curves with increasing savings (see Exhibit 21.12). Yet, given the recent history of MH rates, the media effect is not expected to have a pronounced impact for the first 100bp rally or so, reducing the sensitivity to rate movements in that region.

- In declining-rate scenarios, one-year average projections are higher than lifetime speeds for seasoned deals. Exhibit 21.40 provides a particularly vivid demonstration of this fact. Burnout and the attenuation of the media effect are the main reasons for the decline of speeds with age. The effect is particularly pronounced for large rate declines for deals that are already deeply in the money, such as GT95.2. A 300bp rally would lead to very high speeds that would rapidly deplete the population of fastest borrowers. For very recent deals, such as GT992, the turnover (and, to a lesser extent, the refinancing) seasoning ramp moderates the effects of burnout.

- If interest rates increase, prepayments slow, as would be expected. For deals that are nearly at-the-money, such as GT99.2, the main reason for the slowdown is the lock-in effect—higher MH rates make moving less appealing. For premiums, there is also a decline in refinancing activity. Whether the slowdown is the result of one of these factors or a combination of them, the decline in speeds due to rate selloffs is always smaller than the increase in speeds for the same amount of rate rally. This asymmetry is particularly clear in Exhibit 21.40.

Comments and Caveats

Loan-Level versus Individual Loan Tracking   Interest has recently been rekindled in loan-level modeling of various types of mortgage instruments, although the term loan-level has not been applied consistently. In the context of this work, we use the term to describe two operations. The first is an analysis of the full set of data available for all MH loans originated by Conseco. The second is an application of the results of that analysis to each loan in a given pool, leading to an aggregation of loans into a small number of groups. As we noted, the aggregation is done based on the expected overall prepayment behavior of a loan under a given set of conditions. We do not use the term *loan-level* to imply that prepayments for each loan in a given pool are projected for every month into the future for every interest rate path (as would arise in an OAS calculation). When hundreds of interest rate paths are used in a simulation, as is typical, and the number of loans in the pool reaches or exceeds 20,000, the scope of the calculations is prohibitive. Even in a sophisticated implementation, such a calculation would likely require dramatic simplifications of the model to achieve an acceptable computational speed.

Nevertheless, to gauge the impact of individual loan tracking on the accuracy of prepayment projections, we have constructed a model in which each loan is followed individually. (We used it for static scenario calculations, but not for simulation of interest rate paths.) The conditional probability of voluntary prepayment and default was computed for each loan using the full set of loan attributes and external factors. The cumulative voluntary prepayment and default rates for a pool were then obtained by averaging the prepayment probabilities for individual loans, *weighted by the amortized (and partially prepaid) balances and the probability that a given loan is still outstanding* at the time for which the prepayment is calculated. *A comparison of the results of that individual loan-tracking model with the model described in the text showed no significant differences either in fits or in prepayment projections.* Therefore, in the context of MH prepayments, the use of extensive additional computational resources required to track individual loans along hundreds of interest rate paths is not warranted. It is likely that a far better improvement in model reliability would be obtained from an implementation of a *dynamical model* of external input variables required by the prepayment model.

Although prepayment models are an essential tool for analyzing MBSs, they incorporate a host of assumptions. Users should be aware of their limitations.

Projections Are for a Specified Interest-Rate Scenario To the extent that prepayments vary with interest rates, actual speeds going forward will differ from projections for any static scenario. Although projections over a variety of interest rate scenarios will give an indication of the likely range of speeds, *actual* speeds going forward will depend on future interest rates, which we cannot project.

It goes without saying that the same comments apply to any other economic variables that influence speeds and that are explicitly or implicitly included in the model. Examples include MH inflation and depreciation, personal bankruptcies, the level of MH shipments, loan costs, borrower awareness of refinancing, and opportunities/level of solicitation of borrowers.

Short-Term versus Long-Term Speeds Projections are generally given for some period going forward, such as the next 12 months or the life of the loans. Speeds over the next month or two can differ from longer-term projections for various reasons, such as seasonality and seasoning. Thus care should be taken in using longer-term projections to gauge likely speeds over the near term.

Random Error (or Noise) in Monthly Speeds A projected speed represents an *expected* value for the speed. Even if the model is perfectly accurate and the interest rates and other macroeconomic variables are known with certainty, the presence of statistical sampling error (or noise) implies that actual speeds will fluctuate randomly around projected speeds from month to month.[40] To illustrate the magnitude of the fluctuations we consider a hypothetical pool consisting of 15,000 loans which prepay on average at a constant expected rate of 12% CPR. The 95% confidence interval for the one-month speed is then 10.2% CPR – 13.8% CPR. The width of the confidence interval is approximately inversely proportional to the square root of the number of loans. Pools with few loans exhibit more fluctuation in the month-to-month speed than pools with a large number of loans.

---

[40] See Chapter 5, "Random Error in Prepayment Projections."

21.5 SUMMARY/CONCLUSION

Recently, the nominal spreads on three-, five-, and seven-year triple-A-rated MH securities were 50bp to 75bp wider than the spreads on the same-WAL automobile and credit card securities (see Exhibit 21.42). Do they offer good relative value?

A key part of the answer to this question is an analysis that determines the OAS, effective durations and convexities, compares returns under various interest rate scenarios, and so on.[41] Such calculations, in turn, require a prepayment model that reliably predicts prepayment rates under a variety of interest rate conditions, over long periods of time. Given the wide variation of loan and unit characteristics within the majority of Conseco MH deals, as well as the difference in collateral from deal to deal, it is imperative that the prepayment model be developed from loan-level data.

We have accomplished this by analyzing prepayment patterns on more than 940,000 Conseco MH loans originated since the early 1980s. In the process, we uncovered the main determinants of voluntary prepayments and defaults, and quantified their effect. For voluntary prepayments these include loan type (new versus used versus land-and-home), OLTV, location of unit (in a MH park versus on private land), unit size and loan purpose, as well as external factors, such as the level of MH rates and shipments of new MH units. Defaults were mostly explained by Salomon Smith Barney's credit score and, to a smaller extent, by a combination of loan and unit characteristics. Of external factors, we found that defaults depend on the rate of MH inflation and price depreciation, as well as the national level of personal bankruptcies.

In addition to differential prepayment rates governed by collateral and external factors, we have evaluated the baseline voluntary prepayment and

EXHIBIT 21.42   Representative Secondary-Market Nominal Spreads as of July 30, 1999

Asset Type	Three-Year	Five-Year	Seven-Year
Auto	78 bp	98 bp	95 bp
Credit Card	78	98	95
Manufactured Housing	130	150	170
Home Equity	140	160	180

Source: Salomon Smith Barney.

---

[41] Additional factors that impact the pricing of MH securities include liquidity, structuring considerations, and the investor's valuation of the issuer's financial condition, and servicing capabilities.

default curves. Although the exact seasoning ramp for total prepayments is dependent on the collateral, our analysis indicates that it generally extends to the loan age of three and a half years, substantially longer than the 24 months assumed by the MHP convention. Using these baseline curves and the full collateral composition of recent current coupon deals, our model projects prepayment rates of about 190% MHP, considerably faster than the market's old convention of 100% MHP. Several significant trends have emerged, contributing to these changes: average loan size, term, the percentage of land-and-home loans and double-wide units, the average OLTV, and the debt-to-income ratio have all increased. Although some of these variables have offsetting effects on prepayments and defaults, the combined effect has been an upward shift in voluntary prepayments and in defaults, and a slight increase in sensitivity of speeds to rate movements. The increased sensitivity, however, is still very small compared with residential mortgages, giving rise, generally, to securities with superior convexity characteristics.

MATHEMATICAL MODELING OF DEFAULTS

A Model for Home Prices

We assume that home prices change randomly each month, displaying some volatility around a trend. Denoting the home price at time t by P_t, we assume that the variable

$$\log \frac{P_1}{P_{t-1}}$$

which is approximately the percentage change in the price in month t is normally distributed,

$$\log \frac{P_t}{P_{t-1}} \sim N(\mu_t, \sigma_t^2) \qquad (21.1)$$

where μ_t is the average change in month t and σ_t is the standard deviation of the price change. In other words, percentage changes in home prices are assumed to follow the well-known "Bell Curve."

For site-built homes, the mean increase μ_t would just be the housing inflation rate for month t. For MH, depreciation of the unit adds an extra term. If we let δ_t be the average depreciation in period t, and f_t be the increase in the price of a unit of fixed age (i.e., housing inflation rate for MH in the absence of depreciation), then

$$\mu_t = \delta_t + f_t$$

In other words, the expected change in the price of the unit in period t is assumed to be the sum of its depreciation in that period and the inflation rate for MH unit for that period.[42] We estimate the inflation and depreciation rates directly from Conseco data.

Probability of Default

To model defaults, we assume that the borrower defaults only if the equity in the property is negative, that is, if the loan-to-value ratio is greater than one, *and* an external shock event occurs that jeopardizes the borrower's financial position. Examples of such events are loss of job, divorce, and death of the borrower. We denote the probability per unit time of an external shock event under the baseline scenario[43] by Q. Let L_t be the loan balance at time t (assumed to be a known function of time) and let L_o be the initial loan balance. We note that the LTV at time t, which we denote as LTV_t, is

$$LTV_t = \frac{L_t}{P_t} = \frac{P_o}{P_t} \times \frac{L_o}{P_o} \times \frac{L_t}{L_o} \tag{21.2}$$

Using straightforward algebra, it follows from Equations 21.1 and 21.2 that the probability of default per unit time is

$$Q \times P[LTV_t > 1] = Q \times \Phi \left[\frac{-\left(\sum\limits_{j=1}^{t} \delta_j + f_j\right) + \log OLTV + \log \dfrac{L_t}{L_o}}{\sqrt{\sum\limits_{j=1}^{t} \sigma_j^2}} \right] \tag{21.3}$$

---

[42] Note that δ_t is a negative number.
[43] The baseline scenario specifies borrower, loan, and unit characteristics *and* macroeconomic conditions (see Exhibit 21.28).

EXHIBIT 21.43 Typical Default Seasoning Curve

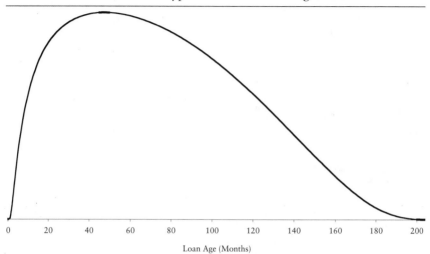

Loan Age (Months)

Source: Salomon Smith Barney.

Here, OLTV is the original loan-to-value ratio L_o/P_o and Φ is the cumulative normal distribution whose values are tabulated or can be easily computed numerically.

If we assume that the quantity Q is constant for a given set of loans, then the seasoning curve for defaults is determined by the probability that $LTV_t > 1$. Exhibit 21.43 illustrates the baseline default curve. OLTV is taken to be 90%, WAC 10.5%, loan term 220 months, and the average price trend −1% per year. The actual curve used for fitting differs in three respects. Projected defaults are weighted by the lag function given in Exhibit 21.26, unit depreciation is a function of loan age as given in Exhibit 21.24, and the default rate levels off at a nonzero value for large loan ages.

The likelihood of default initially increases, peaks after a few years, and then declines, in line with observed historical behavior. The reasons for this pattern are fairly clear: Loans are not extended to people who are going to default straight away, and after many years, loan amortization has reduced to almost zero the chances that the LTV is greater than one. Hence, the danger zone is the early years, when depreciation, coupled with an adverse swing in MH prices in a particular region, can overtake amortization and lead LTVs to climb above one.

Nonmortgage-Related Asset-Backed Securities

CHAPTER 22

Class C Notes

Opening the Next Frontier in Credit Card Asset-Backed Securities

Paul Jablansky and Ronald E. Thompson, Jr.

Over the past several years, the credit card asset-backed securities (ABS) market has broadened for issuers and investors.[1] A large universe of investors has become familiar with credit card structures and has grown comfortable with the collateral risks and performance, allowing issuers to bring increasingly more sophisticated transactions to market.

ERISA-eligible Class C notes offer institutional investors an opportunity to improve yield by participating in triple-B-rated credit enhancement. In our view, sophisticated institutional investors should consider buying these securities for four main reasons:

1. Class C notes offer institutional investors an ability to participate in a credit market that until now was closed to all but a small group of selected banks and insurance companies.
2. These credits have significant structural protections that build enough credit support to withstand loss rates equal to two or more times historical levels under almost all conceivable scenarios.
3. The notes create the opportunity to take advantage of a sector as it becomes more liquid and moves from predominantly private issuance to public issuance.
4. Class C ratings should be less volatile than ratings for comparable unsecured debt.

---

[1] See Chapter 2 for an introduction to credit card ABSs.

Until recently, in many credit card structures, BBB-rated credit enhancement consisted primarily of a receivables interest subordinated to the Class A and to the Class B certificates. The interest was traditionally sold to banks and insurance companies in the form of a collateral invested amount (CIA) on a private-placement basis. Trading restrictions and the lack of ERISA-eligibility, however, prevented a broad market for CIAs from developing.

In May 1998, First USA and Salomon Smith Barney launched the first ERISA-eligible Class C notes. MBNA followed in June with a transaction of its own. Using an owner trust to purchase the equivalent of the CIA and the excess spread, the structure made it possible to offer a triple-B-rated Class C *note,* which was not constrained by any trading restrictions. Class C notes, therefore, offer a much broader group of investors an opportunity to buy lower-rated ABSs while avoiding the ERISA and trading restrictions of prior structures.

In this chapter, we provide background on the development of credit card ABS credit enhancement, a detailed look at the structure and its risks, and a framework for finding relative value in these securities.

22.1 PUTTING CLASS C NOTES IN A HISTORICAL CONTEXT

Over the past several years, the market for credit card credit enhancement has evolved significantly. Institutional investors have become increasingly comfortable with the deal structures, credit card originators' performance as issuers, and the underwriting standards and performance of most credit card collateral. As a result, these investors have grown more willing to purchase more deeply subordinated classes. In addition, traditional buyers of investment-grade corporate debt have developed an interest in purchasing lower-rated ABS as an attractive source of yield and portfolio diversification.

Of course, issuers have always looked to create more cost-effective credit enhancement structures (see Exhibit 22.1). Constant innovation has enabled issuers to lower incremental funding costs, improving shareholder returns. At the same time, issuers have enhanced their own funding liquidity by expanding their investor bases (see Exhibit 22.2). The latest improvements have led to the development of triple-B-rated, ERISA-eligible ABS in the form of Class C notes.

At the inception of the credit card ABS market in 1986, most transactions utilized partial bank letters of credit to create triple-A-rated securities. The rating of this type of structure depended on the rating of the letter of credit provider, and as triple-A-rated banks were downgraded, the transactions backed by letters of credit issued by those banks were downgraded. This created an undesirable degree of event risk. With the downgrades, the group of available credit enhancers shrank.

EXHIBIT 22.1 Evolution of Credit Card Enhancement Structures over Time, 1986–1998

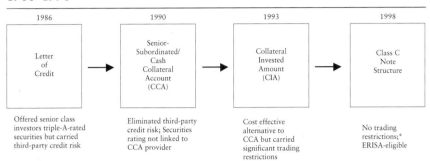

1986	1990	1993	1998
Letter of Credit	Senior-Subordinated/ Cash Collateral Account (CCA)	Collateral Invested Amount (CIA)	Class C Note Structure
Offered senior class investors triple-A-rated securities but carried third-party credit risk	Eliminated third-party credit risk; Securities rating not linked to CCA provider	Cost effective alternative to CCA but carried significant trading restrictions	No trading restrictions;* ERISA-eligible

* Class C notes offered under Rule 144A or Regulation S would be subject to the trading restrictions applicable to those types of offerings.
Source: Salomon Smith Barney.

This situation led to the development of senior/subordinated transactions, in which single-A-rated subordinated Class B certificates absorbed losses on behalf of senior triple-A-rated Class A certificates. However, to achieve the single A rating, the Class B certificate required its own credit enhancement.

To build credit enhancement supporting Class B certificates, issuers eventually introduced the cash collateral account (CCA), which provided a pool of cash available to support the transaction. This pool covered losses on behalf of the Class A and Class B certificates. The CCA was structured as a loan from a bank, effectively isolating third-party event risk from the transaction. However, in almost all cases, cash from the loan was initially deposited with the CCA loan provider. This deposit was only possible so long as the CCA loan provider's short-term deposit rating was A-1+/P-1. As a result, CCA providers were effectively limited to A-1+/P-1-rated banks.

To create more efficiency and expand the universe of credit enhancement providers, the CIA was introduced as a new structure for credit enhancement. This instrument provided a small group of investors with either a triple B-rated or unrated receivables interest that took a first-loss position after excess spread was exhausted. By using receivables of the master trust rather than cash or other eligible short-term instruments as credit enhancement, the CIA structure offered a more cost-effective solution for issuers.

Similar to the CCA, the CIA structure employs a spread account to capture excess spread under certain circumstances. The amount required to be funded in the spread account (including, in some cases, an upfront deposit of cash) depends on the level of excess spread. For CIA providers, there are certain limitations. Any single master trust cannot have more than 100 investors

EXHIBIT 22.2 Evolution of Credit Card Enhancement Structures over Time,
1986–1998

Credit Enhancement Structure	Targete Investors	Constraints	Evolutionary Advantages
Letter of Credit	AAA-Rated Banks	Limited market, ratings under scrutiny; L/Cs carry 100% risk asset weights for banks; Only offer partial coverage	Simple structure; limited negotiation
Cash Collateral Account (CCA)	Banks	Market interest declining, mostly limited to A-1+/P-1 rated banks; Japanese and Europeans were big participants in markets	No dependence on third-party credit risk
Collateral Invested Amount (CIA)	Yankee Banks	Arranged and syndicated like a bank loan; transfer restricted; did not expand universe beyond banks	More cost-effective than CCA
Certificated CIA	Insurance Companies	Privately placed; limited trading flexibility; not ERISA-eligible	Appeal to a broader audience
Class C Note	Institutional Money Managers, Insurance Companies, Banks	Relatively small tranche sizes	No trading restrictions*; ERISA-eligible

* Class C notes offered under Rule 144A or Regulation S would be subject to the trading restrictions applicable to those types of offerings.
Source: Salomon Smith Barney.

in CIAs across all series, and CIAs cannot be freely traded. These constraints are designed to protect the master trust from being characterized as a publicly traded partnership, which could have extremely adverse tax consequences for the master trust.[2] As a result, issuers need to maintain control of the number of CIA investors, and they achieve this control by requiring consent to any transfers.

---

[2] The Internal Revenue Service taxes publicly traded partnerships like corporations.

As new issue volume increased, major issuers looked for ways to diversify their CIA investor bases. They sought not only to broaden the universe of investors participating in three- to five-year CIAs, but also to identify a new segment of players who could buy longer tenors. As a result, issuers began to market a certificated CIA which carried the same risk as a CIA but was structured in a form more acceptable to institutional investors such as insurance companies. The CIA certificate still had the same 100-holder limit and transfer restrictions as regular CIAs and was not ERISA-eligible.

In May 1998, the first Class C Note structure came to market. Class C notes enjoy the same cash flow and credit characteristics of CIA certificates but they are ERISA-eligible, can be freely traded, and can be held by an unlimited number of investors.[3]

22.2 HOW CLASS C NOTES WORK

From the investors' perspective, the Class C note operates essentially in the same manner as the CIA certificate. Each series issued by a master trust generally consists of three components: a senior Class A security, a subordinated Class B security, and collateral interest (see Exhibit 22.3). The collateral interest comprises a subordinated receivables interest and the excess spread remaining after all series expenses are paid.

Under the Class C note structure, an owner trust purchases the collateral interest of the series.[4] The owner trust issues liabilities consisting of the Class C notes and an equity interest. The Class C notes have a soft-bullet maturity, although, as with any other credit card securities, they can amortize early or extend under certain, limited circumstances. In addition, the owner trust holds a reserve account for the *exclusive* benefit of the Class C noteholders. The seller retains the equity interest, through which the seller receives excess spread. The notes are free from any trading restrictions and have no tax-imposed limit on the number of investors because the use of the owner trust does not create any publicly traded partnership concerns.[5]

Cash flow from the collateral interest is used to pay principal and interest on the Class C notes. Any remaining cash flow is characterized as excess spread, which is either released to the seller or used to fund the reserve

---

[3] Class C notes offered under Rule 144A or Regulation S would be subject to the trading restrictions applicable to those types of offerings.

[4] An owner trust is used because it issues securities in note form under an indenture, making the securities ERISA-eligible.

[5] Class C notes offered under Rule 144A or Regulation S would be subject to the trading restrictions applicable to those types of offerings.

EXHIBIT 22.3 Class C Note—Structure

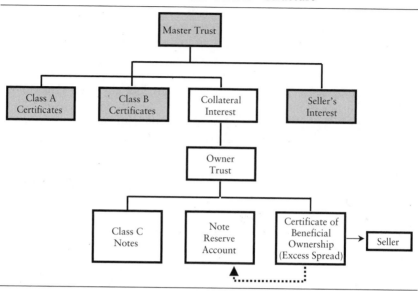

Source: Salomon Smith Barney.

account, depending on the excess spread level. The reserve funding arrangement is designed to protect the Class C notes against a deterioration in collateral credit performance.

The reserve account structure defines a schedule of required reserve funding levels tied to three-month average excess spread (see Exhibit 22.4). If the three-month average excess spread exceeds a predetermined minimum, the reserve account is not required to be funded at all and excess

EXHIBIT 22.4 Example of Dynamic Reserve Account Funding Parameters Based on Excess Spread Levels

Quarterly Excess Spread	S&P's Sample Reserve Account Structure[a]	
	Req. Reserve Amt.	Est. Time (months) to Fund[b]
>4.50%	0.00%	No accumulation
4.00% to 4.50%	1.50	4.0 Mo. to 4.5 Mo.
3.50% to 4.00%	2.00	6.0 Mo. to 6.9 Mo.
3.00% to 3.50%	3.00	10.3 Mo. to 12.0 Mo.
< 3.00%	4.00	Over 16 Mo.

[a] Based on S&P Ratings' Sample Reserve.
[b] Based on a constant excess spread, assuming a zero initial balance.
Sources: S&P Ratings Services and Salomon Smith Barney estimates.

spread is automatically released to the seller. If the average declines through a series of threshold levels, the required funding level increases. If the average subsequently increases above those thresholds, the required funding percentage decreases and the excess cash in the reserve account is released to the seller.

In an example developed by S&P and shown in Exhibit 22.4, no reserve is required as long as the three-month average excess spread equals or exceeds 4.50%. Between 4.00% and 4.50%, the reserve must build to 1.50% of the sum of the Class A, Class B, and Class C securities for the series. For each 50bp (basis points) decline, the reserve must be funded by an additional amount subject to a maximum level of 4.00%. *The rating agencies set trigger levels based on the specific characteristics and historical performance of each pool.* As with virtually all credit card ABS structures, if the three-month average excess spread falls below zero, then the series will begin to amortize early, sequentially paying the Class A certificates, the Class B certificates, and the Class C notes.

22.3 CLASS C NOTE STRUCTURE AND ITS PROTECTIONS

A key issue for investors is the risk profile of the Class C notes. The risk profile depends primarily on collateral performance, which is influenced by four parameters:

1. Portfolio yield
2. Portfolio losses
3. Monthly payment rate
4. Monthly purchase rate

For the purposes of this discussion, we will focus on the sensitivity of the Class C notes to losses and look specifically at structural protections, which are activated as losses rise and which serve to build credit enhancement beneath the Class C notes.

Seasoned credit card portfolios may be viewed as having a range of possible monthly, annualized loss rates described by a probability distribution function. The function reflects the likelihood that a given percentage of borrowers will default in any month. In the current environment, a typical distribution might rise asymmetrically from a very low probability of experiencing no losses to a more prominent likelihood of experiencing 3% to 10% annualized loss rates. The *expected* loss rate might be approximately 6% to 7%, and the probabilities would likely decline quickly for loss rates above 10%.

EXHIBIT 22.5   Securitization Security Loss Protection Design

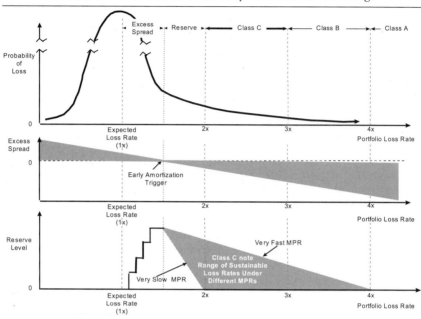

MPR: Monthly payment rate.
Source: Salomon Smith Barney.

Viewed within this context of probabilities, credit card securitizations are best seen as selling off pieces of credit risk. To the extent that portfolio yield, monthly payment rate, and new purchase rates are kept constant, these pieces of risk will correspond to specific points within the loss probability distribution. In Exhibit 22.5, we show a sample loss probability distribution to illustrate conceptually how losses relate to credit risk.

From this perspective, originators' underwriting skills play a key role in shaping the distribution and minimizing the possibility of extreme losses. Nevertheless, transactions enjoy the benefit of several layers of protection against unanticipated losses. Excess spread forms the first level of credit protection. Early amortization triggers, which are designed to shorten investors' exposure to poorly performing collateral, provide the second level. Building cash as excess spread falls, a dynamic reserve account contributes the next layer of protection (and the last for Class C notes).[6]

---

[6] In the unlikely event that either loss rates or certificate and note interest rates spike dramatically, or portfolio yield declines dramatically, over a one- or two-month

Assuming that an early amortization event is triggered when the three-month average excess spread declines to zero, the structure redirects principal collections to pay down first the Class A certificates, then the Class B certificates, and then the Class C notes. During this period of amortization, the reserve account provides a cushion solely for the Class C notes against losses. As the diagram shows, the reserve level is designed to rise as excess spread falls below a schedule of breakpoints. This schedule creates a step function within the reserve account as each level is met.

The structure does not shield the Class C notes (nor the CIA certificates) from a *rapid* deterioration in collateral credit performance. For example, should the portfolio experience an upward spike in charge-offs or a downward spike in portfolio yield (among other possibilities), excess spread might diminish too rapidly for the reserve account to build up sufficient cash. These factors could combine to trigger an early amortization event before the reserve account is adequately funded. Therefore, safeguards built into the Class C note structure (and the CIA certificate structure) provide only limited protection against a highly accelerated deterioration of the portfolio.

The key, then, is to determine how high loss rates must rise before the Class C notes lose any principal. In reality, changes in excess spread are more relevant than changes in the loss rate alone. However, projecting excess spread depends on a projection of portfolio yields, an exercise that involves assumptions regarding not only how borrowers will behave but also how the seller will react to market forces and collateral performance changes. For the purpose of this analysis we assume that portfolio yields remain constant. To the extent that portfolio yields adjust upward to compensate for rising losses, the Class C note sustainable losses would be more robust. Likewise, if portfolio yields were to fall, then the sustainable losses would be lower.

Exhibit 22.6 illustrates the relationship between sustainable constant loss rates (and associated excess spreads) and monthly payment rates for a hypothetical transaction.[7] Given that early amortization is one of the main

---

period (resulting in negative excess spread), the reserve account is available to cover Class C note interest shortfalls regardless of whether early amortization has already been triggered.

[7] For this analysis we assume that collateral performance deteriorates over a two-year period and that the reserve account builds up to approximately 3%, or three-quarters of its fully funded level, before the three-month average excess spread declines to zero and early amortization is triggered. We assume an 18.5% portfolio yield and a weighted average interest rate on the certificates and notes of one-month LIBOR + 40bp. Once early amortization is triggered, we fix the monthly payment rate and solve for the highest annual constant default rate that the Class C note can withstand before losing its first dollar of principal.

EXHIBIT 22.6   Hypothetical Transaction: Sustainable Constant Loss Rates and Associated Excess Spread Levels versus Monthly Payment Rates

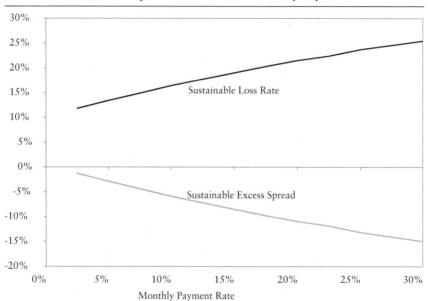

Assumes 18.5% portfolio yield and a constant average interest rate of LIBOR + 40bp.
Source: Salomon Smith Barney.

protections, the rate at which the securities amortize determines how long the securities are vulnerable to high collateral losses. The monthly payment rate determines how quickly the credit card accounts pay down and, therefore, the rate at which the securities amortize.

This example shows that, even at a monthly payment rate as low as 2.5% (which is actually slower than the slowest rate at which the portfolio would pay down if every borrower made only the minimum monthly payment), the Class C note can withstand annual constant loss rates as high as approximately 12%. For a portfolio with an average historical chargeoff rate of 6.5%, this would represent a historical loss multiple of 1.8 times. More typical monthly payment rates are 10% to 18%. At these levels, the Class C notes can withstand annual constant loss rates of approximately 16% to 20%, or loss multiples of 2.5 to 3 times based on the same 6.5% historical average. Clearly, Class C notes carry robust enhancement levels, enabling them to withstand severe performance degradation.

22.4 RATING AGENCY APPROACHES TO SIZING AND RATING CLASS C NOTES

To determine the level of credit enhancement required to support a given rating, the rating agencies use certain benchmark scenarios to evaluate possible future master trust performance under severe stress. As of this writing, S&P and Fitch IBCA are the only two rating agencies that have published methodologies to evaluate these scenarios as they relate to the Class C notes. The methodologies, not surprisingly, are derivatives of how each agency generally views credit card securitization. In addition, each brings a unique approach to evaluating the qualitative aspects of a transaction, including an analysis of the issuer's ability to achieve the objectives of its business strategy within a highly competitive industry.

In Exhibit 22.7 we summarize the key considerations in the rating processes of S&P and Fitch IBCA. Both agencies look at historical collateral performance, both review the originator's operations, and both look at portfolio concentrations.

The rating agencies' quantitative analysis focuses on the portfolio variables we have already identified. For example, Fitch IBCA stresses the portfolio dynamically by assuming large increases in chargeoffs, substantial

---

EXHIBIT 22.7 Rating Class C Notes: Rating Agency Approaches

Fitch IBCA
  Performance of historical collateral
  Cardholder credit scores
  Effects of competition, co-branding, etc.
  Originator's operations
  Concentration
  Seasonality
  Fixed- versus floating-rate investor coupon and interest rates
  Assumes most volatile interest rate environment (early 1980s)

S&P
  Performance of historical collateral
  Legal considerations (bankruptcy, "true-sale")
  Competitive pressures
  Originator's operations
  Concentration
  Fixed- versus floating-rate investor coupon and interest rates

Source: S&P's Ratings Services and Fitch IBCA Inc.

declines in portfolio yield, and substantial declines in monthly payment rates. S&P uses similar benchmark scenarios but also includes stresses to new purchase rates (the amount of new receivables acquired each month) and to series' certificate rates.

Each of the rating agencies performs an interest-rate analysis, particularly on floating rate-based certificates and notes, based on historic dislocations. For example, the early 1980s produced interest-rate spikes, particularly in the short end of the curve. Stress of this sort causes deterioration in excess spreads as certificate rates rise while portfolio yields reset more slowly.

The rating agencies take a holistic approach to examining new master trust series. This approach helps to define interactions among series and classes within each master trust. Exhibit 22.8 shows a summary of the specific stress scenarios that the rating agencies require to be satisfied for triple-A, single-A, and triple-B ratings.

In terms of sizing, the rating agency view the Class C note as an equivalent form of credit enhancement to the CIA certificate, and thus, they essentially require the same amount and structure of credit enhancement for the overall transaction. In MBNA's case for example, the agencies limit up to 85% of the transaction amount to be allocated to the triple-A-rated Class A tranche, with 7.5% allocated to the single-A-rated Class B tranche and 7.5% allocated to the Class C note (see Exhibit 22.9). In the case of First USA, the prescribed levels are up to 83% in a triple-A-rated Class A tranche, 7.5% in a single-A-rated Class B tranche, and 9.5% is allocated to the collateral interest.

EXHIBIT 22.8   Rating Class C Notes: Rating Agency Approaches

Fitch IBCA Base Case Stress Scenarios

	AAA	A	BBB
Charge-Offs (multiple)	4.50x	3.00x	2.30x
Portfolio Yield (decline)	35%	25%	20%
Monthly Payment Rate (decline)	45	35	30

S&P Combined Stress Scenarios[a]

	AAA	A	BBB
Charge-Offs (multiple)	3.00-5.00x	2.00-3.00x	1.50-2.00x
Portfolio Yield	11%-12% Cap	12% Cap	75% of Yield
Payment Rate (of steady state)	45-55%	50-60%	75%
Purchase rate	2-5	2-5	Flat[c]
Certificate Rate[b]	3-4	2	75% of worst[d]

[a] Loss-spike and interest rate-spike stress scenarios are performed.
[b] Example applies to floating-rate issues and is shown as an excess of the certificate rate over the yield. Fixed-rate issues use coupon of the issue.
[c] Purchase rate adjusts downward with payment rate to reflect stable portfolio balance for investment-grade issuers.
[d] 75% of worst case portfolio yield.
Sources: Fitch IBCA and S&P Rating Services.

EXHIBIT 22.9 Recent MBNA Master Credit Card Trust II and First USA Credit Card Master Trust Transactions—Size of Credit Enhancement

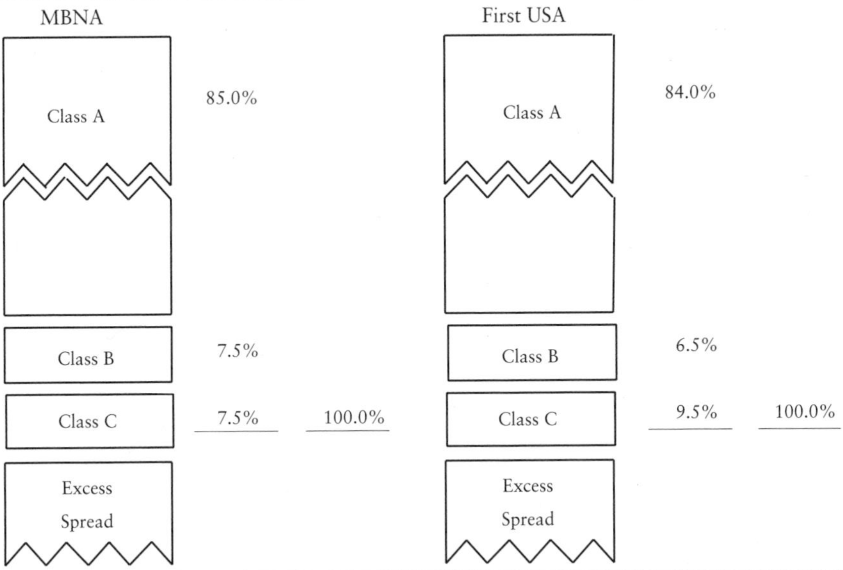

Note: Salomon Smith Barney and/or its affiliates have acted as a manager and/or co-manager of debt issues of MBNA Master Credit Card Trust II and First USA Credit Card Master Trust within the past three years.
Source: Prospectuses.

22.5 DETERMINING RELATIVE VALUE FOR CLASS C NOTES

The introduction of Class C notes is particularly significant in that it has created an entirely new sector: triple-B-rated, ERISA-eligible ABSs. These notes should appeal to new investor bases, including pension funds, which may have had an interest in low-investment-grade asset-backed securities but were precluded from investing by ERISA, and crossover triple-B-rated corporate investors, who may have sought diversification in structured products with simple cash flows and attractive relative value. To date, all Class C notes have been sold privately under Rule 144A. However, there is nothing about the notes that *requires* a Rule 144A offering, and we anticipate that issuers will soon begin to offer publicly registered Class C notes.[8]

---

[8] Issuers have utilized Rule 144A thus far to avoid the potentially long SEC review process associated with the introduction of any new structure.

We expect that as public notes become available, new issue spread levels will tighten, reflecting large incremental demand from money managers who, for one reason or another, cannot participate in or allocate large positions to 144A offerings.

Class C notes are likely to come in fixed- and floating-rate form and in average lives of 3 to 10 years. The market should ultimately price these securities relative to comparable alternatives. Given the novelty of the product, however, the alternatives are not entirely obvious. Investors are likely to compare levels available on Class C notes with those of similar average-life unsecured corporate debt, especially those from finance companies. We would argue that triple-B-rated ABSs enjoy an event risk advantage over triple-B-rated, unsecured debt. The market however has traditionally demanded a novelty premium for new structured products. To the extent that the premium exists, Class C notes will, by definition, offer value relative to unsecured, corporate debt.

More generally, Class C note investors must determine relative value by defining a framework (Exhibit 22.10) that incorporates the following: (1) absolute spread *levels* relative to those of comparable alternatives; (2) spread *differences* between triple-A, single-A, and triple-B ABSs relative to those of comparable alternatives; and (3) spread *differences* between Class C notes of different tenors relative to those of comparable triple-B alternatives. Under this framework, Class C notes offer fair value to an alternative investment class not only when absolute spread levels for Class C notes and the alternative are equivalent (after making adjustments for structure and liquidity), but also when the relationships between triple-A, single-A, and triple-B-rated credit card securities and those of the alternative are comparable, and the term structures of credit spreads are similar.

Based on structure alone, in the case of triple-B-rated sellers, Class C notes should trade at levels that are *tighter* than the seller's unsecured debt. Even though a correlation exists between collateral credit performance and corporate downgrade risk, corporate debt can be downgraded for other reasons as well. For example, the rating agencies may be uncomfortable with the seller's expansion into a new business line or proposed acquisition and take a rating action on the unsecured debt. Such an action would have no impact on the Class C notes. However, structure is not the only relevant consideration. At 7% to 10% of a typical transaction, Class C notes tend to have small tranche sizes. For example, on a $500 million transaction, the size of the Class C note would likely be $35 to $50 million. On a $1 billion transaction, the Class C note might only be as large as $70 to $100 million. As a result, the liquidity of Class C notes tends to be somewhat lower than that of comparable corporates and requires a liquidity premium adjustment to spread levels. The development of the so-called

EXHIBIT 22.10 Three Dimensional Relative Spread Analysis Framework as of October 1998

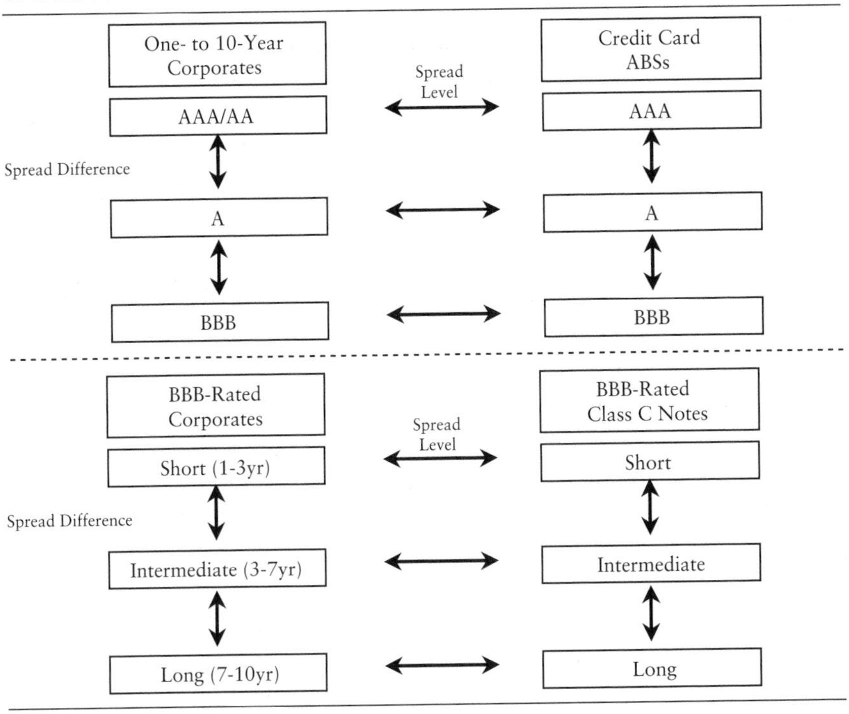

Source: Salomon Smith Barney.

block-and-trap securitization technology will help to enhance liquidity in the sector by increasing investor interest.

Just as with any other revolving ABS, in evaluating this new asset class, investors should examine not just the Class C note structure, but also the details of the collateral including ongoing maintenance of accounts within the collateral pool and the issuer's strategy for adding new receivable into the pool. Investors should also scrutinize a number of issuer-related and master trust-related investment factors. On the issuer side, these factors include such elements as issuer market share, commitment to the business, economies of scale, origination practices and accounting, capital strength and its components, client retention and management, and access to alternative, liquid markets. On the master trust side, factors include master trust cash flow allocations, cash flow components (for example, recoveries, interchange fees, and annual fees), historical and anticipated collateral performance, and structure of dynamic credit enhancement.

Examining issuer origination practices will lead investors to better define potential cash flow streams and to understand the impact of changes in the streams on the master trust. For example, certain issuers spend more time up front developing borrower client profiles during the solicitation and underwriting process. This development expense ultimately leads to better underwriting of borrowers, but it tends to penalize short-term earnings. Therefore, corporate shareholders, rather than master trust noteholders, bear these expenses, resulting in potentially subtle but ultimately significant cash flow differences for series noteholders.

We expect to see a variety of pricing options as the market develops. To date, issuers have sold fixed-rate Class C notes supporting floating-rate and fixed-rate Class A and B certificates, and floating-rate Class C notes supporting floating-rate Class A and B certificates. As investor opportunities develop in particular sectors (for example, nondollar markets), we expect that issuers will create pricing strategies targeted to meet those opportunities.

22.6 CONCLUSION

Credit card Class C notes represent the next logical step in the development of credit card ABS credit enhancement. The rating agencies have sized the structural cash flow protections to withstand severe stresses. As our analysis shows, Class C notes can tolerate historical loss multiples of approximately two times under extremely conservative monthly payment rate assumptions and 2.5 to 3 times under more typical scenarios. For corporate debt buyers, the securities offer a means to engage in structured products with simple cash flows, similar risks, and, arguably, less potential ratings volatility.

For ABS investors, Class C notes offer an opportunity to participate in the triple-B-rated credit sector without being constrained by trading restrictions and with the significant additional advantage of ERISA-eligibility.

CHAPTER 23

A Fresh Look at Credit Card Subordinate Classes

Peter DiMartino and Mary E. Kane

This chapter describes the new technology associated with Salomon Smith Barney's Block and TRAP technology and an overview of 1999 triple-B card issuance. We examine historical new-issue spreads and supply and look at relative values of subordinated cards versus other asset classes and higher-rated ABSs. Finally, we discuss the basics of card analysis and provide an overview of the credit card market. First, a brief description of blocking and TRAPing:

- *Blocking* creates the ability to issue public, ERISA-eligible credit card subordinated classes in larger size than previously issued.
- *TRAPing* (acronym for titanium rapid accumulation of principal) allows issuers to create subordinated classes delinked in maturity from any senior classes of the bond issue. It allows an issuer to create subordinated classes at any time, not necessarily concurrent with a senior bond issuance. Class C notes could mature before the senior classes, if replaced by equal credit enhancement. The C classes will not be repaid before a senior class maturity unless the ability to refinance exists and full principal due to the Cs has fully accumulated. Importantly, the subordinated classes are secured by the same collateral pool that collateralizes the entire Master Trust.

23.1 NEW TECHNOLOGIES IN CLASS C CARDS

The new two-tier structure using Block and TRAP technology will be somewhat modified from historical structures. As seen in Exhibit 23.1, a new

643

EXHIBIT 23.1   Two-Tier Owner Trust

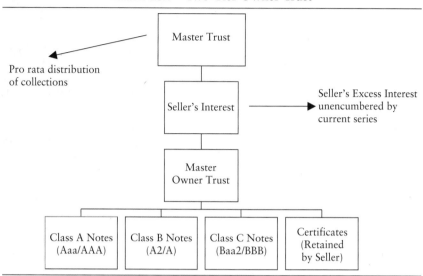

Source: Salomon Smith Barney.

Master Owner Trust is created to purchase the unencumbered seller's interest of the original Master Trust,[1] and *notes* (as opposed to certificates) are issued to *all* traditional classes of investors: triple-A, single-A, and triple-B. This will allow all classes of the notes to be registered at the SEC, publicly issued, and ERISA-eligible. Certificates of the Master Trust will be retained by the seller, allowing them to receive excess spread and cash flows allocated to the seller's interest. The seller's interest will continue to insulate investors from fluctuations in the amount of receivables as a result of seasonality, attrition, disputes, or other factors.

The seller sells a pool of receivables to the Master Trust, which is revolving. Investors and sellers are undivided beneficial interest holders in the receivables of the Master Trust. Principal and interest collections are allocated pro rata among the beneficial interest holders of the Master Trust (the Master Owner Trust will be one such holder). Collections may be shared among the outstanding series in the Master Trust, to the extent not required for that series.

---

[1] For issuers without an existing Master Trust, the two-tier structure will not be necessary.

Block Size

The significant structural enhancement enables issuing larger tranche sizes ($100–$200 million or larger, and seller issuance needs). This is subject to conforming to the credit enhancement requirements of the ratings agencies. We expect that tranche size will be sufficiently large to be eligible for inclusion in aggregate fixed-income indexes. This has obvious appeal for investors seeking improved efficiency and liquidity in ABS subordinates.

TRAPing

This technology enables tailored maturities to meet the needs of issuers and investors, creating the flexibility of an MTN-like program. Therefore maturities need not precisely match notes issued in the senior classes. This provides significant maneuverability for the issuer and may benefit investors who are more likely to be filled on a reverse-inquiry order.

How It Works

An interesting aspect for the Class C investor is that the notes may mature before the senior classes. The C class may not be repaid, however, unless sufficient cash exists to fully repay them. At some time before the maturity of an outstanding triple-B class, a determination will be made concerning the ability to replace the triple-B credit enhancement layer. If there is no ability to replace, an accumulation period will begin for the senior classes that rely on the triple-Bs for credit enhancement. The issuer will begin to accumulate cash in the principal funding account. These funds are for the benefit of the senior notes until sufficient cash exists to repay them and the senior noteholders are, in essence, defeased.

The length of time needed before the refinancing of the triple-B class will depend on the characteristics unique to each issuer's pool. Large issuers with substantial excess unallocated monthly principal collections will benefit from using the new technology. *The senior classes will never be in a position where the triple-B class is repaid without first being replaced.*

23.2 HISTORICAL SUPPLY

Triple-B credit card issues in 1998 aggregated $829 million. A total $1.8 billion was issued in 1999, and year-to-date 2000 issuance amounts to almost $800 million. ERISA-eligible subordinated cards contributed to the market's progress. Maturities ranged from 3 to 10 years, and both floating

EXHIBIT 23.2   1999 Class C Monthly Issuance

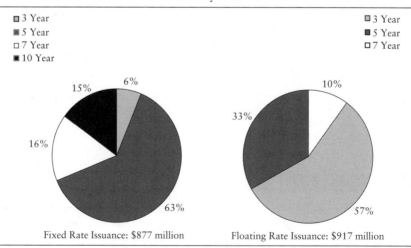

Source: Salomon Smith Barney.

and fixed classes have been issued. We show 1999 monthly issuance activity in Exhibit 23.2.

Total fixed and floating issuance in 1999 was about equal, and the 5-year sector was the most popular maturity, followed by the 3-year sector. Three-years dominated floating-rate issuance, making up 57% of 1999 floater issuance, followed by 5-years, with 33% issued as floaters. In fixed-

EXHIBIT 23.3   C-Piece Maturity and Product Mix for 1999

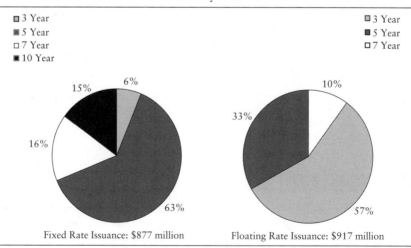

Source: Salomon Smith Barney.

rate issuance, 5-years made up 63%, so it can be inferred that investors' preference is for short- to medium-term maturities, although some demand exists in 7- to 10-years. Exhibit 23.3 illustrates investors' preference for 3- and 5-year paper.

23.3 RELATIVE VALUE ANALYSIS

Given the many attractive credit and structural features of credit cards, the relevant questions to ask are as follows:

- What is the yield on C class credit cards?
- How does it compare to higher-rated credit card classes?
- How does it compare to comparable CMBSs?
- How does it compare to triple-B finance unsecured corporate paper?
- Is this for buy-and-hold investors only, or are there trading opportunities?

To answer these questions, we begin by an examination of historical new-issue spreads of C class credit cards. Interestingly, there has been a fair amount of volatility on new-issue spreads, even discounting the Y2K and fourth-quarter 1998 noise. For trading-oriented accounts, spreads exhibited a fairly wide range, creating an interesting trading opportunity.

It is possible to trade triple-B credit card paper, particularly the new ERISA-eligible unrestricted paper, as it has more liquidity than other triple-B structured paper. Although not as liquid as more senior ABS classes, triple-B cards are more liquid than some triple-B unsecured corporate issues.

Supply seems to correlate closely with spread in the case of the 3- and 5-year sectors, particularly short floaters (the Y2K factor certainly influenced spreads). In the 7- and 10-year sectors, however, it seems as if supply was less influential, and rallying swap spreads drove supply. Exhibit 23.4 illustrates the volatility seen in all new-issue triple-B credit card spreads for the last two years. Each data point represents a new issue with a 3-, 5-, 7-, or 10-year maturity. Three- and five-years dominated class C supply.

We show the five-largest issuers of subordinated credit cards in Exhibit 23.5. Clearly, MBNA has dominated issuance in the class C market in 1999.

Relative Value versus Comparables

The reward for going down-in-credit in the credit card sector appeals to a growing number of investors. The spread pickup between triple-A and triple-B ABSs averages 54bp (basis points) and 87bp in the 3- and 5-year sectors, respectively (Exhibit 23.6).

EXHIBIT 23.4 Spreads and Volume for all New Issue Class C Credit Cards by Maturity May 1998–June 2000

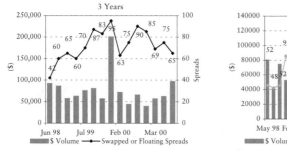

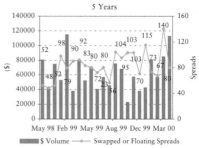

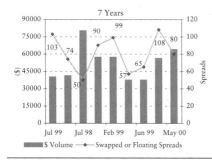

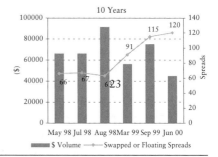

Source: Salomon Smith Barney.

EXHIBIT 23.5 1999 Top Class C Issuers

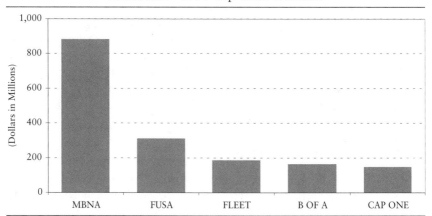

Source: Salomon Smith Barney.

EXHIBIT 23.6 Three- and Five-Year Spread Differentials, Triple-B versus Triple-A ABSs, June 1999–June 2000

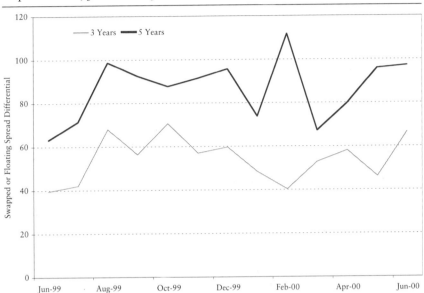

Source: Salomon Smith Barney.

Many investors examine crossover relationships when making investment allocation decisions for portfolio management. Therefore, we looked at some crossover relationships. CMBS and unsecured finance company paper are among the main product competitors for triple-B investment allocations. From Exhibit 23.7, we make the following observations:

■ Unsecured triple-B finance companies and CMBSs trade cheap to comparable C classes in all maturities (however, due to superior pool diversification and structural protection from event risks, ABSs are inherently less risky).

■ Investors wishing to arbitrage the credit curve can pick up cheap triple-B yields from issuers with more highly rated underlying unsecured debt ratings (i.e., investors may purchase triple-B-rated debt from single-A unsecured issuers like Fleet and Bank of America).

■ The average pickup in swapped or floating spreads from 10-year credit cards to 10-year CMBS is 20bp. (Commensurate with that spread advantage, CMBS has less pool diversification and greater extension risk than credit cards.)

EXHIBIT 23.7 Triple-B Comparative Spreads

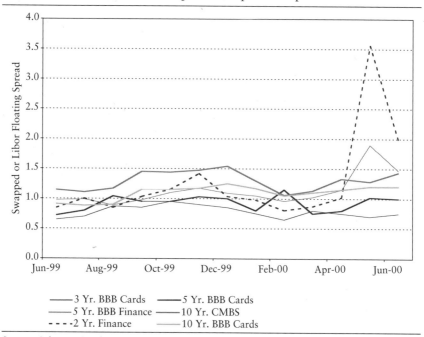

Source: Salomon Smith Barney.

- The average pickup of triple-B finance company paper over triple-B cards is 21bp. (The premium does not appear worth the unsecured nature and event risks prevalent in this sector.) The unsecured spread advantage can vary substantially.

23.4 A FUNDAMENTAL ANALYSIS OF CREDIT CARDS

Our focus on the class C credit card market would be incomplete without some discussion of the basics of card analysis and an overview of the current state of the credit card markets.

Structural Evaluation

The key analytical elements in credit card pool analysis are:

1. Pool yield
2. Excess spread

3. Payment rate
4. Purchase rate

Pool performance is measured and triggers are generally set against defined levels of these four factors. Securitization structures are dynamically credit-enhanced, trapping excess spread and/or early amortizing under adverse pool performance. Understanding these key factors allows the analyst to evaluate the sufficiency of the credit enhancement in relation to the expected loss scenario, maturity, and cash flow of the pool.

Pool Yield As receivables pay down, the trust purchases new receivables. While varying somewhat among issuers, in general, all interest and card annual fees, late charges, and recoveries on defaulted receivables are included in gross pool yield. However, not all issuers include recovery of defaulted receivables in gross pool yield, and this accounts for some of the observable differences among issuers' pool yields.

Excess Spread Servicing fees, interest expense, and credit losses are deducted from gross yield and comprise "excess spread." **Excess spread is the most important and comparable analytical factor in credit card analysis.** The rating agencies heavily weight excess spread to determine required credit enhancement.

Payment Rate Some credit card users will pay the full balance off each month (these are called convenience users), others will pay the minimum required payment, and others pay between the minimum payment and the full balance. The repayment patterns of the customer base (monthly payment rate) are relevant, measuring how quickly the pool could self-liquidate from cash flow.

The strategy of the card originator will result in some differences in payment rates among issuers. High-credit-quality pools tend to pay faster, because there tends to be more convenience usage among these cardholders. (Correspondingly, these pools will have lower yields.) In general, however, regardless of the marketing strategy of the originator, credit card pools have the ability to self-liquidate within 6 to 18 months.

Purchase Rate The replacement of receivables (monthly purchase rate) allows the pool to replace receivables and to revolve for the life of the transaction. When the revolving period is scheduled to terminate, an accumulation period commences, and the pool applies collections to build in a cash accumulation account to defease principal instead of replacing receivables.

Adverse Pool Performance

What happens when a credit card pool experiences adverse pool performance? Several events would probably occur simultaneously:

- Losses would rise.
- The monthly payment rate (due to higher chargeoffs) would decline.
- Yields would increase (more late fees and revolving balances).

The effect on excess spread will depend on the level of pool losses and the ability of the servicer to avoid losses and to improve recoveries. Credit card structures are deliberately robust and are structured to trap excess spread early on to build credit enhancement or to amortize prior to the expected maturity if additional triggers are reached. This makes credit card structures dynamic and deserving of a closer look.

Dynamic Credit Enhancement

Credit enhancement for the class C notes is typically a **note reserve account** and **excess spread.** Exhibit 23.8 provides an example of typical required reserve account levels based on excess spread. Note that the levels require more cash as excess spread declines. This is achieved by trapping excess spread in the deal in lieu of paying it out to the seller. It also illustrates that the lower the excess spread level, the longer it will take to fund the account to required levels.

EXHIBIT 23.8   Example of Dynamic Reserve Account Funding Parameters Based on Excess Spread Levels

	S&P Sample Reserve Account Structure[a]	
Quarterly Excess Spread	Required Reserve Amount	Est. Time to Fund[b]
> 4.50%	0.00%	NA
4.00%-4.50%	1.50	4.0-4.5Mo.
3.50%-4.00%	2.00	6.0-6.9
3.00%-3.50%	3.00	10.3-12.0
< 3.00%	4.00	Over 16

[a] Based on S&P Ratings' Sample Reserve.
[b] Based on a constant excess spread, assuming a zero initial balance.
NA: Not applicable.
Source: Standard & Poor's Corporation and Salomon Smith Barney estimates.

EXHIBIT 23.9 Moody's Credit Card Index, 1Q 1991–1Q 2000

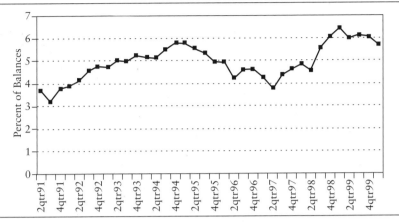

Source: Moody's Investors Service.

Pool Performance Measurement

Credit card pool performance varies among issuers, and factors such as yield, losses, and monthly payment rates are issuer specific. Well-managed, higher loss portfolios are offset by higher yielding accounts, so yields and losses are not necessarily comparable across issuers. However, **excess spread** offers a meaningful measure of comparison across issuers.

Excess spread dipped in the early 1990s as competition intensified among card issuers. It started to rebound in second quarter 1997 and has been stable in recent quarters. Moody's Investor's Service *Aggregate Credit Card Index*[2] is a good source to track how a representative range of major credit card issuers are performing. Moody's 1Q 2000 Credit Card Index calculates three-month average excess spread at 5.73%, which is an industrywide decline in excess spread year-over-year (see Exhibit 23.9). Even so, these levels are well above the levels in 1991 to 1993 when competition and consolidation eroded excess spread to between 3% and 5%.

What is an appropriate level of excess spread? Benchmarking to the industry average excess spread level is a good point of reference. Above all, excess spread levels should demonstrate a proven stable track record. We believe that investors may still be comfortable with certain issuers with excess spreads below the industry average, as long as their performance records are consistent.

---

[2] "Credit Card Indexes: March 2000," *Structured Finance Research,* Moody's Investors Service.

Monitoring Pool Performance

Most of the major credit card issuers report their salient data on Bloomberg monthly, so it is easy for investors to track the relevant parameters. (Type CCR Go to obtain a menu of those issuers posting monthly master trust data.) We believe that it is easier to track the performance of securitizations than that of unsecured corporate notes, where investors must closely watch event and other risks.

Portfolio Comparison of Major Credit Card Issuers

Selected major credit card issuers are shown in Exhibit 23.10. It is helpful to compare and contrast the issuers' differences in portfolio yield, net chargeoffs, and payment rates, as well as the proportion of issuance in relation to the entire portfolio.

23.5 LOSS SUSTAINABILITY

As discussed, adverse pool performance will cause a number of variables to change simultaneously—pool yield, payment rate, and losses. The triggers and credit enhancement levels sized by the rating agencies will take these variables into account and will be appropriate for individual issuers. The structure should amply protect investors. Triple-B rating levels are credit

EXHIBIT 23.10   Major Credit Card Issuer Portfolio Comparison, YTD as of April 30, 2000 (Dollars in Thousands)

	MBNA	Citibank	USA	Fleet	Chase	America	One	Providian
Performance Data								
As Of	31 Mar 00	30 Sep 99	31 Mar 99	31 Dec 99	31 Dec 99	30 Jun 99	31 Dec 99	30 Sep 99
Yield	19.08%	17.49%	20.18%	19.01%	18.40%	19.54%	27.74%	23.34%
Payment Rate	14.44%	21.53%	15.30%	12.06%	13.51%	15.83%	14.23%	9.23%
Net Charge-offs	5.48%[a]	4.83%	5.13%	6.83%	5.70%	6.49%	3.74%	7.32%
Trust Portfolio (000s)	$56,204,213[b]	$45,240,105	$34,986,711	$11,654,324[e]	$19,960,003	$9,785,125	$12,294,601	$8,149,922
Approx Managed Portfolio (000s)[c]	$58,800,000	$73,300,000[c]	$69,000,000[d]	$14,300,000	$33,300,000	$20,000,000[f]	$16,800,000	$10,800,093

[a] Gross charge-offs.
[b] As of June 29, 2000.
[c] Average balance as of March 31, 2000.
[d] As of December 31, 2000.
[e] As of February 29, 2000.
[f] As of March 31, 2000.
Source: 10K and 10Q Reports.

EXHIBIT 23.11 Standard & Poor's Combined Stress Scenarios[a]

	AAA	A	BBB
Chargeoffs (Multiple)	3.00x–5.00x	2.00x–3.00x	1.50x–2.00x
Portfolio Yield	11%-12% Cap	12% Cap	75% of Yield
Payment Rate (of Steady State)	45%-55%	50%-60%	75%
Purchase Rate	2-5	2-5	Flat[b]
Certificate Rate[c]	3-4	3	75% of Worst[d]

[a] Loss-spike and interest rate spike stress scenarios are performed.
[b] Purchase rate adjusts downward with payment rate to reflect stable portfolio balance for investment-grade issuers.
[c] Example applies to floating-rate issues and is shown as an excess of the certificate rate over the yield. Fixed-rate issues use coupon of the issue.
[d] 75% of worst-case portfolio yield.
Source: Standard & Poor's Corporation.

enhanced by a multiple of expected losses. The severity of Standard & Poor's methodology for sizing card credit enhancement can be seen in Exhibit 23.11. The agency simultaneously stresses portfolio yields, payment rates, purchase rates, and the certificate rates, producing loss coverage of 1.5 to 2.0 times for triple-Bs.

Salomon Smith Barney's stress test is similar to the S&P test shown in Exhibit 23.11. Holding portfolio yields constant and stressing monthly payment rates, we determine the losses the notes can tolerate before the class C notes lose any principal. Even at a monthly payment rate of only 2.5% (which is actually slower than the slowest rate at which a portfolio would pay down if every borrower made only the minimum monthly payment), the class C notes loss sustainability is 12%. At higher payment rates of 10% to 18% (more typical), the class C notes can sustain loss rates of approximately 16% to 20%.[3] In our opinion, investors are well-protected.

23.6 CONCLUSION

We believe that on a risk-return basis, subordinate credit cards are justifiably prudent investments for institutional investors. The combination of spread and proven performance, along with robust structure creates a unique asset class worthy of investors' focus. Furthermore, we envision that as issuance and investor participation continue to expand, liquidity in subordinate ABS classes will become less of a concern.

---

[3] See *Class C Notes: Opening the Next Frontier in Credit Card Asset-Backed Securities,* Salomon Smith Barney, November 23, 1998.

CHAPTER 24

Recreational Vehicle and Boat Loan ABSs

A Prepayment Analysis

Ronald E. Thompson, Jr. and Ivan Gjaja

A recent slowdown of prepayment speeds on transactions backed by recreational vehicle (RV) and boat loans, together with the unexpected prepayment behavior of very seasoned RV deals, have brought attention to the prepayment characteristics of these asset classes. The changes from historical patterns and the pricing speeds have been significant, affecting the valuation of longer-dated tranches. In this chapter, we analyze historical evidence from 27 deals to determine three main features of RV and boat prepayments: their *dependence on loan age* (seasoning ramp), *sensitivity to interest rates,* and *seasonal variation.* For comparison, we also examine the loan-age dependence of speeds on automobile loans.

ABS transactions backed by automobile and recreational vehicle (RV) loans are generally priced at issuance to a constant ABS prepayment speed, while transactions backed by boat loans are generally priced at a constant CPR.[1] Exhibit 24.1 shows historical prepayments by loan age for 20 automobile transactions issued by Chrysler and Ford, and Exhibit 24.2 shows historical prepayments by loan age for 22 RV transactions issued by Fleetwood, CIT, Bank of Boston, and Chase.

---

[1] The ABS curve is defined as an increasing sequence of single-monthly mortalities (SMMs). Therefore, when expressed in CPRs, the prepayments following a constant ABS curve correspond to a sequence of increasing CPRs. The relationship between ABS (%) and SMM (%) is given by ABS = $100 \times SMM/(100 + SMM \times (m - 1))$, where m is the age of the collateral in months.

EXHIBIT 24.1   Seasoning of Automobile Prepayments Expressed in ABS

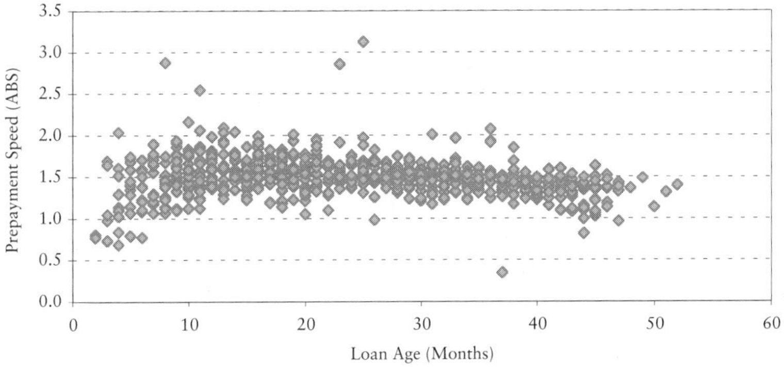

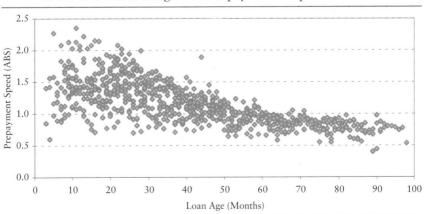

Source: Salomon Smith Barney.

Constant ABS speeds appear to adequately represent prepayments on automobile loans. Although a seasoning effect is discernible for auto loan ages less than 10 months, and prepayments appear to slow down modestly for collateral seasoned more than three years, prepayment speeds cluster around a constant 1.5% ABS through the remainder of the loan life.

In contrast, speeds of RV loans display a strong dependence on loan age. After starting out in the range of 1% to 2% ABS, prepayments on this asset class begin to slow down after about 20 months of seasoning, reaching

EXHIBIT 24.2   Seasoning of RV Prepayments Expressed in ABS

Source: Salomon Smith Barney.

EXHIBIT 24.3   Seasoning of RV Prepayments Expressed in CPR

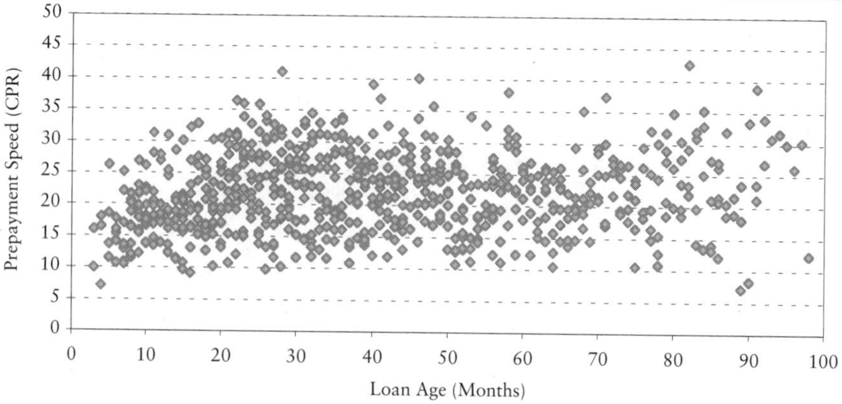

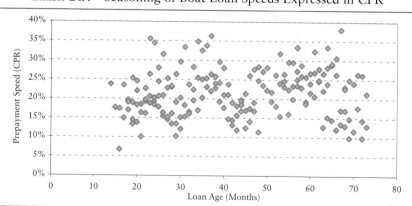

Source: Salomon Smith Barney.

about 0.8% ABS by the loan age of 6 to 7 years. Therefore, the assumption of constant ABS prepayment speed does not appear justified for deals backed by RV loans, despite ABS remaining as a pricing speed convention.

The dependence of RV prepayments on loan age can be reduced by expressing the speeds in CPR units, rather than ABS units. Exhibit 24.3 shows historical speeds on RV loans expressed in CPR. While a seasoning ramp is evident for loan ages less than about 20 months, for greater loan ages, speeds seem to fall generally around the 20% CPR line, with only a small

EXHIBIT 24.4   Seasoning of Boat Loan Speeds Expressed in CPR

Source: Salomon Smith Barney.

increase for very seasoned loans. Therefore, a constant CPR prepayment rate, or a seasoning curve that levels off after about 20 months when expressed in CPR units, is a better prepayment assumption for RV loans than a constant ABS prepayment rate.

A similar pattern exists for boat loan-backed transactions, as shown in Exhibit 24.4. However, in this case, history is more recent and more limited. Most of the boat loan transactions are well seasoned at issuance, which masks any beginning seasoning ramp.

More recently, boat- and RV-backed transactions have appeared to slow down even when expressed in CPR units. Although seasoning plays a major role, it appears that interest rate sensitivity also affects prepayment speeds.

24.1 DEPENDENCE OF PREPAYMENTS ON INTEREST RATES

The solid credit quality of the typical RV and boat loan borrower has an impact on the slight negative convexity found in RV and boat loan-backed bonds. RV and boat purchasers or borrowers tend to be older and have substantially more means than typical consumers (see Exhibit 24.5). Therefore, prepayments due to defaults are generally lower than for comparable securities. However, many of these borrowers tend to have fixed monthly incomes and often compare yields on investments against those paid on borrowings. In a declining rate environment, RV and boat borrowers may find it advantageous to tap other resources to pay off or refinance their loans. Conversely, in rising rate environments, this incentive is reduced.

In Exhibit 24.6, CPR speeds are compared to absolute changes in interest rates, using the three-year Treasury rate as a proxy.[2] Loan payoff/refinancing

EXHIBIT 24.5 Typical Demographic Characteristics for Boat and RV Purchasers

	Boats	RVs
Age	48 Yrs.	48 Yrs.
Income	$71,000	$47,000
Married	86 %	Most*
Retired	38 %	40 %

*According to RVIA research for an average RV owner.
Source: RV Industry Association and National Marine Manufacturers Association.

---

[2] The refinancing incentive is measured by the difference between the month-end three-year Treasury rate at prepayment time and at loan origination.

EXHIBIT 24.6 Effect of Refinancing Incentive on RV Loan Prepayments

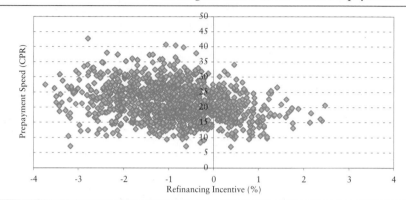

Source: Salomon Smith Barney.

incentives caused by interest rate changes appear to have a modest effect, implied by a small slope in the graph.

To examine the payoff/refinance incentive further, we compare prepayment speeds against differences between the weighted-average coupon for the pool and prevailing Treasury rates.[3] The results are shown in Exhibit 24.7. The distinctive slope of this graph highlights borrower incentives in comparing loan rates with financial alternatives. Greater differences between the pool WAC and prevailing Treasury rates imply greater incentives to pay off or refinance, and therefore, leads to faster speeds. This factor also implies that, holding all other variables constant, investors may expect higher speeds on pools with higher WACs.

Offsetting some of the refinancing and payoff effects are the relatively small sizes of RV and boat loans compared with home mortgages and the depreciating nature of the equipment. The small loan size of boat, RV, and auto loans implies very limited savings in monthly payment should loan rates fall. Furthermore, boats and RVs depreciate in value, implying that borrowers may have to inject cash for refinancing, a negative factor that may dampen a borrower's desire to refinance.

---

[3] Here, the refinancing incentive is the pool WAC minus the month-end three-year Treasury rate at prepayment time.

EXHIBIT 24.7   Effect of WAC-Treasury Spread on RV Loan Prepayments

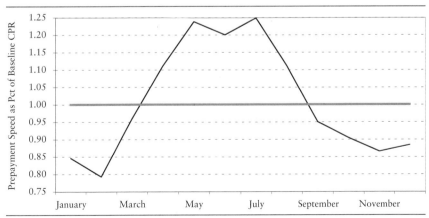

Source: Salomon Smith Barney.

24.2 PREPAYMENT SEASONALITY

Seasonality plays a role, but is generally more pronounced in boat loan-backed transactions. Exhibit 24.8 shows the effect of seasonality on boat loan prepayments. We found only slight patterns in transactions backed by autos and RVs. This factor likely relates to stronger boat sales in spring,

EXHIBIT 24.8   Seasonal Factors of Boat Loan Pool Prepayments Expressed in CPRs

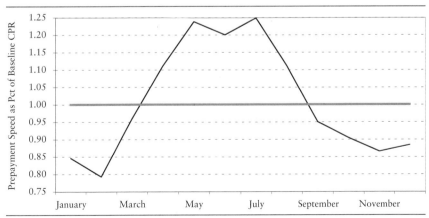

Source: Salomon Smith Barney.

following winter storage. Cars and RVs have some seasonal selling variations, but are actively sold throughout the year.

All of these factors—seasoning, interest rate sensitivity, and seasonality—determine prepayment speed. However, seasoning is the most relevant
for investors, followed by the financial incentives implied by the pool's
weighted-average coupon relative to other interest rates. Seasonality adjustments may be made, but these have only a small effect on long-term speeds.

24.3 IMPLICATIONS FOR INVESTORS

For investors in longer-dated tranches and for secondary trading, prepayment speed deceleration has particular significance. As an example,
we examine a recent market trade of CIT's 1999 RV-backed transaction.
By comparing the effect of different prepayment speeds, the weighted-
average life of the A5 tranche of the transaction shortens from 6.1 years, at
a 0.9 ABS (close to February's speed of 0.92 ABS), to 3.58 years, at the
deal pricing speed of 1.4 ABS (see Exhibit 24.9).

So what is the right prepayment speed to use? As with autos, the pricing
convention for RV-backed securitizations has generally been to use a constant
ABS speed, while boat loan-backed deals use a constant CPR speed. Boat
loan- and, especially, RV loan-backed transactions have longer average lives
than auto deals, to which they are often compared. Our analysis has shown
that a constant CPR curve, or a seasoning ramp, is a more accurate pricing
assumption for RV loans whereas, pricing of boat loans to a constant CPR
curve appears adequate.

EXHIBIT 24.9   Market Pricing of CITRV 99-A A5 Tranche, Effects of
Prepayment Speed on Valuation

	Prepayment Speed (ABS/CPR)					
	0.8%/20%	0.9%/23%	1.0%/26%	1.2%/33%	1.4%/39%	1.6%/45%
Weighted Average Life (Years)	6.87	6.08	5.42	4.38	3.58	3.00
Static Spread (bp)	91	99	109	132	160	193
Mod Duration	5.35	4.85	4.41	3.67	3.08	2.62
Payment Window (Dates)	10/06-6/07	1/06-8/06	6/05-12/05	6/04-11/04	10/03-1/04	3/03-6/03
Payment Window (Months)	9	8	7	6	4	4

Table assumes a cleanup call with a dollar price of 93-30 as of May 12, 2000.
Source: Salomon Smith Barney.

CHAPTER 25

The ABCs of CDO Equity

Glen McDermott

Collateralized debt obligations (CDOs) are formed when asset-backed structuring technology is applied to a pool of corporate credit exposures. Total rated issuance of CDOs has boomed in recent years (see Exhibit 25.1). CDO structures can be segmented into three categories:

1. Cash flow,
2. Market value, and
3. Credit derivative.

Cash flow CDOs, which currently are the most prevalent CDO structures, rely on the cash flow generated from the pool of assets to service the issued debt. This chapter focuses on cash flow CDO income notes. A CDO is created when a special purpose vehicle (SPV) is established to acquire a pool of high yield corporate bonds, bank loans, or other debt obligations (see Exhibit 25.2). To fund the acquisition of the debt obligations, the SPV issues rated and unrated liabilities. Since the majority of the these liabilities are highly rated, the CDO can raise most of its capital cheaply in the investment-grade market and invest it more profitably in other markets including the high yield market.

In a typical cash flow CDO, the rated liabilities are tranched into multiple classes, with the most senior class receiving a triple-A or double-A rating and the most subordinated class above the income note receiving a double-B or single-B. The ratings on the classes are a function of subordination and how cash flow and defaults are allocated among them. Principal and interest cash flow are paid sequentially from the highest rated class to the lowest, but if the cash flow is insufficient to meet senior costs or certain asset maintenance tests are not met, most or all cash flow is paid to the most senior class.

EXHIBIT 25.1 Moody's Rated Volume, 1988–2000

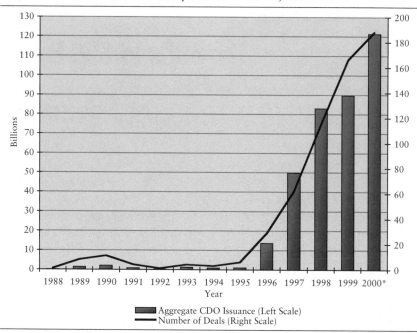

Source: Moody's Investors Service.

25.1 CASH FLOW CDO INCOME NOTES

CDO income notes are typically unrated and represent the most subordinated part of the CDO capital structure.[1] These notes will receive the residual interest cash flow remaining after payment of fees, rated note holder coupon, and the satisfaction of any asset maintenance tests. Factors that will impact the residual interest cash flow include the level and timing of defaults, the level and timing of recoveries, and the movement of interest rates. Income notes returns are generated by capturing the spread differential between the yield on the pool of fixed income assets (the majority of which are high yield bonds and bank loans) and the lower borrowing cost of the investment-grade and the non-investment-grade debt issued by the SPV. This positive spread relationship can produce risk-adjusted returns to income note holders in the range of 15% to 20%.

---

[1] Duff & Phelps Credit Rating Co. has recently developed criteria for rating CDO equity: *DCR's Criteria for Rating "Equity" of Cash Flow CDOs*, January 2000.

Exhibit 25.2   Typical CDO Structure

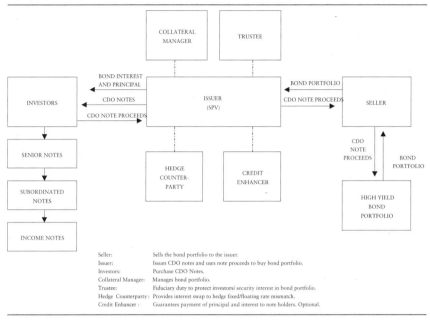

Seller: Sells the bond portfolio to the issuer.
Issuer: Issues CDO notes and uses note proceeds to buy bond portfolio.
Investors: Purchase CDO Notes.
Collateral Manager: Manages bond portfolio.
Trustee: Fiduciary duty to protect investorsi security interest in bond portfolio.
Hedge Counterparty :   Provides interest swap to hedge fixed/floating rate mismatch.
Credit Enhancer :   Guarantees payment of principal and interest to note holders. Optional.

Source: Salomon Smith Barney.

Once a cash flow CDO is issued, the collateral manager will manage
the portfolio according to the investment guidelines set forth in the bond indenture and within parameters necessary to satisfy the rating agencies. Pursuant to these guidelines, the manager will sell and buy assets and, during
the reinvestment period, will reinvest collateral principal cash flows into
new bonds. The investment guidelines typically require that the CDO manager maintain a minimum average rating and portfolio diversity such that
any trading will have a minimal impact on the senior CDO bondholders.

The primary responsibility of the cash flow CDO collateral manager is
to manage the portfolio in a way that minimizes losses to note holders resulting from defaults and discounted sales. To this end, all note holders rely
on the manager's ability to identify and retain creditworthy investments. A
manager's trading decisions can have a substantial impact on the returns
paid to income note holders; the initial asset selection and its trading activity throughout the reinvestment period are critical to achieving high returns. A manager with a deep understanding of the underlying credit
fundamentals of each of its investments can make informed, credit-based
trading decisions, not trading decisions based on price movements.

Cash flow CDO income notes have many favorable characteristics. Among them are:

- *Healthy returns.* The risk-adjusted internal rate of return (IRR) to income note holders can range from 15% to 20%. This return rate compares favorably with that of other investment opportunities (see Exhibit 25.3). We explore the volatility of this return in Section 25.2, "Return Analysis."
- *Lack of correlation with other asset classes.* Although there is no established index for CDO income note returns, the performance of the traditional cash flow CDO income note is directly linked to the behavior of a pool of U.S. high yield bonds. U.S. high yield bonds have not shown a strong correlation to other asset classes (see Exhibit 25.4).
- *Top-tier fund managers.* An income note investment allows an investor to gain exposure to an experienced CDO manager and the healthy returns it can generate, with a smaller initial investment than might otherwise be required.
- *Access to esoteric assets.* An income note investment can be an efficient way for an investor to gain exposure to a variety of esoteric asset classes. Certain asset types, such as leveraged loans, mezzanine loans, and project finance loans, are asset classes to which relatively few investors have access.
- *Cash flow-based returns.* Returns on cash flow CDO income notes are driven by the cash flow generated from the assets, not the market value or the price of those assets. This characteristic enables the investor to mitigate market risk and allows the manager to focus on the underlying

EXHIBIT 25.3   Historical Returns—Various Asset Classes, 1990–2000

Index	10 Year Average (%)	Standard Deviation	Sharpe Ratio	5 Year Average (%)	Standard Deviation	Sharpe Ratio
*Fixed Income**						
SSB Brady Bond Index	17.52	15.98	0.78	17.52	17.88	0.69
SSB HY Market Index	10.94	6.39	0.92	9.71	5.25	0.86
Corporate Bond Index	8.27	4.58	0.70	8.15	4.66	0.63
Intermediate Term Treasury Index	7.89	5.79	0.49	7.95	5.78	0.47
Mortgage Bond Index	7.84	3.17	0.88	7.93	2.87	0.95
SSB Broad Investment-Grade (BIG) Index	7.75	3.88	0.69	7.74	3.74	0.68
AAA Rated Corporate Bond Index	7.65	3.70	0.70	7.46	3.68	0.61
Equities						
Nasdaq Composite	24.50	20.62	0.94	40.17	22.82	1.53
S&P 500	18.27	13.42	0.98	28.72	14.07	1.67
DJIA	16.17	14.26	0.78	24.56	15.65	1.24

*For more information on Salomon Smith Barney indexes, please see *April 2000 Performance, Total Rate-of-Return Indexes,* Salomon Smith Barney, May 2, 2000.
Source: Salomon Smith Barney.

EXHIBIT 25.4 Correlation of Various Asset Classes, 1990–2000

	SSB HY Mkt Index	3 Month Treas. Bill	Brady Bond Index	Corporate	Treasury 7-10 Year	BIG Corporates	AAA Rated Mortgage Index	Mortgage Index	Nasdaq Composite	DJIA
3-Month Treasury Bill	-0.08									
SSB Brady Bond Index	0.47	0.11								
Corporate Bond Index	0.53	0.10	0.34							
Intermediate Term Treasury Index	0.30	0.09	0.19	0.94						
SSB Broad Investment-Grade (BIG) Index	0.41	0.14	0.26	0.98	0.98					
AAA Rated Corporate Bond Index	0.45	0.11	0.28	0.98	0.97	0.99				
Mortgage Bond Index	0.43	0.22	0.29	0.90	0.87	0.94	0.91			
Nasdaq Composite	0.51	-0.05	0.43	0.29	0.16	0.21	0.25	0.21		
DJIA	0.53	0.00	0.59	0.38	0.25	0.32	0.33	0.35	0.71	
S&P 500	0.54	0.00	0.56	0.47	0.35	0.40	0.42	0.42	0.82	0.92

Source: Salomon Smith Barney.

credit fundamentals of the high yield collateral. The investment is especially attractive when there is a dislocation in the high yield market due to technical, not credit, factors (e.g., in fourth-quarter 1998). This stands in stark contrast to high yield mutual fund returns, which are sensitive to market value fluctuations.

■ *Diversification.* A relatively small investment in a cash flow CDO income note can confer substantial diversification benefits. An investor can gain exposure to 50 to 120 obligors across 15 to 25 industry sectors.

■ *Structural protections.* Income note holders benefit from a variety of structural features present in cash flow CDOs. Chief among them is the ability to remove the portfolio manager and the right to call the deal after the end of the noncall period.

■ *Front-loaded cash flows.* Unlike other alternative investments (e.g., private equity) an investment in cash flow CDO income notes will typically generate cash flow within six months of the initial investment.

■ *Transparency.* Income note investments are more transparent than many alternative investments. Every month, the trustee reports, among other things, trading activity, obligor names and exposure amounts, industry concentrations, and compliance or noncompliance with liquidity and asset maintenance tests.

■ *Imbedded interest rate hedges.* Many CDOs are floating-rate obligations backed by pools of fixed-rate bonds. In order to hedge the mismatch between the fixed-rate assets and the LIBOR-indexed liabilities, most CDOs purchase a combination of interest rate swaps and/or caps. Although these hedges are bought for the benefit of the rated note holders, they also benefit the income notes as the residual interest beneficiary.

■ *Taxation.* Non-U.S. investors are not subject to U.S. withholding tax on dividends and gains from sale, exchange or redemption they receive from their investment. Tax-exempt entities are not subject to Unrelated Business Income Tax.

Although CDO equity has many favorable characteristics, prospective note holders should consider the risks associated with ownership. Some risks include:

- *Subordination of the income notes.* The income notes are the most subordinated notes in the CDO capital structure. They receive interest cash flow only after fees and rated coupon interest are paid, and asset and cash flow coverage tests are satisfied. No payment of principal of the income notes is paid until all other notes are retired and, to the extent that any losses are suffered by note holders, such losses are borne first by the income note holders.

  Since the income notes are subordinated, prospective investors should consider and assess for themselves, given the manager's track record, the likely level and timing of defaults, recoveries and interest rate movements. Section 25.2 provides numerous examples that will help investors understand how these variables impact income note returns.

- *Limited liquidity and restrictions on transfer.* Currently, potential income note buyers should not rely on a secondary market for CDO income notes. The investment trades on a "best efforts" basis and in a typical transaction, the income notes will be owned by a relatively small number of investors. Also, before selling an income note in the secondary market, the seller must comply with various regulations that restrict the transferability of certain types of securities.

- *Mandatory principal repayment of senior notes.* If the aggregate asset balance is insufficient to meet the minimum overcollateralization test or the aggregate asset yield is insufficient to meet the minimum interest coverage test, cash flow that would have been distributed to the income notes will be diverted to amortize the most senior notes. If this occurs, the capital structure will de-lever until the test(s) are brought back into compliance. A de-levering structure will have a negative impact on income note returns.

- *Reinvestment risk.* During the reinvestment period the collateral manager will reinvest principal collections in additional bonds and loans. Depending on market conditions and the CDO's investment guidelines, the manager may purchase loans and bonds with a lower yield than the initial collateral (i.e., spread compression), resulting in less cash flow for all note holders.

One way to mitigate some of these risks is to bundle the income note with a zero coupon Treasury STRIP (or other security free of credit risk) and

EXHIBIT 25.5   Principal Protected Units

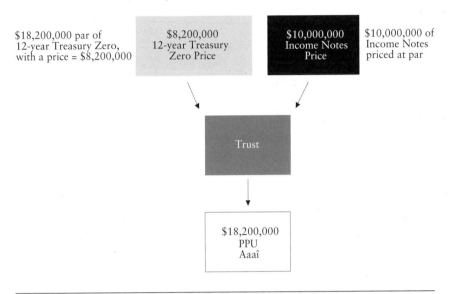

Price (Treasury Zero) + Price (Income Notes) = Par (Treasury Zero)

$18,200,000 par of 12-year Treasury Zero, with a price = $8,200,000

$8,200,000 12-year Treasury Zero Price

$10,000,000 Income Notes Price

$10,000,000 of Income Notes priced at par

Trust

$18,200,000 PPU Aaaî

Source: Salomon Smith Barney.

create a principal-protected structured note or unit (PPU) (see Exhibit 25.5). These units are designed to protect income note holders from the loss of their initial investment while still providing the potential of some yield upside. Moody's can rate PPUs Aaa, thereby allowing insurance company investors to gain NAIC1 capital treatment.

25.2 RETURN ANALYSIS

The vast majority of CDOs are privately placed. As a result, publicly available data on the historical performance of CDO bonds is scarce. This dearth of information makes it difficult to use traditional statistical techniques to analyze CDO income note returns and the volatility of those returns. The lack of historical information, however, does not mean that returns cannot be analyzed under a variety of stress scenarios.

An internal rate of return (IRR) of 15% to 20% is often bandied about in the marketplace, but how robust and predictable is this return? What assumptions underlie such forecasted returns? The answers to these questions depend on the confluence of a number of factors, including:

- ■ Magnitude and timing of defaults and sales at a discount to par,
- ■ Magnitude and timing of recoveries,
- ■ Interest rate movements, and
- ■ Calls and tenders.

Defaults

Since most CDOs are repackagings of high yield corporate bonds and loans, their performance is correlated with the default trends in the high yield market. That default trend has been rising during the last few years, with aggregate defaults reaching 4.15% in 1999, up from 1.6% in 1998 (see Exhibit 25.6). Peters and Altman cite a number of factors contributing to the rising default rate, including heavy high yield bond issuance from 1997 to 1999, a trend toward defaults occurring a shorter period of

EXHIBIT 25.6   Historical Default Rate, High Yield Bond Market, 1971–1999

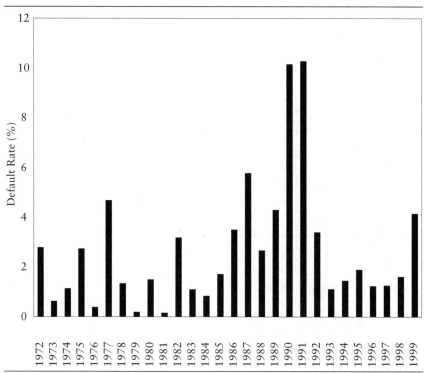

Source: Salomon Smith Barney.

EXHIBIT 25.7   Cash Flow Modeling Assumptions

Base line default rate	2%
Recovery rate	50%
Liability weighted-average cost of funds	10yr UST + 2.25%
Asset yield*	10yr UST + 5.20%
Fees	0.55%
Reinvestment Rate	11%
Interest rate hedge	Notional amount equal to 90% of the initial asset base

*Net of management fees.
Source: Salomon Smith Barney.

time after issuance, deteriorating credit quality of new issues, and significant defaults in certain industries.[2] Over the life of the study, however, defaults have been approximately 3% per year.

It is also important to note that although the performance of the CDO sector is correlated with high yield corporate sector in general, they are far from perfectly correlated. A CDO, after all, does not own all the credits in the high yield universe. It owns a carefully selected, diverse portion. Top-tier portfolio managers have proven that they can consistently experience lower defaults than the marketplace as a whole. Asset selection and the manager's long-term track record are key.

While the average annual default rate for the entire high yield universe has been about 3% over the last thirty years, the relatively small number of obligors in the typical CDO (i.e., 70–120) will result in default behavior that is considerably more volatile than any historical study. Consequently, we question whether the Street CDO equity pricing convention of applying a level 2% annual default rate is valid. It is impossible to predict which default pattern will prove to be the "right" pattern but it certainly will not be a smooth, steady 2% every year for the life of the income note. The prudent investor will take a view on future default behavior and test an income note under varying default assumptions before investing.

Unless otherwise stated in a particular exhibit, the base assumptions listed in Exhibit 25.7 will apply in all exhibits. Exhibits 25.8 and 25.9 illustrate the impact of various default scenarios on equity returns.

Exhibit 25.8 is representative of the current equity pricing paradigm of applying a "smooth" default number over the life of the cash flow scenario. If a CDO's annual defaults match the historical average of 3% described in

---

[2] Gregory J. Peters and Edward I. Altman, *Defaults and Returns on High Yield Corporate Bonds, Analysis through 1999 and Default Outlook for 2000–2002*, January 31, 2000.

EXHIBIT 25.8   CDO Income Note Returns—Sensitivity to Annual Default Rates

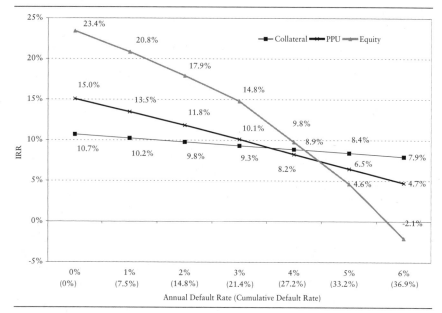

Source: Salomon Smith Barney.

EXHIBIT 25.9   CDO Income Note Returns—Sensitivity to Default Rate Spikes

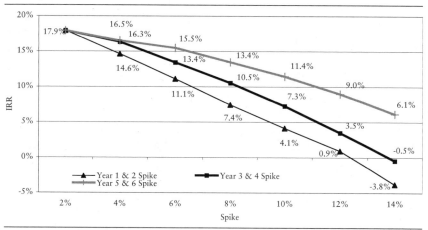

Source: Salomon Smith Barney.

the Peters and Altman study, the equity IRR would equal 14.8%, the Principal Protected Unit (PPU) IRR would equal 10.1% and an unleveraged investment in the pool would return 9.3%. As Exhibit 25.8 illustrates, the annual default rate must exceed 4% over the life of the CDO in order to make the unleveraged investment in the pool of bonds a better value relative to the leveraged equity investment. Interestingly, if annual defaults stay at a 3% rate, the PPU investment returns a paltry 0.8% above the collateral yield (10.1% vs. 9.3%).

Exhibit 25.9 illustrates the impact of default rate "spikes" on the equity IRR. Since small pools of corporate debt obligations have no predictable loss curve, default rate "spike" scenarios are key to understanding potential returns. If default rates remain in the 4% range (i.e., 33% above the historical average) for the next two years and then revert to 2% per annum, Exhibit 25.9 shows an IRR of about 15% (14.6%). If, over the next two years, default rates rise 50% above today's average default rate (4.0% × 1.5 = 6.0%) and then revert to 2% per annum, the equity IRR in Exhibit 25.9 will equal approximately 11.1%. As Exhibit 25.9 illustrates, loss avoidance in the early years is key.

Recoveries

As default rates rose in 1999, recovery rates dropped.[3] The average recovery after default was 28% in 1999, the lowest since 1990 and lower than both the 1998 recovery rate (36%) and the average recovery rate from 1978 to 1999 (42%) (see Exhibit 25.10). This was the case even though less than 40% of the defaulted obligations were subordinated. One reason for the drop in recovery rates in 1999 may be the current glut of distressed and defaulted corporate paper.

Another contributing factor may be how some CDOs treat defaulted bonds. The way a CDO structure treats distressed and defaulted assets can have an impact on its overcollateralization (OC) test as well as on the ultimate recovery that the manager receives on the asset. Both of these can affect returns to the income note holders. For example, for the purpose of the OC test, defaulted assets typically are carried at the lesser of 30% or the market value of the asset. In addition, many structures require the manager to sell defaulted assets at a maximum of one year after default. Distressed corporate market participants are all too aware of these artificial structural constraints and, as a result, we have seen bids for defaulted paper at or slightly above 30 cents on the dollar. Since CDOs have become such huge buyers of high yield

---

[3] Ibid.

EXHIBIT 25.10 Annual Recovery Rates, 1971–1999

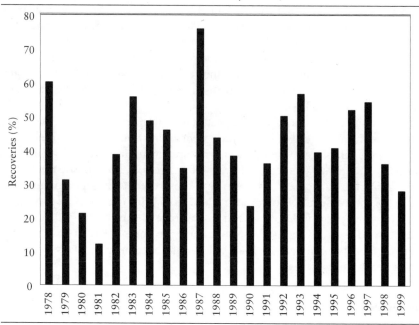

Source: Salomon Smith Barney.

paper and now hold, by our estimates, over 15% of the high yield market, their rules regarding the disposition of defaulted paper may have begun to affect the distressed bond market.

Lower sale prices drive recoveries lower and can ultimately diminish returns to the income note holder. For this reason, when examining an income note opportunity, an investor should put historical recovery studies in the context of the last two years. The recovery paradigm may be shifting. Exhibits 25.11 and 25.12 illustrate the impact of various recovery scenarios on equity returns.

Absolute recovery levels aside, all recovery studies show a tiering in recovery rates based on the defaulted instrument's level of seniority and security.[4] Historically, senior secured bank loans have shown the best recovery

---

[4] Karen Van de Castle and David Keisman, "Recovering Your Money: Insights Into Losses from Defaults," *Standard & Poor's CreditWeek*, June 15, 1999; and David T. Hamilton, *Debt Recoveries for Corporate Bankruptcies*, Moody's Investors Service, Global Credit Research, June 1999.

EXHIBIT 25.11   CDO Income Note Returns—Sensitivity to Recovery Rates and Annual Default Rates

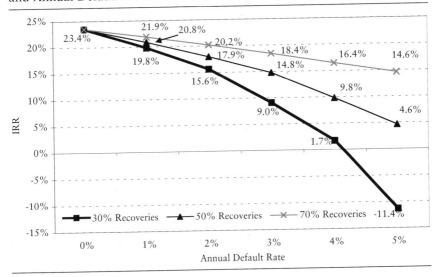

Source: Salomon Smith Barney.

EXHIBIT 25.12   CDO Income Note Returns—Sensitivity to Recovery Rates and Default Rate Spikes

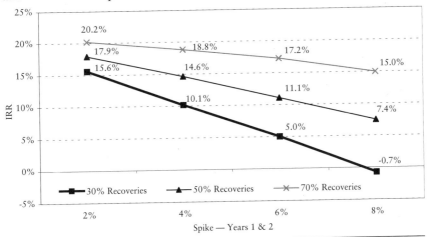

Source: Salomon Smith Barney.

potential, followed in descending order by senior unsecured bank loans, senior secured bonds, senior unsecured bonds, and subordinated bonds. An investor should determine the potential asset mix of a CDO and the assets that are most likely to default before taking a view on the average recovery rate that the CDO may experience. Depending on the mix, the average recovery rate of 42% cited above may be too conservative or too generous. Either way, given the relatively small number of assets in a CDO, the actual recovery experience may differ from the averages cited in industry studies.

Interest-Rate Risk

Many CDOs are floating rate obligations backed by pools of fixed-rate bonds and, to hedge potential interest rate mismatch, most CDOs purchase a combination of interest rate swaps and caps. Hedging is one of the least standardized features of a cash flow CDO and, as a result, it must be analyzed on a deal-by-deal basis.

Most CDOs are not perfectly hedged because such a hedge would be prohibitively expensive. Incremental hedging costs are funded by the issuance of additional income notes, thereby diluting equity returns. Historically, as a result, most equity investors have been willing to accept some interest rate risk in exchange for returns that have not been dampened by excessive hedging costs.

In a typical CDO, the trust pays a fixed rate of interest to the counterparty and the counterparty pays LIBOR to the trust. The swap notional amount amortizes pursuant to a schedule set at closing. Exhibit 25.13 assumes that the notional amount of a hedge is equal to 90% of the CDO capital structure and that the CDO liabilities are floating rate notes indexed to LIBOR.

Call and Tender Premiums

When a high yield bond is called or tendered, the premium paid to bondholders often equals half the annual coupon. Since many CDOs treat this premium as part of asset yield collections, increased call and tender activity can mean increased returns to the CDO income notes. We estimate that call and tender activity in the high yield market, while volatile, has averaged about 8.5% in the last seven years (Exhibit 25.14). Exhibit 25.15 demonstrates the effect of assuming a 2.5% and 5.0% annual call/tender rate. The exhibit assumes the calls/tenders are at a price of 105. At a 3% annual loss rate, a 2.5% call/tender rate can boost the equity IRR by more than 100bp (basis points).

EXHIBIT 25.13 CDO Income Note Returns—Sensitivity to LIBOR Movements

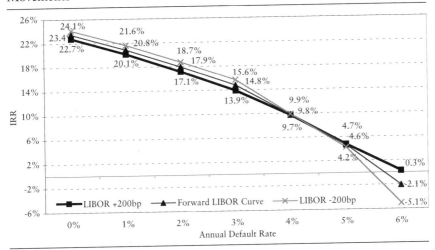

Source: Salomon Smith Barney.

Although it may be tempting to assume call premiums when analyzing CDO equity, we recommend against it for a few reasons. First, call and tender activity is driven by a number of factors including changes in interest rates and company specific events. Over the 12-year legal life of the CDO, it is extremely difficult to predict the movement of interest rates and the effect of those interest rate changes on the high yield market as a whole, much less the impact on the 80 to 150 names that the CDO holds at any point in time. Also, many CDOs today contain a percentage of loans. Typically, loans may be prepaid without penalty at par at any time. Most importantly, while premiums offer some potential IRR upside, credit losses present a much larger threat on the down side. It would take a large number of calls at 105 to outweigh the impact of a few assets defaulting and being liquidated at 40, 20, or 10.

EXHIBIT 25.14 Historical Calls and Redemptions (Dollars in Millions)

	1993	1994	1995	1996	1997	1998	1999	Average
Calls/Redemptions	28,828	17,386	10,664	7,281	16,504	19,195	9,514	
Tender Offers	1,982	2,383	3,660	10,507	20,290	24,716	18,178	
Avge Size of HYM	213,537	237,297	261,453	301,453	363,917	453,047	534,361	
Calls/Redemptions/Tenders as a % of HYM	14.43%	8.33%	5.48%	5.90%	10.11%	9.69%	5.18%	8.45%

Source: Salomon Smith Barney.

EXHIBIT 25.15   Sensitivity to Call and Tender Premiums

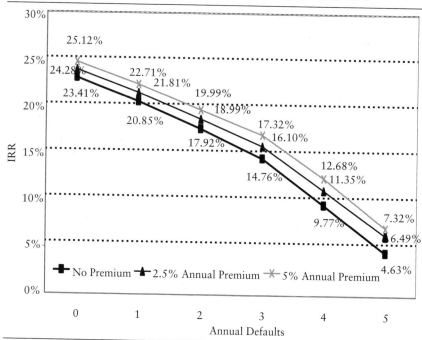

Source: Salomon Smith Barney.

In addition to the numerous quantitative considerations explained above, there are a number of key qualitative factors that will determine relative value among income note investment opportunities. These factors fall into three main categories: (1) collateral manager; (2) asset characteristics; and (3) structural features. The remainder of this chapter will explore these qualitative factors in depth.

25.3 COLLATERAL MANAGER

Collateral Manager Review

An arbitrage CDO is a hybrid-structured finance/corporate instrument whose performance is linked not only to the credit quality of the collateral and the nature of the structure but also to the portfolio manager's trading decisions. The collateral manager's initial asset selection and trading decisions throughout the reinvestment period are crucial.

The key attributes of a manager that investors should examine in depth are:

- Track record,
- Experience managing within the CDO framework,
- Level of institutional support,
- Investment and trading philosophy,
- Expertise in each asset class that the manager is permitted to invest in,
- Importance of CDO product to overall organization, and
- Manager's access to assets.

An asset manager review is the best way for an income note investor to get a firm grasp of a manager's strengths, weaknesses, and historical performance. Some key discussion points and portfolio performance information requirements are listed in Exhibits 25.16 and 25.17.

Asset Selection

A CDO manager can outperform the market depending upon which names and industries it chooses initially and the trading decisions it makes during the reinvestment period.

Investors should be aware, however, that the time period during which the collateral manager purchases its collateral (*cohort* or *time stamp*) can have as much effect on the performance of a CDO as the skill of the manager. For example, as a general matter, CDOs which ramped-up during the spring of 1998 have not performed as well as other CDOs. During early 1998, asset spreads were tight and managers had to venture down the credit curve and invest in marginal credits in order to generate sufficient returns to CDO equity investors. One way CDO equity investors can mitigate the potential risk associated with cohort to identify a list of approved, "blue-chip," CDO managers and invest serially in CDOs issued by those managers.

Time stamp aside, we agree with the thesis that the high yield market is not as efficient as other markets and, as a result, there are opportunities for CDO managers who are well versed in fundamental credit analysis and have access to timely information to outperform their competitors.[5] The high yield market does not price every asset accurately. An experienced manager knows which assets are cheap relative to default probability and which are priced properly. Those CDO managers with strong research teams, good

---

[5] Fitch IBCA, Management of CBOs/CLOs, Robert J. Grossman, December 8, 1997.

EXHIBIT 25.16 Collateral Manager Review Check List

Company Overview

Financial strength of the company
Experience in corporate lending and managing portfolios of high yield bonds and bank loans
How does managing a CDO fulfill the company's strategic objectives?
Importance of CDO to overall organization
Prior history managing CDOs
Is entire CDO managed by a couple of key decision makers ("key person" risk)?
Number of high yield funds under management
Performance results relative to peer group and index benchmarks
Compensation arrangements for the collateral managers
Will the company purchase part of the CDO income note?

Research

Research methodology
Industries covered
Number of analysts and credits per analyst
Depth of analyst contacts with industry participants
Ability to expand research to cover additional industries required in a diversified CDO
Sample research reports

Underwriting and Investment Strategy

Credit and approval policy
Investment style
Facility with and understanding of bond indentures and loan covenants
Decision making process for buy and sell decisions
Pricing sources and policies regarding securities valuation

Credit Monitoring

Procedures to service the CDO and to ensure compliance with the CDO transaction documents
Does the manager have in-house cash flow modeling capabilities or does it rely solely on the trustee and/or underwriter?
Frequency of credit reviews
Technological tools used to monitor the portfolio
Procedures for managing credit-risk and defaulted assets

Sources: Standard & Poor's, Fitch IBCA, and Salomon Smith Barney.

industry contacts, robust deal flow, and sophisticated systems have a good chance of outperforming the market.

Prudent asset selection is crucial because the asset pool supporting a typical arbitrage CDO is granular. Although the trend is toward larger pools and smaller obligor concentrations, the typical high yield arbitrage CDO may have as few as 70 to 120 names. With obligor concentrations ranging from 1% to 3%, a handful of poor investment choices may substantially reduce returns to income note holders.

CDO Investment Guidelines

A good total return high yield manager does not necessarily equate to a good CDO manager. Two major differences exist. Total return arbitrage

---

EXHIBIT 25.17   Portfolio Performance

Defaults and Credit-Risk Sales

Default history

Credit risk sales below 80

Asset specific rationale for each credit risk sale

Where has each credit-risk asset traded after sale? Did it ultimately default?

Length of time between an asset purchase and its sale as a credit-risk asset

Recoveries

Recovery history

Method of disposition: sale after default or buy-and-hold

Recovery timing

Trading

Annual turnover rate for the portfolio

Frequency of credit-improved sales

Credit-improved sales: average premium to purchase price

Returns

Compare annual returns to peer group and index benchmarks

Volatility of annual returns

Source: Salomon Smith Barney.

CDOs are typically leveraged 8 to 12 times, and this leverage greatly magnifies returns and losses to the CDO income notes. Also, managing within a CDO's arcane and cumbersome investment guidelines (which have been crafted to garner investment-grade ratings on the senior notes from the rating agencies) can be challenging.

In a typical CDO, a manager must satisfy more than twenty investment guidelines before making a trade. No trade is easy. Exhibit 25.18 illustrates the guidelines that must be satisfied before a manager can make a purchase.

Given the complexity of these investment guidelines, a manager who currently manages one or more CDOs will have a distinct advantage over a first-time CDO manager, all other factors equal. Although a new CDO manager may have a conceptual understanding of each of these guidelines in isolation, until a manager operates within them and understands the interrelationship among all guidelines, they are difficult to master.

If a CDO collateral manager has mastered the investment guidelines within a CDO, in what ways may this benefit the income note holders? One way involves industry diversification. All rating agencies encourage industry diversification for the benefit of the rated note holders. A manager must seek the optimal amount of industry diversification: diversification that

EXHIBIT 25.18   Typical CDO Investment Guidelines

Minimum average asset debt rating
Minimum percentage of assets rated B3 or better
Minimum percentage of assets in U.S.
Maximum percentage of assets outside U.S., Canada and U.K.
Maximum percentage of synthetic securities
Minimum diversity score
Maximum single issuer exposure
Maximum percentage in any S&P industry group
Maximum percentage in any Moody's industry group
Maximum percentage of zero coupon bonds
Maximum percentage of loan participations
Maximum percentage of floating rate securities
Weighted average life test
Class A, B, and C minimum O/C tests
Class A, B, and C minimum I/C tests
Minimum weighted average recovery test
Maximum percentage of securities maturing after a certain date
Minimum average asset margin test
Minimum average asset coupon test
Maximum annual discretionary trading bucket

Source: Salomon Smith Barney.

maximizes the rating agency "credit" to rated note holders, minimizes forays into unknown industries, and generates a fair risk-adjusted return to income note holders.

Another way that an experienced CDO manager can benefit income note holders is by taking a balanced view of a CDO's asset eligibility parameters. Many modern CDOs allow a manager considerable flexibility to invest in various nontraditional assets, such as emerging market debt and structured finance obligations. These asset types may generate significantly more yield than comparably rated high yield bonds. They present an enticing way for a manager to "juice up" returns to income note holders. But, as with the perils of industry diversification, a manager who is too aggressive in searching for additional yield in nontraditional products may invest in asset types that it does not understand. Enhanced returns to the income note holder may not provide adequate compensation for the additional risk. A prudent CDO manager will resist this urge and instead stick to asset classes that it understands, even if that means forgoing some yield opportunities. In the long run, this should ensure a more stable, risk-adjusted return to the income notes.

CDO Manager Types

CDO managers run the gamut from giant, highly rated banks and insurance companies to small, specialized, high yield portfolio managers. The size of the CDO manager does not, on its own, determine whether a particular income note is a good investment opportunity. For example, a CDO business that is a tiny part of a large insurance company or bank may not receive the same level of attention as a CDO business which is managed by a high yield boutique. In the latter case, the success of the CDO business is crucial to the success of the business as a whole. On the other hand, if an insurance company sponsored CDO falters or a key portfolio manger departs, the insurance company will have greater financial wherewithal to support the CDO business and hire a capable replacement.

An income note buyer should also understand how the portfolio manager makes its investment decisions. An institution that centralizes its investment decisions with one or two key people runs the risk that those key people might leave the institution for other opportunities. For this reason, income note investors should try to ascertain whether the sponsoring institution espouses an investment philosophy and whether this philosophy is shared by a broad cross section of the CDO management team. These team members should participate actively in all trading decisions.

Another key indication of support is whether an institution has issued multiple CDOs. If so, this indicates an institutional commitment to the CDO business. That commitment is further strengthened if the institution is an income note investor in each of its CDOs.

Investment and Trading Philosophy

A CDO manager's investment philosophy and trading style will have a significant impact on returns to the income notes. A key indication of this style is how the manager strikes a balance between the rated notes and the income notes. Although rated note holders and income note holders share many of the same concerns, their interests diverge in some important ways. Their viewpoints often differ as to the optimal investment and trading philosophy for a CDO manager.

Rated note holders occupy the majority of the capital structure of the CDO, and their primary concern is the preservation of principal and a coupon entitlement that is attractive relative to other similarly rated fixed-income instruments. These note holders are concerned with initial asset selection before closing and during the ramp-up period. Once a transaction is ramped up, triple-A note holders are averse to a CDO collateral manager that actively trades the portfolio because they rely upon asset cash flow, not trading gains, to service their debt. As long as assets do not default, they will produce the necessary cash flow to service the rated debt. The market value of the underlying asset pool may be of interest as a leading indicator of credit quality, but it is not of primary importance to rated note holders.

Income note holders do not think in terms of preservation of principal and a fixed coupon payment. They think in terms of cash flow and a return on their initial investment. As we have explained, this return is driven by, among other things, defaults, recoveries, interest rates, premiums, and trading gains and losses. Like rated note holders, income note holders focus on a manager's initial asset selection, because prudent asset selection can minimize losses and benefit all note holders. Unlike rated note holders, however, income note holders are concerned with the market value of the assets in the CDO and the manager's trading decisions, if any, regarding assets that are trading at premiums and discounts.

There are three categories of trades that a manager can make: credit-risk, credit-improved, and discretionary. Rated note holders and income note holders often have differing views as to the advisability of a particular trade. If a manager has a CDO or CDOs outstanding, a potential income note investor can analyze the manager's past trades and infer whether the manager has worked to preserve principal for all note holders or has concentrated on enhancing returns to the income note holders.

1. *Credit-risk sales.* A credit-risk sale is a sale of an asset that has declined in credit quality and that the manager reasonably believes will default with the passage of time. A credit-risk asset is sold at a discount to par and this sale, in isolation, results in the reduction of the asset base supporting the notes. This loss of principal will move the actual overcollateralization (OC) closer to the minimum OC trigger. If the minimum OC trigger is tripped, collections will be used to pay down the senior notes.

   Rated note holders will view credit-risk sales favorably only if: (1) the asset ultimately defaults; and (2) the sale price is greater than ultimate recovery on the defaulted asset. If an asset is sold as credit-risk and does not default before the CDO is retired, the CDO has taken a loss (i.e., sale at discount to par) that it could have avoided if the asset had been held to maturity.

   Income note holders may have differing views concerning credit-risk sales. Some may prefer managers to hold onto credit-risk assets because any discounted sale would push actual OC closer to the minimum OC trigger and increase the risk of de-levering. Other income note investors may prefer early aggressive sales of credit-risk assets at slight discounts rather than waiting for an asset to trade at a steep discount.

2. *Credit-improved sales.* Credit-improved sales can benefit both rated and income note holders. The issue hinges upon how the premium is

treated in the structure. The premium generated from a credit-improved sale may be treated as interest collections and used to enhance returns to the income note holder or it can be used to grow OC through the purchase of additional assets. Clearly, the latter method benefits all note holders. When a manager sells an asset that has improved in credit quality, the rated note holders lose the benefit of upward credit migration but if the sale proceeds (including premium) are reinvested in additional assets, the manger may be able to maintain or increase OC.

3. *Discretionary sales.* Depending on the structure, a CDO manager also has the discretion to trade 10% to 20% of the portfolio annually. Not surprisingly, rated note holders have a bearish view of unfettered discretionary trading: they prefer managers with strong credit fundamentals to execute a long term investment strategy. Any problem credits can be traded under the credit-risk trading rules. In contrast, income note holders favor discretionary trading provisions, because these allow the manager to continually search for assets with the best risk-adjusted returns.

In the final analysis, trading is a two-edged sword. Trading can expose cash flow CDO note holders to market value risk, but it also can be used to improve the credit profile of the pool of assets and could ultimately be a very positive force in mitigating credit risk.

25.4 ASSET CHARACTERISTICS

Collateral Mix

In addition to high yield bonds and bank loans, arbitrage CDOs increasingly include nontraditional investments (see Exhibit 25.19). Most CDOs have certain limitations or "buckets" for these types of assets, but

EXHIBIT 25.19 Nontraditional Assets

Loan participations
Emerging markets sovereign debt
Emerging markets corporate debt
Distressed debt
Credit derivatives
Structured finance obligations
Convertible bonds
Mezzanine loans with warrants
Project finance loans and bonds

Source: Salomon Smith Barney.

the limitations are different for each CDO. Such assets are often included in arbitrage CDOs because their generous yields enhance arbitrage opportunities for the collateral managers and, ultimately, the income notes. Although these nontraditional assets offer enticing yield pickup, the income note holders must be certain that the collateral manger has sufficient investment experience in the particular asset class. If not, enhanced short-term income note returns may be outweighed by significant long-term credit risk.

The inclusion of nontraditional assets also raises a credit question. The credit risk inherent in all cash flow CDOs is analyzed using various corporate default studies. Since these are studies of corporate instruments they are not directly applicable to assets like structured finance obligations and project finance loans. Some have argued, however, that applying corporate default studies to structured finance instruments is overly conservative, given that there have been far fewer structured finance defaults than corporate defaults over the last 10 years.

Some nontraditional investments can be categorized as *bivariate risk* assets. These include loan participations, emerging market corporate debt, and credit derivatives. With respect to each of these assets, the CDO is exposed to the nonperformance risk of more than one counterparty. For example, if a collateral manager invests in a credit derivative, the CDO will not receive payment if either the underlying referenced obligation or the credit derivative counterparty fails to perform. Most CDOs allow a manager to invest up to 20% of a CDO's assets in bivariate risk assets, but many managers do not avail themselves of this opportunity. If the collateral manager plans to utilize the 20% bivariate risk bucket or has used it in past transactions, the income note holders should determine whether they are being compensated for this additional risk.

Finally, the inclusion of nontraditional asset types may have an impact on assumed recovery values. Over the last few years, several large recovery studies have been completed, but each revolves around defaulted U.S. corporate bonds and loans. If a manager aggressively invests in sovereign debt or structured finance obligations, the applicability of these studies becomes questionable.

Time Stamp or Cohort

The period of time during which a CDO is ramped up can have a significant impact on its long-term performance. Depending on market conditions, the collateral manager will purchase assets from both the primary and secondary market. Historically, a large percentage of the assets (10%–50%) emanates from the new-issue calendar, and during the average ramp-up period (3–6 months), that calendar contains a finite number of names. Consequently, arbitrage CDOs that are ramped up during the same period may share a large percentage of the same names. Accordingly, if an investor purchases multiple income notes from CDOs that have concurrent ramp-up periods, there is the risk that the performance of these income notes may be correlated. This risk will decline after the end of the ramp-up period as the manager starts trading the portfolio and the risk may not be as pronounced if one CDO manager is purchasing loans and the other is purchasing high yield bonds.

The prices of high yield bonds and bank loans during the ramp-up period can also have a big impact on the performance of a CDO. As we mentioned earlier in this chapter, during the fall of 1998, prices for high yield bonds dropped and spreads widened considerably for technical reasons, although underlying credit fundamentals were relatively stable. CDO managers that purchased collateral during that time frame were able to buy good credit quality collateral at discounted prices. Discounted prices allowed managers to purchase much more collateral than they had projected without going down the credit spectrum. Many of these deals, consequently, have asset buffers that are significantly above their minimum overcollateralization tests. These managers did not time the market: it was fortuitous that they came to the market during that period.

For these reasons, if an investor is going to build a portfolio of income note investments, we recommend that it purchase income notes that are issued during different time periods or cohorts. Investors can execute this strategy in two ways. They can review the new-issuance calendar for the next quarter or two and select income notes from various CDO issuers. This would give them maximum exposure to different credits and CDO manager investment styles. Alternatively, since the performance of CDO income notes is tied so closely to the skill of the manager, an investor may approve certain "blue-chip" managers and buy income notes from each of their deals over time. An investor who chooses the second strategy will likely be exposed to some of the same credits across all CDOs that a manager issues. A manager tends to buy additional exposure to names it likes.

Diversification

The rating agency methodologies encourage obligor and industry diversity. The theory is simple: since CDO asset pools are lumpy to begin with, the more names in the pool, the less any one obligor default can hurt note holders. Similarly with industries, if one industry is experiencing higher than average defaults, note holders' exposure to that industry is limited. Rated note holders favor broad diversification because they are interested in preservation of principal and the payment of a fixed coupon. Income note holders are less sanguine about zealous diversification because diversification, while limiting credit risk, also limits upside opportunities. The income note holder wants the manager to make a few right "picks" that can have a disproportionately beneficial impact on income note returns.

How does the manager strike a balance between the interests of the rated note holders and the interests of income note holders? At some point, too much diversity can work against all note holders. No note holder benefits if overly restrictive CDO investment guidelines force a manager to invest in obligors and industries that it does not fully understand. Credit risk increases and income note returns decline.

25.5 STRUCTURE

Unlike certain structured finance products (e.g., credit card ABS), CDO structures are far from commoditized. Every CDO underwriter uses a different base structure, and even CDOs underwritten by the same banker can contain significant structural variations that can affect the income note holder. Income note investors who study these features in each CDO before deciding to invest may be able to deduce how the manager intends to strike a balance between the interests of the rated note holders and the interests of the income note holders.

The structure of a CDO is an important consideration for the income note holder because the income notes are structurally subordinated to the other notes issued by the CDO. From a cash flow perspective, the income note holder is not entitled to cash flow until payment of: (1) all fees and expenses (capped and uncapped); (2) interest and principal to more senior notes; and (3) all hedging costs (including termination payments). If these obligations have been paid and the minimum interest coverage (IC) and overcollateralization (OC) tests are in compliance, the income notes are eligible for distributions.

Trigger Levels

All arbitrage CDOs contain two types of coverage tests: an asset coverage test (minimum OC test) and a liquidity coverage test (minimum IC test). If these tests are violated, reinvestment of principal ceases and principal and interest collections are used to accelerate the redemption of the senior notes until these tests are brought back into compliance. These triggers function as structural mitigants to credit risk. Because violation of these coverage tests can result in the payment of all cash flow to the senior note holders (and consequently none to the income note holders), income note holders should have a firm understanding of how they function.

One of the key ways to gauge the robustness of a projected IRR is to compare the actual OC and IC in the transaction to the minimum IC and IC triggers set by the collateral manager and deal underwriter. If the difference between actual and minimum is small, the triggers have been structured "tightly" by the collateral manager and the deal underwriter in an effort to give the CDO issuer a higher degree of leverage (i.e., enhance the projected IRR to the income note). If the relationship between actual and minimum is larger, the triggers have been structured more "loosely." Although it may allow an underwriter to present a higher IRR to potential income note investors, a tight trigger is easier to violate and thus makes the IRR potentially more volatile.

An income note investor should also explore the relationship between the actual levels of OC and IC and the trigger points in the context of the overall credit quality of the portfolio. A portfolio with an average credit quality of single-B should, all other factors equal, have a larger income note and less leverage (as a percentage of the deal) than a portfolio with an average credit quality of double-B. Also, the CDO supported by the single-B portfolio should have a larger buffer between the actual OC level and the minimum OC trigger, since single-B default rates are more volatile than double-B default rates.

Finally, in most CDO structures, each class has its own minimum OC and IC test and the tests associated with the most subordinated rated class should trigger first. Nevertheless, the income note investor should analyze cash flow runs to understand under a variety of stress scenarios which tests trigger the pay down of the deal.

Senior Costs, Swaps, and Caps

Portfolio management fees and the coupon payable to the rated note holders are two costs that can affect the cash flow payable to the income notes. An income note holder should examine the manager's fee in each CDO and compare it to fees payable in other arbitrage CDOs. A typical fee structure will pay the manager 0.25% prior to payment of interest on the rated notes and at least 0.25% after payment of fees and rated note interest and the satisfaction of the IC and OC tests.

More importantly, as we have described in Section 25.2, "Return Analysis," in many arbitrage CDOs the assets are primarily fixed-rated bonds and the liabilities are issued as LIBOR floaters. These deals typically use a combination of swaps or caps to hedge interest rate risk. The swaps and caps usually have notional amounts that amortize on a predetermined basis. This presents the risk that the transaction may be underhedged or overhedged at any point in time (see Exhibit 25.13). If the deal is underhedged, for example, more of the asset cash flow will be used to meet rated note debt coverage and less will be available for the income notes. Moreover, these hedges can terminate, and if the SPV owes a termination payment to the counterparty the payment will be made senior to payment of any residual cash flow to the income notes. Since termination payments can be large, investors should analyze the swap documents for each deal and understand which events can cause the termination of the swap.

Manager Fees and Equity Ownership

There are a few ways that a structure can more closely align a portfolio manager's economic interests with those of the income note holders. One way is through the payment of the portfolio manager's fee. In some older transactions, the manager's fee is paid before payment of rated note holder interest. This senior position is beneficial if the CDO needs to attract a replacement manager but it does not align the interests of the manager and the income notes. Even if the CDO is performing very poorly, the manager still gets paid its full fee. For this reason, most recent deals pay part of the fee at the top of the waterfall (base management fee) and part of the fee after payments of other fees, rated note holder interest and the satisfaction of the IC and OC tests (performance management fee). By subordinating a portion of the manager's fee, these structures encourage the manager to generate enough cash flow to service the rated debt in a fashion that preserves the asset base and does not violate the IC and OC tests. Some structures pay the manager an additional fee if the actual IRR paid to the income note holder hits a certain target. Another way a manager can align its economic interests with those of the income note holders is by purchasing a portion of the income note. This is the case in most CDOs. The theory: Since the manager owns part of the income notes, it will manage the portfolio so as to produce reasonable returns to the income notes while protecting them from unreasonable credit risk. Although many deals do not explicitly prohibit the manager from selling its portion of the income notes, as a practical matter the market for income notes is limited. In all likelihood, if a manager purchases income notes, it will retain them.

Credit-Improved Sales—Treatment of Premium

CDO investment rules allow a portfolio manager to sell an asset that has improved in credit quality and is now trading at a premium (credit-improved sale). What is a credit-improved sale and how are sale proceeds distributed? Definitions vary. Some structures define a credit-improved sale as a sale of an asset that has improved in credit quality and can be sold at a premium to purchase price. Other CDO structures describe a credit-improved sale as a sale of an asset that has improved in credit quality and can be sold at a premium to par.

CDO structures treat gains differently. Some treat premiums as principal proceeds that will be reinvested in new collateral. Rated note holders favor this treatment because premium sale proceeds are used to buy more collateral and enhance overcollateralization in the structure. Some income note holders may favor this treatment for the same reason. Other structures treat premium sale proceeds as interest proceeds that can be distributed to the income note holders if fees and rated coupon have been paid and the IC and OC tests have been satisfied. Rated note holders do not favor this version, because it allows a manager to skim all the credit upside off the pool of assets and stream it to the income note holder in the form of an enhanced IRR. Still other structures give the manager the option of designating premium proceeds as either interest or principal. Finally, another variation weighs the cumulative losses against the cumulative gains that a manager has incurred over the life of the CDO. If cumulative losses exceed cumulative gains, the proceeds of any credit-improved sale are deemed principal proceeds.

25.6 CONCLUSION

During the last few years, demand for CDO equity has broadened substantially from large institutional investors to other investors such as small pension funds and high-net-worth individuals. A CDO equity investment program that purchases income notes from a select group of experienced CDO managers across various periods of time can be an effective way for an investor to diversify its portfolio and improve its risk-adjusted returns. We expect that continued growth in the CDO market will drive increased demand for CDO equity investments in the United States and in overseas markets, including Europe, the Middle East, and Asia.

CHAPTER 26

Student Loans

Frank Tallerico and Ivan Gjaja

Society Student Loan Trust 1993-A issued the first SEC-registered student loan asset-backed security (ABS) in June 1993. Other issuers followed Society's lead, and the basic form of the current student loan ABS market was established by late 1994. In addition, student loan-backed revenue bonds were issued well before the first SEC-registered student loan ABS was issued in 1993, and state educational finance authorities and nonprofit corporations still issue substantial amounts of student loan-backed revenue bonds in the tax-exempt and taxable bond markets. Some of these offerings are structured to look like student loan ABSs.

Student loan ABSs resemble other types of amortizing ABSs. They usually have been issued by an owner trust, with a single series of securities backed by an amortizing collateral pool. Student loan revenue bonds usually have been issued as the direct obligation of a state agency or nonprofit corporation, using master trust-like structures where a single pool of pledged collateral supports one or more series of "parity" bonds that may share collateral cash flows. Appendix 26B lists student loan ABSs issued through October 15, 2000. This list includes several parity bond offerings from frequent issuers, such as Brazos Student Finance Corporation that we think most closely fit within the ABS framework.

In late 1995, the student loan ABS market grew substantially when Sallie Mae issued its first student loan ABS. Between October 1995 and September, 2000, Sallie Mae came with $36.7 billion of new-issue volume in 18 large offerings. Perhaps as important to the market's development as the actual issuance volume, Sallie Mae has repeatedly stated its intention to continue to issue similar volume annually.[1] In 2000, year-to-date (November

---

[1] Sallie Mae held approximately $66.7 billion in student loans as of September 30, 2000, or roughly one-third of the student loan market.

10, 2000) student loan ABS new issue volume reached $16.1 billion, making student loans the fourth largest sector of the ABS market. In addition, the trailing 12-month spread performance has been impressive. Security structure has continued to evolve in response to regulatory and market changes, and investor demand for student loan ABS has steadily increased as almost all transactions are now indexed to the more widely favored three-month LIBOR rate, rather than the 91 day Treasury bill rate.

26.1 PROGRAMS AND PLAYERS

The student loan industry operates through a unique collaboration of federal and state agencies and not-for-profit and for-profit corporations. These entities originate, service, and guaranty student loans under the federally sponsored student loan program, known as the Federal Family Education Loan Program (FFELP). On a smaller scale, privately sponsored supplemental loan programs have developed to fund the gaps in federally sponsored aid. The following section explains in detail the various loan programs and participants.

Student Loan Classifications

- **Federally sponsored loans.** Federally insured student loans have protection against default via principal insurance of 98% or 100%, ultimately guaranteed by the U.S. Department of Education (DOE).
- **Nonfederally sponsored loans.** Privately insured student loans are not guaranteed by the DOE, and only have protection against default via the guaranty of private companies or from reserves pledged to the securitization.

As the majority of student loan-backed securitizations are composed of federally and privately insured loans, we discuss the attributes of these two collateral types.

Federally Sponsored Loans   The FFELP, formerly known as the Guaranteed Student Loan Program, is authorized by Title IV of the Higher Education Act of 1965. Since its inception in 1966, the FFELP has provided students with about $223.8 billion of loan commitments to finance the cost of postsecondary academic and vocational training.

The FFELP has four major types of loans:

1. Subsidized Stafford Loans
2. Unsubsidized Stafford Loans

3. Parental Loans for Undergraduate Students (PLUS)
4. Consolidation loans

The subsidized Stafford loan is the basic FFELP loan type, making up 51.3% of FFELP fiscal year 1999 commitment volume. Because the DOE pays loan interest while borrowers are attending school, students must meet a family income means test to be eligible for the program, and Congress sets annual and lifetime borrowing limits to maximize the number of students able to access the program. The *unsubsidized Stafford* loan program was created in 1992 to serve dependent students with family income or assets that make them ineligible for subsidized Stafford loans, and for dependent and independent students who have exhausted their borrowing capacity under the subsidized Stafford loan program. Except for different loan limits and eligibility for interest-rate subsidies, subsidized and unsubsidized Stafford loans have similar terms.

PLUS loans are loans to parents of dependent students. Parents may borrow up to the sum of their required parental contribution to the student's financial aid package and any unmet financial need remaining after the student's other sources of financial aid are exhausted. Beginning July 1, 1993, parents were required to have a satisfactory credit history to receive a PLUS loan.

Upon leaving school, students can refinance all of their existing FFELP loans with a single *consolidation* loan. Students with high loan balances can use consolidation loans to extend loan maturities from 10, to as much as 30 years. In addition, with the 1998 reauthorization of the Higher Education Act, students with balances greater than $30,000 were given the option of extending the maturity of their Stafford loans up to 25 years.

FFELP Program Philosophy   The FFELP was a broad-based middle-class entitlement program through the 1970s. Rapid inflation of college costs and budgetary constraints during the 1980s, however, increasingly forced the program to concentrate on the borrowing needs of the most needy students. By the 1989/1990 school year, only 16% of American students received Stafford loans, with Stafford loans making up just 25% of the average financial aid package. Extensive program amendments in 1992 and 1993, however, lifted program participation rates to 52.8% of full-time students by the 1995/1996 school year.

Exhibit 26.1 shows FFELP annual commitment volume by loan type. Dollar growth since 1987 has been split between the subsidized Stafford loan program and unsubsidized programs. The volume of unsubsidized Stafford loans, in particular, took off rapidly in 1992, after the introduction of the

EXHIBIT 26.1   FFELP Annual Commitment Volume*

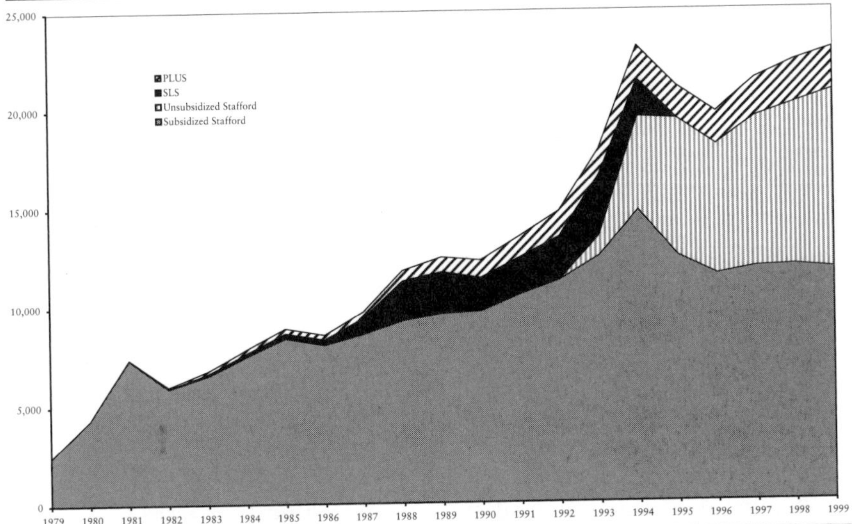

* Federal fiscal year, ending September 30. The SLS program was merged into the unsubsidized Stafford program on July 1, 1994.
Source: US Department of Education.

program. Production of these loans has continued to increase since 1996, even as the production of subsidized Stafford loans has held steady or declined. PLUS loans represented approximately 9.3% of total FFELP volume in 1999. FFELP volume declined in 1982 when students with family incomes in excess of $30,000 lost their eligibility for interest-rate subsidies, and again in 1986, when all borrowers were required to meet a financial needs test. Annual growth accelerated in 1981, 1987, and 1993, after amendments to the Higher Education Act increased lender yield, borrower loan limits and eligibility for interest-rate subsidies. The growth in volume has continued in recent years as the cost of education has continued to increase.

Privately Insured Loan Programs   Students enrolled in expensive private institutions or lengthy graduate or professional degree programs often exhaust their FFELP borrowing capacity and need additional loans to cover their remaining financial need. Parents who wish to spread payment of their required parental contribution over several years or who do not want to liquidate appreciated assets also take out loans to finance their required contribution to student expenses.

A number of "alternative," "private," or "supplemental" loan programs are sponsored by not-for-profit 501(c)(3) corporations[2] affiliated with networks of private universities and graduate and professional schools. Access Group, Inc., a Delaware nonstock corporation based in Wilmington, is a membership organization, whose members include state operated and nonprofit American Bar Association-approved law schools located in the United States. Until July 1, 1998, Access was a loan marketing organization who received marketing fees from a lender for allowing the lender to make loans to students attending Access member schools. Access Program Loans have been securitized by KeyCorp since 1993. Access now retains the right to purchase and finance the loans from the program lender and also entered the bond market in 2000.

Supplemental lenders generally limit themselves to program design and marketing, contracting out underwriting, servicing, and funding to high-volume, third-party servicers, such as PHEAA and USA Group Loan Services, Inc., both of which service FFELP portfolios for a number of student loan ABS issuers.

Exhibit 26.2 shows annual and lifetime Stafford program loan limits over time. Exhibit 26.3 shows how FFELP and private supplemental loans might be used in two representative financial aid packages.

Eligible Lenders   FFELP loans are originated by *eligible lenders*—primarily commercial banks, credit unions, thrift institutions, insurance companies, state agencies, and nonprofit student loan companies. Other originators can participate in the industry through the use of *eligible lender trustees* who hold legal title to the loans on behalf of the lenders.

Historically, competition for origination volume (and secondary market purchase volume) focused on providing school financial aid officers and smaller lenders with value-added services, such as high-speed data-processing links that streamlined the application and disbursement process, specialized software packages that helped financial aid offices manage their paper flow and loan servicing links, and forward sale agreements that helped small

---

[2] Entities organized to support the charitable, cultural, or educational purposes of their members may be exempt from federal income tax under Section 501(c)(3) of the Federal Income Tax Code of 1986. 501(c)(3) not-for-profit corporations are the operating form of many major American charities and cultural organizations and often are substantial economic enterprises. USA Group Loan Services, Inc. had 859 full-time employees and a $17 billion student loan servicing portfolio as of August 31, 2000—an operation larger than many for-profit consumer lenders.

EXHIBIT 26.2 Stafford Loan Annual and Lifetime Loan Limits

	Subsidized Loans		Subsidized and Unsubsidized[c] Since 7/1/93	Independent Students[a]	
Borrower Status	Prior to 1/1/87	Since 1/1/87[e]		Additional Unsubsidized Limit	Total Subsidized and Unsubsidized[d]
Annual Limits					
Freshman Year	$2,500	$2,625	$2,625	$4,000	$6,625
Sophomore Year	2,500	3,500	3,500	4,000	7,500
Other Undergraduate Years	2,500	5,500	5,500	5,000	10,500
Graduate Years	5,000	8,500	8,500	10,000	18,500
Lifetime Limits[b]					
Undergraduate	$12,500	$23,000	$23,000	$23,000	$46,000
Undergraduate and Graduate	25,000	65,500	65,500	73,000	138,500

[a] Independent undergraduates, graduate and professional school student, and dependent students whose parents do not qualify for PLUS loans.
[b] Lifetime limits are higher for students training for certain health professions.
[c] Dependents were limited to the maximum amount set for subsidized loans only.
[d] Independents could borrow the maximum subsidized amount plus the maximum unsubsidized amount. Students that do not qualify for Subsidized Stafford loans can borrow the entire amount in Unsubsidized Stafford loans.
[e] The yearly maximum amounts add to $22,625 for dependent students and $45,625 for independent students, but the maximums stipulated by the regulations are $23,000 and $46,000, respectively.
Source: Student Loan Marketing Association and Salomon Smith Barney.

lenders, such as community banks and credit unions, to originate and warehouse loan production.

Today lenders treat statutory program rates as maximum rates, and are competing for volume by offering borrowers reduced origination fees, rebates of a portion of the lender margin, and flexible repayment terms. This marketing environment favors well-capitalized, high-volume lenders able to

EXHIBIT 26.3 Representative Financial Aid Packages

	Dependent Junior-Year Student	Independent Graduate Student
Total Tuition and Living Expenses	$15,000	$36,000
Required Parental Contribution	(3,500)	None
Financial Need	11,500	36,000
Grants and Scholarships	(3,000)	(10,000)
Subsidized Stafford Loan[a]	(5,500)	(8,500)
Unmet Need	3,000	17,500
Unsubsidized Stafford Loan[a]	(1,500)	(10,000)
Remaining Unmet Need	1,500	7,500
Private Supplemental Loan	(1,500)[b]	(7,500)
	$0	$0
PLUS or Private Supplemental Loan		
Required Parental Contribution	$3,500	
Remaining Unmet Need	1,500	
Total Borrowing by Parent[c]	$5,000	

[a] Based on the maximum annual amount as of September 15, 1996.
[b] Loan to student or parent.
[c] Parents may borrow up to this amount under either a PLUS or private supplemental loan or under a combination of PLUS and private supplemental loans.
Source: Salomon Smith Barney.

devote the fixed resources necessary to develop and support expensive value-added services and with the scale necessary to process volume profitably at reduced yields.

Guaranty Agencies   FFELP lenders are guaranteed payment of 98% of principal and accrued interest due on defaulted loans. (Loans originated prior to October 1, 1993, and loans where the default was due to the death, disability, or bankruptcy of the borrower are guaranteed at 100%.) A loan is generally defined as defaulted when it becomes 270 days past due.

The Higher Education Act requires each state to designate a single guarantor that must guaranty the FFELP loan of any student who is a state resident, or who is attending a school located in the state. The designated guarantor for most states is typically a state agency that administers a number of education finance-related programs for the state. Some states contract with guaranty agencies in neighboring states to serve as the designated guarantor for their state, or with a national guarantor such as USA Funds, Inc. (USAF). Guaranty agencies may guaranty loans from states where they are not the designated guarantor, and many of the larger guarantors compete for loan volume because of the value of lender relationships for related lines of business, such as third-party loan servicing and secondary market activities.

Guaranty agencies fund claims payments to lenders primarily from reinsurance payments received from the DOE. Guaranty agencies generally receive 95% of claims expense paid (loans originated prior to July, 1998 are reinsured at 98%), with reinsurance rates reduced to as low as 75% of claims expense for agencies with excessive default rates.

A number of guaranty agencies expanded their commitment volume in the late 1980s when FFELP regulations were changed, which resulted in increased lending to students attending proprietary trade schools. These loans defaulted at extremely high rates, and a number of guaranty agencies were merged into other guaranty agencies when they could not cover the shortfall between lender claims and DOE reinsurance payments.

To mitigate lender concerns about guarantor solvency, 1992 amendments to the Higher Education Act required the DOE to honor the guaranty obligations of insolvent guaranty agencies. Although the DOE has never drafted regulations that set out the conditions that would cause it to declare a guaranty agency insolvent, the major credit rating agencies believe that clear congressional intent makes it highly likely that the DOE will honor valid lender claims against an insolvent guaranty agency. Passage of the 1992 amendments was critical to the development of the student loan ABS market because it allowed the rating agencies to assume that FFELP loans are guaranteed by a unit of the U.S. government, rather than by a number of thinly capitalized state guaranty agencies. The rating agencies assume delays of up to 540 days for claims payments filed with the DOE because of the lack of written regulations about the direct claims process.

Exhibit 26.4 ranks the largest guarantors by annual commitment volume. The market share of the 10 largest guarantors has not changed much between 1998 and 1999.

Special Allowance and Interest Subsidy Payments FFELP loans have borrower rates that generally adjust annually, on each July 1, subject to rate caps in a range between 8.25% and 11%. The DOE makes quarterly "special allowance payments" (SAP) to lenders when accrued interest on a loan over a calendar quarter at the uncapped lender yield exceeds accrued interest at the capped borrower rate. The DOE also makes quarterly "interest subsidy

EXHIBIT 26.4 Largest FFELP Guarantors—Federal Fiscal Years 1998 and 1999 (Dollars in Millions)

1999 Rank	Name	Amount Guaranteed* 1999	Amount Guaranteed* 1998	Annual Growth	% of Total Volume 1999	% of Total Volume 1998
1	USAF	6,404.8	6,181.1	3.6%	27.9%	27.7%
2	CALIFORNIA	2,066.5	1,948.8	6.0	9.0	8.7
3	PENNSYLVANIA	1,785.6	1,787.2	-0.1	7.8	8.0
4	NEW YORK	1,619.9	1,567.8	3.3	7.1	7.0
5	TEXAS	1,560.2	1,456.4	7.1	6.8	6.5
6	WISCONSIN	1,546.5	1,625.6	-4.9	6.7	7.3
7	MASSACHUSETTS	691.9	656.3	5.4	3.0	2.9
8	NEBRASKA	646.5	626.2	3.2	2.8	2.8
9	FLORIDA	617.6	594.7	3.9	2.7	2.7
10	ILLINOIS	589.7	581.5	1.4	2.6	2.6
11	TENNESSEE	361.1	337.0	7.1	1.6	1.5
12	KENTUCKY	341.0	288.8	18.1	1.5	1.3
13	OKLAHOMA	323.0	330.3	-2.2	1.4	1.5
14	MISSOURI	318.3	306.7	3.8	1.4	1.4
15	WASHINGTON	310.4	305.7	1.6	1.4	1.4
16	COLORADO	304.8	293.1	4.0	1.3	1.3
17	MICHIGAN	280.9	275.8	1.8	1.2	1.2
18	NEW JERSEY	248.1	229.0	8.4	1.1	1.0
19	SOUTH CAROLINA	226.5	229.6	-1.4	1.0	1.0
20	SOUTH DAKOTA	224.2	204.8	9.5	1.0	0.9
21	IOWA	217.5	215.3	1.0	0.9	1.0
22	GEORGIA	207.0	225.9	-8.4	0.9	1.0
23	UTAH	194.5	224.9	-13.5	0.8	1.0
24	NORTH CAROLINA	193.3	185.8	4.0	0.8	0.8
25	LOUISIANA	191.1	191.2	0.0	0.8	0.9
26	CONNECTICUT	187.9	194.8	-3.6	0.8	0.9
27	ARKANSAS	166.3	167.1	-0.5	0.7	0.7
28	RHODE ISLAND	165.9	148.5	11.7	0.7	0.7
29	NEW HAMPSHIRE	155.9	153.6	1.5	0.7	0.7
30	VIRGINIA/ECMC	152.9	149.7	2.1	0.7	0.7
31	MAINE	134.8	140.2	-3.9	0.6	0.6
32	OREGON	115.9	92.0	26.0	0.5	0.4
33	VERMONT	98.6	116.4	-15.3	0.4	0.5
34	MONTANA	97.4	98.3	-0.9	0.4	0.4
35	NORTH DAKOTA	92.1	87.9	4.8	0.4	0.4
36	NEW MEXICO	84.7	83.2	1.9	0.4	0.4
	Total - Ten Largest Guarantors	17,529.3	17,025.4	3.0%	76.5%	76.3%
	Total - Commitment Volume	22,923.3	22,301.0	2.8		

*Amount Guaranteed includes Stafford, SLS, and PLUS loans.
Source: Department of Education—Office of Postsecondary Education Loan Volume Updates.

payments" to FFELP lenders equal to accrued interest on loans to borrowers eligible for federal interest subsidies while they are attending school.

Lender yields on loans originated prior to January 1, 2000, generally equaled the 91-day Treasury bill rate, adjusted weekly, plus a margin. This margin ranges from 2.20% to 3.50%, depending on the loan type, disbursement date of the loan, and whether or not the borrower is attending school. Stafford loans originated after January 1, 2000, still have the interest reset adjusted every July 1st based on the last T-Bill auction in May. However, the SAP paid on these Stafford loans is based on the daily average of the 3-month financial commercial paper (CP) rate for the previous quarter plus a margin ranging between 1.74% and 2.34% dependent of the same characteristics mentioned above. Consolidation and PLUS loans originated after January 1, 2000, also receive SAP based on the above CP calculation, plus a margin of 2.64%.

Eligible Servicers   A guaranty agency can reject a guaranty claim submitted by a lender if the loan was not originated or serviced according to DOE guidelines. This means that lenders bear default risk on FFELP loans to the extent of uncured servicing errors, with loss severity ranging from the loss of accrued interest to full loss of principal and interest. Typical violations include due diligence errors made by originators, such as failure to verify a borrower's eligibility for the program, and servicing errors such as the failure to contact a delinquent borrower within the required time limits.

FFELP reporting and processing guidelines are highly technical, and the penalty for violating a guideline is expensive. To minimize technical violations, the student loan servicing environment is highly automated, and many lenders contract out some or all of their underwriting, disbursement, and collections functions to high-volume, third-party servicers. Third-party servicers must meet solvency and performance standards to be eligible to service FFELP loans.

Secondary Markets   Many lenders hold subsidized loans only while the borrowers attend school and loan collections consist of quarterly federal interest subsidy and special allowance payments. These lenders typically sell loans to specialized investors called secondary markets when borrowers graduate and the loan servicing function shifts from quarterly collection of lump-sum federal payments to monthly collection of principal and interest from individual borrowers.

Secondary markets include Sallie Mae, commercial banks, many of the state guaranty agencies, and a number of nonprofit corporations. Secondary markets either keep the loans on their balance sheet, fund them through the issuance of student loan revenue bonds in the municipal bond market, or sell them into the ABS market. Not-for-profit entities tend to view their secondary market activities as a revenue generating rather than member service function and attempt to earn a positive spread on their financing activities to subsidize other programs.

Sallie Mae was chartered by Congress in 1972 to provide secondary market liquidity to the student loan industry. Sallie Mae executes its mandate by purchasing loans from originators and holding them in portfolio, or more recently, selling them into the student loan ABS market. Like Fannie Mae and Freddie Mac in the residential mortgage market, Sallie Mae was a shareholder-owned, government-sponsored enterprise (GSE) that had federal agency debt status because of the public-purpose nature of its activities. Unlike Fannie Mae and Freddie Mac mortgage-backed securities, however, Sallie Mae student loan ABSs do not carry the corporate guaranty of their sponsor. In October 1996, Congress passed legislation that will effectively privatize Sallie Mae. Today the GSE, known as Sallie Mae, is owned by a holding company called USA Education, renamed from SLM Holdings after the recent purchase of USA Group. Sallie Mae will surrender its GSE status by 2008.

Exhibit 26.5 ranks the largest FFELP originators by annual commitment volume. Note that only a limited number of lenders have annual origination volume large enough to support an efficient ABS program without secondary market purchases from other lenders.

Exhibit 26.6 lists the largest holders of FFELP loans as of September 30, 1999—the most recently available federal data. Note that the groups of originators and holders are distinct, as some of the largest student loan

EXHIBIT 26.5 Largest Originators of FFELP Loans—Federal Fiscal Years 1998 and 1999 (Dollars in Millions)

1999 Rank		Amount Guaranteed[a]		Annual Growth	% of Total Volume	
		1999	1998	Growth	1999	1998
1	Bank One	1,902.0	1,768.4	7.6%	8.3%%	7.9%
2	Citicorp	1,820.5	1,748.0	4.1	7.9	7.8
3	Chase Manhattan Bank	1,725.5	1,653.5	4.4	7.5	7.4
4	Bank Of America	1,591.4	1,560.9	1.9	6.9	7.0
5	Norwest Bank	1,501.3	1,571.1	-4.4	6.5	7.0
6	First Union National Bank	1,269.8	1,324.4	-4.1	5.5	5.9
7	National City Bank	824.2	763.3	8.0	3.6	3.4
8	Education Finance Group[b]	568.1	256.0	121.9	2.5	1.1
9	Pittsburgh National Corp Bank	459.4	558.0	-17.7	2.0	2.5
10	Union Bank & Trust Co.	452.4	396.9	14.0	2.0	1.8
	Total - Ten Largest Originators	12,114.5	11,600.5	4.4%	52.8%	52.0%
	Total - All Originators	22,923.3	22,301.0	2.8%		

[a] Includes Stafford, PLUS, and SLS loans. Does not include consolidation loans.
[b] Includes volume reported for Academic Management Service.
Source: Department of Education—Office of Postsecondary Education Loan Volume Updates.

EXHIBIT 26.6 Largest FFELP Holders (Dollars in Millions), September 30, 1999

1999 Rank		Outstanding Balance*	% of Total Volume
1	Sallie Mae	45,090.5	34.0%
2	Citicorp	9,465.8	7.1
3	USA Group Secondary Market Services	5,236.8	3.9
4	First Union National Bank	4,629.6	3.5
5	Norwest Bank	4,157.0	3.1
6	Nellie Mae	3,576.9	2.7
7	Key Corp	2,926.8	2.2
8	Bank of America	2,642.6	2.0
9	Student Loan Funding Corporation	2,629.1	2.0
10	National City Bank	2,310.3	1.7
	Total - Ten Largest Holders	82,665.4	62.3%
	Total - Outstanding	132,622.3	

*Includes Stafford, PLUS, SLS, and Consolidation Loans. Securitized loans are reported under the original holder.
Source: Department of Education—Office of Postsecondary Education Loan Volume Updates.

originators hold very little collateral in their portfolios. This pattern exists because most private market lenders find it more attractive to sell the loans to Sallie Mae or state guaranty agencies than to fund these loans on balance sheet.

The Federal Direct Lending Program The Omnibus Budget Reconciliation Act of 1993 made major changes to the FFELP, including expansion of the federal direct lending program. The direct lending program requires that the DOE originate FFELP loans directly to its own balance sheet, where loans are funded at Treasury bill rates plus servicing costs. The direct lending program called for direct federal funding of at least 60% of federally sponsored student loan volume by the 1998/1999 school year. In recent years, Direct Lending's market share has been relatively constant at about 33%. The inability of the Direct Lending Program to capture the market share anticipated is generally attributed to customer service to schools that ranks below that offered by private lenders together with aggressive price competition on the part of private lenders. For a brief period of time following the 1998 reauthorization of the Higher Education Act, the direct lending program originated consolidation loans at rates which were more favorable than consolidation loans originated by the private sector. The direct program did see an increase in consolidation volume during this time, but due to limited marketing of these loans, the availability of the favorable rates was not widely known.

Future Market Structure We believe that Congress will support a continued private sector role in the market, as the market share for the federal direct student loan program appears to have peaked (at approximately 30% of all federal lending), signaling potential issues with the direct lending program. In addition, private sector involvement will provide a standard of quality for the federal direct lending program. In addition, we expect to see the following:

- Large, vertically integrated players such as Sallie Mae and several large commercial banks will dominate the generic FFELP sector because of the significant funding and servicing benefits available to large-scale players. Smaller, specialized lenders will take advantage of servicing and funding efficiencies achieved by the large-scale players to create programs for members of their origination networks that fill gaps in the federally sponsored programs.
- Despite significant loss of market share to the federal direct lending program, the private sector will continue to originate increasing annual loan volume due to the continued inflation of college cost, the large increases in student enrollment expected as the 1970s baby bulge generation enters its college years and the preference of schools to work with private lenders. Despite smaller annual origination volume increases in the private sector, we expect the student loan ABS market to grow, as origination volume shifts from small portfolio lenders and tax-exempt revenue bond issuers to large lenders likely to fund themselves in the ABS market.

Consolidation in the student loan industry will continue as the operating environment becomes more competitive and economies of scale become more critical to profitability. Recent major acquisitions/mergers include:

- Sallie Mae acquired Nellie Mae in July 1999.
- Sallie Mae acquired Student Loan Funding in May 2000.
- Sallie Mae acquired USA Group in July 2000 (holding company renamed USA Education).
- Wells Fargo acquired Educap in March 2000.

26.2 STUDENT LOAN ABS MARKET

The beginning of the student loan ABS market usually is dated to the November 1992 adoption of Rule 3(a)-7 of the Investment Company Act of 1940. Rule 3(a)-7 exempted issuers of ABSs backed by a broad class of consumer assets, including federally sponsored student loans, from investment company reporting requirements.

Exhibit 26.7 shows annual and cumulative student loan ABS new-issue volume since market inception. (We define market inception as August

EXHIBIT 26.7 Student Loan ABS New-Issue Volume, October, 1992–2000*

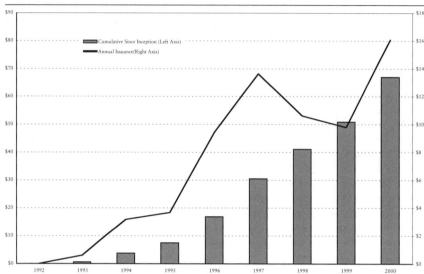

* From August 6, 1992 through October 15, 2000.
Source: Salomon Smith Barney.

1992, to include offerings from several repeat nonprofit issuers that were exempt from the 1940 Act reporting requirements.)

Issuer Composition

Student loan ABS issuers have distinct origination and funding strategies. Sallie Mae and Brazos Student Finance Corporation purchase FFELP collateral from networks of diversified lenders. Supplemental lenders such as Chela Financial USA, Inc. and PNC originate supplemental loans, primarily from students at private, four-year institutions. Access Group provides one-stop shopping to professional school students, primarily law students, originating both their FFELP and private supplemental loans.

Student loans have lower gross margins than credit card or home equity loans, but can generate high gains on sale owing to low expected losses and long maturities. Although these characteristics make student loans prime candidates for securitization, other factors (such as complex security structures and investor reporting requirements, excess capital and liquidity at many potential issuers, and the ability of lenders to sell assets to Sallie Mae and other secondary markets at attractive prices) have limited the value of student loan securitization to many banks. Active securitizers, in addition to Sallie Mae, generally include private nonprofit specialized student loan lenders and for-profit lenders with roots in the nonprofit sector. Consequently, the student loan issuance has been concentrated among few large players. In addition to regular issuers, state education authorities enter the ABS market from time to time, because of IRS caps on the amount of tax-exempt bond issuance allowed to the state, or favorable arbitrage opportunities. Exhibit 26.8 lists the largest student loan ABS issuers, from August 1992 through November 2000.

Collateral Mix

Exhibit 26.9 shows market composition by collateral type. Most securities are backed exclusively by FFELP loans, or a mix of FFELP and supplemental

EXHIBIT 26.8 Largest Student Loan ABS Issuers (Dollars in Millions), 1992–2000

Issuer	New-issue Volume
Sallie Mae Student Loan Trust	36,730.1
SMS Student Loan Trust	6,015.8
KeyCorp Student Loan Trust	5,258.5
Brazos Student Finance Corporation	1,982.6
Nelnet Student Loan Corporation (f/k/a Union Financial Services)	2,410.5
ClassNotes Trust	1,404.0
Student Loan Funding Corporation	1,352.7
EMT Inc	1,336.0
Banc One Student Loan Trust	1,223.8
Education Loans Inc	1,049.8
PNC Student Loan Trust	1,030.0
Access Group Inc	801.5
Education Finance Group	663.5
Chela Financial USA	570.0
Society Student Loan Trust	454.7
Signet Student Loan Trust	428.4
First Union Student Loan Trust	405.6
University Support Services	277.8
Crestar Student Loan Trust	222.9
Educaid Student Loan Trust	203.0
Panhandle Plains Higher Education Authority	200.0
South Carolina Student Loan Corporation	150.0
North Carolina State Education Authority	105.0
	64,276.2

Source: Salomon Smith Barney.

EXHIBIT 26.9   Student Loan ABS New-Issue Volume by Collateral Type, August 6, 1992 through September 30, 1996*

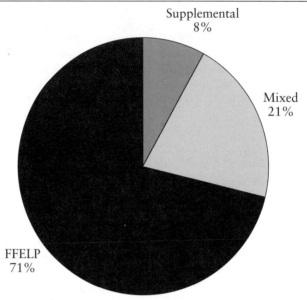

Supplemental
8%

Mixed
21%

FFELP
71%

* Percentages by cumulative principal balance.
Source: Salomon Smith Barney.

loans. Brazos Student Finance Corporation and Access Group have sold loan pools that were a mix of FFELP and supplemental loans.

Credit Ratings

More than 96% of student loan ABSs have been rated triple-A at offering. The high percentage of triple-A-rated balances largely is a result of low levels of required credit support for structures backed by pools of FFELP loans.

Pricing Index

Initial student loan ABSs had floating-rate coupons indexed to one-month LIBOR. Many offerings from July 1995 through 1997 had been indexed to the bond-equivalent yield on the 91-day Treasury bill, adjusted weekly, which provides an almost perfect match with underlying asset yield. Though this posed some basis risk for many investors who typically fund themselves off of LIBOR, the risk was not deemed significant. More recently, as the spread relationship between 91-day T-Bill and 1-month LIBOR became more volatile, issuers were forced to index future debt issuance off of 1-month and 3-month LIBOR to meet investor demand. Sallie Mae, which traditionally issued all of its debt off of 91-day T-Bill, altered its strategy to issuing as much T-Bill based debt as the market would absorb, and issuing the remainder as LIBOR indexed bonds. Many of the other issuers who chose the 91-day T-Bill as the index for their bonds were also forced to follow Sallie Mae's lead. This effectively shifted basis risk away from the investor and to the issuer. Much of the basis risk concern in respect to LIBOR-indexed bonds was alleviated when it was announced that the SAP paid on student loans would become indexed off the three-month financial CP rate. The historical spread relationship between CP and LIBOR has proven more stable than that between 91-day T-Bill and LIBOR. Both the change in the SAP calculation rate and the change in the index away from 91-day T-Bill have added significantly to the attractiveness of student loan ABSs. In 1999, less than 5% of new issue volume was indexed off of the 91-day Treasury Bill. This represents a dramatic change from just three years earlier when 62% of student loan ABSs was indexed to the 91-day T-Bill. Another major development was the increased issuance of auction rate debt, which accounted for 37% of total industry issuance in 1999 compared to less than 19% of the total debt issued in 1996.

Maturity Distribution

Exhibit 26.10 below shows the distribution of student loan ABSs by expected average life at pricing. Larger offerings generally have tranched senior notes into two classes of sequential-pay notes. Some smaller issues, however, have issued only a single class of senior notes.

Recent offerings have been priced at 5% to 7% CPR, resulting in senior notes with expected average lives of one to three years and seven to eight years. Because securities typically have been priced to a 10-year auction call, subordinated certificates generally have been sold with 10-year expected average lives. Some issuers have sold student loan ABSs with short-term A-1+/P-1 rated money market tranches. These securities met money market legal maturity criteria and had actual weighted average lives of two to four months.

26.3 STUDENT LOAN ABS SECURITY STRUCTURE

The generic student loan ABS structure is an owner trust that issues one or more classes of sequential-pay, triple-A-rated notes and a single class of single-A-rated certificates.

EXHIBIT 26.10   Student Loan New-Issue Volume by Average Life at Pricing, August 6, 1992 through December 31, 1996*

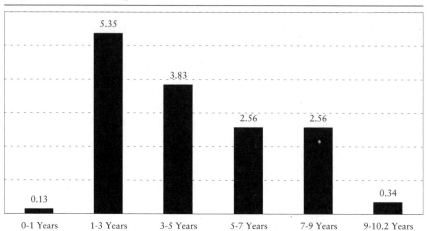

* Cumulative principal balance. Priced to call.
Sources: Salomon Smith Barney and MCM "Corporatewatch."

Entities subject to the federal bankruptcy code generally use a standard two-stage transfer of assets. An operating company sells loans to a wholly owned, bankruptcy remote, special purpose subsidiary, which transfers loans to a trust. Issuers, such as owner trusts, that are not eligible lenders under FFELP regulations must use an "eligible lender trustee" to hold legal title to the loans for the benefit of the trust. The trust holds the beneficial, or economic, ownership interest in the loans and has the following characteristics:

- Note and certificate rates reset monthly to one-month LIBOR, or quarterly to three-month LIBOR, or weekly, to the bond-equivalent yield on the 91-day Treasury bill. Interest on LIBOR-indexed securities is accrued on an actual/360 basis and is paid monthly or quarterly. Interest on Treasury bill-indexed securities is accrued on an actual/actual calendar day basis and is paid quarterly. Both LIBOR- and Treasury bill-indexed securities were typically subject to available funds rate caps, with absolute rate caps rare. However, beginning with SMS' 2000-A transaction, transactions have generally not included an available funds cap.
- The auction rate market has emerged as a very active market for student loan-backed bonds. This market allows issuers to effectively issue long term bonds and investors to have the ability to buy in and out of these

same bonds on a monthly basis without the risk of having to sell the bonds below par. Taxable bonds typically re-price every 7 to 28 days while tax-exempt bonds re-price every 35 days.

■ Principal is paid monthly or quarterly, equal to the sum of principal collections (including guaranty claims payments) and the principal balance of repurchased and liquidated loans. Liquidated loans are defaulted loans written off because of an uncured, rejected claim.

■ Credit support for the triple-A-rated senior notes comes from excess spread, subordination of cash flows from the single-A-rated certificates, and a small reserve fund. Credit support for the single-A-rated certificates is provided by excess spread and the reserve fund.

■ Loan servicers must deposit monthly collections from borrowers to the trust within two business days of receipt. Guarantor claims payments and DOE special allowance and interest subsidy payments are made to the eligible lender trustee, who also must deposit funds to the trust within two business days. Subject to a ratings trigger, most structures allow highly rated administrators—which generally are the parents of the sellers—to commingle collections from the servicer and the eligible lender trustee for up to 90 days.

■ Many student loan offerings have used prefunding accounts. Some structures replace or supplement prefunding accounts with short revolving periods.

■ Most structures have a 10-year auction call or mandatory clean-up call from excess spread.

Exhibit 26.11 illustrates the generic student loan ABS structure. Appendix 26B summarizes the terms of individual student loan ABSs issued through October 15, 2000.

The Available Funds Rate Cap and Excess Spread

Available funds rate caps used to be common in student loan ABSs. If there is a cap, structures accrue any shortfall between interest calculated at the index rate plus reset margin and at the available funds rate, for payment from future excess spread. Payment of carryover amounts usually is not addressed by the ratings on the securities. Due to the desire to market student loan ABS internationally, where some large investors are unable to purchase securities with rate caps, recent student loan transactions have been often marketed without available funds caps.

A structure's available funds rate cap usually is equal to its weighted-average asset yield less servicing and administration fees. Excess spread available for credit support is the available funds rate, less note and certificate

EXHIBIT 26.11   Student Loan ABS Security Structure

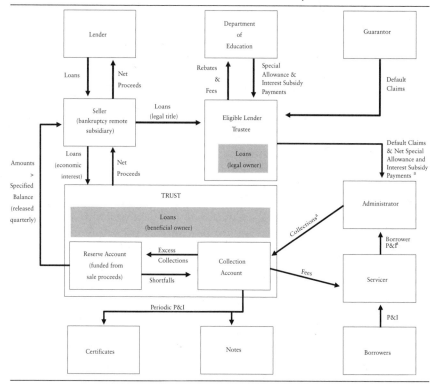

* The administrator can commingle funds up to the quarterly distribution date, subject to satisfaction of short-term ratings triggers. Otherwise, the servicer and the eligible lender trustee must deposit collections to the collection account within two business days of receipt.
Source: Salomon Smith Barney and Moody's Investor Service.

interest. The available funds rate—often called the "student loan rate"—is calculated by summing borrower interest, DOE special allowance, and interest subsidy payments, and investment income on trust accounts due for an accrual period (net of servicing and DOE rebate fees). This sum is then divided into the sum of the pool principal and prefunding account balances at the beginning of the accrual period. Accruals are based on contractual amounts due, not actual collections, and rates should be annualized using the day count convention used for note and certificate interest payments. Available funds and excess spread are affected by a number of structural features.

Collateral Mix   Collateral mix affects asset yield. The lender yield on almost all seasoned FFELP loans equals the weekly average of the 91-day Treasury bill rate plus a gross margin of 2.80% to 3.25%. Stafford loans originated on or after July 1, 1998, however, pay only a 2.20% lender margin on loans when the borrower is still attending school and servicing costs are relatively low. This means that pools with high proportions of recently originated, in-school Stafford loans, will have weaker excess spread and a lower available funds rate cap than pools of seasoned collateral with generic 3.10% to 3.25% margins. Separately, the SAP paid on Stafford Loans originated after January 1, 2000, is based on the daily average of three-month financial CP rate for the previous quarter plus a margin in between 1.74% and 2.34%. PLUS loans are eligible for special allowance payments only if the borrower rate is greater than or equal to the maximum rate at the most recent annual reset date for the loan. In high interest-rate environments, PLUS loans look like generic Stafford pools. In low—but rising—rate environments, pools with high PLUS concentrations will experience weakening excess spread and a tightening available funds rate cap relative to generic Stafford collateral.[3] Appendix 26A describes FFELP loan collateral in detail.

Negative Carry   Asset yield is stressed when pool assets include assets subject to negative carry. Routine sources of negative carry in student loan ABSs include principal collections commingled for up to three months in low-interest-bearing collection accounts; prefunding account balances invested at less than the weighted average of the note and certificate rates; negative equity; accrued capitalized interest that is classified as principal under ABS investor reporting, but that does not generate contractual interest from the borrower until it is converted to principal at loan repayment; and cure periods for rejected claims, if the seller or servicer is not obligated to cover accrued interest lost on the loan during the time it takes for the rejected loan to be cured. (Remember that cured rejected claims usually are loans that are made eligible for loan guaranty payments, not necessarily loans that are restored to current payment status.) Potential, but unlikely, sources of negative carry include delayed payments from the DOE or guaranty agencies.

---

[3] PLUS borrower rates adjust annually to the 91-day Treasury bill rate plus a 3.10%–3.25% margin. Given a generic 3.10% margin and 9%–12% caps, most PLUS loans will be capped when the rate on the 91-day Treasury bill on the annual adjustment date is less than 5.91%.

Servicing Fees   Given relatively homogeneous collateral pools and structures, servicing fees cause some student loan ABSs to be more sensitive to available funds rate caps than other structures and to have less excess spread than other structures. Existing pools have annual servicing fees that range from 23bp (basis points) to 167bp, with average servicing fees of approximately 60bp. This range is material if asset yield also is strained by adverse collateral mix and negative carry. Some structures compensate for early period spread weakness by charging graduated servicing fees over time, or lower servicing fees for loans with in-school status.

Cumulative Impact of Factors Affecting Available Funds and Excess Spread   Exhibit 26.12 calculates available funds and excess spread for three generic student loan ABS structures. Except for a high concentration of low-margin Stafford loans—which have only been originated since July 1, 1998, but which likely will represent the bulk of new origination volume going forward—these structures look very much like existing structures.

Structure 1 is backed by a pool that is 20% lower margin, in-school, post-January 1, 2000 Stafford loans, 20% in-school, pre-January 1, 2000 Stafford loans, 10% post-July 1, 1998 loans in repayment with a 2.80% gross margin, 35% pre-July 1, 1998 loans in repayment with a 3.10% gross margin, and 10% prefunding account balances invested at the weighted average note and certificate rate to yield a zero gross margin. Structure 2 is backed by similar collateral, except that there is no prefunding account. Approximately 5% of the collateral backing Structures 1 and 2 is accrued capitalized interest that has not been converted to loan principal. Capitalized interest has a negative gross margin, because it has no yield, but must be funded at the weighted average of the note and certificate rates. Structure 3

EXHIBIT 26.12   Available Funds Rate Calculation

	Structure 1	Structure 2	Structure 3
91-day Treasury-Bill Rate	6.00%	6.00%	6.00%
Weighted-Average Gross Margin*	1.98	2.26	3.10
Annual Servicing Fee	-1.00	-1.00	-1.00
Available Funds Rate Cap	6.98	7.26	8.10
Weighted Average Note and Certificate Rate	-6.55	-6.55	-6.55
Net Excess Spread	0.43%	0.71%	1.55%

*Weighted-Average Gross Margin Calculations
Structure 1 $20\% \times 2.20\% + 20\% \times 2.50\% + 10\% \times 2.80\% + 35\% \times 3.10\%$
$+ 10\% \times 0\% - 5\% \times 6.50\% = 1.98\%$
Structure 2 $20\% \times 2.20\% + 25\% \times 2.50\% + 10\% \times 2.80\% + 40\% \times 3.10\%$
$- 5\% \times 6.50\% = 2.26\%$
Structure 3 $100\% \times 3.10\% = 3.10\%$
Source: Salomon Smith Barney.

is backed by all pre-1998 Stafford loans, but assumes that all collateral has entered repayment and has a 3.10% gross margin.

Note that Structure 1 generates a slim 43bps of annual excess spread—more than two-thirds less than excess spread generated by Structure 3—and has an available funds rate cap that is 112bp lower than Structure 3's. Exhibit 26.12 suggests that different securities—or the same securities at different points in their lives—may have very different sensitivities to moderate basis shifts or above-average servicing fees. Most collateral pools will look like Structure 3 within one to two years of issuance, assuming that loans in the pool were made mostly to students near their expected graduation dates.

Relatively Limited Credit and Liquidity Risks of Student Loan ABSs Rejected Claims Risk

The primary risk of principal loss in most student loan ABSs backed by FFELP loans is the risk that servicing error will cause uncured, rejected claims. Reporting on servicer performance has improved, but many student loan offerings have not disclosed even minimal information about the size of the servicer's portfolio, historical delinquency and default rates, or the servicer's or the seller's historical rejected and cured claims rates. Interestingly, issuers provide extensive information about guarantor performance, which has not been a credit risk since 1992, likely because the DOE collects and reports this data.

Relatively low required credit support levels for pools of FFELP collateral suggest that rejected claims rates are minimal, as do servicer repurchase obligations. (We assume that repurchase obligations are triggered at levels that are set at or above historical rejected claims rates.) The USA Group's Loan Services, Inc., for example, is obligated to repurchase defective loans from SMS pools when annualized losses from rejected claims exceed 15bp of recent outstanding principal balance. Sallie Mae is obligated to repurchase defective loans from SLM pools when unpaid rejected claims exceed approximately 1% of the outstanding pool balance. Sallie Mae's loan loss provision expense for its on-balance sheet portfolio also suggests that rejected claims are probably less than 10bp annually, as a percentage of outstandings. (Sallie Mae's provision expense, however, reflects only errors that it makes as loan servicer. Lenders who sold the loans to Sallie Mae typically bear the cost of any rejected claims resulting from origination error.)

Most structures have some form of seller repurchase or servicer purchase obligation, a significant strength considering the high credit quality of most student loan sellers and servicers. These purchase obligations generally are not considered a source of ABS credit support by the rating agencies, to isolate the ABS security ratings from corporate downgrade risk. Investors should review the sections of the prospectus that summarize the transfer and servicing agreements because seller/servicer purchase obligations differ materially among structures and different lenders have different servicing contracts with third-party servicers.

Co-Insurance Risk Loans originated on or after October 1, 1993, are insured at 98% of defaulted principal and accrued interest amount. Uninsured losses on these loans are charged to credit support. Some ABS structures lack a mechanism to access credit support to pay this 2% principal loss other than at the final maturity of the security. The most subordinated class of securities in these structures is sensitive to principal loss to the extent that losses on co-insured loans might exceed the reserve fund balance on the final maturity date of the ABS. Investors should review an offering's principal distribution formula to make sure that the amount of the co-insurance loss incurred in a quarter is promised to investors each quarter, thereby triggering a draw on excess spread or the reserve fund.

Negative Equity Student loan ABSs are unique in the ABS market in that some pools have been issued with 1% to 3% negative equity—that is, with 1% to 3% less collateral than the par amount of securities issued. Negative equity usually is a result of purchase of the loan collateral by the trust at a 102% to 104% premium and the financing of issuance costs in the transaction.

We do not believe that moderate levels of negative equity represent a credit risk, given the long time period available to most student loan ABSs to generate sufficient excess spread necessary to cure the shortfall. Purchase of loans at a premium should cease two or three years after issuance, however, to allow the pool time to generate sufficient excess spread to reduce bond principal down to the loan balance.

Basis Risk Available funds rate caps in older student loan ABS structures prevent note and certificate rates from exceeding net asset yield. Basis risk between asset yield and the weighted average of the note and certificate rates is minimal in structures where both asset yield and liability cost are indexed to the same Treasury bill rate. Structures with Treasury bill-indexed Stafford loans funded by LIBOR-indexed notes and certificates, however, are subject to basis risk. This has been partially remedied as of January 1, 2000, after which SAP was indexed to the three-month financial CP rate, an index that tracks more closely to the three-month LIBOR than does the 91-day Treasury bill. Structures with PLUS collateral funded by either LIBOR- or Treasury bill-indexed obligations are subject to both interest-rate risk and basis risk in low and moderate interest-rate environments, when the PLUS loans are effectively capped at the borrower rate. In high-rate environments, when PLUS loans receive uncapped special allowance payments indexed to the 91-day Treasury bill rate, like Stafford loans, structures with PLUS loans have no interest-rate risk, and basis risk only if they have LIBOR-indexed obligations.

The probability that a student loan ABS will hit its available funds rate cap as a result of basis risk is minimal. Historical spreads between 91-day Treasury bill rates over a month (the index for asset yield) and one-month LIBOR at the beginning of the month (the index for note and certificate rates) suggest that there is little risk that a student loan ABS's available funds cap will be hit because of adverse basis movement. This data would also suggest that default risk (the possibility that expenses in a given period would be greater than available funds) associated with transactions that are structured without available funds rate caps is also minimal. Excess spread erosion is a concern, however, for securities that also have high servicing costs or negative carry. Historical spreads also suggest that PLUS collateral does not add substantial risk of hitting the available funds rate cap or potential for excess spread erosion.

To protect themselves against spread erosion and potential downgrade risk, investors in LIBOR-indexed securities may prefer to hold seasoned versus unseasoned collateral or pools with low PLUS concentrations. Investors also should remember that the rating agencies generally incorporate adverse assumptions about basis movement into their rating levels and that actual basis shifts must be more adverse than these expected levels to trigger a ratings downgrade.

Liquidity Risk Student loan ABSs are more subject to liquidity risk than other ABS structures, owing primarily to delayed payments from the DOE and guarantors, to delinquency rates that can ramp up to 18% to 20% of total pool balance over the first months after offering, and to loans in deferral or forbearance payment status that often add up to another 10% to 20% of pool principal. Liquidity risk affects the timing of the payment of interest to subordinated classes, with the risk most extreme immediately after issuance and for structures that pay certificate interest junior to note principal.

It is possible for actual cash collections for a student loan pool in the early periods after sale to be significantly less than the accrued amount due—a risk that the rating agencies are well aware of, and so they size it into their required reserve account levels. As a result, transactions may draw on their reserve accounts or borrow from future period collections to cover liquidity shortfalls. These draws generally are cured within one to two quarters, when high monthly delinquencies and delayed federal support payments, should they occur, cure themselves on a rolling basis.

Many structures can draw on their reserve fund to cover both principal and interest shortfalls. High losses in a single distribution period—possible, but an unlikely scenario—could exhaust reserve funds for several periods, removing liquidity support available to pay subordinated interest until the reserve fund is replenished. Certain supplemental loan structures, such as those from the University Support Services and Nellie Mae, reallocate subordinated certificate interest to make accelerated principal distributions to the senior classes if required overcollateralization levels for the senior classes of securities are breached. Investors concerned about delayed interest payments should purchase subordinated classes where certificate interest is paid senior to note principal, or where reserve fund draws are limited to interest only, such as in the generic Sallie Mae structure.

Credit and Liquidity Support Mechanisms in Existing Structures   Credit support levels for different student loan ABSs differ significantly. Senior classes in generic Sallie Mae offerings, which are backed 100% by FFELP loans and have limited basis and liquidity risk, are rated triple-A based on 3.5% subordination, a 0.25% reserve fund, and net excess spread in the 175bp to 280bp range, annualized. For 1999 and 2000 Sallie Mae deals, for example, the excess spread has averaged 229bp. Older KeyCorp pools, on the other hand, carry a 13.5% to 17.5% triple-A subordination and overcollateralization levels, owing to the presence of 30% to 40% non-FFELP supplemental collateral in their collateral mix.

Single-A-rated student loan subordinated certificates generally have been backed by a minimal reserve fund and excess spread. Although this credit support structure may seem sparse, particularly compared with single-A-credit support structures for credit cards and retail auto collateral, it is similar to credit support for subordinated ABSs backed by other assets with long maturities, such as manufactured housing and recreational vehicle loans. Assets with 15- to 20-year maturities are expected to generate significant excess spread over their lifetimes.

With the exception of TERI, which reports extensive static pool data, supplemental programs have limited static pool loss histories, and required credit support levels for supplemental loans are relatively high compared with other types of ABS collateral. Recent KeyCorp pools that are 50% to 60% FFELP loans by principal balance have triple-A subordination/overcollateralization levels of approximately 11.25%. Assuming a 3.5% level for the FFELP collateral, a 11.25% weighted average level suggests 19% triple-A subordination/overcollateralization levels for the supplemental loans in the pool.

Supplemental loans may or may not be guaranteed by a third party, such as the borrower's school or an affiliated 501(c)(3) corporation. Law school access loans included in Access Group ABSs, for example, are guaranteed by The Education Resources Institute, Inc. (TERI), a nonprofit corporation that administers private scholarship and financial aid programs for affiliated schools. TERI is currently rated Baa3/A by Moody's and Fitch, respectively.

Commingling Risk The presence of highly rated sellers and servicers in the student loan sector introduces commingling risk of a magnitude not typically seen in other ABS sectors. The ability of the administrator in most student loan ABSs to commingle funds over a quarterly collection period means that as much as 5% to 8% of pool balances are subject to short-term corporate credit risk.

The necessity of using eligible lender trustees to hold legal title to federally insured student loans adds a unique commingling risk to student loan ABS structures. The DOE may assume that all loans held by the trustee comprise a single loan portfolio for purposes of calculating special allowance and interest subsidy payments. If monthly rebate and other amounts due to the DOE from a single pool held by the trustee exceed payments due to that pool, cash flows due to other pools also held by the trustee could experience temporary or permanent cash flow shortages until they are reimbursed by the deficit pool. We believe that trustee commingling risk is minor for eligible lender trustees that hold large, diversified loan pools.

Other Structural Risks

Qualitative Servicing Risk Student loan ABSs have servicing risks that may be more significant than rejected claims risk, although these risks are more difficult to quantify. Many servicing contracts, for example, have contract termination fees and task-based fees that are paid senior to note and certificate distributions. These fees may not be trivial. The DOE, for example, could require extensive new due diligence procedures or other servicing requirements that could involve one-time or continuing data processing expense that is paid senior to note and certificate interest. Servicing contracts also may not last the full life of a loan pool, and servicing fees may have to be increased to attract a new servicer.

Although servicing risk is not likely to create a principal loss on a transaction, reduced available funds rate caps could affect security price and weakened excess spread could increase downgrade risk. We believe that servicing risk could cause spread relationships to shift among transactions over time. Investors may prefer to purchase an issue, such as KeyCorp 1999-B, that has a highly rated master servicer committed to servicing the pool over the life of the securities, or issues in which the seller and servicer are owned by the same economic entity, such as in the Sallie Mae and SMS structures.

Regulatory Risk Deficit reduction measures could significantly affect the economics of the student loan industry. To the extent that the industry is highly concentrated, certain sellers or issuers, such as Sallie Mae, could be particularly vulnerable to regulatory action. The federal government could take adverse action without changing the terms of existing loans, for example, by offering attractively priced consolidation loans to current borrowers. A general industry contraction could cause servicers to exit the business or cause unit costs for loan servicing to increase, affecting servicing quality.

We consider regulatory risk to be remote, but not improbable. The only protection investors have is to purchase pools from larger, or repeat issuers that have an incentive to spend their own funds to litigate if necessary to protect the performance of existing pools.

Prefunding and Recycling—Prepayment and Extension Risk

Many student loan ABSs have had prefunding accounts that ranged from 10% to 20% of initial pool assets. Most structures limit prefunding activity to the "purchase" each month of accrued capitalized interest on loans owned by the trust, to the purchase of loans to existing borrowers held outside the trust that must be purchased by the trust to originate a consolidation loan, and to the purchase of "serial loans"—loans to existing borrowers to finance additional years of schooling. Prefunding generally is limited to one year.

Some transactions replace or supplement prefunding accounts with "recycling." Illinois Student Assistance Commission Series 5 and 6, for example, have a short revolving period following its prefunding period, while some SMS pools allow unrestricted purchase of serial loans from principal collections over the full life of the pool. Recycling uses principal collections to purchase loans from existing and new borrowers rather than to pay down principal on the notes.

Most student loan ABSs place extensive restrictions on the type of loans that can be purchased during prefunding and recycling periods. Such restrictions include limits on the maximum amount of consolidation and serial loans that can be purchased (to limit extension risk) and limits on the purchase of loans that may have significantly different remaining terms or margin.

Given restrictions on potential asset purchases, we believe that student loan ABS prefunding accounts and recycling can strengthen a structure. Prefunding and recycling can strengthen liquidity during periods when the structure has a high percentage of loans with capitalized interest, by reclassifying principal collections as current interest for pool accounting purposes. Purchase of serial loans also reduces the likelihood that a borrower will take out loans with a lender other than the trust. This reduces the probability that the borrower will receive a consolidation loan from a lender other than the trust upon graduation, which reduces prepayment risk. Prefunding accounts and recycling complicate prepayment measurement and modeling, however.

Some structures purchase additional loans at a premium. This is not a credit risk if the purchase premium is paid from excess spread that would be released from the structure anyway. Purchase of assets at a premium with principal collections, however, introduces the same risk to a pool as issuance of bond principal in excess of asset value, which is the risk that the loans may be prepaid or called at auction before the pool has generated sufficient excess spread to align asset balances with note and certificate balances.

Collateral Auctions and Other Call Provisions

Many student loan ABS structures have required that the trustee auction the collateral approximately 10 years after the issuance date, with some structures supplementing or replacing this auction call with a mandatory clean-up call from excess spread. Because almost all student loan ABSs have auction calls, auction calls should not affect relative performance within the sector. Absent extended deferral periods, most pool balances also should be significantly reduced by their auction date, giving the auction call the same performance implications as a clean-up call in other ABS sectors.

Principal Payment Rates: Scheduled Payments, Prepayments, and Defaults

Intuition and anecdotal evidence suggest that the following factors affect student loan principal payments:

Refinancing Risk Student loan collateral probably is not subject to interest-rate-related refinancing risk owing to a lack of alternative loan sources. Consolidation loans are made at the same or a higher rate than the weighted-average rate on the student's existing loans.

Collateral Mix Loan type, loan status, and school type are the important collateral characteristics to look at when projecting principal payments. Pools with high concentrations of loans in grace status, for example, may be about to experience a rapid increase in principal payments, as loans enter

EXHIBIT 26.13 Stafford Loan Cohort Default Rates by School Type

Cohort[a]	Default Rate ($'s) [b]					
	Public 4 Year	Private 4 Year	Public 2 Year	Private 2 Year	Proprietary	All Borrowers
1985	12%	11%	29%	11%	45%	18%
1986	11	9	35	14	44	19
1987	12	11	31	19	46	18
1988	12	11	32	20	50	17
1989	12	11	31	24	57	21
1990	13	12	32	27	57	22
1991	7	6	15	15	36	18
1992	7	6	15	14	30	15
1993	7	6	15	14	24	12
1994	7	6	14	14	21	11
1995	7	7	14	14	20	10
1996	7	7	13	14	18	10
1997	7	6	13	12	15	9
1998	6	5	11	9	11	7

[a] Cohorts consist of borrowers who entered repayment status during the federal fiscal year listed. Fiscal year 1985 and 1986 cohorts are random samples. Remaining cohorts consist of all borrowers who entered repayment during the year.
[b] *Default Rate* is the cumulative original principal balance of loans that had defaulted as of the end of the fiscal year following the fiscal year that the cohort entered repayment. The percentage is of the initial principal balance of the loans at the time they entered repayment.
Source: U.S. Department of Education.

repayment. Pools with high concentrations of SLS loans,[4] which industry studies have shown have high expected default rates, could pay down faster than pools made up primarily of subsidized Stafford loans to students from four-year institutions. Loans with high average balances may be more subject to consolidation risk, which could manifest itself in rapid early period repayments in pools that do not have mechanisms to buy loans from outside the pool, or extension risk, in pools able to convert existing collateral to longer-maturity consolidation loans. Low average balance loans could pay down faster than larger loans, because the minimum $600 annual payment will amortize the loans more quickly than 10 years. In high-rate environments, pools of Stafford loans will amortize more quickly than PLUS loans, because the 8.25% to 10% borrower rate caps on the Stafford loans are less than the 9% to 12% caps on the PLUS loans.

Cohort Defaults Numerous industry studies suggest that default risk is highest during a student loan's first three years of repayment, with school type determining the magnitude of the default curve. Exhibit 26.13 shows "cohort default rates" calculated by the DOE for Stafford loans. These cohort default rates represent the cumulative initial principal balance of loans that entered

---

[4] The majority of SLS borrowers have been proprietary school students.

repayment in a fiscal year and defaulted during the next fiscal year, expressed as a percentage of the initial principal balance of all similar loans that entered repayment in the same calendar year. With the exception of rates for proprietary schools and private two-year institutions, the DOE cohort default rates were stable over time, at 9% to 13% cumulatively, and then began falling gradually throughout the 1990s. Proprietary trade schools, however, showed extremely high cohort default rates—in the 44% to 57% range—likely reflecting aggressive student enrollment practices during the late 1980s that since have been limited. Proprietary school default rates have continued to decrease at a much higher rate over time than many of the other loan types, reflecting stricter Department of Education standards. DOE data also suggest that as much as one-half of three-year cumulative defaults are first-payment defaults. This could cause ABSs with concentrated first-payment dates to show very high one-quarter principal payment rates six to nine months after the occurrence of the first payment dates.

DOE cohort default rates cover the period between 1985 and 1998, during the early years of which the loan programs were very different from current programs. The cohorts include students in school during the early 1980s, when all students were eligible for interest subsidies. This may have drawn a higher proportion of wealthier students into the program than in more recent years. The DOE cohort default studies also include proprietary school loans made before significant restrictions were made on the eligibility of schools with excessive default rates.[5] Current proprietary school borrowers may or may not default at historical rates.

Supplemental Loan Programs

Supplemental loans are a hybrid form of unsecured consumer loans and federally sponsored education loans. Static pool data for existing pools generally show cumulative loss rates on pools of parental loans to be similar to, or lower than, loss rates on pools of unsecured consumer loans. This is consistent with the relatively stringent credit standards of the underlying programs and the high credit quality of the borrowers, who typically are parents with incomes or assets that limit their eligibility for federal programs. Extensive static pool data from TERI programs, which are supplemental loans to students, show that TERI's undergraduate borrowers have lower loss rates than its graduate borrowers.

---

[5] The 1992 amendments to the HEA of 1965 included provisions to exclude schools with cohort default rates of 25% or greater from participating in the FFELP.

APPENDIX 26A
FFELP TERMS

Eligible Students and Institutions

Students are eligible to receive a FFELP loan if they are enrolled at least half-time in eligible institutions, have a demonstrated financial need, as calculated by a central federal processing service, and have not reached annual and lifetime borrowing limits or defaulted on existing education loans. "Eligible institutions" are accredited public or nonprofit two-year or four-year colleges or universities. Trade schools with shorter vocational courses also can be eligible institutions if the schools meet conditions that include satisfactory historical default rates.

Guaranty Payments and Federal Reinsurance

FFELP loans are guaranteed by a state guaranty agency and reinsured by the DOE. Lenders receive 100% of defaulted principal and interest on loans disbursed prior to October 1, 1993 and 98% of defaulted principal and accrued interest due on loans disbursed on or after October 1, 1993. Default due to the borrower's death, disability, or bankruptcy is covered at 100%, and default is generally defined as 180 days past due for loans originated before July 1, 1998 and 270 days past due after such date.

A guaranty agency can reject a guaranty claim submitted by a lender if the loan was not originated or serviced according to DOE guidelines. This means that lenders bear default risk on FFELP loans to the extent of uncured servicing errors, with loss severity ranging from the loss of accrued interest, to full loss of principal and interest.

Guaranty agencies fund their claims payments primarily with reinsurance payments received from the DOE. If the amount of reinsurance claims paid by the DOE to a guarantor in a given year exceeds 5% of the original principal balance of the guarantor's loans that were in repayment status at the beginning of the year (the agency's "claims experience"), the guarantor's reinsurance rate drops from 98% and 95% of the claim expense, for loans originated before July 1, 1998 and after July 1, 1998, respectively, to 88% and 85%, for all additional claims submitted during the remainder of the year. If the guarantor's claims experience exceeds 9%, reinsurance payments on remaining claims are reduced to 78% or 75% for loans originated before July 1, 1998 and after July 1, 1998, respectively. (Comparable reinsurance rates are 100%, 90%, and 80% for loans originated prior to October 1, 1993, and for all loans that defaulted owing to the death, disability, or bankruptcy of the borrower.)

Since the 1992 amendments to the Higher Education Act, the DOE has been required by law to honor the guaranty obligations of insolvent guaranty agencies on terms no more stringent than the terms of the original guaranty. This obligation makes guaranty agency performance primarily a liquidity, rather than a credit risk, in student loan ABS structures.

Guarantor performance, however, is still interesting to ABS investors. Some agencies with claims rates near trigger rates have disputed valid claims to defer recognition of the claim until the following fiscal year. Higher claims rates also are correlated with higher rejected claims risk, because the likelihood of committing a servicing error is highest for seriously delinquent and defaulted loans. Finally, pools with loans backed by guarantors with high claims rates may prepay more quickly than pools of loans from guarantors with low defaults. Most student loan ABS offering documents provide extensive loss data for guarantors represented in the collateral pool.

Loan Status

A FFELP loan has a defined life cycle. Generally, loans have "in-school" status when the borrower is enrolled at least half-time in a degree program. Loans enter "grace" status when the borrower graduates or ceases to be enrolled at least half-time. Loans to borrowers who return to school, who are in the Peace Corps or the armed forces, or who are temporarily disabled, have "deferral" status, while loans to borrowers who are unemployed or who are experiencing a temporary financial hardship have "forbearance" status. Grace periods generally equal six months, while deferral for financial hardship or enlistment in the armed forces or the Peace Corps generally is limited to three years.

Interest Subsidy Payments and Capitalized Interest

The DOE makes quarterly "interest subsidy payments" to lenders equal to accrued interest at the borrower rate for eligible borrowers who have in-school, grace, or deferral loan status. Payments are due to the lender 45 to 60 days after the close of each calendar quarter and are backed by the full faith and credit of the United States. Interest subsidy payments are a major program expense and FFELP program changes over time reflect the conflict between maximum student access to interest-rate subsidies and program cost.

Borrowers who are not eligible for interest subsidies must pay interest currently, or may capitalize interest on loans that are not in repayment status. Capitalized interest generally is added to the principal balance of a FFELP loan only when the loan enters or returns to repayment status, meaning that accrued capitalized interest does not bear interest until it is converted to principal at loan repayment. Capitalized accrued interest introduces negative carry into most student loan ABS structures, which typically convert capitalized interest to principal monthly for trust accounting purposes. Interest on FFELP loans accrues on a simple interest basis, with the coupon rate applied on an actual/actual day basis.

Exhibit 26.14 lists interest payment methods for the major FFELP loan types.

Lender Yield and Special Allowance Payments

A FFELP loan has two different rates—a borrower rate and a lender rate. The DOE makes up any difference between the two rates, in the form of quarterly "special allowance payments" made to lenders when lender yield exceeds borrower rate. SLS and PLUS loans pay special allowance only if the borrower rate was at its maximum rate at the most recent annual reset date for the loan, effectively capping SLS/PLUS lender yield at the borrower rate over most low and moderate interest-rate environments.

The quarterly special allowance payment on a loan generally equals the product of the daily average balance of the loan over the calendar quarter and a rate equal to: (Index rate + Margin − Borrower rate)/4, where "Index rate" generally equals the average of the bond equivalent yields on the 91-day Treasury bill at each weekly auction during the quarter for loans originated before January 1, 2000. For loans originated after January 1, 2000, the "Index Rate" is equal to the average of the bond equivalent rates of the quotes of 3-month financial commercial paper rate for the preceding quarter. "Margin" varies by loan program and disbursement date. Special

EXHIBIT 26.14 FFELP Interest Payment Methods

Loan Status	Subsidized Stafford	Unsubsidized Stafford	SLS[a]	PLUS	Consolidation
In-School	Interest Subsidy	Capitalized	Capitalized	NA	NA
Grace	Interest Subsidy	Capitalized	Capitalized[b]	NA	NA
Deferral	Interest Subsidy	Capitalized	Capitalized	NA	Interest Subsidy[c]
Forbearance	Capitalized	Capitalized	Capitalized	[Capitalized]	Capitalized
Repayment	Current	Current	Current	Current	Current

[a] The SLS program was eliminated July 1, 1994.

[b] SLS interest can be capitalized during the grace period for any outstanding Stafford loans, otherwise, interest is due currently.

[c] Consolidation loans with applications received between January 1, 1993 and August 9, 1993 receive interest subsidies during deferral periods. Loans with applications received on or after August 10, 1993 receive interest subsidies during deferral periods if all consolidated loans were eligible for subsidies.

NA: Not applicable.

Source: Salomon Smith Barney and various ABS offering documents.

allowance margins and borrower rates are summarized in Exhibits 26.15 and 26.16.

Special allowance payments are due to the lender 45 to 60 days after the close of each calendar quarter and are backed by the full faith and credit of the United States. Special allowance payments have been relatively small in recent years, but have been a significant program expense in high interest-rate environments.

Borrower Rates

FFELP loan borrower rates are highly complex. Remember that lender yield is the effective asset yield for student loan ABSs, with borrower rate interesting to ABS investors primarily because it affects the loan amortization schedule, potential prepayment risk, and the size of any special allowance payments on the loan.

Monthly Payments

Stafford Loans   Except for different loan limits and eligibility for interest subsidies, subsidized and unsubsidized Stafford loans have virtually identical payment terms. Stafford loans do not require any principal payments until the student leaves school and enters repayment status. The monthly payment amount is set at the time the loan enters repayment, based on an

EXHIBIT 26.15   FFELP Special Allowance Margins, October 20, 2000

Loan Disbursement Date	Subsidized Stafford	Unsubsidized Stafford	SLS[a]	PLUS[b]	Consolidation[c]
To 10/16/86	3.50%	NA	3.50%	3.50%	NA
10/17/86-9/30/92	3.25%	NA	3.25%	3.25%	3.25%
10/1/92-6/30/95	3.10%	3.10%	3.10%[d]	3.10%	3.10%
7/1/95-6/30/98					
In-school, grace or deferral status	2.50%	2.50%	NA	NA	[NA]
Forbearance or repayment status	3.10%	3.10%	NA	3.10%	3.10%
Post 7/1/98					
In-school, grace or deferral status	2.20%	2.20%	NA	NA	[NA]
Forbearance or repayment status	2.80%	2.80%	NA	3.10%	3.10%
Post 1/1/00					
In-school, grace or deferral status	1.74%	1.74%	NA	NA	[NA]
Forbearance or repayment status	2.34%	2.34%	NA	2.64%	2.64%

[a] The SLS program was eliminated on July 1, 1994.
[b] SLS/PLUS loans pay special allowance only if the borrower rate on a loan is at its maximum rate.
[c] Lender owes a 1.05% annualized rebate fee to the DOE on consolidation loans disbursed on or after October 1, 1993. This fee generally is offset against quarterly special allowance and interest subsidy payments due to the lender.
[d] The SLS margin was 280bp during the 1993/94 school year for loans not in repayment status.
NA: Not applicable.
Note: SAP for Post January 1, 2000 loans is indexed to 3-month financial CP.
Source: Salomon Smith Barney and various ABS offering documents.

EXHIBIT 26.16 Borrower Rates, September 15, 1996

Disbursement Date	Stafford Margin and Cap	Disbursement Date	SLS/PLUS[a] Margin and Cap
To 6/30/88 [b]	7%, 8% or 9% Fixed	To 6/30/87	9%, 12%, or 14% Fixed
7/1/88-7/22/92 [b,c]	3.25% / 10%	7/1/87-9/30/92	3.25% / 12%
7/23/92-6/30/98 [d]	3.10% / 7%-10%	10/1/92-6/30/94	3.10% / 11% SLS
10/1/92-6/30/94 [e]	3.10% / 9.00%		10% PLUS
7/1/94-6/30/95 [e]	3.10% / 8.25%	After 7/1/94	3.10% / 9%[f]
7/1/95-6/30/98 [e]			
In-School, Grace or Deferral	2.50% / 8.25%		
Repayment or Forbearance	3.10% / 8.25%		
Index [g]	91-day T-bill	Index [g]	52-week T-Bill
Reset Period	Annual	Reset Period	Annual
Reset Date	July 1	Reset Date	July 1
Post 7/1/98			
In-School, Grace or Deferral	1.70% / 8.25%		
Repayment or Forbearance	2.30% / 8.25%		
Index [g]	91-day T-bill	Index [g]	91-day T-Bill
Reset Period	Annual	Reset Period	Annual
Reset Date	July 1	Reset Date	July 1

[a] The SLS program was eliminated July 1, 1994.
[b] For loans disbursed during this period, the rate on all loans to existing borrowers equals the rate on the first loan made to the borrower.
[c] Rate is fixed at 8% through the first four years following the start of repayment. Loan is variable-rate thereafter with a 10% cap.
[d] New loans to borrowers who were existing borrowers prior to 10/1/92. Cap is the fixed rate that the borrower paid on existing loans at the time the new loan was disbursed with a 10% cap for "8/10" borrowers.
[e] New loans to new borrowers and borrowers who were new borrowers as of October 1, 1992.
[f] The margin on SLS loans disbursed during the 1993/94 school year was 2.80% for loans not in repayment.
[g] Index is the bond-equivalent yield on the relevant Treasury bill at the auction just prior to June 1 of each year.
Source: Salomon Smith Barney and various ABS offering documents.

amortization schedule that in most cases cannot exceed 10 years. Effective with the 1998 reauthorization of the Higher Education Act, if a student has more than $30,000 in outstanding loans, the repayment period can be extended to as long as 25 years. Borrowers, however, must make annual principal and interest payments of at least $600. Principal payments are suspended when a loan enters deferral or forbearance status. For loans to first-time borrowers made on or after July 1, 1995, lenders must offer income sensitive, graduated repayment schedules. (Monthly payments on variable-rate student loans may or may not be readjusted each year to reflect changes in the annual interest rate on the loan. Negative amortization is not allowed on the loans.)

PLUS Loans Monthly principal and interest payments on PLUS loans begin 60 days after disbursement, with amortization over a maximum of 10 years. SLS principal payments begin when the borrower graduates, except that SLS borrowers with outstanding Stafford loans may defer principal repayment until principal repayment begins on their Stafford loans.

Consolidation Loans Payment of monthly principal and interest on consolidation loans begins at disbursement. Consolidation loans made prior to July 1, 1994 bear interest at the weighted-average rate of the consolidated loans, with a 9% floor. Consolidation loans originated on or after July 1, 1994 bear interest at the weighted-average note rate, rounded up to the nearest 1%. Loan originated after July 1, 1998, bear interest at the weighted-average note rate, rounded up to the nearest 1/8%. Loan amortization can be up to 25 years, or 30 years for loans with balances greater than $60,000.

For consolidation loans originated on or after October 1, 1993, lenders who originate a consolidation loan must pay the DOE a 50bp loan origination fee when the loan is made and an annual 1.05% "rebate fee," paid monthly, equal to the sum of the loan balance and accrued interest. The DOE typically offsets origination and rebate fees against interest subsidy and special allowance payments due to lenders.

Borrower Bankruptcy

FFELP loans and supplemental loans made by a nonprofit lender generally cannot be discharged in a bankruptcy proceeding. This was changed with the 1998 reauthorization of the Higher Education, before which loans could be discharged in bankruptcy if they were in repayment for more than 7 years. FFELP guaranty and reinsurance claims are paid at 100% of principal and accrued interest when default is caused by borrower bankruptcy (Exhibit 26.17).

EXHIBIT 26.17 FFELP Principal Payment Terms

Loan Status	Subsidized and Unsubsidized Stafford	SLSb	PLUS	Consolidation
In-School	Deferred	Deferred	Current	NA
Grace	Deferred	Current[c]	Current	NA
Deferral	Deferred	Deferred	NA	Deferred
Forbearance	Deferred	Deferred	Deferred	Deferred
Repayment	Current	Current	Current	Current
Maximum Term[d]	10 years[a]	10 years	10 years	30 years[e]

[a] Students with Stafford loans with balances greater than $30,000 may extend the repayment period to up to 25 years.

[b] The SLS program was eliminated July 1, 1994.

[c] Principal payments on SLS loans to borrowers with outstanding Stafford loans can be deferred until the end of the grace period for Stafford loans.

[d] From commencement of repayment period. Term is increased by any deferral or forbearance periods.

[e] 25-year maximum for principal balance less than $60,000.

NA: Not Applicable.

Source: Salomon Smith Barney and various ABS offering documents.

APPENDIX 26B
RECENT STUDENT LOAN DEALS

Date	Deal	Tranche	Size ($MM)	WAL (years)	Ratings	Pricing Spread
31-Oct-96	Union Financial Services 1996-C	A-5	225.00		AAA	TB+56
		A-6	75.50		AAA	Auction Rate
		B	15.60		N/R	1ML+48
13-Nov-96	University Support Services Inc 1996-A	A	204.30		AAA	1ML+17
		B	31.70		N/R	1ML+45
03-Dec-96	Brazos Student Finance Corporation	A-4	55.00		AAA	TB+50
		A-5	155.00		AAA	TB+65
		B-2	13.00		AA	1ML+45
		C-1	2.00		BBB	1ML+68
19-Dec-96	Signet Student Loan Trust 1996-A	A-1	252.00		AAA	1ML+9
		A-2	161.00		AAA	1ML+15
		A-3	15.00		A2	1ML+45
12-Mar-97	SLM Student Loan Trust 1997-1	A1	1190.00	2.49	AAA	TB+46
		A2	787.40	7.03	AAA	TB+57
		B	71.80	8.85	A+	TB+85
19-Mar-97	The Money Store		299.0			
19-Mar-97	Union Financial Services Taxable Student Loan 1997-1	B4	30.60	11.50	A	1ML+45
20-Mar-97	CHELA Financial Incl 1997-1J	A	50.00	5.18	AAA	TB+58
07-Apr-97	Panhandle Plains Higher Education Authority 1997-A	A1	48.00	1.27	AAA	TB+51
		A2	77.00	4.95	AAA	TB+61
01-May-97	SMS Student Loan Trust 1997-A	A	525.39	7.00	AAA	TB+60
11-June-97	SLMA Student Loan Trust 1997-2	A1	1601.00	2.42	AAA	TB+54
		A2	808.00	6.72	AAA	TB+60
		B	87.45	8.10	A+	TB+83
20-June-97	PNC Student Loan Trust I 1997-2	A1	90.00	0.37	A-1+	1ML-6
		A2	107.00	1.70	AAA	25/5.875 2/99
		A3	107.00	2.70	AAA	26/5.875 2/00
		A4	102.00	3.71	AAA	30/5.625 2/01
		A5	94.00	4.69	AAA	32/6.25 2/02
		A6	72.50	5.69	AAA	34/6.25 2/03
		A7	121.00	7.47	AAA	40/7.875 11/04
		A8	175.00	1.90	AAA	1ML+11
		A9	125.45	8.17	AAA	1ML+18
		B	36.05	10.08	AA	1ML+30
17-June-97	Missouri Higher Education Loan Authority 1997-P	A	100.33	3.80	AAA	TB+62
23-June-97	First Union Student Loan Trust 1997-1	A1	263.64	2.50	AAA	TB+58
		A2	127.76	6.86	AAA	TB+64
		CTFS	14.20	8.24	A3	TB+82
19-Aug-97	SLFC 1997-A	A3	135.00	3.24	AAA	TB+60
		B1	27.75	7.83	A	1ML+33
04-Sep-97	SLMA Student Loan Trust 1997-3	A1	1456.35	2.52	AAA	TB+60
		A2	1028.50	7.20	AAA	TB+64
		B	90.15	9.12	A+	TB+83
04-Nov-97	Student Loan Marketing Association 1997-4	A1	1488.00	2.60	AAA	TB+75
		A2	989.00	7.20	AAA	TB+75
		CTFS	89.90	8.95	A+	TB+105
05-Nov-97	Sallie Mae Student Loan Trust 1997-4	A1	1,488.00	2.58	AAA	TB+75
		A2	989.00	7.20	AAA	TB+75
		B	89.90	8.95	A	TB+105
09-Dec-97	Brazos Student Finance Corp 1997	A1	100.00	2.51		1ML+20
		A2	90.00	7.76		1ML+27
		B	15.00	7.47		1ML+47
11-Dec-97	Crestar Student Loan Trust 1997-1	A1	130.00	1.98	AAA	1ML+16
		A2	84.00	6.85	AAA	1ML+22
		B	8.90	9.36	A	1ML+45
17-Dec-97	Class Notes Trust 1997-2	A4	150.00	2.21	AAA	1ML+17
		A5	57.50		AAA	Auction Rate
		A6	57.50		AAA	Auction Rate
		CTFS	15.00		AAA	Auction Rate
11-Feb-98	Education Loans Incorporated 1998-1	I	185.00	1.44	Aaa	1ML+15
		J	239.60	5.48	Aaa	1ML+20
		L	59.20	3.72	A2	1ML+40

Continued

Date	Deal	Tranche	Size ($MM)	WAL (years)	Ratings	Pricing Spread
05-Mar-98	Chela Financial 1998-A	A	206.80	4.90	Aaa	1ML+18
10-Mar-98	Student Loan Marketing Association 1998-1	A-1	1713.10	2.49	Aaa	TB+71
		A-2	1224.50	7.29	Aaa	TB+76
		B	100.66	9.35	A2	TB+97
16-Mar-98	Classnotes Trust 1998-1		410.00			
9-Apr-98	SFLC, Inc. 1998	A1	56.00	N/A	AAA	Auction Rate
		A2	57.70	N/A	AAA	Auction Rate
		B1	9.90	N/A	A2	Auction Rate
		C	19.20	N/A	A2	Auction Rate
		D	19.90	N/A	A2	Auction Rate
13-Apr-98	Brazos Student Finance Corp 1998-A	A-1	118.00	2.08	Aaa	TB+89
		A-2	269.50	5.78	Aaa	TB+96
		A-3	62.50	Auction	Aaa	Auction Rate
		B-1	50.00	10.11	A2	1ML+43
14-May-98	South Carolina Student Loan Corp		105.70			Auction Rate
			105.70			Auction Rate
20-May-98	SMS Student Loan Trust 1998-A	A-1	150.00	3.05	Aaa	3ML+4
		A-2	433.00	7.49	Aaa	3ML+12
		B	21.35	10.13	Aaa	3ML+27
10-Jun-98	Student Loan Marketing Association 1998-2	A-1	1678.00	2.48	Aaa	TB+68
		A-2	1237.00	7.36	Aaa	TB+73
		Cert	106.00	9.35	A2	TB+95
19-Nov-98	Chela Financial USA, Inc. 1998 CD	C1	58.00	N/A	AAA	Auction Rate
		C2	58.00	N/A	AAA	Auction Rate
		C3	59.00	N/A	AAA	Auction Rate
		C4	70.00	N/A	AAA	Auction Rate
		C5	70.00	N/A	AAA	Auction Rate
		D	35.00	N/A	A	Auction Rate
16-Dec-98	Union Financial Services-1 1998	A-7	125.00	3.93	Aaa	105/5.625 12/02
		A-8	125.00	5.04	Aaa	110/5.75 8/03
		A-9	125.00	6.26	Aaa	120/7.50 2/05
			100.00			Auction Rate
			100.00			Auction Rate
			97.90			Auction Rate
			70.00			Auction Rate
22-Dec-98	Student Loan Funding 1998	A3	400.00	1.95	AAA	1ML + 38
		A4	93.30	N/A	AAA	Auction Rate
		A5	90.00	N/A	AAA	Auction Rate
		A6	90.00	N/A	AAA	Auction Rate
		B3	54.50	5.37	A	Fixed
03-Feb-99	Keycorp Student Loan 1999-A	A-1	260.00	1.38	AAA	3ML+14
		A-2	570.40	6.93	AAA	3ML+33
		B	34.60	10.13	A1	3ML+75
17-Feb-99	Panhandle Plains Higher Education Authority 1999-A2	A-1	35.00		N.A.	
		A-2	165.00	4.17	AAA	1ML+28
04-Mar-99	Brazos Student Finance Corp. 1999-A	A-1	73.80		N.A.	
		A-2	73.80		N.A.	
04-Mar-99	SMS Student Loan Trust 1999-A	A-1	130.00	2.95	AAA	TB+10
		A-2	506.90	7.06	AAA	TB+25
		B	23.10	10.13	A2	TB+55
22-Mar-99	Colorado Student Loan Obligation Bond Authority 1999-A4		209.00	4.90	AAA	1ML+28
17-May-99	SMS Student Loan Trust 1999-B	A-1	150.00	2.89	AAA	3ML+12
		A-2	588.20	7.23	AAA	3ML+24
		B	26.80	10.19	A2	3ML+48
23-Jun-99	SLM Student Loan Trust 1999-1	A-1L	397.52	2.50	Aaa	3ML+8
		A-1T	165.00	2.50	Aaa	TB+87
		A-2L	431.53	7.40	Aaa	3ML+18
		B	36.61	11.40	A2	3ML+45
30-Jun-99	South Carolina Student Loan Corp		150.00	2.90		1ML+27
01-July-99	Union Financial Services-1, Inc.	A13	70.00	N/A	AAA	Auction Rate
		A14	70.00	N/A	AAA	Auction Rate
		A15	70.00	N/A	AAA	Auction Rate
		A16	68.70	N/A	AAA	Auction Rate

(continued)

Continued

Date	Deal	Tranche	Size ($MM)	WAL (years)	Ratings	Pricing Spread
04-Aug-99	SLM Student Loan Trust 1999-2	A-1T	150.00	1.06	Aaa	TB+94
		A-1L	120.00	1.06	Aaa	3ML+8
		A-2	619.00	4.99	Aaa	3ML+20
		A-3	104.50	8.86	Aaa	3ML+28
		CTFS	36.00	8.96	Aaa	3ML+54
30-Sept-99	KeyCorp Student Loan Trust	A1	280.00	1.60	AAA	3ML + 28
		A2	625.00	7.00	AAA	3ML + 43
		M	30.00	N/A	AA	3ML + 70
		Cert	65.00	N/A	A	3ML + 90
28-Oct-99	Student Loan Funding 1999	A1	75.00	N/A	AAA	Auction Rate
		A2	75.00	N/A	AAA	Auction Rate
		A3	75.00	N/A	AAA	Auction Rate
		A4	100.00	N/A	AAA	Auction Rate
		A5	75.00	N/A	AAA	Auction Rate
		A6	95.00	N/A	AAA	Auction Rate
		B	30.00	N/A	A	Auction Rate
01-Dec-99	Education Loans Incorporated 1999-1	1A	78.00	N/A	AAA	Auction Rate
		1B	39.00	N/A	AAA	Auction Rate
		1C	9.30	N/A	A	Auction Rate
21-Dec-99	SLM Funding Corp	A-1	1,201.50	2.36	Aaa	3ML+8
		A-2	787.00	7.00	Aaa	3ML+16
		B	72.30	10.69	Aaa	3ML+40
12-Jan-00	SMS 2000-A	A-1	266.00	3.00	Aaa	3ML+11
		A-2	684.00	7.20	Aaa	3ML+19
		B	35.00	10.00	A2	3ML+TBA
02-Feb-00	SLM Student Loan Trust 2000-1	A-1	1,800.00	2.55	Aaa	3ML+9/TB+85
		A-2	799.00	7.17	Aaa	3ML+18
		A-3	71.70	10.60	A2	3ML+45
09-Feb-00	Access Group. Inc 2000 A1-A4, B1	A1	83.50	N/A	AAA	Auction Rate
		A2	83.50	N/A	AAA	Auction Rate
		A3	83.50	N/A	AAA	Auction Rate
		A4	67.00	N/A	AAA	Auction Rate
		B1	17.00	N/A	A	Auction Rate
15-Mar-00	SLM 2000-2 (Sallie Mae)	A-1L, A-1T	1,210.00	2.65	Aaa	3ML+8/TB+80
		A-2L, A-2T	782.00	7.23	Aaa	3ML+20
		B CTFS	72.30	8.83	A2	TBA
24-Mar-00	Brazos Student Finance Corp. 2000 A1-A7, B1	A1	50.00	N/A	AAA	Auction Rate
		A2	75.00	N/A	AAA	Auction Rate
		A3	75.00	N/A	AAA	Auction Rate
		A4	50.00	N/A	AAA	Auction Rate
		A5	75.00	N/A	AAA	Auction Rate
		A6	75.00	N/A	AAA	Auction Rate
		A7	80.00	N/A	AAA	Auction Rate
		B1	20.00	N/A	A	Auction Rate
13-Apr-00	EMT Corp. 2000 A10-A15, B2	A10	70.00	N/A	AAA	Auction Rate
		A11	70.00	N/A	AAA	Auction Rate
		A12	70.00	N/A	AAA	Auction Rate
		A13	50.00	N/A	AAA	Auction Rate
		A14	50.00	N/A	AAA	Auction Rate
		A15	50.00	N/A	AAA	Auction Rate
		B2	15.00	N/A	A	Auction Rate
14-Apr-00	SLM 2000-3 (Sallie Mae)	A-1L	1,160.50	2.48	Aaa	3ML+7.5
		A-1T	250.00	2.48	Aaa	TB+84
		A-2L	1,064.25	7.25	Aaa	3ML+19
		B CTFS	89.75	9.25	A2	3ML+55
10-May-00	SMS Student Loan Trust 2000-B	A-1	200.00	3.00	Aaa	3ML+8
		A-2	958.00	7.10	Aaa	3ML+20
		B	42.00	10.00	A3	TBA

Continued

Date	Deal	Tranche	Size ($MM)	WAL (years)	Ratings	Pricing Spread
01-Jun-00	NelNet Student Loan Corporation	A1	50.00	N/A	AAA	Auction Rate
		A2	50.00	N/A	AAA	Auction Rate
		A3	50.00	N/A	AAA	Auction Rate
		A4	50.00	N/A	AAA	Auction Rate
		A5	50.00	N/A	AAA	Auction Rate
		A6	50.00	N/A	AAA	Auction Rate
		A7	50.00	N/A	AAA	Auction Rate
		A8	75.00	N/A	AAA	Auction Rate
		A9	75.00	N/A	AAA	Auction Rate
		A10	75.00	N/A	AAA	Auction Rate
		A11	75.00	N/A	AAA	Auction Rate
		A12	100.00	N/A	AAA	Auction Rate
		A13	100.00	N/A	AAA	Auction Rate
		A14	100.00	N/A	AAA	Auction Rate
		B1	50.00	N/A	A	Auction Rate
01-Jun-00	EMT Corp. 2000-I A16-A22, B3	A16	98.00	N/A	AAA	Auction Rate
		A17	98.00	N/A	AAA	Auction Rate
		A18	98.00	N/A	AAA	Auction Rate
		A19	98.00	N/A	AAA	Auction Rate
		A20	98.00	N/A	AAA	Auction Rate
		A21	49.00	N/A	AAA	Auction Rate
		A22	49.00	N/A	AAA	Auction Rate
		B3	48.00	N/A	A	Auction Rate
15-Jun-00	KeyCorp Student Loan Trust 2000-A	A1	100.00	1.70	AAA	3ML + 13
		A2	450.00	7.30	AAA	3ML + 32
28-Jun-00	Access Group. Inc 2000 A5-A9, B2	A5	85.70	N/A	AAA	Auction Rate
		A6	85.70	N/A	AAA	Auction Rate
		A7	85.70	N/A	AAA	Auction Rate
		A8	85.70	N/A	AAA	Auction Rate
		A9	93.00	N/A	AAA	Auction Rate
		B2	31.20	N/A	A	Auction Rate
08-Sep-00	KeyCorp 2000-B	A-1	150.00	1.95	Aaa	3ML+12
		A-2	485.00	7.54	Aaa	3ML+31
12-Sep-00	SLM Student Loan Trust 2000-4	A-1	1290.00	2.47	Aaa	3ML+5
		A-2	691.00	6.99	Aaa	3ML+16
		B	71.00	8.33	Aaa	3ML+55
12-Oct-00	Brazos Student Finance Corp. 2000 A8-A13	A8	43.00	N/A	AAA	Auction Rate
		A9	44.00	N/A	AAA	Auction Rate
		A10	43.00	N/A	AAA	Auction Rate
		A11	100.00	N/A	AAA	Auction Rate
		A12	100.00	N/A	AAA	Auction Rate
		A13	100.00	N/A	AAA	Auction Rate
16-Nov-00	Access Group. Inc. 2000 A10	A10	109.50	N/A	AAA	Auction Rate

bp basis points. 1ML one-month LIBOR. 3ML three-month Libor. TB weekly average of the 91-day Treasury-bill rate.

Source: Salomon Smith Barney.

Non-U.S. Markets

The Mortgage Market in the United Kingdom

Lakhbir Hayre and Ronald E. Thompson, Jr.

The last few years have seen continued growth in the issuance of mortgage- and asset-backed securities outside the United States, as lenders seek balance sheet efficiency and new funding sources. As shown in Exhibit 27.1, growth has been particularly strong in Europe, where issuance volume almost doubled from 1998 to 1999, to roughly $83 billion.

As in the United States, residential mortgages form a particularly important asset class. In fact, 41% of European issuance was collateralized by residential mortgage loans in 1999. The United Kingdom continues to provide the largest share of European MBS issuance, and in this chapter we give an overview of the British mortgage market. We discuss the primary mortgage market, prepayment and default patterns, and the growth of the secondary mortgage market. We also describe structuring issues germane to the United Kingdom, and finish with a detailed examination of an important recent structuring innovation, the Bank of Scotland's Mound Financing No. 1 plc transaction. This deal was priced as a series of soft bullets and callable, pass-through securities, using the master trust structure common in credit card deals, but here applied to prime mortgages.

27.1 THE PRIMARY MORTGAGE IN THE UNITED KINGDOM

The United Kingdom has the second-largest primary mortgage market in Europe, after Germany. The market has grown steadily in recent years, with the current outstanding volume of mortgages close to £500 billion. Exhibit 27.2 shows year-end amounts outstanding from 1989 through 1999.

EXHIBIT 27.1   Issuance Volume of Non-U.S. Mortgage and ABS
Instruments, 1995–1999

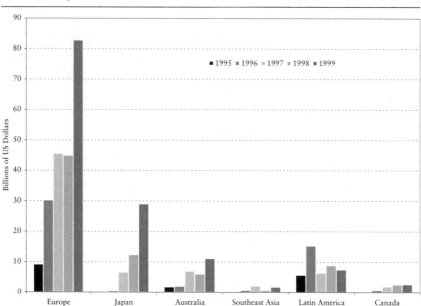

Source: Moody's Investors Services and Salomon Smith Barney.

The primary factor responsible for the increase in mortgage debt has
been a steady rise in home prices. A secondary factor has been an increase
in the homeownership rate, partly due to the government encouraging
council home tenants to buy their homes.

Basic Loan Characteristics

Loan Terms   Most loan terms in the United Kingdom are 25 years.

Coupon Rates   Mortgage loans in the United Kingdom are classified as either
variable rate or *fixed rate*. Variable-rate loans carry coupons that typically
change in line with the borrowing costs of the lending institution.[1] Fixed-rate
loans are not truly fixed rate in the U.S. sense; rather, in U.S. terminology,

---

[1] Because the coupon for most variable loans can be changed at any time by the lender,
it is an **administered rate,** comparable to, for example, the prime rate in the United
States.

EXHIBIT 27.2 U.K. MBS Market—Amount of Mortgages Outstanding at Year-End, 1989–1999

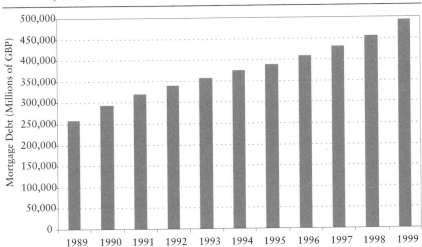

Source: Bank of England.

they are hybrids, with a coupon that is fixed for a specified period (generally two to five years), after which it adjusts according to market interest-rate levels.

As might be expected, the market share of variable- and fixed-rate mortgages varies with interest rates. Recently, variable-rate loans have constituted about 65% to 70% of originations, an increase from about 40% in the spring of 1998. This increase is the result of more attractive initial coupons on variable-rate loans.

Principal Payment Schedule It is a salient feature of the U.K. mortgage market that a substantial fraction of mortgages are not *self-amortizing.*[2] *Interest-only mortgages* often comprise more than 50% of originations. Many of these interest-only mortgages are *endowment loans,* so called because the borrower makes regular payments into an investment plan or endowment policy, which pays off the principal at the maturity of the loan. Amortizing loans, referred to as *repayment mortgages* in the United Kingdom, have increased in popularity in recent years, because of problems with poorly managed endowment funds.

---

[2] A self-amortizing mortgage is one whose monthly payments comprise interest and principal, such that the loan balance is paid down to zero over the term of the loan.

Within these broad interest and principal payment categories, there is a range of options available to borrowers. For example, variable-rate loans can be capped or uncapped, can have an initial teaser rate, or give cash back to the borrower at closing. A recent innovation is the *flexible mortgage,* which gives the borrower the option to increase the mortgage balance, up to a specified limit, by means of "drawing," similar to a home equity line of credit, and to make extra payments (and redraw up to scheduled principal balances) or even to skip payments (again, within limits) without penalty.

A British insurance company, Standard Life, introduced a low, fixed-rate 30-year mortgage, but the degree of lender appetite for this type of mortgage product is unclear at this writing. However, we believe that this development, if it proves popular, will cause more lenders over the long term, to look to securitization to avoid asset/liability mismatches.

27.2 PREPAYMENT AND DEFAULTS

Prepayment rates in the United Kingdom are much more stable than in the United States. Exhibit 27.3 shows aggregate prepayment rates for loans originated by building societies from 1963 through 1999. Speeds have

EXHIBIT 27.3   U.K. Building Society Aggregate Prepayment Speeds, 1963–1999

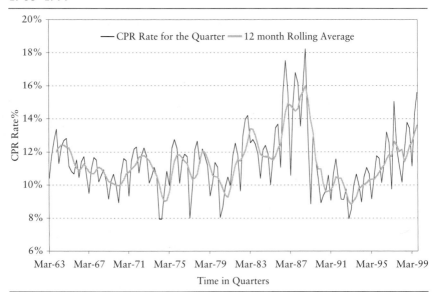

Source: Council of Mortgage Lenders.

remained remarkably stable for the past 37 years, generally above 8% CPR and rarely exceeding rates in the low teens. In contrast, aggregate speeds in the United States have been close to 40% CPR during major refinancing waves. Several factors explain the relative stability of U.K. speeds, including the following:

- The coupons on variable loans track prevailing mortgage rates, and hence there is little incentive to refinance.
- Fixed-rate loans usually carry prepayment penalties if the loan is refinanced, typically ranging from three to six months of interest.
- There is a lack of attractive refinancing vehicles, because long-term fixed-rate mortgages are generally not available.

A useful statistic published by the Bank of England is the aggregate refinancing (or *remortgaging*) rate. This has varied between 3% CPR and 7% CPR over the past eight years with an average of between 5% and 6% CPR in the past few years. These refinancing rates, combined with the overall speeds shown in Exhibit 27.3, imply that the housing turnover rate has averaged around 6% CPR, comparable to U.S. levels.

The narrow range for refinancing rates over the past eight years—a period during which mortgage rates have, as in the United States, varied by several hundred basis points, ranging from a low of about 6.5% to about 9%—indicates that they have been relatively insensitive to interest rates. As indicated, there is limited economic incentive to refinance most loans, so the refinancings that do occur may mostly involve loans that initially start off with below-market, or teaser, rates, which are refinanced once the coupon rises to market levels.

There are indications that refinancing rates are increasing, particularly for "fixed-rate" loans, which may see a sharp jump in the coupon at the end of the fixed period (remember that the CPRs shown in Exhibit 27.3 are aggregate speeds). The increased availability of loans with coupons fixed for a period of time (and potentially with the introduction of true fixed-rate loans such as those recently offered by Standard Life), along with a more competitive lending environment and increasing borrower awareness of refinancing opportunities, may be leading to a systematic increase in refinancing rates in the United Kingdom.

Default Rates

Loan-to-value (LTV) ratios in the United Kingdom tend to be higher than in the United States, with the majority of loans having LTV ratios above 90%, reflecting a tradition in the United Kingdom for home buyers (especially first-time buyers) to put a low downpayment. This fact, along with the prevalence of interest-only loans, might indicate high levels of defaults. However, while delinquency rates seem to be higher than in the United States (although comparable to rates on FHA/VA loans), the percentage of properties ending up in foreclosure has been comparable to that in the United States, and even a little lower in recent years, as a strong housing market has resulted in a sharp decline in default rates. Exhibit 27.4 shows the percentage of properties taken into possession each year since 1989,

EXHIBIT 27.4   Percentage of Properties Taken into Possession (Top Panel) and Home Prices in the United Kingdom and Greater London (Bottom Panel), 1989–1999

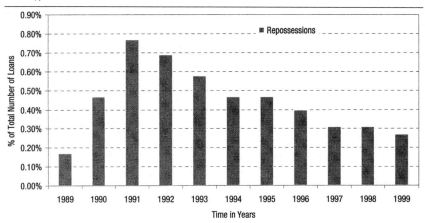

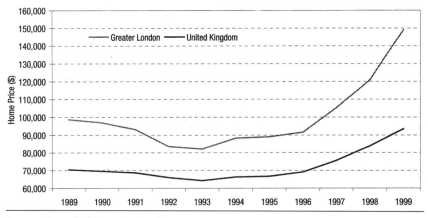

Source: Council of Mortgage Lenders.

along with average home prices in the United Kingdom and, to illustrate regional variations, home prices in London.

A couple of factors likely explain the low foreclosure rates relative to the level of delinquencies. First, there is probably a greater stigma attached to bankruptcy in the United Kingdom than in the United States, so mortgagors will go to great lengths to avoid it. Second, lenders would rather work with borrowers to avoid default and will foreclose on a home only as a last resort.

The Alternative Mortgage Sector

The past few years has seen the development of an "alternative," or subprime, mortgage sector, which caters to borrowers who for one reason or another cannot qualify under traditional underwriting policies. Examples of such borrowers[3] are those with a history of poor employment, self-employed individuals with irregular income, those with high levels of debt, and those who have been delinquent on mortgage payments in the past.

Estimates for the percentage of potential borrowers who fall into these categories are as high as 25%, so the market clearly has considerable potential for growth. This potential, in fact, has attracted entrants from the more established U.S. market, such as Ocwen and RFC, who have entered the U.K. subprime market in the past few years. As the list of deals in Appendix 27A shows, many of the MBS deals in the United Kingdom in recent years have used subprime mortgages as collateral.

27.3 THE DEVELOPMENT OF THE U.K. MBS MARKET

The first European MBS deals were issued in the United Kingdom in 1987, and the United Kingdom has continued to be the leader in European MBS issuance, although issuance in other countries has grown sharply in recent years.[4] Exhibit 27.5 shows estimated annual issuance of MBSs for the United Kingdom and for Europe (not including the United Kingdom).

Reflecting the nature of the collateral and the preferences of U.K. and European investors, most U.K. MBSs have variable-rate coupons, typically spread to three-month LIBOR. Spreads have been generally wider than those on credit cards—for example, five-year WAL, triple-A MBS tranches have been priced at 25bp (basis points) to 30bp in the past year or two.

---

[3] These are examples from the Office of Fair Trading, a government agency.
[4] For a discussion of the early development of the U.K. MBS market, see *U.K. Mortgage-Backed Securities*, Richard Pagan, Salomon Brothers, May 1989.

EXHIBIT 27.5   European and U.K. MBS Issuance, 1988–2000YTD

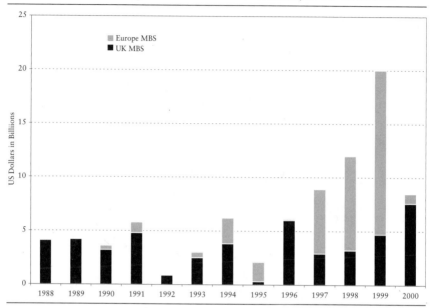

Source: Salomon Smith Barney.

Secondary Market Trading

Liquidity has been limited, particularly in subordinated tranches, and in fact, buy-and-hold investors have bought many European MBSs. However, there are signs that liquidity will improve. One reason is simply the sheer growth in the market, which inevitably leads to more bonds eventually being reoffered in the secondary market. A second reason is more focus by dealers on secondary trading, in response to investor demands. Last, but not least, the availability of updated deal information (prepayments, collateral performance) is improving, for several reasons including the following:

- Underwriters and issuers are making more of an effort to report information in response to investor requests.
- The dealer community is also getting involved in the effort to increase the flow of information. For example, the Bond Market Association, a trade group of bond dealers, has set up a committee, the European Securitization Forum, which has published guidelines for standardized reporting of updated deal information.
- Commercial vendors are beginning to offer updated collateral information.

27.4 GENERAL FEATURES OF U.K. MBS DEAL STRUCTURE

Much of the evolution of mortgage securitization in Europe has taken its cues from the development of ABS structuring technology in the United States, but with modifications to handle differences in the laws, customs, and practices of the issuer's country. We first briefly review a standard securitization structure, and then discuss issues specific to the United Kingdom.

The two principal goals of an ABS structure are to create (1) a bankruptcy-remote vehicle and (2) a true sale of securitized assets. The first goal insures that securitized assets are not included in the assets of the issuer or sponsor in the event of bankruptcy. The second goal ensures that investors have all rights and remedies to the assets in the structure.

In Exhibit 27.6, we show a simplified version of a typical securitization structure. The seller creates a special purpose vehicle (SPV) that exchanges

EXHIBIT 27.6 Simplified ABS Structure

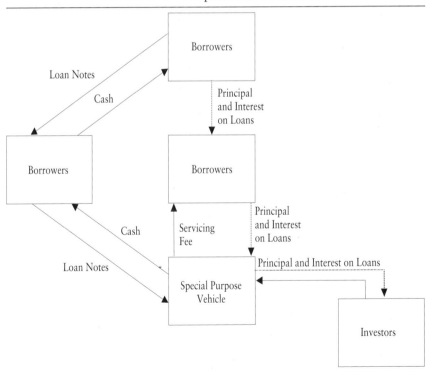

Source: Salomon Smith Barney.

cash raised from investors for the assets (loans, in this case). The seller will also typically establish an initial cash reserve to act as credit enhancement. An appointed servicer—generally the seller acts as servicer—collects the cash from the borrowers, which is paid to investors. Any excess spread income is passed back through the reserve and, if not needed to meet the requirements of the structure, is paid to the seller.

As the credit quality of the collateral to be securitized may be less than the desired ratings of the ABSs, bonds may receive credit enhancement to add support. This credit enhancement may take several forms, including reserves, excess spread, liquidity support, subordination, and surety wraps.

Structural Issues Germane to U.K. MBSs and ABSs

U.K. deal structures are based on the standard ABS model described previously, though U.K. laws and the desire to create more marketable transactions increase structural complexity. Three issues stand out in U.K. securitization law:

- Sale of assets without incurring stamp duty;
- Legal assignment of interest in collateral; and
- Reduction of the risk of set-off.

The first issue, concerns over stamp duty, does not exist in mortgage securitization as mortgages are exempt from stamp duty under English law. For other securitized assets, this duty could be punitive and usually transactions are structured to insulate against this risk.

The second issue arises when interest in collateral is assigned without notifying borrowers. Under U.K. law, issuers may use *equitable assignment* to transfer mortgages to an SPV. This well established principal meets true-sale criteria under English law and satisfies all rating agency requirements to achieve desired ratings. However, as full legal title is not transferred, interest in collateral is not fully perfected. If the lender becomes insolvent, borrowers are immediately notified, thereby transferring full legal title and fully perfecting interests in the collateral. Certain issuers have further mitigated this risk by creating a mechanism to notify borrowers in the event of a ratings downgrade. This additional action protects investors against delays in enforcing the assignment in the event of issuer insolvency.

As a result of equitable assignment, the last major issue arises if the seller files for bankruptcy holding a liability of a borrower that has been used to satisfy the loan obligation. For example, if a borrower of $100 has a deposit of $10 with a bank, the borrower may use the deposit to set off the

$100 loan. Other limited circumstances—such as the seller denying a contractually obligated redraw provision on a flexible mortgage—may also create a risk of set-off claim. If borrowers assert set-off claims prior to full legal title transfer, these claims could reduce the value of the collateral. Sellers are generally required to undertake steps related to legal proceedings, and notification to each borrower eliminates any further right of set-off.

Enforcing legal title through notification (either through an insolvency trigger or a ratings trigger) and the likely amount of set-off claims make this risk very small.

Other Parties to U.K. Mortgage Securitization

As the market has evolved, U.K. residential mortgage deals have often incorporated a variety of features to meet different investor targets or to achieve certain funding goals. This often involves various third parties.

Interest Rate and Currency Swaps The coupons on the mortgage loans are either fixed or variable rate, in which case they are tied to some base rate set by the lending institution. Bond coupons, on the other hand, are typically set at a spread to LIBOR. To offset the resulting basis risk between mortgage and bond coupons, deals generally include an interest-rate swap, generally provided by the seller.

In many recent deals, some bonds are offered in currencies other than British pounds. To remove the resulting currency basis risk, a currency swap is integrated into the deal structure.

Swap providers are typically required to maintain high credit ratings and, should ratings fall, may need to be replaced or required to post collateral to support the swap.

Mortgage Insurance Loans with LTVs greater than a specified limit, typically 75%, usually carry mortgage insurance policies from a mortgage indemnity provider. The policy proceeds are generally assigned to the trust. The mortgage indemnity provider may be related to the seller, if the seller's credit ratings are sufficiently high, or it may be a third party.

Liquidity Providers and Backup Servicers As a guard against disruption of cash flows from insolvency of the mortgage servicer or against revenue shortfalls from collateral, deals may include a separate liquidity provider. Often, as in similar U.S. deals, a backup servicer may be required for subprime issuers. Similar to swap providers, these liquidity providers and backup servicers must meet certain rating standards or take actions to remedy the risk (such as replacement of the servicer or provider).

Deal Tranche Features

Most of the structures used for U.K. MBSs have been akin to U.S.-style, CMO-type transactions, but with some differences. Deals typically include short and long tranches, supported by sequential-pay, amortizing subordinate tranches and other credit enhancements.

To increase the securities' attractiveness to investors, many of the mortgage deals have incorporated call features, with step-up coupons at the beginning of the call period. Coupon step-ups act as economic incentives for issuers to call securities, though we note that the incentive has generally been limited to a doubling of the spread[5]—a feature regulated by the FSA—to limit possible preferential treatment of the trust structure by MBS issuers. More recently, transactions have included soft bullets with relatively short legal final maturities, using ABS structuring technology.

Credit Enhancement

Early U.K. mortgage transactions used mortgage pool insurance to support transactions. These structures were insured by an indemnity against catastrophic collateral losses. However, the expense and credit dependence on third-party insurers caused issuers to seek alternative forms of credit enhancement.

More recently, securitizations have used subordination, reserve funds and excess spread for credit enhancement. A number of the older transactions incorporated static credit enhancement to achieve desired ratings, but later transactions have employed more dynamic mechanisms, primarily in the form of increasing reserves. Building reserves have helped to offset the risk of rapidly paying collateral. If collateral pays too quickly, the value of excess spread is diminished, and, therefore, higher credit enhancement may be required.[6] However, investors in longer-dated tranches may receive a benefit as shorter-dated tranches pay down if increasing credit enhancement offsets the falling value of excess spread. From the seller's perspective, this dynamic reserve is more efficient as sellers must hold capital against the reserve.

To illustrate the evolution of deal structures in the United Kingdom, we next describe recent transactions from two prime-quality mortgage securitizers—Abbey National and Northern Rock—and then take a detailed look at the recent Mound transaction from the Bank of Scotland.

---

[5] More recently, the step-up has been limited to 100bp.
[6] Excess spread is trapped to build reserves. If excess spread is not required, it is then released to the issuer.

27.5 A LOOK AT TWO PRIME-QUALITY MORTGAGE SECURITIZERS

Two issuers help to illustrate the rapid structural evolution taking place in U.K. MBSs.[7] Abbey National Group and Northern Rock plc rank among the most visible issuers in the securitization of high-quality prime, U.K. mortgage collateral. Thus far, through midyear 2000, Abbey National and Northern Rock have completed five transactions, totaling the equivalent of $5.8 billion. These transactions shared common elements, but they are also evidence of the structural evolution of U.K. MBSs as investors have grown more comfortable with assessing U.K. mortgage collateral.

Abbey National

Thus far, Abbey has completed three MBSs, using seasoned first mortgages as collateral. Over time, Abbey made structural advances on each of its subsequent deals after gaining experience and looking to access alternative markets.

Abbey completed its first term mortgage securitization in 1998 in the form of ILSE No. 1 plc, a £247.5 million securitization (equivalent to $407.1 million at the deal pricing) of nearly 5,000 loans. ILSE incorporated a simple two-class sequential structure—denominated in Sterling—using only loans originated in 1995 to 1996. The Class A and B tranches were structured as balloons, with average lives of 5.0 years and 6.9 years, respectively, based on a 15% CPR; the balloons resulted from a call provision in the seventh year of the structure. These tranches were supported by an initial 1% reserve, which increased over time to 2.6% by trapping excess spread.

On a larger scale, Holmes Funding No. 1 transaction was completed in February of 1999, a £1 billion ($1.6 billion) deal consisting of approximately 22,000 loans. To increase investor penetration, the deal incorporated a sizable Euro-denominated senior tranche in addition to Sterling-denominated tranches. Two of the three senior tranches paid sequentially, and all of the three senior and two subordinated tranches were callable in the seventh year of the deal. Though less seasoned than that for ILSE, 64% of the collateral pool was originated in 1997 or earlier. Based on increased comfort with expected collateral performance, Moody's upgraded each of the two subordinated tranches in October 1999, when the Holmes No. 2 plc was rated.

---

[7] In Appendixes 27A and 27B, we list deal features from transactions completed by two prime-quality MBS issuers—Abbey National and Northern Rock—including tranche detail and credit enhancement.

Abbey's most recently completed transaction—Holmes Funding No. 2 plc—was another £1 billion transaction consisting of over 20,000 loans. Similar to Holmes No. 1, Holmes No. 2 incorporated euro-denominated tranches. This structure was innovative as it allowed substitution, based on controlled CPRs, and the deal could be priced with tranche maturities more akin to bullets. Less seasoned than the preceding two deals, Holmes No. 2's collateral pool consisted of loans mostly originated between 1995 and 1998, but nearly 44% were originated in 1999. However, credit enhancement in the form of reserves were initially set at 25bp, building to 120bp.

Northern Rock

Though a smaller mortgage lender in the United Kingdom compared with Abbey, Northern Rock has completed two securitizations—one in 1999 for £600 million ($987.9 million) and one earlier this year for £750 million.

In 1999, Northern Rock completed Granite Mortgages 99–1 plc, a £600 million ($987.9 million) securitization. This transaction included 12,053 first mortgages, over 60% of which were seasoned over 24 months with a low, average of 66% LTVs. Structured as a simple two-class deal priced at 17.5% CPR, the Class A tranche was amortizing and the Class B tranche was to be paid sequentially. The tranches were callable in seven years, otherwise incurring a step-up in spread, effectively creating a balloon maturity for the Class A and a bullet for the Class B. Reserves provided nondeclining support at 1.5% of the original deal amount. If Northern Rock's ratings fell below A3, excess spread would be trapped in a liquidity reserve.

Earlier this year, Northern Rock returned with Granite Mortgages 00–1 plc, a £750 million ($1.2 billion) securitization. Priced at a 17.5% CPR, the deal consisted of an amortizing security and two subordinate classes. Similar to the 99-1 transaction, this deal had a call in seven years, with a coupon step-up.

The five transactions by the two issuers illustrate the structural evolution that is in large part mirroring an evolution in the mortgage origination business.

27.6 A CASE STUDY: THE MOUND STRUCTURE

We finish by taking a detailed look at a recent structuring innovation. The Bank of Scotland Mound transaction securitizes mortgages using a master trust structure similar to that employed in credit card securitizations.[8]

---

[8] Salomon Smith Barney has acted as an underwriter for issues from and sponsored by the Bank of Scotland within the past three years.

EXHIBIT 27.7 Bank of Scotland's Mound Financing No. 1 plc (Principal Amounts in Millions)*

Class	Ratings	Rating Agencies	Principal Amount	% of Series	Expected Maturity	Legal Maturity	Maturity Type
Class A-1	Aaa/AAA	Moody's/S&P	$208.0	17.3%	3 Yrs.	5 Yrs.	Soft bullet
Class A-2	Aaa/AAA	Moody's/S&P	$208.0	17.3%	5	7	Soft bullet
Class A-3	Aaa/AAA	Moody's/S&P	$208.0	17.3%	7	10	Soft bullet
Class A-4[a]	Aaa/AAA	Moody's/S&P	£285.0	38.0%	7	42	Callable PT
Class B[a]	A1/A+	Moody's/S&P	£37.5	5.0%	7	42	Callable PT
Class C[a]	Baa2/BBB	Moody's/S&P	£37.5	5.0%	7	42	Callable PT

*The Class A-4, B, and C tranches were offered with step-up coupons, in the event that securities were not called.
PT: Pass-through securities.
Source: Salomon Smith Barney.

Exhibit 27.7 shows the structure for the Mound Finance deal, where the expected maturities are the bullet principal payment dates for the bonds.

The bullet structure is achieved by (1) using a collateral pool of loans much larger than the amount of bonds issued, and (2) *substitution;* that is, the addition of new mortgages to the pool during a specified revolving period as principal is collected or prepayments occur. Substitutions to the pool are subject to specified guidelines and restrictions and changes in the size of the pool are absorbed by the seller's interest. During this substitution period, all principal paid is directed to the seller. Prior to each of the soft-bullet payments, principal is accumulated in a funding account for the benefit of the investor interest. Following each bullet payment, principal is again directed to the seller. Once the specified substitution period is completed, the pool begins to amortize, paying down any remaining bonds. Exhibit 27.8 shows the main features of the structure.

The pool of assets is larger than the amount of bonds issued, and hence, the master trust consists of a *seller's interest* and an *investors' interest,* as illustrated in Exhibit 27.9. A minimum seller's interest is sized to absorb prepayment fluctuations and provide sufficient cash flow to pay bullets as scheduled, even under slower-than-expected prepayment scenarios. Held by the issuer, this seller's interest represents a co-investment in the master trust pool alongside the investors' interest. Shortly before each of the bullet payments (an *accumulation period*), principal amortization and prepayments accumulate in a funding account.

In the Bank of Scotland's structure, the longer tranches, Classes A-4, B, and C, were offered as callable securities with step-up coupons, increasing the economic desirability of a call for the issuer, and thus helping to ensure a bullet-like maturity.

EXHIBIT 27.8   Main Structural Features of a Mortgage Master Trust and
Their Purposes

Structural Feature	Purpose
Common pool	One pool of mortgages supports all issuance of securities.
Substitution period	The seller adds new mortgages to the pool, changing the share of the seller's interest, subject to prespecified minimums.
Accumulation period	Collected principal and prepayments are accumulated in a funding account and used to pay off the soft bullet on its expected payment date.
Early amortization period	Occurs when payout events happen. Either the revolving period or the accumulation period ends and all principal accumulated or collected thereafter is paid to investors to retire bonds.*
Payout events	Various events that trigger an early amortization.
Types of securities	A variety of security types can be issued from this new structure, including: • Fixed- and floating-rate soft bullets • Fixed- and floating-rate pass-throughs • Step-up coupon securities • Non-local currency denominations (hedged through currency swaps within master trust)
Seller's interest	Investors and the seller jointly own the pool of assets. The seller's ownership interest is the total amount of mortgage assets in the pool minus the amount of outstanding bonds. The seller's interest absorbs a variety of risks.

*Depending on the type of triggering event.
Source: Salomon Smith Barney.

Stability of Bullet Structure against Prepayment Variability

For MBSs, borrowers' ability to prepay typically leads to average life volatility. If prepayments are too slow, bonds could extend. If prepayments are too fast, bonds could shorten. Hence, reliable estimates of the range of likely prepayment rates over the term of the bonds are important.

The master trust structure significantly reduces these risks in two ways. First, and most important, the master trust's ability to substitute, or add, collateral helps to eliminate much of the risk of the bullet bond's shortening. Second, the structure will allocate all principal collected (both investors' and seller's shares) to pay off bullet bonds. Also, the seller is required to maintain a minimum aggregate amount of outstanding mortgages to support the structure. These factors mitigate extension risk. Another factor mitigating average life volatility is the relative stability of prepayments in the United Kingdom, as discussed previously.

These factors help to increase the desirability of this structure for investors and issuers. For investors, bonds may be structured for investors and issuers. For investors, bonds may be structured as bullet securities with short legal final maturities, regardless of the life of the collateral. For issuers, swaps to hedge the basis risk have limited optionality based on the bullet structure of the bonds, thereby reducing hedging costs.

EXHIBIT 27.9 Example of a Typical Mortgage Pool Master Trust Bullet Structure*

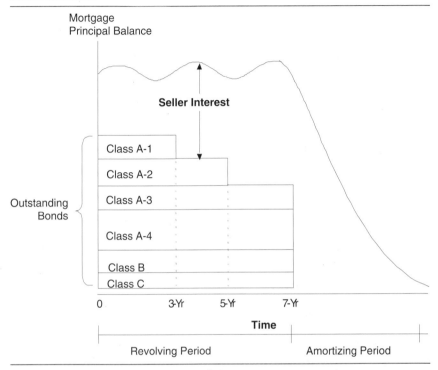

* Assumes that Classes A-4, B, and C are called at note coupon step-up date.
Source: Prospectus.

To determine if bonds were subject to extension risk, Bank of Scotland's structure underwent extensive stress tests to determine what CPR scenarios would cause the bonds to extend. This stress analysis included several CPR scenarios and assumed that, concurrently, the bank was unable to substitute new collateral from the closing date (an extremely unlikely event). Exhibit 27.10 shows the CPR scenarios at which the bullet payments are still made, even assuming no substitution.

The stress tests included prepayments slower than historical U.K. experience, and speeds faster than historical experience during the revolving period (during which time principal is directed to the sponsor under the terms of the transaction), after which prepayment rates were assumed to suddenly plummet. These results should reassure investors about the solidity of the bullet structure, as the scenarios required that both events occur simultaneously.

EXHIBIT 27.10   Bank of Scotland's Mound Financing No. 1 Stress Analysis*

CPR Scenario	Event 1	AND	Event 2
Shock slowdown	No new mortgages added to pool		CPR Rates are 5% for the life of the deal.
Short whipsaw	No new mortgages added to pool		CPR Rates are 24% for the first 2 years then 7% for the life of the deal.
Normal, then shock slowdown	No new mortgages added to pool		CPR Rates are 15% until 6 months before the first bullet then 6.25% for the life of the deal.
Long whipsaw	No new mortgages added to pool		CPR Rates are 20% until 6 months before the first bullet then 7.6% for the life of the deal.

*Bonds meet scheduled expected payment dates under the following stress tests, assuming that Event 1 and Event 2 occur simultaneously.
Source: Salomon Smith Barney.

The prepayment assumptions shown in Exhibit 27.10 are outside the range of historical U.K. experience. In addition, the probability that a large institution like the Bank of Scotland with access to a large pool of available collateral would be unable to substitute new collateral seems quite remote.

Credit Concerns for Investors

Servicer concerns typically present risks in ABS structures, and the mortgage master trust structure is not immune. These risks manifest themselves in several forms: (1) the ability to service existing mortgages in a timely and efficient manner to prevent increased credit defaults and delinquencies; and (2) the ability to substitute new collateral that meets the specified guidelines. This second risk, although significant, is generally less for well regarded mortgage lenders with embedded infrastructures.

   Other collateral risks include credit risk of underlying mortgagees and the ability of the mortgage collateral to be liquidated to satisfy obligations.

Why Issue a Bullet Structure?

A prime motivation behind bullet structures is that many investors (especially those outside the United States) generally prefer bullet securities to amortizing ones, and issuers have sought ways to create securities targeted to those preferences. The evolution of credit cards and, more recently, auto loans to restructure cash flows, creating bullet securities, have been well received by investors.

   Another key motivating factor for issuers is to achieve a lower average cost of funding. An issuer's all-in cost consists of a weighted-average of all of the bonds supporting the structure. The shape of the term and credit curves makes longer average life and credit support bonds cheap to shorter ones. If prepayments increase, the shorter, lower-coupon (and hence, from the issuer's point view, cheaper) tranches pay down, leaving the longer, more expensive bonds outstanding. In the bullet structure, the cheaper shorter classes will remain outstanding until their maturity dates, so that the issuer's cost is less subject to prepayments.

In Exhibit 27.11, we compare the all-in cost of the Bank of Scotland structure against typical amortizing structures at varying prepayment speeds. Under traditional mortgage financing using pass-throughs or pay-throughs, the deal is paid down as prepayments occur, and the issuer must find new financing to fund new originations. By issuing a series of bullets that form a stable funding platform, Bank of Scotland can use prepayments to finance new originations. This reinvestment ability, without turning to new funding sources, enhanced the cost efficiency of the structure.

Recent mortgage product trends in the United Kingdom and in Australia have created an appetite for issuers to obtain more flexible funding vehicles. Many of the primary mortgage products offered outside the United

EXHIBIT 27.11   Soft Bullet Cost in Basis Points versus Amortizing Pass-Through Structures

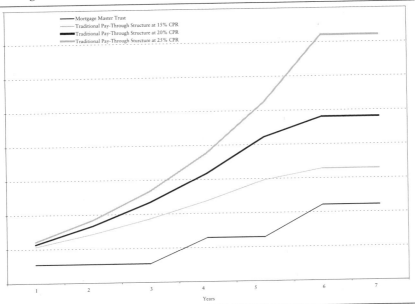

Source: Salomon Smith Barney.

States combine options such as principal redraws and payment holidays (e.g., the *flexible mortgage* described previously). These instruments require lenders to fund these principal extensions or subject investors to more payment volatility. Alternatively, lenders have looked for ways to optimize capital relief using stable funding bases. These factors led to the development of soft bullet securities in a master trust format. We believe issuers will likely use this master trust type of vehicle to grow over time.

APPENDIX 27A
RECENT MBS TRANSACTIONS BY NORTHERN ROCK PLC

	Granite Mtg. 99-1		Granite Mtg. 00-1		
Amount (MM):	£564.0	£36.0	£694.8	£32.7	£22.5
Ratings at Issue (Moody's/S&P):	Aaa/AAA	A1/A	Aaa/AAA	Aa3/AA	Baa2/BBB
Expected Average Life:	3.8	7.0	3.7	7.0	7.0
Maturity:	Balloon	Bullet (Call)	Balloon (Call)	Bullet (Call)	Bullet (Call)
Legal Final:	September 13, 2033		September 13, 2032		
Basis:	3-Month £ LIBOR		3-Month £ LIBOR		
Margin:	+0.28%	+0.75%	+0.25%	+0.45%	+1.30%
Step-Up Margin:	+0.56%	+1.50%	+0.50%	+0.90%	+2.60%
Step-Up Date:	September 13, 2006		February 13, 2007		
Collateral					
Principal amount (MM):	£672.3		£911.0		
Number of loans:	12,053		15,958		
Avg. Loan Size:	55,777		57,085		
Avg. LTV:	66.4%		67.5%		
Interest Rate:	100% SVR		80% SVR, 20% Fixed-Rate		
3 Largest Geog Conc.:	SE 30.1%; North 18.8%; NW 12.0%		SE 21.0%; London18.2%; North 17.7%		
Seasoning					
6-12 months	1.9%		7.1%		
12-18 months	9.0%		6.6%		
18-24 months	26.6%		21.0%		
24-30 months	41.7%		15.3%		
30+ months	20.9%		50.0%		
Pricing Date:	September 27, 1999		February 8, 2000		
Pricing Speed:	17.5% CPR		17.5% CPR		

SVR: Standard value rate. Rate is fixed in a period of time (generally 3–5 years) then reads to SVR plus a margin.
Source: Salomon Smith Barney.

APPENDIX 27B
RECENT MORTGAGE TRANSACTIONS BY ABBEY
NATIONAL GROUP PLC

See Table on page 756.

	ILSE No. 1 plc		Holmes Funding No. 1					Holmes Funding No. 2				
Amount (MM):	£232.5	£15.0	£210.0	EU700.0	£210.0	£52.5	£47.5	EU575.0	£315.0	EU300.0	£40.0	£45.0
Ratings at Issue (Moody's/S&P):	Aaa/AAA	A1/A	Aaa/AAA	Aaa/AAA	Aaa/AAA	Aa3/AA	Baa2/BBB	Aaa/AAA	Aaa/AAA	Aaa/AAA	Aa2/AA	Baa1/BBB
Expected Average Life:	5.0	6.9	0.9	4.0	7.0	7.0	7.0	2.4	5.0	5.0	5.0	5.0
Maturity:	Balloon (Call)	Balloon (Call)	Amort.	Amort.	Callable PT	Callable PT	Callable PT	Amort.	Callable PT	Callable PT	Callable PT	Callable PT
Legal Final:	December 15, 2024		December 15, 2025					September 15, 2035				
Basis:	£ LIBOR		£LIBOR	Euribor	£LIBOR	£LIBOR	£LIBOR	Euribor	£LIBOR	Euribor	£LIBOR	£LIBOR
Margin:	+0.15%	+0.35%	+0.10%	+0.20%	+0.27%	+0.55%	+1.60%	+0.24%	+0.28%	+0.27%	+0.50%	+1.50%
Step-Up Margin:	+0.30%	+0.70%	+0.20%	+0.40%	+0.54%	+1.10%	+3.20%	+0.48%	+0.56%	+0.54%	+1.00%	+300.00%
Step-Up Date:	September 13, 2006		March 15, 2006					November 15, 2004				
Collateral												
Principal amount (MM):	£255.0		£1,031.2					£1,032.4				
Number of loans:	4,992		21,818					20,633				
Avg. Loan Size:	51,082		47,263					50,035				
Avg. LTV:	87.8%		92.1%					90.6%				
Interest Rate:	100% SVR		100% SVR									
3 Largest Geog Conc.:	SE 22.4%; E Anglia 10.9%; London 8.5%		SE 27.9%; North West 14.7%; South West 17.7%					SE 35.3%; North West 12.6%; West Midlands 9.8%				
Seasoning (Year Origination)												
1995	67.0%		3.9%					0.3%				
1996	33.0%		11.3%					0.5%				
1997	0.0%		48.7%					7.6%				
1998	0.0%		36.0%					47.7%				
1999	NA		0.0%					43.9%				
Pricing Date:	February 23, 1998		February 23, 1999					October 18, 1999				
Pricing Speed:	15.0% CPR		15.0% CPR					10.0% CPR				

Source: Salomon Smith Barney.

CHAPTER 28

The CMBS Market in the United Kingdom

Darrell Wheeler

Since 1992, the United Kingdom (U.K.) has experienced stable economic conditions. Exhibit 28.1 indicated that price inflation and economic growth have been relatively stable, in the 2% to 4% range since 1993, while the base lending rate has been in the low 6% to 7% range. This stable growth/negligible inflation environment has combined with limited real estate construction to create a very strong commercial real estate market.

Beyond economic conditions, the established British legal system provides for strong mortgage security, Special Purpose Vehicles,[1] and other features that give investors faith in bonds backed by secured U.K. assets. The key strength of the U.K. legal system is demonstrated when there is a default. In a default, the appointment of a receiver cannot be blocked. This standard default mechanism is better than the system in the United States where a borrower's filing for bankruptcy protection may delay secured creditors from realizing on their collateral.

The typical CMBS bond structure is almost identical to the North American structure, but with a rated liquidity facility providing advancing of initial bond debt service during an asset cash flow shortfall, rather than a loan servicer. This chapter reviews the favorable factors that should lead to a rapid expansion of the securitization of U.K. commercial real estate.

---

[1] Special purpose vehicles are separate corporate companies that have the sole purpose of holding the asset being securitized. By restricting the holding company's activities in the operating covenants, the asset is prevented from incurring further liabilities and prevented from incurring liability for any other related company liability.

EXHIBIT 28.1   U.K. Macroeconomic Indicators, 1985–2000

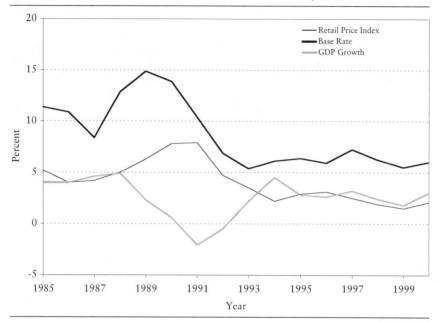

Source: Salomon Smith Barney.

28.1 LANDLORD/TENANT LEASE STRUCTURE

The U.K. real estate market has established one of the most landlord-favor-
able leasing markets in the world. Commercial leases have a contractual
term of 15 or 25 years and provide the landlord with "five-year, upward-
only rent reviews." This means that the rent is bumped up to the greater of
market or the previous rental rate every five years. When we review the office markets, the advantage of this leasing structure will be clear, in that
many tenants are still paying rents established in the 1988 real estate market boom.

In addition, commercial leases are usually *fully repairing and insuring*
(FRI), which means that the tenant is responsible for paying the cost of fully
repairing and insuring the property, in addition to the operating cost and
taxes that would be covered under a typical North American triple-net lease.
The tenant's requirement to maintain, repair, and insure the property removes most of the capital expenditure cost that a landlord might incur on
a standard triple-net lease. Furthermore, at lease termination, the tenant is

responsible for returning his or her space to a base building standard. *This means that tenants who have made substantial improvement investments are more likely to renew their lease at expiry to preserve their "sunk build-out costs."*

Landlords may also benefit from "Privity of Contract," which is a lease feature that preserves the original tenant's obligations, even after he or she may have assigned his or her lease. For leases signed after the introduction of the Landlord and Tenant (Covenants) Act in 1995, this feature extends only to the first two occupants, but many leases now contain additional provisions designed to maintain the benefits provided by "Privity of Contract." Thus, for commercial properties, an original tenant's covenant can usually be relied upon to continue for the duration of the lease. *Preserving the original credit guarantee is a unique lease feature that makes the property's future cash flow more creditworthy and securitizable.*

The Rating Agencies' U.K. CMBS Methodology

All of the major rating agencies have been involved in rating U.K. commercial real estate transactions over the past few years. The agencies have found that they have to adjust their models in each European real estate market to reflect the term of the lease, the sharing of property obligations between tenant and landlord, the mortgage security, and the strength or volatility of the real estate market. In the case of the United Kingdom, the long lease terms have caused most CMBS issues to be structured to fully amortize during the tenant's lease, and as a result, the agencies focus on the tenant default probability, rather than balloon refinance risk.

Unfortunately, default and loss data in the United Kingdom are not widely available to predict future portfolio defaults and losses. Without historical data, the agencies use the tenant rent roll to project a transaction's cash flow under a set of conditions such as a triple-A economic-stress scenario, a double-A stress scenario, a single-A stress scenario, and so on down the rating scale. The triple-A stress scenario has the toughest set of cash flow projection assumptions for tenant retention, rental rate decline, releasing costs, property vacancy, and property underlying value. Similar to North American guidelines, the rating agencies use a benchmark such as the 1990–1992 recession which may be considered to be a single-A stress scenario. The agencies then gear their stress assumptions up from 1990–1992 distressed property parameters using a commercial property valuation data source such as the Investment Property Databank (a U.K. property performance database).

The resulting stressed cash flows are then compared to each loan's required mortgage debt service to determine if a property has sufficient cash flow to service the mortgage. For a case in which there is insufficient cash flow, the loan is assumed to default and a loss is calculated based on the property's stressed value. This stressed value may be derived from the stressed cash flow, divided by a stressed valuation yield that is based on historical property performance. The rating agencies also adjust the defaulted loan's recovery proceeds to account for legal procedures and property disposition costs. Using this methodology, the rating agencies determine the absolute amount of triple-A proceeds that they consider to be triple-A recession-proof using their triple-A recession assumptions; the same analysis is performed for each additional class.

North American CMBS rating agency methodology, such as stressed debt service at an expected refinance constant and stabilized loan-to-value calculations, is not commonly used in the U.K. CMBS market. This is because the bonds are usually structured to match amortization with the longer-term real estate leases. When a property has a publicly rated tenant, the rating agency simply adjusts the property's default probability to reflect the expected corporate default rate of the underlying tenant rating. Many of the transactions benefit from a liquidity facility, from which the issuer can pay bond interest if the underlying property experiences a shortfall in the cash flow. The rating agency will give subordination credit for the liquidity facility, to the extent that the rating agency projects that it will enable a transaction to make it through one of the agencies' stress scenarios without incurring a loss at the sized certificate class. Most transactions require some form of liquidity facility, because the U.K. market has not yet fully developed the concept of loan servicers or servicers advancing to the bonds in times of cash flow shortfall. To date, U.K. transactions have usually had a trustee with limited decision-making discretion that services the transaction. The concept of a loan servicer with loan workout discretion has emerged only in the past couple of years.

Although the agencies and issuers size the transaction to match the underlying leases, a transaction may have an earlier anticipated bond repayment date, created by allowing prepayment combined with a significant step-up in the required bond coupon if the loan is not repaid early. In this case the rating agencies still focus on the full term of the bond as though the bond is not repaid at the early repayment date. This approach ensures the property's cash flow can service the bond's higher interest cost after the interest rate step-up.

28.2 A REVIEW OF U.K. CMBS ISSUANCE

To review U.K. CMBS issuance, we break up the issuance into three categories:

1. Operating companies, such as nursing home operators;
2. Multiborrower conduit transactions; and
3. Single-asset/issuer.

Operating Companies

The operating companies were the first form of securitization to use commercial real estate to support bonds. Since 1994, we have detailed information on 11 different pools of operating company CMBSs that have raised more than US$3.7 billion in issuance (see Exhibit 28.2). Citibank was one of the early issuers, using CMBS to finance two different nursing home pools in 1994 and 1995. Operating companies have been early CMBS product adopters, because their corporate cost of debt is usually higher than traditional mortgage finance rates. The CMBS market has enabled the nursing home operators to access the mortgage finance market by financing a sale-leaseback of their assets with a secured mortgage.

U.K. issuers have also utilized the CMBS type structure to finance large pub portfolios. These pub operating companies receive revenues from rents from owned pubs leased to smaller local operators (the typical lease term is 10 to 20 years), from beer sales and other revenues from the pubs they operate directly, and from beer sales to the pubs they rent to other operators. Pub transactions typically use a secured loan from the issuer to the operating company rather than a true sale of the assets to the issuer. This enables the financing to be based on the operating company's revenues, as well as the underlying property's rental revenues. The issuer will have fixed and floating charges over all the assets of the operating company. Under the British legal system, this structure enables the issuer to gain control of the operating company and the related real estate assets relatively quickly in the case of a loan default. The underlying borrower is usually not a SPE, but the actual operating company structured with restrictions on dividend payments, a minimum initial equity requirement, and operation limitations. Therefore, rating agencies and pub transaction investors are required to access the underlying business operating risks.

By April of 2000, pub CMBS transactions had raised more than £2.5 billion in financing, demonstrating strong investor confidence in the stability of the British pub industry. Pub transactions are usually structured to fully amortize the loan over a 20- or 25-year period, achieving spreads that are attractive relative to the borrower's other long-term financing options. Given the financing advantage and the competitiveness of the pub operating environment we expect to see significant further pub-based CMBS issuance in 2000. The British pub industry is a regulated competitive business environment, with complexities beyond the scope of this chapter. Investors interested in pub-related CMBSs should review old pub

EXHIBIT 28.2 United Kingdom CMBS Issuance—Operating Company Issuance

Issuer/Date Closed	US $MM	Class	US$	UK £	S&P/Moodys/Fitch/Duff	Sub %	Mature	Ave. Life	Bond Rate	Net Spread
Sonar 1 PLC,	$169.6	A	146.3	109	Aaa	13.7%	05/15/21	4.25	2 mo LIBOR +30	+30
Closed: 12/15/94		B	20.2	13	Baa2	1.8%	05/15/21		2 mo LIBOR +115	+115
		C	3.1	2						

Mortgages on nursing homes and residential-care facilities in England and Wales. The loans were originated by Citibank International. Citibank International arranged the transaction to remove mortgages from its balance sheet. The notes carried step-up coupons, which were initially set at 6.58% for Class A and 7.43% for Class B. The senior notes were to pay 30bp over two-month LIBOR until February 1995, when the benchmark was to change to three-month LIBOR plus 30bp. In February 2002, the coupon was to step up to three-month LIBOR plus 60bp. The bonds were eligible for redemption at par value beginning in February 2002.

Issuer/Date Closed	US $MM	Class	US$	UK £	S&P/Moodys/Fitch/Duff	Sub %	Mature	Ave. Life	Bond Rate	Net Spread
Sonar 2 PLC	$78.70	A	62.9	40.0	Aaa	20.0%		4.30	3 mo LIBOR +22.5	+22.5
Closed: 10/17/95		B	15.7	10.0				7.00	3 mo LIBOR +110	+110

Mortgages on nursing and residential-care homes in England and Wales. The loans were originated by Citibank International's consumer services group. The securities were listed on the London exchange. The senior notes were to pay 22.5bp over three-month LIBOR until January 2003, when the rate was to step up to 50bp over three-month LIBOR. The subordinate notes were to pay 110bp over three-month LIBOR until October 2002, when the spread is to step up to 230bp.

Issuer/Date Closed	US $MM	Class	US$	UK £	S&P/Moodys/Fitch/Duff	Sub %	Mature	Ave. Life	Bond Rate	Net Spread
Craegmoor Finance PLC	133.8	A	85.6	51.2	//AA/AA	36.0%	12/31/08	8.50	3 mo LIBOR +50	+50
Closed: 12/20/96		B	18.7	11.2	//A/A	22.0%	12/31/08	10.00	3 mo LIBOR +70	+70
		C	29.4	17.6	//BBB/BBB		12/31/08	10.00	3 mo LIBOR +125	+125

Mortgages on 41 residential-care and nursing homes (total of 1,964 beds). The properties were concentrated in Wales (25% of net operating income for the pool) and the London area (22%). Craegmoor, an owner and operator of residential-care and nursing homes in the United Kingdom used $57 million of the proceeds to pay off debt. The rest was to be held in a reserve account and advanced to Craegmoor as it made acquisitions. The securities were listed on the London exchange. The spread on each class was to step up on January 1, 2007 (to 250bp for Class A, 270bp for Class B and 325bp for Class C). Craegmoor was required to make only interest payments until September 2000.

Issuer/Date Closed	US $MM	Class	US$	UK £	S&P/Moodys/Fitch/Duff	Sub %	Mature	Ave. Life	Bond Rate	Net Spread
Care Homes No. 1 Ltd.	159.8	A-1	95.9	60.0	///AAA	40.0%	04/09/21	24.00	24 yr UK 8.0	+60
Closed: 4/9/97		A-2	62.9	40.0	///BBB		04/09/21	24.00	24 yr UK 8.5	+115

Leases on 39 nursing homes located throughout the UK. The transaction enabled Nursing Home Properties PLC, a London-based owner of nursing homes, to raise long-term financing at attractive terms (issuer paid a blended all-in spread of 82bp over the 8% UK government bond due June 7, 2021). The securities were listed on the Luxembourg exchange.

Issuer/Date Closed	US $MM	Class	US$	UK £	S&P/Moodys/Fitch/Duff	Sub %	Mature	Ave. Life	Bond Rate	Net Spread
PHF Securities No. 1 Ltd.	252.8	A-1	168.5	100.0	AAA///AAA	33.3%	07/10/25	7.19	8% UKT 6/21	+80
Closed: 12/12/97		A-2	84.3	50.0	BBB///BBB		07/10/27	8.13	8% UKT 6/21	+170

Leases on 99 high-quality nursing homes in the United Kingdom. Principal Healthcare acquired the collateral properties from seven nursing-home operators and then leased the properties back to the operators. The principal on Class A-1 was expected to be redeemed in a single payment from the proceeds from a zero-coupon swap guaranteed by Merrill Lynch. The coupon on Class A-2 was to step up on July 10, 2025, to the higher of 9.125% or six-month LIBOR plus 150bp.

Issuer/Date Closed	US $MM	Class	US$	UK £	S&P/Moodys/Fitch/Duff	Sub %	Mature	Ave. Life	Bond Rate	Net Spread
Punch Taverns Finance PLC	856.0	A1, 2, 3, 4,	696.0	435.0	A/A2//	18.7%	10, 15, 20, 25 yr		3 mo LIBOR +60, +75, +95, +135	
Closed: 24/3/98		B	160.0	100.0	BBB/Baa2//		3/23/2026 5/2024		UK Govt. +165	+165

A loan to Punch Taverns Ltd. Secured by fixed and floating charges on freehold and leasehold interest in 1,190 leased and 238 managed pubs bought from Bass PLC. Transaction was structured with a liquidity facility to amortise over 28 years, with A classes maturing every five years (floating rate classes had interest caps).

Issuer/Date Closed	US $MM	Class	US$	UK £	S&P/Moodys/Fitch/Duff	Sub %	Mature	Ave. Life	Bond Rate	Net Spread
Unique Finance PLC	1,296	A1,2,3	1,096.0	685.0	A///A	15.3%	Staggered		3-mo LIBOR +75, +112, gilt+200	
Closed: 3/99		B	125.0	100.0	BBB///BBB		3/2024 12/2022		UK Govt. +290	+290

A £815 million loan secured by fixed and floating charges on freehold and leasehold interests in 2,614 pubs. Transaction was structured with a liquidity facility and amortizes over a 25-year period. A classes had staggered maturities after 2010 (floating-rate classes were fully swapped).

Issuer/Date Closed	US $MM	Class	US$	UK £	S&P/Moodys/Fitch/Duff	Sub %	Mature	Ave. Life	Bond Rate	Net Spread
Care Homes Ltd., No. 2	434.6	A	295.2	180.0	AAA///AA	32.1%	02/15/23	24.00	8% U.K. Govt. 5.75	+135
Closed: 2/15/99		M	98.4	60.0	A///A	9.4%	02/15/23	24.00	8% U.K. Govt. 6.65	+225
		B	41.0	25.0	BBB///BBB		02/15/23	24.00	8% U.K. Govt. 7.65	+325

The offering financed a series of sale-leaseback transactions. Nursing Home Properties bought 103 nursing-home and long-term care properties in the United Kingdom from their operators and leased them back to the sellers. The London firm financed the acquisition by securitizing 25-year leases on the properties. The bonds were offered in London and denominated in pounds.

Issuer/Date Closed	US $MM	Class	US$	UK £	S&P/Moodys/Fitch/Duff	Sub %	Mature	Ave. Life	Bond Rate	Net Spread
Tiara Securities Issuer B.V.	198.9	A	133.7	82.0	AAA///AA	32.8%	07/10/27	28.00	U.K. Govt. 5.90	+140
Closed: 3/23/99		M	48.9	30.0	A///A	8.2%	07/10/29	28.00	U.K. Govt. 6.90	+240
		B	16.3	10.0	BBB///BBB		07/10/29	28.00	U.K. Govt. 7.90	+340

The lease-backed offering provided long-term financing on 76 nursing homes in England that were acquired by Principal Healthcare. Principal, a unit of Omega Health Care Investors, a REIT based in Ann Arbor, Michigan, bought the properties from nursing-home operators, which then leased them back. Principal used the proceeds to reduce the balance of credit facilities that it tapped to close the acquisitions. The bonds were denominated in pounds.

Issuer/Date Closed	US $MM	Class	US$	UK £	S&P/Moodys/Fitch/Duff	Sub %	Mature	Ave. Life	Bond Rate	Net Spread
Westminster Health Care Finance Ltd.	322.2	A	214.8	130.0	AA//AA/	33.3%	07/05/28	19.90	UK 8/21 6.89	+190
Closed: 11/5/99		B	90.9	55.0	BBB//BBB/	5.1%	07/05/30	30.00	UK 6/28 8.05	+330
		C	16.5	10.0	BB//BB/		07/05/30	30.00	UK 6/28 12.26	+750

Westminster Health Care of London securitized mortgages on 84 health-care facilities that it owns and operates. The properties were located throughout the United Kingdom. The bonds were denominated in pounds and acquired primarily by UK pension funds.

Issuer/Date Closed	US $MM	Class	US$	UK £	S&P/Moodys/Fitch/Duff	Sub %	Mature	Ave. Life	Bond Rate	Net Spread
U.K. Care No. 1 Ltd	322.2	A-1	282.2	175.0	AAA//AAA	12.4%	10/01/31		UK 12/28 6.30	180
Closed: 2/17/00		A-2	96.7	60.0	A//A		10/01/31		UK 12/28 7.50	300

BUPA Care Homes securitized a 35-year loan on 116 nursing homes that it owns. The properties contain 4,200 units and are operated by BUPA.

Total Operating Co. CMBS	$3,785 ($4,993 million including transactions for which we have insufficient information)

Sources: Commercial Mortgage Alert and Salomon Smith Barney.

presale material available from the rating agencies and current industry-specific research.

The first Citibank deal, Sonar 1 plc in December 1994, demonstrated a significant capital markets financing advantage, with 86% of the loans rated triple A at a cost of LIBOR plus 30bp (basis points). The issue had a 25-year term, with the coupon stepping up after six years to LIBOR plus 60bp, creating a classic early anticipated repayment date. In recent years, operating company issuers have moved to fixed-rate classes. A recent transaction, U.K. Care No. 1 Ltd. (February 2000), was a £322 million issue with 87% rated triple A at a yield of 6.3%. The £60 million single-A rated class had a coupon of 7.5% (300bp over the U.K. bond).

With single-A rated CMBSs at a 300bp spread, the U.K. market appears to offer significant value relative to North American CMBS spreads. However, on an all-in-yield basis, the yields are about the same, because the long-term gilt had been trading 50bp–150bp lower than U.S. Treasuries. Overall, CMBS represents a very efficient method for U.K. operating companies to raise long-term funding. We expect to see further growth in U.K. operating company CMBS issuance in the next few years.

Multiborrower Conduit Transactions

Several issuers have attempted multiborrower CMBS transactions, with limited success. In total, we track eight transactions containing US$1.98 billion in issuance (see Exhibit 28.3). The early issues between 1995 and mid-1998 all achieved pricing in line with North American floating-rate CMBS. These early issues achieved triple-A pricing of 15bp to 35bp over LIBOR, with single-A rated paper pricing at sub-100bp.

Since the 1998 capital markets crisis, multiloan CMBS transactions have priced triple-A floating classes at roughly LIBOR plus 50bp with the single-A rated floating notes pricing at 100bp to 125bp over LIBOR. At these levels, it is hard for multiloan CMBS issuance to make economic sense. This is especially true in the United Kingdom, where the mortgage loan pricing of some European banks is not tied to the capital markets. In many instances, cheap mortgage financing is available from institutions that are not required to assess a significant capital risk allocation to mortgage loans, or because government finance guarantees subsidize the mortgage rate being offered on commercial properties. The net effect is that U.K. and European mortgage rates are often significantly below North American mortgage rates, while North American floating-rate CMBS spreads have been 10bp to 20bp tighter than U.K. CMBS spreads (triple A through triple B) (see Exhibit 28.3). Since the first quarter of 2000, this floating-rate CMBS gap has widened as North American CMBS spreads have tightened to 20bp to 25bp over LIBOR for triple-A paper.

EXHIBIT 28.3 United Kingdom CMBS Issuance—Multi Borrower Conduit Pools

Issuer/Date Closed	US $MM	Class	US$	UK £	S&P/Moodys/ Fitch/Duff	Sub %	Mature	Ave. Life	Bond Rate	Net Spread
Acres (No. 1) PLC	175.3	A	147.3	91.4	Aaa	16.0%	03/15/05	2.10	1 mo LIBOR +25	+20
Closed: 3/29/95		M1	19.3	12	Aa2	5.0%	03/15/05	4.00	1 mo LIBOR +95	+90
		M2	8.7	5.4	Baa2				+130	

35 loans on mixed commercial properties in England and Wales. The mortgages were originated by United Bank of Kuwait. The offering enabled the bank to remove assets from its books, thereby gaining fresh funds for new loans. All of the properties had tenants with long-term leases. One-third were investment-grade or governmental tenants. The notes were listed on the London exchange. Class M2 was retained by the United Bank of Kuwait but was expected to be sold to private clients of the bank.

Acres (No. 2) PLC	186.7	A	151.5	98.45	AAA///	18.9%	04/28/07	3.15	3 mo LIBOR +15	+15
Closed: 6/28/96		M1	26.3	17.1	A///	4.8%	04/28/07	4.95	3 mo LIBOR +45	+45
		M2	8.9	5.75	BBB///					

Loans on mixed commercial properties in Great Britain. The mortgages were originated by United Bank of Kuwait. The Eurobonds were listed on the London exchange. Class M2 was retained by the issuer.

PARCS Ltd.	229.4	1	208.0	128.9	AA-/Aa3//	9.3%	04/30/04	3.58	3 mo LIBOR +24	+24
Closed: 5/14/97		2	6.0	3.7	A-/A2//	6.7%	04/30/04	4.83	3 mo LIBOR +40	+40
		3	6.1	3.8	BBB/Baa2//	4.1%	04/30/04	4.83		
		4	9.4	5.8			04/30/04			

Citibank International securitized mortgages from its portfolio recycle funds for new originations. Mortgages were backed by office buildings (96%) and retail properties. The 24 properties were located in England and Wales, with a concentration in the London area. Each property had a different owner. Twenty of the properties had one tenant. Most of the leases had a maturity date before 2009. The collateral balance was actually $328 million. Citibank retained a 30% interest in the pool, divided proportionately among each of the deal's classes. The securities were listed on the Luxembourg Exchange.

Acres (No. 3) PLC	193.2	A	160.3	97.8	/Aaa//	17.0%		4.15	3 mo LIBOR +15	+17
Closed: 6/24/97		M-1	23.2	14.1	/A1//	5.0%		4.99	3 mo LIBOR +40	+42.25
		M-2	9.7	5.9	/Baa2//			4.91	3 mo LIBOR +62.5	+64.5

Mortgages on 96 retail, office and industrial properties in the United Kingdom. United Bank of Kuwait securitized the mortgages to recycle funds for new originations. The bonds were listed on the London exchange.

SASCO Europe PLC, 1998-C1	170.1	A	133.2	79.7	AA/Aa2/AA/	21.7%	03/15/23	3.00	1 mo LIBOR +35	+35
Closed: 4/3/98		M	16.5	9.9	BBB/Baa2/B BB/	12.0%	03/15/23	6.10	1 mo LIBOR +140	+140
		B-1	8.9	5.3	BB/Ba2/BB/	6.8%	03/15/23	6.10	1 mo LIBOR +300	+300
		B-2	11.5	6.9	NR	0.0%	03/15/23	6.10	1 mo LIBOR +400	+400

Mortgages originated from 1988 to 1991 by Barclays Mercantile Business Finance. The pool consisted of performing (79.9% of the pool balance), subperforming (1.3%), and nonperforming (18.8%) loans. There was also a reserve fund and a liquidity account. All of the properties were located in the United Kingdom. A Lehman entity, Platform Commercial Mortgage, acquired the loans in April 1997 and cashed out of part of its investment through the securitization.

European Loan Conduit BV, No. 1	272.4	A	217.9	136.2	AAA///	20.0%	01/27/08	4.50	3 mo LIBOR +55	+55
Closed: 8/27/99		B	16.3	10.2	AA///	14.0%	01/27/08	6.50	3 mo LIBOR +75	+75
		C	10.9	6.8	A///	10.0%	01/27/08	6.50	3 mo LIBOR +120	+120
		D	27.2	17.0	BBB///	0.0%	01/27/08	6.20	3 mo LIBOR +225	+225

Morgan Stanley securitized conduit-style mortgages that it had originated in the previous year. All of the loans carry fixed rates. An interest-rate swap was used to ensure that there were sufficient payments for the floating-rate securities.

European Loan Conduit BV, No. 2	574.5	A	448.1	280.4	AAA///	22.0%	10/22/08	5.07	3 mo LIBOR +55	+55
Closed: 12/8/99		B	43.1	27.0	AA///	14.5%	10/22/08	6.62	3 mo LIBOR +75	+75
		C	31.6	19.8	A///	9.0%	10/22/08	6.62	3 mo LIBOR +125	+125
		D	34.5	21.6	BBB///	3.0%	10/22/08	6.87	3 mo LIBOR +250	+250
		E	17.2	10.8	BB///	0.0%	10/22/08	6.24	3 mo LIBOR +450	+450

Morgan Stanley securitized conduit-style mortgages that it had originated in the previous year on 105 commercial properties and 272 pubs in England, Scotland, Wales, and Northern Ireland. About 30% of the underlying properties were located in the London area. All of the loans carry fixed rates. An interest-rate swap was used to ensure that there were sufficient payments for the floating-rate securities.

Paternoster Securitization PLC, No.1	178.2	A	146.1	88.9	/Aaa/AAA/	18.0%	02/15/09	2.32	3 mo LIBOR +50	+50
Closed: 11/8/99		B	20.4	12.45	/A2/A/	6.6%	02/15/09	4.53	3 mo LIBOR +100	+100
		C	11.7	7.1	/Baa2/BBB/		02/15/09	4.53	3 mo LIBOR +225	+225

London-based Charterhouse Bank, a unit of Credit Commercial de France, securitized mortgages it had originated, as well as future originations. The loans, backed by properties in Great Britain, had a weighted-average seasoning of 1.2 years. The collateral pool included a reserve to purchase future originations. The collateral for the loans was a mix of industrial, office, retail, restaurant, pub, hotel, and garage properties. A third of the properties were concentrated in the London area.

Total Multi Loan CMBS	$1,980									

Sources: Commercial Mortgage Alert and Salomon Smith Barney.

Many institutions believe that multiborrower CMBS pools are not economically feasible, given the tight mortgage spreads and the wide CMBS issuance spreads. Originators blamed the tight mortgage spreads on European banks that have liberal capital allocation rules for commercial mortgages. We would expect this factor to disappear with the increasing alignment of EC banking legislation and continuing banking consolidations. *The future of multiborrower CMBS issuance in the United Kingdom will depend on whether U.K. floating-rate CMBS spreads tighten sufficiently following the recent moves in North American CMBS spreads. Relative to North American floating-rate CMBS spreads, U.K. spreads look cheap, and this in and of itself should result in a tightening of U.K. floating-rate CMBS spreads in the near term.*

Single-Asset/Issuer CMBS

A significant focus of U.K. CMBS issuance has been single-asset issuance (see Exhibit 28.4). Since 1997, there have been five transactions totaling more than US$5.7 billion. These first transactions were based almost entirely on the credit rating of a single tenant or entity. The early-1997 transactions were smaller issues financing assets that could have been financed by a single lender. In early 1997, single-asset CMBS issues had a significant financing cost advantage versus traditional mortgage rates, with transactions such as Mooncrest Funding PLC achieving a triple-A cost of LIBOR plus 17.5bp. This Citibank transaction was issued as one £205 million triple-A class guaranteed by CAPMAC. However, since 1998, CMBS pricing has not been interest rate competitive with the portfolio mortgage lending market. Single-asset transactions since late 1997 have only taken place if the underlying assets have been too large for any one lender to finance, leaving the CMBS market as the most efficient method to share participation in the loan.

Recent transactions have all been backed by trophy assets on prime real estate, which real estate lenders view as stable, safe investments:

1. *MS Mortgage Finance (Broadgate) PLC* was a large, $2.5 billion issue that financed a 3.3-million-square-foot office complex near London's financial district. This transaction stands out, because it was structured as £100 million of secured notes that were not permitted to prepay (even in default) before £1.4 billion of unsecured notes. The British legal system's strong creditor rights enabled the agencies and investors to feel comfortable with the loan's unsecured structure.
2. *Trafford Centre Finance Ltd* was a $983.5 million regional mall that achieved subordination of 36% at the triple-A level, indicating the

EXHIBIT 28.4 United Kingdom CMBS Issuance—Single Asset/Borrowers

Issuer/Date Closed	US $MM	Class	US$	UK £	S&P/Moodys/ Fitch/Duff	Sub %	Mature	Ave. Life	Bond Rate	Net Spread
Northavon Investments Ltd., 3/14/97	124.3	A	124.3	77.6	//AA-		8.120	24.20	24 yr UK 8.26	+74

A mortgage and a 30-year lease on a 320,000-sq.-ft. office building in Bristol, England. The property was the headquarters for Sun Life Assurance, a unit of AXA-UAP, the large French insurance company. The financing was part of a sale-leaseback transaction. Sun Life sold the building to Dana Credit of Toledo, Ohio. Dana then leased it back to the insurer. The sale removed the asset from Sun Life's balance sheet, easing the insurer's capital requirements. Fitch's rating was tied to the long-term debt rating of Sun Life, which had a triple-net lease on the property. The securities were denominated in pounds. The notes were priced off of the 8% UK government bond due in June 2021, which was yielding about 7.425% on the pricing date.

Issuer/Date Closed	US $MM	Class	US$	UK £	S&P/Moodys/ Fitch/Duff	Sub %	Mature	Ave. Life	Bond Rate	Net Spread
Mooncrest Funding PLC, 3/19/97	204.9	A	204.9	128.1	AAA/Aaa//		07/18/12	9.20	3 mo LIBOR +17.5	+17.5

A mortgage and net lease on a 350,000-sq.-ft. London office building occupied by Coopers & Lybrand. The transaction helped an unidentified party finance the acquisition of the property. The notes, offered in the Euromarket, were denominated in pounds (128.1 million). The securities were guaranteed by CapMAC. In July 2002, the spread was to increase to 45bp.

Issuer/Date Closed	US $MM	Class	US$	UK £	S&P/Moodys/ Fitch/Duff	Sub %	Mature	Ave. Life	Bond Rate	Net Spread
Canary Wharf Finance PLC Closed: 4/12/97	939	A	456.6	270.0	AAA///AAA	51.3%	22/10/27	16.30	8% UKT 2/15 7.23	+72
		B	135.3	80.0	AA///AA	36.9%	22/10/27	20.10	8% UKT 2/15 7.43	+92
		C	202.9	120.0	A///A	15.3%	22/10/27	23.00	8% UKT 2/15 +125	+125
		D	143.7	85.0	BBB///BBB		22/10/27	5.00	3 mo LIBOR +110	+110

A mortgage on 2.1 million sq. ft. of office space in five buildings at the Canary Wharf complex in London, plus $76 million of reserves. The properties, which had an estimated value of $1.2 billion, were: 1 Canada Square, 25 North Colonnade, 30 South Colonnade, 7 Westferry Circus, and two floors of 10 Cabot Square. There was also a $110 million liquidity facility to ensure that timely payments would be made to bondholders. The Reichmann partnership issued the bonds to refinance debt and raise working capital. The securities were denominated in pounds. The coupon on Class A was to step up to 6.25% in October 1999, to 7.75% in October 2000 and to an unspecified level after October 2006. The coupon on Class D was to step up to LIBOR plus 310 bp in January 2003. Barclays de Zoette Wedd and Hongkong and Shanghai Bank served as co-managers. The notes were listed on the London Stock Exchange.

Issuer/Date Closed	US $MM	Class	US$	UK £	S&P/Moodys/ Fitch/Duff	Sub %	Mature	Ave. Life	Bond Rate	Net Spread
MS Mortgage Finance (Broadgate) PLC Closed: 5/14/99	2,520	A-1	532.0	325.0	AAA/Aaa/AAA/AAA	49.0%	07/05/26	8.50	3 mo LIBOR +55	+55
		A-2	507.5	310.0	AAA/Aaa/AAA/AAA	49.0%	07/05/31	19.30	U.K. Gov't Bond 5.93	+122
		A-3	245.6	150.0	AAA/Aaa/AAA/AAA	49.0%	07/05/33	31.10	U.K. Gov't Bond 5.91	+132
		B	368.3	225.0	AA/Aa2/AA/AA	34.4%	07/05/34	29.10	U.K. Gov't Bond 6.29	+170
		C-1	286.5	175.0	A/A2/A/A	23.0%	07/05/14	9.10	3 mo LIBOR +130	+130
		C-2	286.5	175.0	A/A2/A/A	11.7%	07/05/38	31.10	U.K. Gov't Bond 6.65	+207
		D	294.7	180.0	BBB/Baa2/BBB/BBB		07/05/14	3.50	3 mo LIBOR +165	+165

The transaction enabled British Land to refinance debt on its 3.3 million-sq.-ft. Broadgate Estates complex in London. The bonds were technically backed by £100 million of secured notes, which were not permitted to prepay before £1.4 billion of unsecured notes issued by British Land entities. The transaction also contained a large $200 million liquidity facility sized to allow for a longer workout schedule that might occur because of the unsecured nature of the collateral. Class A-1 was priced at 55bp over LIBOR through October 2007. After that date, the issuer had the option to reissue a similar amount of new bonds at a spread of 150bp over LIBOR. The bonds were denominated in pounds. The bonds were sold to European investors.

Issuer/Date Closed	US $MM	Class	US$	UK £	S&P/Moodys/ Fitch/Duff	Sub %	Mature	Ave. Life	Bond Rate	Net Spread
Trafford Centre Finance Ltd. Closed: 2/28/00	983.5	A-1	80.6	50.0	AAA//AAA/	36.1%	07/05/26	8.50	3 mo LIBOR +51	51
		A-2	548.2	340.0	AAA//AAA/	36.1%	07/05/31	19.30	U.K.T 12/28 6.50	170
		B	193.5	120.0	AA//AA/	16.4%	07/05/33	31.10	U.K. T 6/21 7.03	200
		D-1	80.6	50.0	BBB//BBB/		07/05/34	29.10	3 mo LIBOR +165	165
		D-2	80.6	50.0	BBB//BBB/		07/05/14	9.10	U.K. T 6/21 +320	320

Peel Holdings raised long-term finance on Trafford Centre, a 1.4 million-sq.-ft. regional mall in Manchester. The mall was appraised at £810 million, making this a 75% LTV investment-grade loan. Peel will use some of the proceeds to refinance £340 million of pounds of debt on the property, which opened in September 1998. Peel Holdings originally launched the offering last fall, but delayed because of weak demand for the fixed-rate portion.

| Total Single Asset CMBS: | $5,710 | | | | | | | | | |

Sources: Commercial Mortgage Alert and Salomon Smith Barney.

mall's strong retail position. *With the successful placement of Trafford Centre, the U.K. CMBS market has evolved from investing in the underlying tenants' credit rating to relying on the underlying commercial property value.*

The two recent U.K. office single-asset CMBS issues had strong investment-grade tenants and long-term leases that make purchasing them akin to buying a diverse pool of investment-grade corporate bonds—only in this case, the investors were also secured by the underlying value of the real estate. The subordination levels on these assets at the triple-A level are slightly higher than what we would expect to see on a trophy North American asset, but then credit-enhancement levels decline below the average North American levels at the single-A and triple-B levels. *This subordination difference is mostly due to the fact that the credits backing the U.K. asset are usually long-term and investment-grade, whereas a typical North American securitization would likely contain nonrated tenancy and balloon exposure at maturity, which requires more credit support subordination in the lower classes.* Given the strong investor demand for this premium product, we expect to see more of this type of issuance in the near term.

28.3 THE U.K. COMMERCIAL REAL ESTATE MARKET

Similar to the 1991–1992 North American recession, the U.K. recession had a severe impact on commercial real estate. Therefore, it is not surprising that the U.K. commercial real estate recovery has mirrored the North American recovery. *Primarily, while the economy has been exhibiting tremendous growth, funding of commercial real estate development has been on a prelet, no-risk basis. This conservative development funding has created a situation in which current commercial property vacancy rates are at their lowest levels in a decade, while valuation yields remain relatively high.*

Readers of our U.S. research are familiar with the comfort we take from commercial real estate yields being 300bp greater than those of long-term government bonds. A similar U.K. analysis demonstrates a positive 200bp differential (see Exhibit 28.5).

From a historical perspective, the current 200bp property yield advantage suggests that commercial property values are conservative. Prior to the last recession, U.K. properties were yielding 300bp to 400bp less than the long-term gilt rate, suggesting that U.K. property investors were counting on long-term property appreciation to make up their property's return shortfall. *The current commercial property yield advantage of 200bp plus over gilts suggests that U.K. commercial property investors have built healthy positive current-yield expectations into their property valuations.* Specifically, if the U.K. economy were to enter into a recession in the near term, we would expect the property valuation yield to remain constant or follow gilt yields down, while property cash flows should remain stable, owing to the market's long-term lease structure and low vacancy rate. Alternatively, if the economy were to continue to grow, pushing up interest rates, the gilt yield could rise 200bp before it would apply significant upward pressure on property valuation yields (during the depths of the

EXHIBIT 28.5   Ten-Year Gilt Yield versus IPD Equivalent Yield*

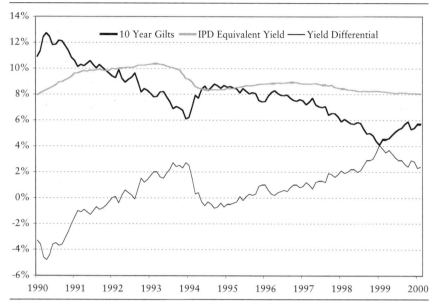

* IPD Equivalent Yield is defined as the rate that discounts the property's projected cash flow
(allowing for reviews and expires but not rental growth) to the capital value.
Sources: Investment Property Databank and Datastream.

previous recession, the IPD yield reached a high of 10%). *Overall, we expect that U.K. commercial property will demonstrate excellent value stability over the next few years.*

The London office market provides a good data source to investigate typical U.K. commercial real estate supply and demand dynamics and good
background for our office transaction overview. The London office market
can be divided into three distinct submarkets, all with unique characteristics.

The West End Office Market

The West End office market is London's largest. It comprises 120 million
square feet, 30 million of which are Class A. The West End market demonstrates significant tenant diversity, with tenants ranging from public service,
professionals, manufacturing, insurance, and finance. However, city planning restrictions limit the submarket's supply, because any new product requires significant site redevelopment. These strong planning restrictions
typically create prime office buildings with no more than five to eight

floors, a small floor plate, and total area of less than 200,000 square feet. This restricted supply and the prestige of the office market has created a low 4% vacancy rate in the West End (see Exhibit 28.6).

Most London research firms are projecting that in the near term (2000 to 2003), new office supply will range from 0.5 to 2 million square feet per annum, with demand being two to three times that amount (the 1999 West End take-up was 3.9 million square feet). This demand/supply imbalance is expected to push West End prime rents above 1988/1989 levels over the next several years (see Exhibit 28.7).

City of London Office Market

The City of London office market has traditionally constituted London's financial district, with 81 million square feet of office space, of which 44 million square feet is Class A. This office market is somewhat less diverse than the West End market, with insurance and banking tenants taking the majority of space. However, in recent years, technology and manufacturing tenants have taken more space. Similar to the West End market, City

EXHIBIT 28.6   London Office Vacancy Rate by Submarket, 1987–1999

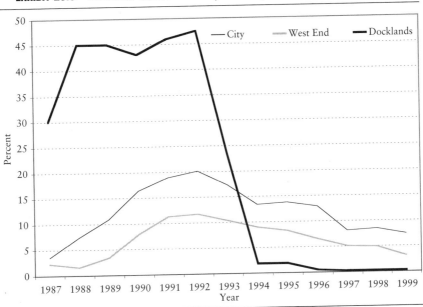

Source: FPD Savills International Property Consultants.

EXHIBIT 28.7   Historical and Projected Prime Office Rents, 1981–2003*

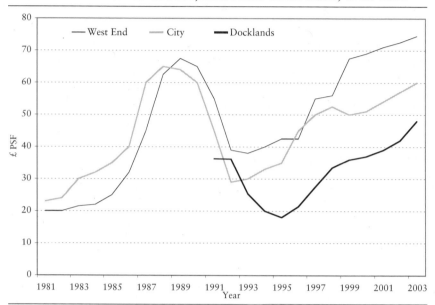

* The prime rent relates to the best rent payable for grade-A quality accommodation in the best
location within any given market.
Source: FPD Savills International Property Consultants.

planning restrictions have limited the market's growth, forcing new development at the northern edge of the City market. The four million square
foot Broadgate office complex that was securitized in 1999 is a prime example of office development's being forced north, away from the Thames
River. Office developers have been able to offer larger buildings in this market, but still face severe restrictive planning guidelines (i.e., buildings cannot
affect the view of St. Paul's Cathedral). So, while buildings can offer larger
blocks of space than the West End market, office buildings offering more
than 500,000 square feet of space are rare. *As a result, the current City office market has only one location available that can accommodate a tenant
requirement greater than 200,000 square feet.*

City real estate brokers and appraisers expect that 2 to 5 million square
feet of space could be added annually to this market for the next few years,
as sites such as Broadgate still have a few development sites. This level of development is needed to meet the historic City demand, which has run at a
take-up rate of 4 to 4.5 million square feet since 1996. In Exhibit 28.6, we
show that the City has the highest vacancy rate of the three submarkets, at

7%. Even so, this tight vacancy rate means *prime office rents should edge up to the £60 per square foot range by 2003* (see Exhibit 28.7).

Docklands Submarket

The Docklands submarket is dominated by the Canary Wharf office complex. This market evolved from a government enterprise zone set up in the east Docklands area of London some 2.5 miles east of the city. Since 1995, Canary Wharf has pushed this submarket to tremendous growth, with roughly 500,000 square feet being added to the market each year and vacancy rates declining to less than 0.5%. In December 1999, the Jubilee metro line was completed to Canary Wharf, putting the submarket on a transportation-access footing even with the other London office markets. Commuter access to the Docklands is now 12 minutes from the City market and 19 minutes from the West End market. Currently, Docklands is London's third-largest office market, with one ownership group controlling more than 6 million square feet of office space.

Unlike London's other two office submarkets, the Docklands are not inhibited by restrictive planning policies. The density plan has been approved to allow further development of 7.5 million square feet and bring the total stock to 13.5 million square feet. The ability to accommodate large users in state-of-the-art specified space at a discount to City and West End rentals continues to draw tenants away from traditional locations. Additions to supply will largely be driven by pre-leasing, and we do not expect a significant element of speculative construction. This will likely drive rental growth and keep the Docklands in balance for the next few years. *Exhibit 28.7 shows that Docklands prime office rents are expected to tighten to City submarket office rents over the next three years.*

London Office Conclusions

A review of London's office market paints a tight supply picture, which is pushing market office rents up. As further backup to this strong real estate story, BH2, a research firm, undertook a study to estimate the highest possible supply pipeline for London office space over the next five years. Under BH2's study, no further space leasing was assumed to take place, and all space that could be developed was developed. The BH2 study determined that the maximum possible office completions would be 4.0 million square feet by the end of 2002, reaching 13.2 million square feet by the end of 2004. *BH2's maximum available space analysis projects a significant office space shortfall, given that office take-up in London has been running at an annual pace of 6.6 million square feet. Overall, the London office market demonstrates very strong underlying fundamentals.*

EXHIBIT 28.8 Retail Warehouses, Shopping Centers, and Standard Shops—
Rental Growth (YoY)

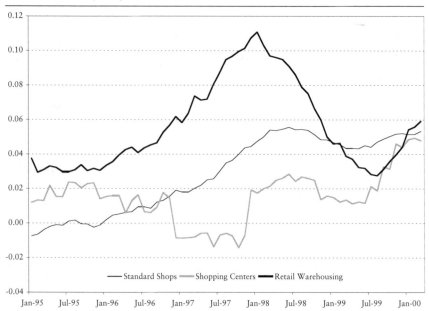

Source: Investment Property Databank.

The U.K. Retail Market

The retail property market outlook is similar to that for the office market. While the U.K. economy has been experiencing a strong retail growth environment, construction has been limited. In Exhibit 28.8, we present retail rental growth on a year-over-year basis. The low retail supply has been further restricted by out-of-town planning departments, which have curtailed retail development. We are aware of no new regional shopping malls that are currently planned. In Exhibit 28.9, we show that the retail development pipeline is at its lowest level in 10 years.

In the *Salomon Smith Barney UK Property Sector Review,*[2] Georgina Browning predicted that annual shopping center completions for 2000 to 2002 would stay at roughly 300,000 square meters and that the retail landlord position would remain strong, unless some significant retailer liquidations freed up large portfolios of vacant retail units. *This low level of retail*

---

[2] *UK Property Sector Review, Who Loves Ya, Baby?,* Georgina Browning, et al., Salomon Smith Barney, February 23, 2000.

EXHIBIT 28.9   Shopping Center Development Pipeline, 1990–1999

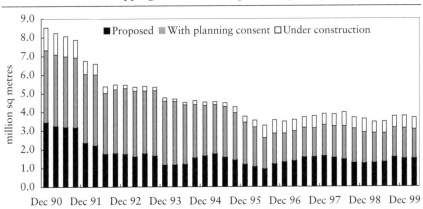

Source: CB Hillier Parker.

supply should support very stable retail property cash flows in the future, providing excellent candidates for CMBS investors.

28.4 U.K. CMBS MARKET CONCLUSIONS

The U.K. CMBS market demonstrates several characteristics that should make it an ideal environment for CMBS issuance and provide improving CMBS performance for investors:

- *CMBS investors can rely on the U.K. legal system to maintain tenants' obligations and preserve the bondholders' security claim on the property.* Specifically, the mortgage claim on an asset in most cases has lender creditor rights that are stronger than many of the laws in the United States. The original tenant covenants are preserved through at least one tenant assignment of the space and usually contractually preserved in the leasing agreement back to the original tenant. Given these legal features, CMBS investors should experience strong creditor rights in any economic stress scenario that may transpire.
- *The underlying collateral fundamentals of commercial real estate are very solid by any measure.* Vacancy rates are at new lows, while property yields exceed long-term gilt rates by more than 200bp. The 1991/1992 recession has definitely had an impact on the funding and development of potentially competitive commercial real estate supply. In the near term, we expect that supply will remain restricted. However,

if the U.K. economy continues to grow at its current pace, we would expect speculative development to start to have an impact on the underlying real estate fundamentals. Therefore (just as in North America), U.K. CMBS investors should review the strength of the underlying tenant roll, the tenure of the leases, and the value of the underlying real estate.

- *Recent U.K. triple-A CMBS floating-rate spreads are 20bp to 30bp wide of U.S. floating-rate spreads, suggesting strong relative value for pound or Eurodollar-based investors.* Relative to triple-A U.K. floating-rate credit cards, floating-rate CMBSs have a 20bp to 30bp differential, 10bp to 15bp wide of the usual 10bp to 20bp U.S. CMBS/credit card differential. Converting these spreads to U.S. dollars, for dollar-based investors, has a cost of 1bp to 2bp, suggesting a U.K. net spread advantage of 12bp to 17bp.

- *Relative to long-term U.K. government debt, fixed-rate triple-A and double-A CMBSs seem to offer significant excess spread relative to U.S. CMBS fixed-rate spreads.* This is to be expected given that a shortage of gilt issuance has inverted the U.K. yield curve to the point where long-term gilts are trading 150bp tight of the U.S. Treasury curve. This shortage of long-term, highly rated U.K. bonds is causing triple-A and double-A U.K. CMBSs to trade tight relative to comparable U.S. CMBSs. However, lower-rated single-A and triple-B fixed-rate CMBSs are trading wider than similarly-rated U.S. CMBSs, making their all-in yields similar. There has not been enough U.K. CMBS issuance to draw an overall conclusion on fixed-rate spreads. Rather, potential CMBS investors should compare government benchmark spreads and all-in yields at the time of purchase.

- *Given that CMBSs are a fairly new product, the market demands a liquidity premium.* While limited secondary trading does take place, we expect the market to have a wide bid-ask spread as long as issuance volume remains low and no homogeneous issuance standards exist. Investors in this market should anticipate a buy-and-hold strategy in the short term. For the long term, we expect the U.K. CMBS market to become more liquid in three to five years.

In conclusion, the U.K. CMBS market offers similar or better collateral than U.S. CMBSs, while providing collateral exposure to a different economic cycle. In the long run, we expect that U.K. CMBS spreads will decrease as the U.K. CMBS market demonstrates strong collateral performance and increasing liquidity. Asset-backed investors with U.K. or international investment allocations should consider U.K. CMBSs as a good asset diversification allocation, with the potential for improving price performance.

CHAPTER 29

The Mortgage
Market in Australia

Peter DiMartino and Robert Young

Securitization activity in Australia has increased significantly in recent years with mortgages being the dominant asset-type securitized. Australian MBS securitization has quadrupled since 1996; mortgages accounted for 56% of Australia's total securitized issuance volume in 1998 and 62% in 1999 (see Exhibit 29.1).

EXHIBIT 29.1　New Issuance in Australia (by Sector), 1999

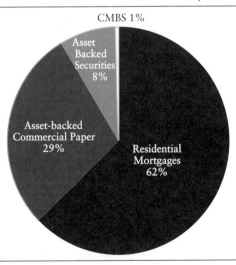

Source: S&P Australia and New Zealand Structured Finance 2000.

Australian mortgage lenders underwrite about 400,000 to 500,000 loans each year, according to S&P. The most common mortgage loan is a 25-year fully amortizing variable rate product secured by first-lien residential property. Banks have traditionally dominated the Australian mortgage origination market, but have been challenged by nonbank competitors, mortgage managers in particular, since the early 1990s.

29.1 AUSTRALIAN OFFSHORE ISSUERS AND VOLUME

The advent of Australian MBS offshore securitization took place in 1997 as issuers sought to diversify their funding sources. In 1999, more Australian MBSs were issued offshore than domestically, as volume topped US$8 billion (of that total, only US$4 billion was issued domestically). Most of Australia's offshore MBSs were originally marketed in Europe. However, U.S. investors are playing an increasingly important role in Australia.

Westpac issued the first global transaction (WST 1998-1G) in June 1998.[1] Global securitizations, typically, are marketed to European and U.S. investors. After a repeat global issuance from Westpac in May 1999, St. George Bank (Crusade Global Trust No. 1 of 1999) was the second issuer to complete a global deal, in September 1999.[2] In March 2000, Commonwealth Bank of Australia (CBA) issued its first global transaction (Series 2000-1G Medallion Trust). Exhibit 29.2 shows historical Australian MBSs issued domestically, in Europe, and globally, since 1995.[3]

The largest issuers of combined domestic and cross-border Australian MBS in 1999 were PUMA, with a 16% market share, followed by Westpac, at 15%, and RAMS, with 14%. In 2000, however, the largest issuers (combined domestic and cross-border) to date are Interstar, with 16% market share, followed by Medallion (CBA), with 15%, and AMS, with 14%. These institutions have laid the foundation for programmatic issuance. Exhibit 29.3 shows issuance volume outstanding for the top Australian MBS lenders.

The rate of growth in offshore issuance is subject to currency swap-pricing considerations. However, domestic demand in Australia remains robust, albeit for a smaller volume of issuance. As Australian issuers continue to seek further diversification of funding sources, the U.S. market, in particular, will become increasingly relevant.

---

[1] By global, we mean that the transaction is SEC-registered and listed on the London Stock Exchange.
[2] See Appendix 29H or a detailed description of Australia's global MBS transactions.
[3] See Appendix 29I for a complete list of Australia's domestic, offshore, and global MBS transactions and selected other data.

EXHIBIT 29.2   Australian MBS Issuance, 1995–Present*

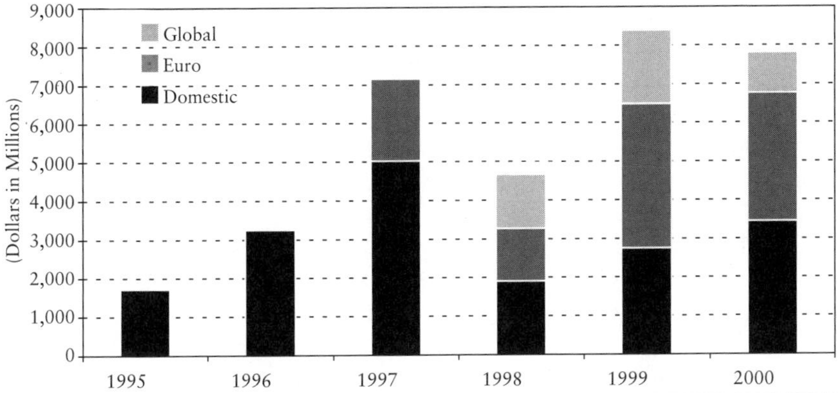

* Up to August 15, 2000.
Source: S&P ABS Performance Watch May 2000, Salomon Smith Barney.

EXHIBIT 29.3   Australian Issuer's Outstanding Issuance Volume and Market Share

Issuer	Number of Deals	Amount of Deals Outstanding (A$)	% of Total Deals Outstanding
Macquarie Securitisation Ltd.	9	7,105,552,151	26.28
RAMS Home Loans	8	3,836,933,016	14.19
Westpac Banking Corp	5	3,565,744,184	13.19
St. George Bank Ltd.	4	2,425,700,000	8.97
Interstar Securities Ltd.	4	1,918,126,586	7.09
Australian Mortgage Securities Ltd.	6	1,611,609,072	5.96
Citibank Ltd.	6	1,014,219,918	3.75
Colonial State Bank	3	1,005,935,272	3.72
National Mutual Funds Management	12	996,297,206	3.69
Commonwealth Bank of Queensland	5	769,733,710	2.85
Fanmac Limited	3	665,507,717	2.46
Adelaide Bank	4	611,845,868	2.26
Priority One (AMP)	1	469,530,950	1.74
FAI Loans	3	384,731,915	1.42
Wide Bay Capricorn	2	244,718,173	0.91
Suncorp Metway Ltd.	1	179,568,949	0.66
The Rock Building Society	1	174,077,756	0.64
Bendigo Bank	1	55,395,263	0.20
Total Outstanding (A$):		27,035,227,707	

Source: S&P ABS performance Watch, February 2000.

29.2 BANK AND NONBANK ISSUANCE

Although Australia's major and regional banks have pursued securitization[4] as an alternative to funding in the unsecured corporate and equity markets, nonbank mortgage originators rely on securitization as their principal source of funding. However, Australia's domestic investor base has at times been constrained in its ability to absorb new supply. As an alternative strategy, Australian issuers began marketing their MBSs in Europe in 1997, completing three such transactions that year. Global Australian MBS issuance is in its infancy, but it is building momentum—Australian MBS issuers completed six offshore transactions in 1998. Exhibit 29.4 shows Australia's major bank and nonbank issuers, as well as the year of their first offshore issuance.

Nonbanks dominated Australia's MBS market early on. With the exception of 1998, nonbanks have issued more MBSs than banks every year since 1995. One reason for this is that Australia's nonbanks do not have a balance sheet that allows them to warehouse loans in the same manner as banks do. However, as shown in Exhibit 29.5 banks have been responsible for a meaningful share of issuance volume in recent years. With two of Australia's four major banks preparing to issue into the U.S. market before year-end, the banks' market share is expected to be larger in 2000 than that of nonbanks.

EXHIBIT 29.4 Australia's Major Bank and Nonbank Lenders

Bank Lenders	First Offshore Issuance
Westpac Banking Corp (Westpac)	1997
Commonwealth Bank of Australia (CBA)	2000
St. George Bank Ltd. (SGB)	1998
Australia & New Zealand Banking Group (ANZ)	2001[a]
National Australia Bank	2000[b]

Nonbank Lenders	First Offshore Issuance
PUMA Management Ltd. (PUMA)	1997
Registered Australian Mortgage Securities (RAMS)	1999
Australian Mortgage Securities (AMS)	1999
Members Equity	2000
Interstar	2000
Residential Mortgage Acceptance Corp. (RESIMAC)	1999

[a] Anticipated issuance in 2001.
[b] Anticipated issuance in 2000.
Source: Salomon Smith Barney.

---

[4] Historically, Australian banks have securitized a small portion of their mortgage originations. We believe, on average, the securitization rate to be between 10% and 20%.

EXHIBIT 29.5   Australian MBS Issuance—Banks versus Nonbanks

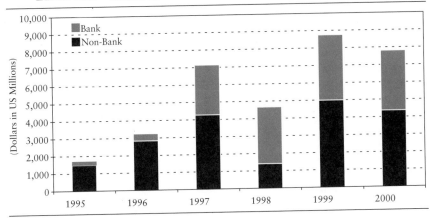

Source: S&P ABS Performance Watch May 2000, Salomon Smith Barney.

In the meantime, U.S. investor demand for international spread products has grown, helping to pave the way for Australia's burgeoning global MBS market. Australian MBSs provide U.S. investors with an alternative investment choice and an opportunity to obtain high-quality mortgage assets from lenders seeking to diversify their funding sources. We believe that the market for global Australian MBSs will accelerate in the next year, with debut and repeat issuance from bank and nonbank issuers endeavoring to take advantage of the deep U.S. investor base.

29.3 PRIMARY MORTGAGE MARKET

Australia boasts a home ownership rate of approximately 70% (as shown in Exhibit 29.6). Nearly 40% of homes are owned without a mortgage. Of all homeowners, about 22% purchased their houses within the past three years (as of 1995). Of those, 38% were first-time homebuyers.

The strong home ownership culture is accompanied by very low default rates and prepayment rates that are significantly less reactive to interest rates than prime mortgages with similar balances originated in the U.S. market. *Contributing to low delinquency rates is the fact that more than 60% of the mortgage borrowing population in Australia make their monthly mortgage payment via direct debit. Another 10% to 20% have their mortgage payment deducted from their paycheck.*

EXHIBIT 29.6   Profile of Australian Residential Housing

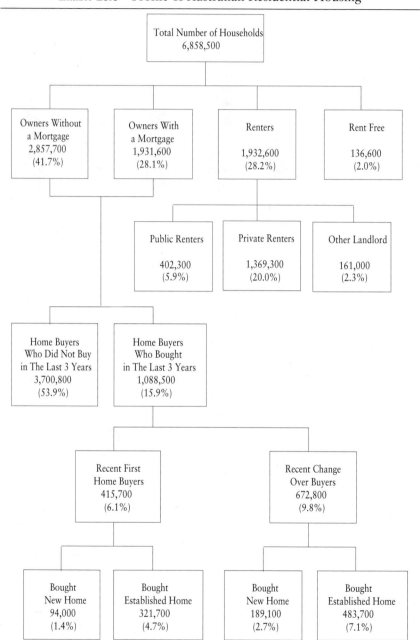

Source: "Australian Residential MBS Criteria," Standard & Poor's.

Loan Types

The Australian mortgage market is complicated, as competitors offer various features as a way to attract customers. In this section, we describe Australia's loan types.

Variable-Rate Loans   These make up the *majority* of mortgages in Australia. For a *wholly variable loan*, the lender determines the floating interest rate. For a *bank bill rate loan*, which is far less common, the interest rate is set by reference to the professional money market, via either a fixed margin or a variable margin. Interest rates on bank bill rate loans normally vary more frequently than wholly variable loan rates. The main determinant of variable mortgage rates is the cash rate set by the Reserve Bank of Australia. When the Reserve Bank alters the official cash rate, most variable rates change by a similar amount. There are two common variable-rate loans:

- *Standard.* This is the most popular loan type in Australia. Most of them have a term of 25 to 30 years and more features and flexibility than other types of loans.
- *Basic.* Although this type has fewer features and less flexibility than standard loans, these loans offer lower rates, typically about 50bp (basis points) lower than standard loan rates.

Variable-rate loans usually do not have prepayment penalties.

Fixed-Rate Loans   These loans are actually what are called *hybrids* in the United States. In most cases, the rate is fixed for one to five years (7-, 10-, and 15-year fixed-rate periods also exist, but are rare) before automatically converting to a standard variable rate loan. Their biggest advantages: (1) protection against rising interest rates; and (2) level payments during the entire fixed-rate period. A disadvantage in a period of decreasing interest rates is the locked-in rate; *prepayment penalties* (called *break costs* or *exit fees*) often apply to these loans. Usually *break costs* are only payable if market interest rates fall during the fixed-rate term, as they are designed to compensate the lender for having to reinvest repayments at lower interest rates. Under the Consumer Credit Code, lenders can only charge an amount that reflects the cost of early termination. When early repayment benefits the lender (when interest rates increase), some lenders actually compensate borrowers, paying the break cost to them. Recently, fixed-rate loans without prepayment penalties or with only limited penalties (for example, some fixed-rate loans allow the borrower to make additional repayments of up to $20,000 per year without penalty) have become available.

Exhibit 29.7 shows representative Australian and U.S. mortgage rates. *Australian mortgage rates during the past several years appear to have been just as volatile as U.S. mortgage rates.* Yet, Australian mortgage prepayments, as will be discussed, appear to have been very stable during this time.

Other Loan Types   *Introductory "Honeymoon" Loans* start with lower teaser rates (50bp–100bp lower), usually for the first year of the loan, to attract new borrowers, and after the introductory period they convert to standard variable-rate loans. Some restrictions or penalties may apply to refinancing or switching loan types within a certain time period after the honeymoon period.

All-in-One Loans work like bank accounts and often provide a cost-effective means of repaying a mortgage. All of the borrower's income (like salary and rent) is paid directly into this mortgage account. After interest due is deducted, any additional funds offset the outstanding principal. This has the effect of reducing the interest charged on the outstanding principal each day. Additional money is left in the mortgage until it is needed. Access to funds is available via a debit card.

Capped Loans are variable-rate loans that have a preset interest rate ceiling usually valid for one year. These loans not only provide borrowers with protection against rising interest rates, but also allow borrowers to benefit from a decreasing rate environment. In some cases, the variable rate applied after the capped period may be higher than standard variable rates.

EXHIBIT 29.7   Australian and U.S. Mortgage Rates

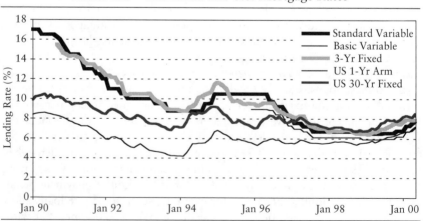

Source: Reserve Bank of Australia, Freddie Mac.

These loans are not common and are normally not included in the collateral for deals because they are difficult to hedge.

Professional Packages are special mortgage packages aimed at attracting professionals and low credit risk borrowers. The packages normally offer reduced interest rates and waive or reduce fees. They may also offer free financial advice and reduced insurance premiums. These loans are not typically found in collateral for deals.

Combination Loans (or Split Loans) allow borrowers to split their loans into fixed- and variable-rate loans to better manage the risks arising from the changes in interest rates. "Splitting" their variable-rate loan into two loans, one variable and one fixed, is how some borrowers have responded to recent rises in interest rates. While not a prepayment from the borrower's perspective, some deals do not allow the new fixed rate loan to remain as part of the collateral, so its balance may show up as a partial prepayment to the investor.

Features of Australian Mortgages

The Australian mortgage is an innovative product that provides borrowers with several vehicles to accommodate their financial needs over the term of the loan. Mortgages can incorporate many of the following features:

- *Redraw* is probably the most notable feature, as it is not a characteristic of typical U.S. mortgages, and it has a significant impact on the cash flow received from the borrower. Redraw gives a borrower the option to withdraw an amount up to the difference in the scheduled and the actual loan balance (so past additional repayments of principal form a sort of savings account that the borrower can tap). This is a feature usually available to borrowers of standard variable-rate loans. It can be conceptually thought of as a negative prepayment since the loan balance increases.

  Redraw loans are often included in MBS transactions and **a redraw does not typically result in the loan being removed from the collateral pool for a deal** (so the negative prepayment concept still applies to securitized collateral). Borrowers typically have to apply to the lender for a redraw. The lender's decision to grant the redraw is at the lender's discretion, but is usually conditional on the two following items: (1) the redraw will not cause the loan to exceed the scheduled principal balance; and (2) the borrower is not currently in arrears. The lender cannot refuse a customer's request to redraw simply because the loan is part of the collateral for a deal. The lender, in turn, is typically entitled to be reimbursed from collateral principal collections received in each period, which are normally more than sufficient to fund the redraws. If the principal collections are insufficient, then the redraws are normally funded by a redraw facility from the lending bank or, in the case of a nonbank, from an adequately rated institution. If still insufficient, re-draw-funding securities may be issued.

■ *Interest-only* is a feature that allows interest-only payments for a spec-ified period and subsequent conversion to an amortizing payment schedule, or interest-only payments for the entire loan term and a lump-sum payment of the principal at the end of the loan term. It is usually chosen by residential property investors to fully utilize the fa-vorable tax treatment they receive (interest is tax-deductible for in-vestor loans). These loans are normally a small proportion of the loans found in deal collateral.

■ *Portability* allows borrowers to keep their loans when they sell their home or investment property and then purchase another home or in-vestment property for which they still need a mortgage. This increas-ingly common feature saves borrowers thousands in discharge costs on the old loan, as well as establishment fees, stamp duty tax, and lender's mortgage insurance[5] on the new one. However, there are significant re-strictions on the use of this facility. Generally, the loan amount must not change, the new property must be of the same or greater value as the old one, and settlement on the sale/purchase of the old/new home must occur on the same day. The fee for making use of this facility varies, but normally is in the neighborhood of a few hundred dollars.

■ *Interest offset* is a feature that allows borrowers to offset interest earned on deposit balances against interest credited to their home loan. By crediting the interest on deposits to the loan account, there is no in-terest income for tax purposes. Redraw and 100% interest offset pro-duce essentially the same results for the borrower and compete against one another as product features.

■ *Payment holiday* is a feature that allows borrowers to prepay and then not send in any payments for some period of time. The payment holiday can continue as long as the sum of the outstanding principal and the ac-crued interest is less than the scheduled principal balance. This feature is also conceptually similar to the redraw feature.

■ *Line of credit (or home equity loan)* allows a borrower to withdraw any amount up to the difference of a preset credit limit and the current loan balance. The credit limit is usually set as a percentage of the property value. These loans are typically not mixed with the more common amor-tizing/interest-only loans found in deal collateral.

■ *Further advances (or top-up facilities),* unlike redraws, result in the borrower's loan balance exceeding the scheduled principal balance. A

---

[5] Lenders mortgage insurance is normally charged as a one-time premium.

borrower typically uses this option to finance home improvements at an interest rate far less than that for an unsecured personal loan. Because a further advance requires the borrower to go through the underwriting process once again, the loan is typically removed from a securitized collateral pool (and so appears as a prepayment to MBS investors). However, some deals include provisions for accommodating further advances. Further advances that take the new LTV ratio above 80% are penalized by S&P in the same way that cash-out refinances are when LTVs rise above 80%.

■ *Parental leave* is a feature that comes with variable loans, and allows eligible borrowers on maternity or paternity leave to reduce their payments for a period of time (typically up to six months).

■ *Switching to fixed rate* is a feature allowing a variable-rate borrower to switch over to a fixed-rate loan, often at no cost.

■ *Repayment frequency* can be weekly and biweekly, as well as monthly. In addition, monthly payment loans are not necessarily due at the beginning of each month as in the United States. For example, if a loan settles on the fifth of a month, a lender can elect to have future repayments due on the fifth of each month.

Mortgage Originators

Banks, regulated by the Australian Prudential Regulatory Authority (APRA),[6] dominate the mortgage market, accounting for roughly 80% of the housing loan market. They have, however, been challenged since the early 1990s by competitors that often do not have the costly branch infrastructure that the banks have. Banks have had a perceived negative image of being large, impersonal corporations, but they have responded to this competition by cutting their rates and being more flexible. This has resulted in reduced lending margins (from 4% to about 1.2%–1.6%) and product innovations (redraw, portability, and interest offset).

Mortgage managers are specialists who generally obtain their funds from securitization, selling the resulting MBSs to investors, as superannuation funds, for example.[7] Besides offering competitive rates, mortgage managers generally try to offer superior customer service. In return for receiving a fee taken from mortgage payments received,[8] they are responsible for arranging

---

[6] The Australian Prudential Regulatory Authority is similar in nature to the Federal Reserve in the United States.

[7] These are retirement funds.

[8] A trustee company receives borrower payments, is responsible for seeing that MBS investors are paid, and also pays the mortgage manager their fee.

the funds for the loan and managing the loan, including credit assessment, monitoring of loan repayments, insurance renewals, interest-rate adjustments, and loan variations. Aussie Home Loans, founded in 1992, started the nonbank home loan industry and is Australia's largest nonbank lender. It offers, for example, the same rates to both homeowners and investors, mobile service with free home visits seven days a week, and a credit card. Aussie Home Loans currently receives 50% of its funding from a subsidiary of ANZ and 50% from PUMA.

Mortgage brokers, not to be confused with mortgage managers, act as an intermediary in helping borrowers choose an appropriate loan, assisting in the application process, and introducing borrowers to lenders in exchange for a commission from the lender. The commission can be an upfront fee of around 0.5% to 0.7% of the loan amount, a trailing commission of about 0.2% to 0.25% of the outstanding balance, or a combination of these. As in the United States, lenders save on the costs associated with directly originating loans by obtaining loans through mortgage brokers. It is estimated that roughly 15% to 20% of all home loans are arranged by mortgage brokers. Mortgage Choice is the largest mortgage broker, operating via hundreds of franchised outlets. Its centralized call center arranges for a broker to visit the borrower at home or at work.

Credit Unions are cooperatives owned and controlled by customers. Member deposits fund loans to other members. They offer a wide range of services, but, unlike banks, are nonprofit organizations.

Building Societies share some of the characteristics of banks (being similarly regulated by the APRA) and credit unions, funding their loans from member deposits. Home loans are their main business.

Internet or online originations are a promising area of future growth, as in the United States. However, as in the United States, online mortgage brokers and lenders face hurdles, such as the requirement that physical documentation must be provided.

Competition in the Mortgage Industry

Competition from nonbank lenders, especially mortgage managers, first pressured bank lenders to offer low-rate mortgage products to new borrowers, such as honeymoon and basic variable-loan products. As more and more bank borrowers refinanced with mortgage managers—because of the lower rates offered by mortgage managers in the mid-1990s—bank lenders responded by making two major rate reductions, in June 1996 and February 1997. These two cuts significantly narrowed the rate gap between bank and nonbank lenders. Mortgage managers, on average, lend at rates just slightly below the banks (see Exhibit 29.8), but this varies when comparing rates offered by specific individual companies. Banks have also adopted

EXHIBIT 29.8   Australian Mortgage Rates

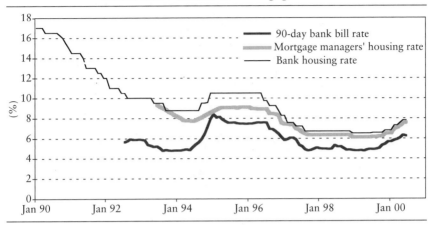

Source: Reserve Bank of Australia.

some of the successful strategies first employed by mortgage managers, such as mobile lending, where the lender comes to the borrower.

According to the Reserve Bank of Australia, as of December 1999, *banks had a 77% share of the market* (57% for major banks, such as West-pac, Commonwealth, ANZ, National, and St. George). The rest of the market is left to mortgage managers (8%), building societies (3%), and other lenders (12%).

29.4 MBS STRUCTURAL FEATURES

Much of the evolution for mortgage securitization outside the Unite States has taken its cues from the development of ABS technology, and differences in the laws, customs and practices of the issuer's country.

Simply, the two principal goals of an ABS are to create: (1) a bank-ruptcy-remote vehicle; and (2) a true sale of securitized assets. The first goal ensures that securitized assets are not included in the assets of the issuer or sponsor in the event of bankruptcy. The second goal ensures that investors have all rights and remedies to the assets in the structure.[9] Exhibit 29.9 illustrates a typical Australian mortgage pass-through structure and how it operates.

---

[9] See "The Mortgage Market in the United Kingdom," Salomon Smith Barney, July 2000.

EXHIBIT 29.9 Australian Mortgage Pass-Through Structure

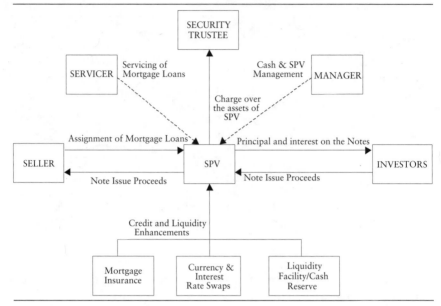

Source: Salomon Smith Barney.

Credit Enhancement

As the credit quality of the collateral to be securitized may be less than the desired ratings of the ABSs, bonds may receive credit enhancement to add support. Credit enhancement can be achieved through (1) issuance of mezzanine or subordinate debt, (2) trapping or reserving excess spread, and (3) insurance or guarantees.

Like U.S. mortgage transactions, Australian MBS deals use step-down tests following a three-year lockout, which if passed, permits an increasing percentage of prepayments released to the subordinates. Typically, the step-down test calls for the satisfaction of (1) rolling average delinquency thresholds; and (2) a credit enhancement multiple (for example, when credit enhancement equals or exceeds two times the initial setting).

Transfer of Assets

Under Australian law, the assets transferred to a special purpose vehicle (SPV) should only be available to investors in the SPV and should not be a part of the seller assets in the event of the seller's insolvency. Australia's bank issuers use equitable assignment to transfer loans into an SPV from their balance sheet. This transaction is free of stamp duty. The mechanism meets true-sale criteria under Australian law and, if the lender becomes insolvent, borrowers are immediately notified, perfecting the SPV's interest in the collateral. Mortgage managers, on the other hand, typically do not need to transfer loans, because their loans are usually originated in the name of the SPV or the trustee that issues the MBS. Hence, no stamp duty is incurred.

Bank and Nonbank Structures

Australian MBSs, especially those issued offshore, have been quarterly pay structures. Because of the swap cost, quarterly pay deals are more cost effective. Under present conditions, Australian MBS issuers will continue to issue quarterly pay deals into the United States. Most domestic issuance, however, pays monthly. From an asset/liability management perspective, monthly pay structures clearly work better for Australian issuers.

There are generally two types of securitization structures used in Australian MBS transactions. The first is employed by banks, the second by nonbanks.

Bank Structures Banks use equitable assignment and pass-through principal and interest right away. Credit enhancement typically includes a combination of individual and pool mortgage insurance, excess interest, and subordination. Bank structures will use pool mortgage insurance policies because it is generally their practice not to insure loans that are originated with an LTV less than 80%. The pool policy is purchased by the bank for these loans if they are included as collateral for the deal. Bank structures need to comply with Prudential Statement C2—Funds Management and Securitization (prescribed by the regulatory authority APRA), which administers rules for the sponsoring bank that provides facilities to the structure. This means that liquidity facilities (interest-rate swaps, etc.) provided by the sponsoring bank have to comply with guidelines to ensure that it is not providing credit enhancement. *Banks typically issue floating-rate pass-through securities with a 10% cleanup call* (although specific call dates and step-up margins are not uncommon). The largest banks may employ the soft bullet structure, taking a cue from recent U.K. mortgage issuance.

Nonbank Structures Nonbank transactions differ from bank structures. Nonbanks typically originate loans in the name of the issuing entity, either a trustee or corporation, and thereby avoid the need for equitable assignment. Like European securitizations, nonbanks issue structures with a call date and step-up coupons (which are initiated if the securities are not called). Call dates vary, but they are usually around seven years. Because of the structure and economics of the nonbank transaction, it is likely that the calls will be exercised. *Most nonbank structures allow substitution for up to two years before passing principal through.* The substitution period serves as a warehouse-funding mechanism for nonbank originators. *The substitution along with the step-up call enhances the convexity of the nonbank structure.* Credit enhancement in nonbank structures differs from bank structures in that all loans in the transaction have individual mortgage insurance, as well as excess interest and subordination. Because of a lack of balance sheet capacity, mortgage managers need to mortgage insure every loan at origination. Hence, nonbank structures will typically have each loan individually mortgage-insured.

Generally, nonbank mortgage transactions have required slightly higher credit enhancement than bank-issued transactions. The main reason is that *nonbank loans are often less seasoned* than those of banks, because banks can carry loans on their balance sheet for a period of time. Nonbanks, on the other hand, rely on securitization for funding and need to securitize as soon as possible. LTV is another reason for higher credit enhancement in nonbank transactions. LTV, on average, is higher than LTV in bank pools.

General Features

- *SPVs* are usually trusts rather than companies as in U.K. transactions. The trust is the favored vehicle because it is easier to achieve off-balance-sheet treatment. In addition, the trust makes it easier to segregate assets to satisfy the rating agencies.
- *Interest-rate swaps* essentially are basis swaps. To offset basis risk between mortgage collateral revenues and liability costs, transactions generally include an interest-rate swap provider and, to provide for multiple-currency deals, may integrate a currency swap provider. For bank transactions, the sponsoring bank provides the basis swaps. The use of swaps permits the banks the flexibility of setting their interest rates at their discretion without interfering with outstanding securitizations. A bank's mix of funding means that the variable-rate loans are a true administered rate, which does not necessarily have a correlation to the movements in benchmark indexes. Swap providers are typically required to maintain high credit ratings and, should ratings fall, may be replaced or required to post collateral to support the swap.
- Most mortgage managers use a *threshold rate mechanism* prescribed by the rating agencies. Nonbanks typically do not rely on basis swaps for interest-rate management (principally because they are not highly rated

entities). In order to ensure that there are sufficient funds to cover the expenses of the securitization, interest rates on the loans must be monitored regularly. If interest rates are not sufficient to cover securitization expenses, the servicer is obligated to raise rates on its mortgages. Nonbanks are typically funded by securitization, so the interest rates on their mortgages closely correlate to the funding benchmark.

- *Liquidity facilities* provide for the payment of interest in full on each coupon date. In bank transactions, liquidity facilities are usually provided by the sponsoring bank. The liquidity facility must be for the term of the notes (up to 31 years) and can only be drawn upon for performing loans (less than 90 days in arrears). Nonbank transactions generally utilize a mixture of cash reserve and timely payment coverage provided by mortgage insurers. Under timely payment cover, the mortgage insurer agrees to pay defaulted interest payments to the beneficiary under the policy for up to 12 or 24 months, depending on the agreement. This form of liquidity support must be supplemented by a cash reserve because of the time delay between when the claim is made and when the insurer honors the claim.

- *Set-off* is a feature in Australia that operates in the same way in the United Kingdom. A borrower may have the right to set off payments it owes to the originator of the mortgage loan against money due from the originator. This is often the case when the originator is a deposit-taking institution. For example, if a borrower of $100 has a deposit of $10 with a bank, the borrower may use the deposit to offset the $100 loan and create a $90 obligation. If the loan were securitized, the trust would become an unsecured party to the bank for the $10, in the event of the bank's insolvency. The risk of set-off is generally small, as it is contingent on both borrowers wishing to set off and issuer insolvency. Most mortgage agreements in Australia have a waiver of set-off clause, which is signed by the borrower. Rating agencies require (1) waiver of set-off in the mortgage agreements; and (2) a legal opinion from deal counsel that states that the signed set-off waiver is sufficient to remove the risk of exposure to the SPV. If both of these requirements cannot be met, the rating agencies are likely to require cash reserves for set-off risk.

- *Substitution periods* are incorporated into several Australian MBS transactions. During the substitution (or revolving) period, the MBS issuer reinvests principal received to purchase new mortgage loans, with the intention of adding these loans to the securitization. Substitution is useful to issuers in that it can help them manage their origination pipeline in a way similar to a warehousing line of credit. In addition, substitution stabilizes the prepayment profile. Because substitution can change the credit profile of the mortgage pool, substitutions must meet strict criteria and may have to be approved by the rating agency that rated the transaction initially. Substitution is monitored over time in order to prevent deterioration in the credit quality of the pool relative to the credit quality of the original pool.

Rating Agency Treatment

S&P, Moody's, and Fitch play important roles in the Australian MBS market. Regardless of which rating agency assigns ratings to an MBS pool,[10] there are many transaction-specific factors that must be examined before the rating agency can determine its required level of credit enhancement. Each rating agency analyzes current macroeconomic conditions, housing market value trends, and issuer/servicer performance trends.

Although the rating agencies' models are somewhat unique, there are adjustments made by each to account for borrower profile and loan characteristics, such as debt-to-income ratio, documentation, geographic location, loan size and purpose, LTV, and so on.[11] However, a transaction-specific examination reveals several pivotal factors in the determination of an Australian MBS class rating. The rating agencies aim to set the credit-enhancement requirement at a level adequate to protect investors from underlying asset defaults. *The rating process includes an assessment based on the strength of the following structural mechanisms and third-party involvement:*

- The credit rating of the currency swap provider(s);
- The credit rating of the issuer/servicer (providing a facility);
- Individual and pool mortgage insurance, including
- The credit rating of the insurer (see Mortgage Insurance in Australia section for details) and percent of loss coverage;
- Excess interest coverage;
- The liquidity facility;
- The legal and structural protections related to the equitable assignment; and
- The documents that stipulate obligations by various parties in the transaction.

Another consideration that rating agencies make concerns delinquency tracking. It is common for many Australian lenders (typically banks) to manage their collections using an arrears identification method based not

---

[10] S&P has garnered the highest ratings market share in Australia.
[11] Appendix 29E for S&P's Australian Benchmark Residential Loan Pool.

on a missed-payment basis, but rather on one that identifies a delinquency once the borrower falls behind their scheduled principal balance. In other words, if a borrower is sufficiently ahead of their scheduled principal balance (by making additional principal payments for example), *the Australian arrears method does not flag a delinquency if the borrower misses a payment.* In addition, a feature common to Australian mortgages known as a payment holiday allows a borrower to skip a payment under certain circumstances. *To assess properly the borrower's true payment performance, rating agencies require servicers to modify their reporting systems to provide delinquency data on a missed-payment basis.*

Finally, because most Australian MBS transactions include mortgages with a redraw facility and top-ups, the rating agencies assume these features are fully drawn at closing. They will size the credit and liquidity supports assuming the loan pool equals the closing pool's size plus the redraw facility limits.

S&P, Moody's, and Fitch each have published ratings criteria specifically for rating residential Australian MBSs.

29.5 CREDIT PERFORMANCE

Australia is lender-friendly in that the enforcement of a loan in default takes place efficiently. Unlike in the United States, there are no formal foreclosure proceedings, and the courts have less discretion in delaying the lender's claim on the property.

In Australia, mortgage interest on owner-occupied housing is not tax deductible. As a result, borrowers have a considerable incentive to pay their mortgages ahead of schedule (assuming prepayment penalties do not apply). *Because homeowner equity is a strong deterrent against default, the lack of a tax deduction on mortgage interest has contributed to Australia's superior mortgage credit performance relative to the United States.* In addition, Australia's strong mortgage performance is thought by many to be the result of one or more of the following:

- Australian's cultural desire to own their homes free and clear of a mortgage.
- Australia's practice of enforcing recourse; borrowers accept the mortgage as a personal obligation.
- Reasonable consumer debt and firm property values.
- Historically strong underwriting standards.
- An ingrained credit culture that surpasses that of the United States and United Kingdom.

■ Mortgage insurance coverage (which provides an extra layer of credit and underwriting diligence).

Home Ownership Culture

The predominant culture of pride in home ownership in Australia advocates paying back a loan as soon as possible, normally via partial repayments of principal. It is also part of the reason for the excellent credit performance of Australian mortgages. *Commonwealth Bank reported 98% of its home-loan customers taking advantage of partial repayments in 1998.*

As noted earlier, about 70% of people in Australia live in their own home and, among them, only 40% have mortgages. Housing loans are a personal obligation in Australia. If a borrower defaults, the lender has the right to recover from the borrower any shortfall after the sale of the property to satisfy the loan balance. It is likely that this has provided strong motivation for Australians to repay their mortgage obligations even in the event that their mortgage is "out of the money."

Australian homeowners are less likely than U.S. homeowners to fall behind in their scheduled mortgage payments. Exhibit 29.10 shows Australian mortgage credit performance as measured by 60+ day delinquencies since 1996 (data from S&P). The figure also shows U.S. 60+ day delinquency data on conventional loans as reported by the Mortgage Bankers Association for the same period. Exhibit 29.10 shows that *delinquency frequency is*

EXHIBIT 29.10   Comparison of Mortgage 60+ Day Delinquencies in Australia versus United States

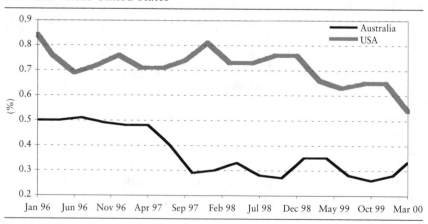

Source: S&P and MBA.

significantly lower in Australia. Since 1998 in fact, the frequency of 60+ day delinquencies has been more than two times greater in the United States than for Australia. In the first quarter of 2000, however, delinquencies have converged significantly (to about 22bp) because of a decrease in U.S. delinquencies and a rise in Australian delinquencies. This trend warrants watching.

Bankruptcies

By most standards, Australians have been responsible users of credit. Bankruptcy rates in Australia, while greater than those in the United Kingdom, have been approximately 20% to 30% of those in the United States over the last 15 years (see Exhibit 29.11). Australian bankruptcies have been steadily increasing since 1995, however, despite a strong domestic economy. From 1995 to 1999, Australian bankruptcies have increased by about 50%, while U.K. bankruptcies remained flat. During the same period, **U.S. bankruptcies jumped 75% and still outpace Australian bankruptcies at a rate of more than 3 to 1.**

Australia's growing credit card debt has been a factor in the rise in bankruptcies, as well as in its recent interest-rate hikes. In the 12-month period ended March 2000, household credit had risen by 16%, mostly because of the Australians' increased use of credit cards. (Similar to cardholders in the

EXHIBIT 29.11 Personal Bankruptcies in Australia, the United States, and the United Kingdom (per 1,000 of Population)

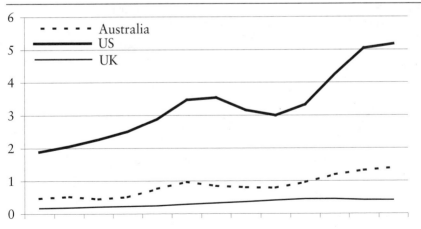

Source: Fitch IBCA, "Offshore Investors Guide to Australian Residential Mortgages."

United States, more Australian cardholders are using credit cards for convenience items like gasoline and groceries, as well as utility payments, and so on.) During the past five years, Australian credit card purchases and advances have risen in terms of annual growth rates from less than 15% to almost 40%. During the same period, Australia's annual savings rate has fallen significantly from more than 5% to almost 2%. Exhibit 29.12 illustrates the credit card and savings phenomenon since 1995.

By comparison, the U.S. savings rate recently hit an all-time low as consumers spent more than they earned. The U.S. savings rate was −0.2% in July 2000, compared with a mark of +0.1% in June. Consumer spending in the United States rose twice as fast as personal income in July. Hence, while *Australia's increased use of credit and reduction in savings seems alarming at first glance, it remains far superior to comparable indicators in the United States.*

Credit card rates for Australian cardholders average about 14% for prime quality borrowers. Credit limits are growing, but recent sources show an average of about A$3,000. Opposing the increasing consumer credit trend, income growth stands at approximately 4% in Australia.

Credit Reporting in Australia

In the United States, credit bureaus play a significant role in the lender's decision to grant credit to a loan applicant. U.S. credit bureaus maintain detailed information on a borrower's credit history. Essentially, the information is

EXHIBIT 29.12   Annual Growth in Australian Credit Card Transaction versus Australian Savings Ratio

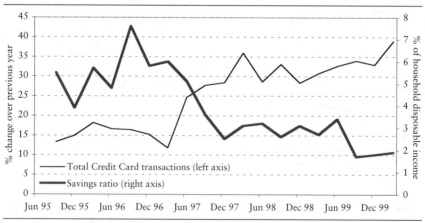

Source: Reserve Bank of Australia.

EXHIBIT 29.13 Reported Credit Events

	Australia	US	UK
Late Payments	Not reported	At 30 days	Sometimes
Defaults	Usually reported	Reported	Reported
Bankruptcies	Reported	Reported	Reported
Current Outstanding Balances	Not reported	Reported	Reported
Judgments	Reported	Reported	Reported
Credit Applications	Reported	Reported	Reported
Credit Granted	Not reported	Reported	Reported
Credit Availability	Not reported	Reported	Sometimes

Source: Offshore Investors Guide to Australian Residential Mortgages, April 17, 2000, Fitch.

used to determine a borrower's default probability. *In Australia and the United Kingdom, credit reporting has not developed to the same extent as in the United States.* Because there is a general lack of credit data relative to the United States, credit reporting in Australia does not play a major role in credit decisions because it is not an accurate indicator of default.

Because delinquencies often are not reported until payments are 120 days or more past due, only borrowers that have shown severe delinquency patterns are identified.[12] (By U.S. standards, these are C and D class borrowers.) Among the U.S. equivalent of A and B borrowers, it is difficult to distinguish between a borrower with a slightly below-average credit history and a borrower with a clean credit history. Also, some lenders, according to Fitch, will not check credit reports on a borrower unless the LTV is greater than 80%. These reporting procedures mean that A and B borrowers are likely commingled in most mortgage pools. Exhibit 29.13 shows how Australia, the United States, and the United Kingdom differ in their reported credit events.

The Australian MBS market does not distinguish between prime and subprime loans as the U.S. MBS market does. In the United States, investors prefer segregating prime, alt-A, and subprime loans into their own subsectors, where pricing conventions and analytical/valuation tools account for the behavioral differences in each group.[13]

Australian MBS does distinguish the differences between conforming and nonconforming loans. Loans that have standard features and meet established

---

[12] A borrower who is habitually 30 to 90 days late in making payments likely will not appear as a chronic delinquent on a credit report.
[13] Certain U.S. issuers have filed separate shelf registrations in order to clearly identify the collateral type.

credit underwriting parameters are conforming loans. *Nonconforming loans are those made to high-risk borrowers (who may lack full-time employment history, have erratic income and/or adverse credit history).* To date, there has been just one publicly issued, nonconforming mortgage transaction. That transaction was issued by Liberty Funding Pty., Ltd. (A$100 million issuance).

Home Prices in Australia

The Australian housing market is composed primarily of single-family detached housing. Only 20% of housing is made up of semidetached houses, townhouses, flats, and so on. More than 70% of home purchases are made on existing housing. According to the Australian Bureau of Statistics, housing prices rose by almost 85% in the 10 years between June 1986 and June 1996. At the same time, the consumer price inflation index rose by 58%. Since then, house prices have risen 5% to 10% annually. Exhibit 29.14 tracks the annualized percent change for Australian consumer and housing price indexes.

Australian house prices have risen fairly steadily in the 1990s. U.K. house prices have shown considerably more volatility during the past 10 years than Australian prices. Aggregate U.S. house prices have experienced less percentage volatility during the same period. Exhibit 29.15 compares annualized percent changes for Australia, United Kingdom, and United States house price indexes.

EXHIBIT 29.14 Australian Consumer (CPI) and Housing (HPI) Prices—2Q87–1Q00

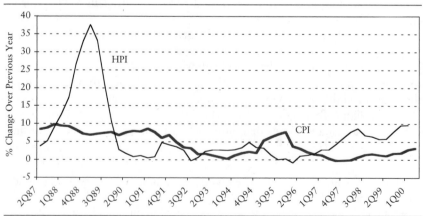

Source: Australian Bureau of Statistics and Salomon Smith Barney.

EXHIBIT 29.15 Housing Price Indexes in Australia, the United Kingdom, and the United States—1Q90–1Q00

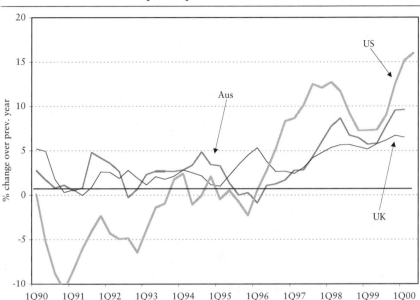

Source: Office of Federal Housing Enterprise Oversight, Nationwide Building Society, and Salomon Smith Barney.

Most of Australia's major cities have experienced strong house price appreciation since the late 1970s. Exhibit 29.16 shows *median* house prices for the six major cities since 1977.

As the 1980s ended, increasing interest rates accompanied by high property values cooled demand in the Australian housing market. The 1990s began with an economic recession. A slowdown in migration reduced new household growth and led to slower economic activity. This pricing phenomenon is shown in Exhibit 29.16, and is most pronounced in Sydney, Melbourne, and Perth.

Declining property values exacerbate the incidence of borrower default. In Australia, the most common events that cause borrowers to default are loss of employment, (or loss of a second job), a decrease in earnings (commissions), a personal crisis (death, illness, and divorce), and increased debt ratios caused by rising interest rates.

The Australian economy has experienced several boom periods, which fueled demand for housing and caused substantial price appreciation. These booms were often followed by bust periods resulting from interest-rate increases to control the overheated real estate market. Less demand and

EXHIBIT 29.16   Australian Median Home Prices by State

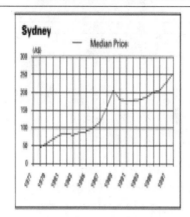

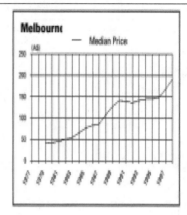

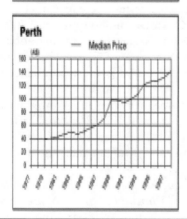

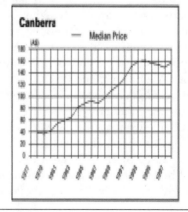

Source: Real Estate Institute of Australia.

consumer confidence resulted in lower property prices, which, in turn, increased the frequency of default and higher loss severity for those mortgages underwritten during the real estate boom period.

Considering the historical pattern of Australia's real estate market, mortgage performance has nonetheless been stable. *Going forward, we do not foresee deterioration in credit performance based on current housing price trends.*

Loan Performance

Loan performance is sensitive to changes in interest rates as well as to changes in housing values. Looking forward, Australian loan performance will be tested by recent increases in rates (1.50% since November 1999) and the possibility for a softer housing market. Nonetheless, Australians have demonstrated discipline in maintaining their mortgages through several economic cycles. As a result, Australian MBS credit performance exceeds its U.S. and U.K. counterparts historically. Looking ahead, loss performance may worsen somewhat because of weakened credit underwriting standards. In the event that housing prices fall, the weaker credit is more susceptible to default. Therefore, LTV remains a key collateral statistic and house prices a key determinant in performance. *For Australian MBS investors, mortgage insurance coverage and other credit-enhancement protections have been more than adequate to protect against credit losses.*

Australia's residential housing loan loss curve appears similar to that in the United States, but upon closer inspection, is different enough to warrant a discussion (see Exhibit 29.17). Essentially, Australian losses appear sooner than U.S. losses (possibly because of the many real estate boom and bust cycles experienced in Australia). Approximately 63% of all losses, according to Australian mortgage insurance data over the last 30-plus years, occurred two to four years from origination. About 15% of the losses appear earlier, in the first two years. About 12% of the losses appear in year four, with another 10% incurred after year four. Historical loss experience in the United States reveals a more evenly distributed loss pattern in years three through seven for prime quality mortgages. *In addition, historical aggregate losses (as a percentage of original principal balance) in Australia have been on average about one-quarter to one-half of those in the U.S. prime mortgage market in the 1990s.* During the decade, both the United States and Australian economies were fairly strong and house prices were stable or rising.

The timing of defaults in Australia also appears more front-loaded than defaults in the United States (see Exhibit 29.18). About 90% of homeowner defaults in Australia happen one to five years from origination; 60% occur

EXHIBIT 29.17   Timing of Losses

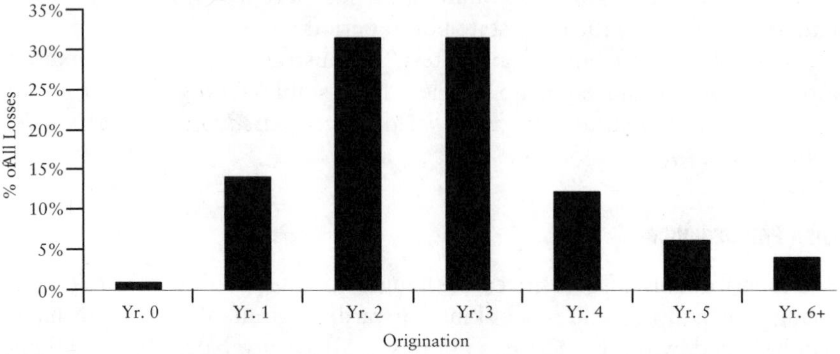

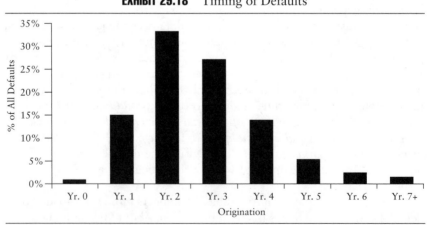

Source: Standard and Poor's Australian Residential MBS Criteria.

two to four years from origination. U.S. defaults are more evenly distributed through year seven, as are the associated losses.

Mortgage Insurance in Australia

Private mortgage insurers provide much of the protection against credit risk in the Australian mortgage market. *Mortgage insurance is usually provided for the full value of the loan rather than just a percentage of the loan* (or "top cover" policy—coverage on the first 20% of the loan, for example). This is in

EXHIBIT 29.18   Timing of Defaults

Source: Moody's Analysis of Australian Mortgage-Backed Securities, September 8, 1995.

contrast to the United States and the United Kingdom, where top-cover policies are the norm. In addition, in the United Kingdom and the United States, mortgage insurance for less-affluent borrowers is available from government programs (ISMI and FHA, respectively), whereas in Australia, the corresponding program, HLIC, was privatized in 1997 (it was acquired by GE Capital).

Australian MBSs typically are protected by individual mortgage insurance (for loans with LTVs greater than 80%), as well as pool insurance for loans with LTVs up to 80%. In most cases, the insurers perform their own credit analysis and underwriting diligence before approving a loan. *Credit loss experience is minimal in the Australian mortgage market even though the market is composed almost entirely of adjustable-rate loans (ARMs).* In the United States, ARMs have been shown to experience higher frequency of default, mostly attributable to payment shock.

Since its introduction by the Australian government in 1965, mortgage insurance has been a fixture in the mortgage lending industry. Insurance-claims data supports the proclamation that Australia has superior credit performance. According to S&P, the average insurance claims frequency on securitized pools was 0.73%, with a resulting loss severity of 0.17% of the total value of insured loans between 1985 and 1999.

Australia's mortgage insurers have aided in (and benefited by) the low incidence of default. Mortgage insurers are involved in virtually every MBS transaction produced by Australian issuers in the form of primary mortgage insurance and/or pool policies. *Often there are three or more mortgage insurers involved in any transaction.* Exhibit 29.19 shows the distribution of mortgage insurers in Australian MBSs.

EXHIBIT 29.19   Mortgage Insurance Distribution, Weighted Average

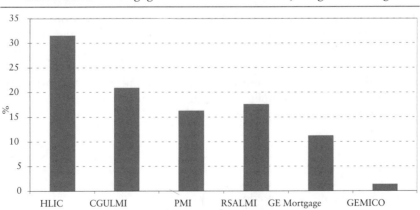

Source: S&P ABS Performance Watch, May 2000.

EXHIBIT 29.20 Australia's Major Mortgage Insurers and Credit Ratings

	Credit Rating			
Mortgage Insurer	S&P	Moody's	Fitch	Parent Company
GE Mortgage Insurance Pty Ltd (HLIC)	AAA	Aa1	AAA	GE (US)
GE Capital Mortgage Insurance Corp of Australia Pty Ltd.	AA	Aa2	AA	GE (US)
CGU Lenders Mortgage Insurance, Ltd.	AA	A2[1]	AA	CGU (UK)
PMI Mortgage Insurance Ltd.	AA-	A1	AA	PMI (US)
Royal & Sun Alliance (RSALMI)	AA-	A2	NR	RSA (UK)

Source: S&P, Moody's, Fitch, and Salomon Smith Barney.

For investors, the presence of several insurers diversifies their exposure to any single insurer. **At present, five mortgage insurers have a credit rating AA– or better from S&P.** Exhibit 29.20 lists the five major Australian mortgage insurers, as well as their credit ratings by S&P, Moody's, and Fitch. Mortgage insurer ratings in Australia have been stable. Moody's, for example, has never downgraded an insurer. In fact, its only ratings action was an upgrade to CGU Lenders Mortgage Insurance from A3 to A2 (Moody's currently has CGU under review for possible upgrade).

Mortgage insurance provides protection against loss in the event of a shortfall from the sale of a property. In most cases, the borrower pays the mortgage insurance premium. In the event that a deficiency results from the sale of a mortgaged property and the mortgage insurer pays the deficiency by a claim, the borrower is obliged under the personal covenants of the mortgage documentation to repay this deficiency to the mortgage insurer.

Typically, the insurance policies provide 100% loss coverage against the loan balance, unpaid interest, and liquidation costs. Rating agencies increase credit-enhancement requirements when a mortgage insurance policy provides less than 100% coverage. For loans with LTVs up to around 80%[14] (and sometimes with a limit on the loan size), the lender pays the insurance premium,[15] but for higher LTV loans, the borrower pays the premium. Loans must first be processed and approved by the lender and are contingent on the approval of the mortgage insurer to underwrite the insurance. This method essentially duplicates the underwriting process. For mortgage managers, the underwriting process is a function of the mortgage insurer's

---

[14] The LTV maximum varies. For average loan sizes, the cutoff may be 80%, but for larger loans, the cutoff may be 70%.

[15] Banks typically do not insure loans with an LTV less than 80%, but mortgage managers will usually require the borrower to pay the insurance premium irrespective of LTV.

underwriting guidelines, because mortgage managers require mortgage insurance on all loans regardless of LTV.

Another method of underwriting private mortgage insurance is done via the "open policy." The use of open policies has decreased as mortgage insurers react to aggressive price competition. In an open policy, the lender is assured that the mortgage insurance underwriter will insure the loan. However, the lender must underwrite to the insurer's guidelines. The open policy reduces the amount of time that is necessary for loan approval. Open policies are deemed by the rating agencies to have more credit risk because a layer of underwriting diligence has been removed (relative to the individual mortgage insurance policy).

Pool policies can operate in one of two different ways. The pool policy can be purchased by the lender to cover 100% of the loss against the loan balance, unpaid interest, and liquidation costs. This practically involves the mortgage insurer underwriting each individual loan. The lender must give the insurer a schedule of all the loans needing to be insured, and the insurer goes through each individual loan to insure it. The other way in which a pool policy can operate is for the lender to pay an insurance premium based on a maximum aggregate claim amount. This claim amount is typically sized to the triple-A level of expected loss. If the maximum claim amount is exhausted, then the policy ceases to pay claims and the other credit enhancements available to investors are utilized.

Whether the mortgage loans have individual mortgage insurance or the securitized pool has a pool insurance policy, the borrower, as always, is in the first-loss position.

Default Management

Every effort is made by the lender to restore a delinquent loan before action is taken to obtain possession of the mortgaged property. Contact with the borrower is attempted in the early stages of default, before arrears become too burdensome to make a satisfactory arrangement to bring the account up to date. Counseling, forbearance plans, repayment plans, and loan modifications are some of the courses of action taken.

Lenders are required to keep insurers advised of any material fact that alters the initial risk taken by the insurer. Once a default is reported to the mortgage insurer, the lender must regularly update the insurer on collection activities and balances in arrears. In addition, the lender must apprise the insurer if it learns of physical damage to the property, and if the borrower files a bankruptcy petition.

The lender and the insurer work together in resolving a default. If the effort to preserve home ownership fails, then the lender reaches an agreement with the insurer on matters including method of sale of the property, sale price, presentation of the property, and so on. After the sale of an insured property, the assignment of mortgage documents are returned to the mortgage insurer to enable recovery of deficiency from the borrower.

If it is discovered that a loan was made based on fraudulent information, the lender has the right to expect that claims on that loan will be paid by the insurer if the lender was not a party to the fraudulent loan application. However, if any of the lender's employees or third parties are party to the fraud, the mortgage insurance policy will not cover the lender.

The Impact of Mortgage Insurer Ratings

A mortgage insurer's rating plays a significant role in the sizing of the rating agency's required credit enhancement. Rating-agency loss estimates will vary based on the assumptions used (this typically depends on the collateral type). However, the insurer's rating directly impacts the required level of credit enhancement. Exhibit 29.21 shows the level of credit given by S&P and Fitch for the mortgage insurer's rating.

To explain the importance of the insurer's rating, Exhibit 29.22 illustrates a representative Australian residential MBS pool. Exhibit 29.22 lists the stress assumptions used to determine the loss severity for triple-A and assumes an average LTV of 80%. The credit enhancement for a class of securities is determined by multiplying the frequency of default (shown in the figure as Benchmark Default Probability) and loss severity. For the triple-A scenario, 10% × 56.6% equals credit enhancement of 5.66%. *Once the credit enhancement is determined, it is reduced by an amount based on the average rating of the mortgage insurers in the pool.* If we assume that the entire pool is covered by a double-A rated insurer, then 75% credit is given

EXHIBIT 29.21 Rating Agency Credit Given to Mortgage Insurers by Rating

	Rating Agency	
Credit Rating	S&P	Fitch
AAA	100%	100%
AA	75	75
AA-	75	68
A	50	50
BBB	25	25
Below (or Not Rated)	0	0

Source: S&P and Fitch.

EXHIBIT 29.22 Credit Enhancement Calculations on Representative Australian RMBS Pool

Description	Triple-A
Default Frequency	10%
LVR Adjustment	—
Other Adjustments	—
Benchmark Default Probability	10%
Original Property Value	$100,000
Loan Amount	$80,000
Market Value Decline	$45,000
New Market Value	$55,000
Market Loss on Loan	($25,000)
Accrued Interest	($12,500)
Selling Costs	($7,750)
Total Loss	($45,250)
Loss Severity	56.6%
Credit Enhancement	5.66%
"AA" Mortgage Insurer (75%)	1.42%

Source: Salomon Smith Barney.

(based upon S&P's and Fitch's criteria in Exhibit 29.18). Hence, the triple-A credit enhancement requirement becomes 1.42% (= 5.66% × (1 − 75%). The same exercise would be performed on any other class rating given the appropriate assumptions.

Australian mortgages and their MBS ratings are largely dependent on mortgage insurance. As a result, a downgrade of a mortgage insurer may result in a downgrade of the MBS transaction (depending on the performance and seasoning of the pool, the downgraded insurer's distribution in the pool, and whether there is additional credit enhancement in the transaction, such as excess spread). *Investors of subordinate MBS classes in a pool-insured MBS transaction run a greater risk of being impacted by the insurer's downgrade,* because the insurer's rating (as shown) is one of the factors that go into sizing the subordinate classes.

29.6 PREPAYMENT BEHAVIOR

A number of factors influence prepayment rates of Australian loans. We describe these factors in this section, and then attempt to develop a modeling framework in the following section. The most notable feature is that *Australian prepayments are very stable.* Important influences on prepayments include the following:

■ *Competition.* Given the competitive nature of the Australian mortgage market, actions of individual lenders to attract more customers can cause refinancings to increase.

■ *Culture.* The "Great Australian Dream" of home ownership contributes to higher curtailments (partial repayments) and full payoffs on Australian mortgages.

■ *Taxes.* Owner-occupied loans are not tax-deductible, which is a positive contributor to prepayments, as borrowers in this category pay off their mortgages as soon as possible. Property investors, however, can deduct the interest component of their loan as an expense, so investment loans tend to display slower prepayment rates.

■ Interest rates. Prepayments of variable-rate loans are at most weakly dependent on rates.

■ *Variable-rate loans.* Given the home ownership culture and tax regulations in Australia, one could argue that curtailments and full payoffs increase as interest rates go down. Assuming the average borrower keeps making roughly the same loan payments as before (rather than choosing to reduce the payment), higher curtailments would result in the case of declining rates, for example. However, in practice, it is difficult to observe much correlation between rates and prepayments, at least partly because the prepayment effects resulting from competitive actions by lenders tend to obscure any changes in prepayments resulting from rates.

■ *Fixed-rate loans.* Because of prepayment penalties, decreasing interest rates do not spark the prepayment surges seen in the United States. Rising interest rates do tend to reduce prepayments because of a lock-in effect. Collateral for deals often contain some fixed-rate loans mixed in with variable-rate loans. The proportion of borrowers taking out fixed-rate loans in the primary mortgage market typically might vary from less than 10% to just over 20%.

■ *Legal (full recourse).* Unlike in the United States, all of the borrower's assets, not only the property itself, are potentially available to the mortgage lender in the case of default. For borrowers, this is a strong disincentive to default on their mortgages and partly explains low default rates on Australian mortgages.

■ *Geographic.* Higher mobility in metropolitan areas leads to higher housing turnover.

■ *LTV.* Similar to the United States, higher LTVs imply slower prepayment rates.

■ *Loan Purpose.* See taxes.

■ *Redraw-type features.* This may tend to increase curtailments relative to the United States as Australian borrowers have more flexibility to prepay and withdraw previous prepayments when needed. However, given that redraw is essentially a negative prepayment, this feature also gives borrowers the opportunity to reduce prepayments.

■ *Portability.* This can act to reduce housing-turnover-related prepayments if the conditions for using this facility are met. However, because the requirements described earlier for using this feature are not easy to meet, it is likely a small factor in reducing turnover-related prepayments.

■ *Deal structure.* Some of the features associated with Australian mortgages can cause a loan to be removed from the collateral backing a deal. For example, for at least some deals, top-ups, which cause the principal balance to exceed the scheduled balance, result in loans being removed from the pool of mortgage collateral backing the deal. Although this is not a prepayment from the point of view of the lender, it is a prepayment for the investor. "Splitting" (see the heading: Loan Types in Section 29.3) can also show up as a partial prepayment to the investor.

Australian Prepayment Decomposition

We categorize unscheduled principal repayments into five types, the sum of which is the total prepayment rate. Note that in addition to the usual components found in the U.S. case, we subtract a redraw component from the Australian version of the basic prepayment formula:

$$\text{Total prepayment} = \text{Turnover} + \text{Refinancings} + \text{Partial repayments}$$
$$+ \text{Defaults} - \text{Redraws}$$

Turnover More precisely, these are home-purchase-related prepayments. This component is closely linked to the housing turnover rate, which in turn is related to the strength of the housing market in Australia. We can roughly estimate the housing turnover rate from Exhibit 29.6, which shows that out of a total of 4.37 million homeowners (not including first-time homeowners), 0.67 million bought their homes in the last three years, implying a turnover rate of about 5.4%.[16] This compares with the turnover rate of roughly 6% to 7% recorded recently by the strong U.S. housing market.[17] The housing turnover rate is different from the turnover prepayment rate, because the

---

[16] $5.4\% = 1 - (1 - 0.67/(4.79 - 0.42))^{\wedge}(1/3)$

[17] In Australia, it is not uncommon to buy a house by bidding at an auction. Also, in general, the term *gazumping* refers to when an offer on a home is accepted, but another party makes a higher offer, which secures the sale of the home.

turnover rate for homeowners with mortgages can be different from the rate for homeowners who own their homes outright. In fact, recent figures from the Australian Bureau of Statistics indicate that this difference can be substantial, with the borrower turnover rate possibly reaching up to almost three times that of the outright owner turnover rate (these figures are from an October 1999 study of population mobility in Victoria). In addition, portable mortgages reduce the turnover prepayment rate from the housing turnover rate, although this is likely a small factor, as indicated in the previous section. Exhibit 29.23 gives some indication of how high the turnover prepayment rate might be as well as roughly what the turnover seasoning ramp looks like. It suggests that the turnover rate for homeowners with mortgages is significantly higher than our estimated overall turnover rate of about 5.4%.

In the United States, the housing turnover rate is assumed to depend weakly on interest rates. This is likely the case for the Australian housing turnover rate, but the effect is probably even weaker than in the U.S. case. Although, as in the United States, higher rates mean lower levels of affordability, because of the large number of variable-rate loans, fixed-rate loans with prepayment penalties, and portability, there will be less of a lock-in type effect that affects American borrowers with a discount mortgage rate.

Refinancings As indicated, this is more dependent on lender actions usually taken for competitive reasons than interest rates, which are the main driver of this type of prepayment in the United States. For example, the number of

EXHIBIT 29.23 Sample Australian Mortgage Prepayments—Three-Month CPRs for Second-Quarter 2000

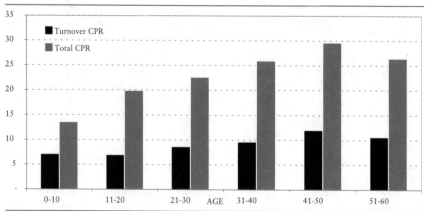

Source: S&P.

refinancings increased in April 1997, partly because of Commonwealth Bank's offer of $1,000 toward refinancing costs. For fixed-rate loans, refinancings should decrease as rates rise, since there is some financial disincentive to getting out of a relatively low fixed-rate loan.

For variable-rate loans, in theory, there should not be much of a link between interest rates and prepayments. Although any connection would be at most weak, one possibility is a link between prepayment speeds and rate volatility. In other words, prepayments might see a slight uptick if rates go up or down substantially. As in the United States, borrowers like to lock in a fixed rate after interest rates fall. But when rates go up, some borrowers like to lock in a fixed rate (at least on part of their loan) to protect against even higher rates. In any case, even if this kind of behavior were to exist, the fact that the *switching* feature allows a variable-rate borrower to switch over to a fixed-rate loan (often at no cost) would tend to make any relationship weak.[18]

Partial Repayments   These payments—also called curtailments—are much higher than in the United States. As stated earlier, Commonwealth Bank reported 98% of its home-loan customers taking advantage of partial repayments in 1998. This category includes full payoffs where no new loan is taken out.[19]

For variable-rate loans, we might assume that Australian borrowers, on average, attempt to keep their periodic payments fixed. So when interest rates decline, for example, curtailments would increase because the required payments would decrease, but the borrowers choose to continue making the same payments as before (so more principal is paid down). This might reflect a particular individual's behavior, but, in practice, it is difficult to determine whether such a relationship holds in aggregate.

Redraws   Redraws are essentially negative partial prepayments.[20] One question concerns how the availability of the redraw feature affects the volatility of prepayment speeds. In theory, redraws could make speeds more volatile. For example, if rates were to skyrocket, variable-rate borrowers might not

---

[18] Assuming it does not trigger removal of the loan from the deal collateral.

[19] These full payoffs are still considered partial repayments because they do not involve a move or refinancing. Alternatively, these full payoffs can be thought of as very large partial repayments, where the borrower pays off all but a tiny portion of the loan.

[20] Redraw being a positive quantity is the sign convention used (so it is subtracted from the sum of prepayments in computing a total prepayment rate).

only stop making partial repayments, but also redraw on principal already prepaid, resulting in even more extension in mortgage average lives than would be the case if the redraw feature were not available. However, putting aside these extreme scenarios, in practice, it appears that redraws tend to stabilize prepayment speeds, since things average out over a large group of borrowers. Some borrowers make use of the redraw facility, but normally the partial repayments made by others more than cancels out these negative prepayments (in which case, there is no issue concerning a lack of principal available to pay bondholders[21]).

Defaults Defaults are very low and so a decent approximation (for prepayment analysis) is to assume this to be zero.

Exhibit 29.23 shows prepayment speeds for a sample of Australian MBS deals reported on by S&P. The data is grouped by age. In addition, estimates for the turnover component of speeds are shown.

Prepayment Analysis

Based on a study of limited loan level data from a major Australian lender and available industry data, we can make some rough observations:

- Prepayments are generally stable at around 20% to 30% CPR, which is representative of Australian prepayment speeds in general.
- Loans season very fast with newer loans prepaying as high as over 20% CPR in some cases. Part of the reason for the fast initial speeds could be deal-structure-related prepayments, as discussed. The steepness of the seasoning ramp varies (Exhibit 29.23 gives some indication of seasoning). In general, initial prepayment speeds and the rate of seasoning will depend to some degree on particular collateral and deal characteristics.
- Variable-rate loans have been prepaying much faster than fixed-rate loans. Since the limited data analyzed is from a period of rising interest rates, it is not clear to what degree the slower fixed-rate speeds reflect the financial disincentive of higher rates or self-selection by borrowers.
- The loan rate does not appear to have a large effect on prepayment speeds. On variable-rate loans, speeds can at times actually be higher on low-rate loans. Partial repayments do not appear to explain this.

---

[21] The other prepayment components would provide additional principal to draw on if needed.

- The breakdown of prepayments appears to be roughly 5% to 9% CPR for partial repayments,[22] over 20% CPR for full payoffs, and approximately 4% CPR for redraws.
- The breakdown of prepayments for fixed-rate loans is fairly subdued, at roughly 0% to 3% CPR for partial repayments, approximately 10% CPR for full payoffs, and around 0% CPR for redraws (as should be the case since redraw is generally not a feature of fixed-rate loans).
- The breakdown of prepayments for variable-rate loans appears to be roughly 7% to 11% CPR for partial repayments, approximately 20% to 30% CPR for full payoffs, and about 4% to 5% CPR for redraws.

The breakdowns given in the last three items only apply to the particular collateral that was studied and would in general vary depending on particular collateral and deal characteristics.

An Australian Prepayment Model

One approach to modeling Australian prepayments is to use a modified PSA curve. For example, a straight-line seasoning ramp (not starting at zero in most cases) could be assumed for the first few years, followed by a constant prepayment rate assumption. This was done for the limited set of data we examined and probably is good enough for some purposes, given the relative stability of Australian mortgage prepayments.

But what more can we say about interest-rate sensitivity? Our feeling is that interest rates may have a limited impact, but it is difficult to isolate the effect of changing interest rates from historical data, because of other industry changes that have occurred simultaneously in the Australian mortgage market. Also, as described earlier, there is limited financial incentive to refinance most loans. Furthermore, the dynamic nature of the Australian market is likely to continue, meaning that being able to predict the effect of future interest-rate changes may be less important than, say, recognizing that a new round of intense mortgage-lender competition for borrowers is about to occur, which might raise prepayments substantially. (But actually, after all of the competition during the past several years, a round of consolidation might be more likely than competition.)

---

[22] Here, partial repayments do *not* include any full payoffs since lender data normally do not give the reason for a full payoff.

APPENDIX 29A
DEMOGRAPHICS

Australia is divided into six states and two territories. Approximately 60% of Australia's 19 million people live in the capital cities of: Sydney (New South Wales), Melbourne (Victoria), Brisbane (Queensland), Perth (Western Australia), and Adelaide (South Australia), as shown in Exhibits 29.24 and 29.25. New South Wales is the most populous and demographically diverse region in Australia. However, each of these capital cities is economically diverse and contains the majority of Australia's housing stock. New South Wales produces one-third of Australia's gross domestic product (GDP). Brisbane, however, is showing the fastest economic growth, primarily through mining and manufacturing. Melbourne has an energy-rich economy and has the largest industry concentration among the major cities with almost 20% of the economy supported by the manufacturing sector.

EXHIBIT 29.24 Australia's States

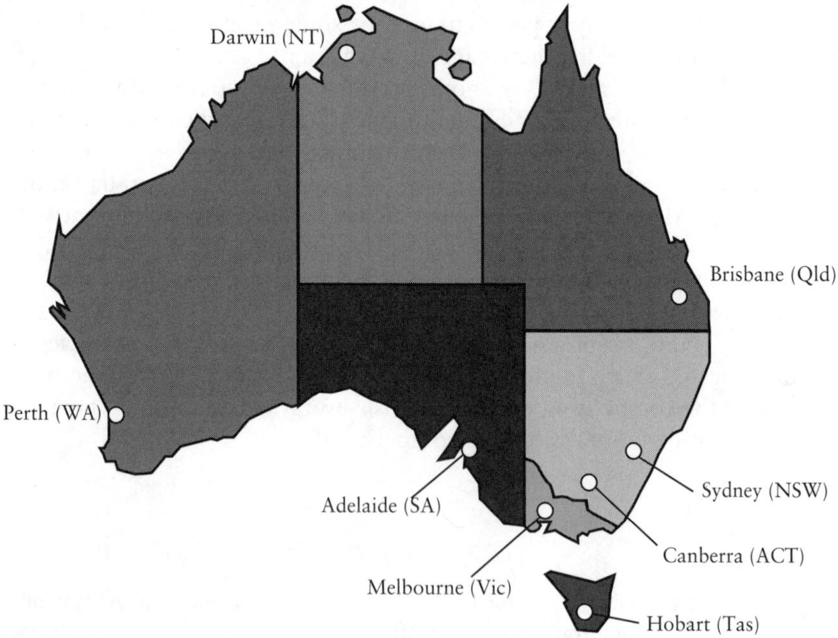

Source: S&P Australian Residential ABS Criteria.

EXHIBIT 29.25 Australia's 19 Million Residents by Region and Population

State/Territory	Capital City	Currency Rating	Population	Notes
New South Wales (NSW)	Sydney	AAA/A-1+	6,173,000	Most populated; 33% of Australia's GDP
Victoria (Vic)	Melbourne	AA+/A-1+	4,453,300	Energy-rich economy; 27% of Australia's GDP
Queensland (Qld)	Brisbane	AAA/A-1+	3,339,000	Fastest economic growth; mining and agriculture
South Australia (SA)	Adelaide	AA/A-1+	1,477,700	Weak industrial base; increasing average age
Western Australia (WA)	Perth	AA+/A-1+	1,755,500	Rich in natural resources; 1M of 1.7M live in Perth
Tasmania (Tas)	Hobart	AA-/A-1+	473,200	Smallest state; dependent on Commonwealth grants
Australian Capital Territory (ACT)	Canberra	AAA/A-1+	306,400	Relies heavily on government-sector activities
Northern Territory (NT)	Darwin	Not Rated	177,500	Lacks metropolitan industrial base

Source: S&P Australian Residential ABS Criteria and Moody's Analysis of Australian MBS.

The typical Australian mortgage borrower earns an approximate average of A$45,000 per annum. Dual-income households earn about A$70,000 (these averages are higher in Australia's largest cities like Sydney and Melbourne). Income peaks for the 45- to 54-year-old group at $A61,000 (as shown in Exhibit 29.26), about 25% more than most first-time house purchasers in the 25- to 34-year-old group. The average mortgage balance at origination is approximately A$175,000. On average, Australians own their homes for about eight years.

Australia's population growth is slow relative to the United States. Its population growth rate in 1997 and 1998 was less than 2% each year.

EXHIBIT 29.26 Household Income by Age Group

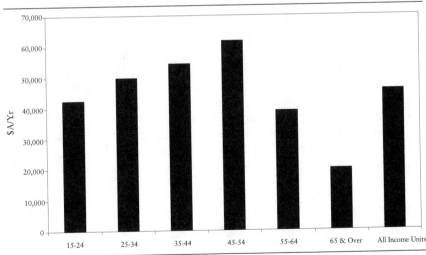

Note: The age groups are for the "reference person" in the household.
Source: Australian Bureau of Statistics and Salomon Smith Barney.

EXHIBIT 29.27   Population Growth Is Changing

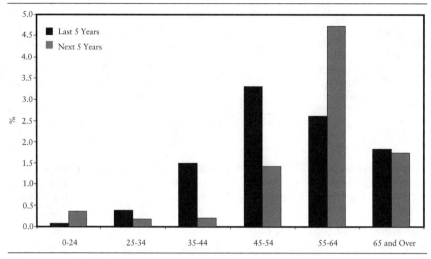

Source: Australian Bureau of Statistics and Salomon Smith Barney.

Aside from its natural population growth, immigration plays a role as well. Asia is the largest source of new entrants into Australia. Each year approximately 90,000 immigrants from Asia settle in Australia's most populous areas, Sydney and Melbourne. Approximately one-third of Australia's arrivals intend to start a business. To achieve business-immigration status, applicants must provide a business plan and verification of start-up capital. Another third of the immigrants come to Australia to rejoin families. The final third are considered refugees.

Demographic trends will change significantly during the next five years. Growth in the 45- to 54-year-old age group is expected to halve to 1.5% per year. The 55- to 64-year-old age group is the only bracket that is expected to grow faster during the next five years, as shown in Exhibit 29.27. This age group will grow by approximately 4.5% per year.

The decline in population growth of the younger, more mobile population groups (except for the 0- to 24-year-old age category) implies a possible slight slowdown in housing turnover and related prepayments in the future.

APPENDIX 29B
AN OVERVIEW OF AUSTRALIA'S GST AND TAX REFORM

On July 1, 2000, the Australian government introduced a major tax reform for individuals and businesses. The reform includes the introduction of a broad-based consumption tax, as well as income and corporate tax cuts. Our colleagues at Salomon Smith Barney Australia believe that these reforms should have long-term positive impacts on business investment, exports, and the Australian dollar.

The tax reform contains the elimination of many indirect taxes, as well as the commencement of a 10% goods and services tax (GST) on all goods except basic food. The GST will be partnered by substantive income tax cuts, including a reduction in capital gains taxes. The business tax reform includes a phased reduction of the corporate tax rate from 36% to 30%, and the elimination of accelerated depreciation. The net effect of these changes, we believe, will be an economic stimulus.

Since November 1999, interest rates in Australia have risen by 150bp. The conventional view is that these monetary tightenings were not directly based on the changes in the GST. Rather, the objective has been to slow the economy to reduce the potential inflationary impact of the GST in the approaching months. At the same time, the rate increases have been a reaction to stronger global economic growth and the falling value of the Australian dollar.

We view the GST and the tax reform as a net wash for the Australian mortgage market at this time, because the promised boost to disposable income from the tax cuts has been eroded by recent interest-rate increases. The GST may, however, cause an increase in the cost of repairing or replacing damaged property. In the event that the mortgage trust takes ownership of a property (by way of default), the expenses incurred, if any, to repair and liquidate the property may increase. To put it another way, loss severity may increase slightly. If liquidation proceeds do not sufficiently meet the outstanding loan balance at liquidation, the shortfall becomes a personal obligation of the borrower. Remaining principal losses generally would be absorbed by the mortgage insurance provider, the excess spread, or the first-loss bondholder.

The interest-rate increases have caused a 30-year A$150,000 mortgage to cost the borrower an additional A$155 per month. Furthermore, an additional 25bp to 50bp of tightening may occur in the third quarter of 2000, with the main inflationary risk originating from a tight labor market and the effects on wages from the GST. For first-time home buyers purchasing houses in value up to A$250,000, the Australian government provides a A$7,000 grant to help offset the expected increase in the cost of a new house under the tax reforms.

In the long run, the tax-reform package should not be problematic for inflation and interest rates, in our opinion. The reduction in capital gains and corporate taxation adds to the likelihood that, overall, the changes will have a positive impact on Australia's equity market. For the Australian

EXHIBIT 29.28 Annual Growth in Real GDP of Australia, the United Kingdom, and the United States, 1Q91–2000

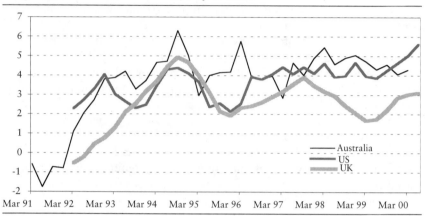

Source: Australian Bureau of Statistics and Reserve Bank of Australia.

dollar, the impact of the tax reform will come from the stimulus that the tax-reform package will provide to the economy and its support to the export sector. In Exhibit 29.28 we show the annual growth rate in Australian GDP versus GDP for the United States and the United Kingdom since 1991.

Consumer confidence in Australia improved dramatically in the mid-1990s and remained fairly bullish throughout the remainder of the 1990s. It

EXHIBIT 29.29 Consumer Confidence (in Units of Standard Deviation from Ten-Year Average)

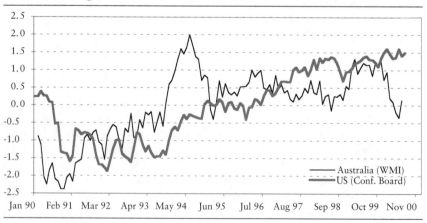

Source: Reserve Bank of Australia and Conference Board.

EXHIBIT 29.30   Exchange Rates—U.S. Dollar versus Australian Dollar

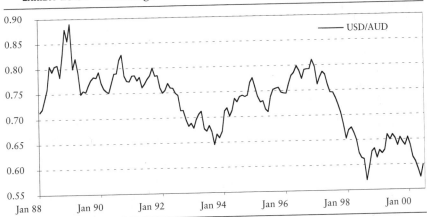

Source: Reserve Bank of Australia.

was not until the end of 1999 and into 2000 that consumer confidence in Australia fell sharply as a reaction to interest-rate increases and a weak domestic currency, which recently hit a historic low versus the U.S. dollar (see Exhibit 29.29). By comparison, consumer confidence in the United States has grown steadily since 1992. Exhibit 29.30 compares consumer confidence in Australia and the United States since 1990.

APPENDIX 29C
THE UNIFORM CONSUMER CREDIT CODE

The Uniform Consumer Credit Code (the code) was enacted in 1996. Its primary purpose is to govern the provision of personal credit. The code applies to owner-occupied home mortgages, but not to investment property loans. The scope of the code is very wide and is uniform across Australian jurisdictions. All mortgage lenders must comply with the code by providing full disclosure of fees, charges, and loan terms associated with the mortgage. As a result of the code, mortgage lenders now use standardized documents in the lending process. Other than the aforementioned, the code has little relevance to MBS structures.

   The code requires that lenders determine that a borrower has the ability to repay the loan. The code calls for the enforcement of its provisions by imposing monetary penalties, reduction or cancellation of debt, or the actual loss of collateral for lenders that do not comply. The code also regulates the means by which lenders pursue borrower obligations. Some examples of the code's provisions:

- The borrower can pay out the contract at any time.
- The credit provider may not charge any amount to the borrower unless it is authorized by the contract.
- The credit provider cannot make any profit on fees and expenses passed on to third parties.
- The borrower has the right to negotiate a deferral or reduction of payments if the borrower cannot make scheduled payments (however, interest continues to accrue under the contractually required rate).
- Courts are allowed to reopen and remedy unjust loan contracts if they can determine (for example) whether unfair pressure, undue influence, or unfair tactics were used, or whether the credit provider knew or could have known that the debtor was unable to pay off the debt without substantial hardship.

APPENDIX 29D
AGGREGATE COLLATERAL BREAKDOWNS: ALL RATED DEALS 1995–1Q00

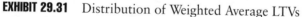

EXHIBIT 29.31   Distribution of Weighted Average LTVs

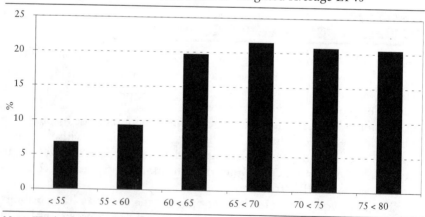

Note: Weighted Average LTV for Securitized Mortgages is 67.5%. Graph excludes HLC Trust 1999–1 (weighted avg. LTV = 97.3%).
Source: S&P Australian and New Zealand ABS Performance Watch, May 2000.

EXHIBIT 29.32   Loan Balance Distribution

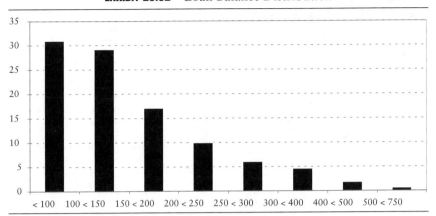

Source: S&P Australian and New Zealand ABS Performance Watch, May 2000.

EXHIBIT 29.33   Weighted Average Geographic Distribution

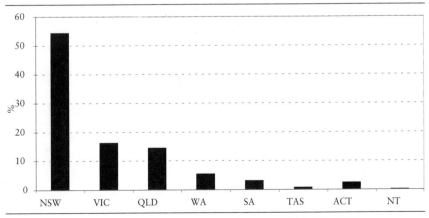

Source: S&P Australian and New Zealand ABS Performance Watch, May 2000.

APPENDIX 29E
S&P AUSTRALIAN BENCHMARK RESIDENTIAL MORTGAGE
LOAN POOL

EXHIBIT 29.34   S&P Australian Benchmark Residential Mortgage Loan Pool

Pool size	Minimum of 300 loans
Loan seasoning	Minimum one payment made
Loan size	Maximum individual loan size A$400,000
	Maximum weighted average loan size A$150,000
LTV	80%
Loan type	Level pay, fully amortizing, variable-rate
Loan term	25 years
Security	First registered mortgage over freehold land or crown lease holds with a lease term at least 15 years longer than the loan term
Security property	Residential property, detached, semi-detached, townhouses, strata title flats, apartments, units
Geographic dispersion	Geographically diverse; metropolitan areas
	State concentration limits:
	– New South Wales/Australian Capital Territory 60%
	– Victoria 50%
	– Queensland 40%
	– Western Australia 25%
	– South Australia 25%
	–Tasmania/Northern Territory 10%
	Maximum inner-city exposure —10%
	Maximum nonmetro exposure —10%
Performance	Not delinquent, strong performance over last 12 months
Borrower employment status	PAYE employee or professional
Borrower status	Australian resident
Affordability	Within market standards and standard imposed by UCCC
Loan purpose	Purchase or refinance without equity release
Property insurance	Fully insured against fire and other major hazards
Underwriting standard	Full

Source: S&P.

APPENDIX 29F
RESIDENTIAL MORTGAGE RATES (AS OF AUGUST 11, 2000)

EXHIBIT 29.35 Residential Mortgage Rates, August 11, 2000

	Total Entry Fees	Standard Variable	Basic Variable	Introductory/ 1 yr Fixed	5 yr Fixed
AMP Banking	600	7.80	7.65	6.65 (9m)	7.99
ANZ Bank	600	7.80	7.20	7.30	7.89
Adelaide Bank	595	8.25	—	7.24	8.09
Aussie Home Loans	820	7.95	7.47	—	7.99
Bank West	500	7.80	7.24	6.80	7.99
Citibank	590	8.39	—	7.79	7.89
Colonial State Bank	750	7.82	7.22	—	7.80
Commonwealth Bank	450	7.82	7.26	7.35	7.80
FAI	600	7.65	7.30	—	8.19
HSBC	750	7.70	—	6.95	7.79
National Aust Bank	600	8.06	—	7.46	7.90
RAMS	690	7.79	7.14	6.60	8.09
St. George Bank	600	8.07	7.22	5.99	7.99
Suncorp Metway	700	7.80	7.35	6.59	7.95
Westpac Bank	600	8.07	7.51	6.74	7.99

Note: Total entry fees include application fee, establishment fee, valuation fee, and any other fees involved to set up a loan. *Source: Your Mortgage Magazine.*

APPENDIX 29G
AUSTRALIAN MORTGAGE FEES

To more easily compare different loans, a **comparison rate** (also called the true rate or AAPR), which incorporates the fees associated with each loan, is often computed similar to the APR (annual percentage rate) used in the United States. However, it should be noted that the comparison rate does not incorporate loan features and repayment flexibility.

EXHIBIT 29.36 Australian Mortgage Fees

Upfront Fees ($100K mortgage in NSW)		
Application Fee	Up to $200	
Establishment Fee	Up to $600	
Valuation Fee	Up to $250	
Mortgage Insurance	$0–$1,700	80% ~ 95% LTV
Legal Fees	Up to $300	
– Settlement Fees		
– Mortgage Preparation Fee		
– Document Preparation Fee		
– Securitization Fee		
Stamp Duty Tax on Loan	$341	
Stamp Duty Tax on Purchase	$2,865–$2,176	80% ~ 95% LTV
Transfer Fee (Government)	Around $60	
Total	**$4,200–$5,200**	
Other Fees		
– Ongoing Administration Fee	$0–$8	Monthly
– Refixing Fee	$500	
– Redraw Fee	$10–$50	
Portability Fee	$300	
Exit Fee/Break Cost	Varies	
Discharge Fee	$90–$250	
(To cover the administrative cost of winding up the loan)		

Source: Your Mortgage Magazine and Westpac Bank.

APPENDIX 29H
GLOBAL AUSTRALIAN MBS TRANSACTIONS

EXHIBIT 29.37 Global Australian MBS Transactions

	Westpac Securitization Trust 1998-1G		Westpac Securitization Trust 1999-1G		Medallion Trust 2000-1G			Crusade Global Trust 1999-1			
	A	B	A	B*	A1	A2	B	A1	A2	A3	B
TRANSACTION SUMMARY											
Amount (MM)	$1,372.7	$32.3	$883.9	A$33.75	$995.0	A$150.0	A$15.0	$300.0	$589.0	$125.0	A$9.5
Rating @ Issue	AAA	AA-	AAA	N/A	AAA	AAA	AA	AAA	AAA	AAA	
Average Life	3.35	5.67	3.4	N/A	3.3	3.3	5.7	0.68	3.56	7.15	
Maturity	10% Call		10% Call		Earlier of 10% Call or July 2007			Earlier of 10% Call or November 2006			
Legal Final	19-Jul-29		19-May-30		12-Jul-31			15-Feb-30			
Basis	3mLIBOR		3mLIBOR	3mBBSW	3mLIBOR	3mBBSW	3mBBSW	3mLIBOR			
Spread	0.14%	0.265%	0.20%	0.63%	0.23%	0.39%	0.70%	0.25%	0.33%	0.42%	
Step-Up Margin	Not Applicable		Not Applicable		2 x Spread (Class A1 only)			2 x Spread			
Pricing Date	6/4/98		5/7/99		21-Mar-00			9/17/99			
Pricing Speed	22.5% CPR		21.0% CPR		22.0% CPR			22.0% CPR			
CREDIT ENHANCEMENT											
Sub Amount		2.30%		2.20%			0.86%				0.60%
Type	HLIC Ins, Liq Facility, Excess Spread, Sub		HLIC/MGICA Ins, Liq Facility, Excess Spd, Sub		GE Cap Ins, HLIC, Excess Spread, Liq Fac., Sub			HLIC Ins, Excess Spread, Liquidity Facility, Sub			
COLLATERAL SUMMARY											
Principal Amount (MM)	A$2,252.8		A$1,383.2		A$2,735.2			A$1,544.5			
Number of Loans	21,132		12,886		16,583			15,433			
Avg. Loan Size	A$129,434.03		A$212,261.37		A$164,940.			A$177,230.61			
Avg. LTV	70.00%		69.59%		71.24%			68.10%			
Interest Rate	74.7% Var, 25.3% FX		70.97% Var, 29.03% FX		45.4% Var, 24.9% Econometrics, 29.8% FX			Not Available			
Geographic Concentration	36.70%, Victoria Metro 15.69%		38.47%, Victoria Metro 13.79%, W. Australia Metro 12.48%		Metro 25.4%, NSW Metro 23.4%, W. Australia Metro 12.62%			NSW Metro 60.79%, NSW Nonmetro 19.91%			
Seasoning	297.11 mo – 288.41 mo = 8.7 months		310.00 mo – 300.89 mo = 9.11 months		W.A. Seasoning = 16 months			W.A. Seasoning = 27 months			

*Private placement.
Source: Salomon Smith Barney.

APPENDIX 29I
AUSTRALIAN MBS DEALS 1995–2000

See pages 826 to 831.

EXHIBIT 29.38 Australian MBS Deals 1995–2000

Issue Date	Transaction Name	Issuer	Issue Type	Sr/Sub	Cur.	Size	Fitch	MDY	S&P	Mortgage Insurance Provider [a]
15 Aug 00	REDS Trust 2000-2	Bank of Queensland	Domestic	A	AUD	194.8	AAA		AAA	GEMICO, PMI
15 Aug 00	REDS Trust 2000-2	Bank of Queensland	Domestic	B	AUD	5.2	AA-		AA-	GEMICO, PMI
15 Aug 00	Kingfisher Trust No. 1	Aussie Home Loans (ANZ Banking Group)	Domestic	A1-3	AUD	485.0			AAA	CGULMI, GE Mortgage, PMI, RSALMI
15 Aug 00	Kingfisher Trust No. 1	Aussie Home Loans (ANZ Banking Group)	Domestic	B	AUD	15.0			AA-	CGULMI, GE Mortgage, PMI, RSALMI
28 Jul 00	WB Trust 2000-1	Wide Bay Capricorn	Domestic	A	AUD	138.0	AAA		AAA	"unrated captive mortgage insurer"
28 Jul 00	WB Trust 2000-1	Wide Bay Capricorn	Domestic	B	AUD	27.0	A		A	"unrated captive mortgage insurer"
28 Jul 00	WB Trust 2000-1	Wide Bay Capricorn	Domestic	C	AUD	35.0	NR			"unrated captive mortgage insurer"
22 Jun 00	Banksia Trust 2	Bendigo Bank	Domestic	A1-2	AUD	169.0			AAA	PMI, CGULMI, GEMICO, RSALMI
22 Jun 00	Banksia Trust 2	Bendigo Bank	Domestic	B	AUD	4.0			AA-	PMI, CGULMI, GEMICO, RSALMI
16 Jun 00	SMHL Global Fund No. 1	National Mutual Funds Management	Euro	A1-3	USD	700.0	AAA	Aaa	AAA	HLIC, GE Mortgage, GEMICO
16 Jun 00	SMHL Global Fund No. 1	National Mutual Funds Management	Euro	B	AUD	10.5	AA	Aa2	AA	HLIC, GE Mortgage, GEMICO
14 Jun 00	RMT Securitisation Trust 4	FAI Loans	Domestic	A1	AUD	135.0			AAA	HLIC, PMI, GEMICO
14 Jun 00	RMT Securitisation Trust 4	FAI Loans	Domestic	A2	AUD	139.0			AAA	HLIC, PMI, GEMICO
14 Jun 00	RMT Securitisation Trust 4	FAI Loans	Domestic	B	AUD	6.0			AA-	HLIC, PMI, GEMICO
14 Jun 00	Torrens Trust 2000-1G	Adelaide Bank Ltd	Euro	A	USD	730.5	AAA	Aaa	AAA	GEMI, GEMICO, CGULMI, PMI
14 Jun 00	Torrens Trust 2000-1G	Adelaide Bank Ltd	Euro	B	AUD	46.9	AA-		AA-	GEMI, GEMICO, CGULMI, PMI
13 Jun 00	Interstar Millennium Trust 2000-3E	Interstar Sec. Ltd	Euro	A2	USD	465.0	AAA		AAA	HLIC, GEMICO, CGULMI, PMI, RSALMI
13 Jun 00	Interstar Millennium Trust 2000-3E	Interstar Sec. Ltd	Euro	B	USD	60.0	AA-		AA-	HLIC, GEMICO, CGULMI, PMI, RSALMI
08 Jun 00	ARMS II Fund VII	Australian Mortgage Securities	Domestic	A	AUD	98.0			AAA	CGULMI, GEMICO, PMI, RSALMI
08 Jun 00	ARMS II Fund VII	Australian Mortgage Securities	Domestic	B	AUD	3.0			AA-	CGULMI, GEMICO, PMI, RSALMI
29 May 00	RAMS Mortgage Corp 8	RAMS Home Loans Pty Ltd	Domestic	A1-2	AUD	570.0	AAA	Aaa	AAA	CGULMI, GE Mort., GEMICO, PMI, RSALMI
29 May 00	RAMS Mortgage Corp 8	RAMS Home Loans Pty Ltd	Domestic	B	AUD	30.0	AA-	Aa3	AA-	CGULMI, GE Mort., GEMICO, PMI, RSALMI
04 May 00	Interstar Millennium Trust 2000-2	Interstar Sec. Ltd	Domestic	A2-4	AUD	651.0	AAA		AAA	HLIC, GEMICO, CGULMI, PMI, RSALMI
04 May 00	Interstar Millennium Trust 2000-2	Interstar Sec. Ltd	Domestic	B	AUD	49.0	AA-		AA-	HLIC, GEMICO, CGULMI, PMI, RSALMI
12 Apr 00	PUMA Masterfund P-6 b	Macquarie Capital Markets Ltd	Domestic	1	AUD	332.0	AAA	Aa1	AAA	HLIC, CGULMI, PMI, RSALMI, GE Mortgage
28 Mar 00	Crusade Trust 2000-1A	St. George Bank	Domestic	T1F-2	AUD	600.0	AAA		AAA	GE Mortgage
21 Mar 00	Medallion Trust 2000-1G	Commonwealth Bank of Australia	Global	A1-2	USD	1105.0	AAA	Aaa	AAA	PMI, CGULMI, GEMICO,GE Mortgage
21 Mar 00	Medallion Trust 2000-1G	Commonwealth Bank of Australia	Global	B	AUD	15.0	AA	Aa2	AA	PMI, CGULMI, GEMICO,GE Mortgage
21 Mar 00	Interstar Millennium Trust 2000-1	Interstar Sec. Ltd	Domestic	A2-4	AUD	334.0	AAA		AAA	HLIC, GEMICO, CGULMI, PMI, RSALMI
21 Mar 00	Interstar Millennium Trust 2000-1	Interstar Sec. Ltd	Domestic	B	AUD	26.0	AA-		AA-	HLIC, GEMICO, CGULMI, PMI, RSALMI
06 Mar 00	ARMS II Eurofund II	Australian Mortgage Securities Ltd	Euro	A1-2	USD	725.0	AAA	Aaa	AAA	CGULMI, PMI, GEMICO, RSALMI, HLIC
06 Mar 00	ARMS II Eurofund II	Australian Mortgage Securities Ltd	Euro	B	AUD	24.5	AA-		AA-	CGULMI, PMI, GEMICO, RSALMI, HLIC
18 Feb 00	REDS Trust 2000-1	Bank of Queensland	Domestic	A	AUD	153.9	AA-		AAA	HLIC, PMI, GEMICO

Date	Issue	Originator	Market	Class	Currency	Amount	S&P	Moody's	Fitch	Insurers
18 Feb 00	REDS Trust 2000-1	Bank of Queensland	Domestic	B	AUD	4.0			AA-	HLIC, PMI, GEMICO
16 Feb 00	Polar Finance 2 (FABS Trust)	Macquarie Sec. Ltd	Domestic	A1-3	AUD	133.0			AAA	HLIC, CGULMI, GEMICO, PMI
16-Feb-00	Polar Finance 2 (FABS Trust)	Macquarie Sec. Ltd	Domestic	B	AUD	7.0			AA-	HLIC, CGULMI, GEMICO, PMI
14 Feb 00	SWAN Trust 2000-1E	Bank of Western Australia	Euro	A1-3	USD	640.0	AAA	Aaa	AAA	PMI
14 Feb 00	SWAN Trust 2000-1E	Bank of Western Australia	Euro	B	USD	29.4	AA		AA-	PMI
14 Feb 00	Puma Masterfund P7	Macquarie Sec. Ltd	Domestic	A1-2	AUD	724.0		Aaa	AAA	HLIC, CGULMI, PMI, RSALMI, GE Mortgage
14 Feb 00	Puma Masterfund P7	Macquarie Sec. Ltd	Domestic	B	AUD	26.0			AA-	HLIC, CGULMI, PMI, RSALMI, GE Mortgage
14 Feb 00	WB Warehouse Trust No.1	Wide Bay Capricorn	Domestic	A	AUD	51.0			AAA	
14 Feb 00	WB Warehouse Trust No.1	Wide Bay Capricorn	Domestic	B	AUD	19.0				
07 Feb 00	Rock Trust	Rock Building Society	Domestic	A	AUD	50.0			AAA	
07 Feb 00	Rock Trust	Rock Building Society	Domestic	B	AUD	1.0				
31 Jan 00	ARMS II Fund VI	Australian Mortgage Securities	Domestic	A1-2	AUD	290.0	AAA	Aaa	AAA	PMI, RSALMI, CGULMI
31 Jan 00	ARMS II Fund VI	Australian Mortgage Securities	Domestic	B	AUD	11.0	AA-		AA-	PMI, RSALMI, CGULMI
21 Jan 00	Puma Masterfund P5B1b	Macquarie Sec. Ltd	Domestic	B1F	AUD	148.0			AAA	HLIC, CGULMI, PMI, RSALMI, GE Mortgage
08 Dec 99	ARMS II FUND V	Australian Mortgage Securities	Domestic	1	AUD	97.5		Aaa	AAA	GEMICO, PMI, RSALMI, CGULMI
08 Dec 99	ARMS II FUND V	Australian Mortgage Securities	Domestic	2	AUD	2.5			AA-	GEMICO, PMI, RSALMI, CGULMI
03 Dec 99	Interstar Millennium 1999-1	Interstar Sec. Ltd	Domestic	A2-4	AUD	372.0			AAA	GEMICO, PMI, RSALMI, CGULMI
03 Dec 99	Interstar Millennium 1999-1	Interstar Sec. Ltd	Domestic	B	AUD	28.0			AA-	GEMICO, PMI, RSALMI, CGULMI
24 Nov 99	Liberty Funding 1999-1	Liberty Funding Pty Ltd	Domestic	A1-2	AUD	90.0		Aaa	AAA	RSALMI
24 Nov 99	Liberty Funding 1999-1	Liberty Funding Pty Ltd	Domestic	B-C	AUD	10.0				RSALMI
26 Oct 99	Gold Star Trust	Trust Bank	Domestic		AUD	250.0			AAA	HLIC
21 Oct 99	RAMS 7E	RAMS Home Loans Pty Ltd	Euro	A	USD	503.4	AAA	Aaa	AAA	HLIC, CGULMI, GEMICO, RSALMI, MGICA
21 Oct 99	RAMS 7E	RAMS Home Loans Pty Ltd	Euro	PTN	EUR	228.0	AAA	Aaa	AAA	HLIC, CGULMI, GEMICO, RSALMI, MGICA
08 Oct 99	ARMS II Fund IV	Australian Mortgage Securities	Domestic	1	AUD	130.0	AAA	Aaa	AAA	HLIC, CGULMI, GEMICO, RSALMI, MGICA
08 Oct 99	ARMS II Fund IV	Australian Mortgage Securities	Domestic	2	AUD	112.5	AAA	Aa3	AAA	HLIC, CGULMI, GEMICO, RSALMI, MGICA
08 Oct 99	ARMS II Fund IV	Australian Mortgage Securities	Domestic	3	AUD	7.5	AA-		AA-	HLIC, CGULMI, GEMICO, RSALMI, MGICA
17 Sep 99	Crusade Global Trust 1999-1	St. George Bank Ltd	Global	A1-3	USD	994.0	AAA	Aaa	AAA	HLIC
17 Sep 99	Crusade Global Trust 1999-1	St. George Bank Ltd	Global	B	USD	6.0			AAA	HLIC
08 Sep 99	Compass Master Trust 1999-04	Citibank Ltd	Domestic	A	AUD	100.0		Aaa	AA	HLIC, RSALMI
08 Sep 99	Compass Master Trust 1999-04	Citibank Ltd	Domestic	B	AUD	4.0		A2	A	HLIC, RSALMI
18 Aug 99	REDS Trust 1999-2	Bank of Queensland	Domestic	A1-2	AUD	171.6			AAA	HLIC, MCIGA, GEMICO
18 Aug 99	REDS Trust 1999-2	Bank of Queensland	Domestic	B	AUD	3.4			AA-	HLIC, MCIGA, GEMICO
23 Jul 99	RESIMAC MBS 1999-1	Residential Mortgage Acceptance Corp	Domestic	A1-2	AUD	504.1	AAA		AAA	HLIC, GEMICO, CGU, MGICA, RSALMI
23 Jul 99	RESIMAC MBS 1999-1	Residential Mortgage Acceptance Corp	Domestic	B	AUD	14.0	AA-		AA-	HLIC, GEMICO, CGU, MGICA, RSALMI
23 Jul 99	RESIMAC ACE 1999-1	Societe Generale Australia Ltd	Euro	A1	EUR	175.0	AAA		AAA	HLIC, GEMICO, CGU, MGICA, RSALMI
23 Jul 99	Puma Finance E32A	Macquarie Bank Ltd	Euro	A1-3	USD	482.5	AAA	Aaa	AAA	HLIC, MCIGA, CUAMIC, RSALMI

continued

EXHIBIT 29.38 Continued

Issue Date	Transaction Name	Issuer	Issue Type	Sr/Sub	Cur.	Size	Fitch	MDY	S&P	Mortgage Insurance Provider[a]
23 Jul 99	Puma Finance E32A	Macquarie Bank Ltd	Euro	2B	USD	17.5	AA-		AA-	HLIC, MCIGA, CUAMIC, RSALMI
15 Jul 99	ARMS II Eurofund 1	Australian Mortgage Securities Ltd	Euro	A1-2	USD	482.0	AAA	Aaa	AAA	HLIC, CGULMI, PMI, RSALMI, GE M., GEMICO
15 Jul 99	ARMS II Eurofund 1	Australian Mortgage Securities Ltd	Euro	B	USD	18.0	AA-		AA-	HLIC, CGULMI, PMI, RSALMI, GE M., GEMICO
13 Jul 99	Compass Master Trust 1999-03	Citibank Ltd	Domestic	A	AUD	100.0		Aaa	AA	HLIC, RSALMI
13 Jul 99	Compass Master Trust 1999-03	Citibank Ltd	Domestic	B	AUD	4.0		A2	A	HLIC, RSALMI
13 Jul 99	CATS 1999-E1	Colonial State Bank	Euro	A	USD	492.0	AAA	Aaa	AAA	HLIC, PMI
13 Jul 99	CATS 1999-E1	Colonial State Bank	Euro	B	AUD	12.2	AA		AA-	HLIC, PMI
11 Jun 99	Torrens Trust 1999-1	Adelaide Bank	Domestic	A1-2	AUD	243.7			AAA	HLIC, CGULMI, MGICA, GEMICO
11 Jun 99	Torrens Trust 1999-1	Adelaide Bank	Domestic	B	AUD	4.9			AA-	HLIC, CGULMI, MGICA, GEMICO
10 Jun 99	SMHL 8	National Mutual Funds Management	Domestic	A	AUD	230.0		Aaa	AAA	HLIC
10 Jun 99	WB Trust	Wide Bay Capricorn	Domestic	A	AUD	50.0			AA	HLIC, GE Mortgage
Jun 99	Interstar Pool VT30 Master Trust	Interstar Sec. Ltd	Domestic	A	AUD	632.0			AAA	HLIC, CGULMI, PMI, RSALMI, GEMICO
Jun 99	Interstar Pool VT30 Master Trust	Interstar Sec. Ltd	Domestic	B	AUD	48.0			AA-	HLIC, CGULMI, PMI, RSALMI, GEMICO
10 May 99	Compass Master Trust 1999-02	Citibank Ltd	Domestic	A	AUD	100.0		Aaa	AA	HLIC, RSALMI
10 May 99	Compass Master Trust 1999-02	Citibank Ltd	Domestic	B	AUD	4.0		A2	A	HLIC, RSALMI
07 May 99	WST 1999-1G	Westpac Banking Corp	Global	A	USD	883.9	AAA	Aaa	AAA	HLIC, MGICA, RSALMI
07 May 99	WST 1999-1G	Westpac Banking Corp	Global	B	AUD	33.8			AAA	HLIC, MGICA, RSALMI
28 Apr 99	RAMS Mortgage Corp 6E	RAMS Mortgage Corp	Euro	A1-2	USD	475.0	AAA	Aaa	AAA	HLIC, CGULMI, RSALMI, GEMICO, MGICA
28 Apr 99	RAMS Mortgage Corp 6E	RAMS Mortgage Corp	Euro	B	USD	25.0	AA-		AA-	HLIC, CGULMI, RSALMI, GEMICO, MGICA
22 Apr 99	REDS Trust 1999-1	Bank of Queensland	Domestic	A	AUD	155.6			AAA	MCIGA
22 Apr 99	REDS Trust 1999-1	Bank of Queensland	Domestic	B	AUD	4.4			AA-	MCIGA
07 Apr 99	ARMS II Fund III	Australian Mortgage Securities	Domestic	1	AUD	242.5	AAA	Aaa	AAA	HLIC, GEMICO, MGICA, RSALMI, CGU
07 Apr 99	ARMS II Fund III	Australian Mortgage Securities	Domestic	2	AUD	7.5	AA-		AA-	HLIC, GEMICO, MGICA, RSALMI, CGU
25 Mar 99	NMHL 4	National Mutual Funds Management	Domestic	A	AUD	120.0		Aaa	AAA	HLIC
22 Mar 99	Puma Finance E31A	Macquarie Sec. Ltd	Euro	A1	USD	772.0		Aaa	AAA	HLIC, MGICA, CGULMI, RSALMI
22 Mar 99	Puma Finance E31A	Macquarie Sec. Ltd	Euro	1B	USD	28.0			AA-	HLIC, MGICA, CGULMI, RSALMI
01 Mar 99	Compass Master Trust 1999-01	Citibank Ltd	Domestic	A	AUD	100.0		Aaa	AA	HLIC, RSALMI
01 Mar 99	Compass Master Trust 1999-01	Citibank Ltd	Domestic	B	AUD	4.0		A2	A	HLIC, RSALMI
19 Feb 99	HLC 1999-1	Home Loan Company Pty	Domestic	A	AUD	42.0	A		A	Not Insured
19 Feb 99	HLC 1999-1	Home Loan Company Pty	Domestic	B	AUD	5.0				Not Insured
19 Feb 99	HLC 1999-1	Home Loan Company Pty	Domestic	E	AUD	3.0				Not Insured
12 Feb 99	Apollo Trust	Suncorp-Metway Ltd	Domestic	A1-2	AUD	220.0	AAA		AAA	HLIC
14 Dec 98	RMT Securitisation 3	FAI Loans	Domestic	A1	AUD	191.0			AAA	HLIC, PMI
14 Dec 98	RMT Securitisation 3	FAI Loans	Domestic	B	AUD	3.0			AA-	HLIC, PMI
08 Dec 98	Torrens Trust 1998-2	Adelaide Bank	Domestic	A	AUD	197.0			AAA	HLIC, CGULMI, PMI, GEMICO

Date	Trust	Originator	Market	Class	Currency	Amount			Rating	Mortgage Insurers
Nov 98	Rock Trust	Rock Building Society	Domestic	A	AUD	88.0			AAA	HLIC, CGULMI, PMI, GE Mortgage, GEMICO
Nov 98	Rock Trust	Rock Building Society	Domestic	B	AUD	2.0			AA-	HLIC, CGULMI, PMI, GE Mortgage, GEMICO
28 Sep 98	RAMS 5E	Registered Australian Mortgage Sec.	Euro	A1-2	USD	384.0	AAA	Aaa	AAA	HLIC, CULMI, MGICA,RSALMI
28 Sep 98	RAMS 5E	Registered Australian Mortgage Sec.	Euro	B	USD	16.0	AA-		AA-	HLIC, CULMI, MGICA,RSALMI
23 Sep 98	Medallion Trust 1998-1	Commonwealth Bank	Domestic	A	AUD	300.0		Aaa	AAA	HLIC
23 Sep 98	Medallion Trust 1998-1	Commonwealth Bank	Domestic	B	AUD	3.0		Aa1	AA+	HLIC
22 Sep 98	Crusade Euro Trust 1998-2	St. George Bank	Euro	A	USD	314.0	AAA	Aaa	AAA	MCIGA, CUAMIC, HLIC
22 Sep 98	Crusade Euro Trust 1998-2	St. George Bank	Euro	B	USD	11.0	AA	A2	AA-	MCIGA, CUAMIC, HLIC
10 Sep 98	CATS Trust 1998-1	Colonial State Bank	Domestic	A1-2	AUD	248.0	AAA	Aaa	AAA	MCIGA, CUAMIC, HLIC
06 Aug 98	Puma Finance E22A	Macquarie Bank Ltd	Euro	A1-2	USD	450.0		Aaa	AAA	MCIGA, CUAMIC, HLIC
22 Jul 98	RAMS 4	RAMS Home Loans	Domestic	A1-2	AUD	192.0			AAA	HLIC, CGULMI, MGICA
22 Jul 98	RAMS 4	RAMS Home Loans	Domestic	B	AUD	8.0			AA-	HLIC, CGULMI, MGICA
13 Jul 98	1998-2	Home Owner Mortgage Enhanced Sec.	Domestic	A1-3	AUD	126.0			AA	HLIC, CGULMI, MGICA
10 Jul 98	Interstar MBS Pool	Interstar Sec. Ltd	Domestic	A2-3	AUD	170.0			AAA	HLIC, CGULMI, PMI
10 Jul 98	Interstar MBS Pool	Interstar Sec. Ltd	Domestic	B	AUD	18.0			AA-	
Jul 98	Jemstone Trust	Australian Mortgage Securities	Domestic							
23 Jun 98	Torrens Trust 1998-1	Adelaide Bank	Domestic	A	AUD	243.0			AAA	HLIC, CGULMI, PMI, MAC
23 Jun 98	Torrens Trust 1998-1	Adelaide Bank	Domestic	B	AUD	3.7			AA-	HLIC, CGULMI, PMI, MAC
04 Jun 98	WST 1998-1G	Westpac	Global	A	USD	1372.7	AAA	Aaa	AAA	HLIC, PMI, RSALMI
04 Jun 98	WST 1998-1G	Westpac	Global	B	USD	32.3			AAA	HLIC, PMI, RSALMI
06 May 98	SAM Trust 1998-1	Citibank Ltd	Domestic	A	AUD	214.8		Aaa	AAA	HLIC, RSALMI
06 May 98	SAM Trust 1998-1	Citibank Ltd	Domestic	B	AUD	2.4			AA-	HLIC, RSALMI
May 98	NMHL_3	National Mutual Funds Management	Domestic	A	AUD	110.0			AAA	HLIC
May 98	Resimac Trust 1998-1	Fanmac	Domestic	A	AUD	193.2			AAA	HLIC, CGULMI, PMI, GE Mortgage
May 98	Resimac Trust 1998-1	Fanmac	Domestic	B	AUD	8.8			AA-	HLIC, CGULMI, PMI, GE Mortgage
May-98	WB Trust 1998	Wide Bay Capricorn	Domestic	A	AUD	141.3			AA	HLIC, CGULMI, PMI, GE Mortgage, GEMICO
Apr-98	SMHL_7	National Mutual Funds Management	Domestic	A	AUD	180.0		Aaa	AAA	HLIC
11 Mar 98	Crusade Euro Trust 1998-1	St. George Bank	Euro	A	USD	496.0	AAA	Aaa	AAA	GE Mortgage
11 Mar 98	Crusade Euro Trust 1998-1	St. George Bank	Euro	B	USD	4.0	AAA	Aa1	AAA	GE Mortgage
Mar 98	Banksia Trust 1	Bendigo Bank	Domestic	A	AUD	122.0			AAA	HLIC
24 Feb 98	REDS Trust 1998-1	Bank of Queensland	Domestic	A	AUD	189.4			AAA	MCIGA
24 Feb 98	REDS Trust 1998-1	Bank of Queensland	Domestic	B	AUD	10.6			AA-	MCIGA
27 Nov 97	Interstar MBS Pool	Interstar Sec. Ltd	Domestic	A2-3	AUD	280.0			AAA	HLIC, CGULMI, RSALMI, MGICA
27 Nov 97	Interstar MBS Pool	Interstar Sec. Ltd	Domestic	B	AUD	32.0			AA-	HLIC, CGULMI, RSALMI, MGICA
12 Nov 97	PUMA Finance E21A	Macquarie Sec. Ltd	Euro	A1-2	USD	846.0	AAA	Aaa	AAA	HLIC, PMI, RSALMI, CGULMI
12 Nov 97	PUMA Finance E21A	Macquarie Sec. Ltd	Euro	B	USD	54.0	AA-		AA-	HLIC, PMI, RSALMI, CGULMI

continued

EXHIBIT 29.38 Continued

Issue Date	Transaction Name	Issuer	Issue Type	Sr/Sub	Cur.	Size	Fitch	MDY	S&P	Mortgage Insurance Provider [a]
06 Nov 97	SAM Trust 1997-2	Citibank Ltd	Domestic	A	AUD	163.0		Aaa	AAA	HLIC, RSALMI
06 Nov 97	SAM Trust 1997-2	Citibank Ltd	Domestic	B	AUD	5.2			AA-	HLIC, RSALMI
Nov 97	SMHL 6	National Mutual Funds Management	Domestic		AUD	150.0		Aaa	AAA	HLIC
28 Oct 97	CATS Trust 1997-1	Colonial State Bank	Domestic	A	AUD	202.0		Aaa	AAA	HLIC
20 Oct 97	Medallion Trust 1997-1	Commonwealth bank	Domestic	A	AUD	277.2		Aaa	AAA	HLIC
03 Oct 97	RAMS 3	RAMS Home Loans	Domestic	A1-2	AUD	288.0		Aaa	AAA	HLIC, CGULMI, PMI, RSALMI, GEMICO
03 Oct 97	RAMS 3	RAMS Home Loans	Domestic	B	AUD	12.0			AA	HLIC, CGULMI, PMI, RSALMI, GEMICO
Oct 97	Progress Trust 1997-1	Priority One (AMP)	Domestic	A1-3	AUD	485.0			AAA	PMI, GE Mortgage
Oct 97	Progress Trust 1997-1	Priority One (AMP)	Domestic	B	AUD	15.0			AA-	PMI, GE Mortgage
26 Sep 97	WST 1997-4E	Westpac Banking Corp	Europe	A	USD	499.0		Aaa	AAA	HLIC, RSALMI
26 Sep 97	WST 1997-4E	Westpac Banking Corp	Europe	B	USD	17.6			AA-	HLIC, RSALMI
Aug 97	RMT Sec. Trust No. 2	FAI Loans	Domestic	A	AUD	228.0			AAA	HLIC, PMI
Aug 97	RMT Sec. Trust No. 2	FAI Loans	Domestic	B	AUD	12.0			AA-	HLIC, PMI
Aug 97	NMHL 2	National Mutual Funds Management	Domestic	A	AUD	110.0			AAA	HLIC
29 Jul 97	Crusade Trust 1997-1	St. George Bank	Domestic	A	AUD	500.0	AAA		AAA	HLIC
08 Jul 97	WST 1997-3	Westpac Banking Corp	Domestic	A1-3	AUD	681.0		Aaa	AAA	HLIC, RSALMI
08 Jul 97	WST 1997-3	Westpac Banking Corp	Domestic	B	AUD	13.9			AA-	HLIC, RSALMI
06 Jul 97	SAM Trust 1997-1	Citibank Ltd	Domestic	A	AUD	225.1		Aaa	AAA	HLIC, RSALMI
06 Jul 97	SAM Trust 1997-1	Citibank Ltd	Domestic	B	AUD	7.0			AA-	HLIC, RSALMI
Jul 97	Interstar Pool RD25 Master Trust	Interstar Sec. Ltd	Domestic	A	AUD	900.0			AAA	HLIC, CGULMI, PMI, RSALMI, GEMICO
Jul 97	Interstar Pool RD25 Master Trust	Interstar Sec. Ltd	Domestic	B	AUD	100.0			AA-	HLIC, CGULMI, PMI, RSALMI, GEMICO
27 Jun 97	Interstar MBS Pool	Interstar Sec. Ltd	Domestic	A2-3	AUD	270.0			AAA	HLIC, CGULMI, RSALMI, MGICA
27 Jun 97	Interstar MBS Pool	Interstar Sec. Ltd	Domestic	B	AUD	30.0			AA-	HLIC, CGULMI, RSALMI, MGICA
06 Jun 97	Puma Fund P6B	Macquarie Sec. Ltd	Domestic	B1-3	AUD	473.0			AAA	HLIC, CGULMI, PMI, RSALMI, GE Mortgage
06 Jun 97	Puma Fund P6B	Macquarie Sec. Ltd	Domestic	SUB	AUD	27.0			AA-	HLIC, CGULMI, PMI, RSALMI, GE Mortgage
Jun 97	SMHL 5	National Mutual Funds Management	Domestic		AUD	180.0		Aaa	AAA	HLIC
29 Apr 97	WST 1997-2	Westpac Banking Corp	Domestic	A	AUD	591.1		Aaa	AAA	HLIC, RSALMI
29 Apr 97	WST 1997-2	Westpac Banking Corp	Domestic	B	AUD	13.3			AA-	HLIC, RSALMI
26 Mar 97	PUMA Finance E-1	Macquarie Sec. Ltd	Euro	A1-2	USD	665.0		Aaa	AAA	HLIC, CGULMI, PMI, RSALMI
26 Mar 97	PUMA Finance E-1	Macquarie Sec. Ltd	Euro	B1	USD	35.0			AA-	HLIC, CGULMI, PMI, RSALMI
13 Feb 97	Puma fund P6A	Macquarie Sec. Ltd	Domestic	A1-3	AUD	475.0		Aaa	AAA	HLIC, CGULMI, PMI, RSALMI, GE Mortgage
13 Feb 97	Puma fund P6A	Macquarie Sec. Ltd	Domestic	SUB	AUD	25.0			AA-	HLIC, CGULMI, PMI, RSALMI, GE Mortgage
Dec 96	SMHL 4	National Mutual Funds Management	Domestic		AUD	180.0		Aaa	AAA	HLIC
20 Nov 96	ARMS II Fund II	Australian Mortgage Securities	Domestic	1	AUD	485.0		Aaa	AAA	HLIC, PMI, GE Mortgage, GEMICO
20 Nov 96	ARMS II Fund II	Australian Mortgage Securities	Domestic	2	AUD	15.0		A1	AA-	HLIC, PMI, GE Mortgage, GEMICO
24 Sep 96	Puma Fund P5B	Macquarie Sec. Ltd	Domestic	B1-3	AUD	475.0		Aaa	AAA	HLIC, CGULMI, PMI, RSALMI, GE Mortgage

Issue Date	Transaction Name	Issuer	Issue Type	Sr/Sub	Cur.	Size	Fitch	MDY	S&P	Mortgage Insurance Provider[a]
24 Sep 96	Puma Fund P5B	Macquarie Sec. Ltd	Domestic	SUB	AUD	25.0			AA-	HLIC, CGULMI, PMI, RSALMI, GE Mortgage
Aug 96	NMHL 1	National Mutual Funds Management	Domestic	A	AUD	110.0			AAA	HLIC
Jul 96	SMHL 3	National Mutual Funds Management	Domestic		AUD	150.0		Aaa	AAA	HLIC
Jul 96	RMT Sec. Trust No 1	FAI Loans	Domestic	A	AUD	187.0			AAA	HLIC, PMI
Jul 96	RMT Sec. Trust No 1	FAI Loans	Domestic	B	AUD	13.0			AA-	HLIC, PMI
07 May 96	Puma fund P5A	Macquarie Sec. Ltd	Domestic	A1-2	AUD	756.0		Aaa	AAA	HLIC, CGULMI, PMI, RSALMI, GE Mortgage
07 May 96	Puma fund P5A	Macquarie Sec. Ltd	Domestic	SUB	AUD	44.0			AA-	HLIC, CGULMI, PMI, RSALMI, GE Mortgage
01 May 96	RAMS 2	RAMS Home Loans	Domestic	A1-B	AUD	1000.0			AAA	HLIC, CGULMI, RSALMI
17 Apr 96	SAM Trust 1996-1	Citibank Ltd	Domestic	A	AUD	310.3		Aaa	AAA	HLIC
17 Apr 96	SAM Trust 1996-1	Citibank Ltd	Domestic	B	AUD	10.0			AA-	HLIC
Feb 96	SMHL 2	National Mutual Funds Management	Domestic		AUD	150.0		Aaa	AAA	HLIC
Feb 96	Torrens Trust 1996-1	Adelaide Bank	Domestic	A	AUD	182.2			AAA	HLIC, CGULMI, RSALMI, MAC
Feb 96	Torrens Trust 1996-1	Adelaide Bank	Domestic	B	AUD	13.2			AA-	HLIC, CGULMI, RSALMI, MAC
05 Oct 95	SAM Trust 1995-1	Citibank Ltd	Domestic	A	AUD	306.3			AAA	HLIC
05 Oct 95	SAM Trust 1995-1	Citibank Ltd	Domestic	B	AUD	9.5			AA	HLIC
22 Sep 95	Puma fund P4	Macquarie Sec. Ltd	Domestic	1F-A3	AUD	803.3		Aaa	AAA	HLIC, CGULMI, PMI, RSALMI, GE Mortgage
22 Sep 95	Puma fund P4	Macquarie Sec. Ltd	Domestic	A4	AUD	46.8			AA-	HLIC, CGULMI, PMI, RSALMI, GE Mortgage
26 May 95	ARMS II Fund I	Australian Mortgage Securities	Domestic	T1-2	AUD	144.0			AAA	HLIC, PMI
26 May 95	ARMS II Fund I	Australian Mortgage Securities	Domestic	T3	AUD	6.0			AA-	HLIC, PMI
25 May 95	Puma fund P3	Macquarie Sec. Ltd	Domestic	1-3	AUD	660.0		Aaa	AAA	HLIC, CGULMI, RSALMI
25 May 95	Puma fund P3	Macquarie Sec. Ltd	Domestic	4	AUD	40.0			AA-	HLIC, CGULMI, RSALMI
08 Feb 95	Puma fund P2	Macquarie Sec. Ltd	Domestic	1-3	AUD	280.0		Aaa	AAA	HLIC, CGULMI, RSALMI
08 Feb 95	Puma fund P2	Macquarie Sec. Ltd	Domestic	4	AUD	20.0			AA	HLIC, CGULMI, RSALMI

[a] HLIC: Housing Loans Insurance Corp. Ltd. (subsidiary of GE Capital Australia), GEMICO: GE Capital Mortgage Insurance Corp., PMI: PMI Mortgage Insurance Ltd. (formerly MGICA Ltd.), CGULMI: CGU Lenders Mortgage Insurance Corp., RSALMI: Royal & Sun Alliance Lenders Mortgage Insurance Ltd. [b]Repurchased and reissued under the same name by Puma. *Source:* Standard & Poor's ABS Performance Watch, May 2000, and Salomon Smith Barney.

glossary

Lakhbir Hayre and Robert Young

ABS In addition to being an acronym for **asset-backed security,** this term is used to denote **absolute prepayment rate,** a prepayment measurement convention used to price ABS deals backed by car loans. As opposed to SMM and CPR, which measure prepayments in terms of the current remaining balance, ABS measures prepayments as a percentage of the *original* balance; thus, 1.5% ABS means that 1.50% of the original balance prepays each month.

amortization The repayment of principal over the term of a loan, rather than in one lump sum at maturity. For a fixed-rate mortgage loan, the (constant) monthly payment is calculated so that the loan is fully paid off over the loan term.

adjustable rate mortgage (ARM) In the United States, the coupon on an ARM typically resets once a year, usually at a specified spread over the one-year Treasury rate, subject to periodic caps (usually 100bp or 200bp) and a lifetime cap (usually 500bp or 600bp) above the coupon at origination.

average life See **WAL.**

Bond Market Association (BMA) A trade association of fixed-income securities dealers, formerly known as the Public Securities Association (PSA). The BMA establishes rules for fixed-income settlement procedures (such as good delivery requirements), deals with issues that affect the bond markets, and publishes brochures on fixed-income securities (see Appendix A for some examples).

book-entry securities Book-entry securities are also known as wireable securities. U.S. Treasury and agency securities (including Fannie Mae and Freddie Mac MBSs) are book-entry securities that are transferred from one entity to another through Fedwire. Ginnie Mae MBSs are wireable through the Participants Trusts Company system.

bounce This operational term refers to sending securities back to where they were originated on the trade date because (a) cash was not received, (b) the dollar amount was not the same as expected, (c) the seller switched the securities, or (d) there is discrepancy in trade information.

Buy-In The process of repurchasing a security previously bought from a customer or broker-dealer who failed to deliver the security to the purchaser within 60 calendar days of the settlement date. Any losses incurred in closing the original transaction are passed along to the original seller who failed to deliver. (Also see **fail**.)

callout date The callout date is also referred to as **48-hour day**. In a TBA trade, information about the actual pools that will be delivered from the seller to the buyer is only provided two days before the actual settlement date (by 3:00 P.M.).

carry The spread between the yield on an MBS and the rate at which money is borrowed to finance the MBS equals the cost to "carry" the security. When the financing rate is greater than the yield, the security has **negative carry**. When the financing rate is less than the yield, the security has **positive carry**.

clearing agent An organization that provides various services for customers and customers' accounts, such as holding inventory positions, receiving and delivering securities, and disbursing funds.

collateralized mortgage obligation (CMO) A common term for a structured mortgage security and used interchangeably with **REMIC**. See Appendix B of the *Guide to Mortgage-Backed Securities* for definitions of common CMO bond types, such as PACs (planned amortization classes).

conforming loans Mortgage loans that satisfy (or conform to) agency underwriting criteria, in terms of maximum loan balance, loan-to-value (LTV) ratio, debt-to-income requirements, and so on.

constant prepayment rate (CPR) An annualized prepayment rate assuming monthly compounding. It is the fraction of the current principal balance, after accounting for scheduled amortization, that would be prepaid over the next 12 months for a given constant monthly prepayment rate (see also **SMM**).

controlled accumulation Accumulation of principal collections in a principal funding account (PFA) and the repayment of principal in a single **soft-bullet** payment on the expected payment date.

controlled amortization Investors receive repayment of principal in a fixed number of *equal* payments. The principal repayment schedule is established at issuance, based on current and historic principal payment rates for the portfolio.

conventional loans Mortgage loans that are *not* insured by the U.S. government (i.e., by the FHA or VA). Conventional loans can be **conforming** or **nonconforming**.

current face   The current principal balance on a security. It is equal to the original balance times either the current pool factor (for pass-throughs) or bond factor (for structured MBSs).

CUSIP   A unique nine-digit identification number for each publicly traded security. CUSIP also stands for the Committee on Uniform Securities Identification Procedures, which assigns the numbers.

custodian   In the clearing process, an organization that holds securities under its own name or under its control on behalf of its customers. In addition to custody, custodians also offer their clients cash management and securities lending services. For example, custodians can help their institutional clients earn incremental income on their portfolios by lending securities from this portfolio to broker-dealers who wish to borrow them.

delay   The principal and interest payments due on an MBS are passed through to investors with a delay to allow servicers time to process mortgage payments. For example, the stated delay on a Ginnie Mae pool is 45 days; thus, the principal and interest for September is paid on October 15, rather than October 1.

dollar roll   In a dollar roll transaction, a pass-through investor agrees to sell securities in the current month and buy back the same amount of substantially similar securities in a forward month at a second, lower price. The second price is specified as a difference, or **drop,** from the first price. The investor forgoes principal and interest payments over the term of the roll and is compensated by the interest earned on the cash proceeds of the initial sale and by the lower repurchase price at the future date. The transaction is favorable to the investor when the drop is large enough to reduce the implied financing rate below short-term reinvestment rates.

early amortization   Revolving period will terminate early pursuant to certain trigger events, and principal collections will be distributed to investors as collections are received.

factor   The fraction of the original balance that is still outstanding. For example, a factor of 0.65 means that the current balance is 65% of the original; that is, scheduled principal payments (amortization) and prepayments have led to 35% of the original balance being paid down. For bonds in structured MBSs and ABSs, the term **bond factor** denotes the remaining principal balance of the bond as a fraction of the original. Collateral and bond factors are updated each month and used to determine principal payments to investors. The three agencies update pool factors near the beginning of each month (see Exhibit 3.4).

fail   A failure to deliver securities versus payment on the settlement date. The originator of the delivery is held liable.

Fannie Mae (formerly the Federal National Mortgage Association, or FNMA) A private corporation originally created by the U.S. government to facilitate the flow of mortgage capital by purchasing and creating a secondary market in such loans. It still has close ties with the U.S. government and is usually referred to as an **agency** or a **Government-Sponsored Enterprise (GSE)**. (See its Web site http://www.fanniemae .com for more details.)

fedwire Connects the Federal Reserve offices, depository institutions, the U.S. Treasury, and other government agencies. Fedwire is typically used to transfer large dollar payments and book-entry securities electronically from one institution to another on behalf of investors.

Freddie Mac (formerly the Federal Home Loan Mortgage Corporation, or FHLMC). A private corporation originally created by the U.S. government to facilitate the flow of mortgage capital by purchasing and creating a secondary market in such loans. It still has close ties with the U.S. government and is usually referred to as an **agency** or a **Government-Sponsored Enterprise (GSE)**. (See its Web site http://www.freddiemac.com for more details.)

Ginnie Mae (formerly the Government National Mortgage Association, or GNMA) An agency of the U.S. government that securitizes mortgages insured by the U.S. government agencies, the **Federal Housing Administration**, the **Veterans Administration**, and the **Rural Housing Service**. Ginnie Mae MBSs carry the full faith and credit of the U.S. government and, hence, have the same credit quality as U.S. Treasuries. (See its Web site http://www.ginniemae.com for more details.)

haircut A percentage of the price of a security used to establish a margin account. This margin account is used to provide the cash lender with a hedge against a decline in the market value of the security. Haircuts are commonly used in repurchase (repo) transactions.

interchange Fees accruing to the credit card processor and credit card issuing bank in return for processing and approving the credit card sale. Credit card issuers typically derive 1% to 2% p.a. in additional interchange fees.

investor interest Share of master trust allocated to investors.

IO An **interest-only** structured MBS, which is entitled to interest payments only from the collateral cash flows (see also **PO**).

master trust Issuance of more than one series backed by a single pool of assets. Each series is entitled to a pro rata share of the assets and cash flows of the trust.

netting When two parties enter into offsetting trades (a pair-off), there is no need to receive/deliver securities. Instead, only the net gain/loss needs to be accounted for. Netting takes this one step further by performing a similar function with many participants simultaneously. For example, if A sells a security to B and B already has a sell position to C for the same amount of the same security, then B has no resulting net position and does not need to receive/deliver any securities for these transactions.

pair-off See **Netting.**

par amount The principal balance of an MBS at issuance. Used synonymously with **face amount.**

percent PSA A prepayment measurement convention. A 100% PSA means that the prepayment rate increases linearly from 0% CPR at loan age 0 to 6% CPR at loan age 30 months, and then remains at 6% CPR, while 150% PSA means that the CPR is 1.5 times the CPR at a 100% PSA, and so on (see Chapter 1 for more details). CMO deals are usually priced at a percentage of PSA.

PO A **principal-only** structured MBS that is entitled to principal payments only from the collateral cash flows (see also **IO**).

pool A collection of individual mortgages that are grouped together by primary lenders (banks, thrifts, mortgage bankers) to constitute the collateral for an MBS.

pool yield All income to master trust, including interest income, interchange and all fees. Many issuers also include recoveries on charged-off loans.

prime broker Prime brokers facilitate the clearance and settlement of securities trades. Prime brokerage involves three parties: (1) The *customer,* typically a substantial retail or institutional investor; (2) The *executing broker,* which executes the trade for the customer; and (3) The *prime broker,* which settles, clears, and finances the customer trades executed by one or more executing brokers.

Prime brokerage allows the customer to utilize the services of several executing brokers, while maintaining one account (with the prime broker) and receiving one consolidated account statement.

principal payment rate Proportion of principal of the master trust that repays in one month, that is, if a master trust has a 20% payment rate, the cash flows will repay investors' principal in five months (100/20 = 5).

Public Securities Association (PSA) See **Bond Market Association.**

record date The date used to note ownership of a security, to determine the distribution of the next payment. For agency MBSs, it is the last day of the month; on this date, the owner receives the principal and interest payment for the month (usually paid the next month). For other MBSs and ABSs, the prospectus specifies the record date.

Real Estate Mortgage Investment Conduit (REMIC) A tax vehicle used to issue structured MBSs, but now the term is used synonymously with **CMO** to denote such securities.

repurchase transaction (repo) Repurchase transactions are securities lending transactions in which one party agrees to sell securities to another party against the transfer of funds, with a simultaneous agreement to repurchase the same securities at a specific price at a later date.

revolving period: Period in which the master trust buys newly charged receivables. Only interest is paid to investors during this period.

seller interest Required by the rating agencies to absorb dilution (amounts related to disputes or returns). The rating agencies require the issuer to allocate an amount of the trust to absorb dilution, that is typically 6% to 10% of the pool balance, depending on historical dilution numbers.

single monthly mortality (SMM) The percentage of remaining principal that, after accounting for scheduled amortization, pays down in a month. The annualized value of the SMM is the **CPR**. (See Appendix A for a mathematical definition.)

soft bullet Single repayment of principal to investors. The structure requires the accumulation of sufficient investor principal collections, prior to the expected final payment date, to retire the certificates. The collections accumulated will be deposited in an account for the benefit of the certificate holders, and the funds in this account will be invested into eligible investments (generally A-1 + /P-1 commercial paper) until the expected final payment date.

weighted-average coupon (WAC) The average coupon on the loans in a pool, weighted by the loan balances. The difference between the WAC and the pass-through coupon paid to investors is termed the **servicing spread.**

weighted-average life (WAL) A measure of the investment life of a fixed-income security that returns principal over a period of time, rather than in one lump sum at maturity. It is the average time until a dollar of principal is returned. (See Appendix A of the *Guide* for a mathematical definition.)

weighted-average loan age (WALA) The average age of the loans in a pool, weighted by the loan balances.

weighted-average maturity (WAM) The average time until maturity of a pool of loans, weighted by the loan balances.

Mortgage Mathematics

Lakhbir Hayre

CASH FLOWS ASSUMING NO PREPAYMENTS

First, we define some terminology. For a level pay mortgage,

let WAC = Gross coupon in percent (for example, 9%)
G = WAC/1200 = Monthly coupon (for example, 9/1200 = 0.0075)
$U = 1/(1 + G)$ = Monthly discount factor for rate G
N = Original loan term in months
n = Age of loan in months
$R = N - n$ = Remaining loan term in months

Then, for each dollar of mortgage, in month n,

$$\text{Monthly payment} = \text{PAY}_n = \frac{G}{1 - U^N}$$

$$\text{Remaining balance (end of month)} = \text{BAL}_n = \frac{1 - U^R}{1 - U^N}$$

$$\text{Principle portion of payment} = \text{PRIN}_n = \frac{GU^{R+1}}{1 - U^N}$$

$$\text{Interest portion of payment} = \text{INT}_n = \frac{G\left(1 - U^{R+1}\right)}{1 - U^N}$$

Because this is a level pay mortgage, the total monthly payment is constant; the subscript n in the formula is for convenience in extending the results in the case of prepayments.

PREPAYMENT TERMINOLOGY

For a given pool of mortgages, let

B_n = Remaining principal balance per dollar of original balance after the nth monthly payment assuming zero prepayments

F_n = Pool factor (the actual remaining balance per dollar of original principal)

$Q_n = F_n/B_n$ = Fraction of the pool that has *not* yet prepaid

While F_n incorporates both scheduled and unscheduled principal payments, Q_n is "normalized" so that changes in Q_n reflect prepayments only.* Thus, for month n,

$$\text{SMM}_n = \frac{\text{Fraction of pool outstanding at beginning}}{\text{of month that is prepaid during the month}}$$

$$= \frac{Q_{n-1} - Q_n}{Q_{n-1}} = 1 - \frac{Q_n}{Q_{n-1}} \tag{A1}$$

The survival factor Q_n and the monthly prepayment rates $\text{SMM}_1, \text{SMM}_2, \ldots$ are related through the equation:

$$Q_n = (1 - \text{SMM}_1)(1 - \text{SMM}_2)\ldots(1 - \text{SMM}_n)$$

For the period from month k to month n, the constant SMM that is equivalent to the actual prepayments experienced is given by

$$(1 - \text{SMM})^{n-k} = \frac{Q_n}{Q_k}$$

The **CPR** corresponding to a given SMM is given by

$$1 - \text{CPR} = (1 - \text{SMM})^{12} \tag{A2}$$

If AGE is the loan age in months, then the **PSA** and the CPR are related to each other according to the following formulae:

_____

* If we think of the pool as consisting of a very large number of $1 mortgages, then Q_n can be interpreted as the fraction of mortgages that have survived (not prepaid) to month n.

$$PSA = CPR \times \frac{100}{6} \times \max\left(1, \frac{30}{Age}\right) \qquad \text{(A3)}$$

$$CPR = PSA \times 0.06 \times \min\left(1, \frac{Age}{30}\right) \qquad \text{(A4)}$$

MORTGAGE CASH FLOWS WITH PREPAYMENTS

The survival factor Q_n links MBS cash flows with and without prepayments. With PAY_n, $PRIN_n$, INT_n, and BAL_n defined as above in the case of zero prepayments, let PAY'_n, $PRIN'_n$, INT'_n, and BAL'_n be the corresponding quantities with prepayments, and let PP_n be the principal prepaid in month n. It is not difficult to show that, given Q_{n-1}

$$PAY'_n = \text{Scheduled monthly payment} = PAY_n \times Q_{n-1}$$
$$PRIN'_n = \text{Scheduled principal payment} = PRIN_n \times Q_{n-1}$$
$$INT'_n = \text{Scheduled interest payment} = INT_n \times Q_{n-1}$$
$$PP_n = \text{Principal prepaid} = (BAL'_{n-1} - PRIN'_n) \times SMM_n$$
$$BAL'_n = BAL'_{n-1} - PRIN'_n - PP_n = BAL_n \times Q_n$$

The total cash flow to the pass-through holder for month n is

$$CF_n = PRIN'_n + PP_n + \left(\frac{C}{WAC}\right) \times INT'_n$$

where C is the pass-through rate and WAC is the weighted average coupon on the underlying loans. In other words, the pass-through holder receives all principal payments, but interest at a rate C rather than the loan rate WAC.

YIELD

For a given prepayment projection and resulting cash flows CF_1, CF_2, . . . , the **mortgage yield** is the discount rate x that equates the present value of the cash flows to the price of the MBS. It is the solution of the equation

$$\text{Price} + \text{Accrued} = \sum_{t=1}^{M} \frac{CF_t}{\left(1 + \dfrac{x}{1200}\right)^{t+a-1}} \qquad \text{(A5)}$$

where Accrued is accrued interest, M is the number of remaining cash flows, a is the number of days from settlement to the first cash-flow date *divided by* 30, and the yield x is stated as an annualized percent.

Yields on MBSs are generally quoted on a bond-equivalent basis (i.e., assuming semiannual compounding) to make them comparable to Treasuries and corporate bonds. The **bond equivalent** yield y can be obtained from the mortgage yield x using the following relationship

$$\left(1+\frac{x}{1200}\right)^{12} = \left(1+\frac{y}{200}\right)^{2}$$

so that

$$y = 200\left[\left(1+\frac{x}{1200}\right)^{6} - 1\right]$$

WEIGHTED-AVERAGE LIFE

The weighted-average life (WAL) is defined as the average time a dollar of principal is outstanding. For a given prepayment rate, it is defined as

$$\text{WAL (in years)} = \frac{1}{12}\sum_{t=1}^{M}(t+a-1)p_{t} \tag{A6}$$

where a is as defined above, and p_t is the fraction of original principal returned in month t under the projected prepayment rate. (Note that $p_1 + p_2 + \ldots p_M = 1$.)

DURATION AND CONVEXITY

Traditional durations are given by the following formula:

$$\text{Macaulay duration} = \frac{1}{12\times P}\times\sum_{t=1}^{M}\frac{(t+a-1)\text{CF}_{t}}{\left(1+\dfrac{x}{1200}\right)^{t+a-1}} \tag{A7}$$

$$\text{Modified duration} = \frac{\text{Macaulay duration}}{\left(1 + \dfrac{y}{200}\right)}$$

where P denotes the full price, or the right-hand side of equation A5. If the security cash flows are fixed, then

$$\text{Modified duration} = \frac{-100}{P} \times \frac{dP}{dy} \qquad (A8)$$

and hence, the modified duration provides a measure of relative price sensitivity with respect to interest rate changes.

For MBSs, cash flows vary with interest rates, so that we cannot use Equation A7. Instead we approximate the right-hand side of Equation A8 directly by **effective duration,** defined as

$$\text{Effective duration} \approx \frac{-100}{P} \times \frac{\Delta P}{\Delta y}$$
$$= \frac{100}{P} \times \frac{P(-\Delta y) - P(\Delta y)}{2 \times \Delta y} \qquad (A9)$$

where $P(-\Delta y)$ and $P(\Delta y)$ are the projected prices if the yield curve is shifted in parallel by small amounts $-\Delta y$ and Δy, respectively. The standard convention is to obtain projected prices by holding OAS constant; however, nothing in the definition of effective duration (A9) stops us from using projected OASs to obtain the prices. We also can consider nonparallel yield curve shifts; for example, *partial durations* with respect to a particular part of the yield curve are obtained by changing only that part of the yield curve.

Convexity is calculated in a similar manner for MBSs:

$$\text{Convexity} = \frac{100}{P} \times \frac{d^2 P}{dy^2}$$
$$\approx \frac{100}{P} \times \frac{\left(\dfrac{P(-\Delta y) - P}{\Delta y} - \dfrac{P - P(\Delta y)}{\Delta y}\right)}{\Delta y} \qquad (A10)$$
$$= \frac{100}{P} \times \frac{P(\Delta y) + P(-\Delta y) - 2P}{(\Delta y)^2}$$

Standard Agency Definitions of CMO Bond Types

Agency Acronym	Definition
Principal Types	
AD	**Accretion Directed (or Stated Maturity).** Classes that are designed to receive principal payments from accretion on specified Accrual Classes. These Classes may also receive principal payments from principal paid on the underlying collateral.
CPT	**Component.** Classes consisting of "Components." The Components of a Component Class may have different principal and/or interest payment characteristics but together constitute a single class. Each Component of a Component Class may be identified as falling into one or more of the categories this chart.
NPR	**No Payment Residual.** Residual Classes that are designed to receive no payments of principal.
NSJ	**Non-Sticky Jump.** Classes whose principal payment priorities change temporarily upon the occurrence of one or more "trigger" events. A Non-Sticky Jum Class "jumps" to its new priority on each Payment Date when the trigger condition is met and reverts to its original priority (does not "stick" to the new priority) on each Payment Date when the trigger condition is not met.
NTL	**Notional.** Classes having only a notional principal amount. A notional principal amount is the amount used as a reference to calculate the amount of interes due on an Interest Only Class that is not entitled to any principal.
PAC	**Planned Amortization Class.** Classes that are designed to receive principal payments using a predetermined schedule derived by assuming the underlying Mortgages will prepay within a range bounded by two constant prepayment rates. A PAC schedule will produce a wide "structuring range" both above and below the Prepayment Assumption for the related Series. The PAC Classes in any series may include two or more "Types." The PAC Class or Classes with any Type have a single structuring range. The different Types have different principal payment priorities. In cases where there is more than one Type, the PAC Classes are designated as Type I PAC Classes, Type II PAC Classes and so forth (standard abbreviations: PAC I, PAC II a so forth).
SCH	**Scheduled.** Classes that are designed to receive principal payments using a predetermined schedule, but that are not designated as PAC or TAC classes. Classes using both PAC and TAC Components are also designated as Scheduled Classes.
SEQ	**Sequential Pay.** Classes that receive principal payments in a prescribed sequence, that do not have predetermined schedules and that under all circumstanc receive payments of principal continuously from the first Payment Date on which they receive principal until they are retired. Sequential Pay Classes may receive principal payments concurrently with one or more other Sequential Pay Classes. A single Class that receives principal payments before or after all other Classes in the same Series may be identified as a Sequential Pay Class.
SJ	**Sticky Jump.** Classes whose principal payment priorities change permanently upon the occurrence of one or more "trigger" events. A Sticky Jump Class "jumps" to its new priority on the first Payment Date when the trigger condition is met and retains ("sticks" to")that priority until retired.
STP	**Strip.** Classes that receive a constant proportion, or "strip" of the principal payments on the underlying collateral.
SUP	**Support (or Companion).** Classes that receive principal payments on any Payment Date only if scheduled payments have been made on specified PAC, T and/or Scheduled Classes.
TAC	**Targeted Amortization Class.** Classes that are designed to receive principal payments using a predetermined schedule derived by assuming that the underlying Mortgages will prepay at a single constant prepayment rate. The TAC Classes in any Series may include two or more "Types." The different Ty have different principal payment priorities and/or have schedules that are derived from different assumed prepayment rates. In cases where there is more th one Type, the TAC Classes are designated as Type I TAC Classes, Type II TAC Classes and so forth (standard abbreviations TAC I, TAC II and so forth).
XAC	**Index Allocation Class.** Classes whose principal payment allocations are based on the value of an index.
Interest Types	
ARB	**Ascending Rate.** Classes that have predetermined Class Coupons that change one or more times on dates determined before issuance.
DLY	**Delay Class.** Floating Rate or Inverse Floating Rate Class for which there is a delay between the end of the interest accrual periods and related Payment Da
EXE	**Excess.** Residual Classes that receive any principal and interest paid on the underlying collateral in excess of the amount of the prescribed principal and interest to be paid on all Classes in the Series. Excess Classes sometimes have specified principal amounts but no specified Class Coupon.
FIX	**Fixed Rate.** Classes whose Class Coupons are fixed throughout the life of the Class.
FLT	**Floating Rate.** Classes with Class Coupons that are reset periodically based on an index and that vary directly with changes in the index.
INV	**Inverse Floating Rate.** Classes with Class Coupons that are reset periodically based on an index and that vary inversely with changes in the index.
IO	**Interest Only.** Classes that receive some or all of the interest payments made on the underlying collateral and little or no principal. Interest Only Classes ha either a nominal or a notional principal amount. A nominal principal amount represents actual principal that will be paid on the Class. It is referred to as nominal since it is extremely small compared to other Classes. A notional principal amount is the amount used as a reference to calculate the amount of interest due on an Interest Only Class that is not entitled to any principal.
NPR	**No Payment Residual.** Residual Classes that are designed to receive no payments of interest.
PO	**Principal Only.** Classes that do not receive any interest.
PZ	**Partial Accrual.** Classes that accrete a part of their interest, which is added to the outstanding principal balance, and simultaneously receive payments of tl remainder as interest.
W	**Weighted-Average Coupon.** Classes whose Class Coupons represent a blended interest rate that may change from period to period. WAC Classes may consist of Components, some of which have different interest rates.
Z	**Accrual.** Classes that accrete all of their interest, which is added to the outstanding principal balance. This accretion may continue until the Class begins receiving principal payments, until some other event has occurred or until the Class is retired.
LIQ	**Liquid Asset.** Classes intended to qualify as "liquid assets" for certain savings institutions. Liquid Asset Classes have Final Payment Dates not later than fi years from their dates of issuance.
RTL	**Retail.** Classes designated for sale to retail investors. Retail Classes frequently are sold in small "units" or other increments and may receive principal payments in accordance with special priorities and allocation procedures.
TBD	**To Be Defined.** Bonds that do not fit under any of the current definitions.

Source: Standard Definitions for REMIC and CMO Bonds, Freddie Mac Publication Number 160, December 1992.

Risk-Based Capital Standards

Lakhbir Hayre and Robert Young

Institutional investors need to be cognizant of their supervisory agencies' capital standards before investing in MBSs and ABSs. These capital requirements will likely be based on standards for capital adequacy that were initially formalized in the 1988 Basle Accord. The Accord was established by the Basle Committee on Banking Supervision of the Bank for International Settlements. The committee consists of senior representatives of bank supervisory authorities and central banks from the Group of Ten (G-10) countries (Belgium, Canada, France, Germany, Italy, Japan, Luxembourg, the Netherlands, Sweden, Switzerland, the United Kingdom, and the United States).

The 1988 Accord was primarily concerned with credit risk and instituted a **minimum ratio** of capital to assets for internationally active banks. The Accord takes into account the relative risk of an asset by relating capital requirements for a particular asset to the credit risk of this asset. Assets are assigned to five different risk buckets with weights of 0%, 10%, 20%, 50%, and 100%. The four risk categories used in the U.S. risk-based regulatory regime are:

Risk Weight	Financial Instrument Characteristics	Examples
0%	Unconditionally backed by the national government in one of 30 economically developed countries	Cash, US Treasuries, Ginnie Mae pass-throughs
20%	Low default risk, easily liquidated	Freddie Mac, Fannie Mae mortgaged-backed securities; federally insured banking deposits
50%	Low to moderate default risk, well collateralized	Many private-label mortgage-backed securities, single-family mortgages with down payments of 20% or, if less, mortgage insurance
100%	Ineligible for lower risk-weight categories	Single-family mortgages with down payments of less than 20% and no mortgage insurance, some second mortgages, commercial loans, asset-backed securities

Source: Federal Reserve Board, Office of Thrift Supervision. Adapted from "Risk-Based Ratios: Getting Closer," Edward L. Golding and Carol A. Wambeke, *Secondary Mortgage Markets*, July 1998, pp. 29–31.

The authors gratefully acknowledge the invaluable contributions of Scott Benedict of Cleary, Gottlieb, Steen, & Hamilton and Steve Rehm at Salomon Smith Barney in putting this Appendix together.

Total risk-weighted assets are calculated by assigning balance-sheet assets (such as those listed in Exhibit D.1) to specified categories and multiplying the amounts by risk weights used for the category. In general, banks and thrifts are required to maintain a capital to risk-weighted asset ratio of at least 8%. The capital reserves calculation for Fannie Mae and Ginnie Mae pass-throughs is:

Security	Risk-Weight	Risk-Weighted Assets	Required Capital Reserves
$100 Fannie Mae Pass-Throughs	20%	20% * $100 = $20	8% * $20 = $1.6
$100 Ginnie Mae Pass-Throughs	0%	0% * $100 = $0	8% * $0 = $0

Since 1988, the Basle Committee has amended the capital accord several times. In particular, in January 1996, the Accord was supplemented with a *market risk measure* that calculates capital requirements separately for the trading portfolios of banks with large equity, debt, foreign exchange, or commodity operations. In June 1999, the Basle Committee published a consultative paper, *A New Capital Adequacy Framework,* which provides a framework for replacing the 1988 Accord. The new capital framework consists of three "pillars," minimum capital requirements,* a supervisory review process, and the "effective use of market discipline."

Banking supervisors of each of the participating G-10 countries—as well as several countries that are not members of the Basle Committee—interpret and apply the Accord standards through their own regulations and directives. In the United States, two years after the Accord and in the aftermath of the thrift crisis, the Financial Institutions Reform, Recovery, and Enforcement Act (FIRREA) required thrifts to adopt a risk-based capital ratio that was based on the Basle recommendations. Currently, the Federal Reserve System (Fed) and other federal banking regulators** apply these standards to all U.S. banks, thrifts, and (although not mandated by the Basle Accord) bank holding companies.***

---

* The current risk-weighting system will be replaced by a system that relies on external credit ratings.

** Namely, the Federal Deposit Insurance Corporation (FDIC), the Office of the Comptroller of the Currency (OCC), and the Office of Thrift Supervision (OTS).

*** In addition to the Basle Accord standards, U.S. institutions are required to maintain non-risk-weighted "leverage ratios" (Tier I capital divided by balance-sheet assets) of at least 3% to 4%. Tier I capital refers to the permanent equity capital of a bank, consisting of equity capital and disclosed reserves. Equity capital includes cumulative preferred stock, noncumulative perpetual preferred stock, and other instruments that cannot be redeemed at the option of the holder.

EXHIBIT C.1   International Risk-Based Capital Weights

Security Type	US Banks	US Thrifts	UK Banks	EU Banks	Japanese Banks	Example of Mortgage Pool or CMO/ABS Trust
Ginnie Mae Pass-Throughs	0[a]	0[a]	0	0	0	Ginnie Mae Pool #482736
CMOs Backed by Ginnie Mae Collateral	20[a]	20[a]	[20][b]	[20]	[20][c]	Fannie Mae CMO 1992-G35
Fannie Mae/Freddie Mac Pass-Throughs	20[a]	20[a]	20	[20]	20	Freddie Mac Pool #181991
Fannie Mae/Freddie Mac CMOs	20[a]	20[a]	20	[20]	20	Freddie Mac CMO 1758
Qualifying Residential Mortgage Loans[d]	50[a]	50	50	50	50	
Nonagency MBSs	50[a]	20 if SMMEA; otherwise 50[a]	50	50	50[c]	NASCOR 1998-12
Asset-Backed Securities	100	100	100	100	100	Citibank Credit Card 1999-2

[a] Except for IO and PO strips, residuals and subordinated classes, which are assigned a 100% risk weight regardless of issuer or guarantor. However, the OTS is in the process of deciding whether lower risk weights may be appropriate for agency IOs and POs.

[b] The UK Financial Services Authority (FSA) assigns a 10% risk weighting to OECD government securities (and CMOs backed by GNMA or other government collateral) that have (i) a fixed rate and one year or less left to maturity, or (ii) a floating rate (and any remaining maturity).

[c] As of the time of publication, the Japanese Ministry of Finance capital regulations are not clear on these specific securities. Japan's large banks tend to follow US risk-based capital regulations by analogy.

[d] The regulations are not completely precise on this point, but most current residential mortgage loans with LTVs of 80% or less or backed by approved mortgage insurance if their LTVs are higher would fall in this category. Nonqualifying mortgage loans include those with LTVs greater than 80% and no private mortgage insurance. These loans are assigned a risk weight of 100%. FHA-insured or VA-guaranteed loans are exceptions to both of these rules and are assigned risk weights of 20% by US banks and thrifts. *Source:* Salomon Smith Barney.

Exhibit C.1 summarizes international risk-based capital credit risk weights for securities held in the banking book. Positions held in trading portfolios are not risk-weighted separately, but are included in portfolio-wide market risk capital calculations. This summary also assumes that there has been no transfer with recourse by the investing bank or thrift. We have left a few risk weights in brackets because the text of the written U.K., EU, and Japanese capital regulations that we have been able to find are just not clear on these items.

RECOMMENDED INTRODUCTORY REFERENCES

Investors should find the following publications useful in understanding some of the intricacies involved in risk-based capital management and regulation:

"Special Issue on Capital," *Secondary Mortgage Markets,* July 1998, Vol. 15, Nos. 1 and 2, Freddie Mac.

"A New Capital Adequacy Framework," Consultative paper published by the Basle Committee on Banking Supervision, Basle, June 1999. (http://www.bis.org/publ/)

Settlement Dates

Lakhbir Hayre and Robert Young

TBA AGENCY PASS-THROUGHS

There are four categories in the Bond Market Association (BMA) settlement date schedule:

Class A. 30-year conventional
Class B. 15-year conventional
Class C. 30-year Ginnie Mae
Class D. Balloons, ARMs, other

Examples of some actual settlement dates include:

	Dec 99	Jan 00
Class A	13th (Mon)	19th (Wed)
Class B	16th (Thu)	24th (Mon)
Class C	20th (Mon)	25th (Tue)
Class D	22nd (Wed)	26th (Wed)

The BMA generally publishes the settlement dates about six months in advance. No formula is used to determine the dates, but general guidelines are that the dates must be after pool factors become available, should not occur too close to the end of the month, and should not fall on a Friday (to help avoid a fail occurring over a weekend).

CMOs/ABSs

CMOs and ABSs traded in the secondary markets use *corporate settlement*. These securities settle three days after the trade date ($T + 3$). Exceptions to this might occur if securities are held through the depositories Cedel or Euroclear. New issues normally settle when the deal settles (issue date).

INTEREST-ONLY/PRINCIPAL-ONLY STRIPS (SECONDARY TRADING)

The settlement date convention for STRIPs is a little more complicated. The settlement convention for STRIPs is given by the following three rules:

1. First part of the month before the 48-hour day is reached, use TBA settlement date (for current month).
2. On the 48-hour day, when TBA settlement date coincides with skip-day settlement (settlement two days after the trade date [$T + 2$]), convert to skip-day settlement at this point and for most of the rest of the month (see 3).
3. Very near the end of month, when skip-day settlement falls into the next month, switch to next month's TBA settlement date and continue with 1.

Examples of IO/PO Settlement Dates (Dec 99)*

Trade Date	Settlement Date
Dec 1–9	Dec 13 (Mon)
Dec 10–29	Skip-Day (T+2)
Dec 30–31	Jan 19 (Wed)

*December 13 and January 19 are BMA TBA settlement dates.
Source: Salomon Smith Barney.

Resources for MBS and ABS Investors

Lakhbir Hayre and Robert Young

In this appendix, we compile some key sources of information on mortgage securities for investors. In particular, Fannie Mae, Freddie Mac, and Ginnie Mae have a number of knowledgeable professionals available to answer questions about their own securities. For ease of reference, we have listed some of the resources they offer in this regard. In addition, commercial vendors, such as Bloomberg®, serve as sources of information on agency and non-agency securities.

As a pioneer in the trading and development of valuation models for mortgage- and asset-backed securities, SSB offers investors unmatched expertise in these areas. The SSB section touches on just some of the facilities that we offer investors. For further details, please contact your salesperson or one of the authors.

SALOMON SMITH BARNEY

- SSB's **Fixed-Income Prime Broker** effectively serves clients in all sectors of the U.S. fixed-income market, including U.S. Treasuries, agencies, mortgage- and asset-backed securities, high yield bonds, and credit-sensitive securities. SSB Prime Broker also provides clearing, custody, and financing services for sovereign and corporate debt in many major and emerging markets. For further information regarding SSB Fixed-Income Prime Broker, please call (212) 723-2846.
- *Salomon Smith Barney DIRECT® (SSB DIRECT)* is an institutional fixed-income communication tool created to deliver research, trade ideas/color, market coverage, and bond offerings to customers over the

Internet. All our research publications and manifolds (including the Key Issue Package MB725) are available on DIRECT. Call your salesperson for a password to SSB DIRECT, or contact (212) 723 9474 or +44-[0]171-721-2920.

■ *Trade Processing and Settlement.* For queries about operational issues, please send e-mail to mbsoperations@ssmb.com.

■ **Yield Book™** (http://yieldbook.com/). The Yield Book is SSB's delivery system for fixed-income analytics, and supports our industry standard mortgage prepayment and valuation models. All SSB mortgage- and asset-backed research may be accessed on the Yield Book. The Yield Book is the premier fixed-income analytics system and is used by all of the top 10 U.S. fixed-income money managers and by 80 of the top 100. For more information, look at the Web site, call (212) 816-7120, or e-mail Sales@YieldBook.com.

FANNIE MAE

■ *Fannie Mae on Bloomberg®.* MBSenger® is an electronic newsletter published by Fannie Mae and available on Bloomberg. It can be accessed by typing *MBSN <GO>.* The newsletter reports on economic, housing, and mortgage market news, among other areas of interest to investors.

■ *Helplines.* This service provides answers to nonroutine questions about Fannie Mae securities (9:00 A.M. to 5:00 P.M., Eastern time, every business day). Call (800) BEST-MBS, or (202) 752-6547. Routine questions, such as inquiries about pool CUSIPs and factors, are answered through PoolTalk®.

■ *MORNET® MBS Bulletin Board.* MORNET, Fannie Mae's electronic mail system, allows investors to receive information and exchange messages with other subscribers. Through the MORNET Bulletin Board, MBS investors have access to information about MBS settlements, new issues, auctions, SMBS factors, Fannie Majors® pools, and ARMs. For more information contact the MORNET Hotline at (800) 752-6440, or (202) 752-6000.

■ *PoolTalk®.* Investors in Fannie Mae MBSs have 24-hour access to pool information (CUSIPs, pool factors, WACs, WAMs, etc.) through PoolTalk, Fannie Mae's voice response information system. An account can be set up by calling (800) BEST-MBS, or (202) 752-6547.

■ *Web Site (http://www.fanniemae.com).* This Web site contains useful information about Fannie Mae and its mortgage and debt securities programs.

FREDDIE MAC

- *Freddie Mac on Bloomberg®.* Freddie Mac Almanac on Bloomberg® (Type *FMAC <GO>*) contains housing news, the *Securities Bulletin* newsletter, and a variety of other financial and product information.
- *Investor Inquiry.* This service provides answers to questions about Freddie Mac securities and disclosure (9:00 A.M. to 5:00 P.M., Eastern time, every business day). Call (800) 336-3672, or e-mail Investor_Inquiry@freddiemac.com.
- *Mortgage Securities Marketing.* This department is available to answer nonroutine questions about Freddie Mac securities. Please contact (703) 903-3805, or e-mail patricia_hand@freddiemac.com.
- *Web Site (http://www.freddiemac.com).* Freddie Mac has special sections of its Web site devoted to mortgage securities and debt securities. The mortgage securities site contains, among other things, Freddie Mac's monthly *Securities Bulletin* newsletter, product information, offering circulars, new-issue announcements, and all single-class and multi-class disclosure for Freddie Mac PCs and REMICs. Freddie Mac's debt Web area also contains product literature and announcements, offering circulars, and disclosure information. The *Financial Research News* (http://www.freddiemac.com/news/finance) section of the Web site contains a number of very useful economic data series for mortgage market participants. In particular, the site contains a weekly survey of mortgage rates (PMMS), a home price index, an economic housing forecast, and a housing refinance survey. It also contains *Secondary Mortgage Markets,* a highly regarded Freddie Mac publication that offers analysis of key business, economic, and public policy issues affecting the housing and mortgage finance markets. Freddie Mac's Web site is accessible 24 hours a day, seven days a week, with no password or access restrictions.

GINNIE MAE

- *Capital Markets.* This service provides answers to questions about Ginnie Mae securities (9:00 A.M. to 6:00 P.M., Eastern time, every business day). Call (212) 668-5180, or (202) 401-8970.
- *Factor Information.* An automated pool factor information service can be accessed at (212) 638-6509. For REMIC factors (and questions about operational issues) contact (800) 234-GNMA.
- *Ginnie Mae on Bloomberg®.* Investors can access information about Ginnie Mae Platinum® securities, Multiple Issuer Pools, REMICs, and Callable Trusts on Bloomberg by typing *GNMA <GO>.* The

information provided on Platinum pools is particularly comprehensive and includes an overview of the program, a fee schedule, and a list of all Platinum pools issued.

- *Web Site (http://www.ginniemae.gov).* The *Ginnie Mae Guides* are among the most useful resources available on the Web site. The *Guides* provide an in-depth description of the Ginnie Mae I and Ginnie Mae II programs. Changes to Ginnie Mae programs (and, therefore, to the *Guides*) are usually announced by *All Participants Memoranda,* which can also be found on the Web site.

THE BOND MARKET ASSOCIATION

The Bond Market Association represents securities firms and banks that underwrite, trade, and sell debt securities (including mortgage- and asset-backed securities) domestically and internationally. The association speaks for the bond industry and advocates its positions. The association also keeps members informed of relevant legislative, regulatory, and market-practice developments.

- *Publications.* The association publishes books, brochures, manuals, and other educational materials. Investors who are new to the ABS and MBS markets will find the following publications especially useful: (1) *Uniform Practices for the Clearance and Settlement of Mortgage-Backed Securities and Other Related Securities;* (2) *An Investor's Guide to Asset-Backed Securities (ABS);* (3) *An Investor's Guide to Collateralized Mortgage Obligations (CMOs);* (4) *An Investor's Guide to Mortgage-Backed Securities;* (5) *Standard Formulas for the Analysis of Mortgage-Backed Securities and Other Related Securities.* For information about ordering these publications, contact Publications at (212) 440-9430, or look at the organization's Web site.
- *Web Site (http://www.bondmarkets.com).* The BMA Web site is a mine of useful information on regulatory, legislative, and market-practice developments relevant to all U.S. fixed-income sectors. However, some parts of the Web site are only accessible to BMA members. Other useful items include a list of MBS settlement and notification dates, and helpful publications for new investors in mortgage- and asset-backed securities.

COMMERCIAL VENDORS

Several commercial vendors serve as a source of data and news on mortgage securities. Perhaps the best known is Bloomberg®; others include Telerate (a division of Bridge Information Systems) and Reuters.